I0818100

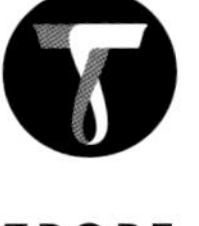

TROPE

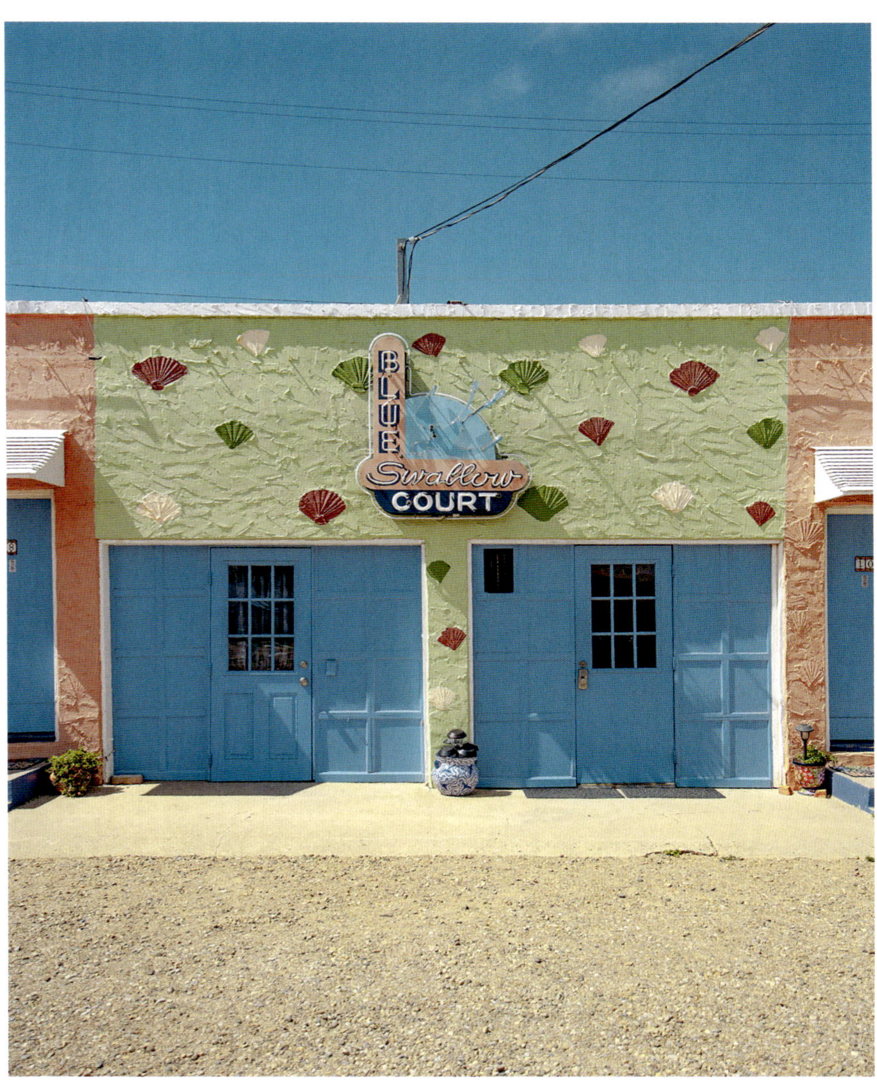

Blue Swallow Motel • Tucumcari, New Mexico

BEN GEIER

VIEWING HOURS

AMERICA'S VANISHING CULTURE

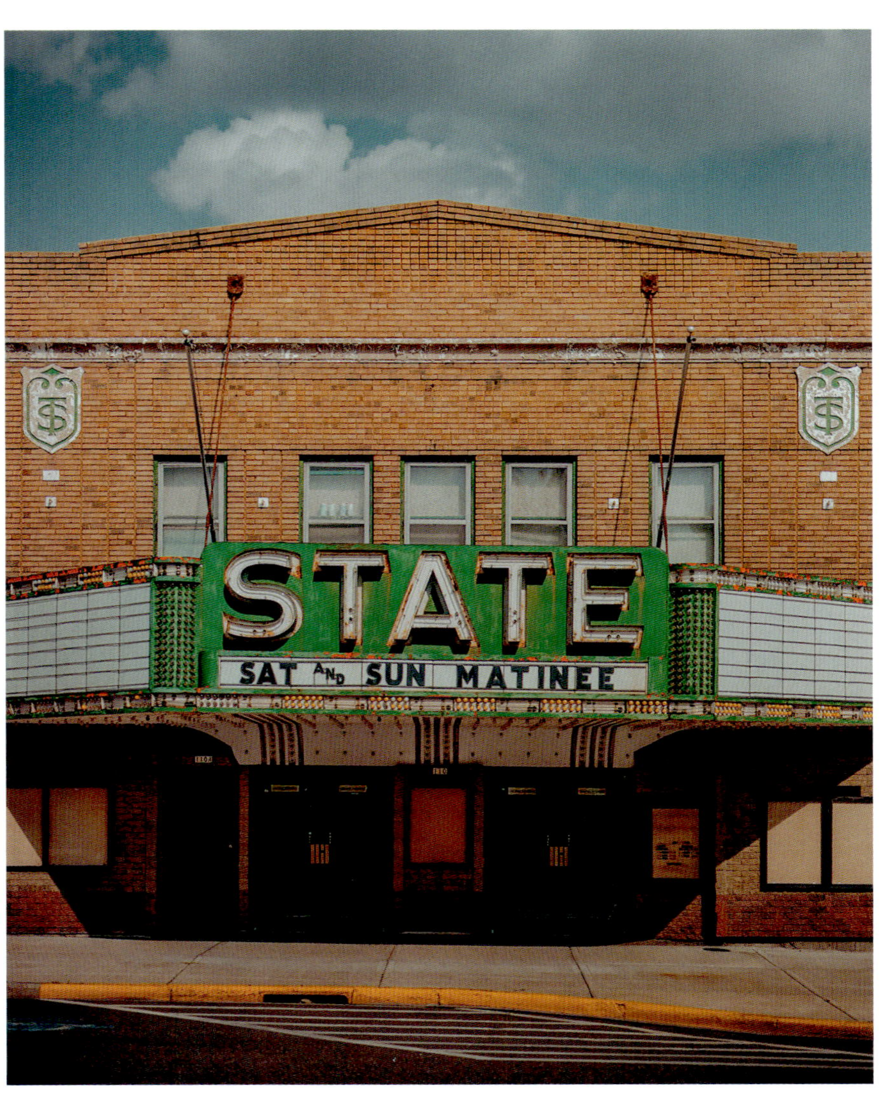

State Theatre • Rhinelander, Wisconsin

FOREWORD

I'm an amateur. I get by on enthusiasm. From the earliest of ages, I remember singing and dancing, playing air guitar, and pretending to be a pop star. The radio was always on, and the Top 40 was my soundtrack. In fifth grade I got my first tape recorder. I started forming semi-fictional music groups; writing lyrics, titles, and, in some cases, designing album covers. When I had saved up enough money, I bought a guitar at the mall for $99. I grew up immersed in the punk/indie music scene in Washington, D.C. I wanted to write and play music. Punk is all about DIY. No training. Just doing. Ben had a very similar experience growing up in the Chicago area. We were both inspired by musicians like the kids at Dischord in Washington, D.C., who were releasing their own records around the ages of 18 or 19 in the early 1980s. Before I learned that local music existed—before I knew there were people my age in bands, making records—I assumed all music came from corporate giants like Warner Brothers, Elektra/Asylum, Sire, and a host of others, distributed through stores like Best, Korvette's, G.C. Murphy's 5 & 10, and Drug Fair. I was so excited to discover this that I formed my own band, Unrest, and record label, Teenbeat. This is Ben's very own album. It has no music, but it makes noise. It makes music. This is a masterwork that has been eight years in the making. We should consider it a greatest hits collection—maybe even a boxed set with six albums, each focusing on a theme: Storefronts, Restaurants, Roadside, Motels, Signs, Theatres. And, of course, it includes a booklet. Or, in this case, a book. Even better. His signs are as good as Black Flag's *Damaged*. His motels are better than The Motels (no offense intended to either motels or the band The Motels). Some motels are just better than others. Ben is Dieter Rams, perhaps the most famous and important industrial designer of our time—if not of all time. Rams created beautiful masterpieces in the form of record players, clocks, and electric shavers. Like Rams, Ben's images are meticulously crafted, with every element fitting together perfectly. Ben is Peter Saville, the innovative graphic designer who changed the world of album covers. In fact, all the photographs in this book could be album covers. They're so good you wouldn't even have to put the name of your band on the front. Ben is Shellac, the power trio fronted by Chicago record producer extraordinaire, Steve Albini. Powerful. Loud.

FOREWORD

Striking. Sometimes melodic. Often mind-blowing. Ben is Cindy Sherman, the fine art photographer who immerses herself in her scenes. He not only takes photographs; he puts a lot of himself into them. You can't see him the way you can see Sherman in her self portraits, but you can feel his presence in every image. Ben is Ian MacKaye, the archivist and co-founder of Dischord Records. While MacKaye saves, catalogues, and classifies every letter he's ever received, Ben is cataloguing the world that was, the world that is, and halfway between the two. Old things somehow become more magical with age and he catches every drop of that magic with his camera. His photography isn't just fascinating because of what's inside the frame. It's how he sets up the shot: where he places the camera, the lighting, the F-stop setting, and a multitude of other intangibles I may never fully understand. That same elusive, unknowable artistry that a musician, painter, or choreographer uses to create is what we see reflected in the pages of this book. Of all the photographers I follow on the popular media platforms of the day, Ben is my favorite. There's never a dud and never a dull moment—just pure beauty. Skills developed over years of creating and just doing, not sitting in the back of a classroom. P.S. News flash. Spoiler alert: Ben shoots digitally. I know. Insane. He somehow captures the most analog-looking photographs we've ever seen with modern, computerized, non-film technology and equipment.

Mark Robinson

Musician, designer, and founder of the Teenbeat label

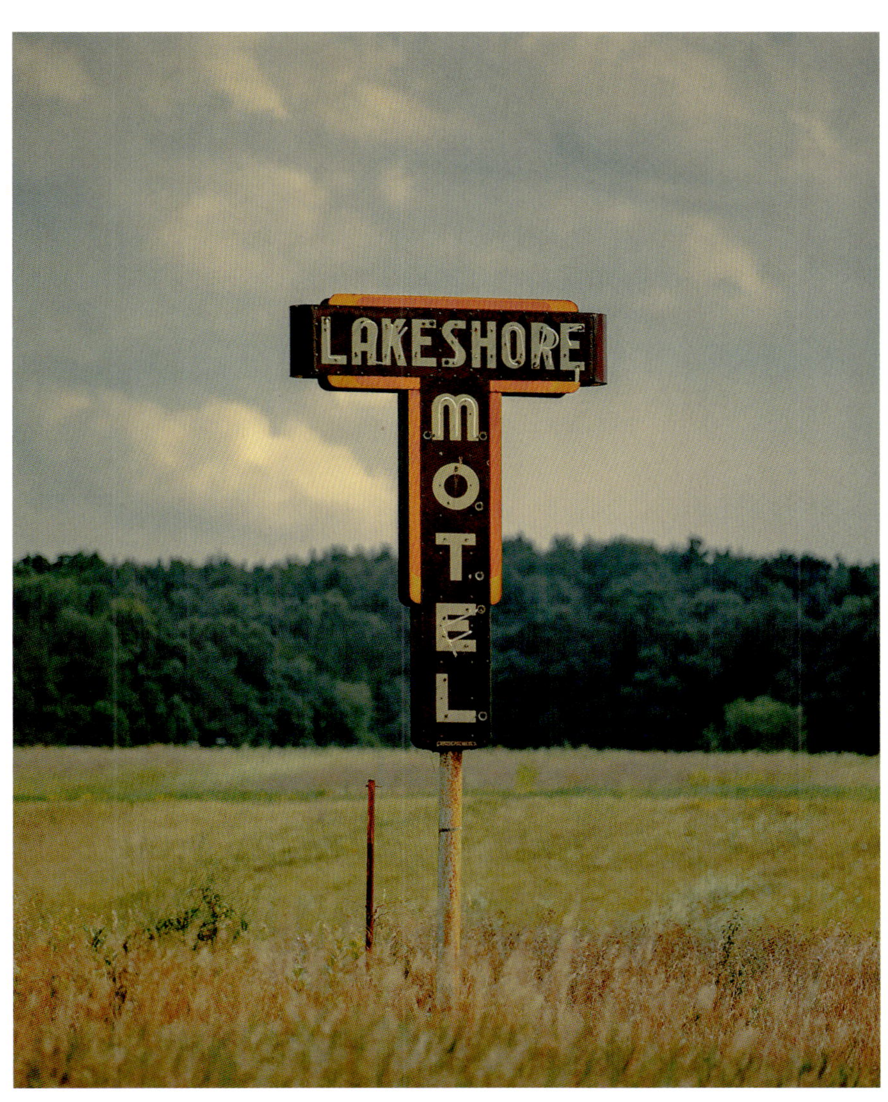

Abandoned Lakeshore Motel Sign • Weyauwega, Wisconsin

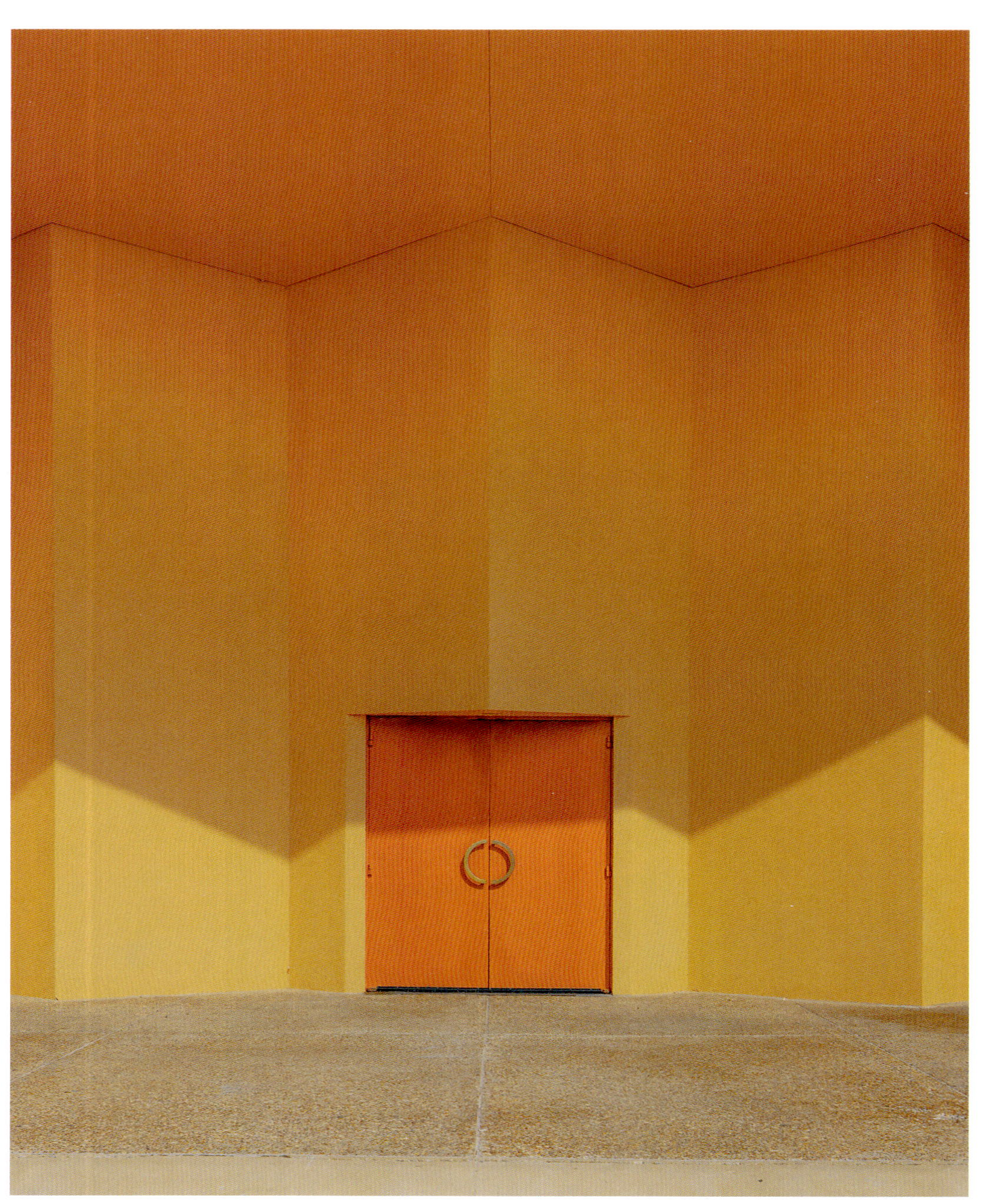

Bartlesville Community Center • Bartlesville, Oklahoma

INTRODUCTION

Welcome to *Viewing Hours*—a collection of photos I've spent nearly a decade capturing and curating.

"Viewing hours" is a slightly unusual term that originates from funeral receptions—a moment when you have the chance to view your loved one for the final time and pay your respects. I think this sentiment is the common thread throughout this book: traveling to see these iconic, and perhaps lesser-known locations, to pay my respects before they're possibly gone forever.

I got my start in photography through my background as a musician and out of necessity. I grew up in the Chicago music scene in the late '90s, attending all-ages shows at the infamous Fireside Bowl, an unlikely music venue for punk and indie bands. Over time, the bowling lanes were used less and less, and shows were put on almost nightly. I typically filmed every show I attended with my Sony Handycam, copied them to VHS tape, and then traded those tapes with people all over the world. I became quite the archivist and still hoard that entire collection to this day. In terms of my contribution to the music scene, I played drums in the band Mt. St. Helens, and because I was obsessed with art and design, I was usually tasked with album layouts and flyer designs. My process was pretty typical—I would conceptualize the artwork and then go out and shoot the photography I needed for it. I took many of my creative cues from the music scene. Some of my favorite musicians were also designers: Mark Robinson from the band Unrest, Jason Farrell from Bluetip, and Jay Ryan from Dianogah, to list a few. I would shoot everything on 35mm, and while I wasn't very knowledgeable about photography at the time, the DIY mindset of the music scene made it all feel experimental and fun, even if I didn't know exactly what I was doing. Creating artwork for bands cemented my love for design and it seemed like a natural extension of the energy and creativity I was surrounded by in the music scene. There was a certain liberation in not worrying too much about rules or technical perfection that allowed me to create work that was genuine and personal.

I find endless inspiration and creativity in the things that truly resonate with me—design, architecture, music, films, history, food, and beyond. When I discover something I love, I almost obsess over it. I want to immerse myself in it, research it, experience it, and document it. I eventually noticed my photography had evolved from a practical tool for band flyers and show documentation, to something deeper, an exploration of places and moments that felt fleeting or on the brink of disappearing. I found myself spending my weekends driving around to find scenes that evoked a sense of nostalgia and solitude. I became consumed with finding architectural and design relics from another era, some long abandoned and forgotten, and some preserved and steeped in history.

Around this time, the mid 2000s, cameras started to advance so much that I put down my 35mm camera and started shooting all of my photos digitally. My new format allowed me to work quickly, which was necessary when I was shooting in areas where I was not always welcome. The most exciting part, however, was how digital photography opened up a world of opportunity in terms of color and editing. This allowed me to incorporate my love of design into my work. As I shifted to this new medium, I noticed a change in my approach. What started as a way to document events transformed into something more profound. I found myself seeking out places and moments that felt transient, on the verge of disappearing. I spent all my time chasing remnants of another era. Old buildings, forgotten landmarks, and spaces where time had left its mark; these were places embedded in history. Some decaying, some preserved, but all connected in a sense of solitude. Many of the places I capture through my photography might seem ordinary or even insignificant to a local who's driven past them countless times. But when does a place become nostalgic? Is it only after we've created memories there? Or does nostalgia kick in once that place is no longer part of our world?

Viewing Hours is my tribute to these places. It's a collection of images that honors the impermanence of time. It is a means of archiving our culture and of preserving stories. These are small moments I wanted to capture before they faded into memory or were erased entirely. The photos are my way of paying respect to the places and stories that both inspired and shaped me.

Each image in this book is a memento, a document in time, much like the VHS tapes I traded in my youth. For me, what started as an act of documentation turned into a way of honoring things that are often overlooked, taken for granted, and too soon forgotten.

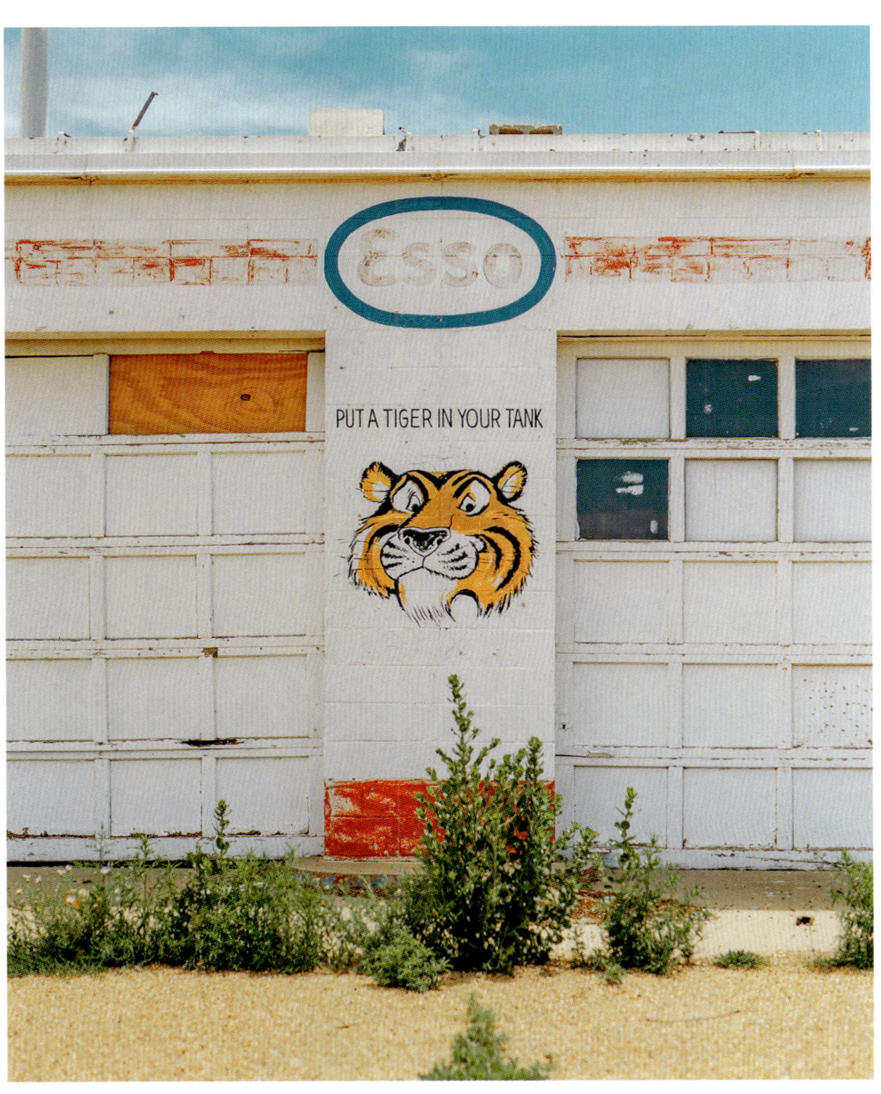

Esso Service Station • Tucumcari, New Mexico

STOREFRONTS

There's a timeless allure in a well-designed storefront. I remember obsessing over the unique exteriors of the Venture discount stores as a kid. I found the black and white diagonal striped buildings with the massive three-dimensional type were such a striking design. Stores and malls became the hangouts for me and my friends; they would later spark my fascination with the forgotten and the abandoned. In the early '90s, the mall that had once been the epicenter of our hangouts closed its doors. Years later, when a back door was found ajar, my friends and I couldn't resist the urge to go in and explore. We ventured inside to discover a ghostly version of the place we had once known—stores, restaurants, and the theater, all decaying, neglected, and crumbling under the weight of time. What stood out most to me, however, was how the signage remained largely intact—faded, but still proudly standing, an echo of our collective memories, frozen in time. A few years later, the mall was completely demolished and the plot of land sat vacant for two decades.

I suppose this is where my love for classic storefronts originated. The few that remain have a rare power: they transport us to a time we never lived through, evoking a kind of nostalgia for a world we never experienced.

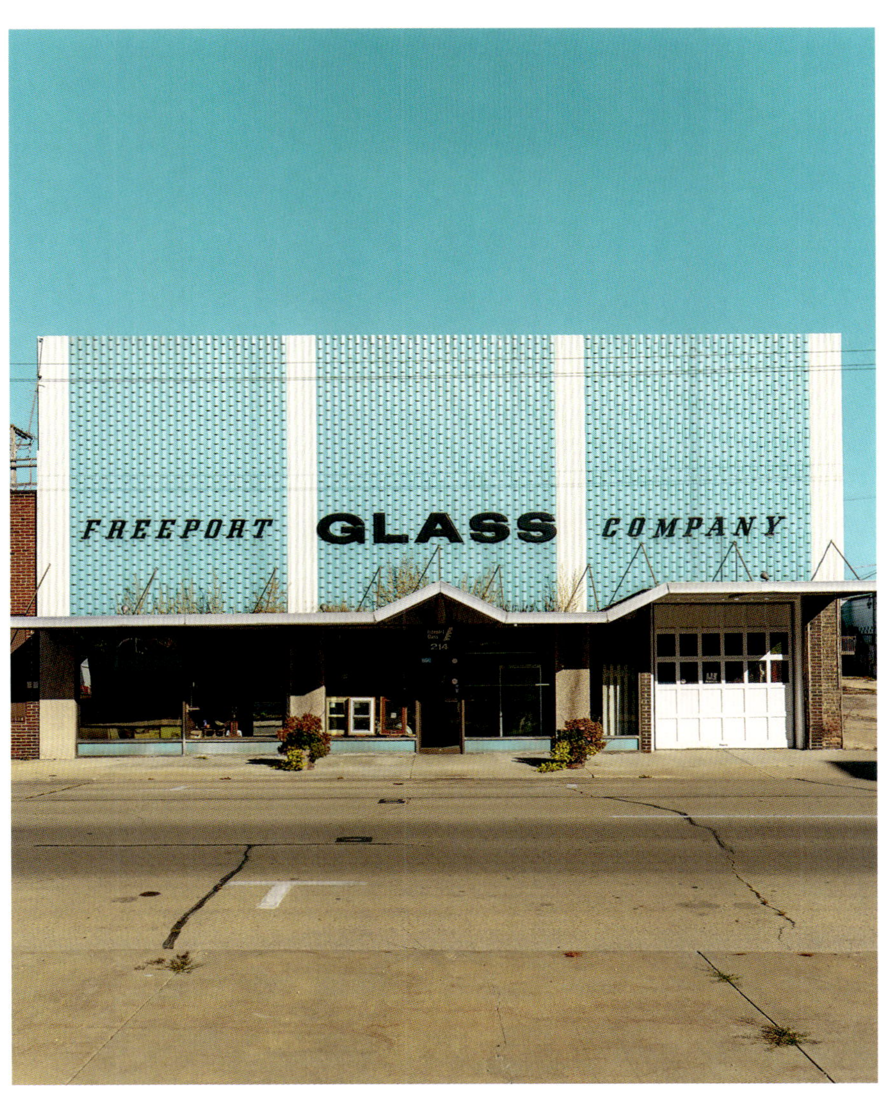

Freeport Glass Company • Freeport, Illinois

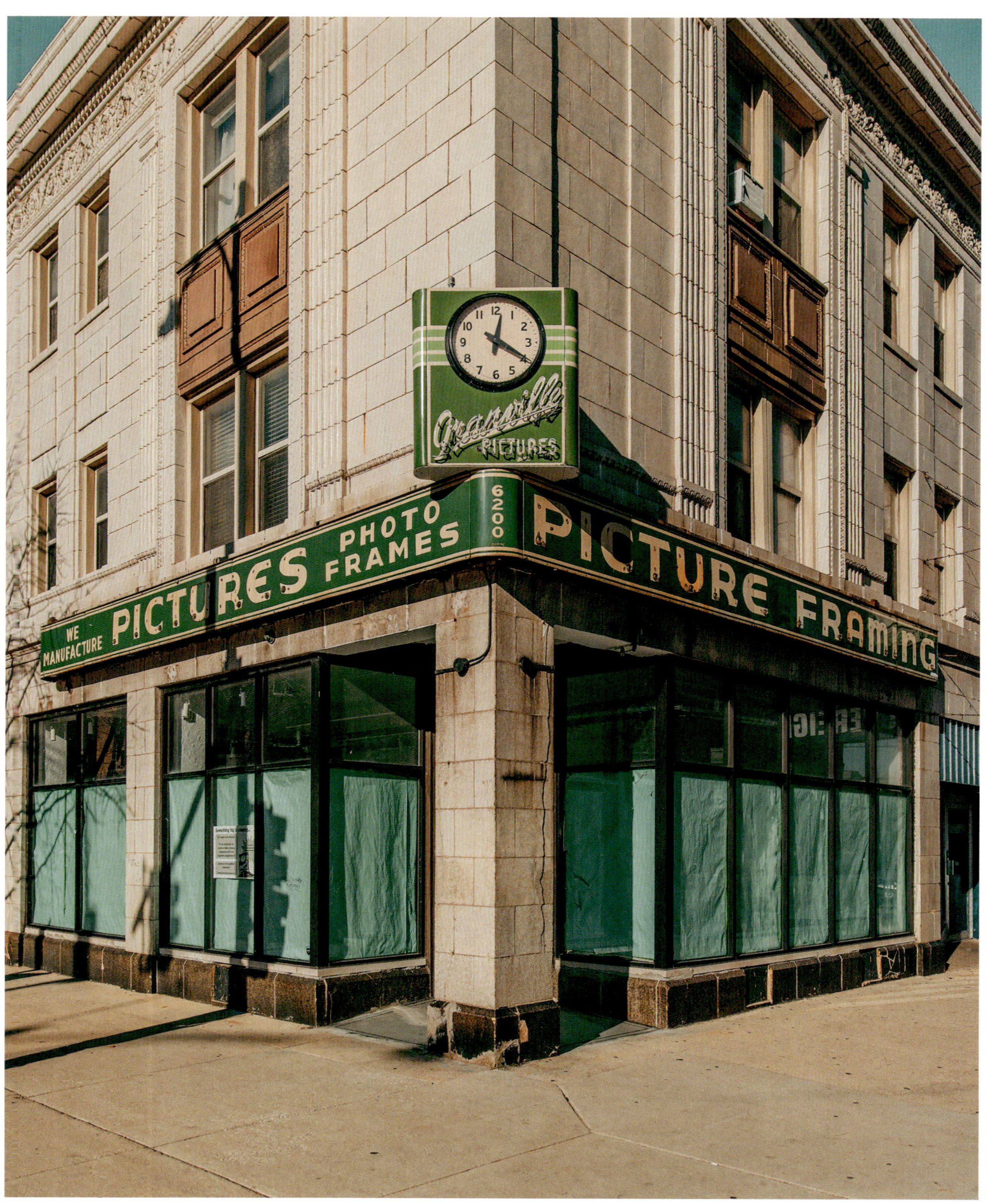

Granville Picture Framing • Chicago, Illinois

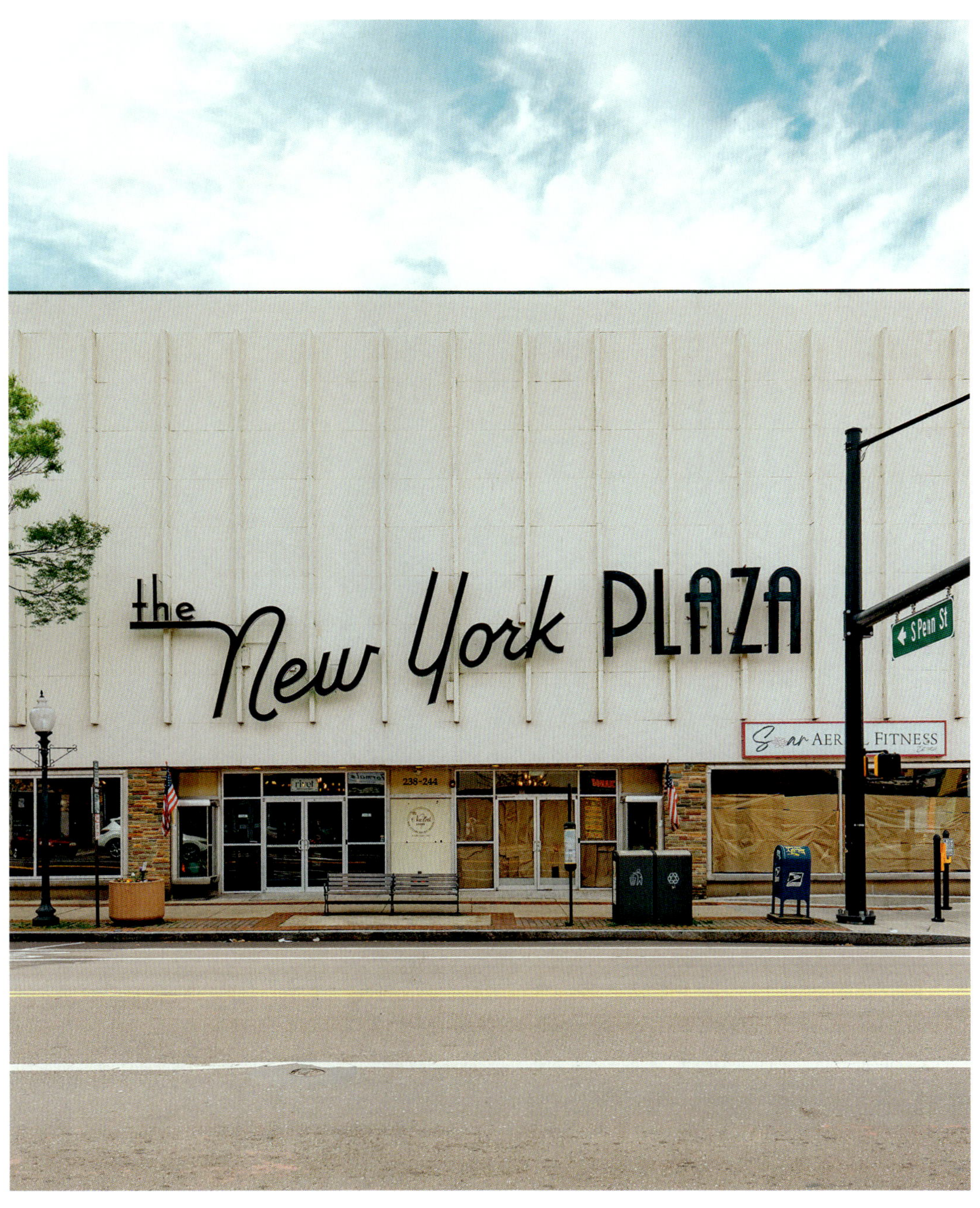

The New York Plaza • Pottstown, Pennsylvania

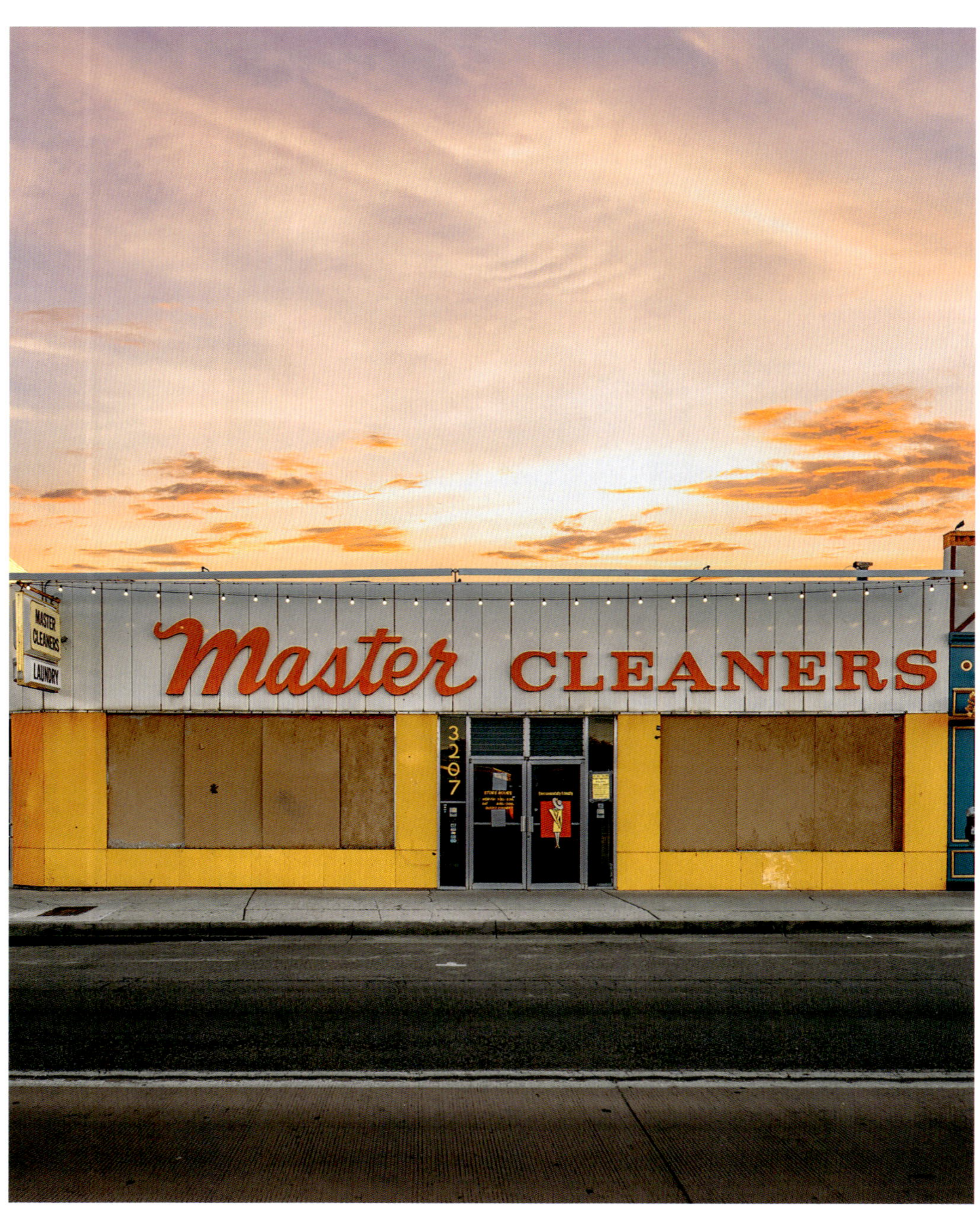

Master Cleaners • Albuquerque, New Mexico

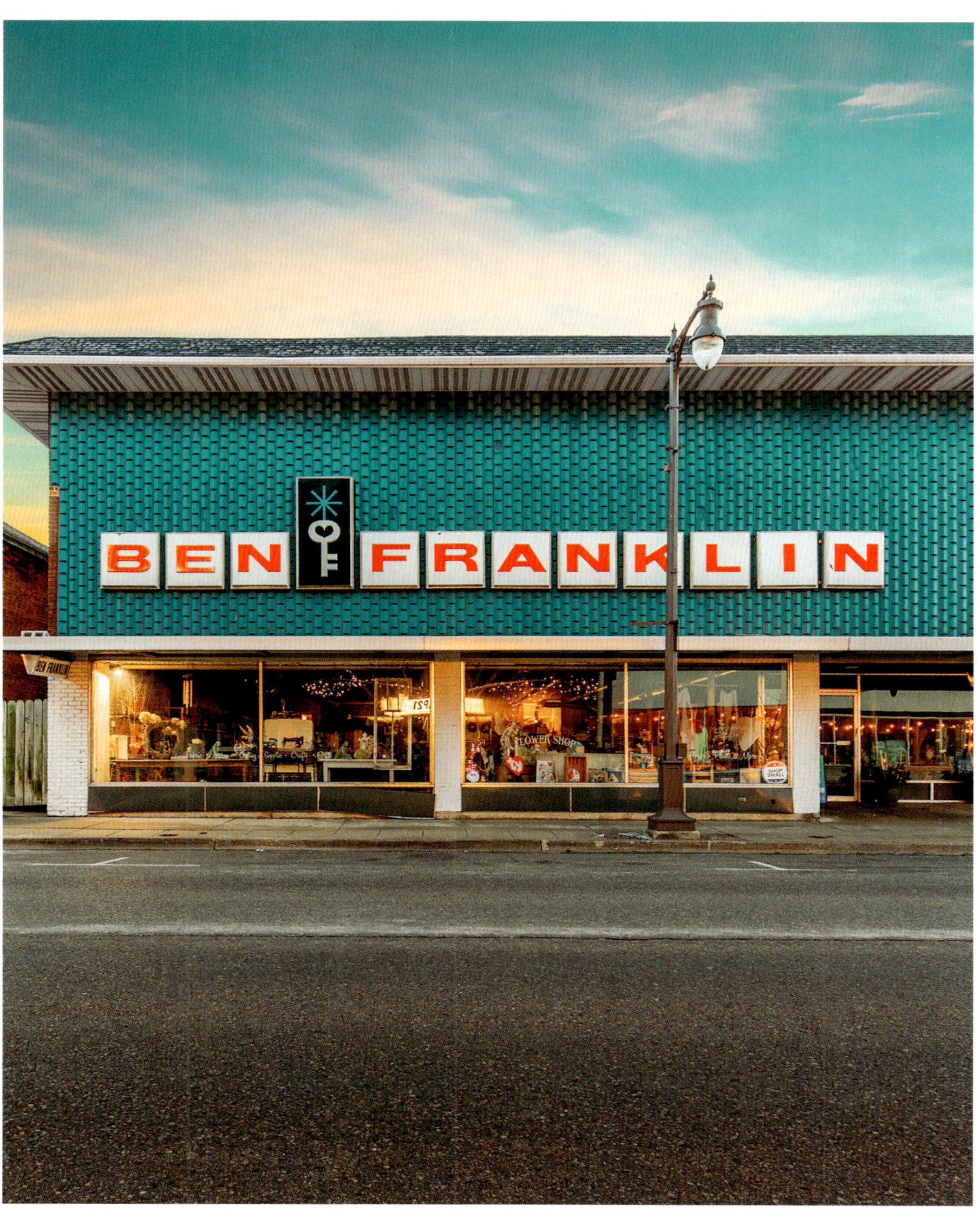

Ben Franklin • Manistique, Michigan

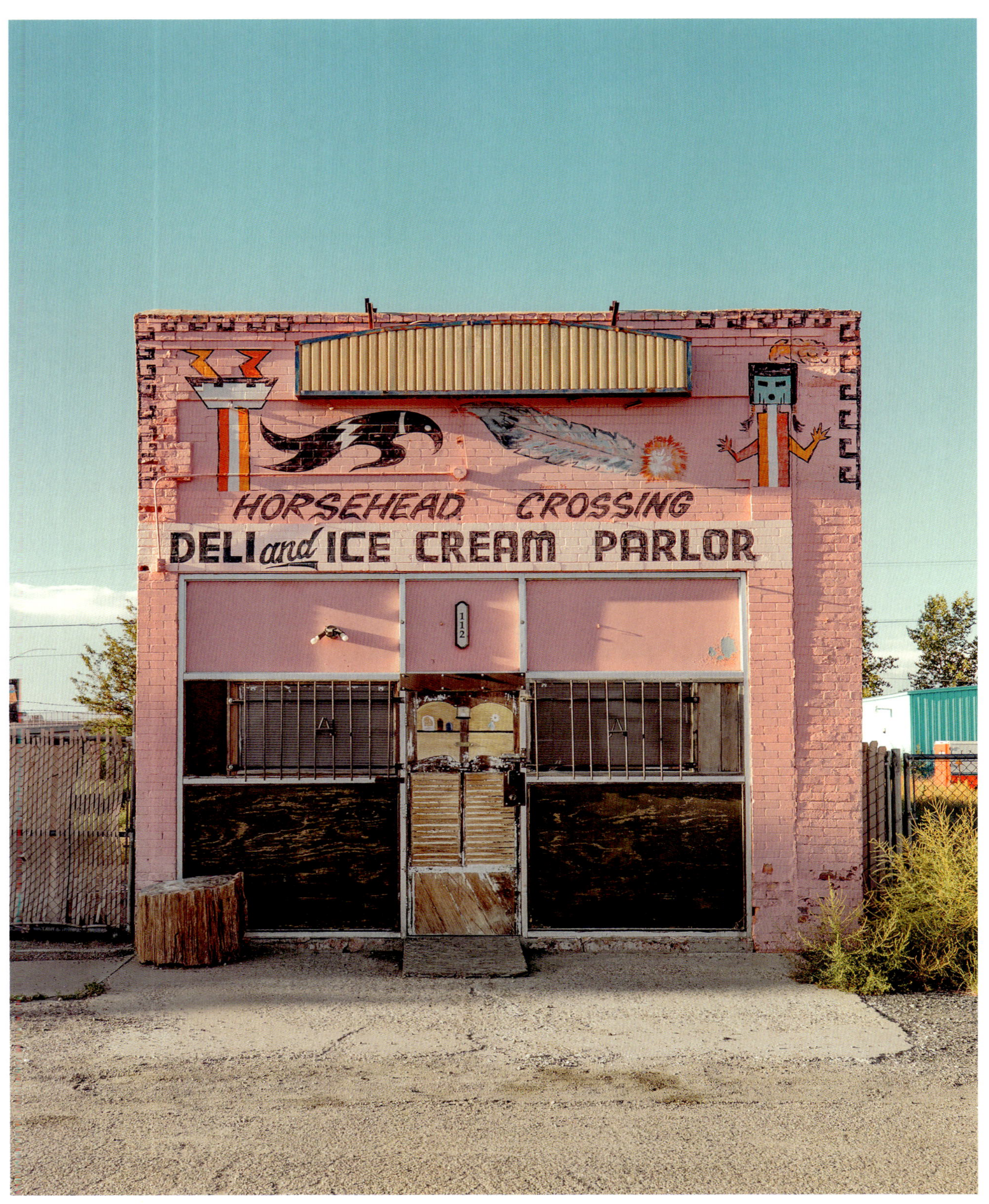

Horsehead Crossing • Holbrook, Arizona

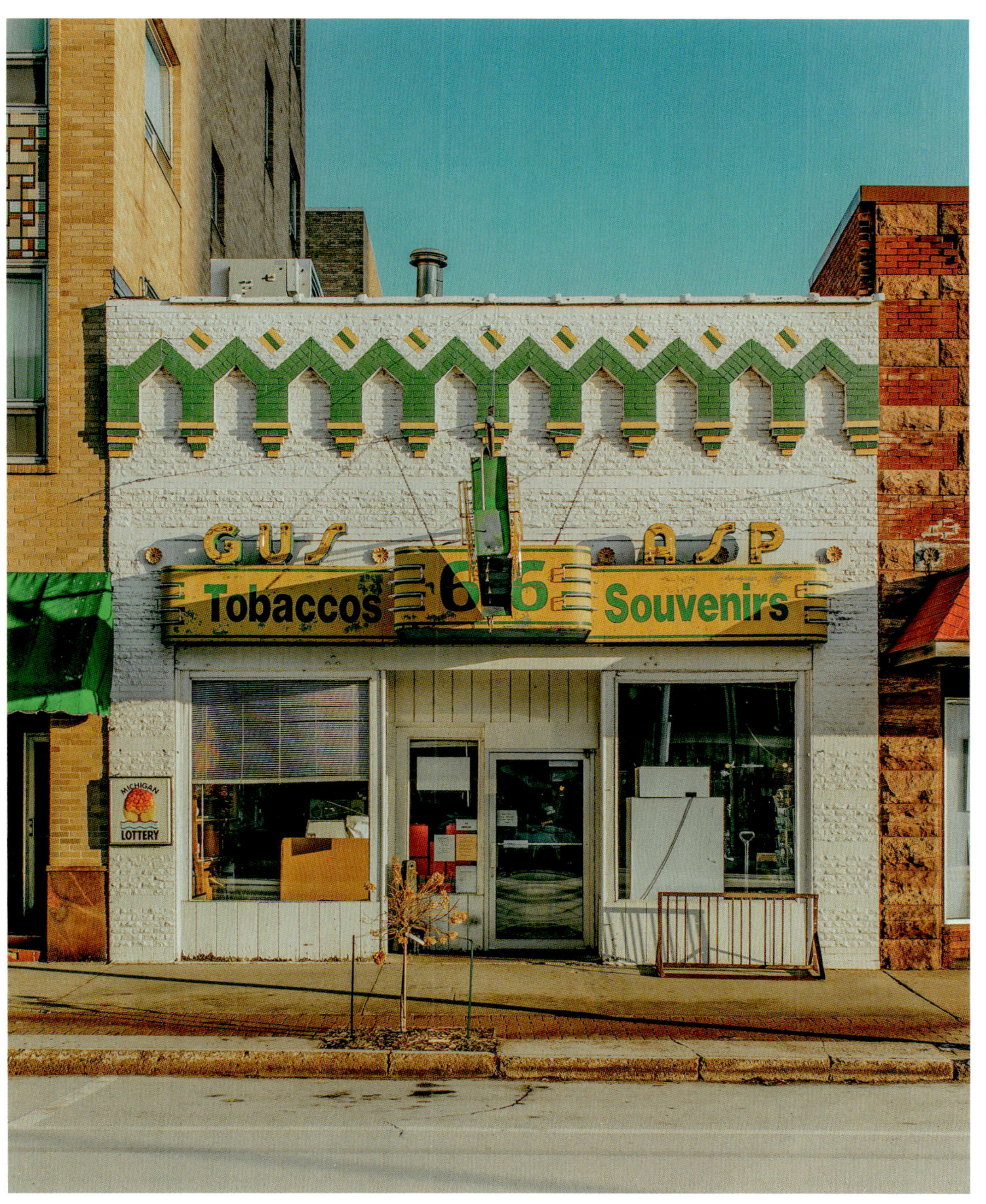

Gus Asp Party Store • Escanaba, Michigan

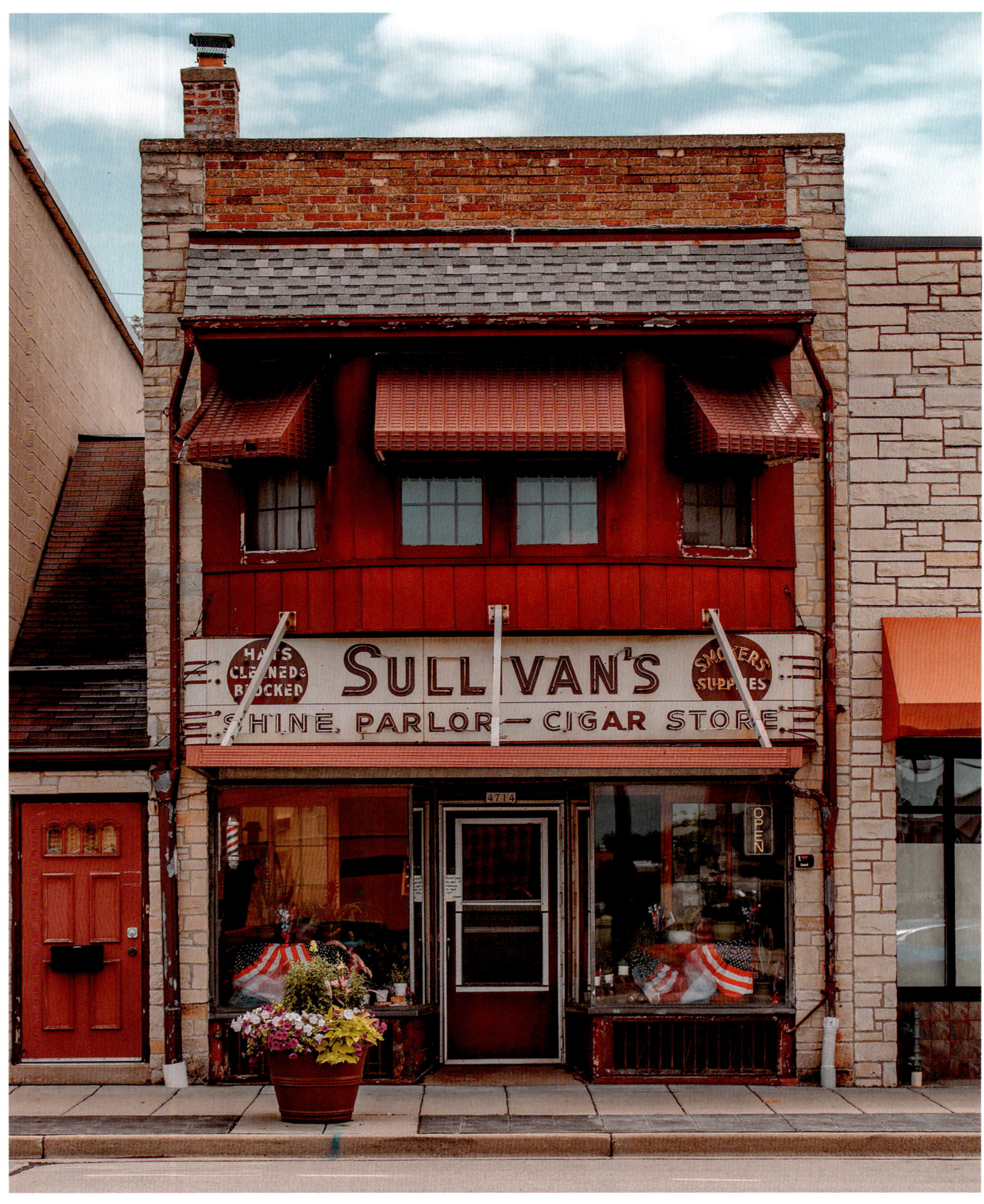

Sullivan's Cigar Store • Milwaukee, Wisconsin

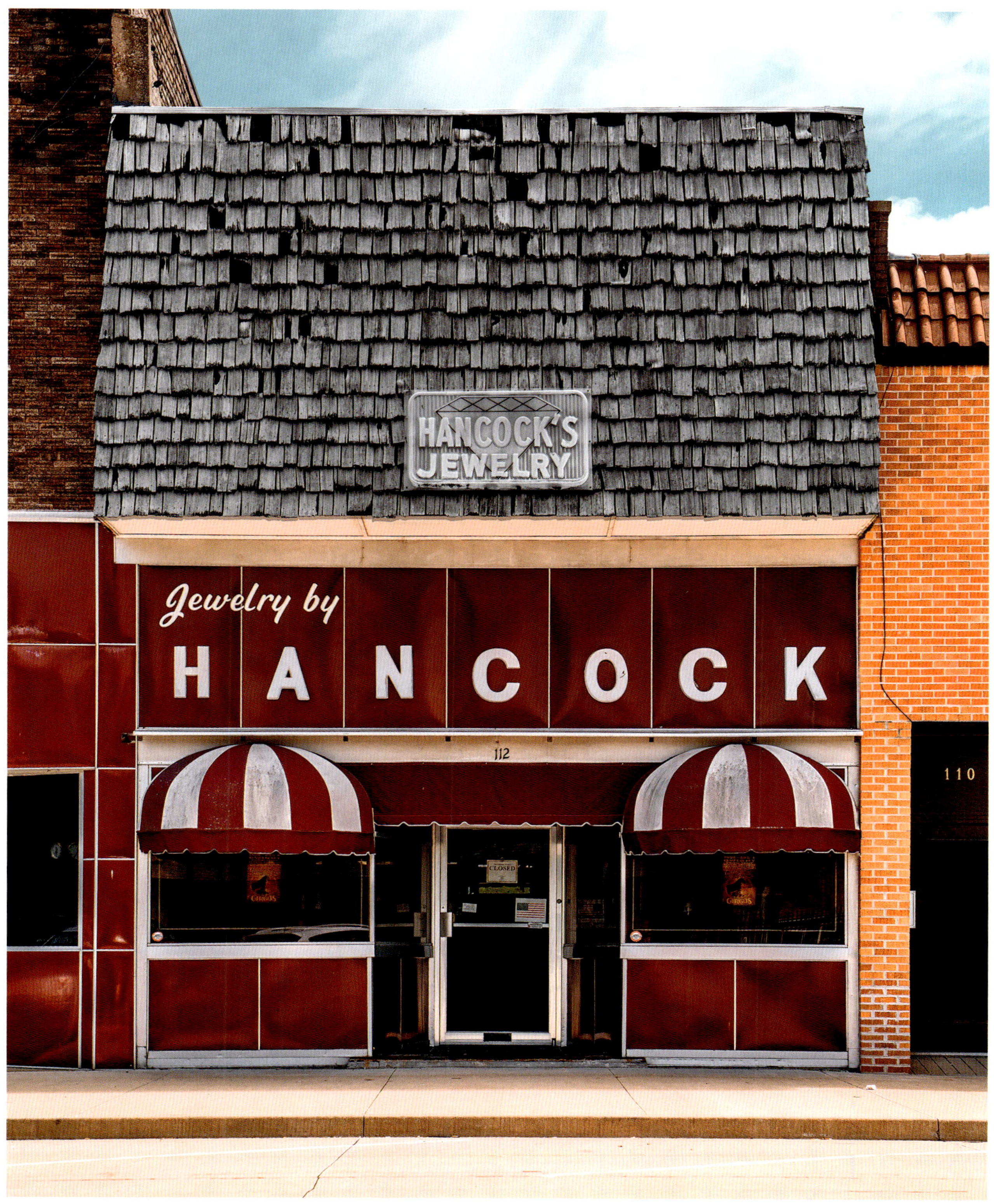

Hancock's Jewelry • Dwight, Illinois

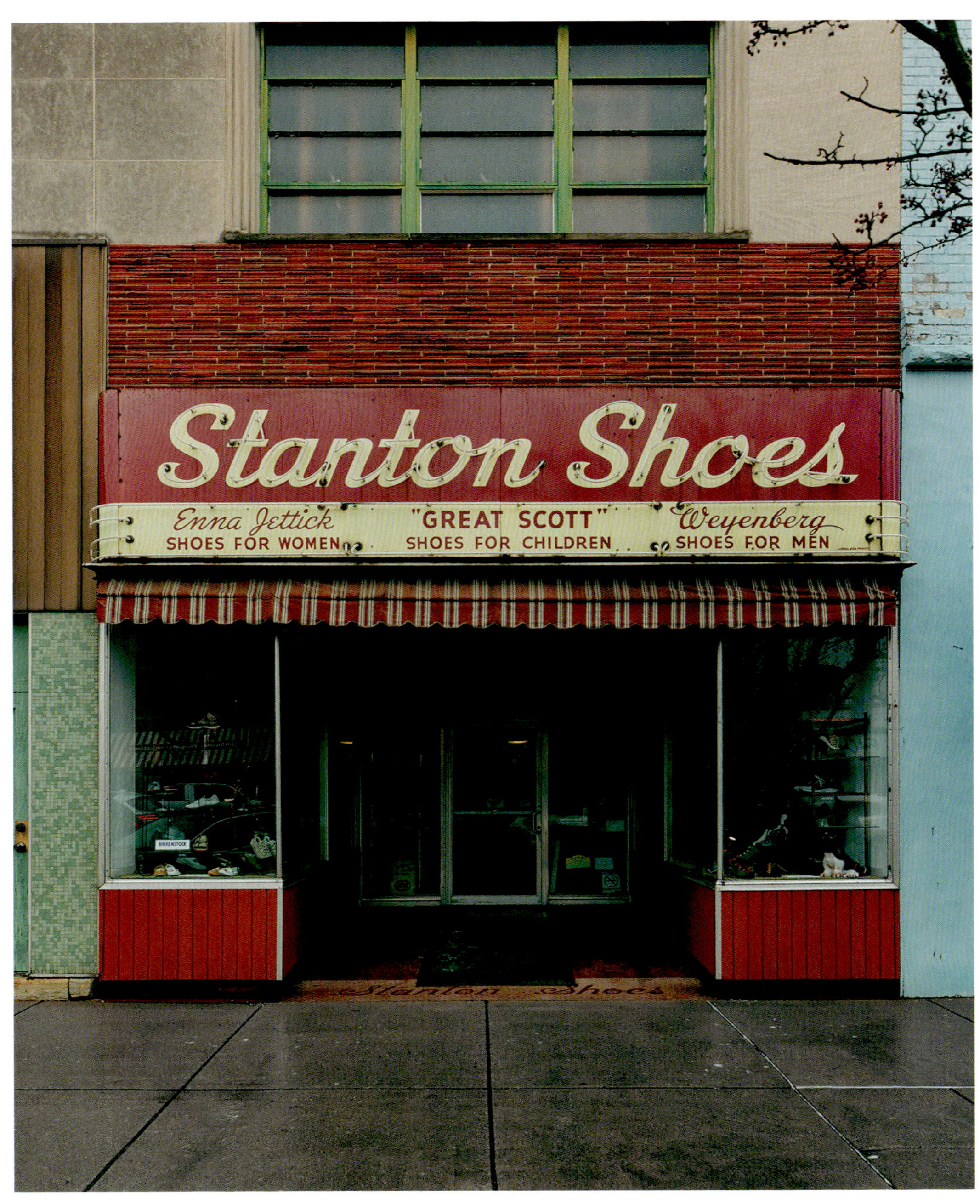

Stanton Shoes • Beloit, Wisconsin

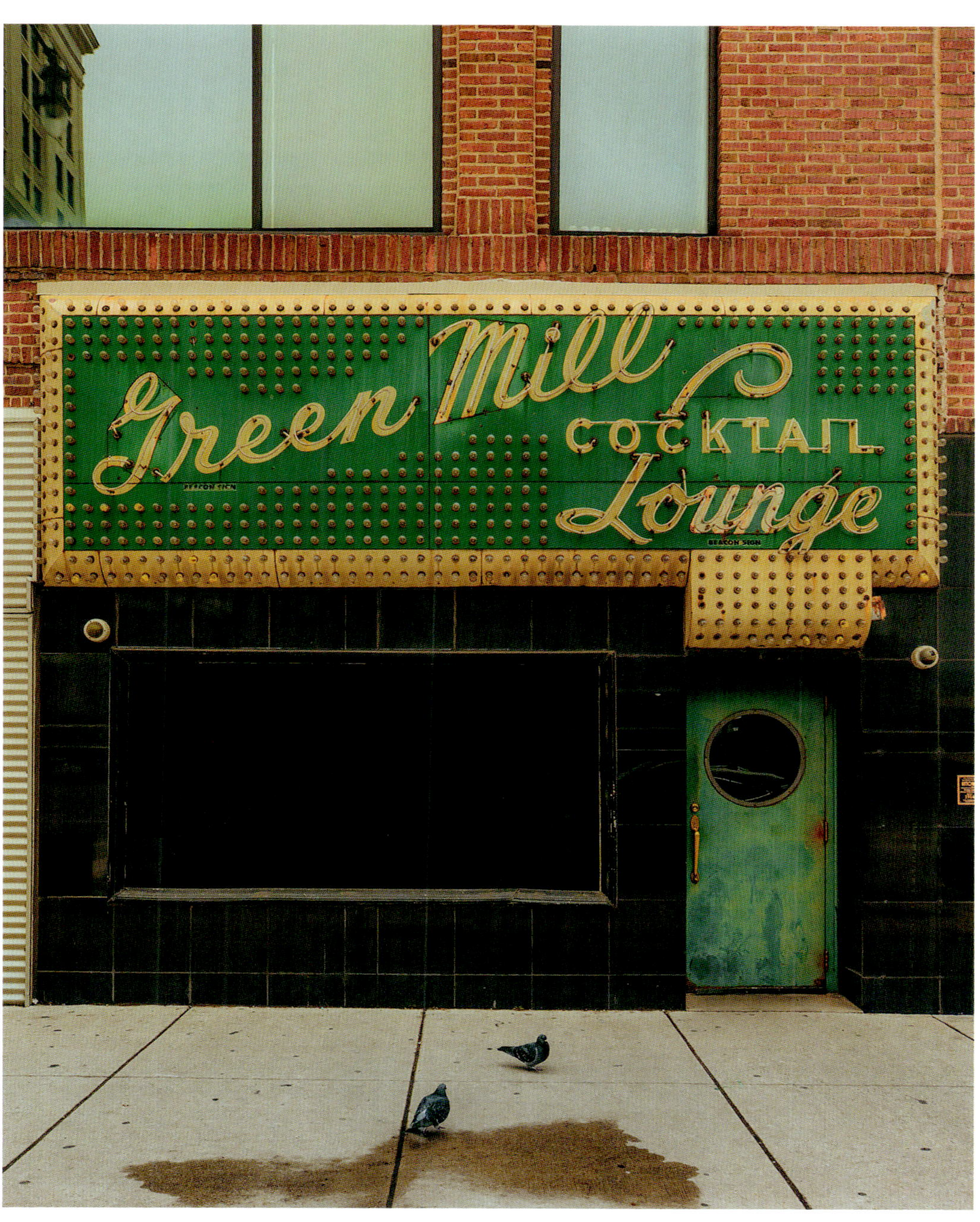

Green Mill Lounge • Chicago, Illinois

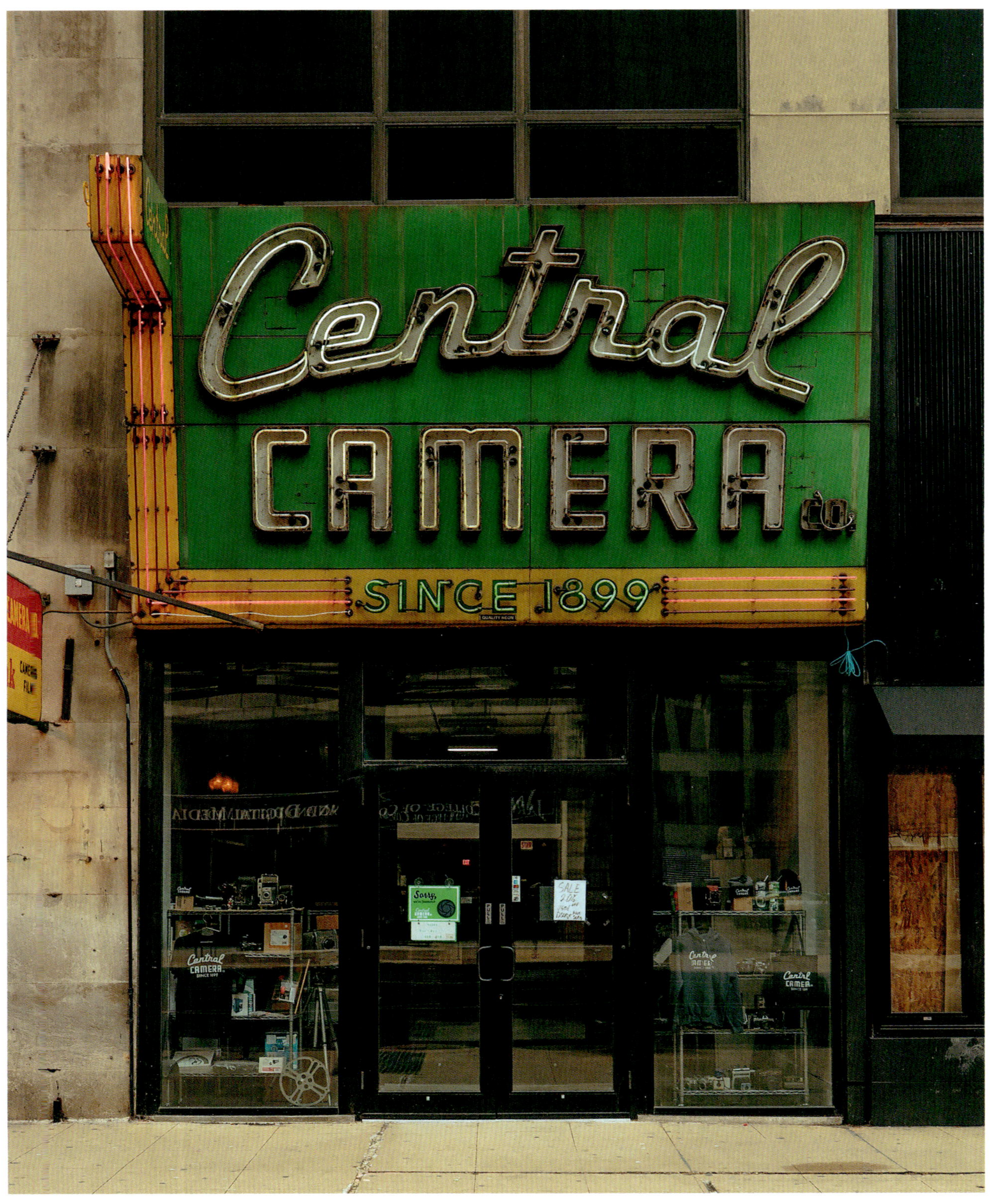

Central Camera • Chicago, Illinois

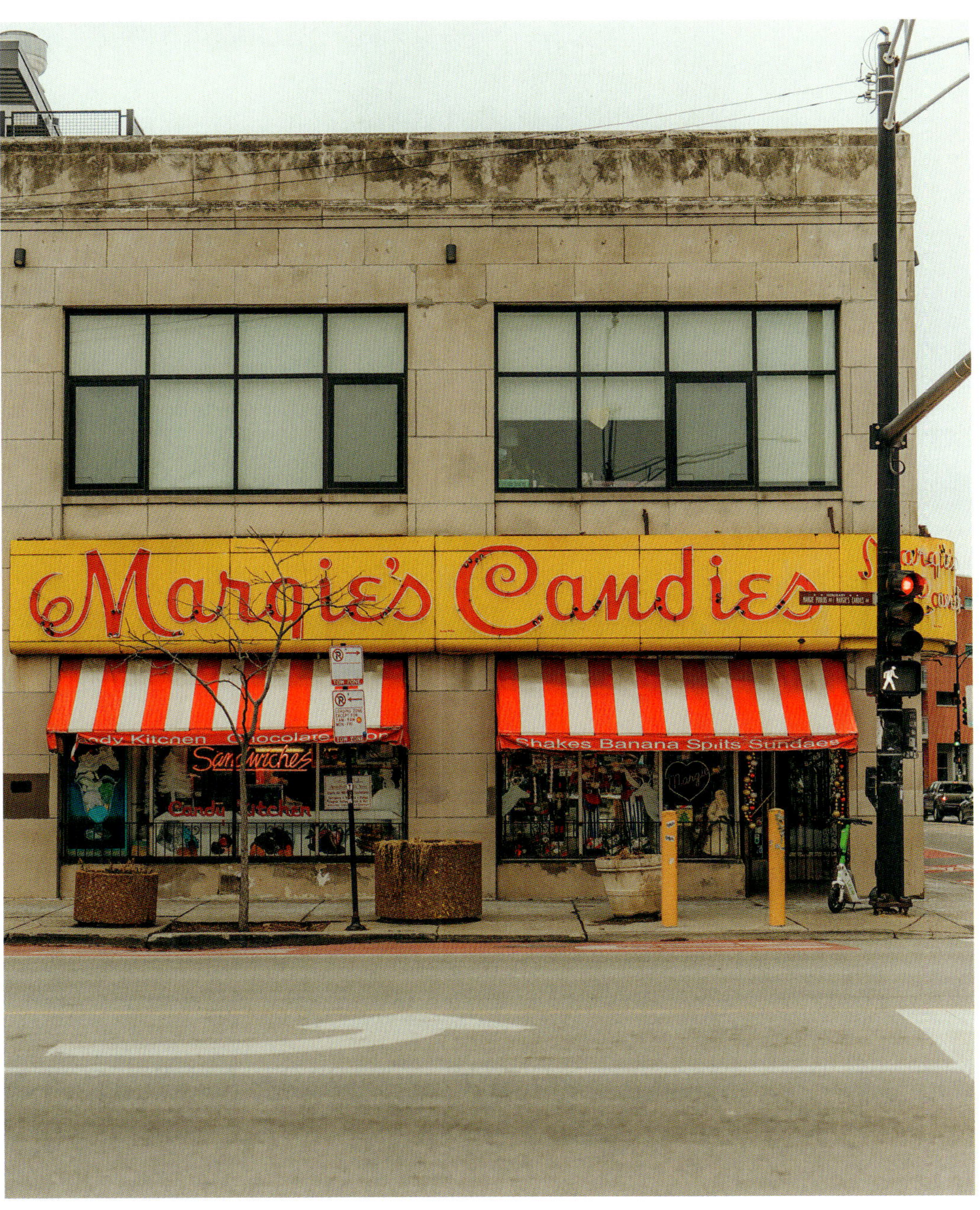

Margie's Candies • Chicago, Illinois

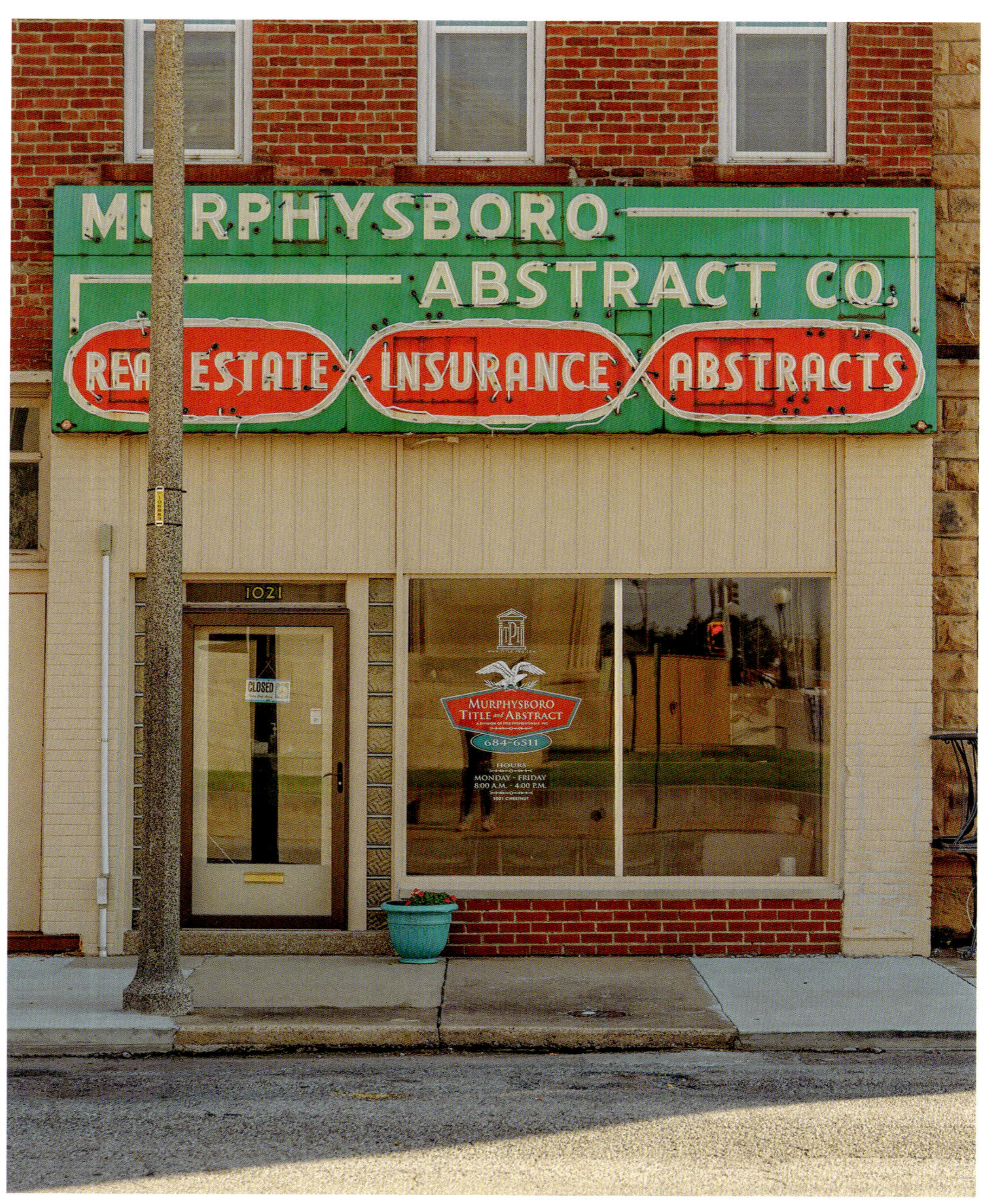

Murphysboro Abstract Co. • Murphysboro, Illinois

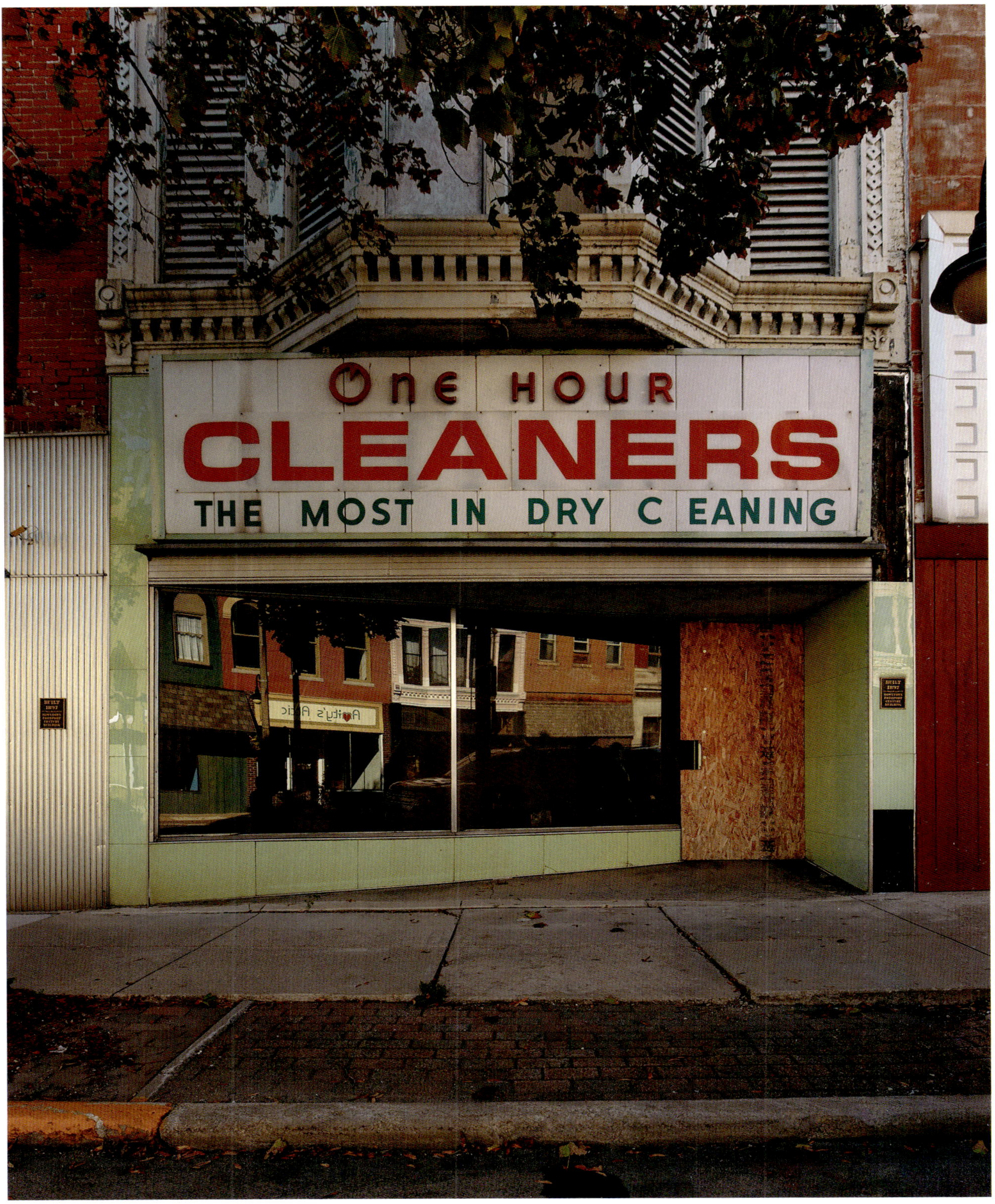

One Hour Cleaners • Freeport, Illinois

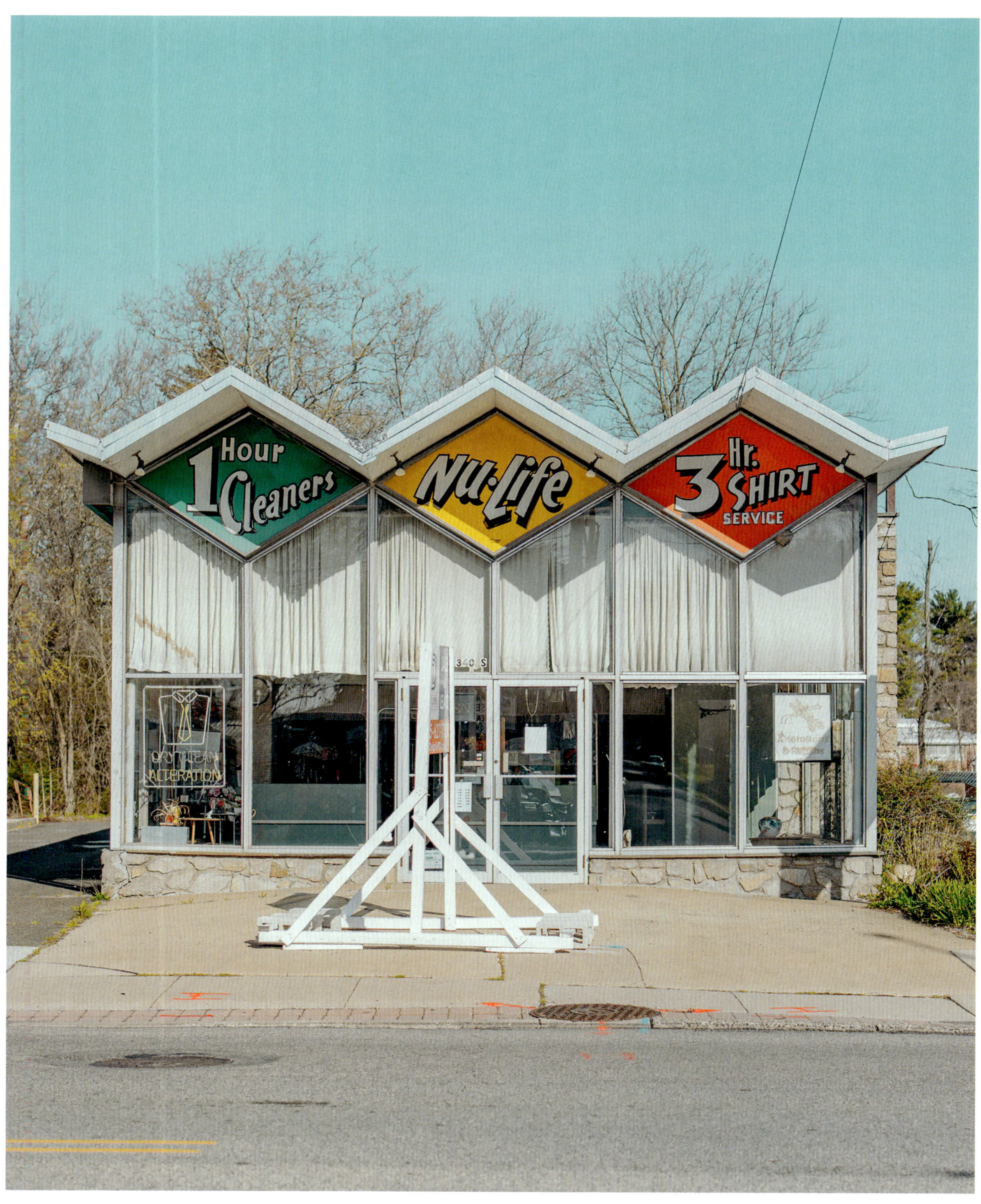

Nu-Life Cleaners • Hatboro, Pennsylvania

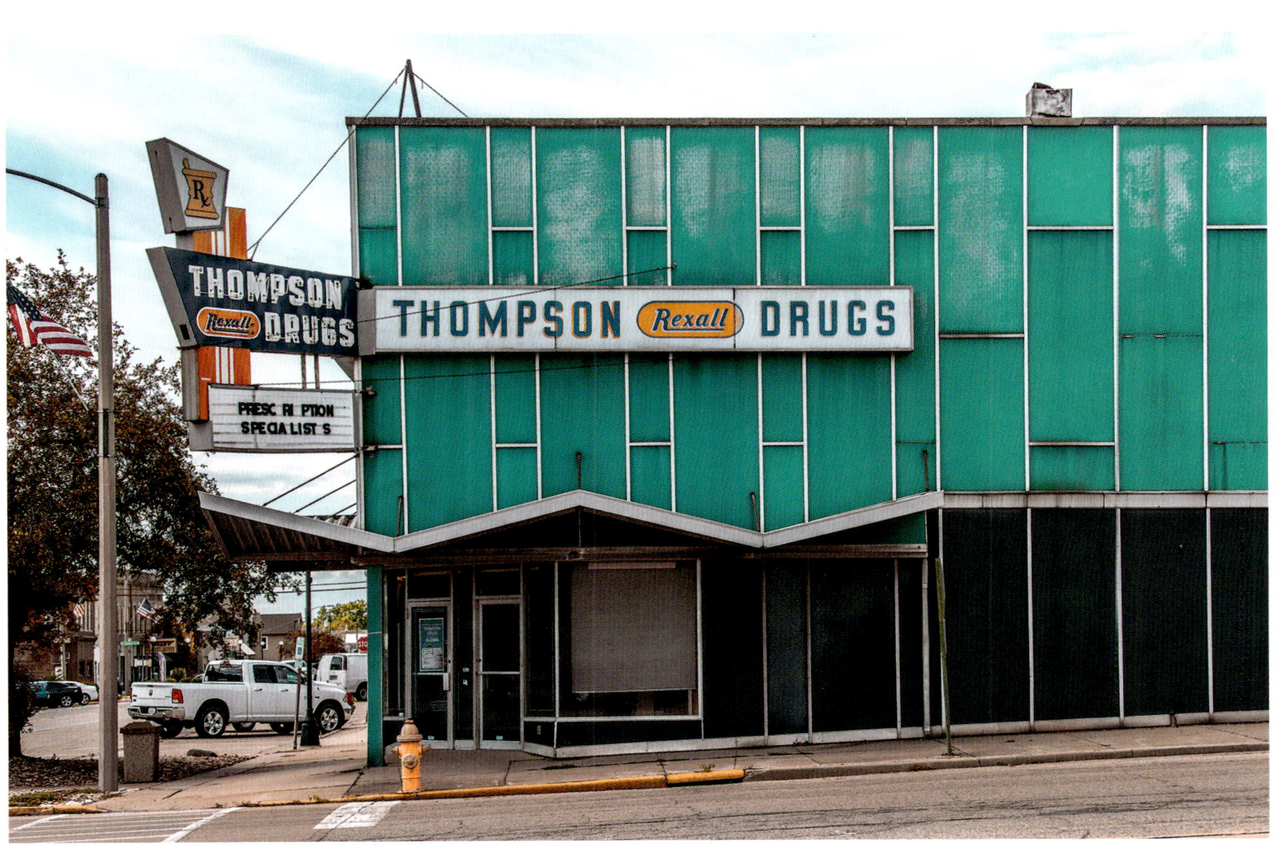

Thompson Rexall Drugs • Spring Valley, Illinois

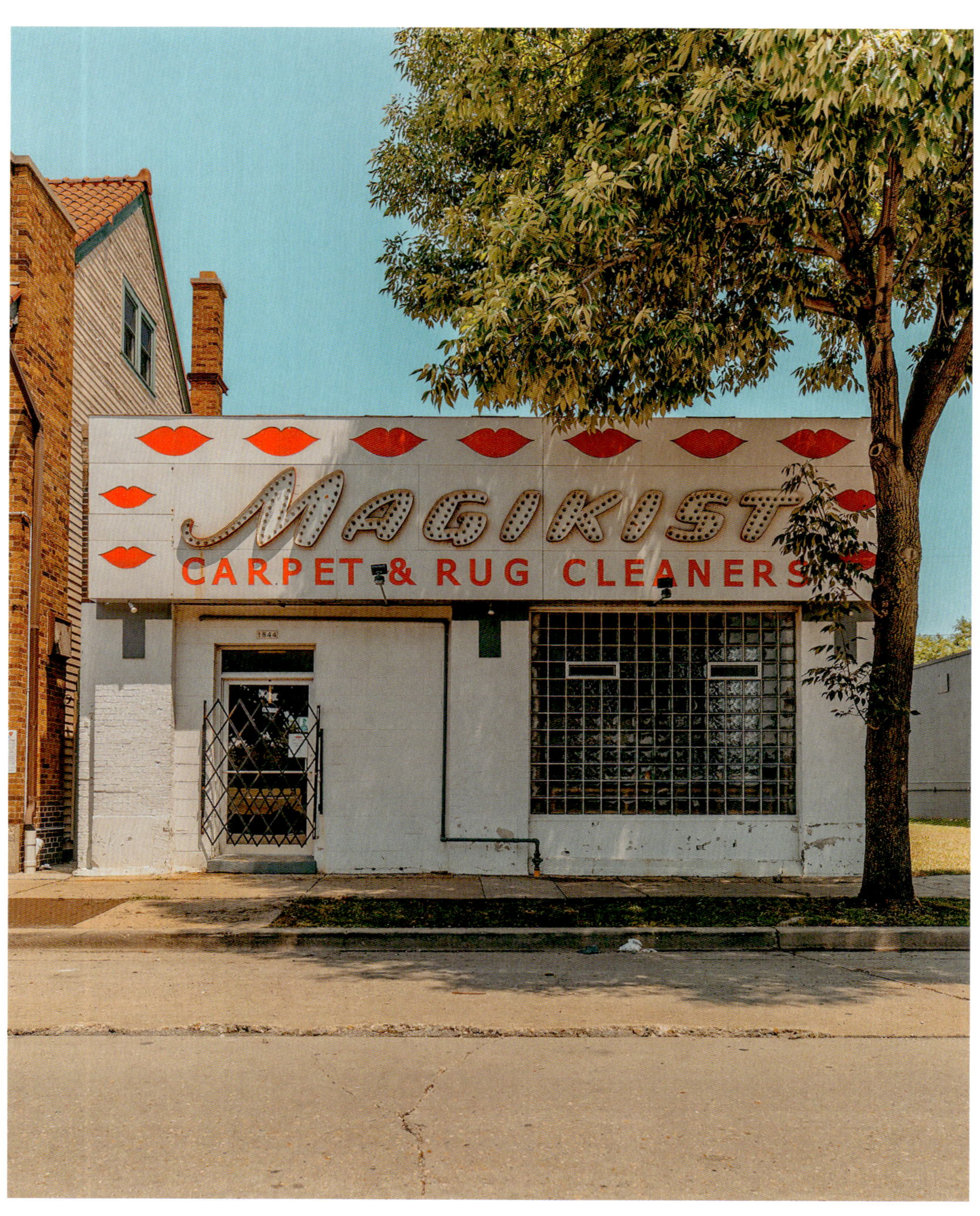

Magikist Cleaners • Milwaukee, Wisconsin

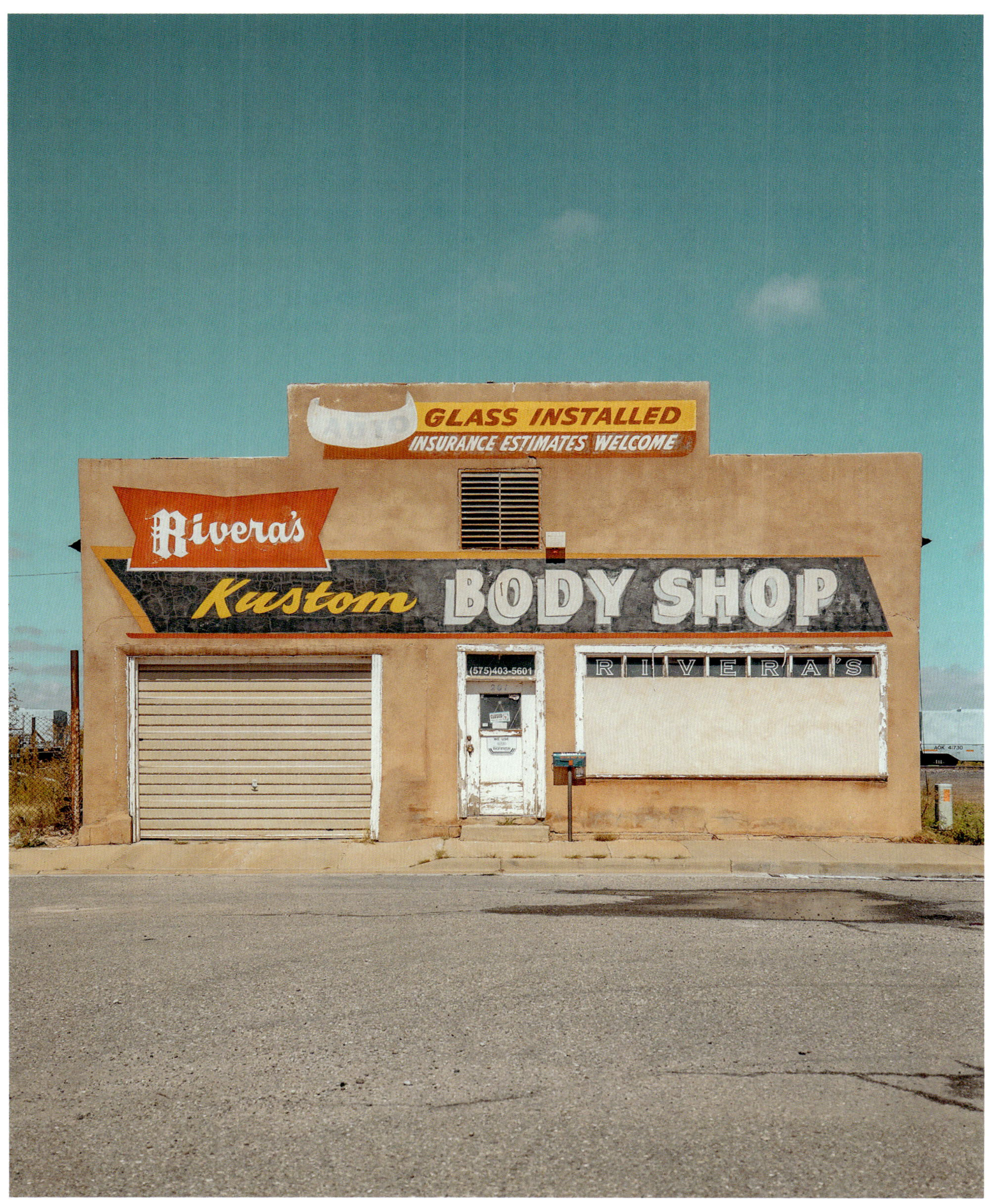

Rivera's Body Shop • Tucumcari, New Mexico

RESTAURANTS

My typical travel itinerary is a bit overwhelming and packed with stops at neon signs, historical sites, architectural landmarks, and abandoned spots, but at the top of my list is always the best restaurants, diners, and bars. Places like Kewpee Hamburgers in Lima, Ohio, Sid's Diner in El Reno, Oklahoma, and Working Man's Friend in Indianapolis, are perfect examples of how food and iconic signage tell a story of American heritage. You can't beat the signage at places like these. The Googie style, characterized by futuristic shapes and bold typography, became synonymous with mid-century American restaurants. The style's atomic motifs, sharp angles, and neon glow draws attention to all these diners, drive-ins, and restaurants. They're more than just landmarks—they are symbols of the era's fascination with space age and modernist design. It's not just about the kitsch at these restaurants for me. A fried onion burger, also known as the Depression Burger, from Sid's Diner is probably the greatest burger you'll ever have, and it's because they've been doing it since the Great Depression. These spots are about much more than a meal; they're a way to connect with the past—whether it's through the iconic neon signs, the architecture, or the rich culinary traditions. These places are treasures, preserving a piece of the American landscape and its food culture for future generations to appreciate.

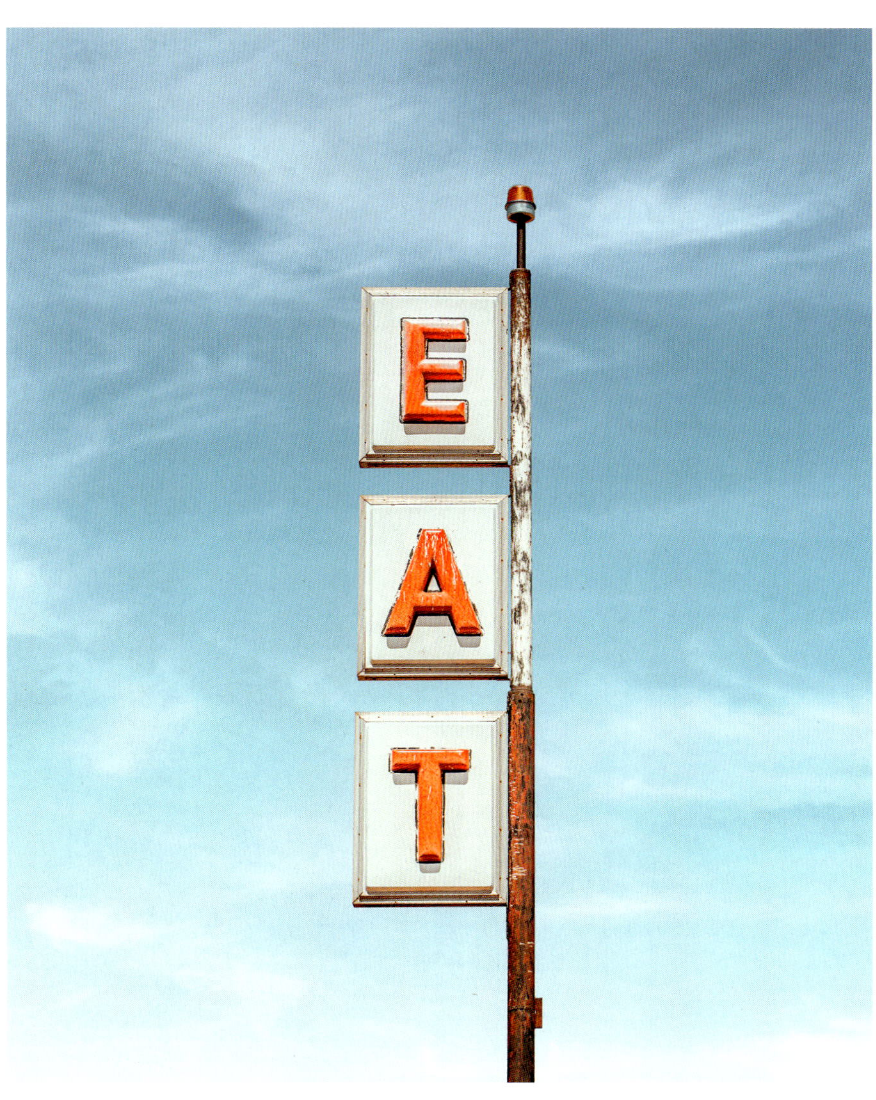

Abandoned Restaurant Sign • San Jon, New Mexico

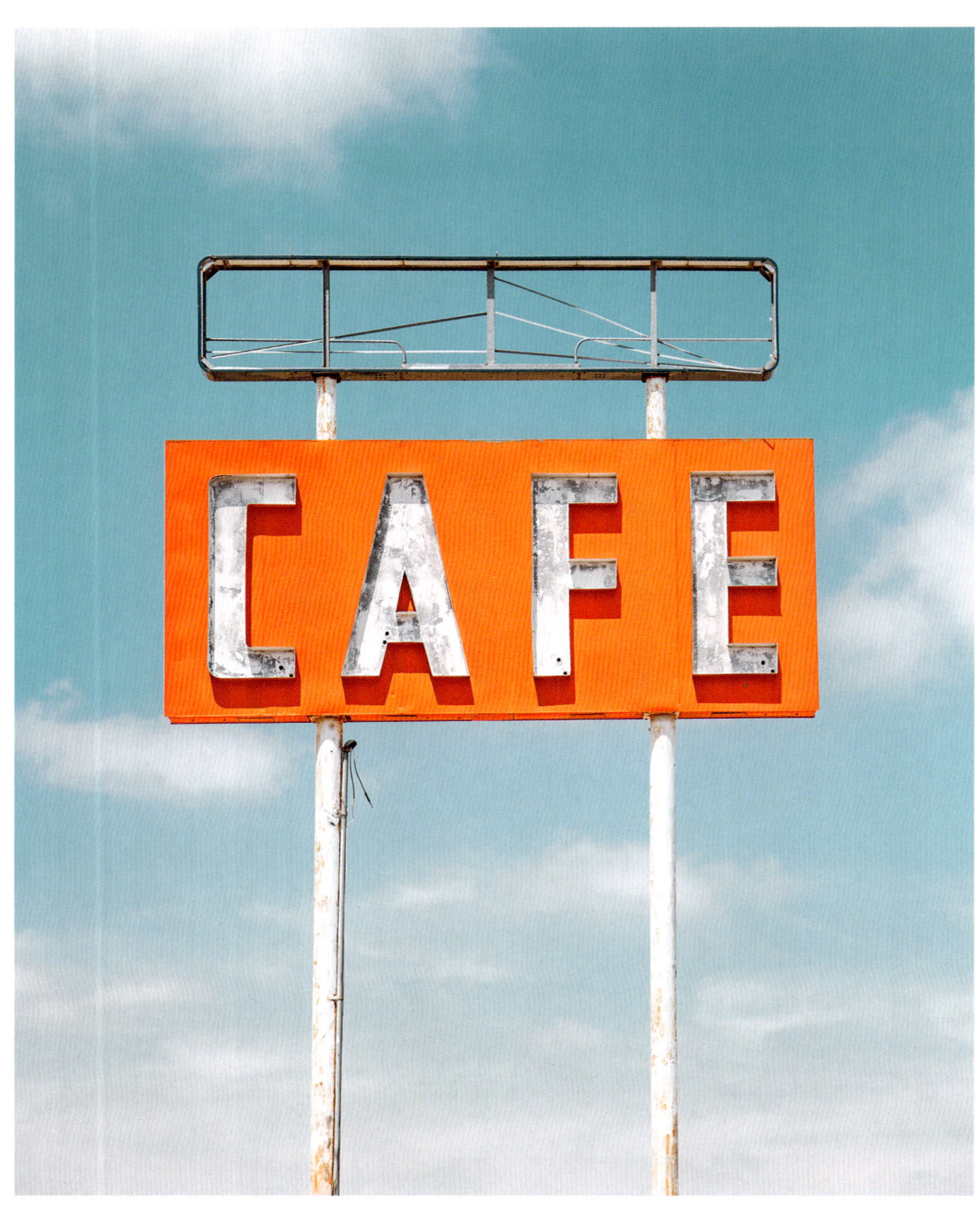

Abandoned Cafe Sign • Adrian, Texas

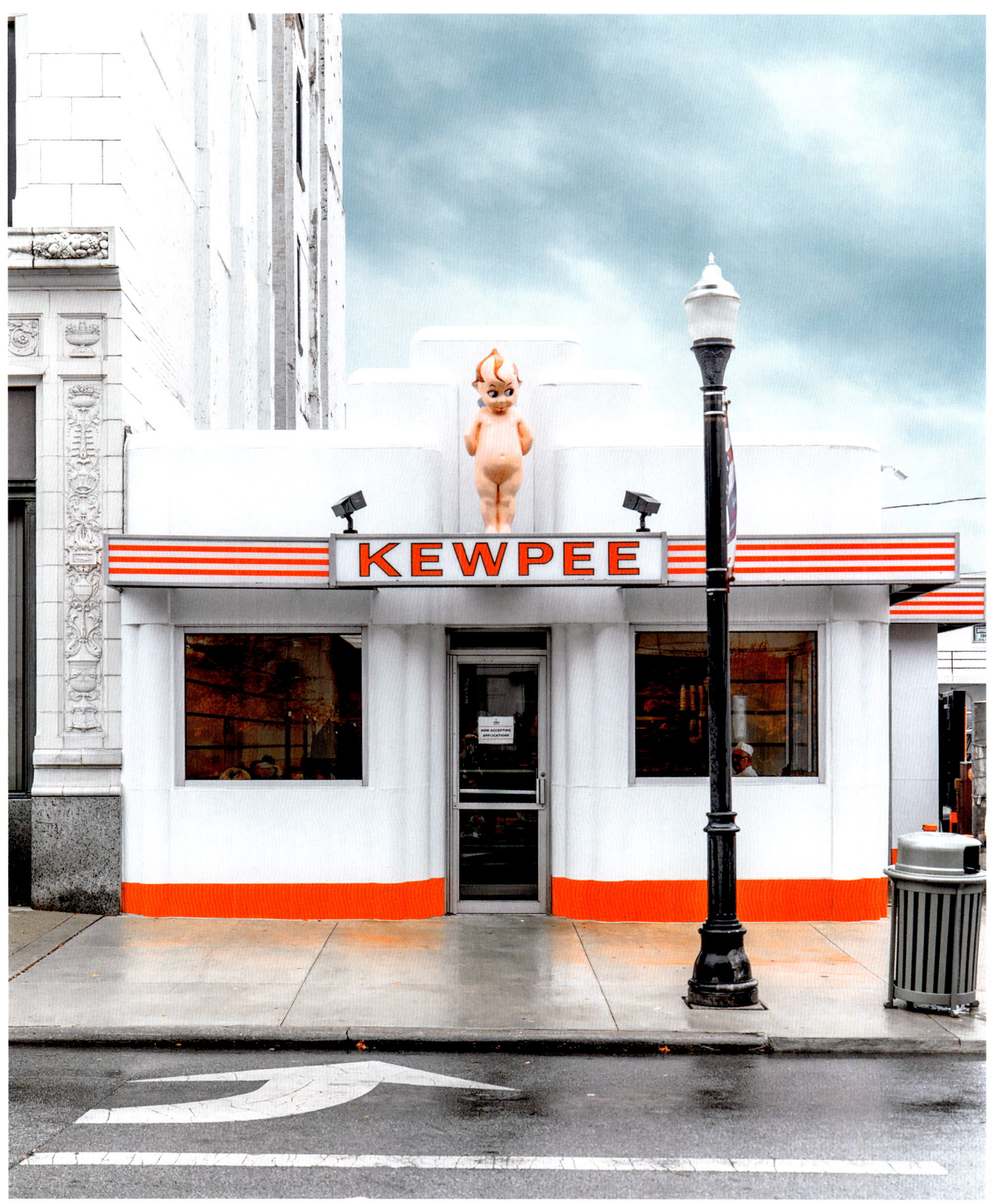

Kewpee Hamburgers • Lima, Ohio

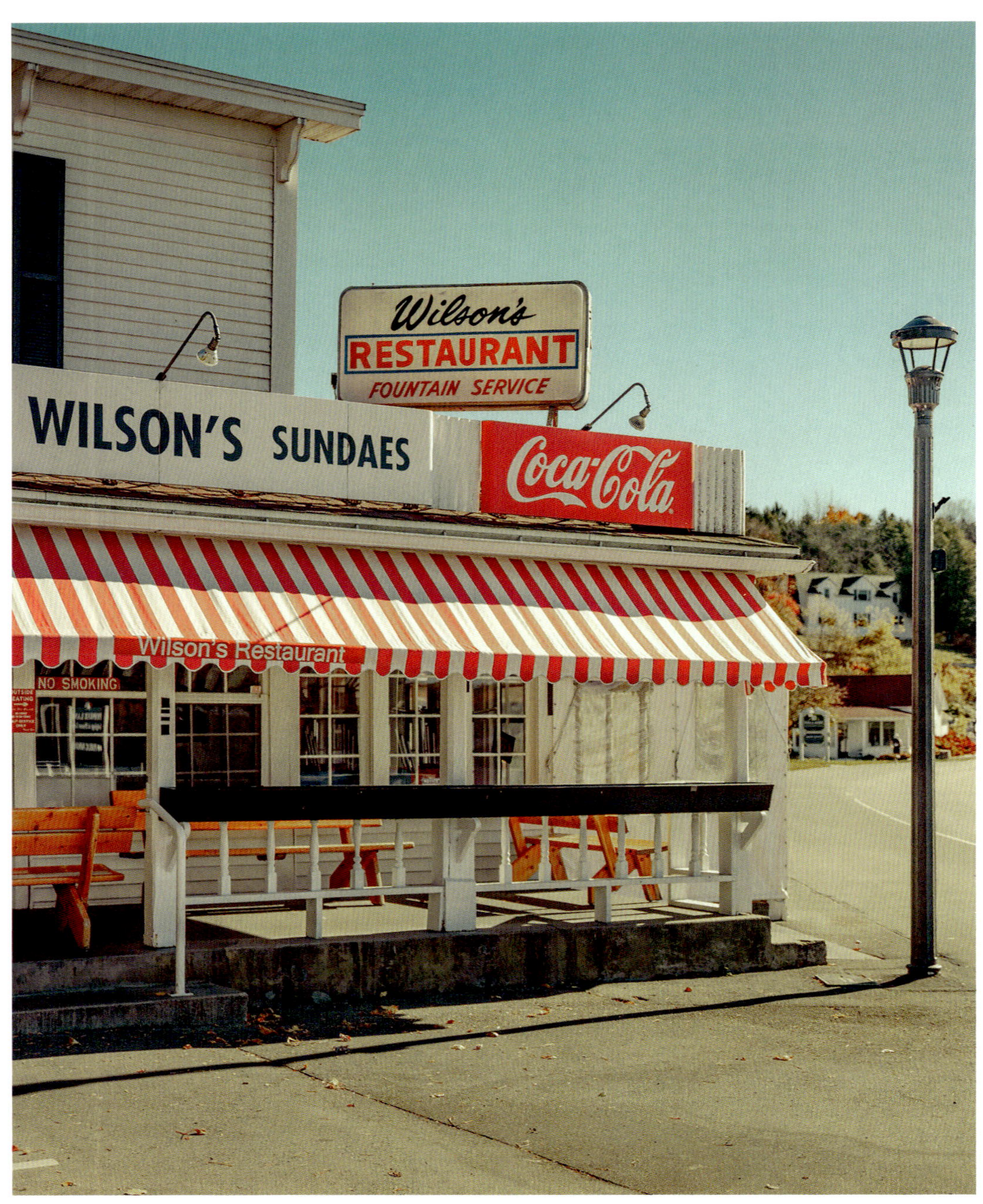

Wilson's Restaurant • Ephraim, Wisconsin

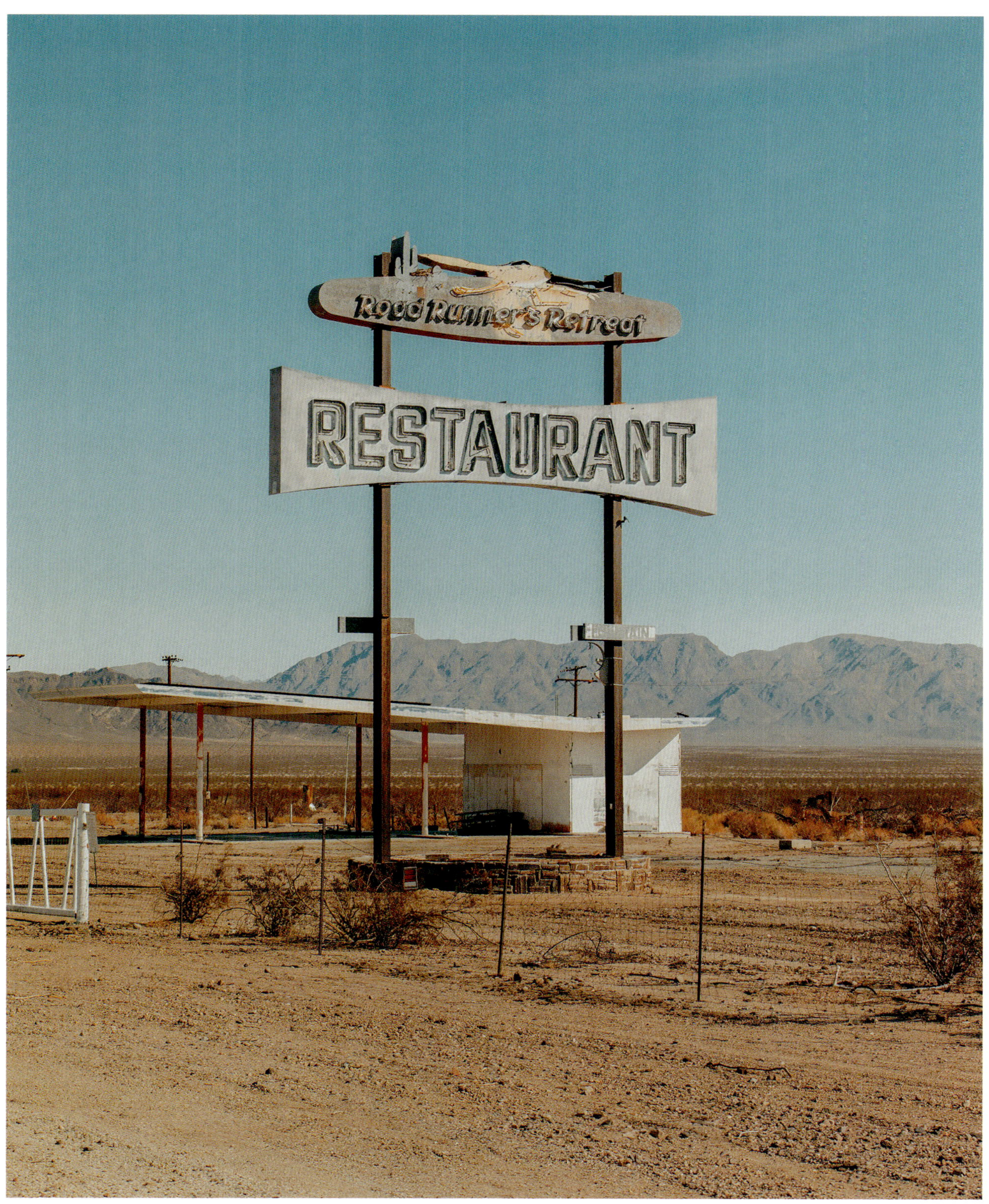

Road Runner's Retreat • Amboy, California

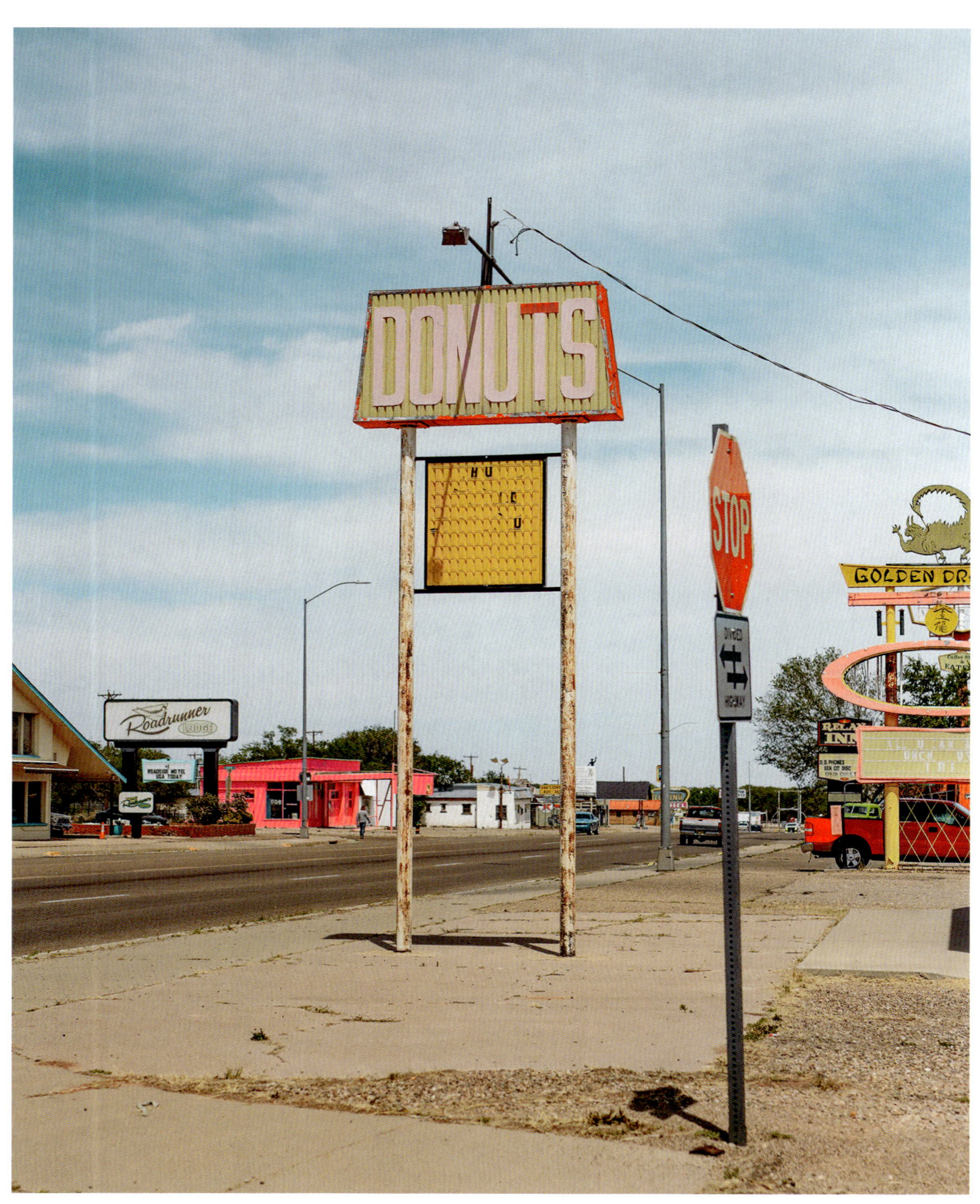

Abandoned Donut Shop Sign • Tucumcari, New Mexico

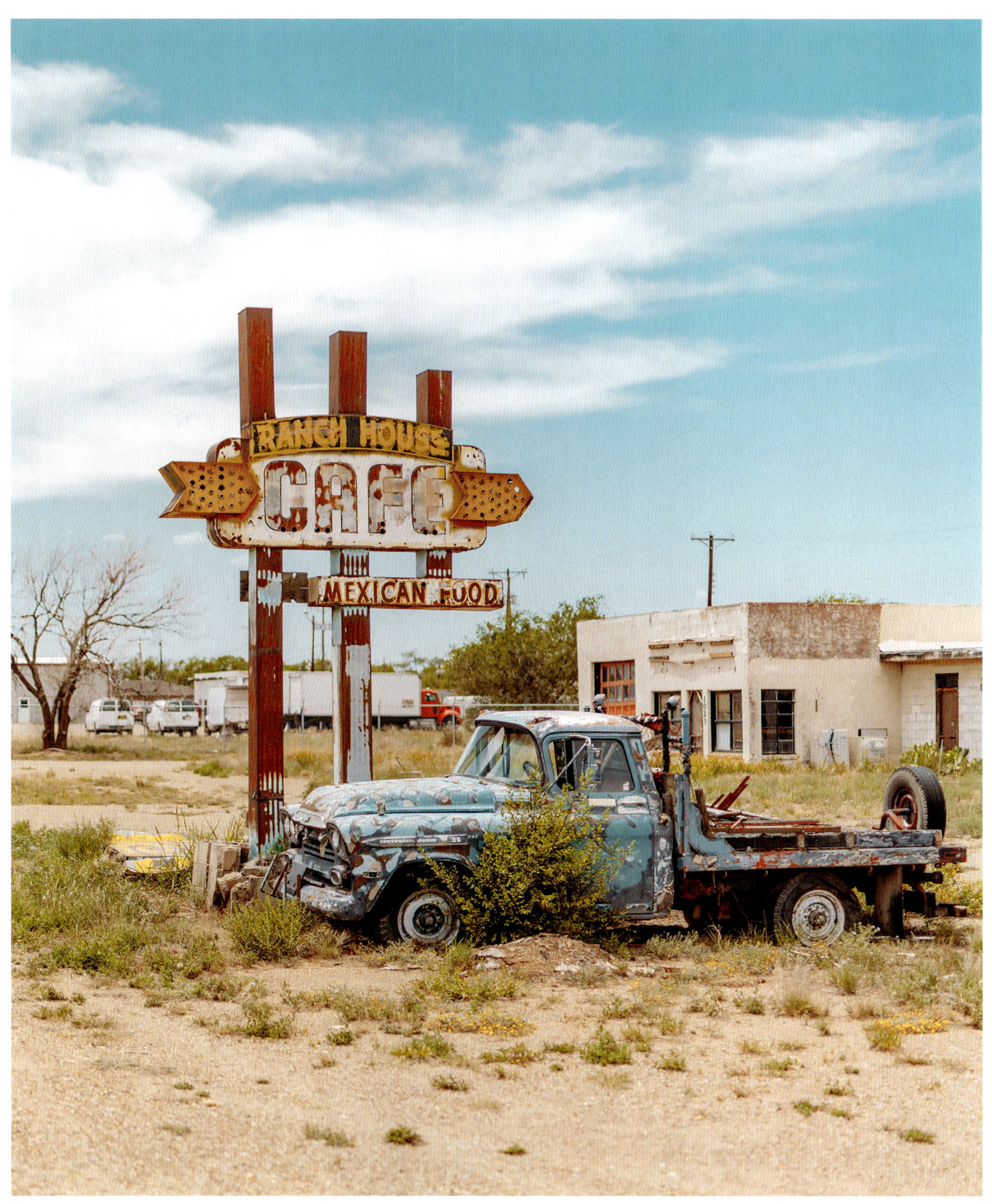

Abandoned Ranch House Cafe Sign • Tucumcari, New Mexico

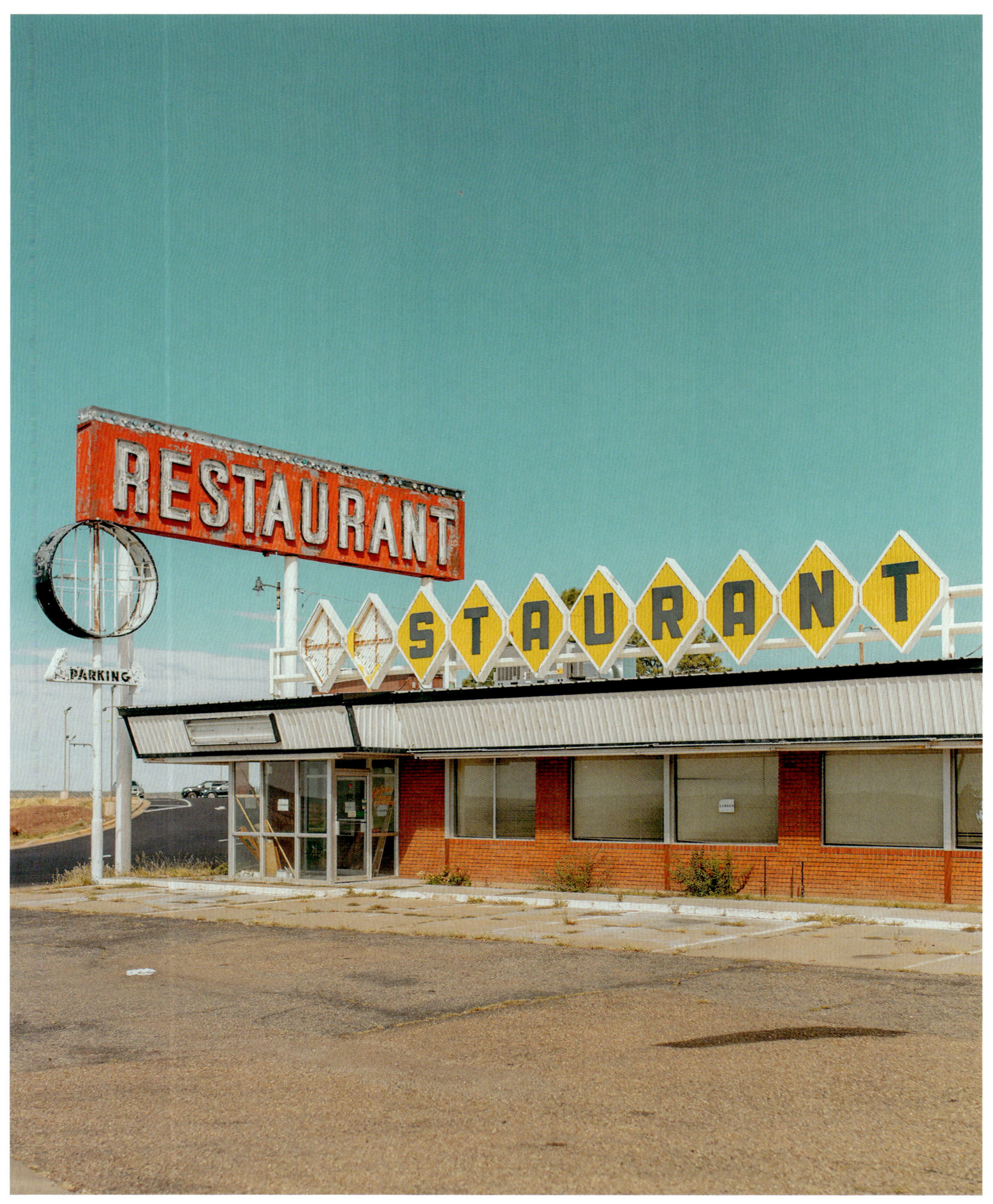

Abandoned Restaurant • Santa Rosa, New Mexico

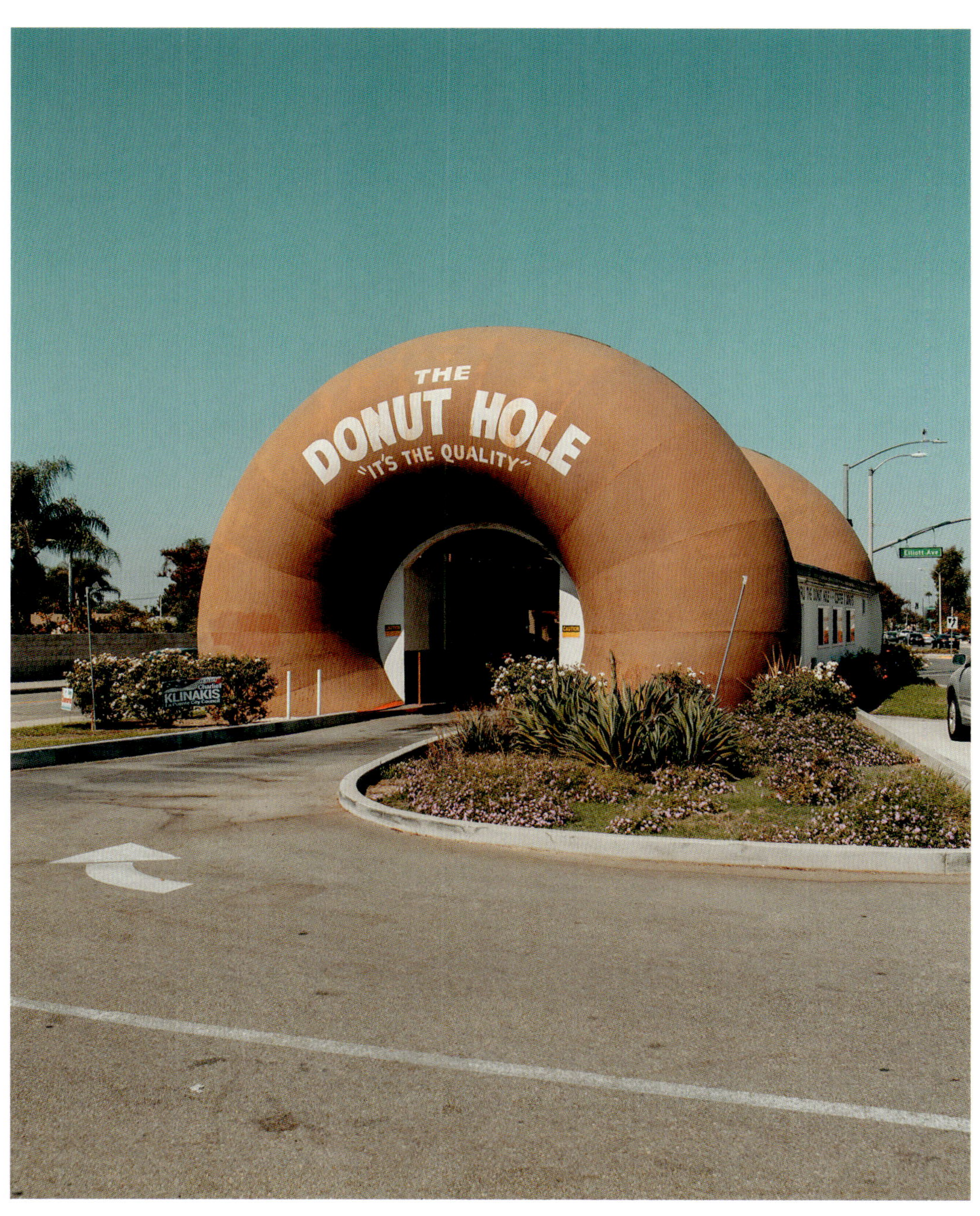

The Donut Hole • La Puente, California

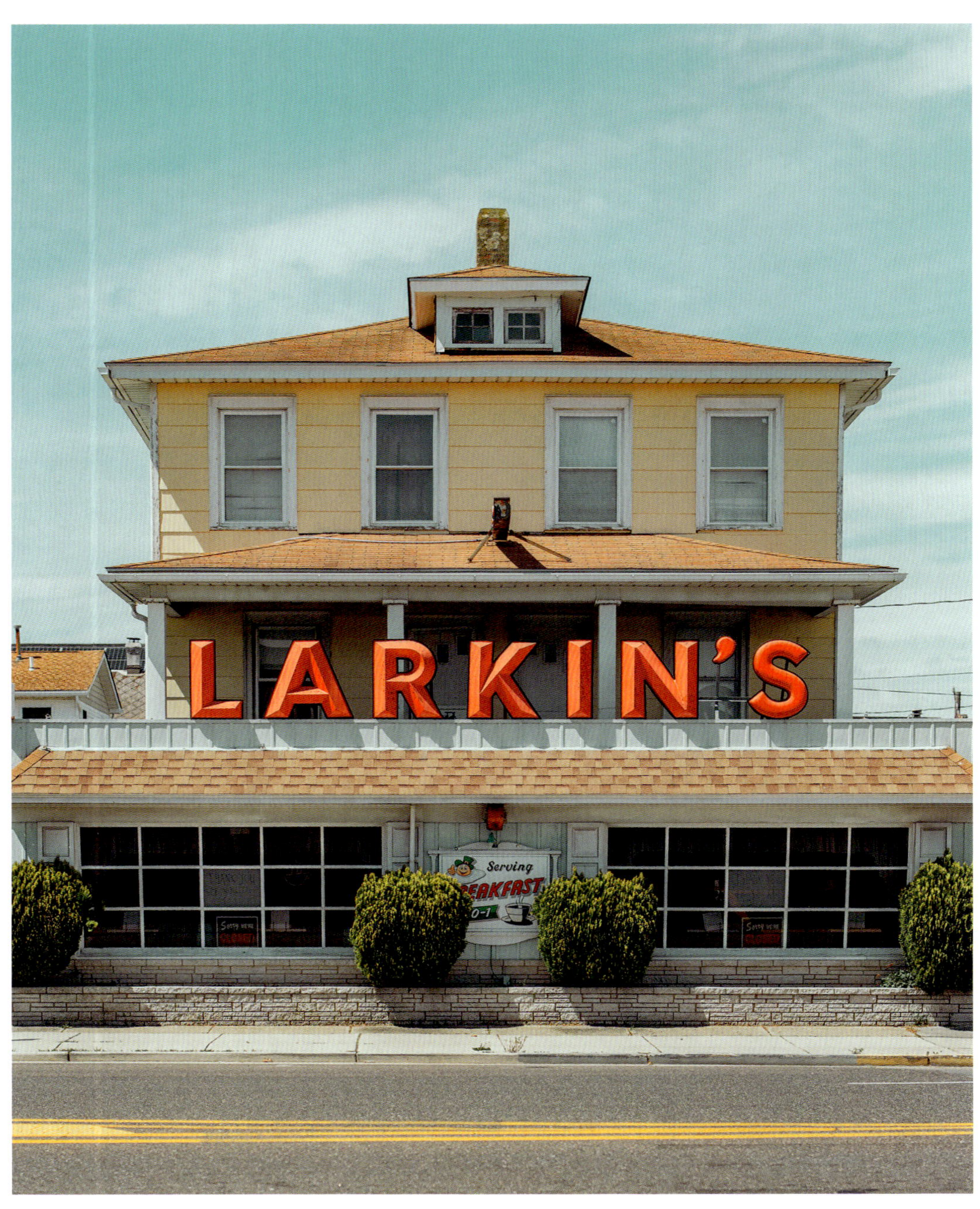

Larkin's Restaurant • North Wildwood, New Jersey

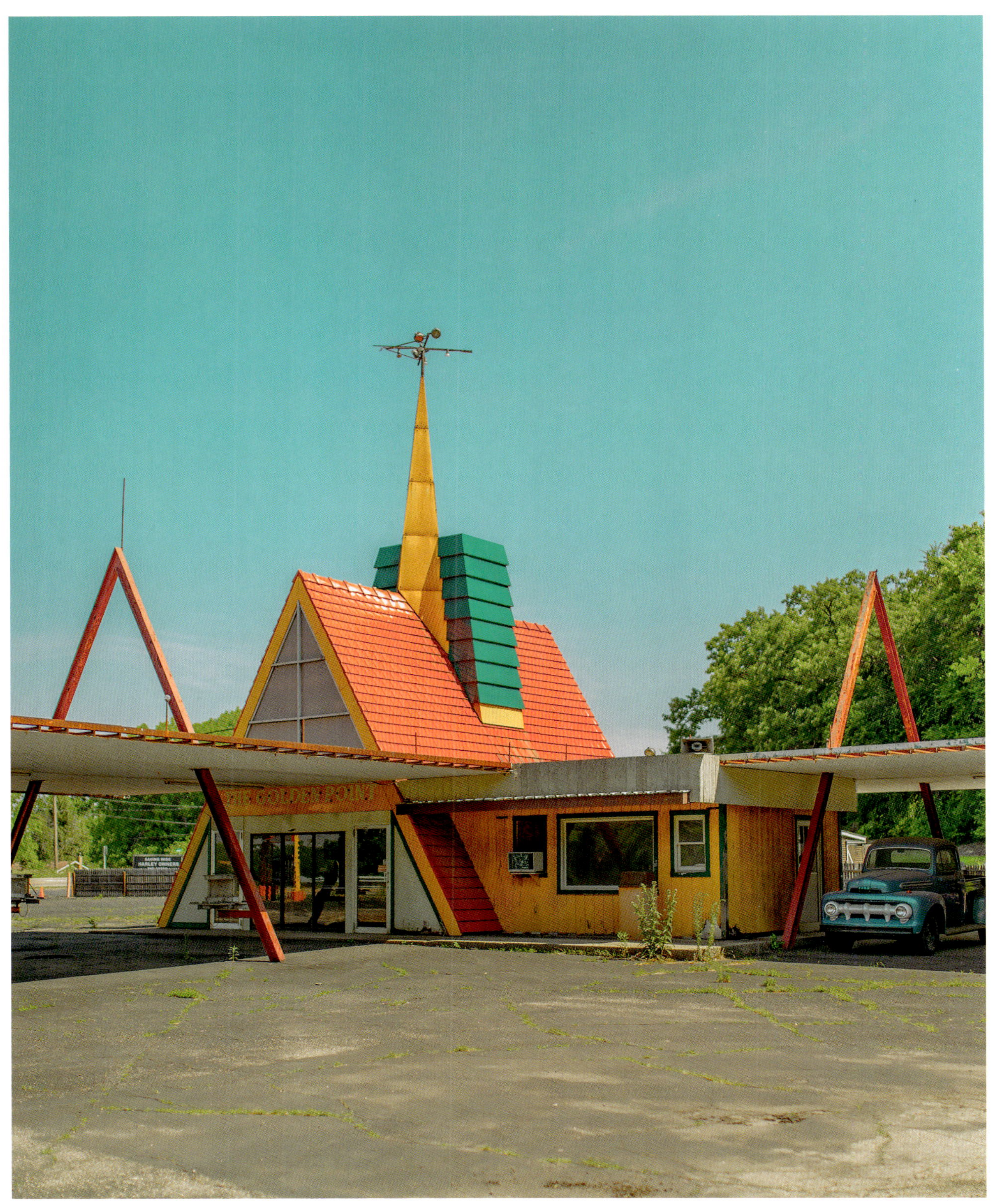

The Golden Point • Beloit, Wisconsin

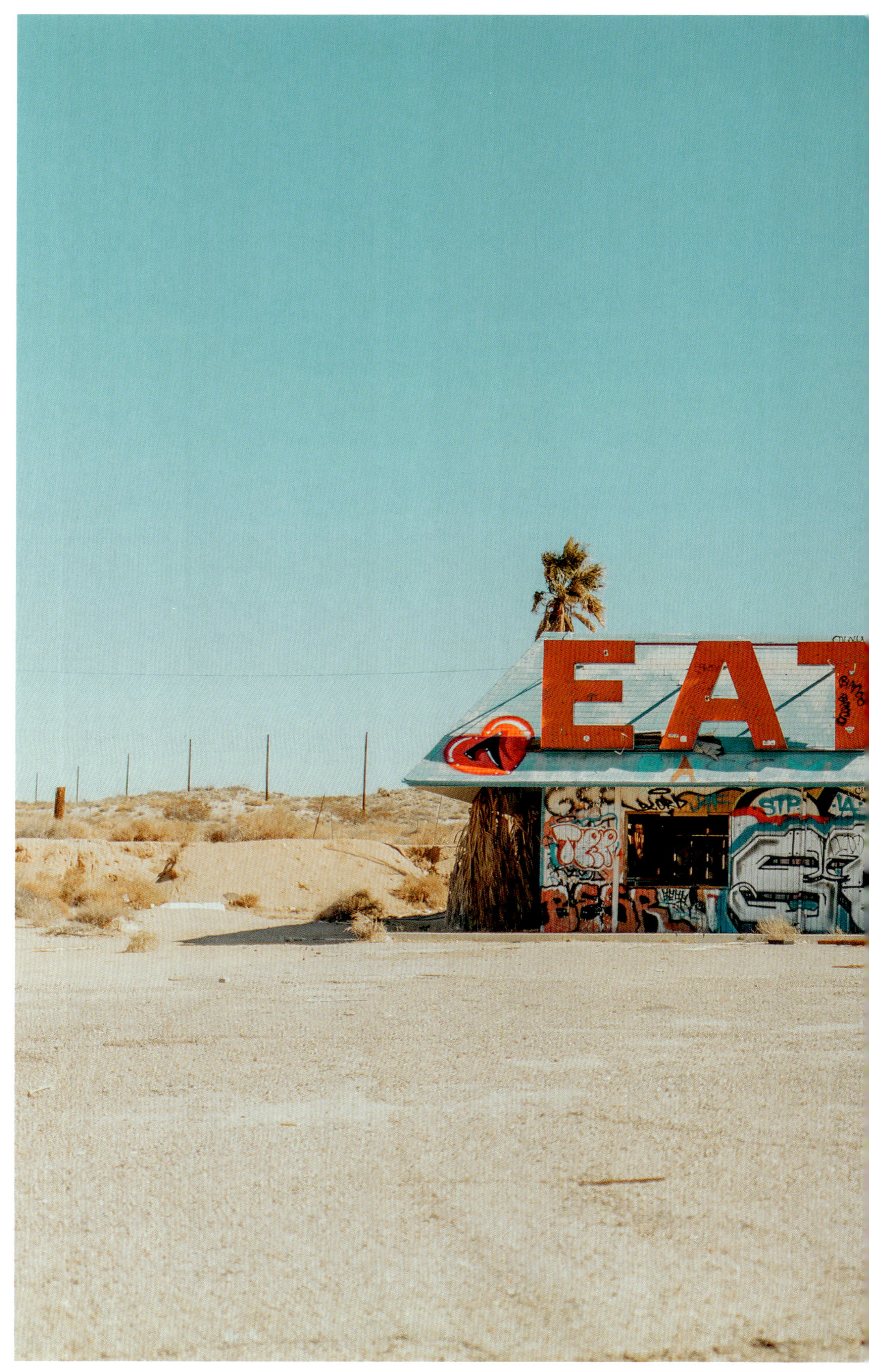

Abandoned Roadside Diner
Halloran Springs, California

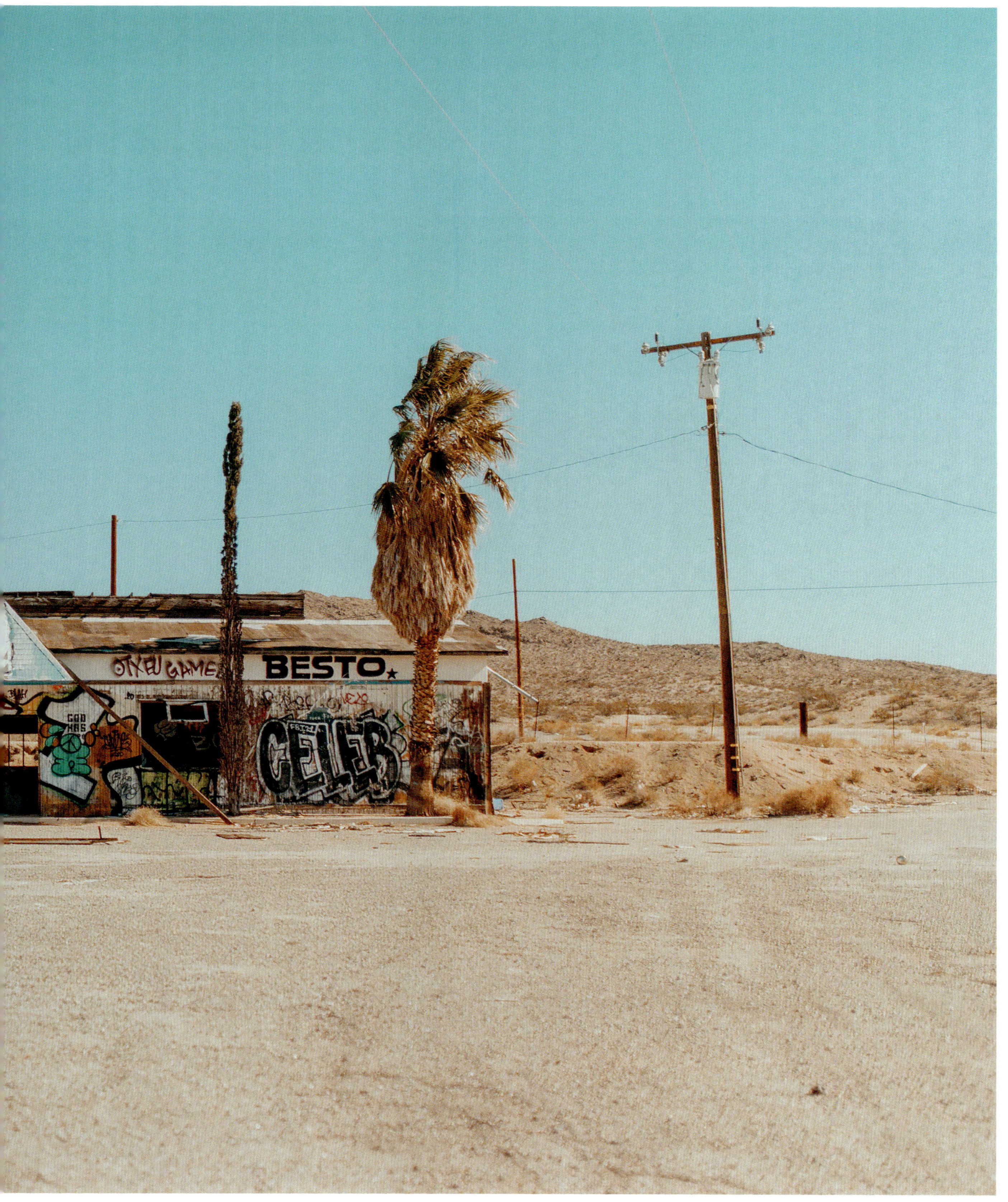
BESTO

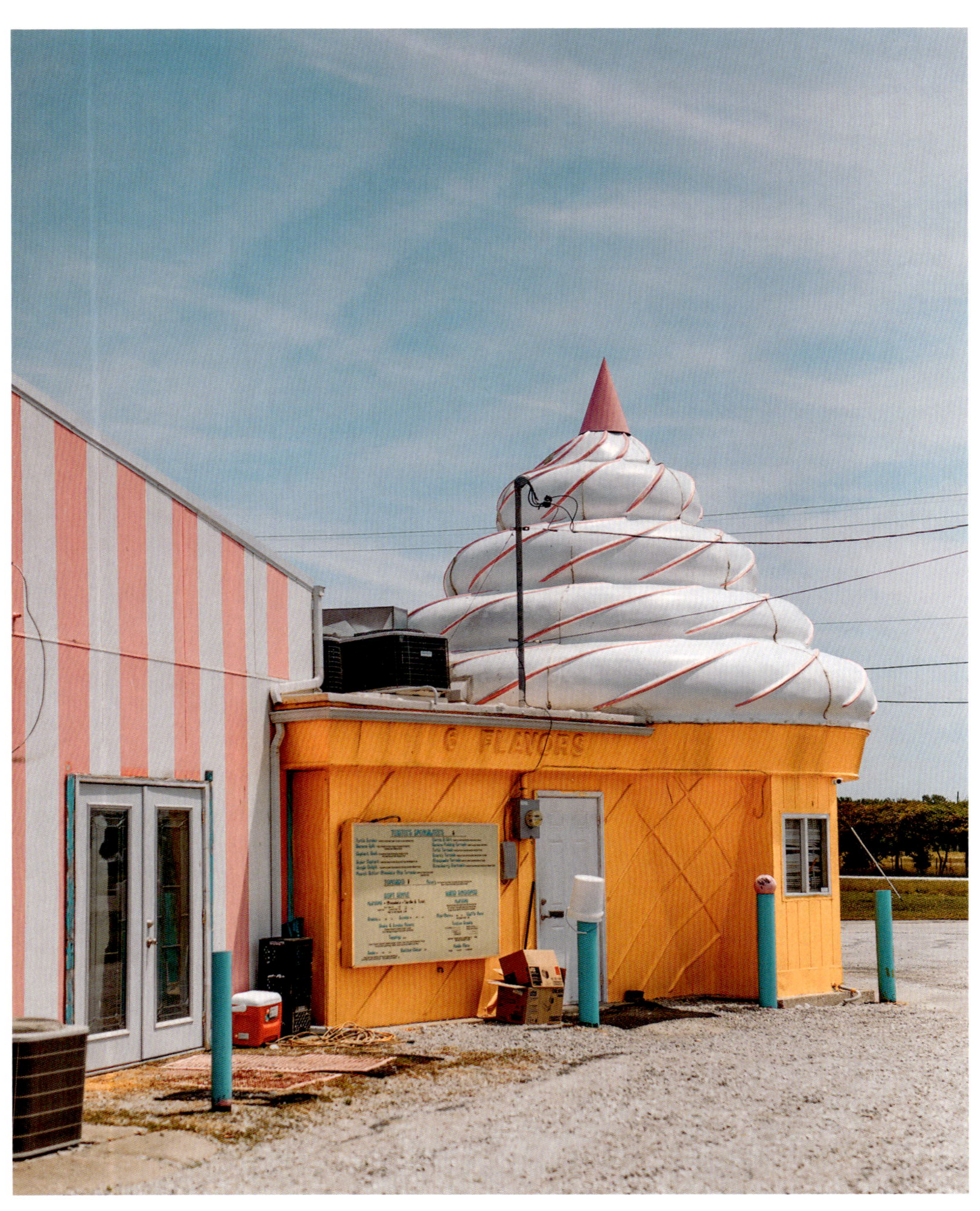

Twistee Treat Diner • Livingston, Illinois

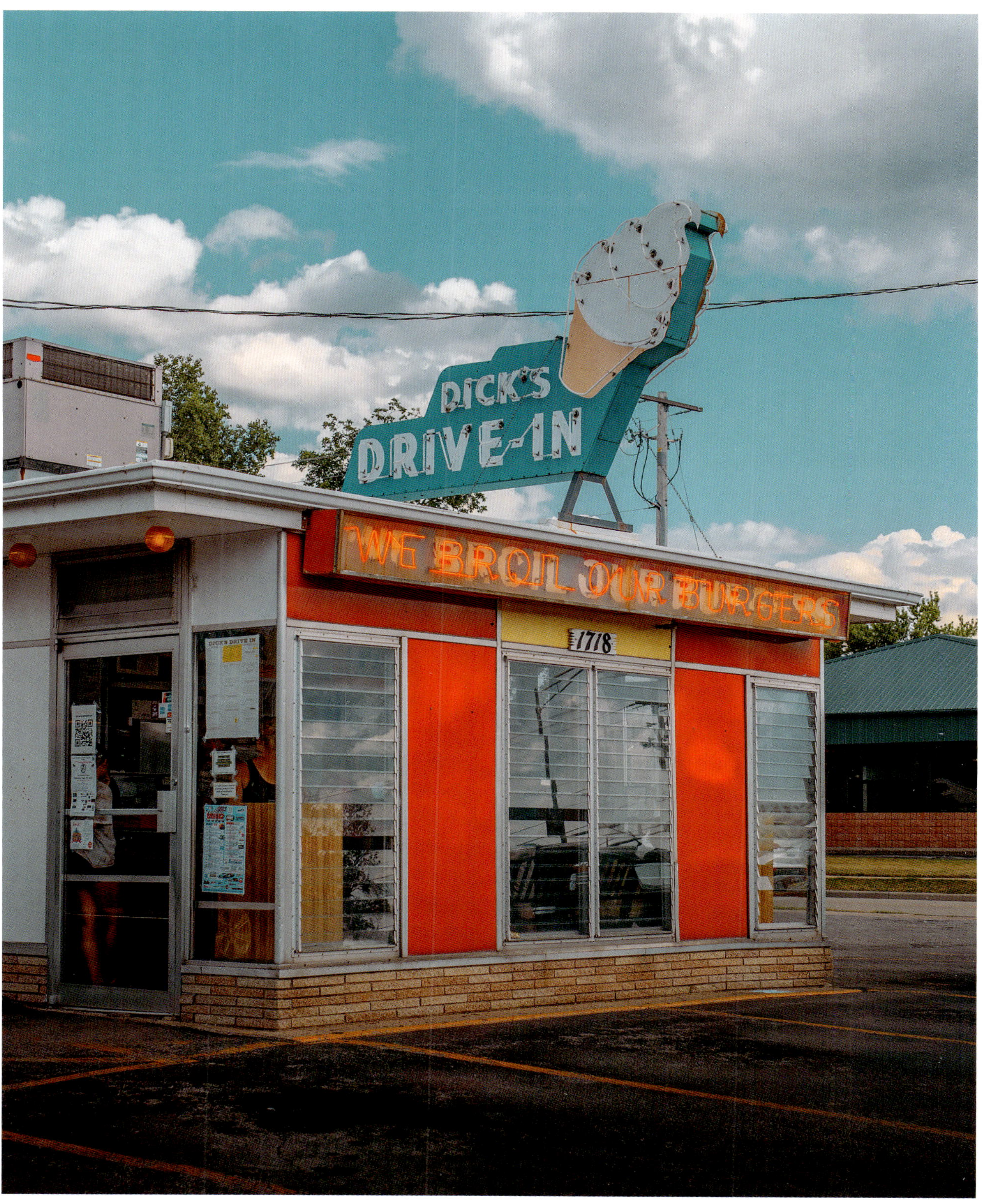

Dick's Drive-In • Kaukauna, Wisconsin

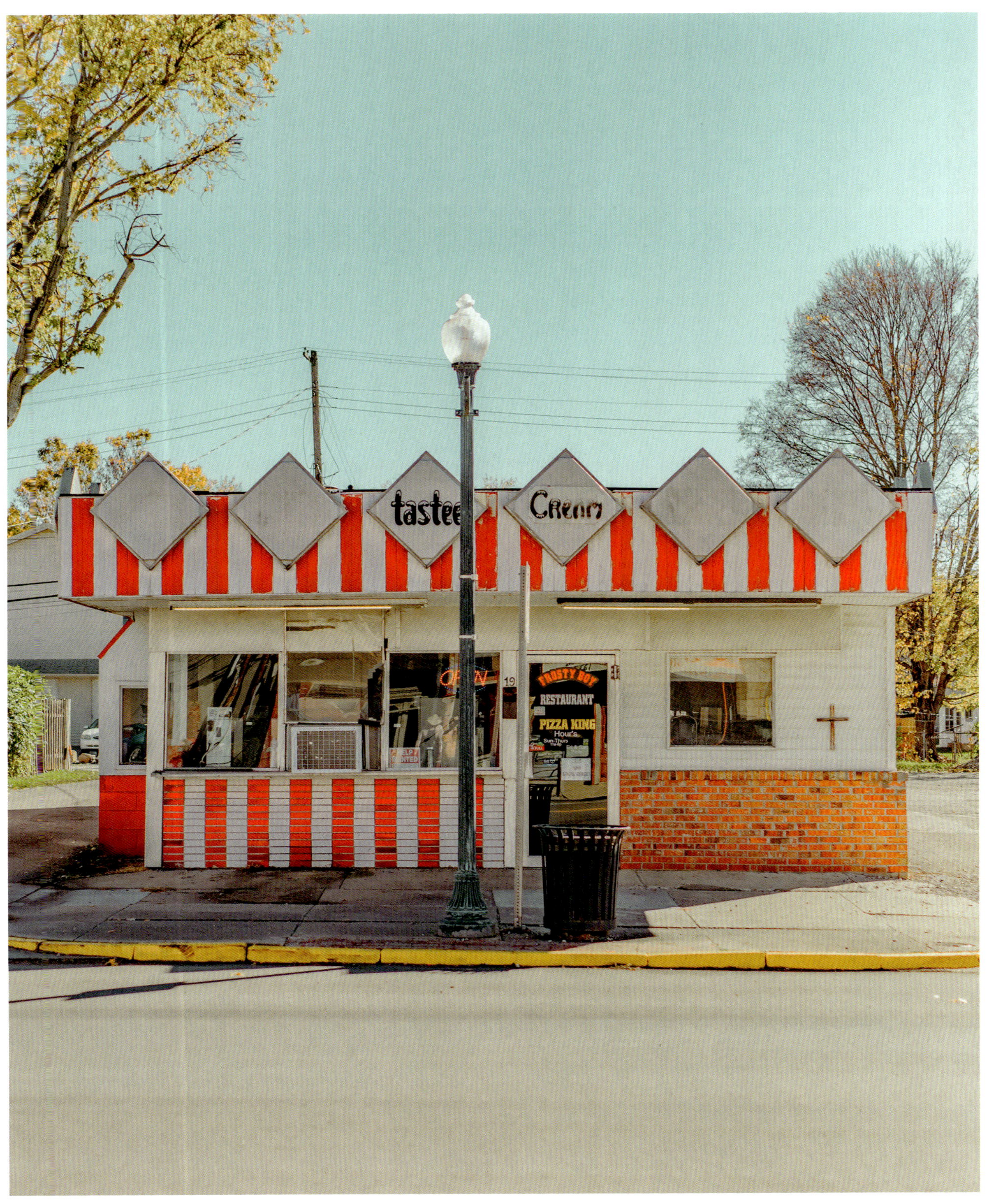

Frosty Boy Restaurant • Knightstown, Indiana

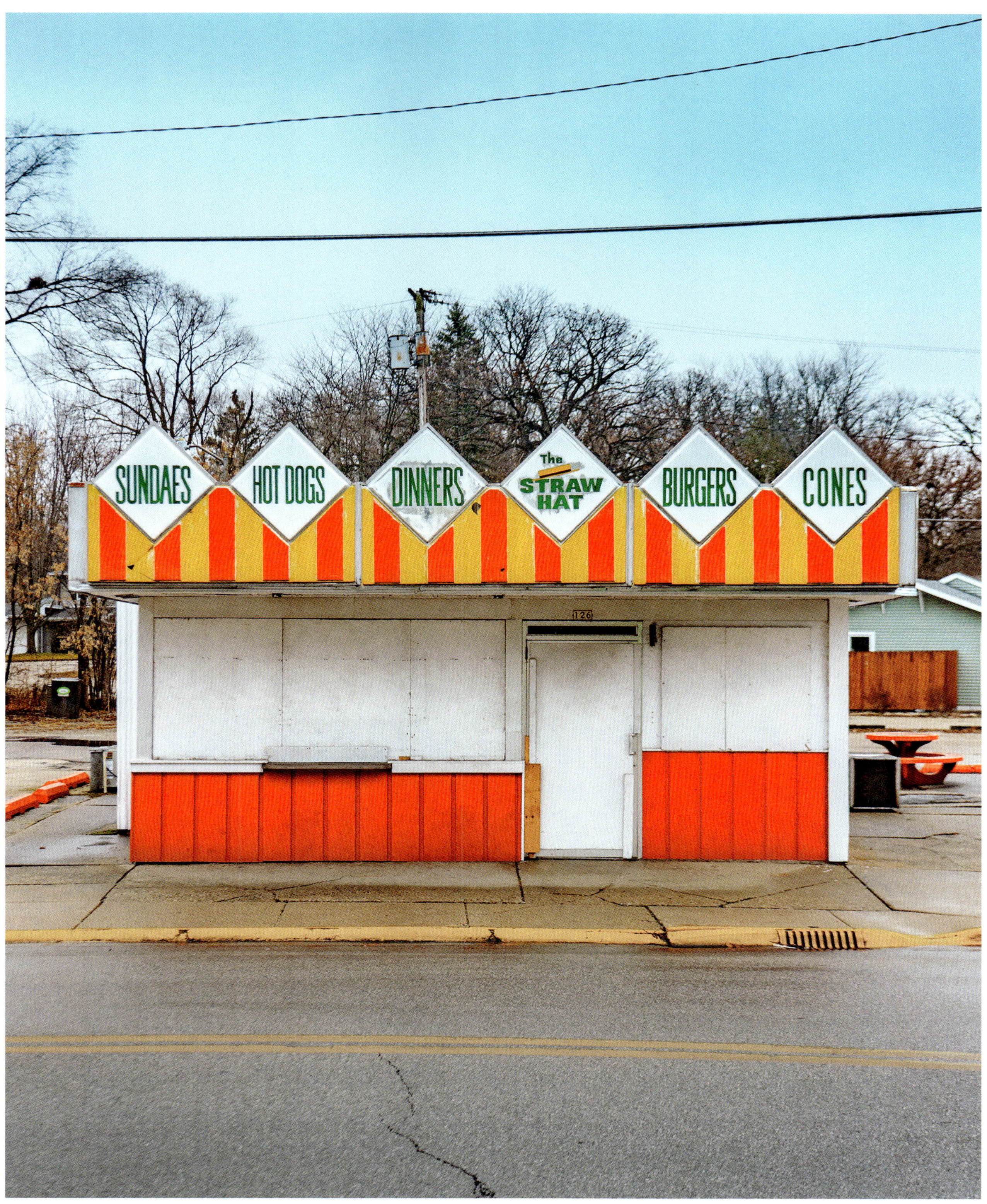

Tom's Straw Hat • Twin Lakes, Wisconsin

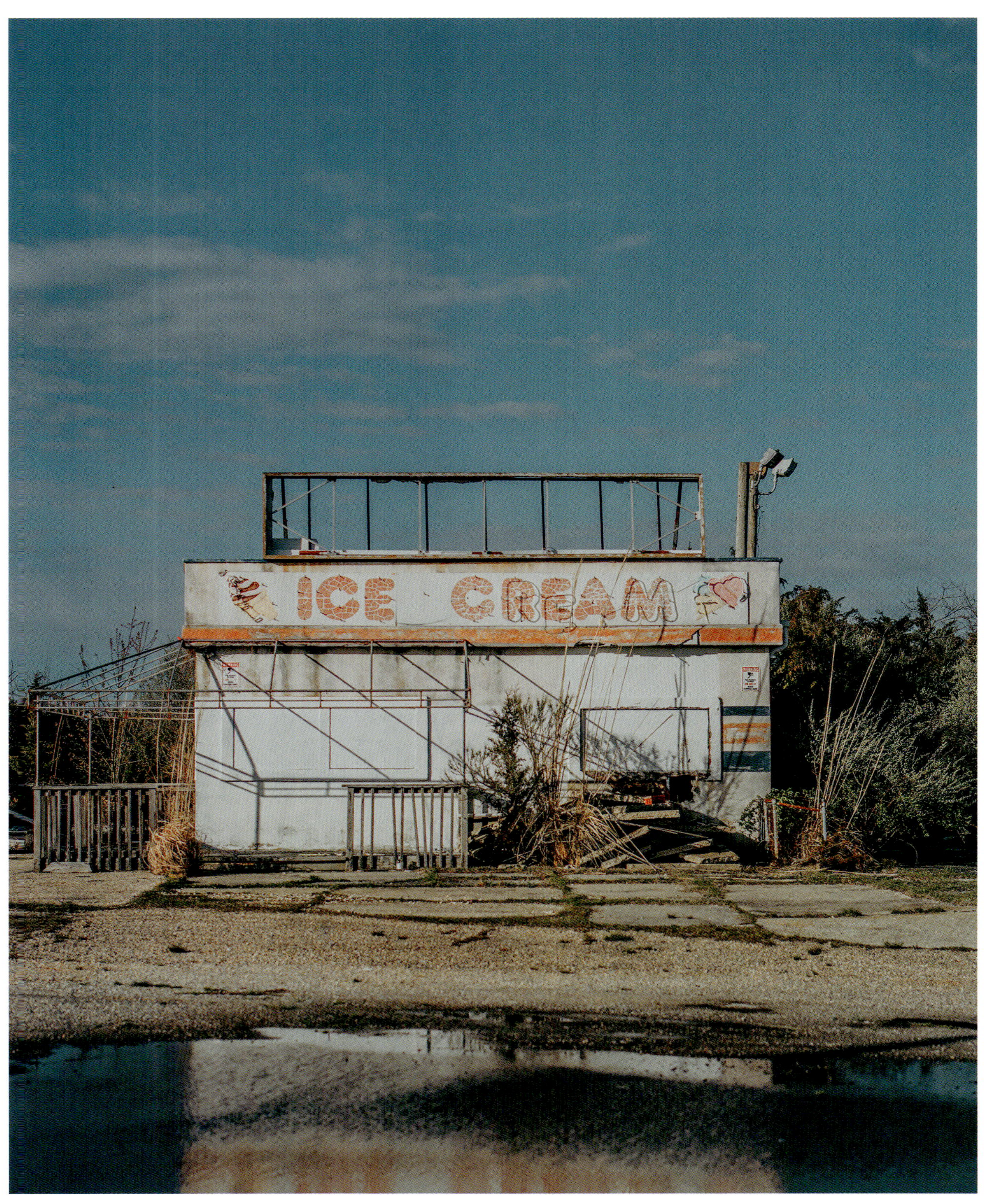

Abandoned Ice Cream Stand • Wildwood, New Jersey

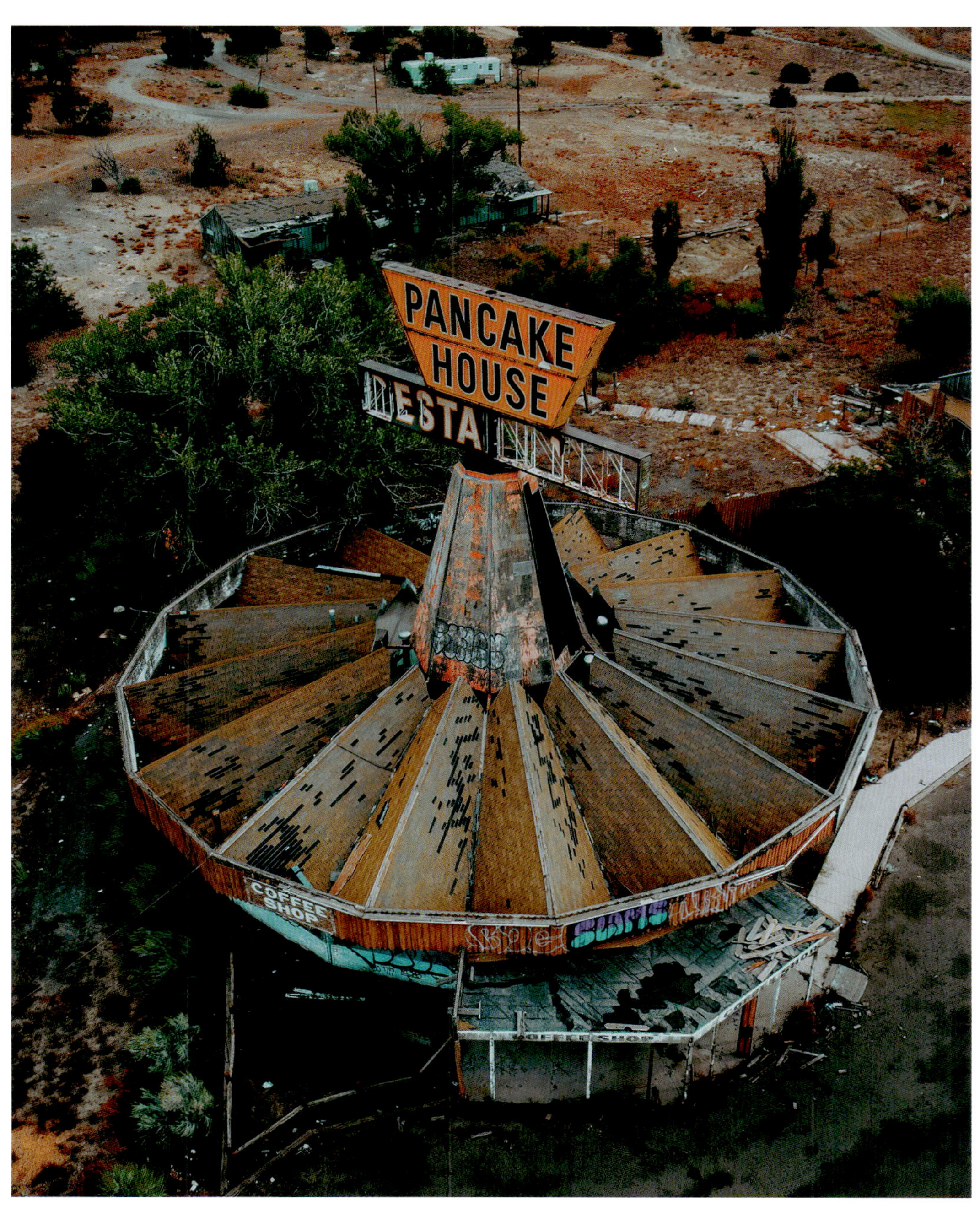

Fort Courage Restaurant • Houck, Arizona

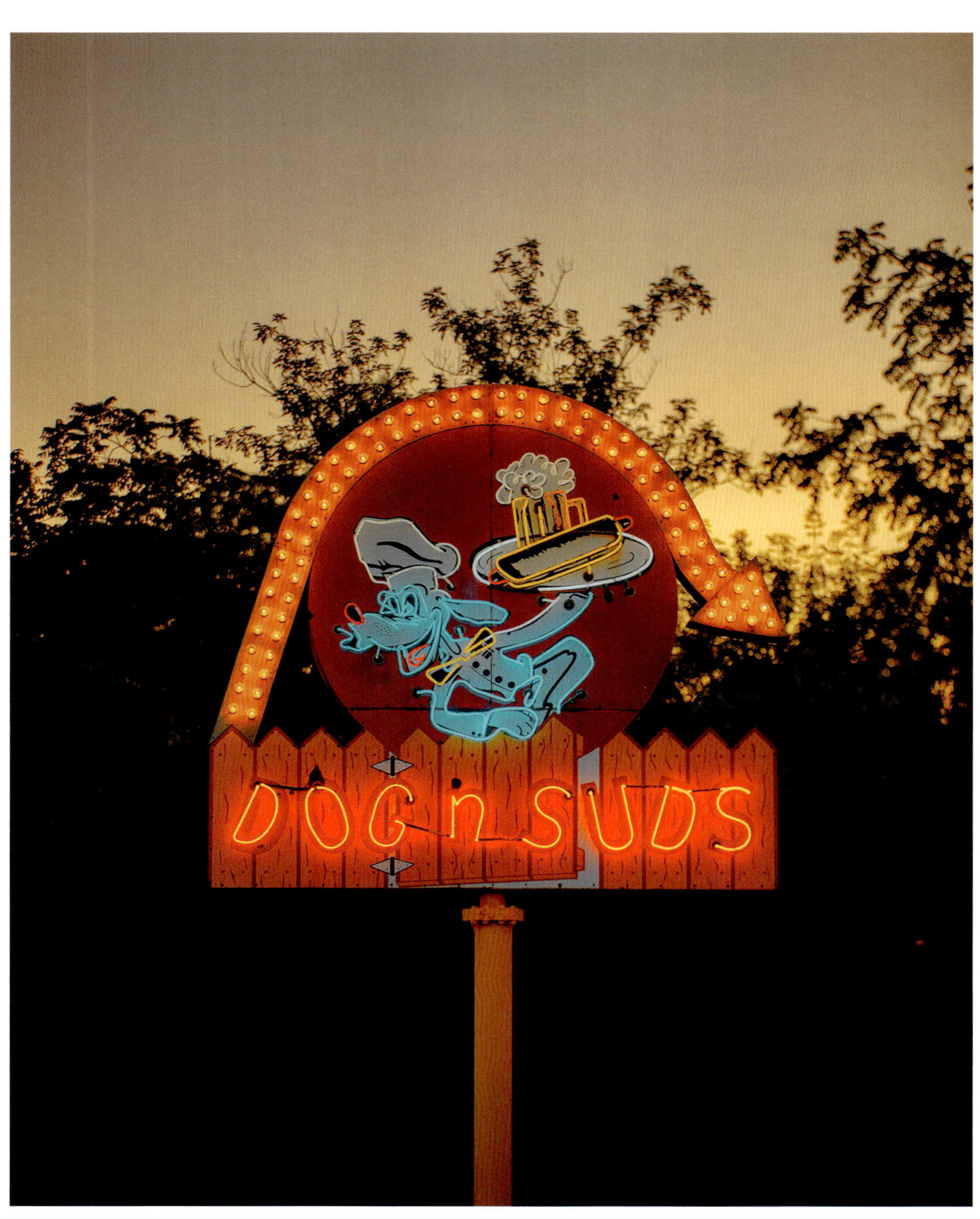

Dog N Suds • Richmond, Illinois

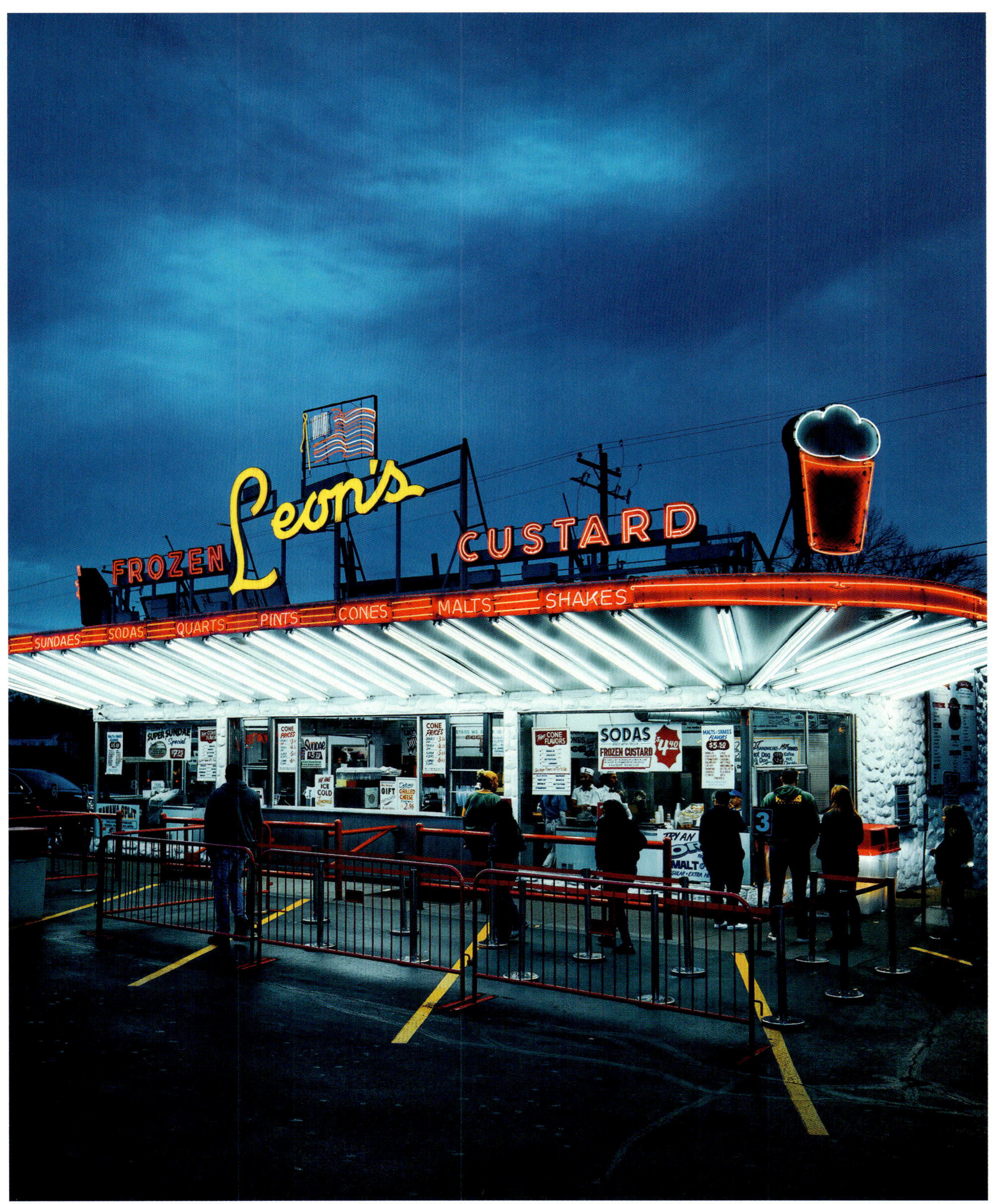

Leon's Frozen Custard • Milwaukee, Wisconsin

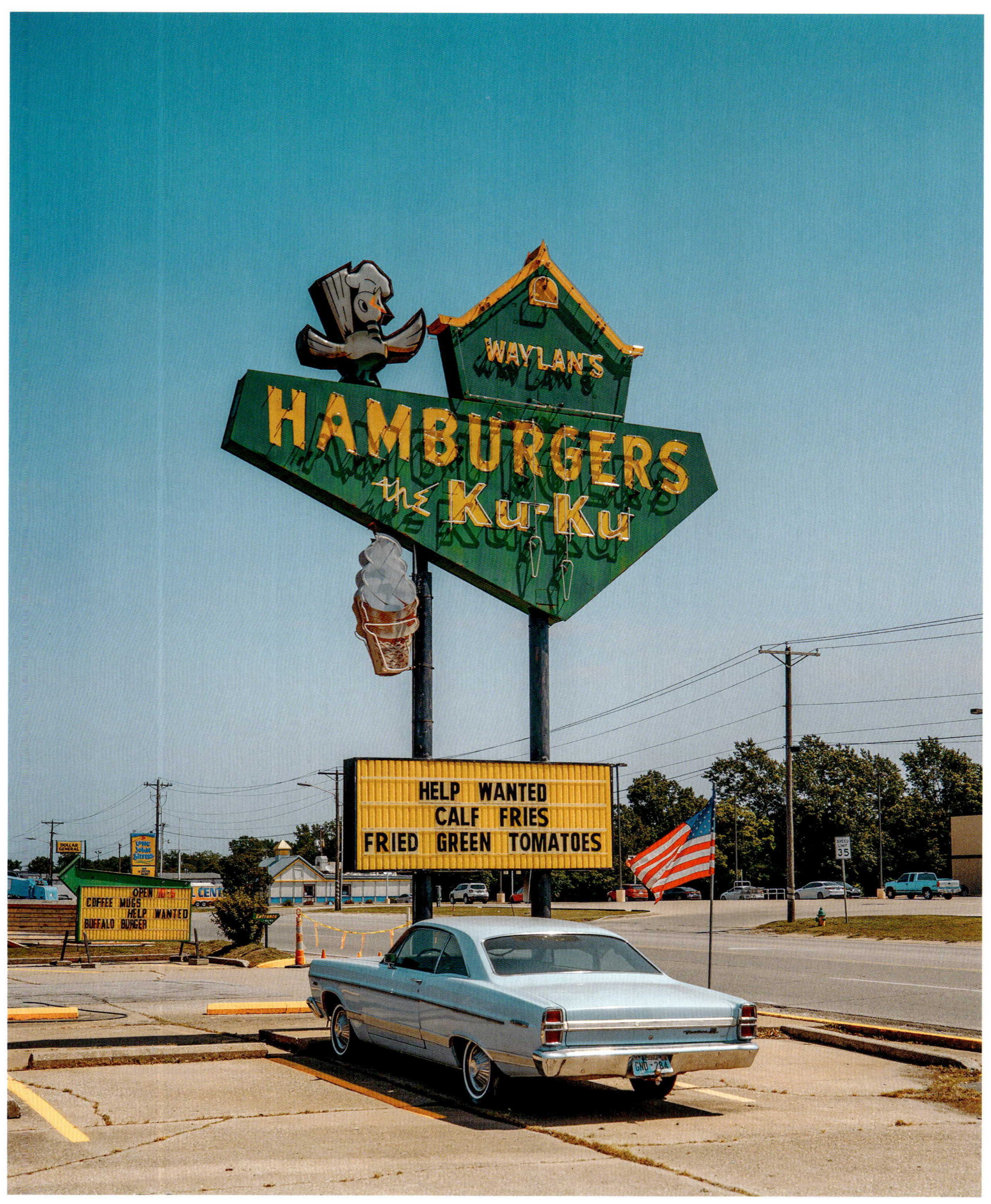

Waylan's Ku-Ku Burger • Miami, Oklahoma

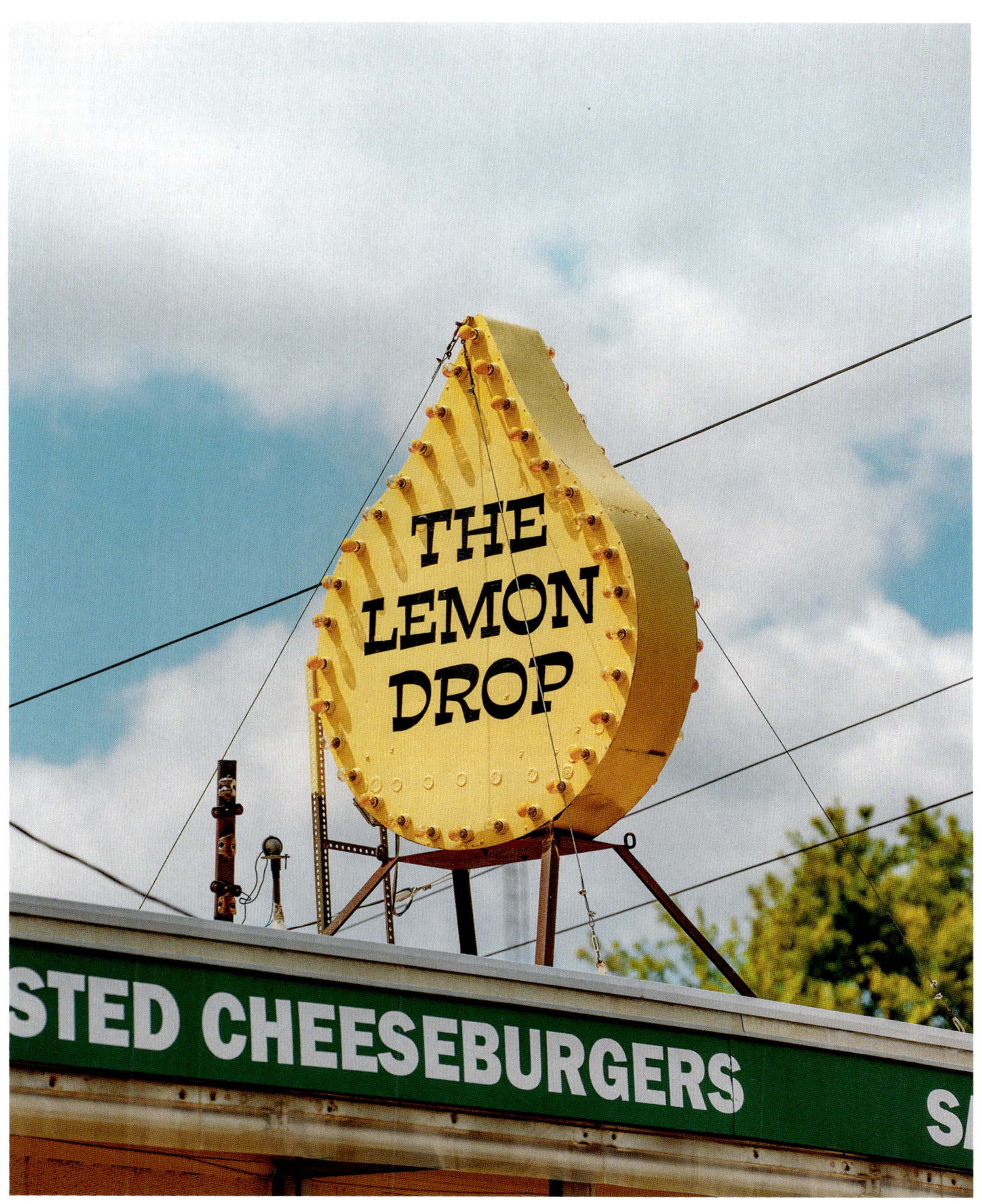

The Lemon Drop Drive-In • Anderson, Indiana

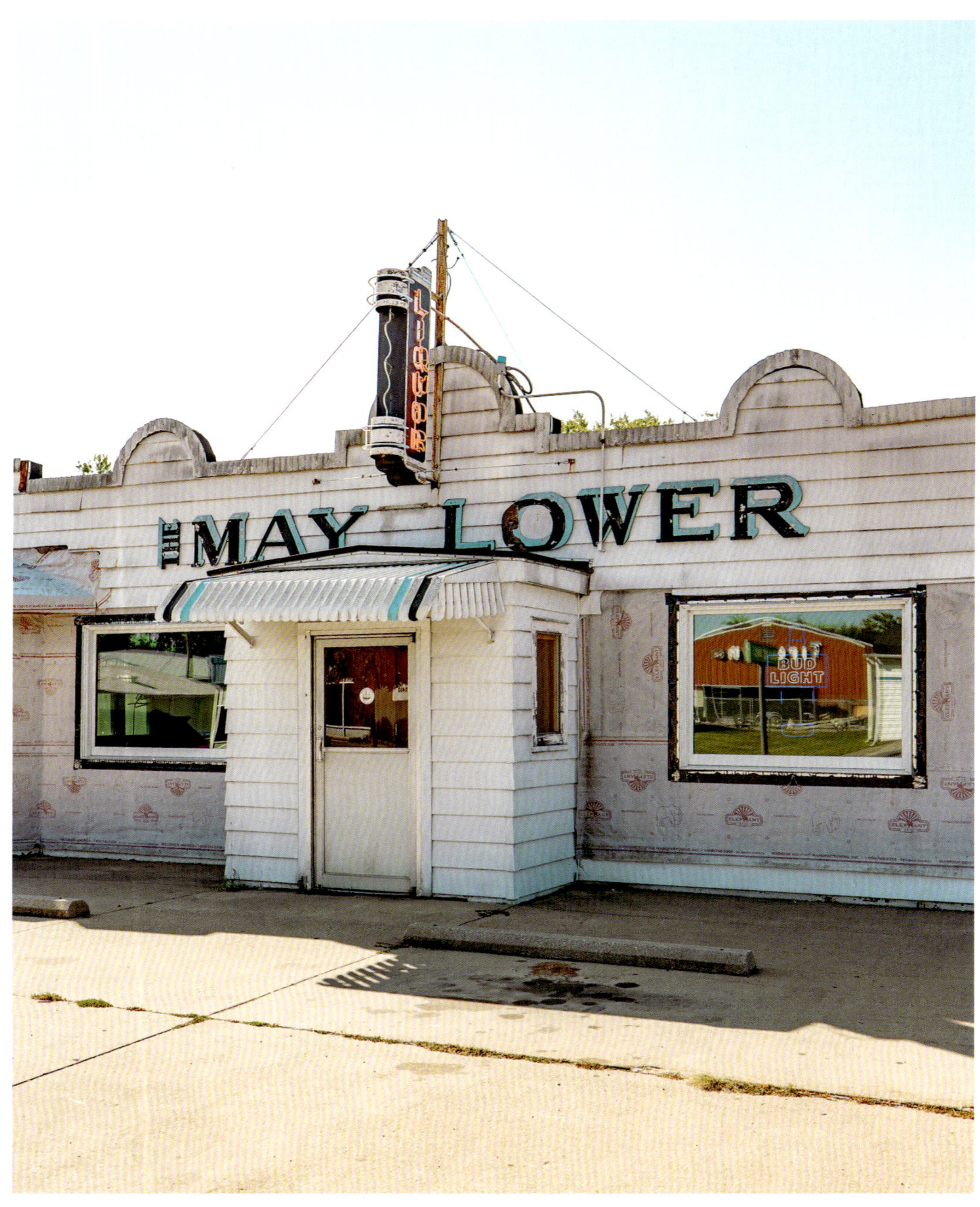

The Mayflower • Plymouth, Indiana

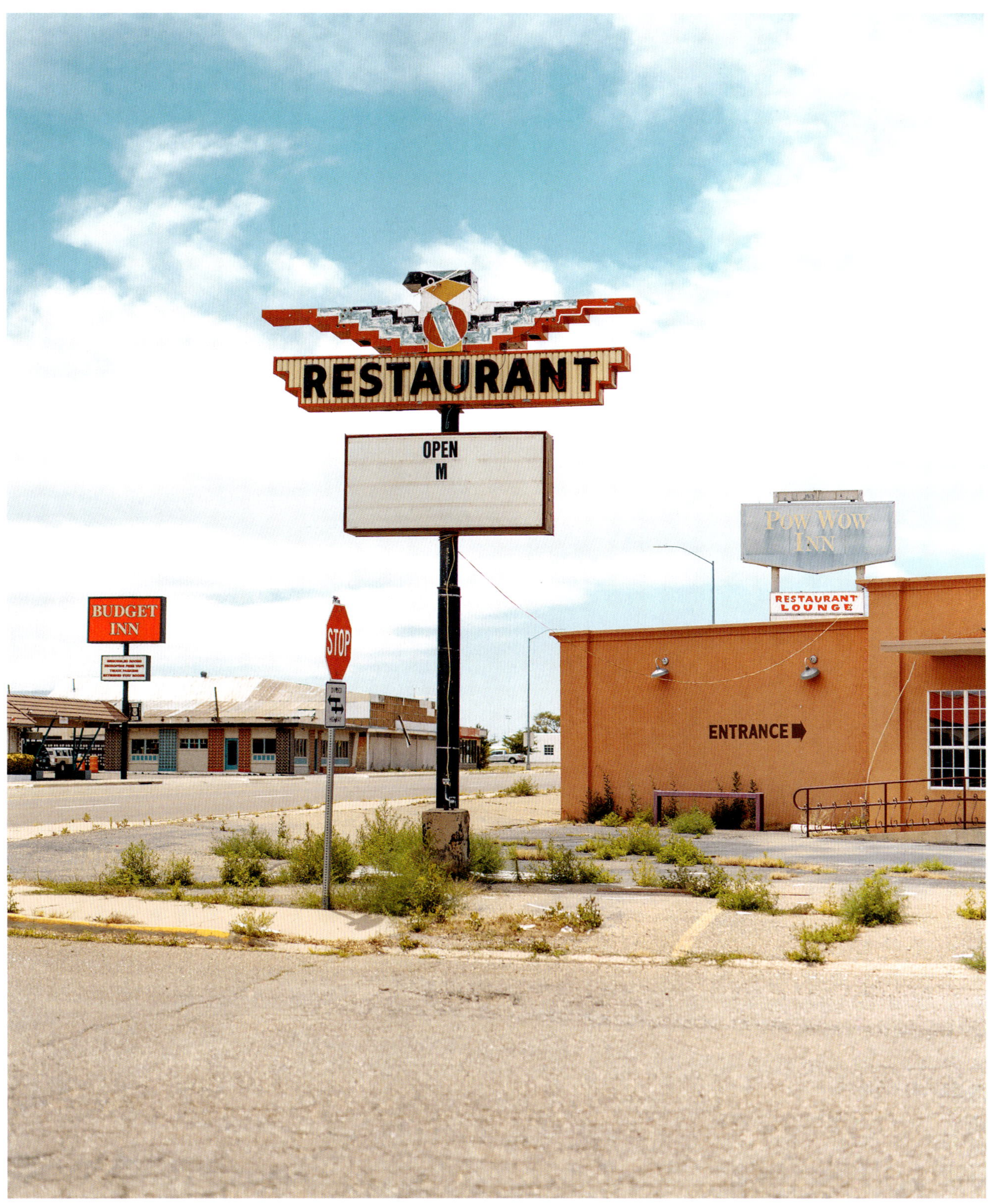

Pow Wow Restaurant & Lounge • Tucumcari, New Mexico

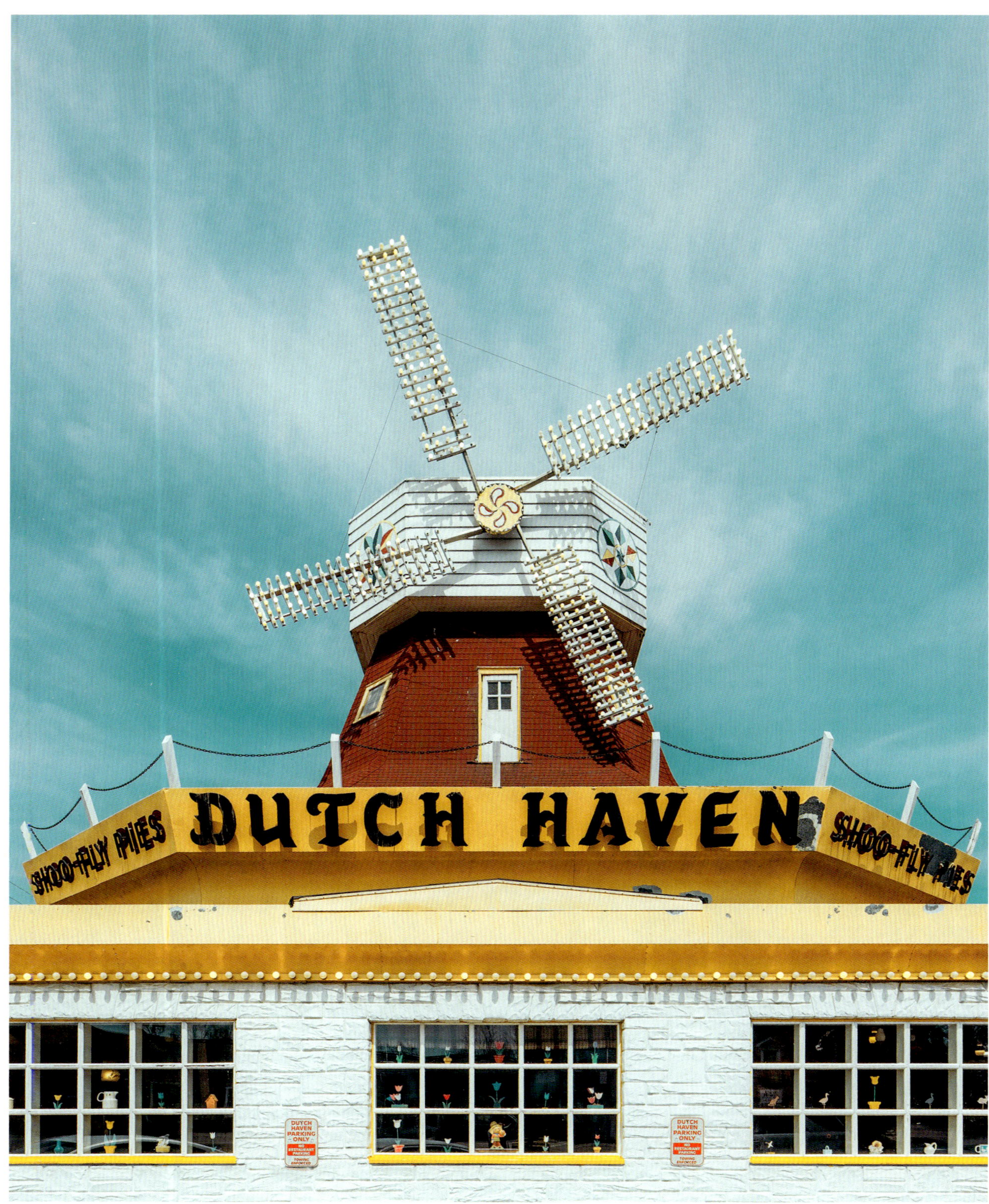

Dutch Haven • Soudersburg, Pennsylvania

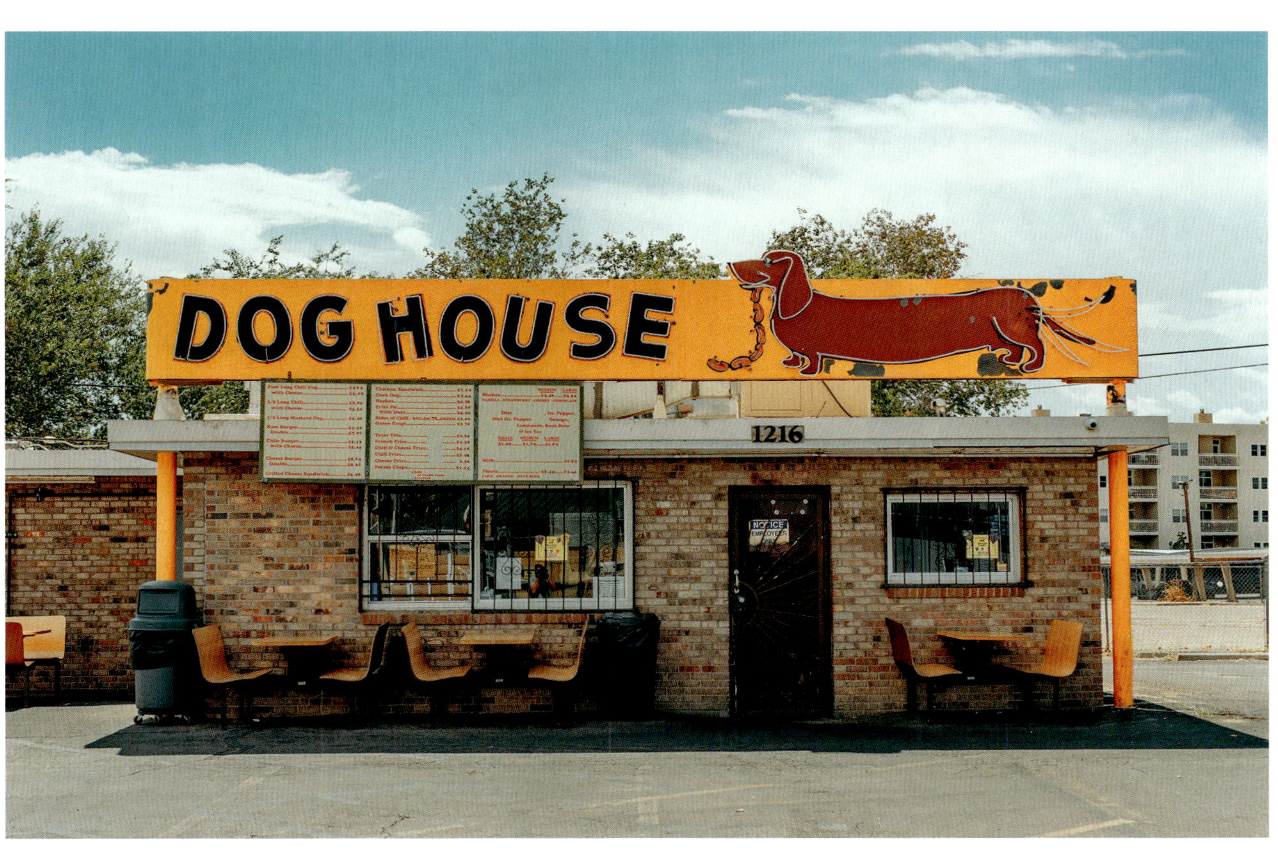

Dog House Drive-In • Albuquerque, New Mexico

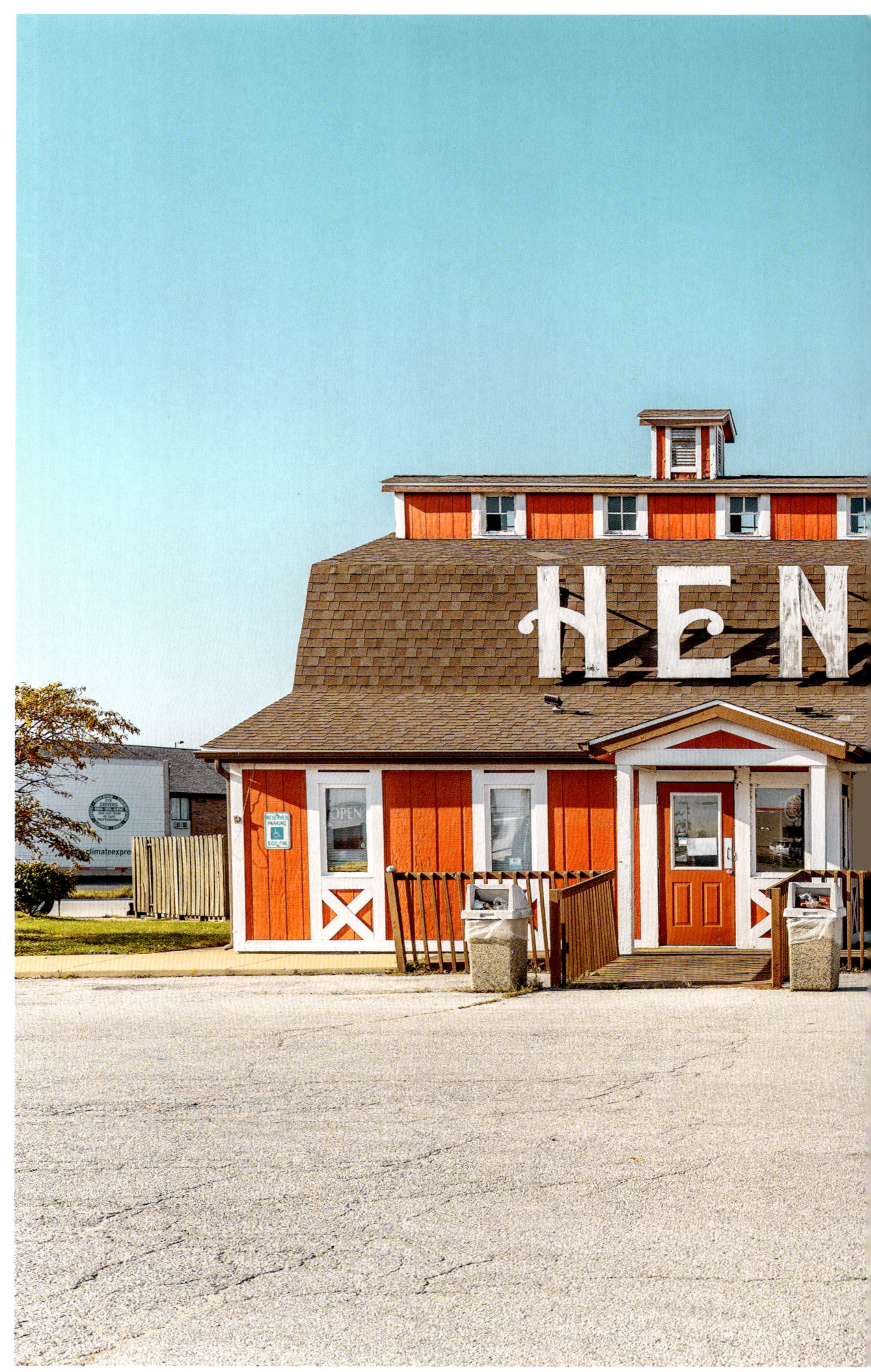

Hen House Restaurant
Arcola, Illinois

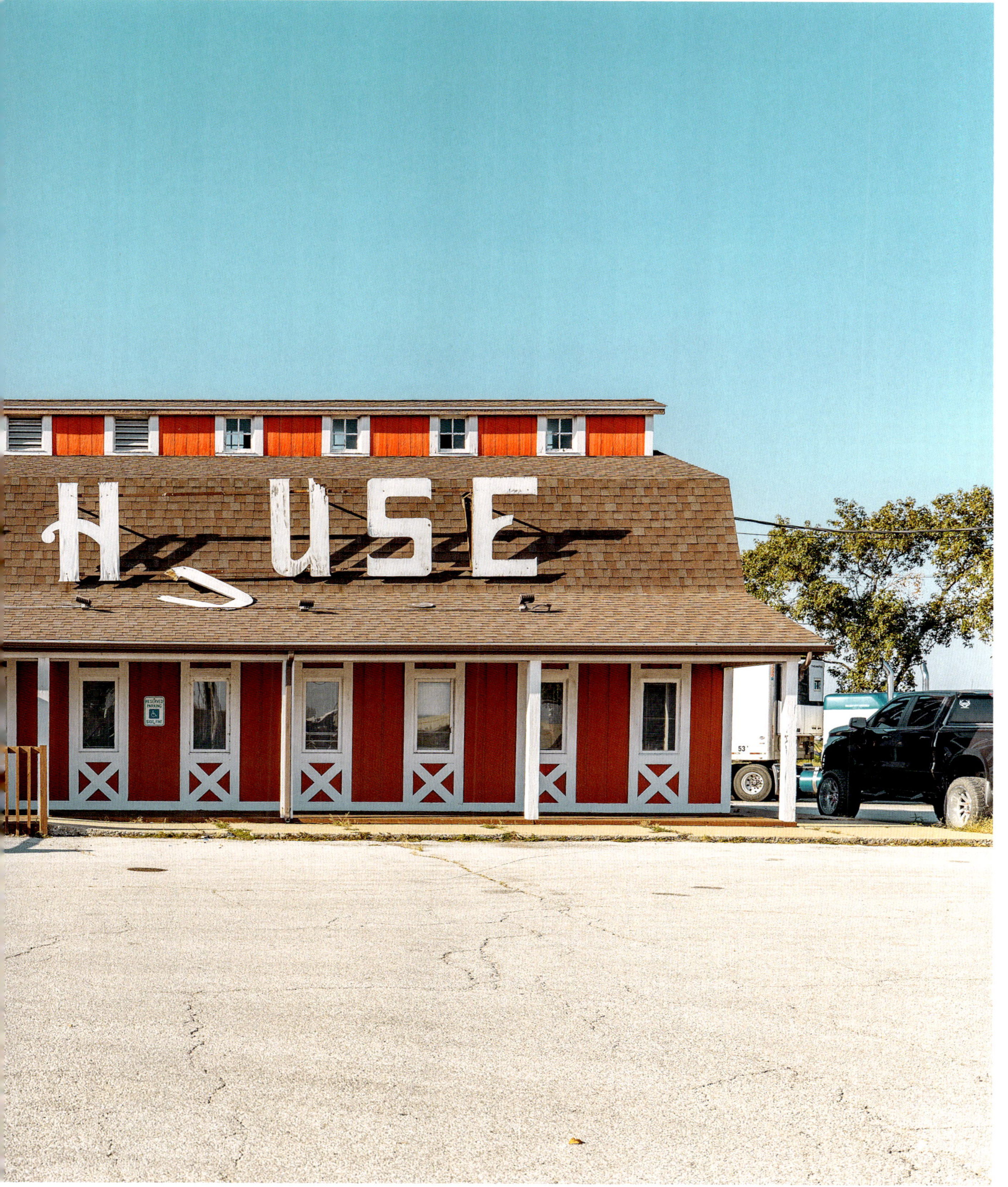
H USE

ROADSIDE

My love for roadside attractions began alongside my passion for road trips. Over the years, I've taken countless long drives with my three children, where frequent stops are essential—not just to stretch our legs, but to break up the monotony of the journey. I'd strategically plan our stops at strange attractions, knowing full well that the kids would groan and complain. And yet, every single time, something surprising would happen. As soon as we stepped out of the car and started exploring, the groans turned into curiosity. The oddities of the places we visited—whether bizarre statues, obscure historical sites, or unusual museums—always sparked conversation, and by the time we were back in the car, my kids couldn't stop talking about it.

One of the first times I truly saw the magic of these stops unfold was at the site of the Buddy Holly plane crash. Buddy Holly is one of my favorite musicians, and visiting the site felt like a pilgrimage. My kids were initially indifferent, but once we were there, something clicked. They learned about the tragic crash and the profound impact it had on music history. The experience left them obsessed not only with Buddy Holly's story, but also with his music. From that moment on, it became the soundtrack of our road trips.

What's remarkable is how these stops, which once served only to break up the journey, have evolved into destinations of their own. Take, for instance, the iconic Blue Whale of Catoosa. In May 2023, I drove over 700 miles just to see it—a pilgrimage in its own right—stopping in small towns and visiting offbeat sites along the way. For me, the Blue Whale wasn't just a pitstop; it was the destination. And this is what makes these roadside treasures so enduring. They captivate not only nostalgic travelers but also new generations who crave something more meaningful than the faceless chain restaurants and fast-food joints that dominate the modern highway.

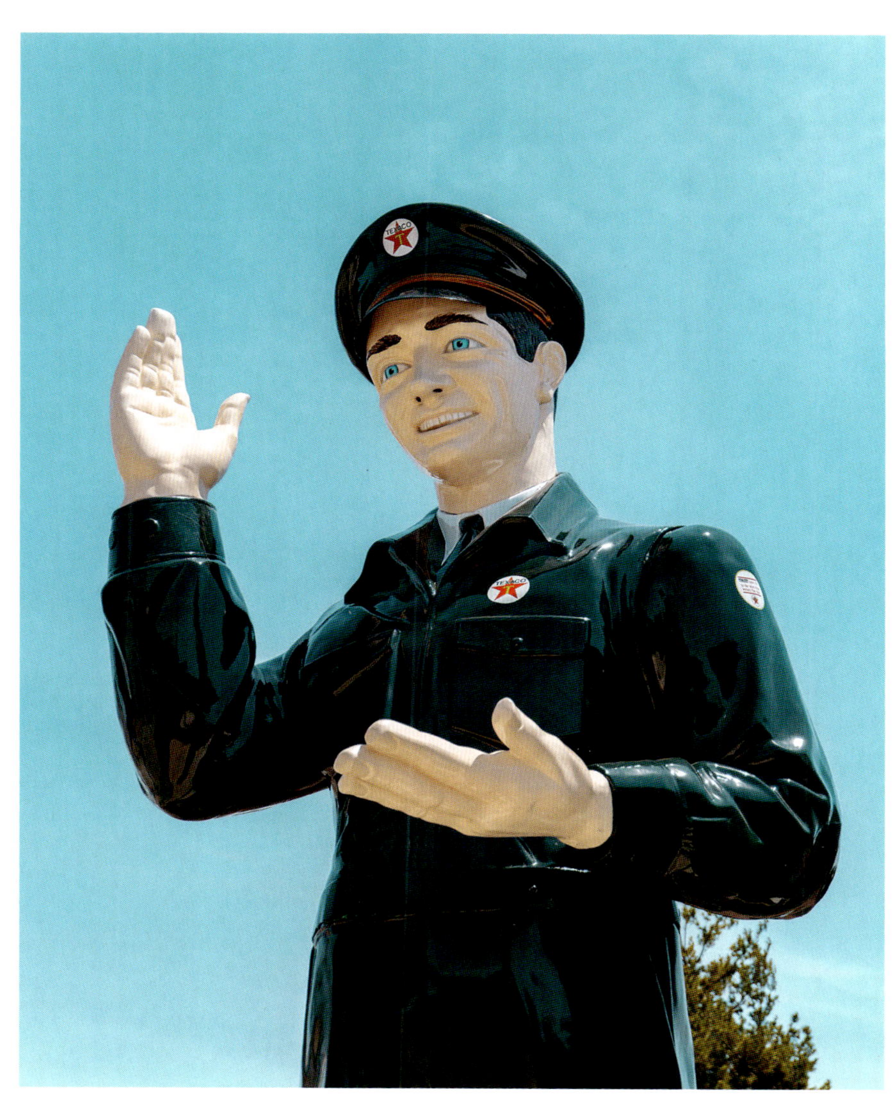

Texaco Big Friend at the American Giants Museum • Atlanta, Illinois

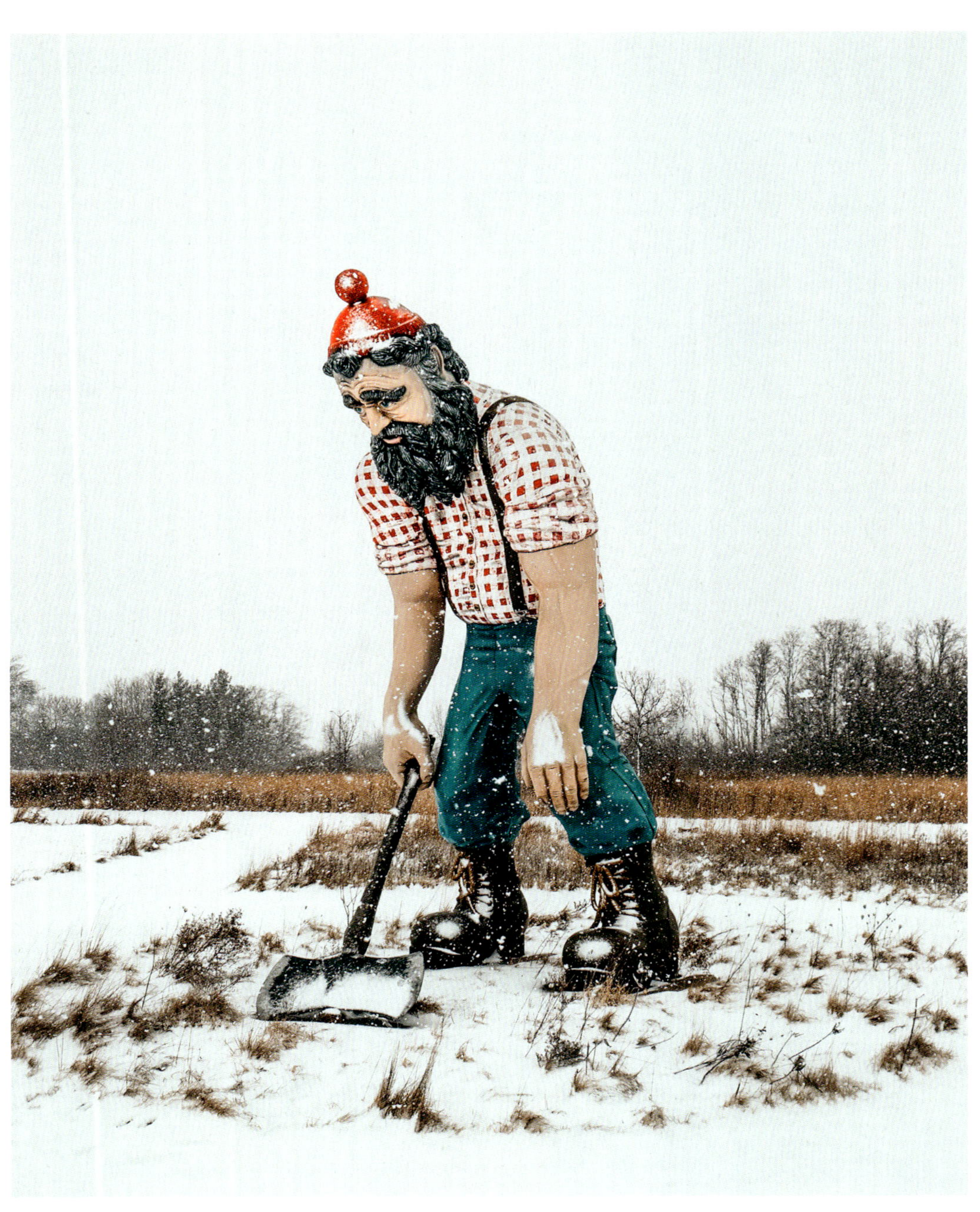

Paul Bunyan Statue • University Park, Illinois

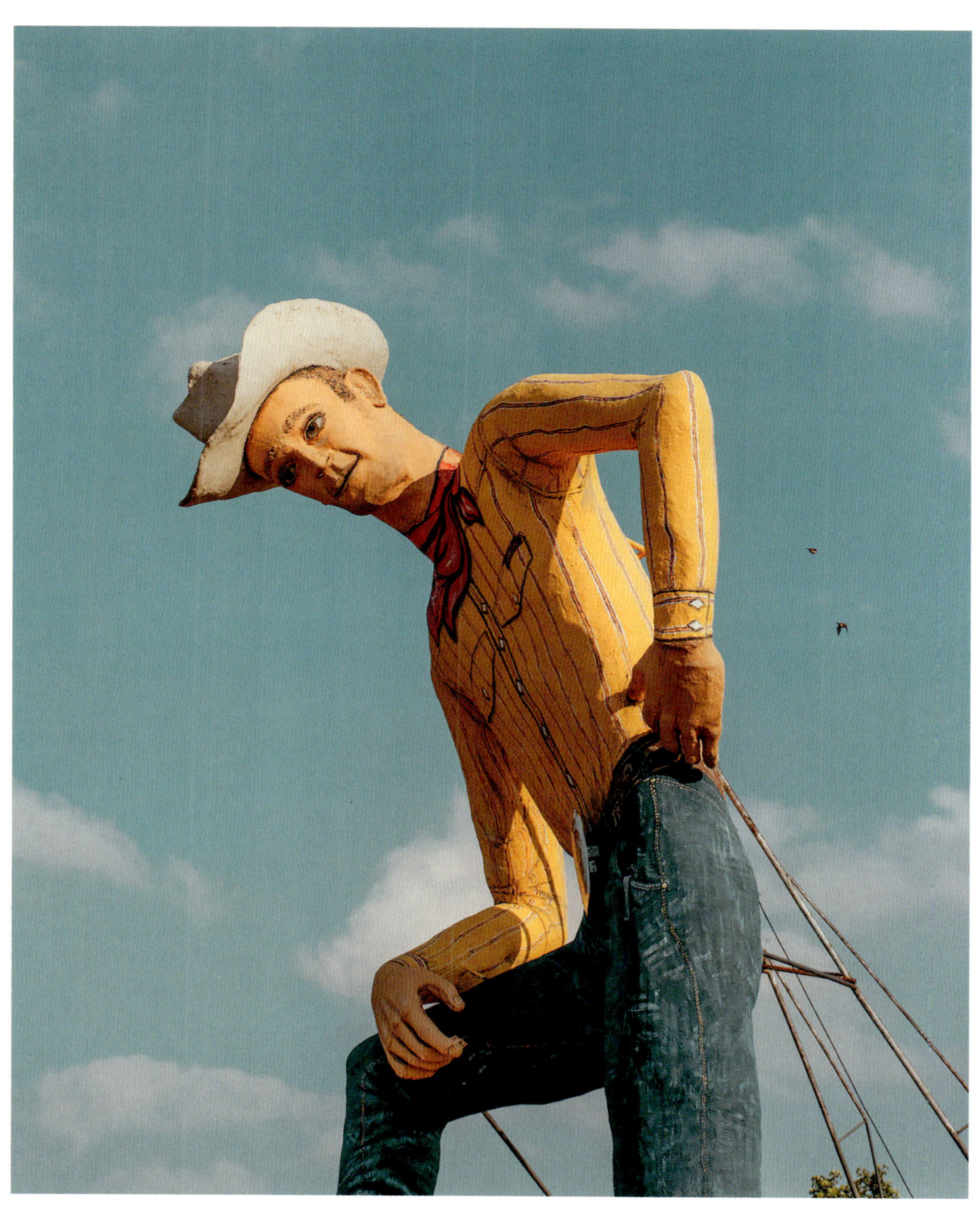

Tex Randall Statue • Canyon, Texas

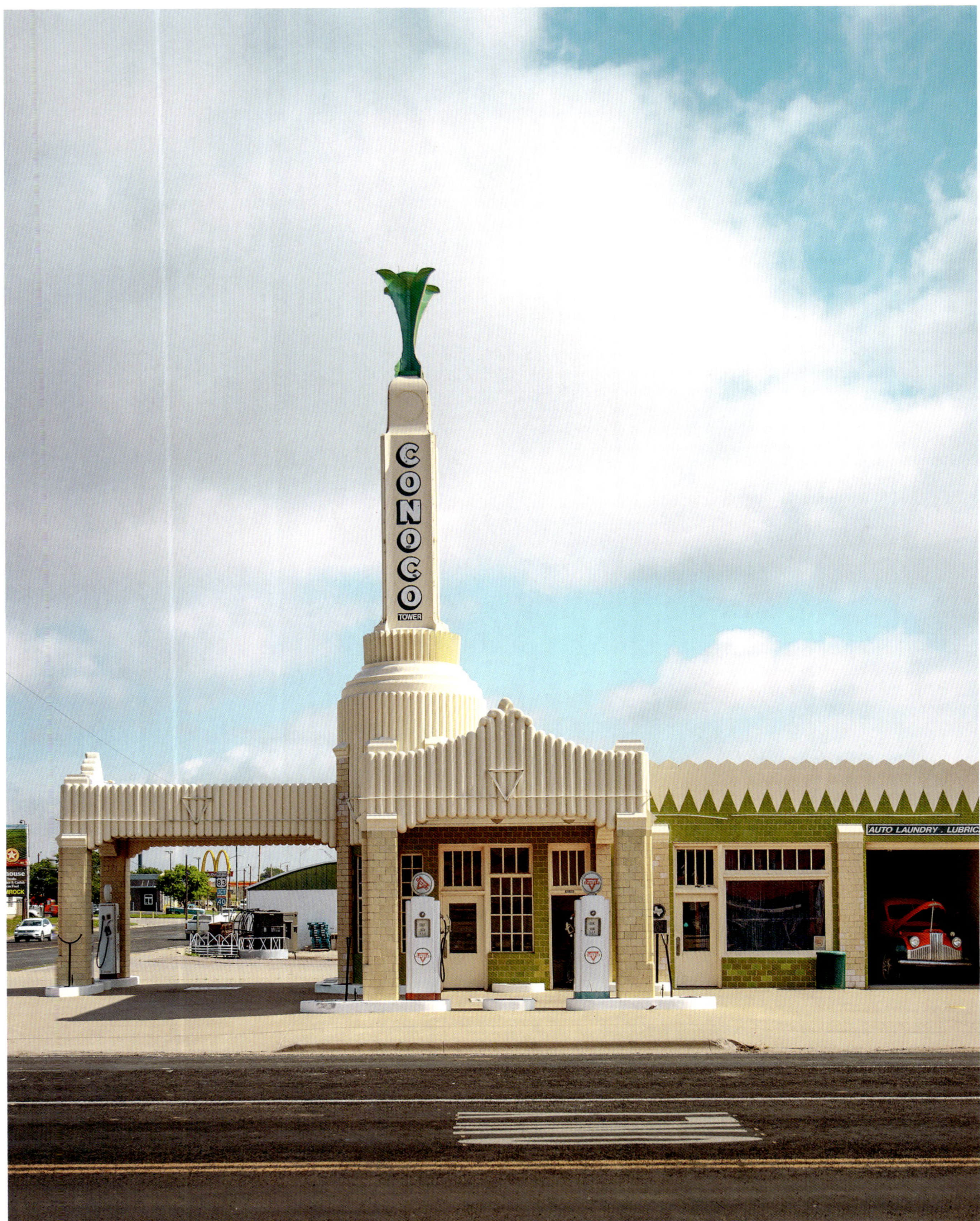
CONOCO
TOWER
AUTO LAUNDRY . LUBRIC

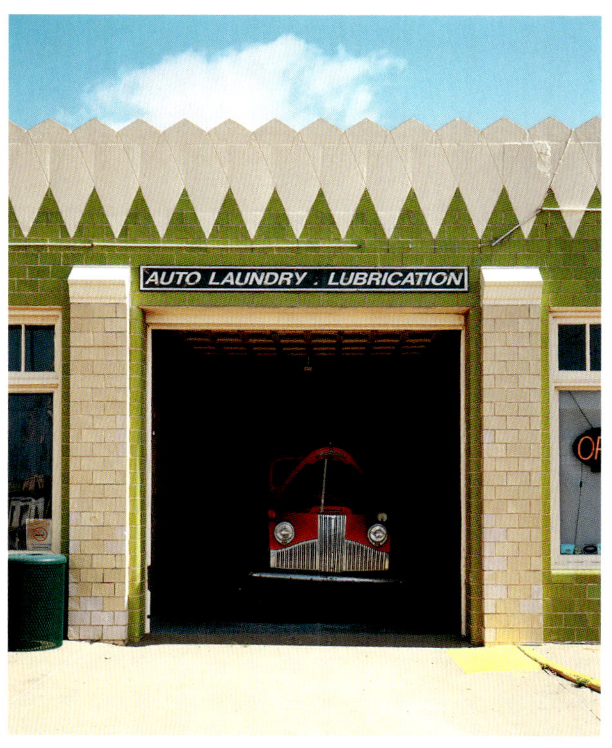

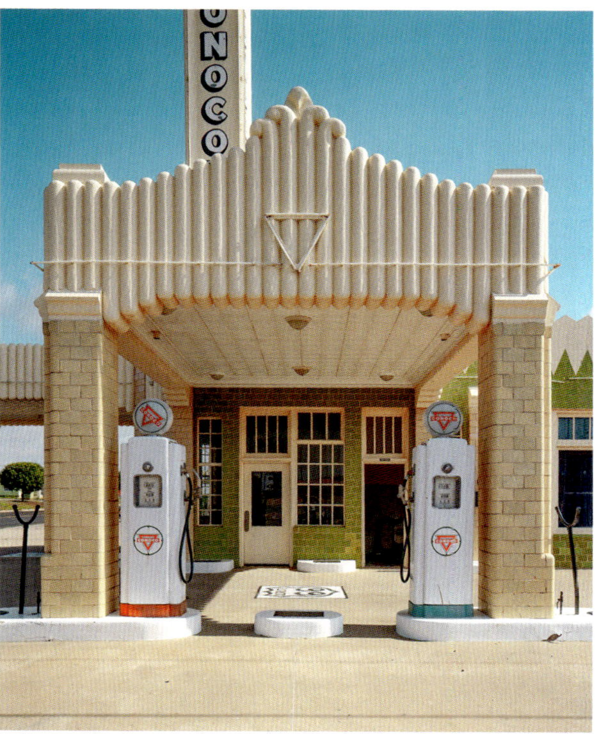

Tower Conoco Station • Shamrock, Texas

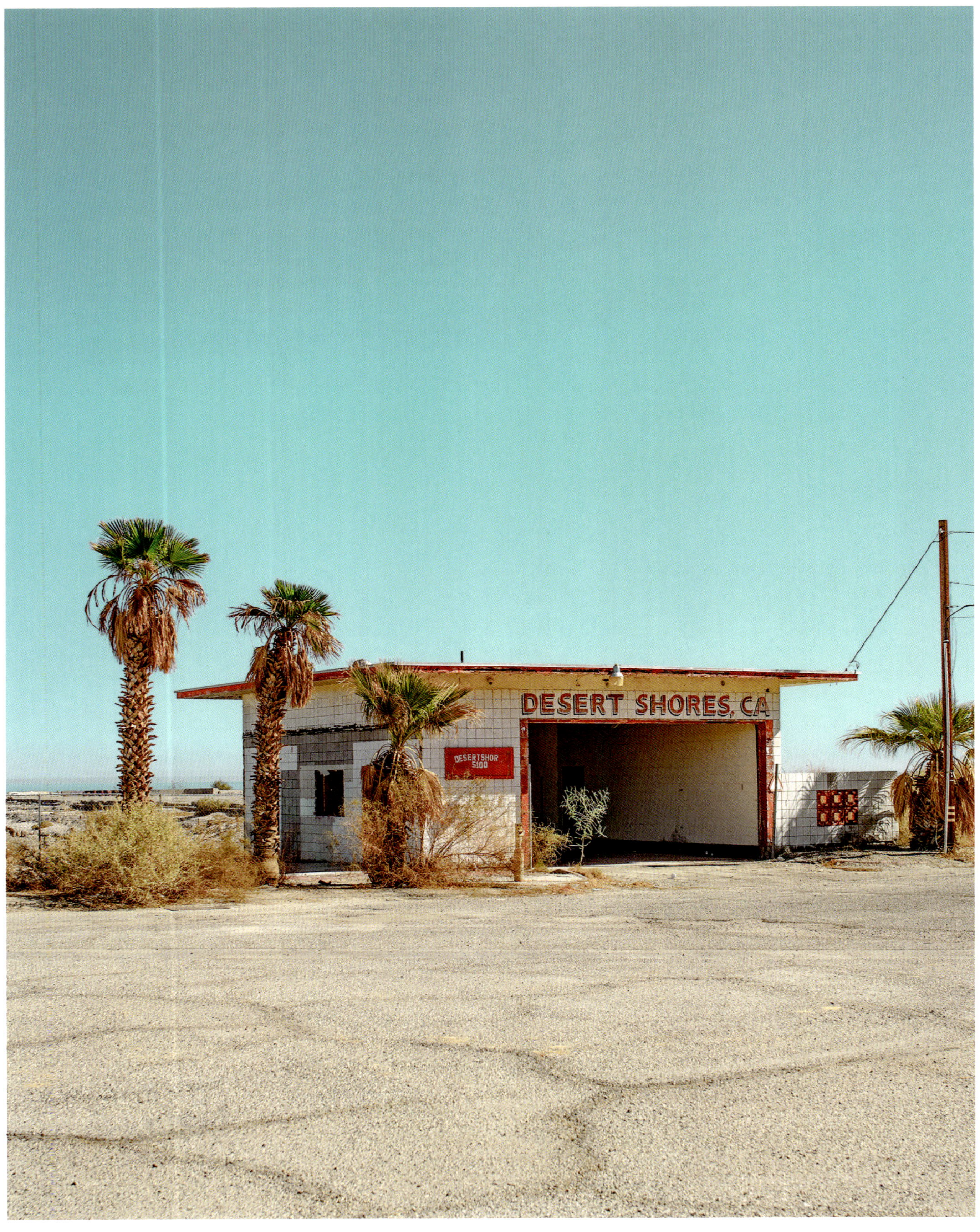
DESERT SHORES, CA
DESERTSHOR
5100

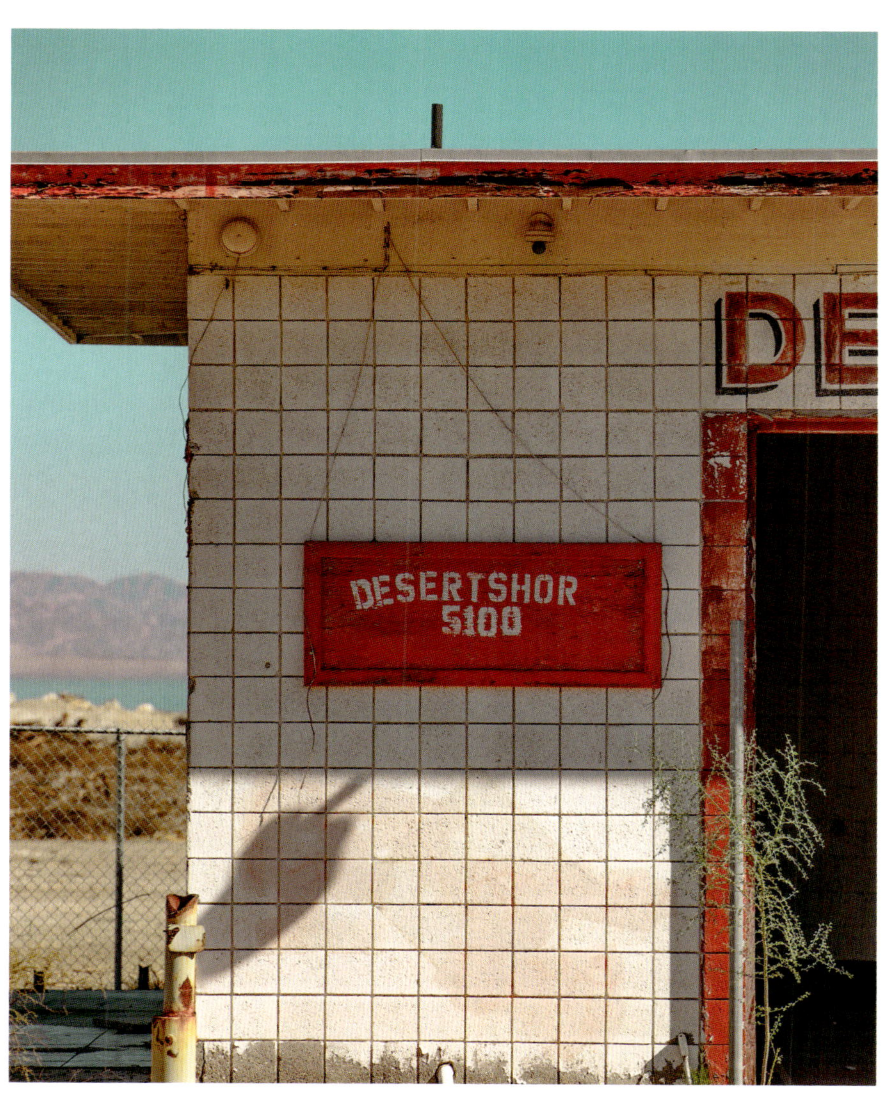

Abandoned Fire Station • Desert Shores, California

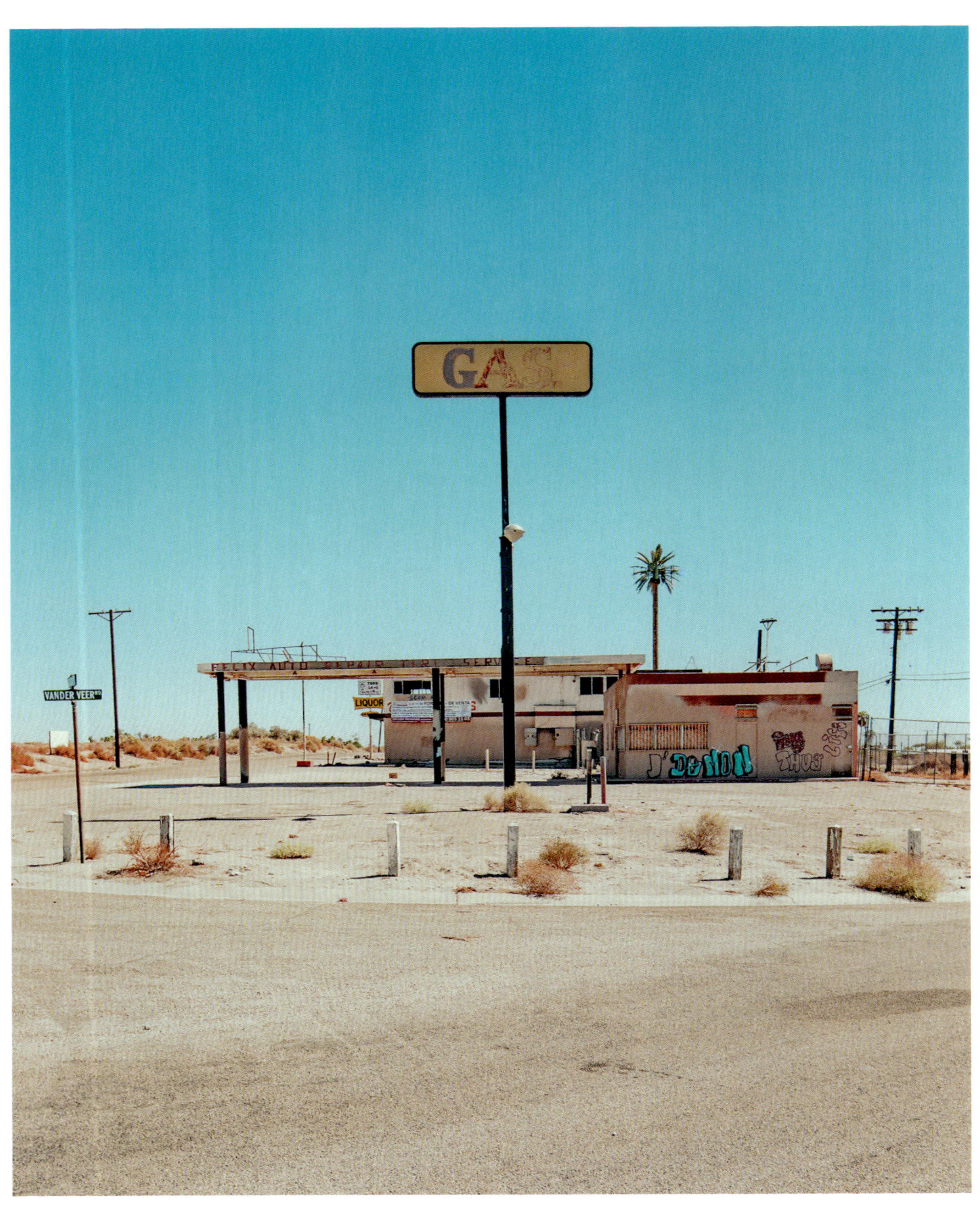

North Shore Service Station • Mecca, California

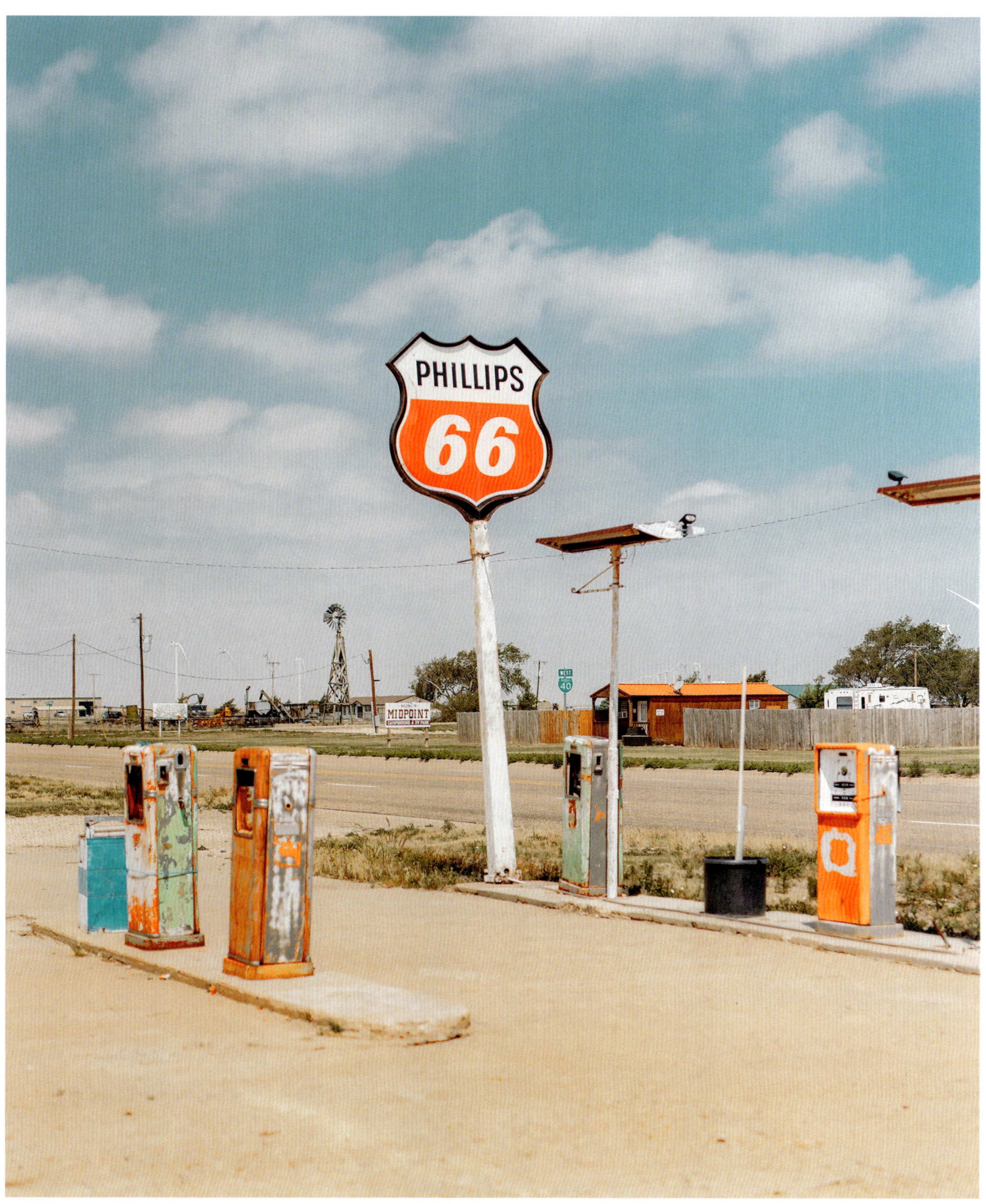

Bent Door Service Station • Adrian, Texas

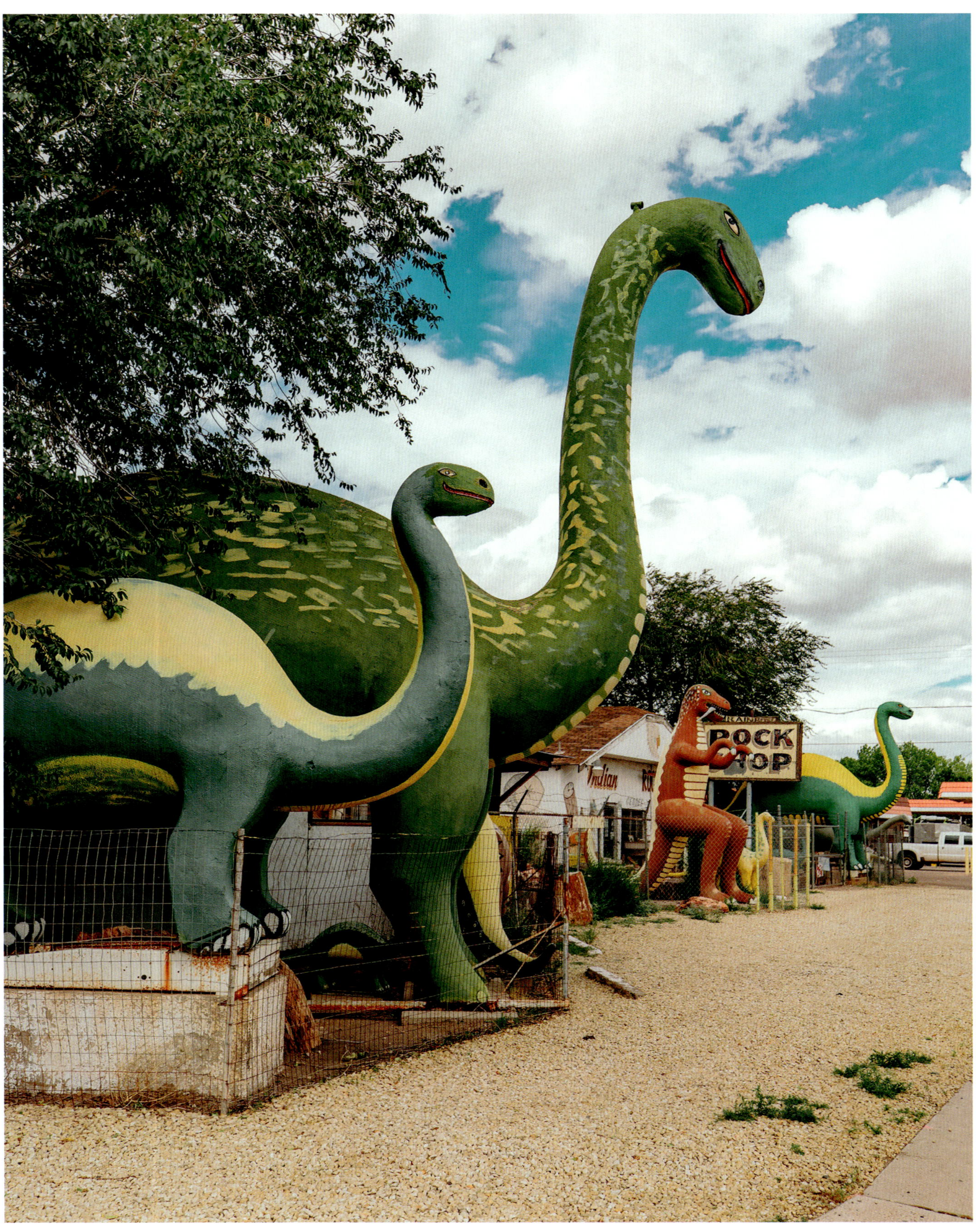
ROCK
Indian

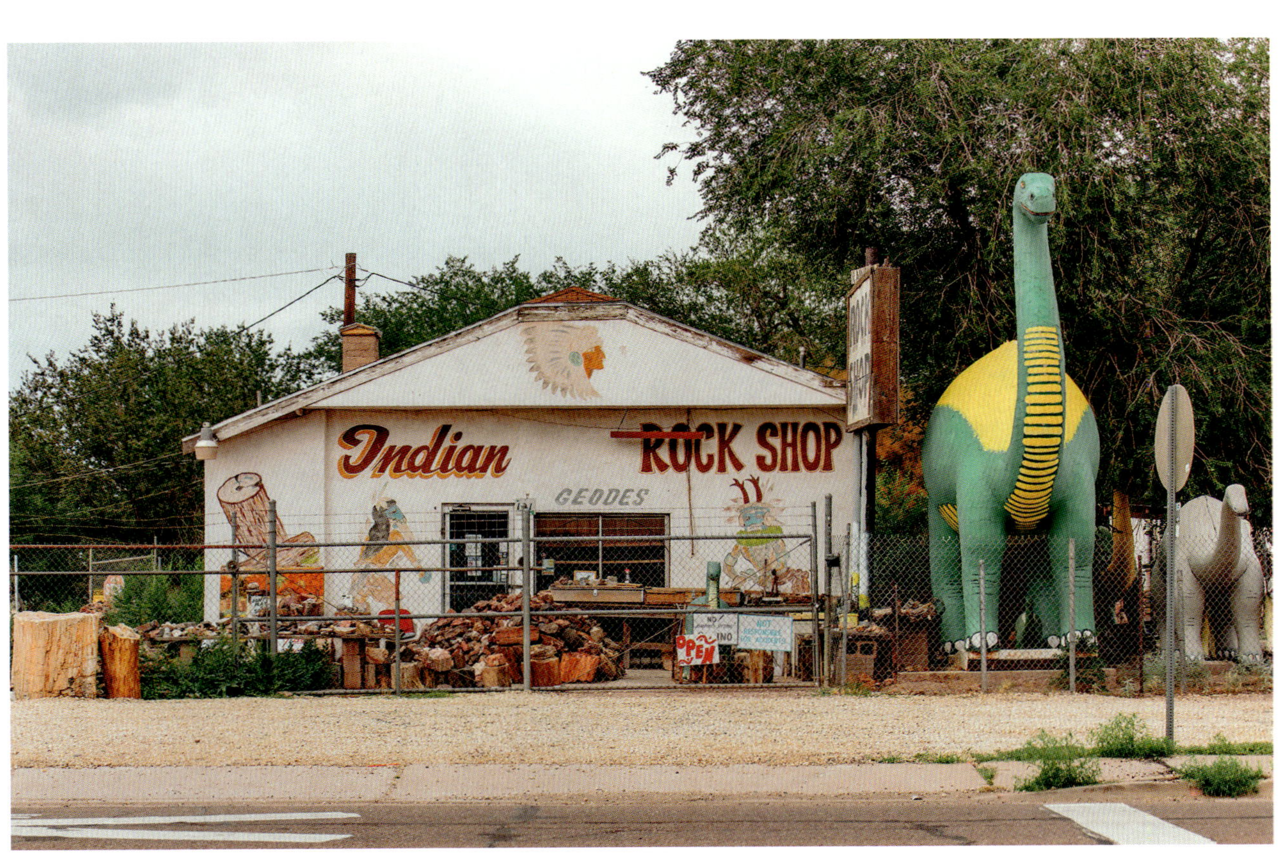

Rainbow Rock Shop • Holbrook, Arizona

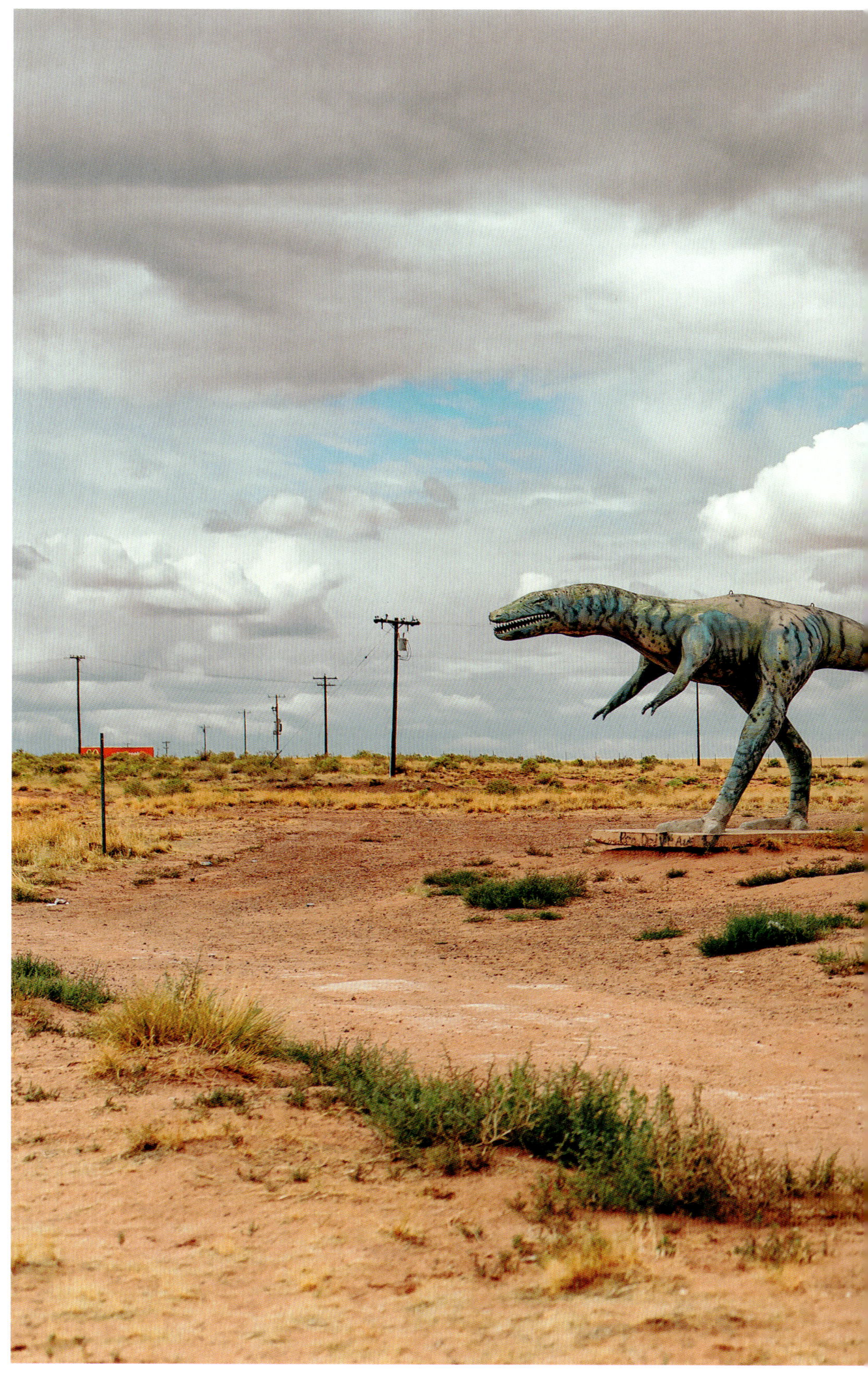

Truck Stop
Holbrook, Arizona

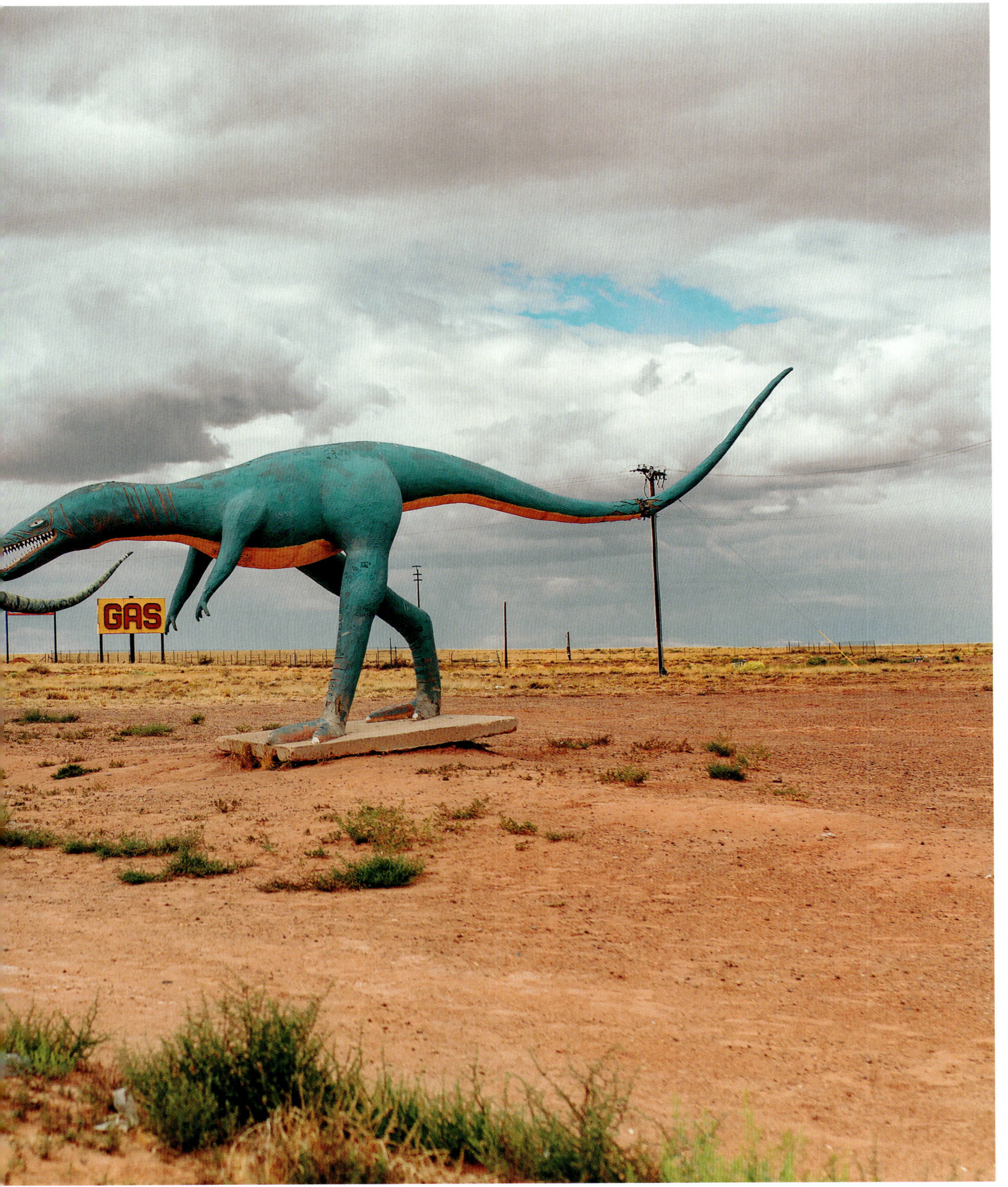
GAS

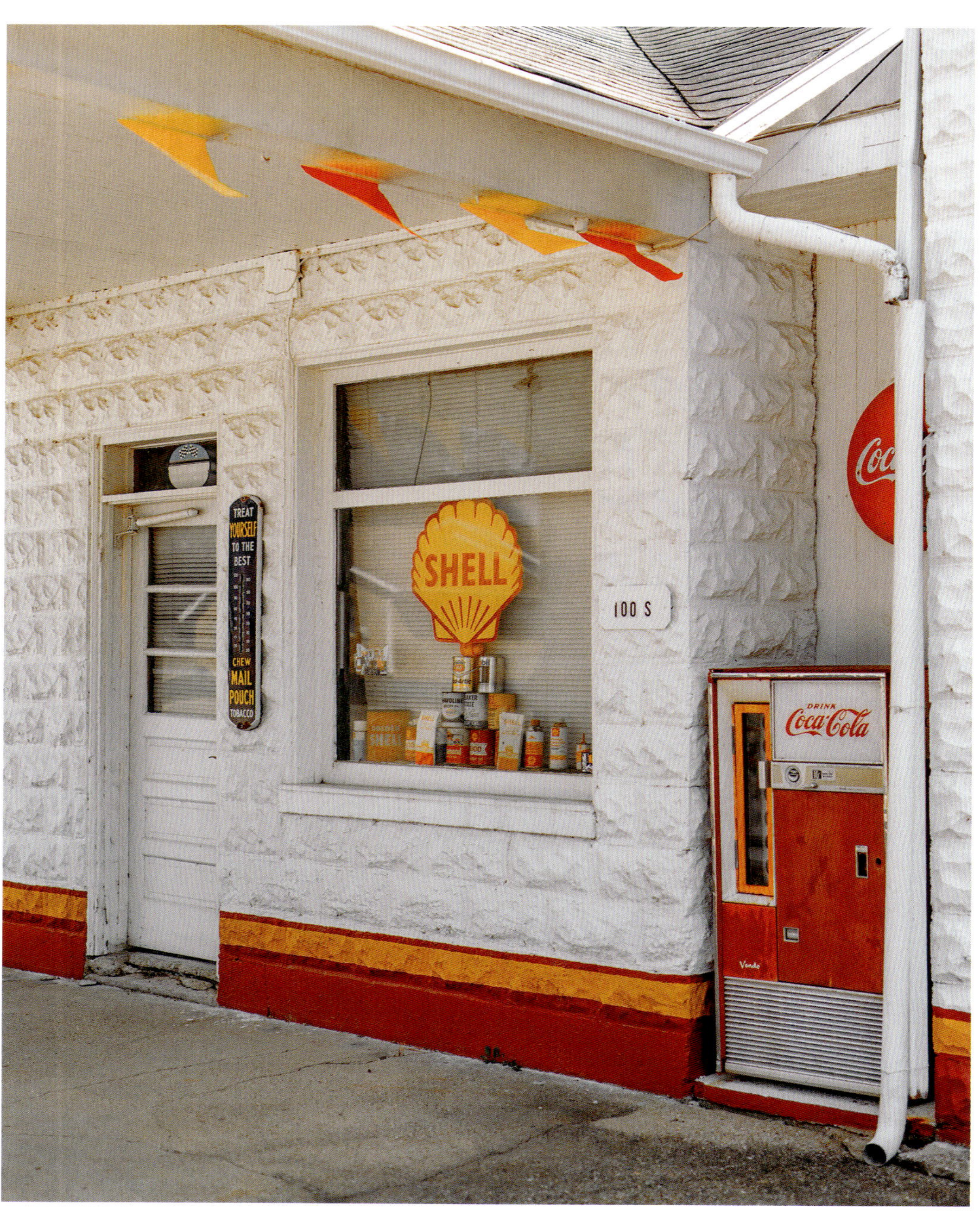

Shell Service Station • Sigel, Illinois

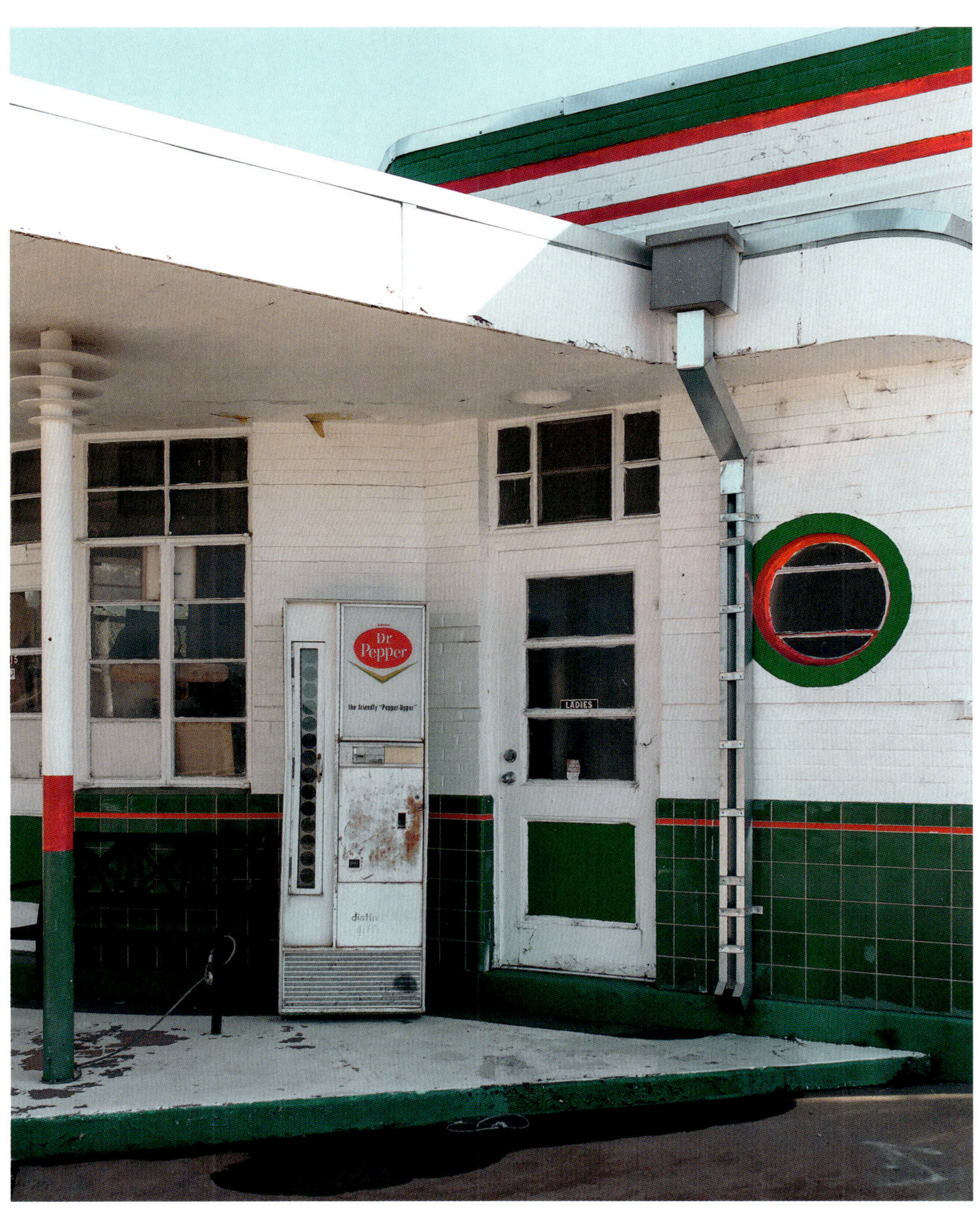

Sinclair Service Station • Raton, New Mexico

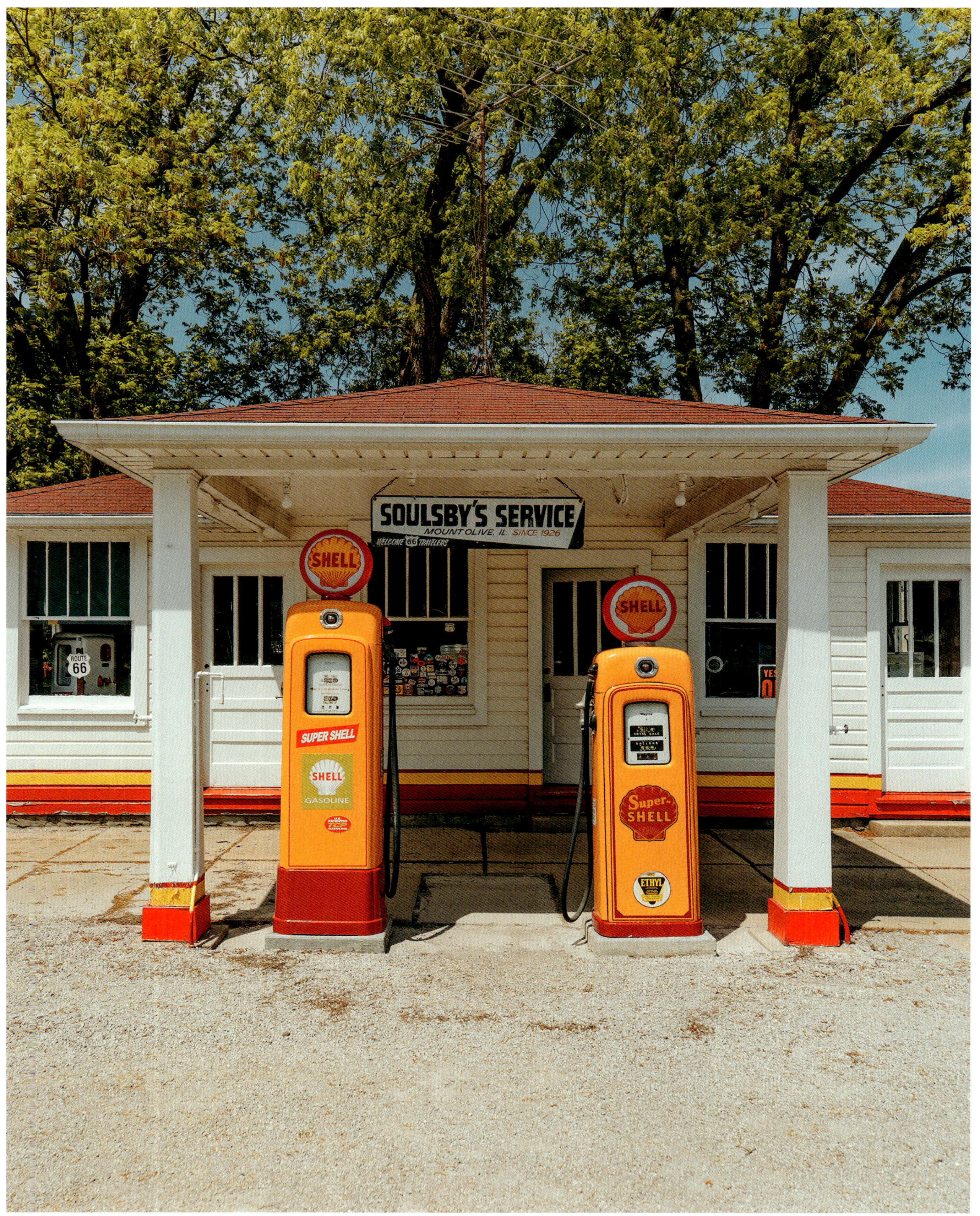
SOULSBY'S SERVICE
MOUNT OLIVE, IL. SINCE 1926
WELCOME 66 TRAVELERS
SHELL
SUPER SHELL
SHELL
GASOLINE
ROUTE 66
SHELL
Super-SHELL
ETHYL

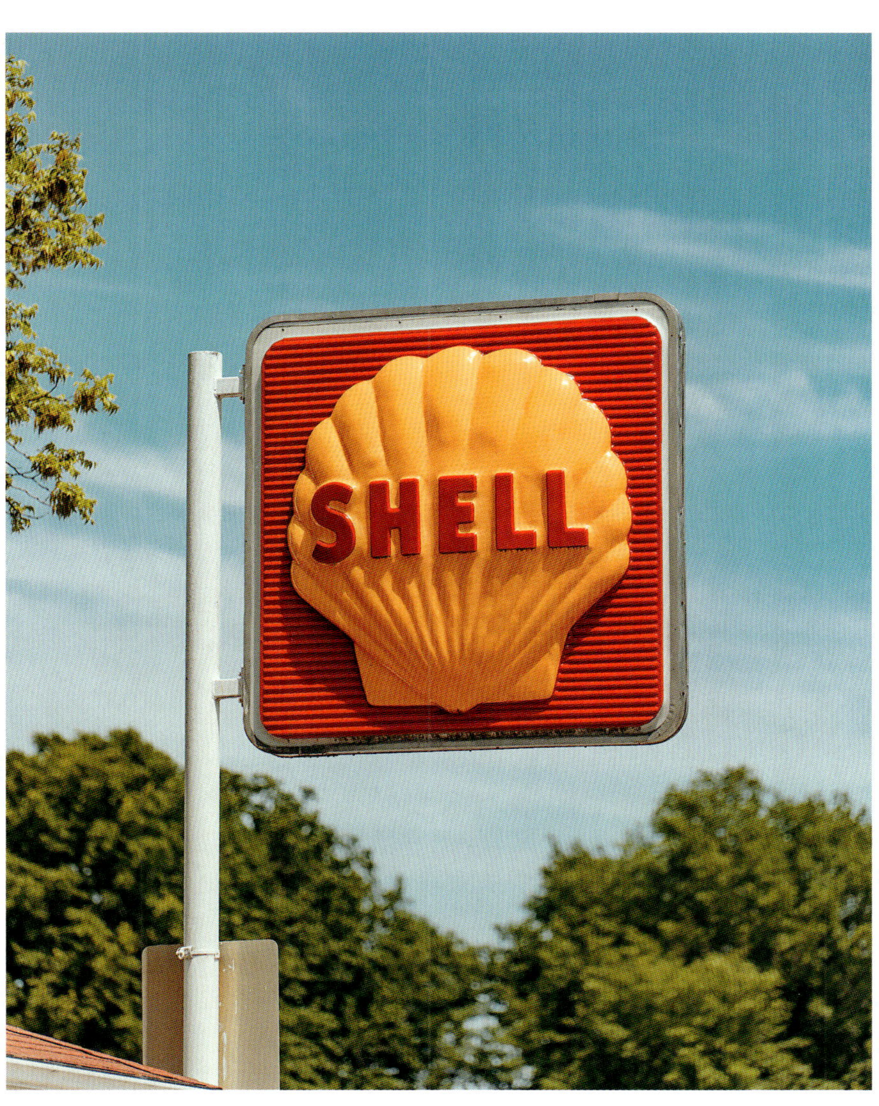

Soulsby's Service Station • Mt. Olive, Illinois

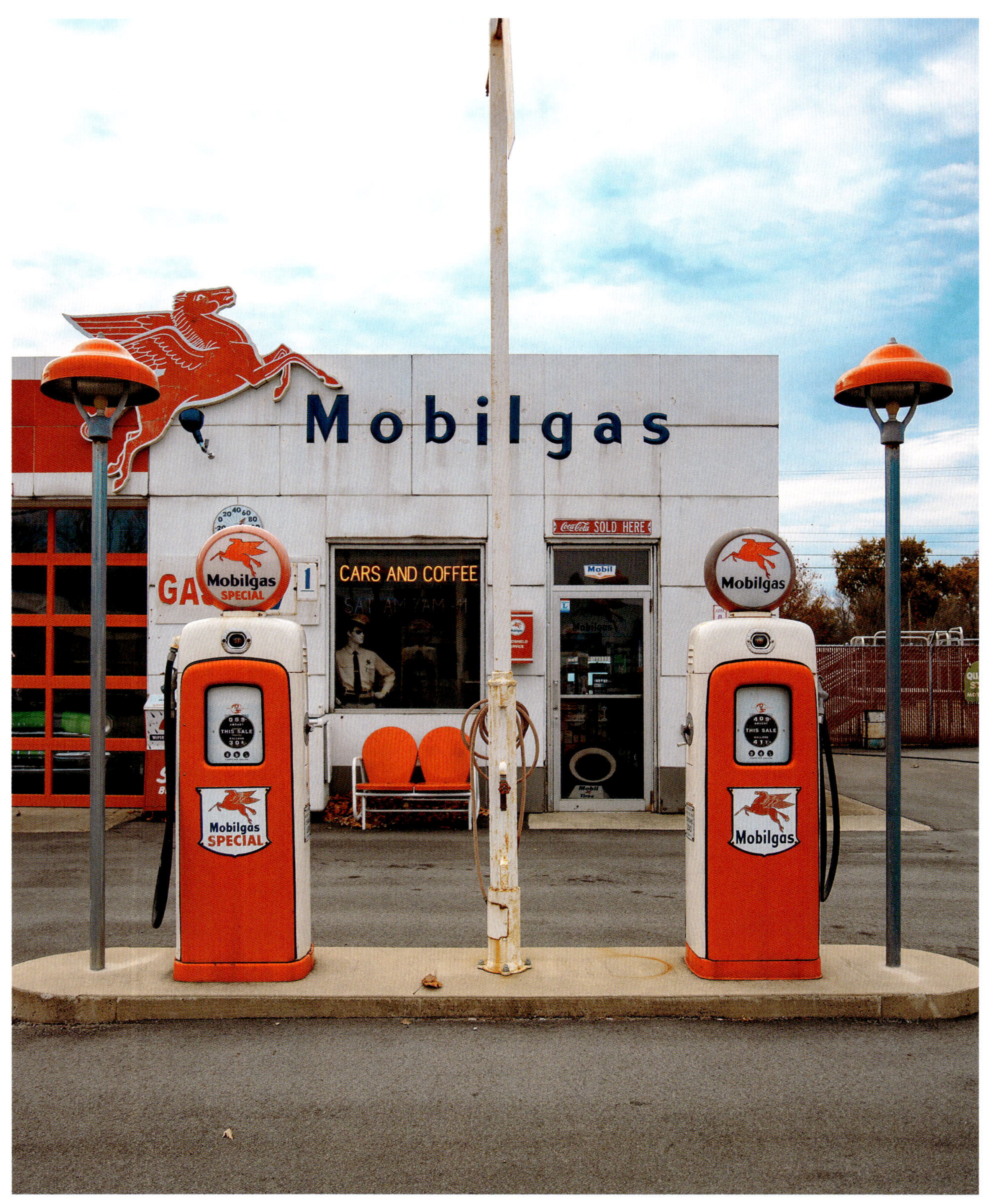

Mobil Gas Station • Plymouth, Indiana

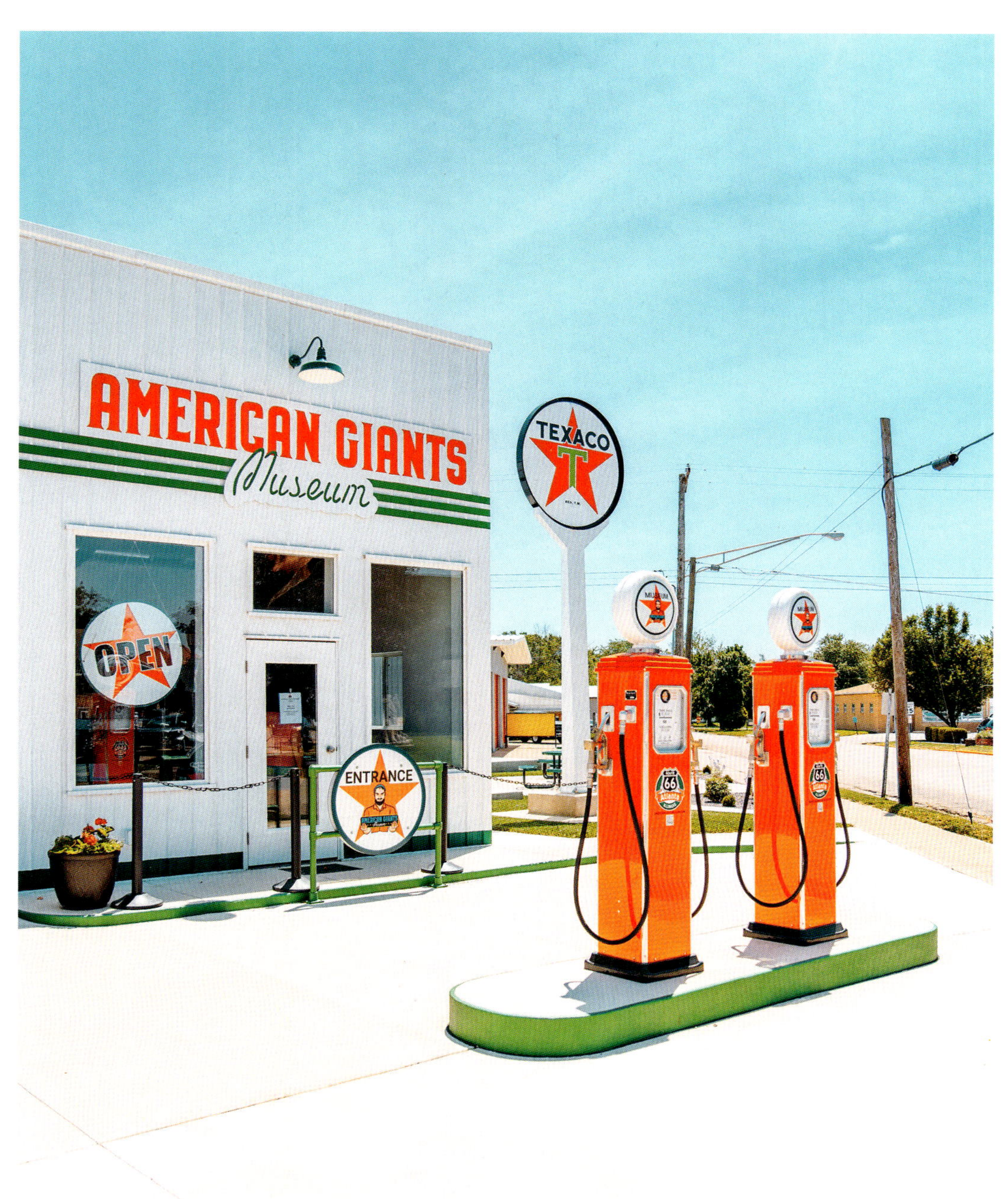

American Giants Museum • Atlanta, Illinois

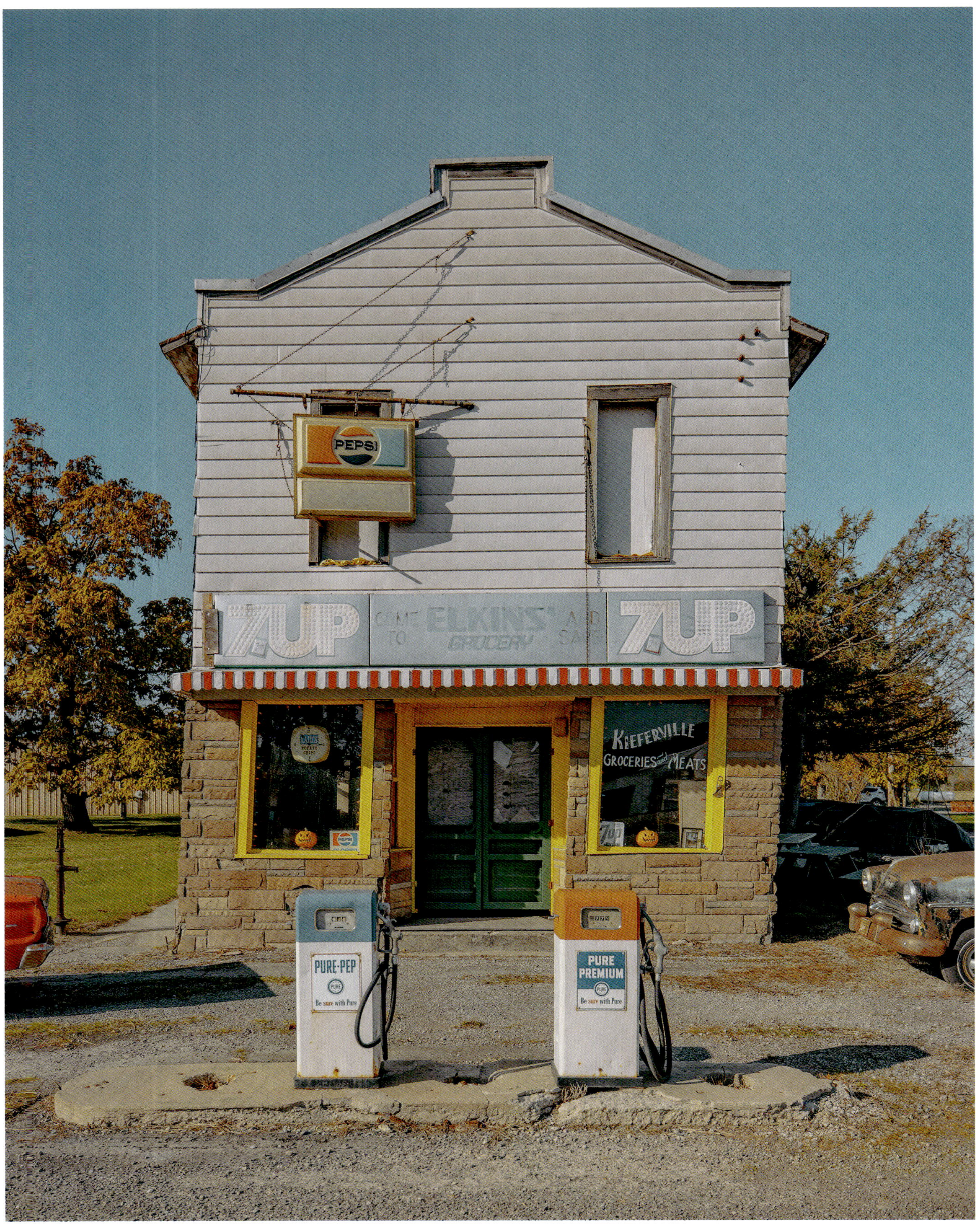
PEPSI
7UP
COME TO ELKINS' GROCERY AND SAVE
7UP
KIEFERVILLE
GROCERIES and MEATS
PURE-PEP
Be sure with Pure
PURE PREMIUM
Be sure with Pure

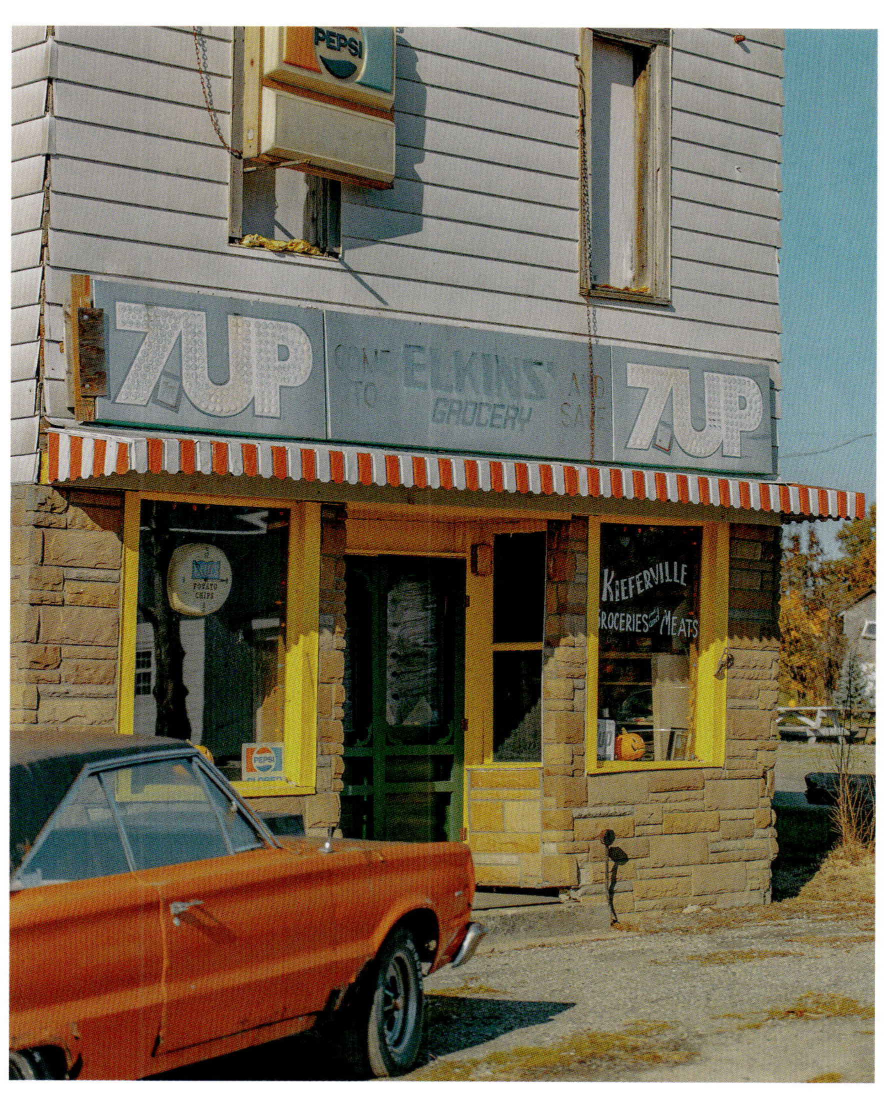

Kieferville Service Station • Kieferville, Ohio

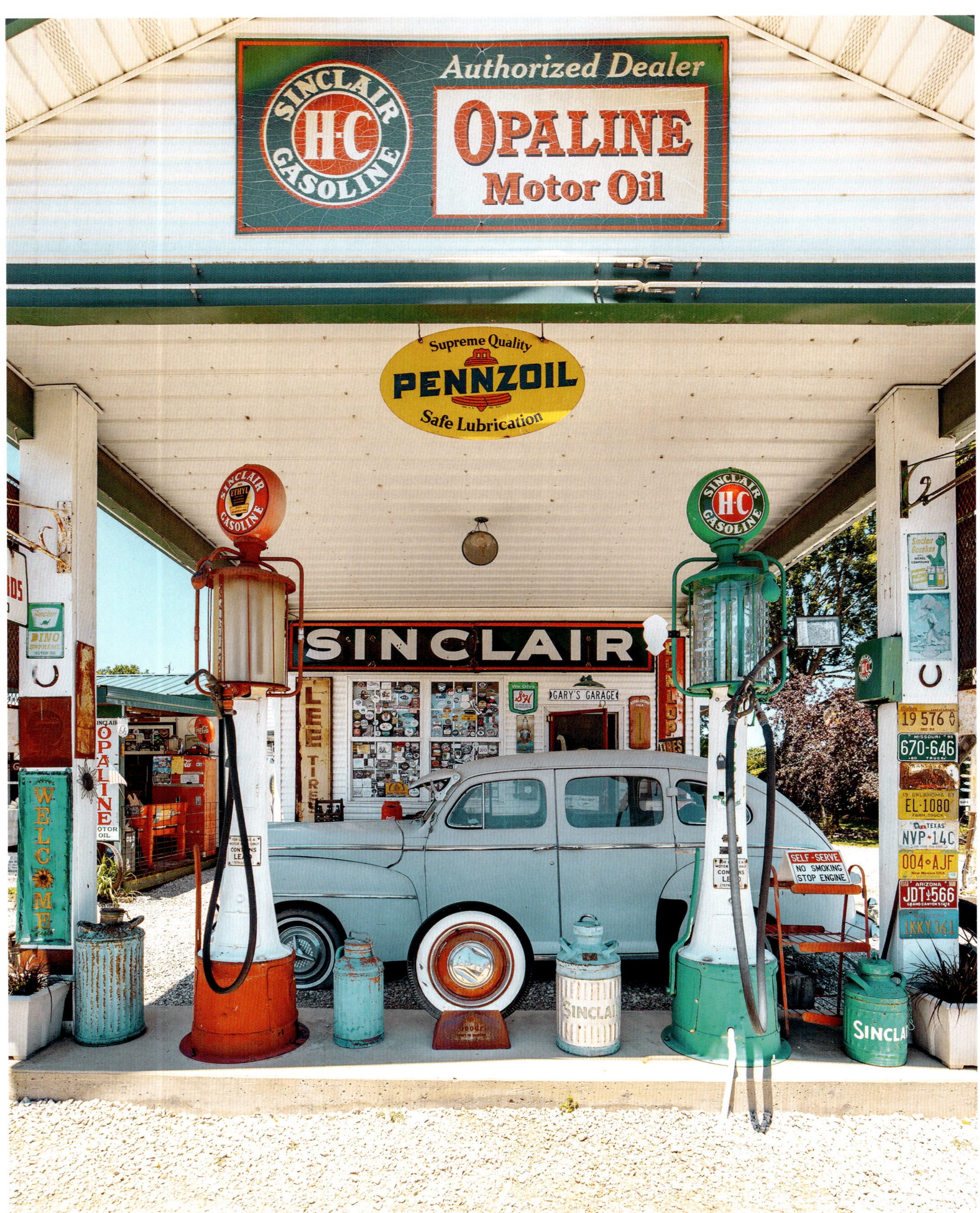
Authorized Dealer
SINCLAIR H-C GASOLINE
OPALINE Motor Oil
Supreme Quality
PENNZOIL
Safe Lubrication
SINCLAIR
GARY'S GARAGE
LEE TIRES
WELCOME
OPALINE
SELF-SERVE
NO SMOKING
STOP ENGINE
670-646
EL-1080
NVP-14C
004-AJF
JDT 566
SINCLAIR

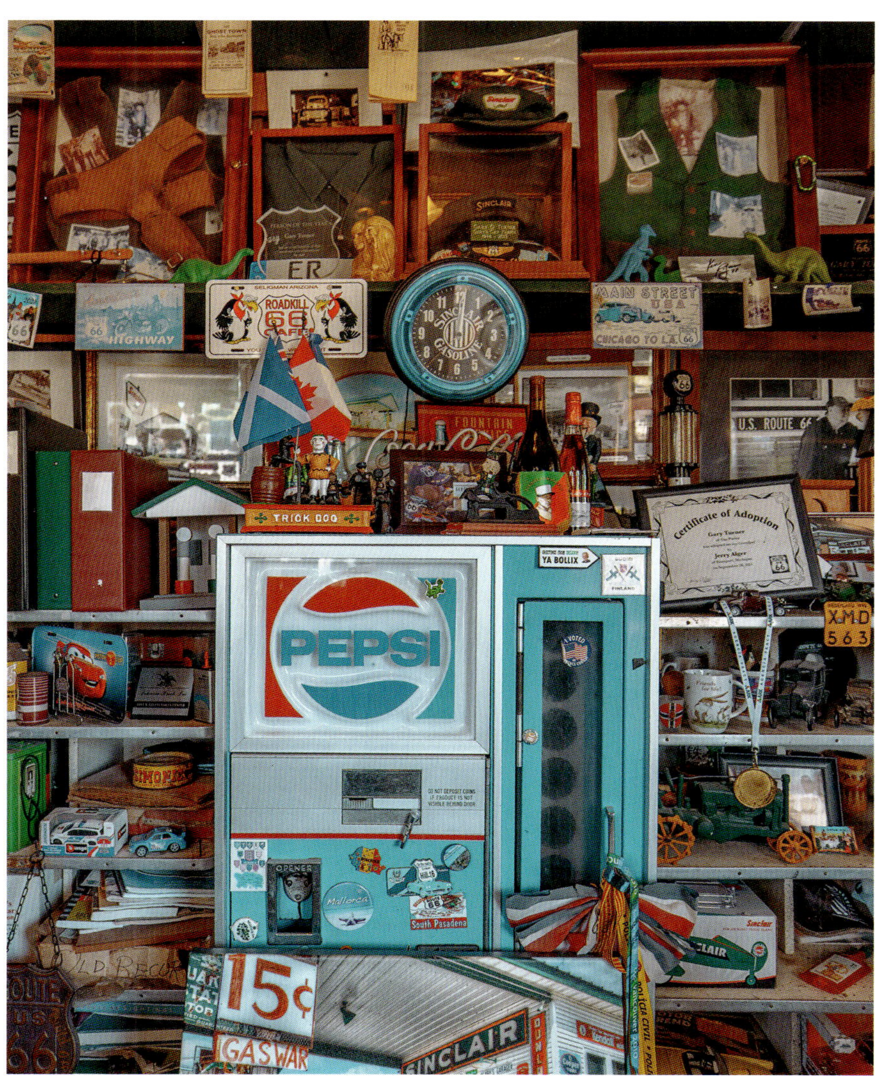

Gary's Gay Parita Service Station • Ash Grove, Missouri

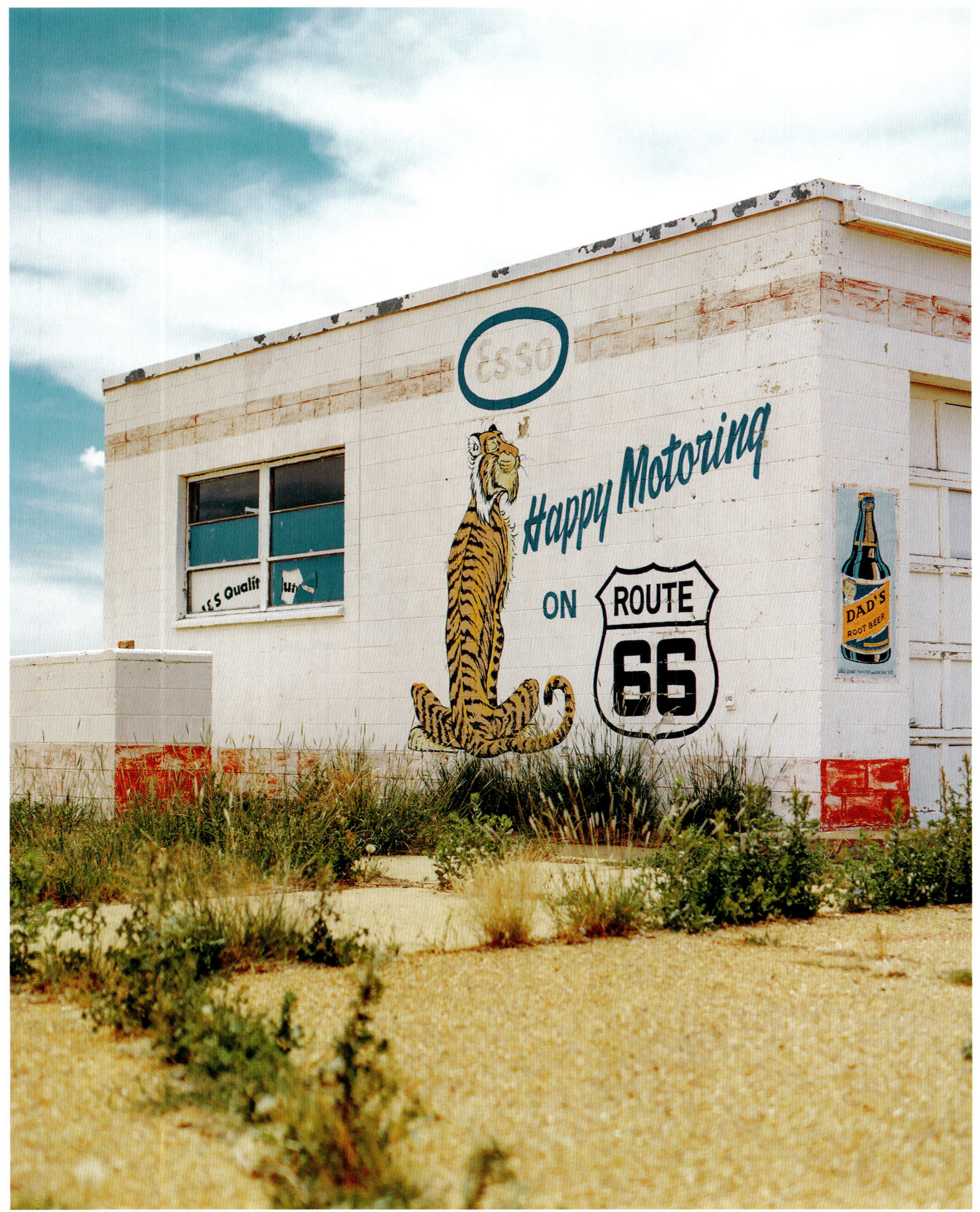
Esso
Happy Motoring
ON
ROUTE
66
DAD'S
ROOT BEER

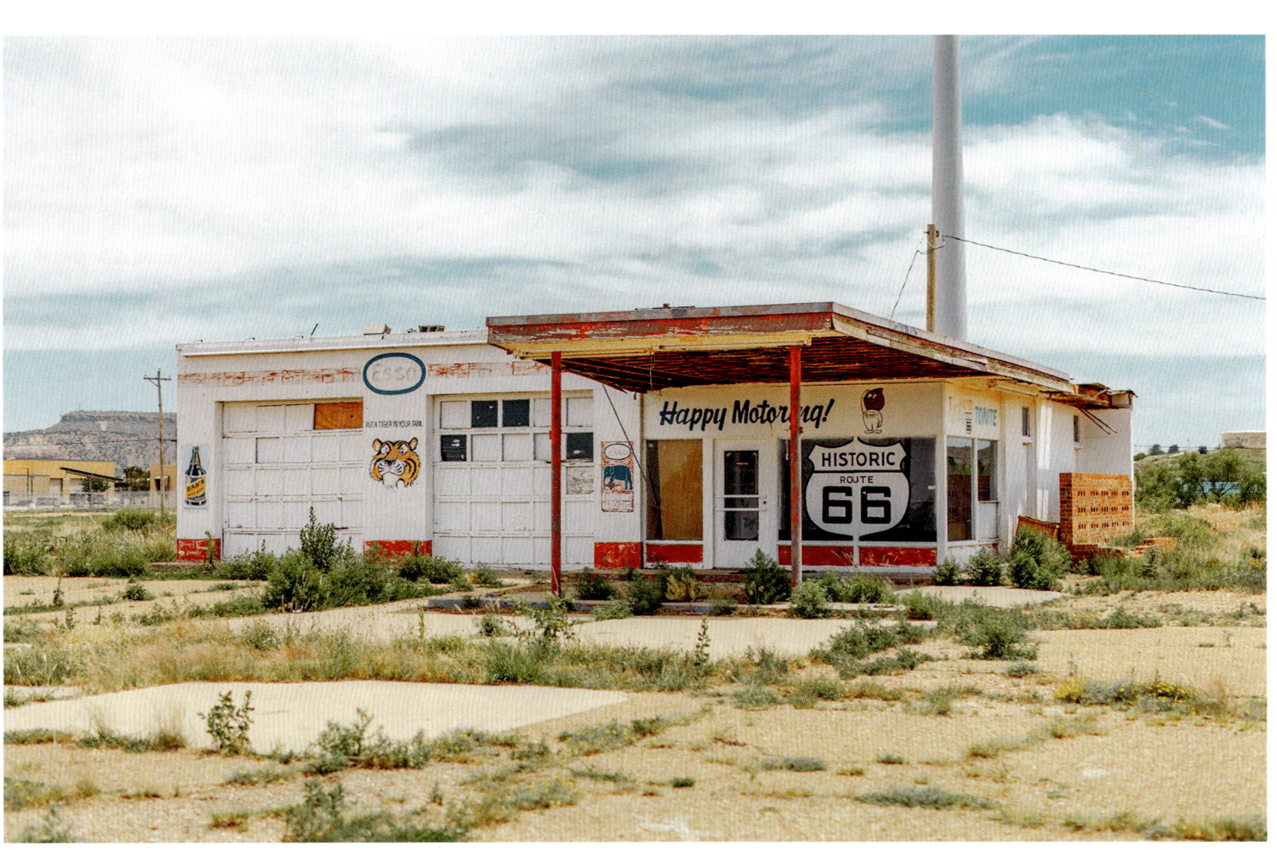

Esso Service Station • Tucumcari, New Mexico

MOTELS

I think the Blue Swallow Motel in Tucumcari, New Mexico, is the first place that comes to mind for most people when they think of Route 66. It's an icon, which is one reason I chose to include it in this collection of photographs. The current owners, Rob and Dawn, are Chicago natives, and I felt an instant Midwest connection with them, spending 90 minutes chatting with Rob over coffee in the front office.

I've stayed in a few different rooms at the Blue Swallow, but on my most recent visit, I stayed in Room #6, the Lillian Redman Suite. Lillian Redman owned the motel from 1958-1998. During my stay, I met a family from Utah staying in the room to my left—a wife, husband, and their two kids—traveling in a vintage Chevy that got about 10-15 miles per gallon. I can't even imagine traveling with my family that way, but I completely respect their dedication to the retro road trip. They were headed to an art show in Austin. In the room to my right was a widower who had lost his wife a couple years earlier. He was traveling to West Virginia by motorcycle, and we talked about life and travel well into the night. The next morning, I woke up early to catch the sunrise and said goodbye to him before he set off for West Virginia.

Motels are such an essential part of any road trip, and if you're lucky enough to stop at one like the Blue Swallow, it's the perfect chance to slow down and connect with like-minded travelers.

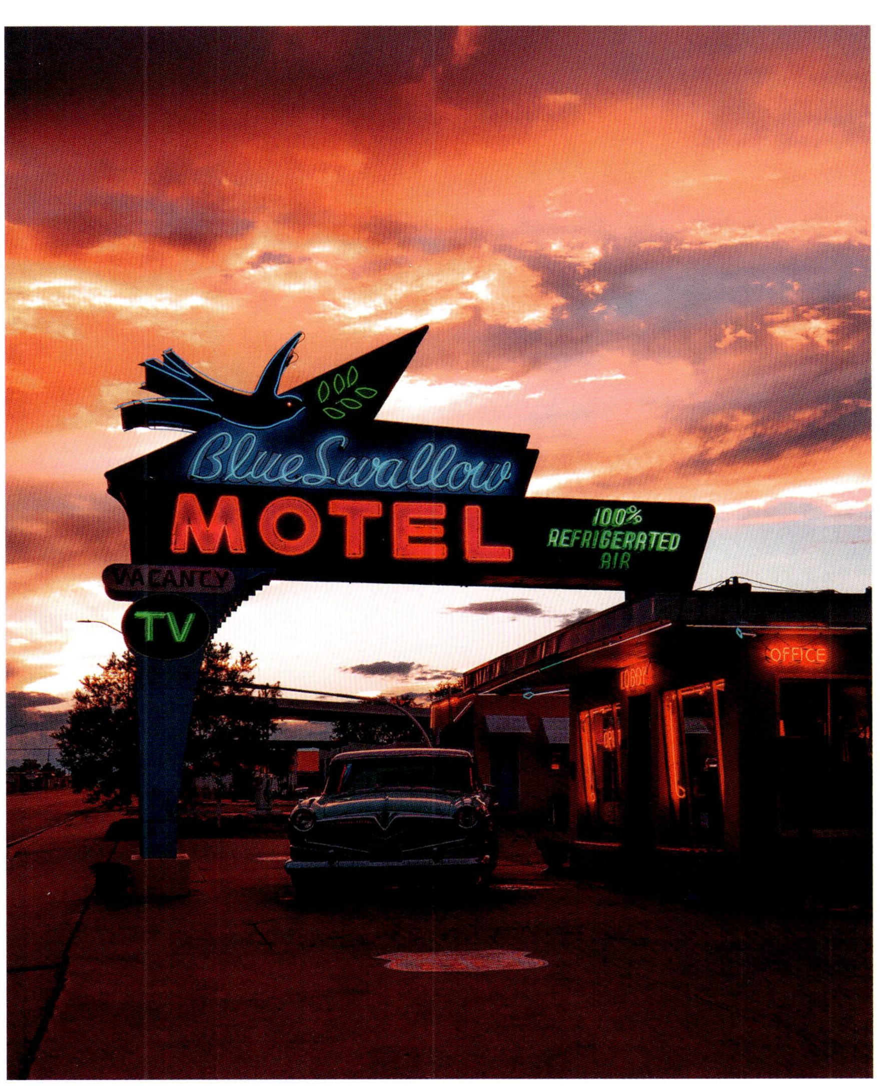

Blue Swallow Motel • Tucumcari, New Mexico

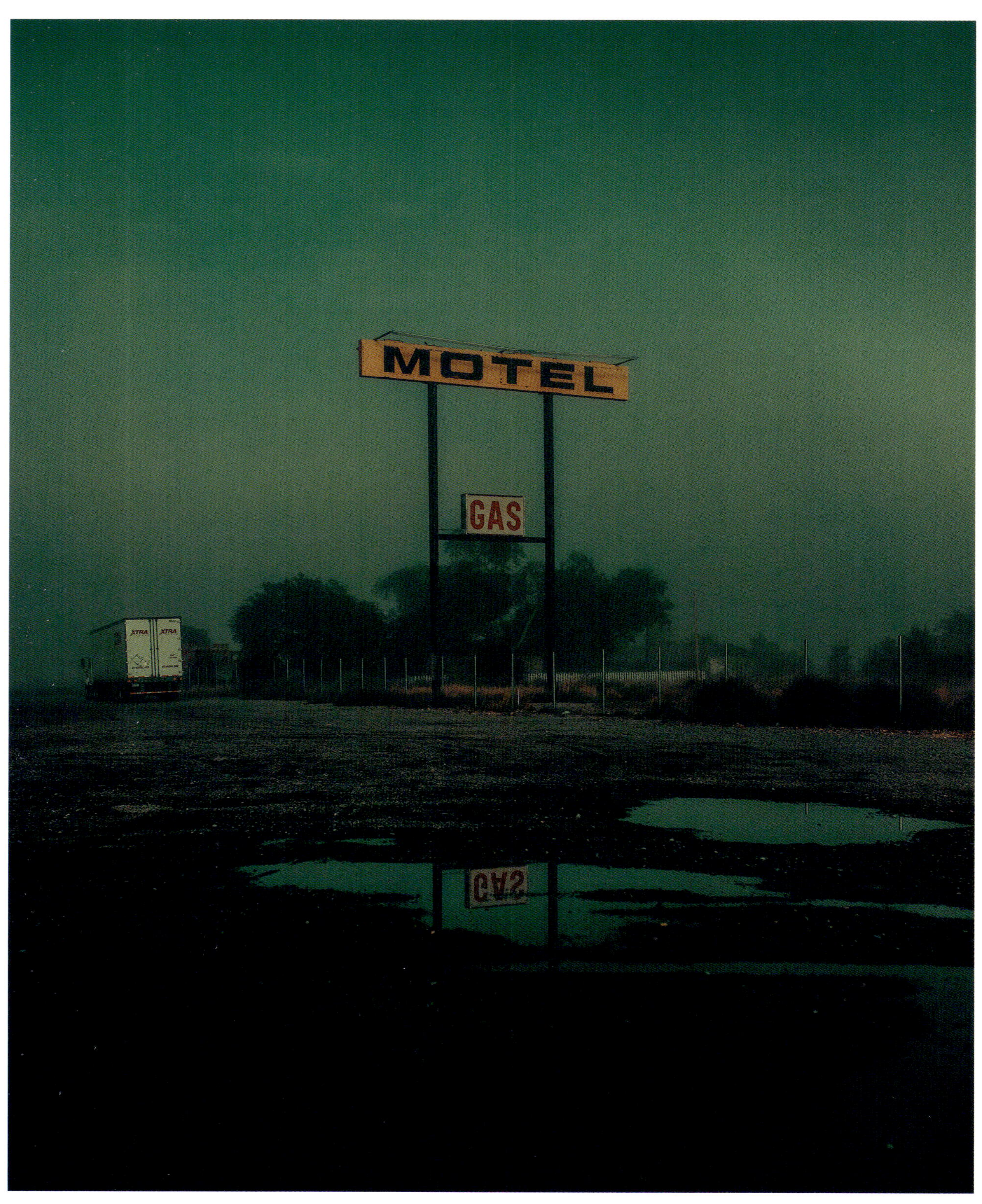

Abandoned Motel Sign • Moriarty, New Mexico

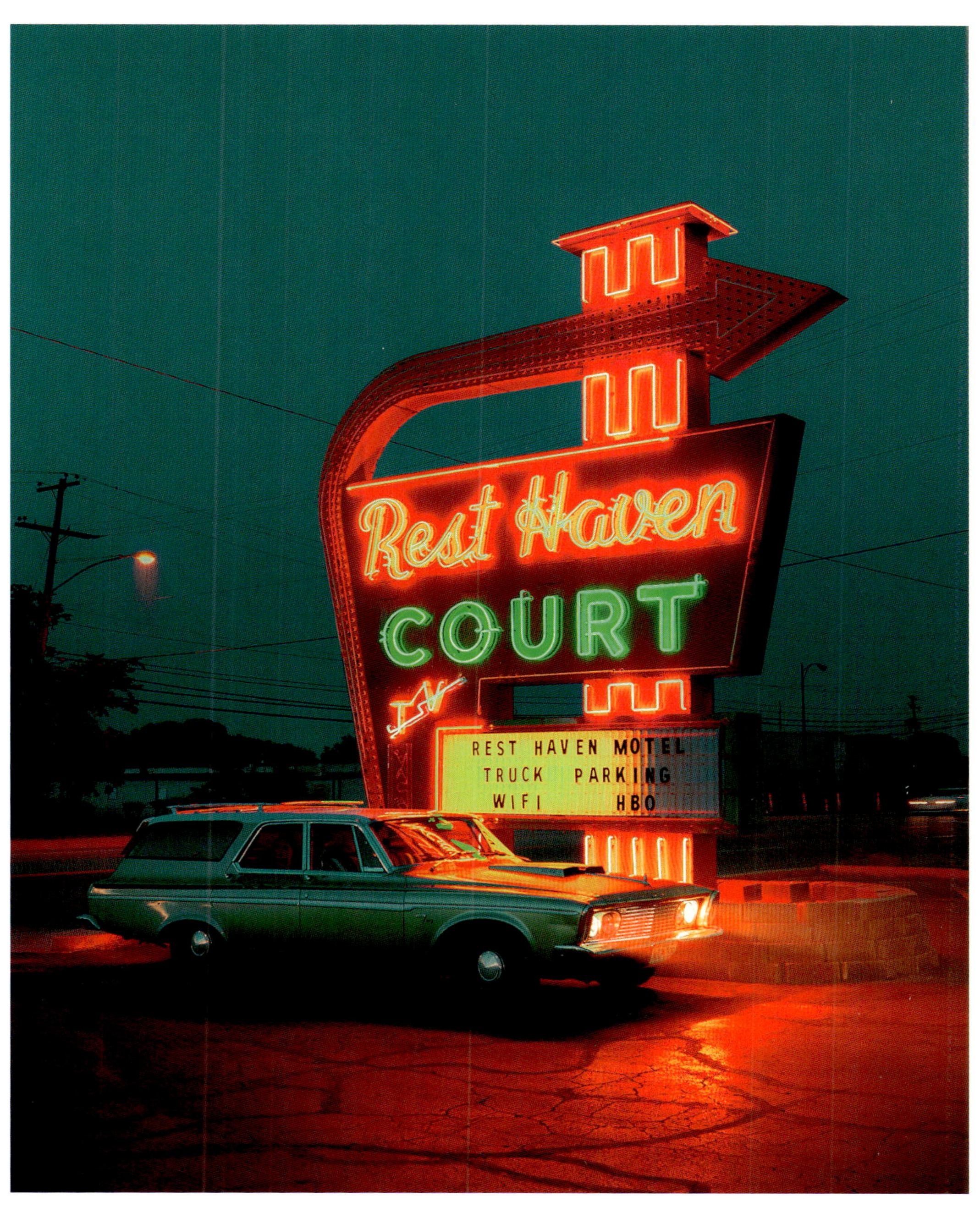

Rest Haven Motel • Springfield, Missouri

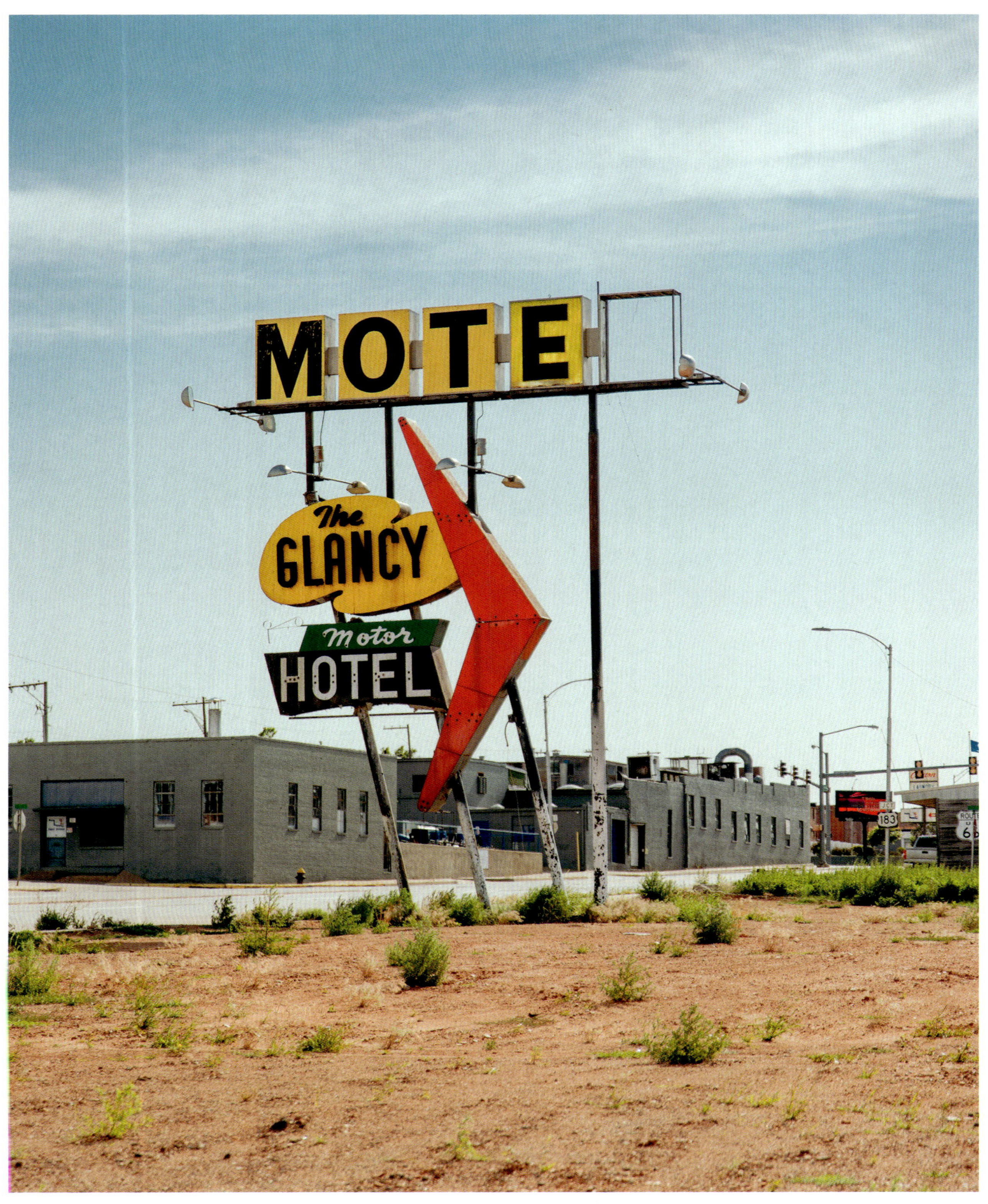

Abandoned Glancy Motel Sign • Clinton, Oklahoma

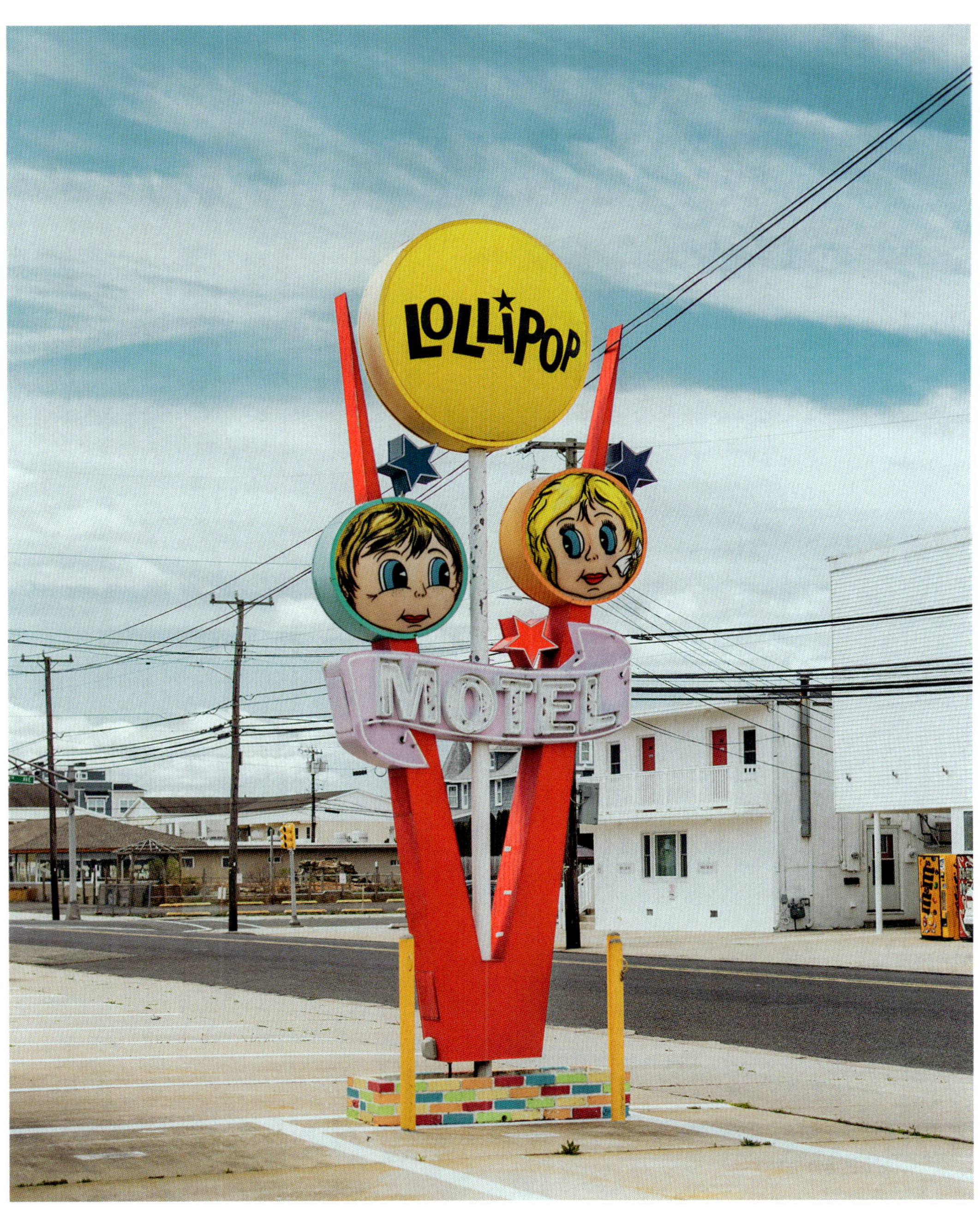

Lollipop Motel Sign • North Wildwood, New Jersey

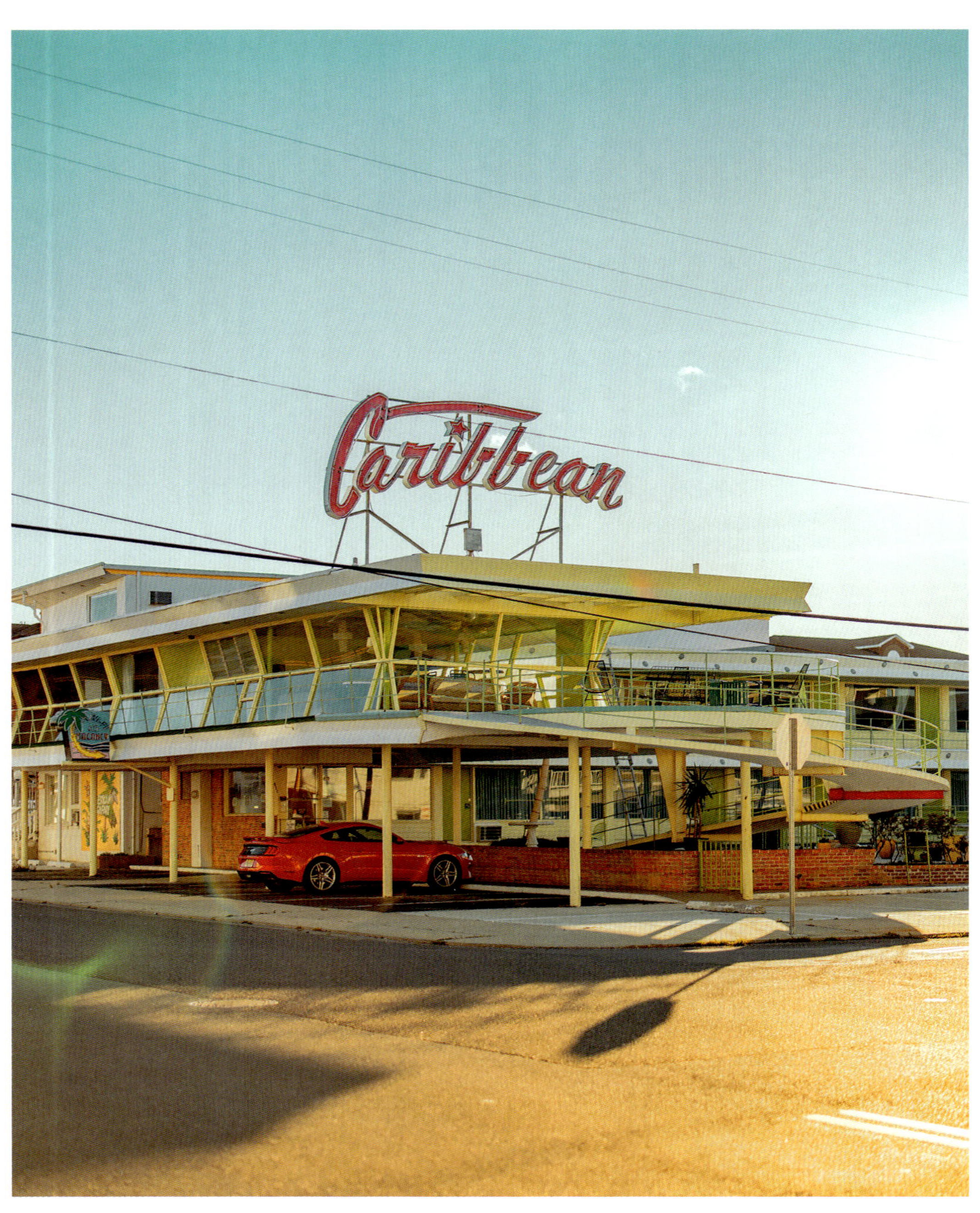

Caribbean Motel • Wildwood Crest, New Jersey

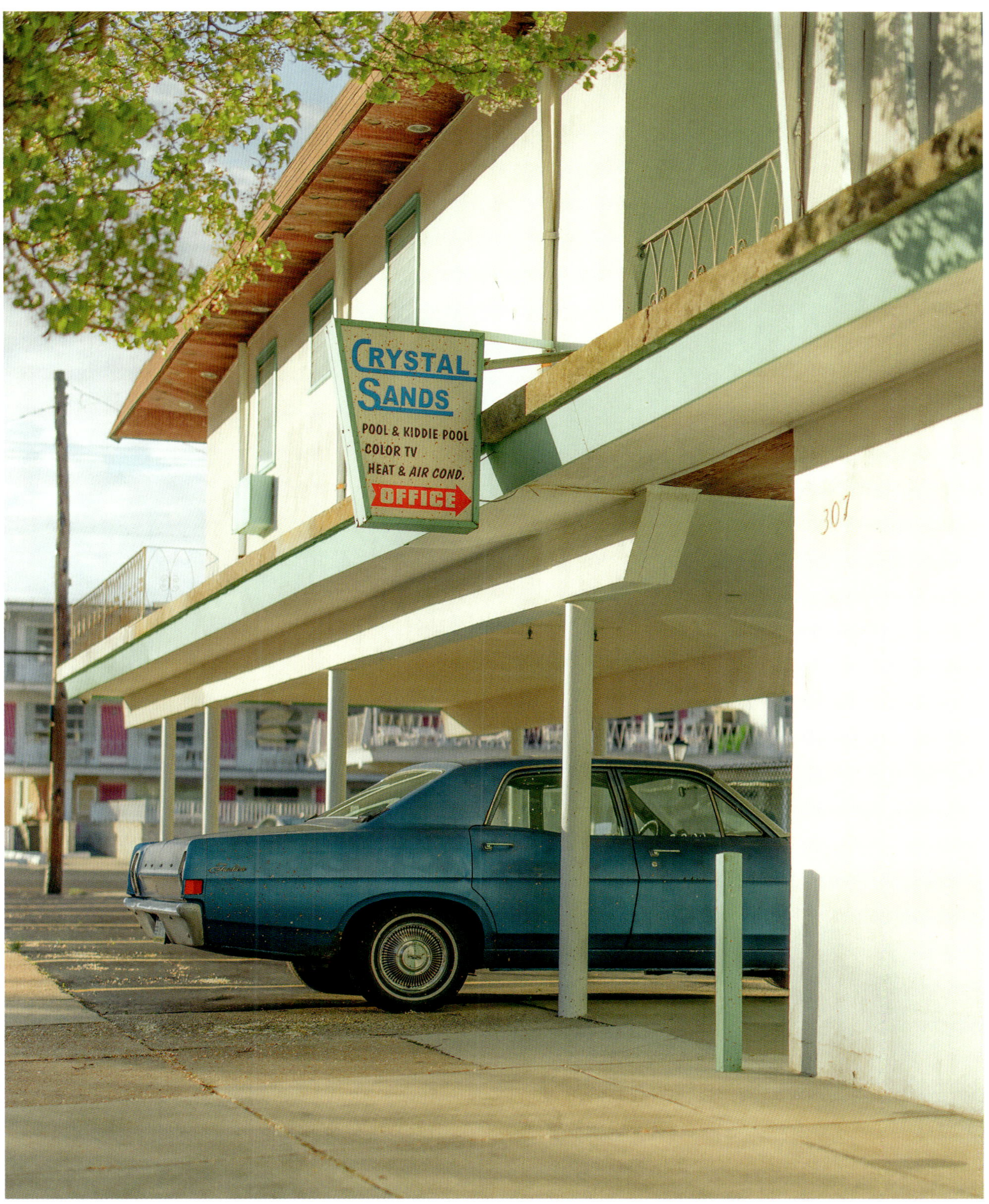

Crystal Sands Motel • Wildwood, New Jersey

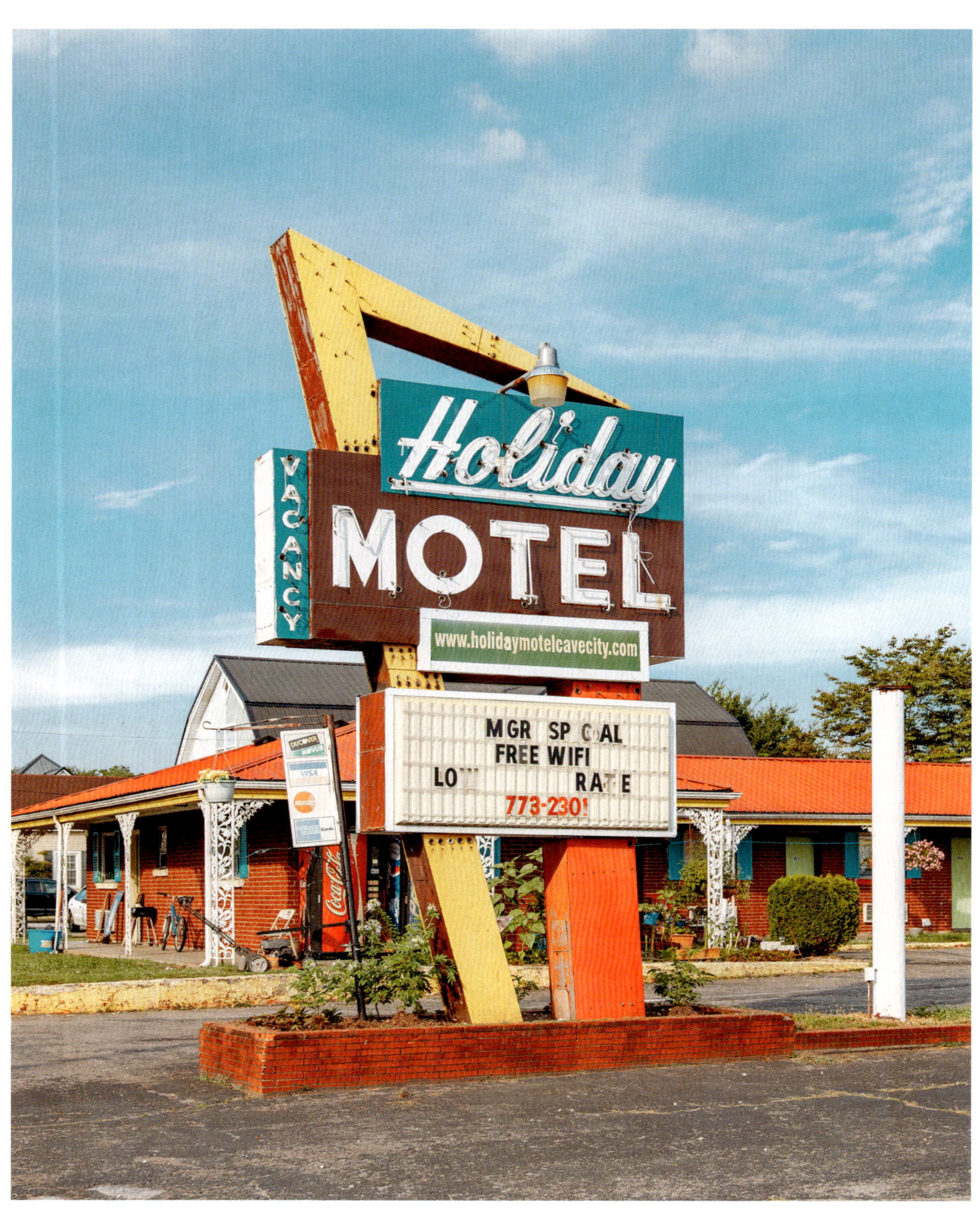

Holiday Motel • Cave City, Kentucky

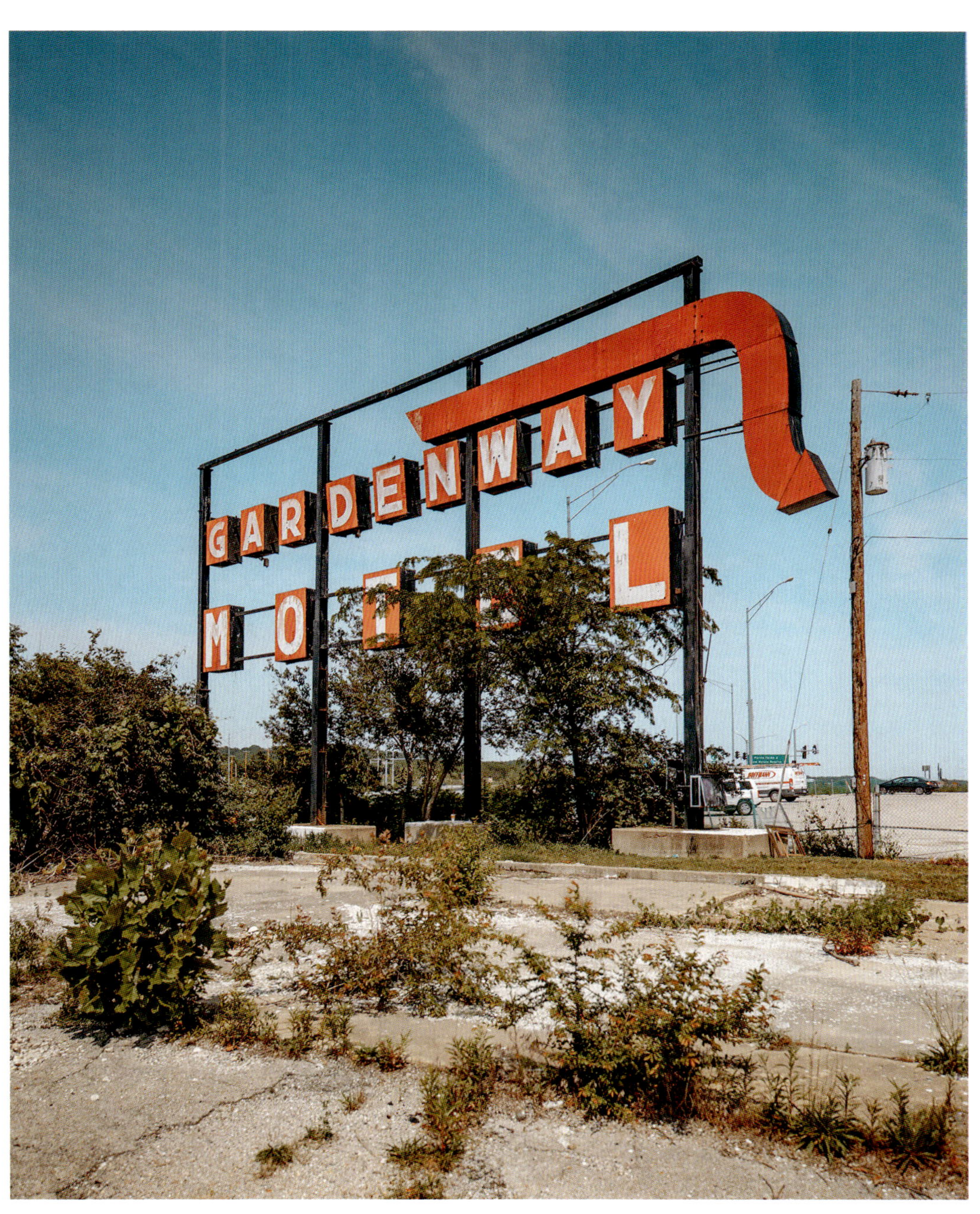

Abandoned Gardenway Motel Sign • Gray Summit, Missouri

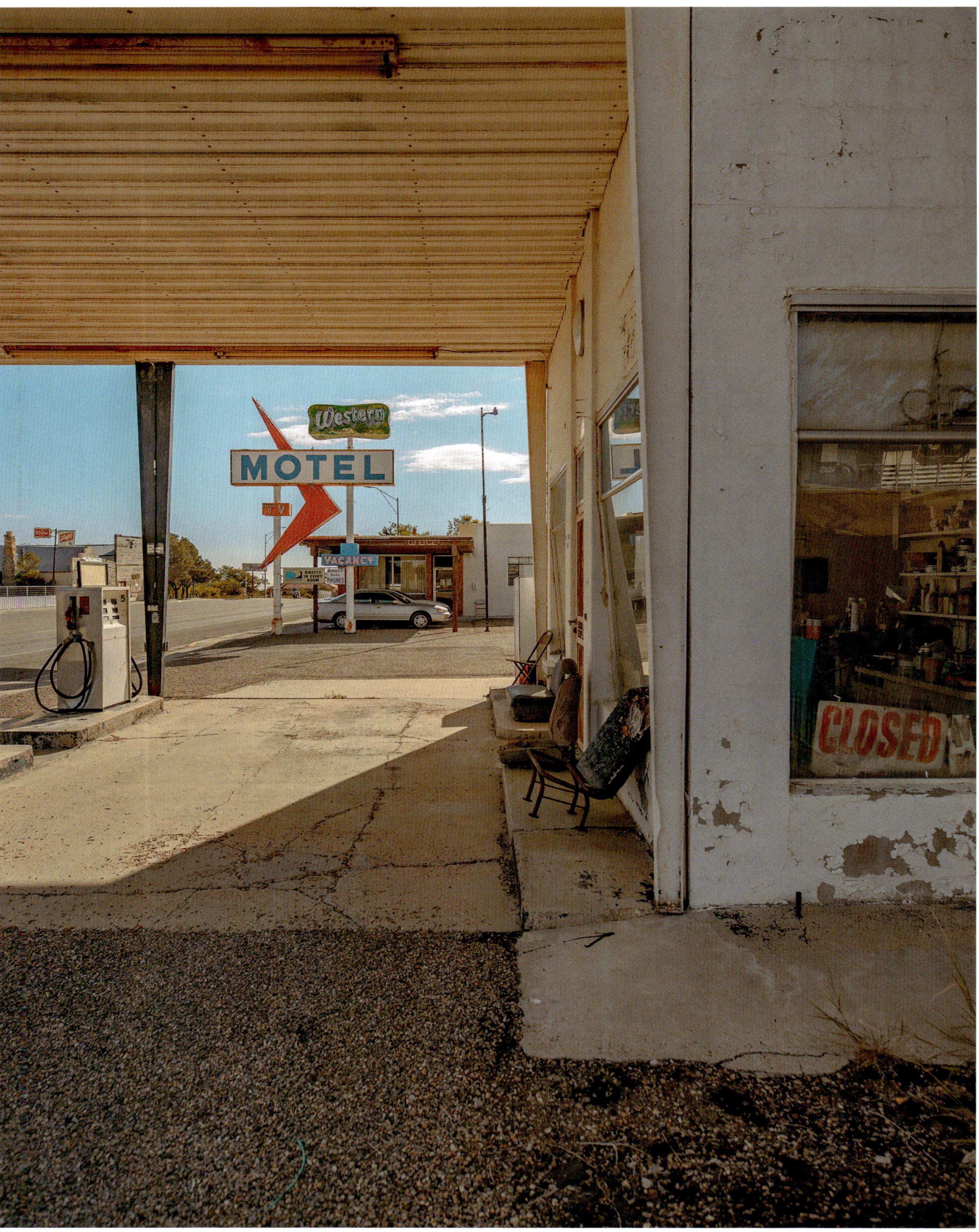
Western
MOTEL
TV
VACANCY
CLOSED

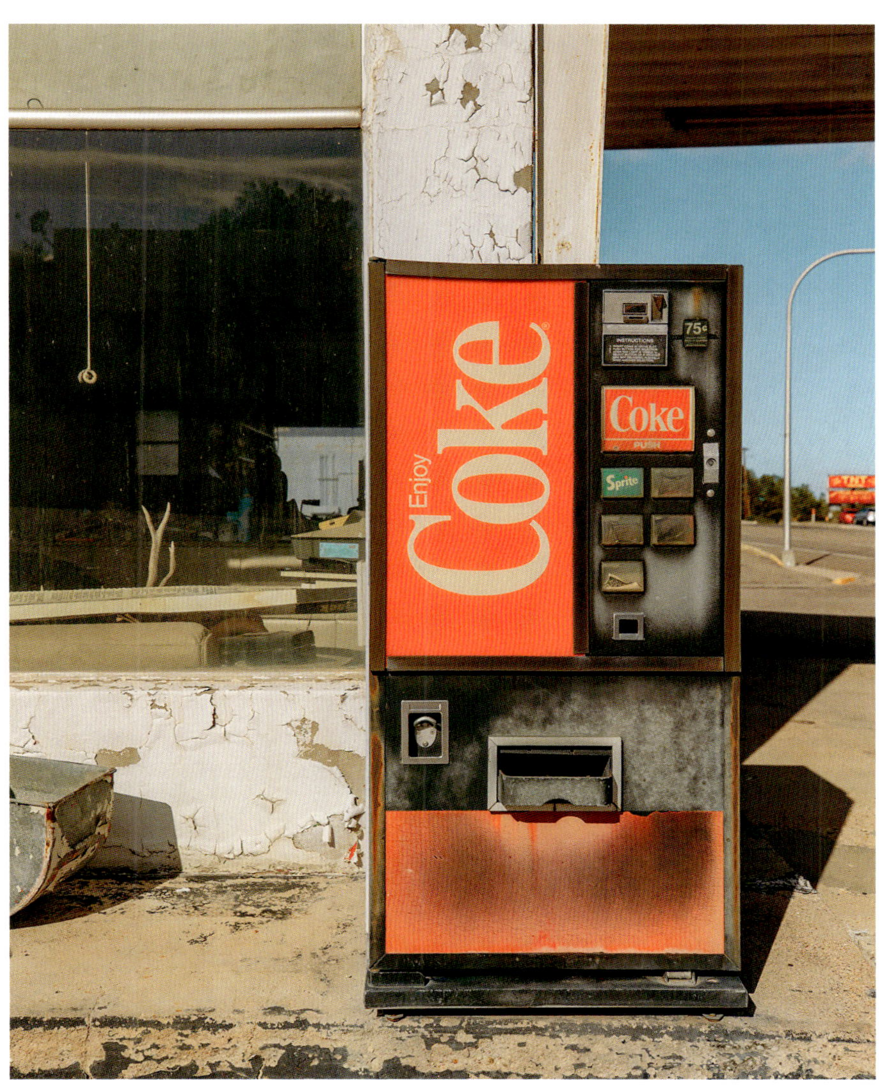

Western Motel • Vaughn, New Mexico

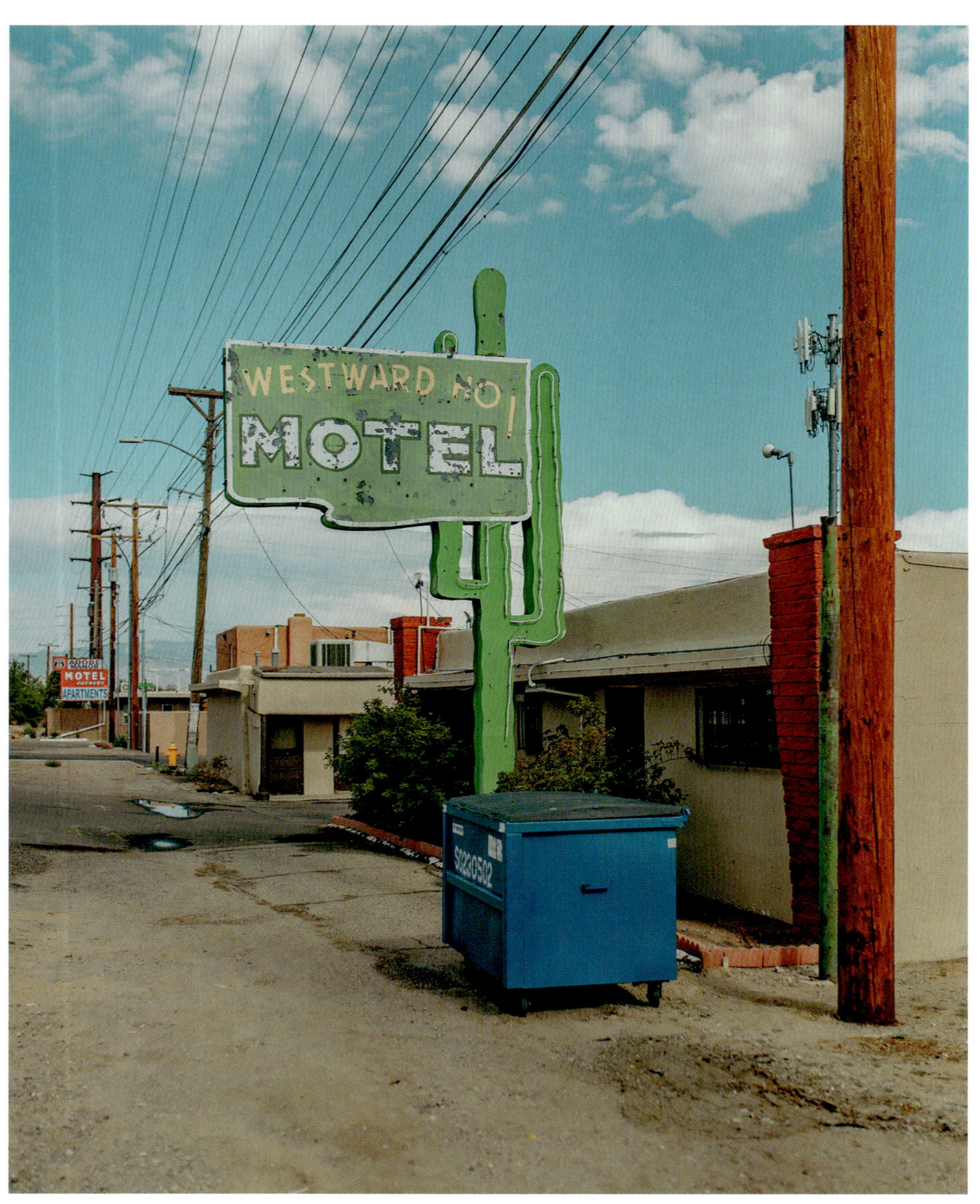

Westward Ho Motel • Albuquerque, New Mexico

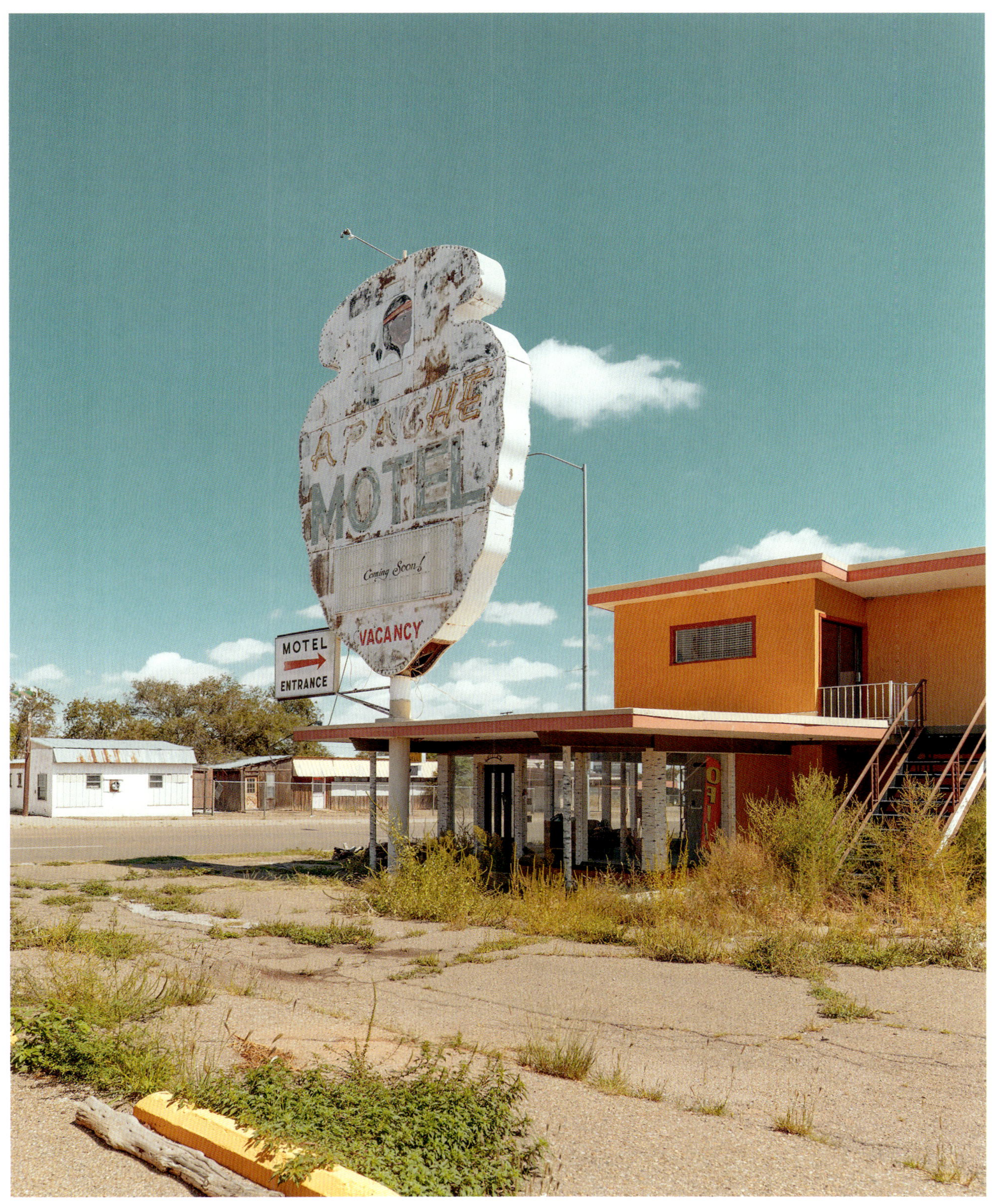

Apache Motel • Tucumcari, New Mexico

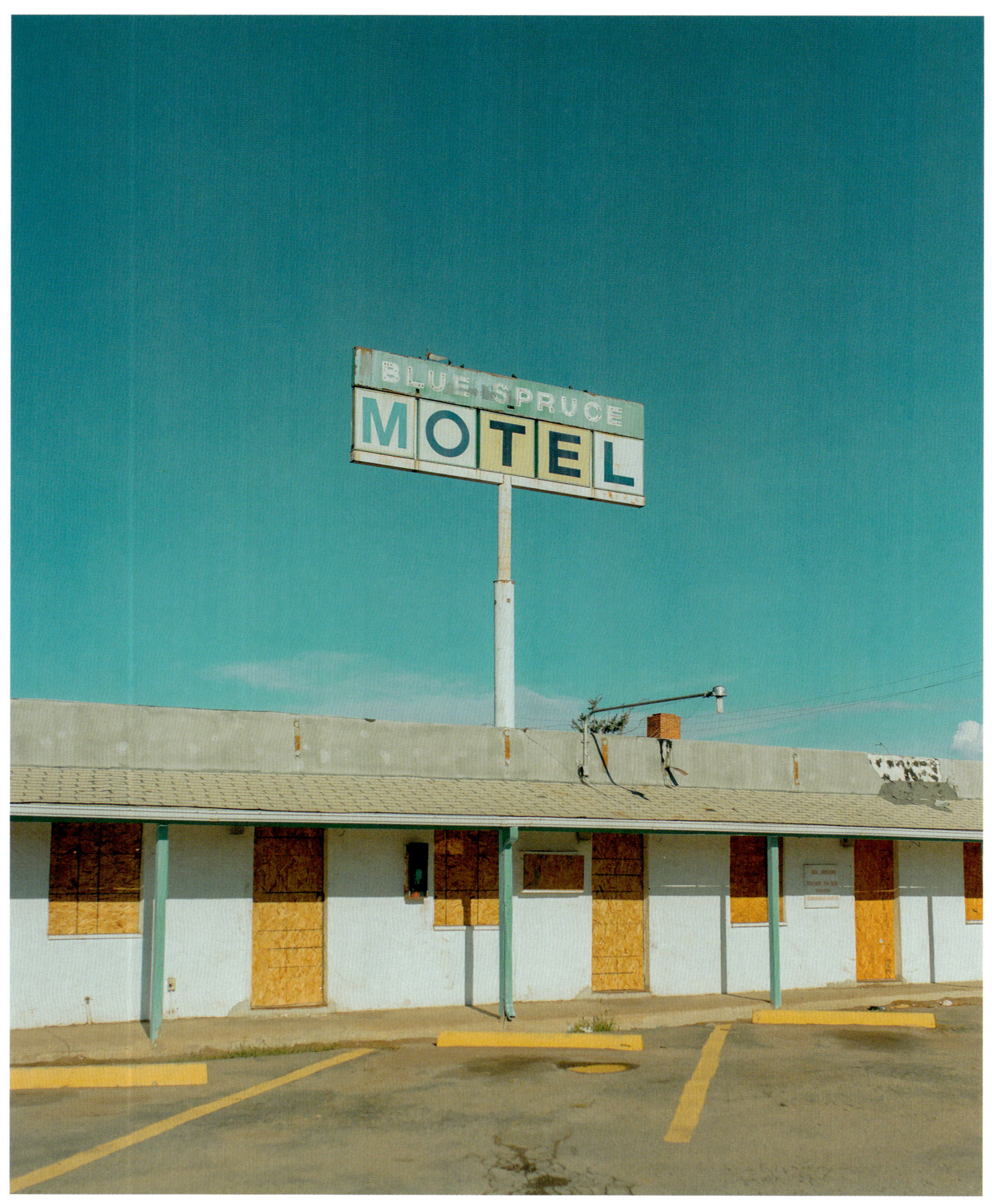

Blue Spruce Motel • Gallup, New Mexico

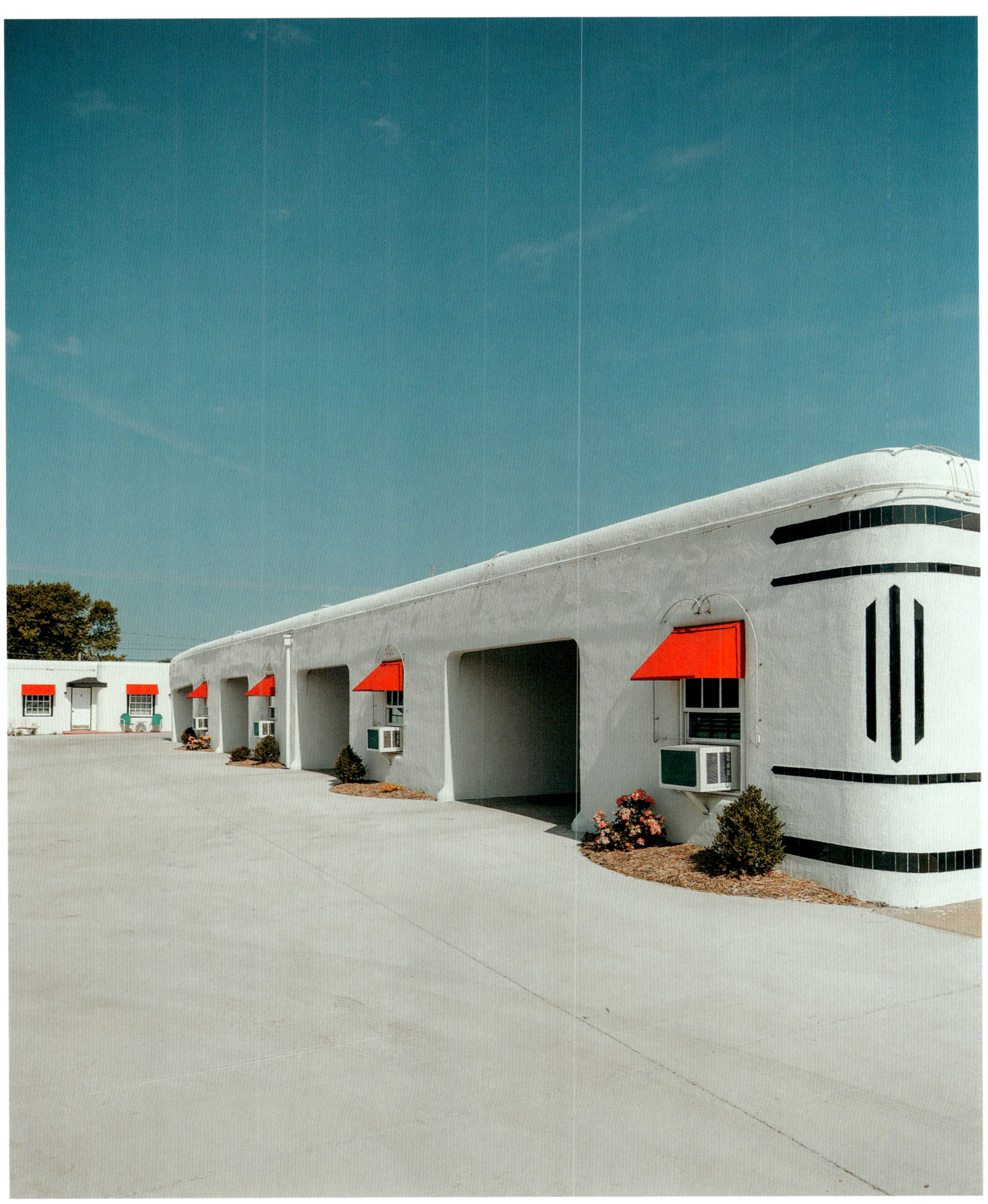

Boots Court Motel • Carthage, Missouri

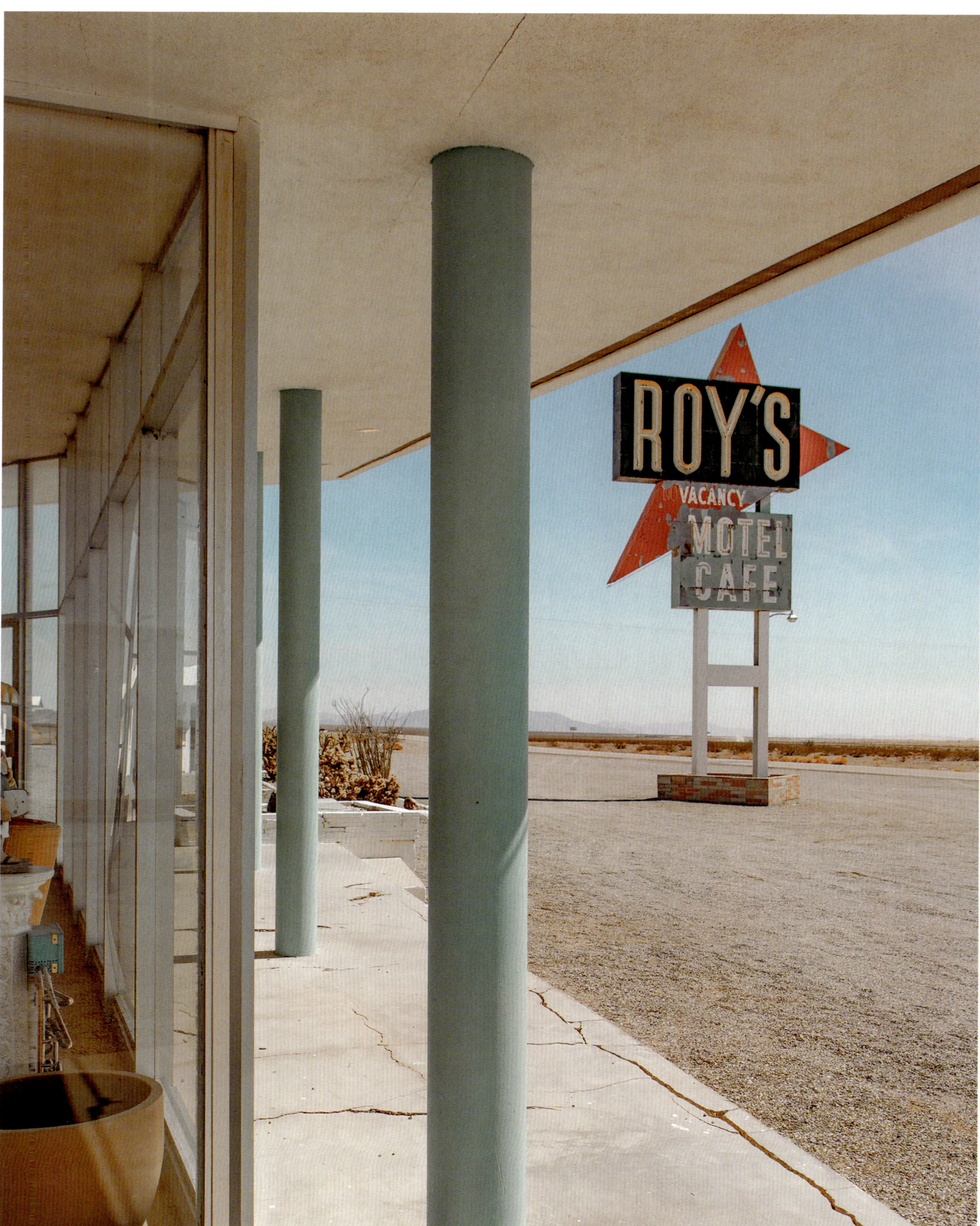
ROY'S
VACANCY
MOTEL
CAFE

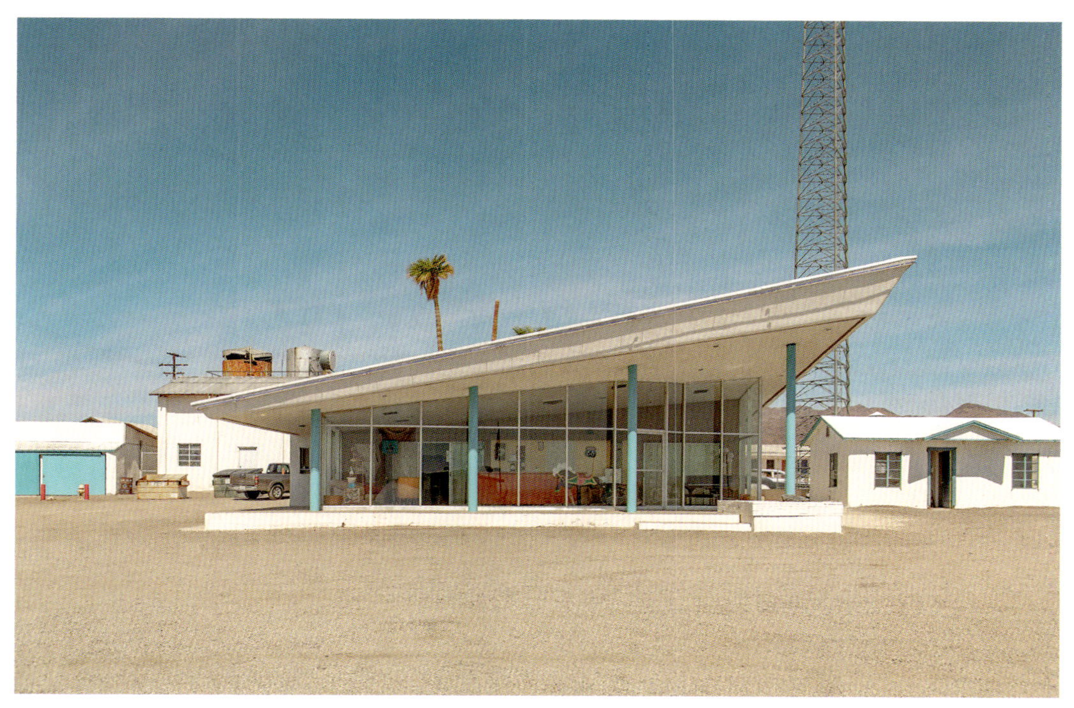

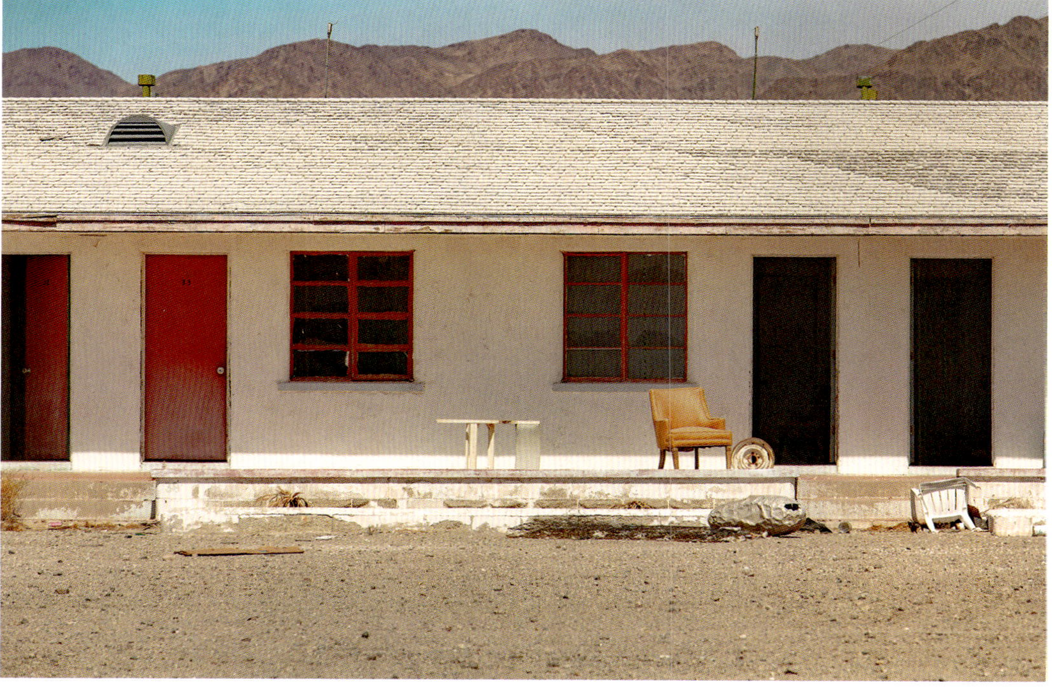

Roy's Motel & Cafe • Amboy, California

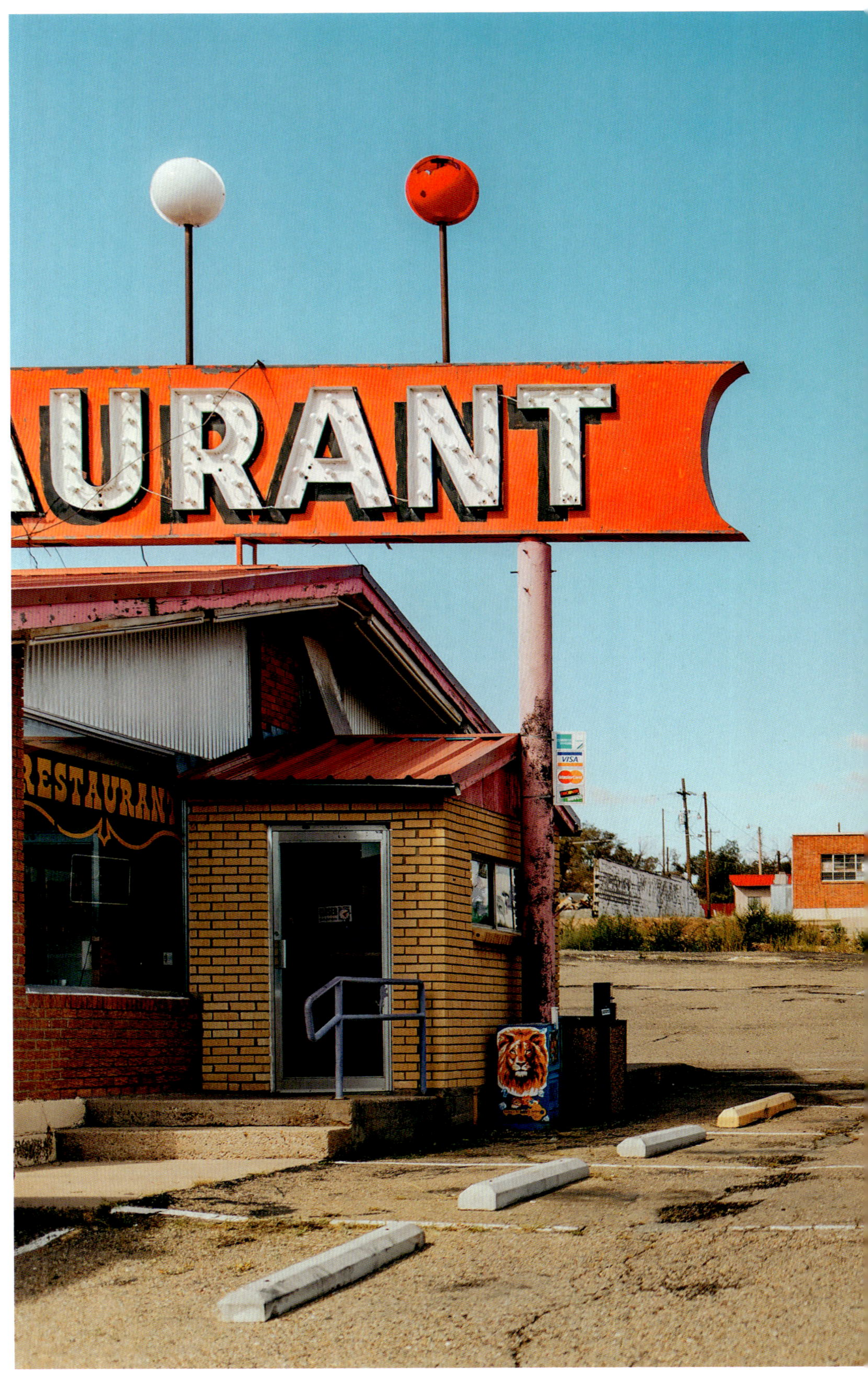

Sun 'n Sand Motel
Santa Rosa, New Mexico

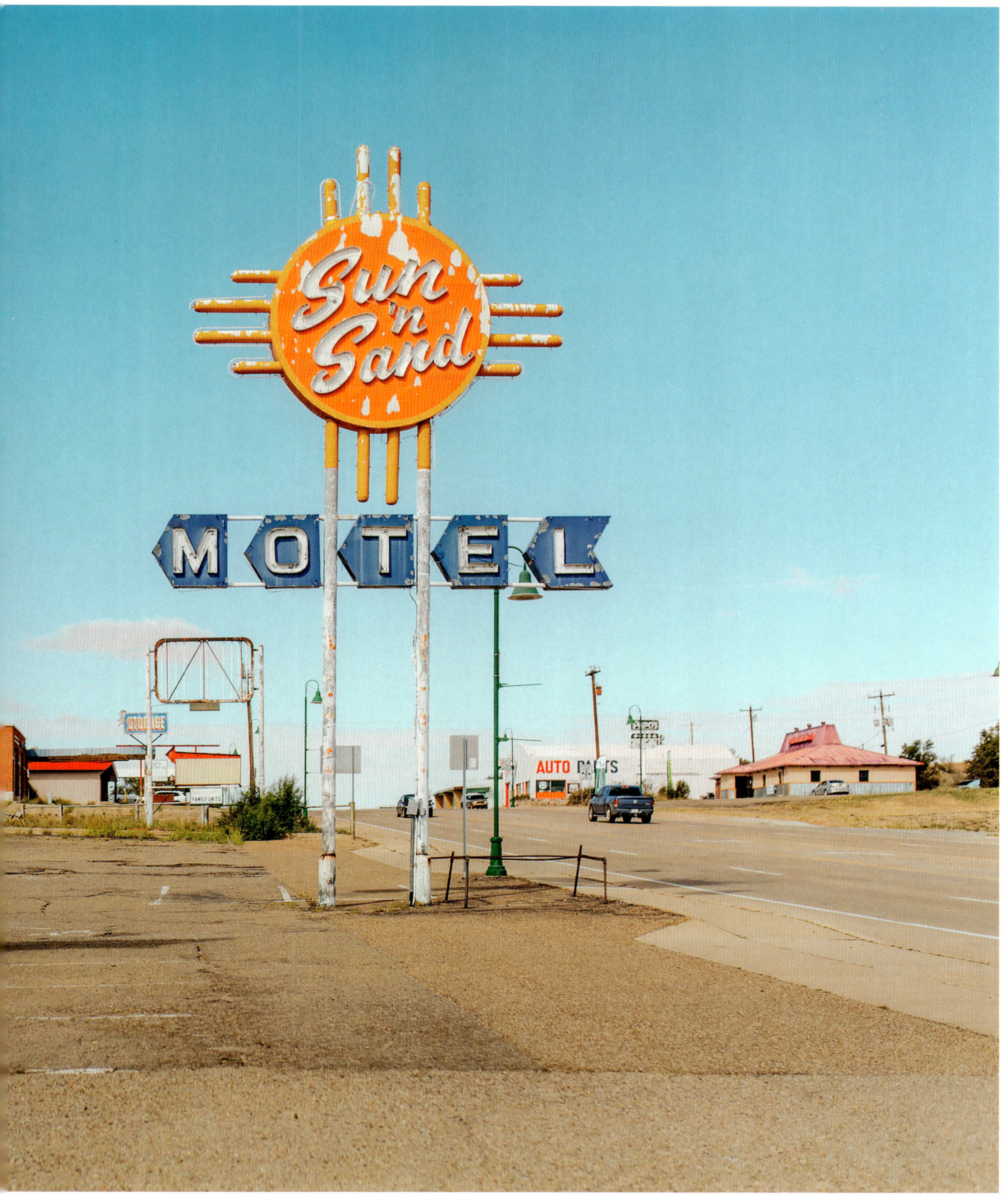
Sun 'n Sand
MOTEL
STORAGE
AUTO PARTS

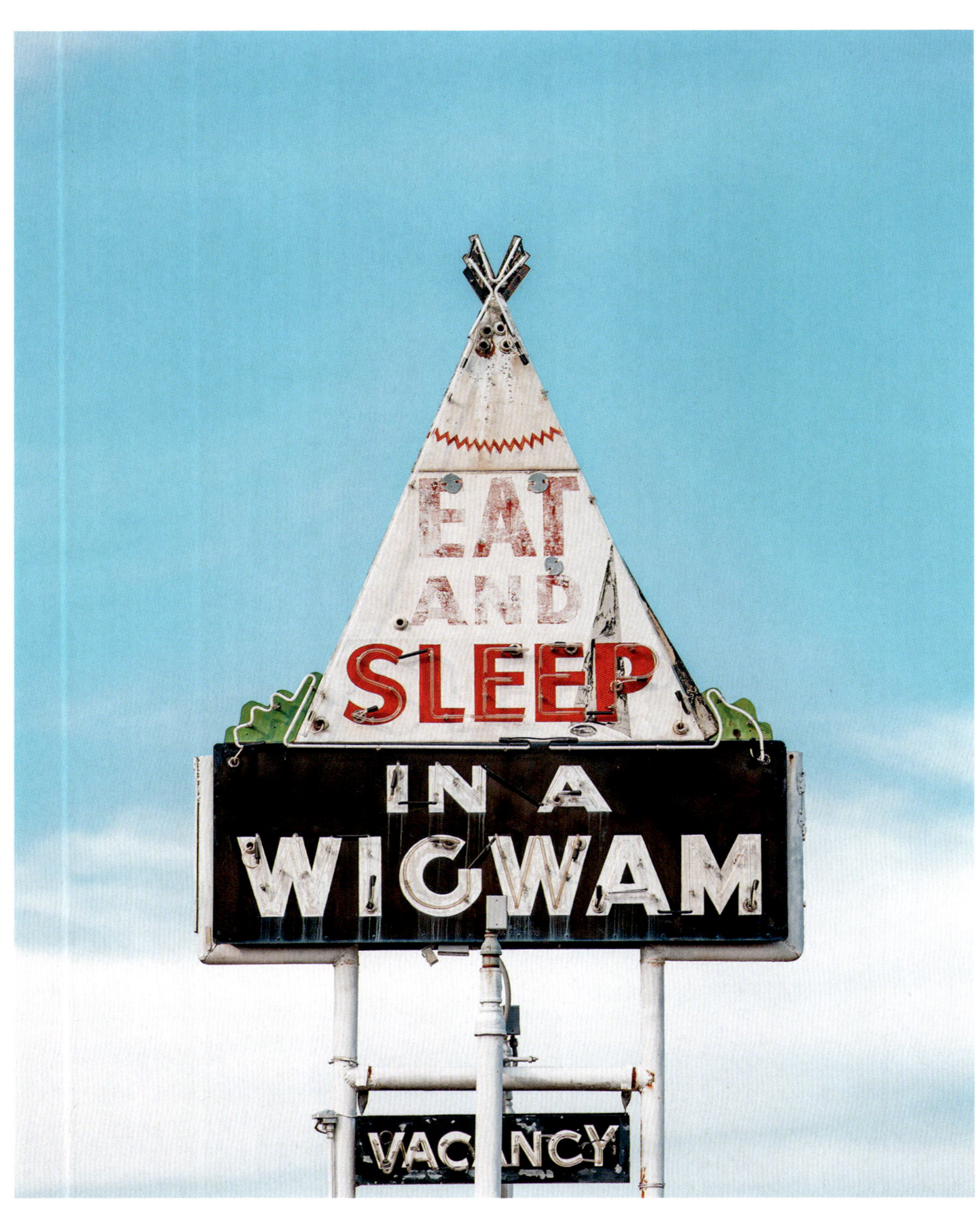

Wigwam Village No. 2 • Cave City, Kentucky

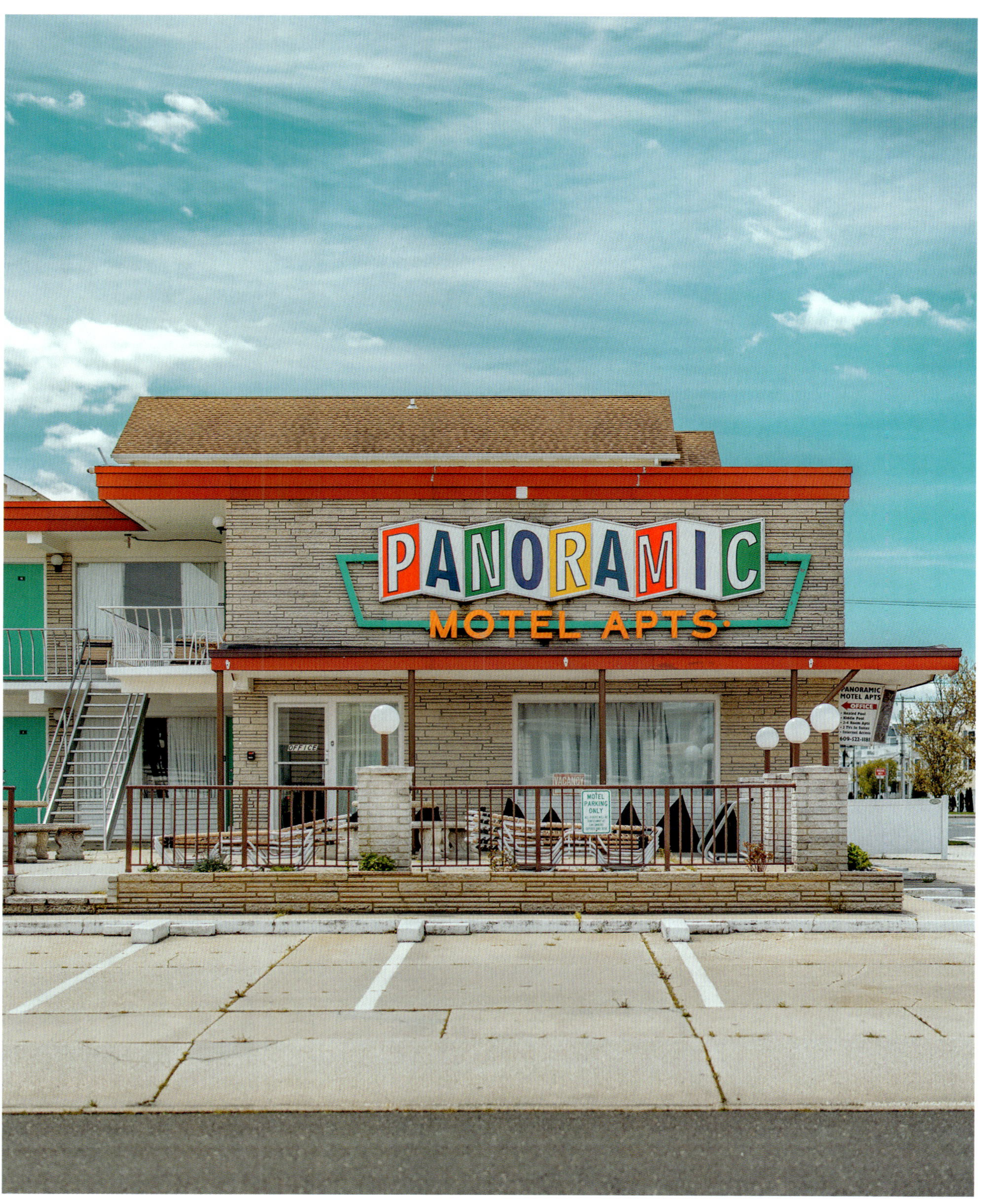

Panoramic Motel & Apartments • North Wildwood, New Jersey

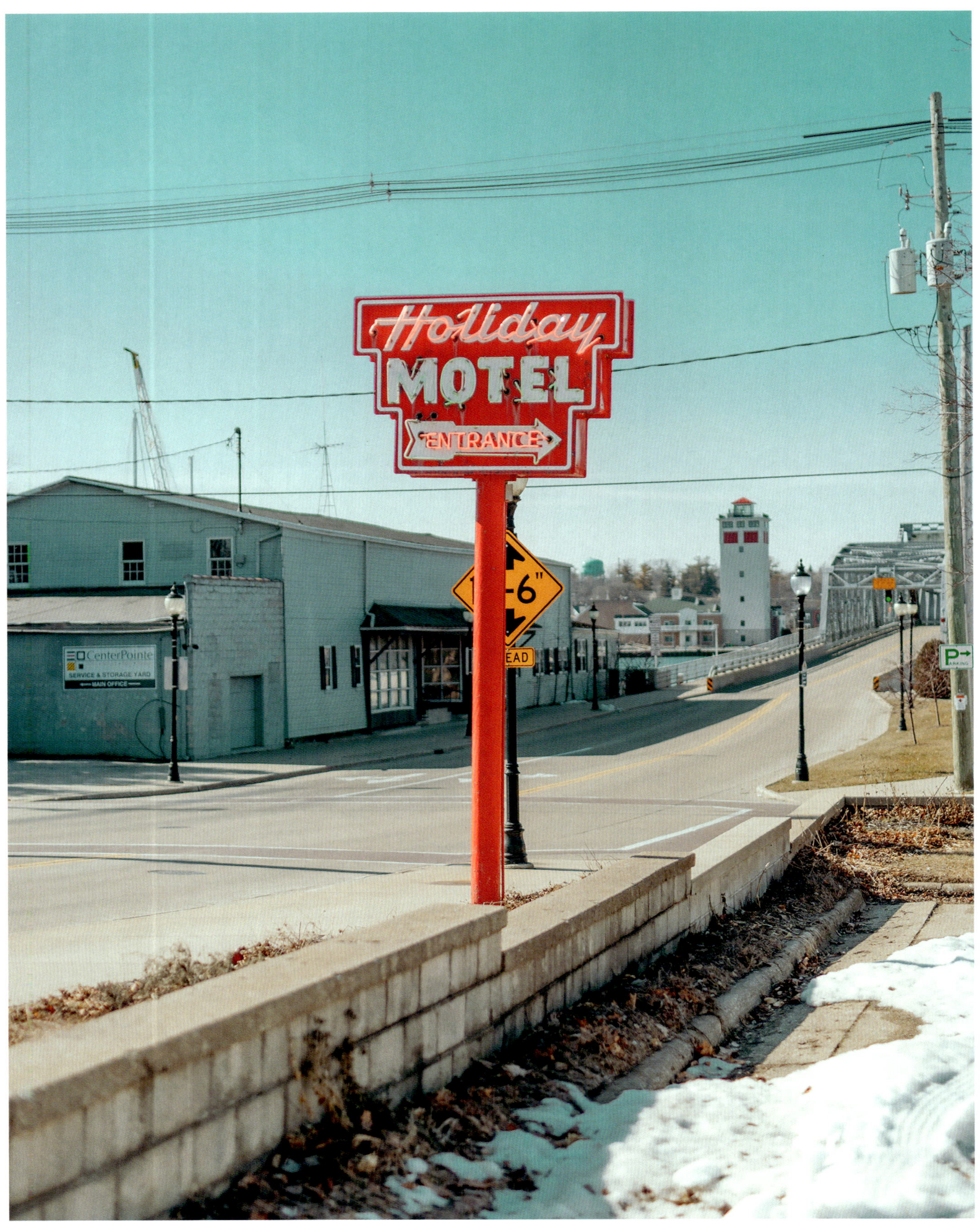
Holiday
MOTEL
ENTRANCE
CenterPointe
SERVICE & STORAGE YARD
MAIN OFFICE

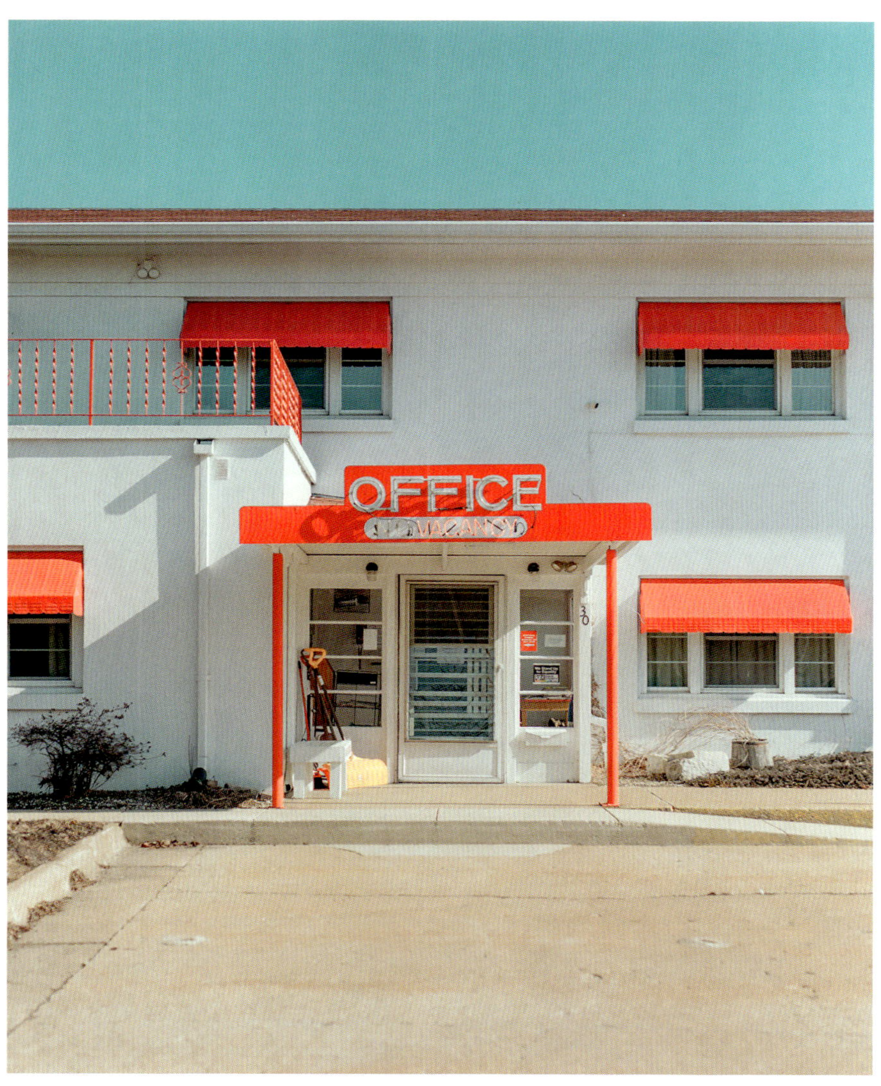

Holiday Motel • Sturgeon Bay, Wisconsin

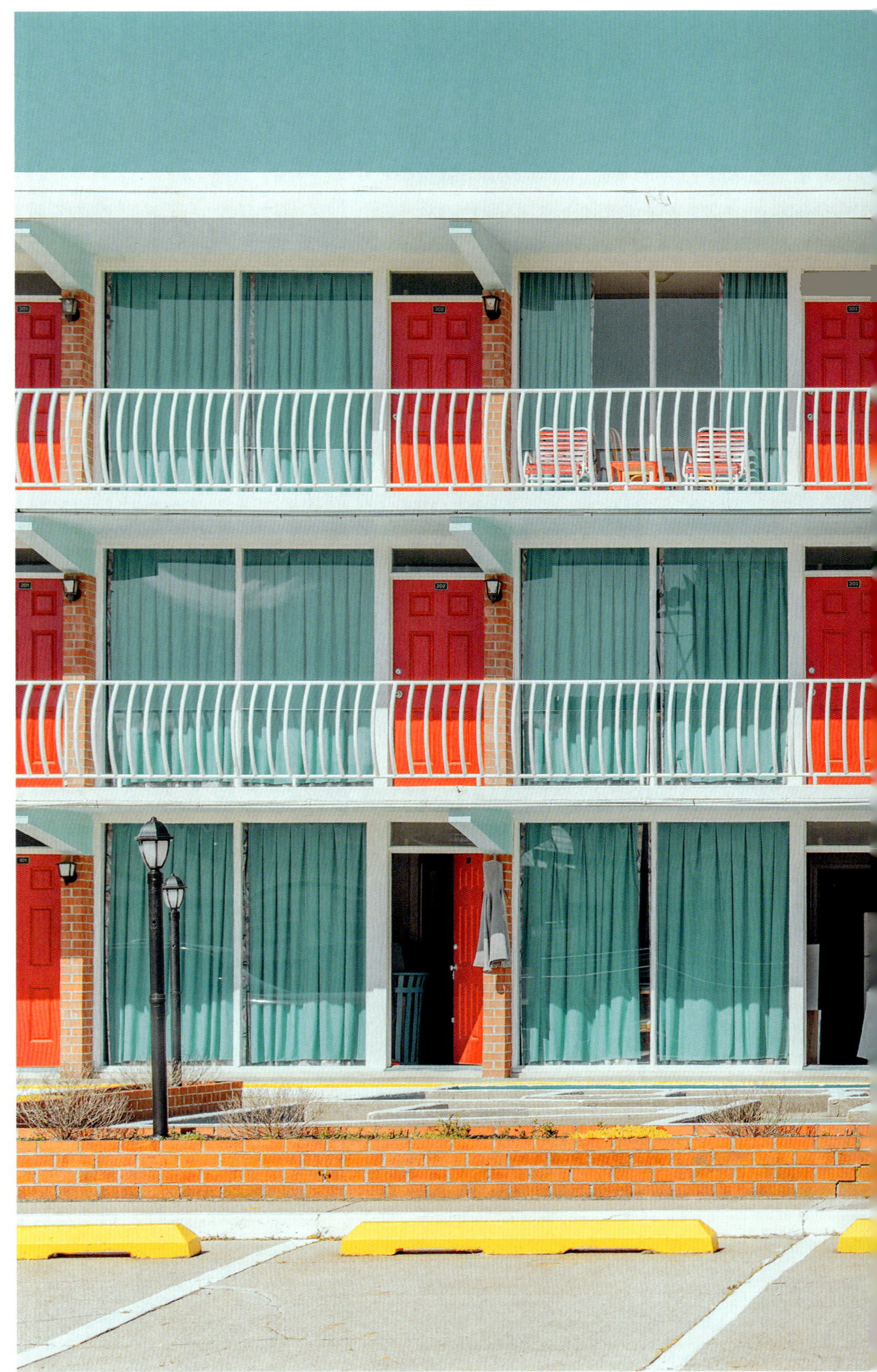

Gold Crest Motel
Wilcwood Crest, New Jersey

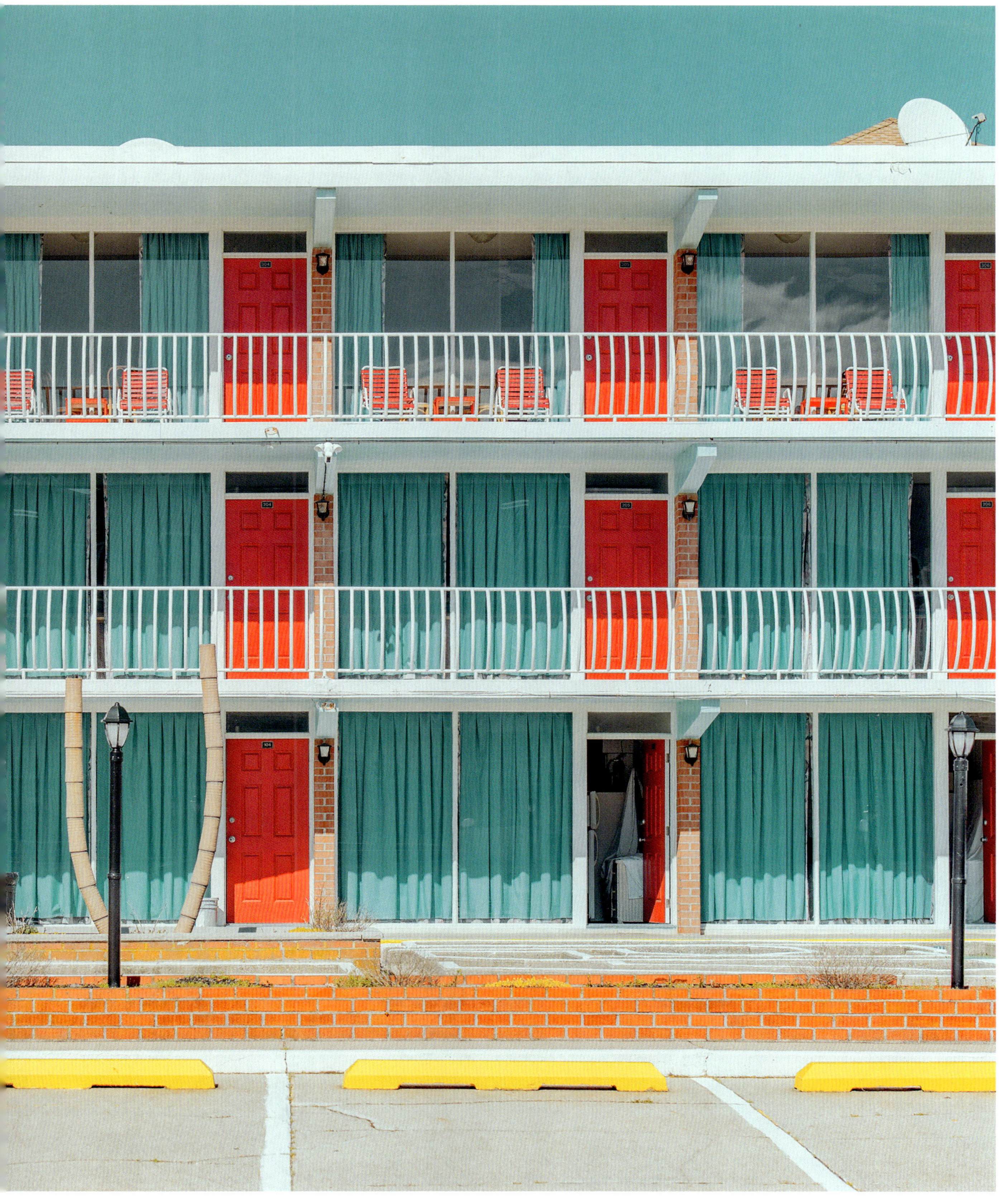

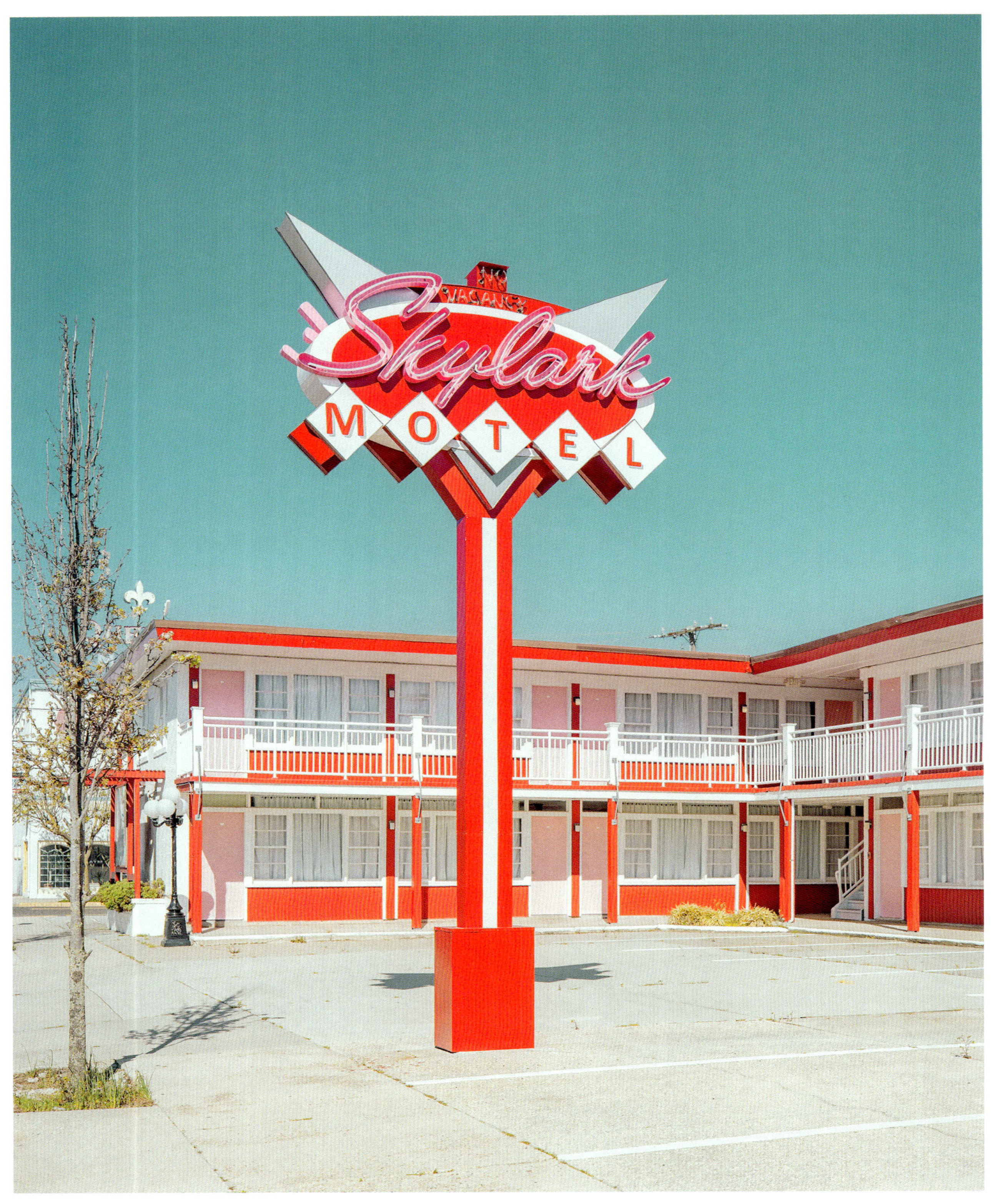

Skylark Motel • Wildwood, New Jersey

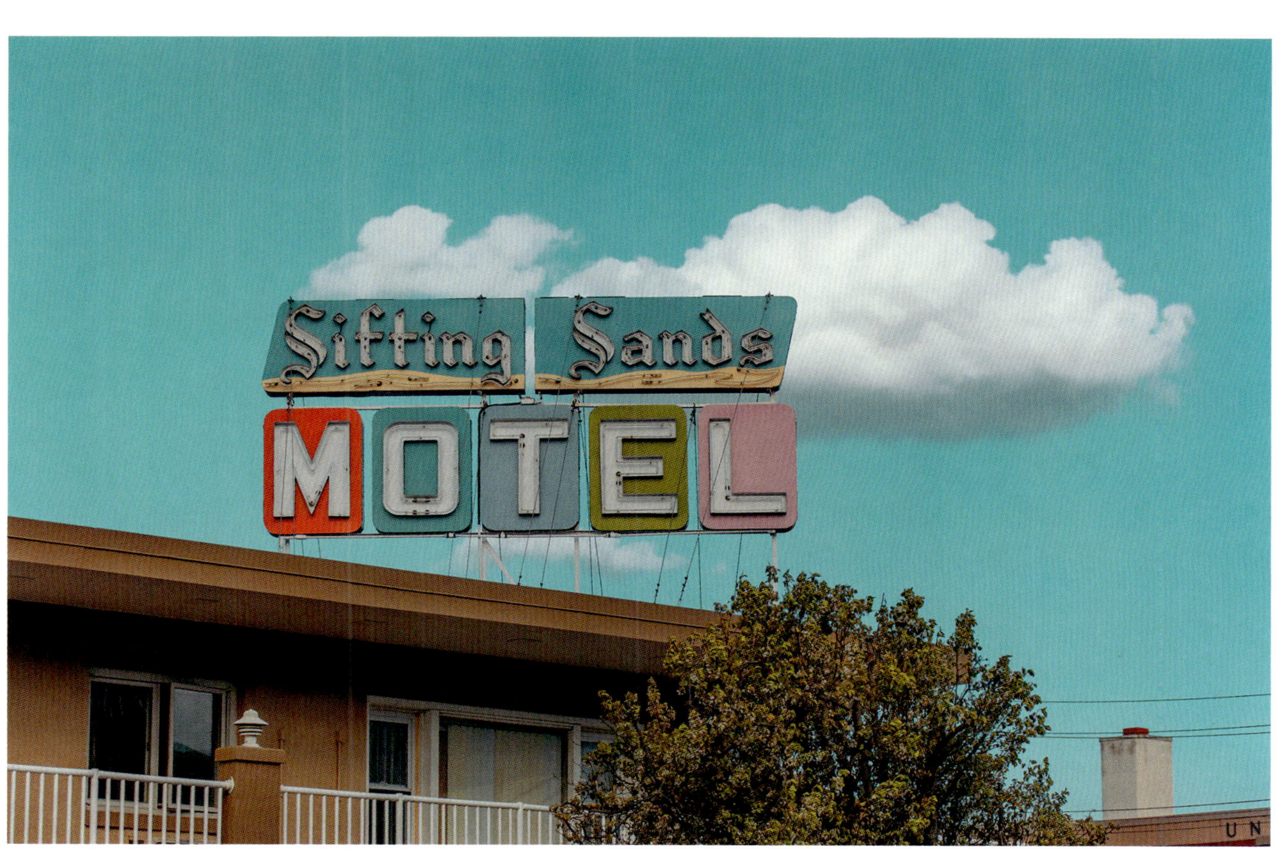

Sifting Sands Motel • Ocean City, New Jersey

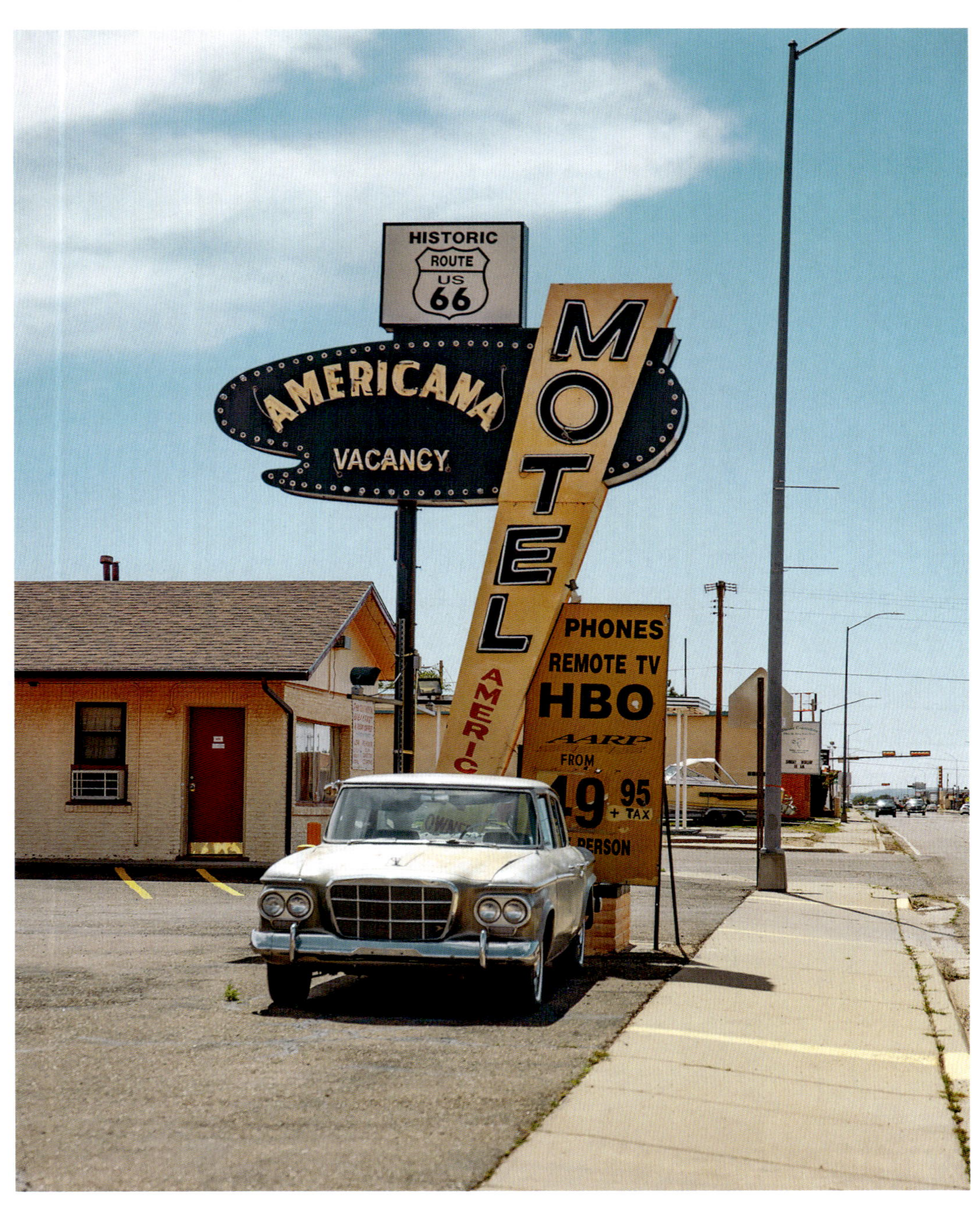

Americana Motel • Tucumcari, New Mexico

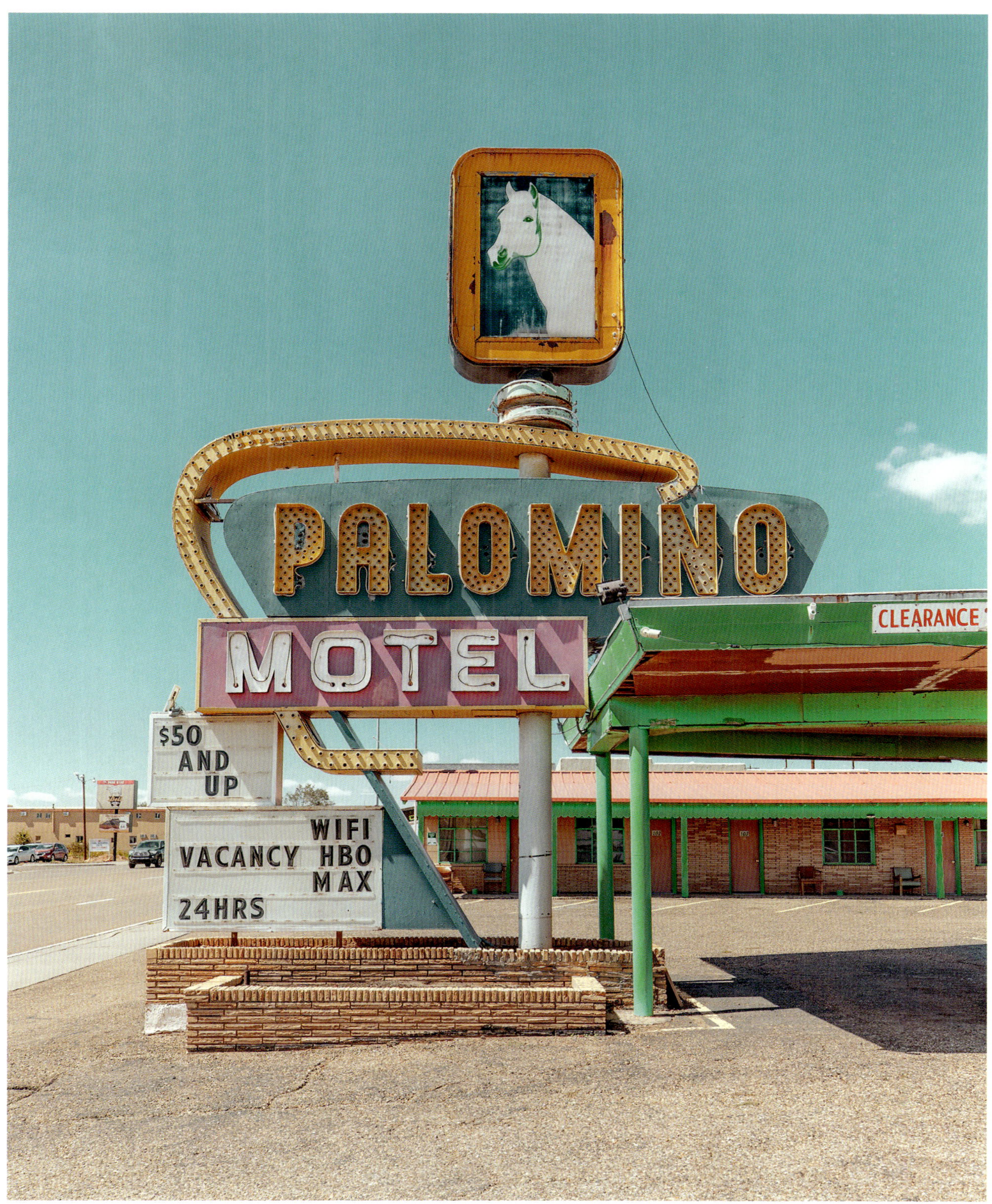

Palomino Motel • Tucumcari, New Mexico

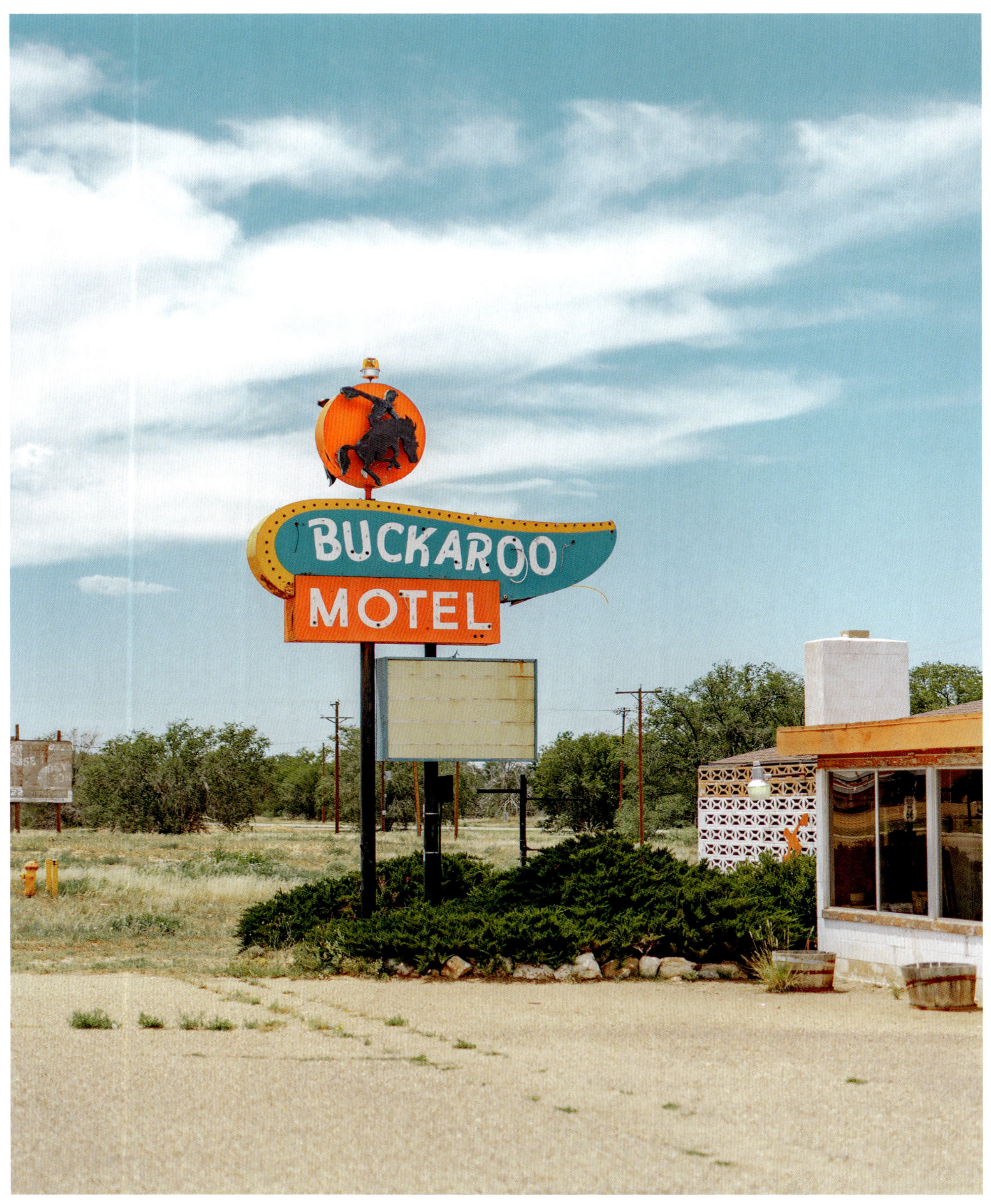

Buckaroo Motel • Tucumcari, New Mexico

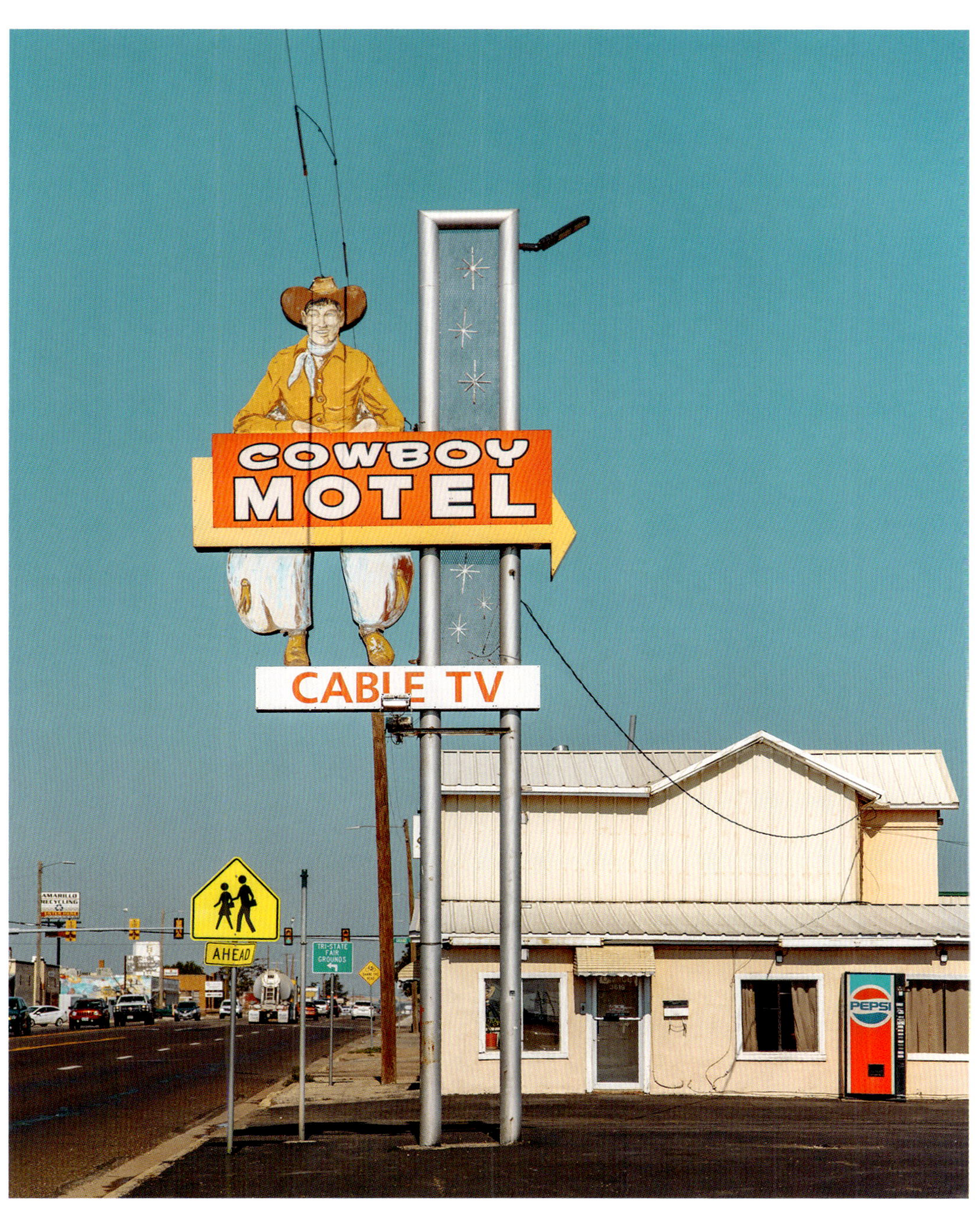

Cowboy Motel • Amarillo, Texas

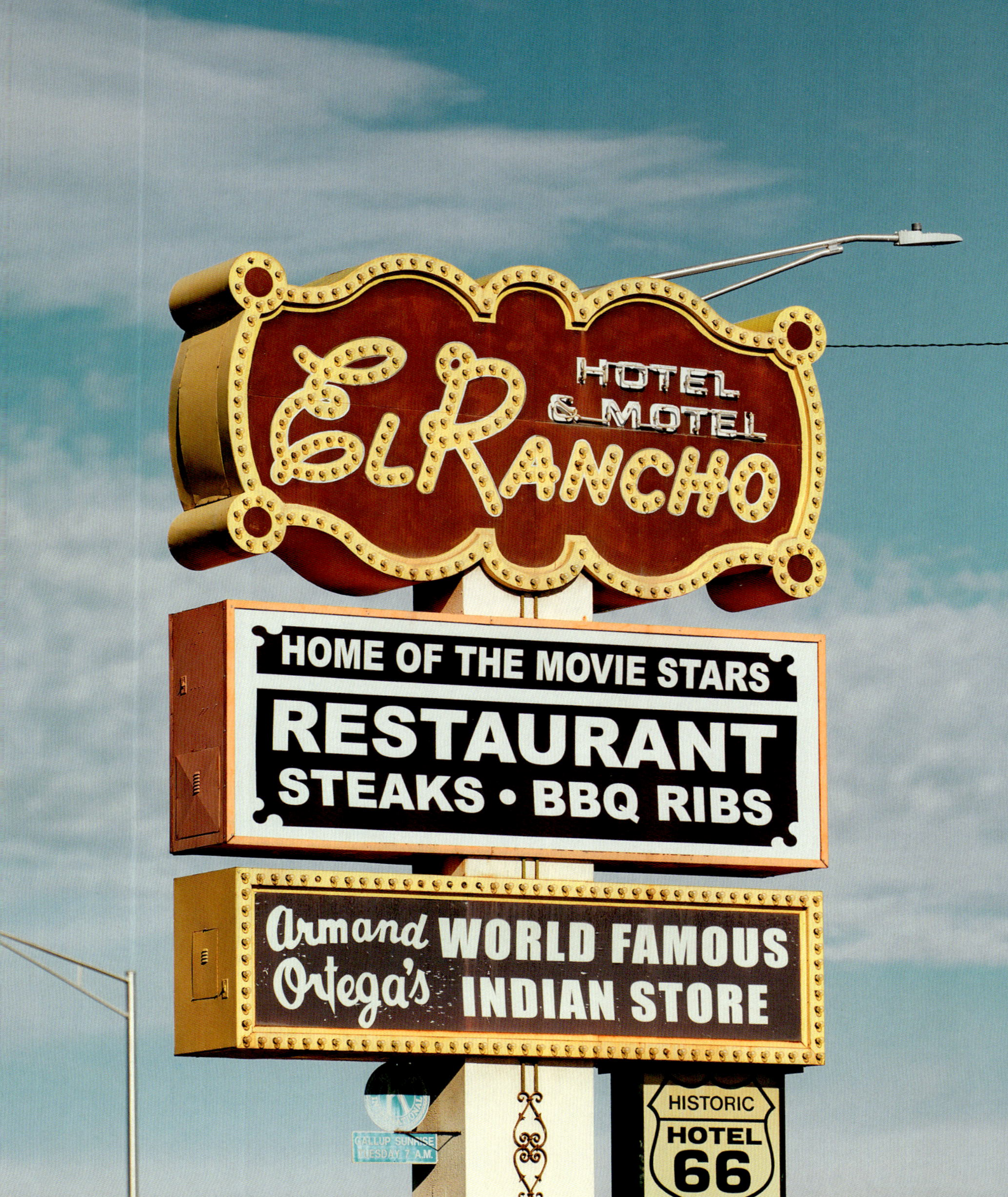
El Rancho
HOTEL
& MOTEL
HOME OF THE MOVIE STARS
RESTAURANT
STEAKS • BBQ RIBS
Armand Ortega's
WORLD FAMOUS
INDIAN STORE
GALLUP SUNRISE
HISTORIC
HOTEL
66

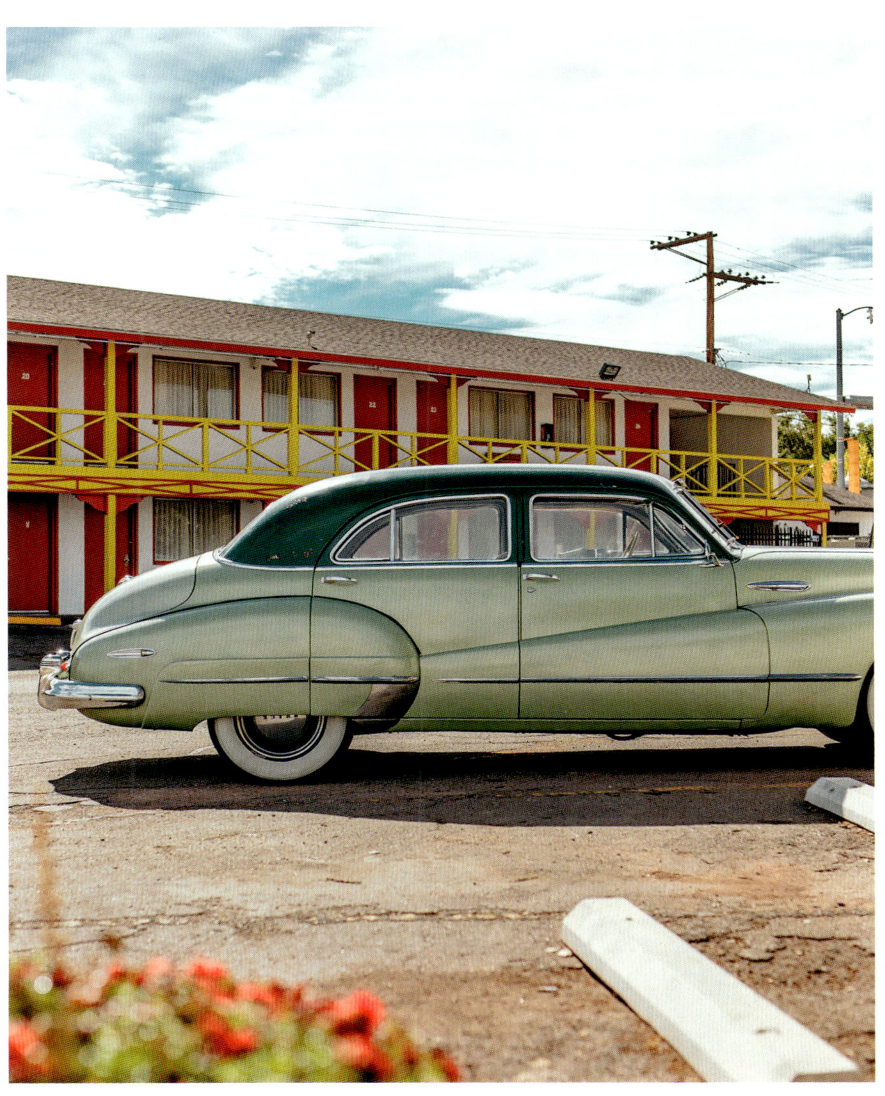

El Rancho Hotel & Motel • Gallup, New Mexico

SIGNS

I've always been drawn to retro signage—the dying craft of bending the glass into intricate lettering and shapes, the neon glow, the bold color palettes, the retro patterns, and the mid-century typography. The atomic-inspired shapes, with their futuristic appeal, have always attracted me. Yet, it wasn't until the pandemic that I began to photograph them.

Stuck indoors, I revisited a few of my favorite films, like *Paris, Texas* and *Nebraska*. While the stories in these movies are moving, I found myself fixated on the small towns the characters passed through. Those fleeting views from a moving car sparked an interest in the forgotten corners of America, especially the signage along the road—whether for motels, restaurants, attractions, or stores. This newfound fascination got me out of the house, and I began tracking down signs within a weekend's drive. Eventually, I started traveling for weeks at a time, photographing signs across various states.

Some of these locations have remained, frozen in time, while others have disappeared over the decades. During those quiet, solitary days, hunting down these signs became my reason to step outside—to explore eerily empty streets and document these fading icons, all while the world seemed to stand still.

What began as a temporary escape during the pandemic has evolved into a deep, ongoing obsession. To date, I've photographed over 1,000 locations, with many more still on my growing list.

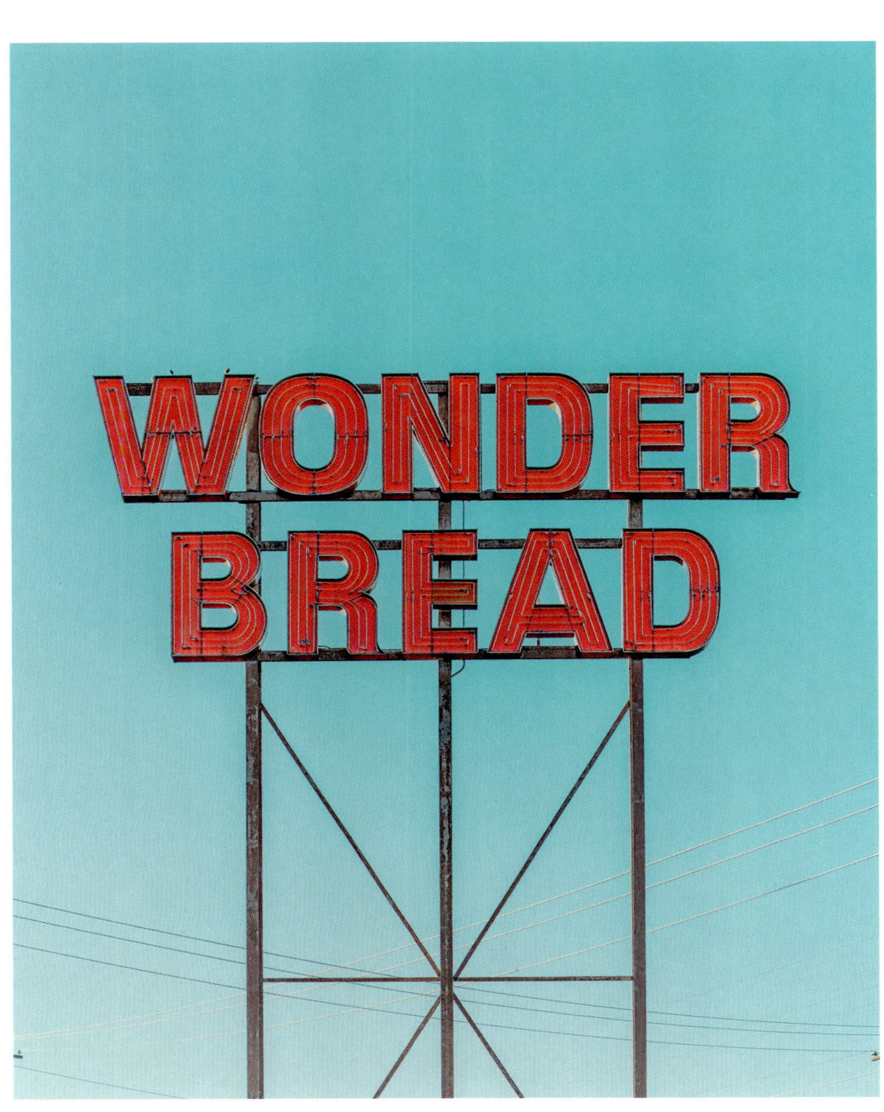

Wonder Bread Sign • Columbus, Ohio

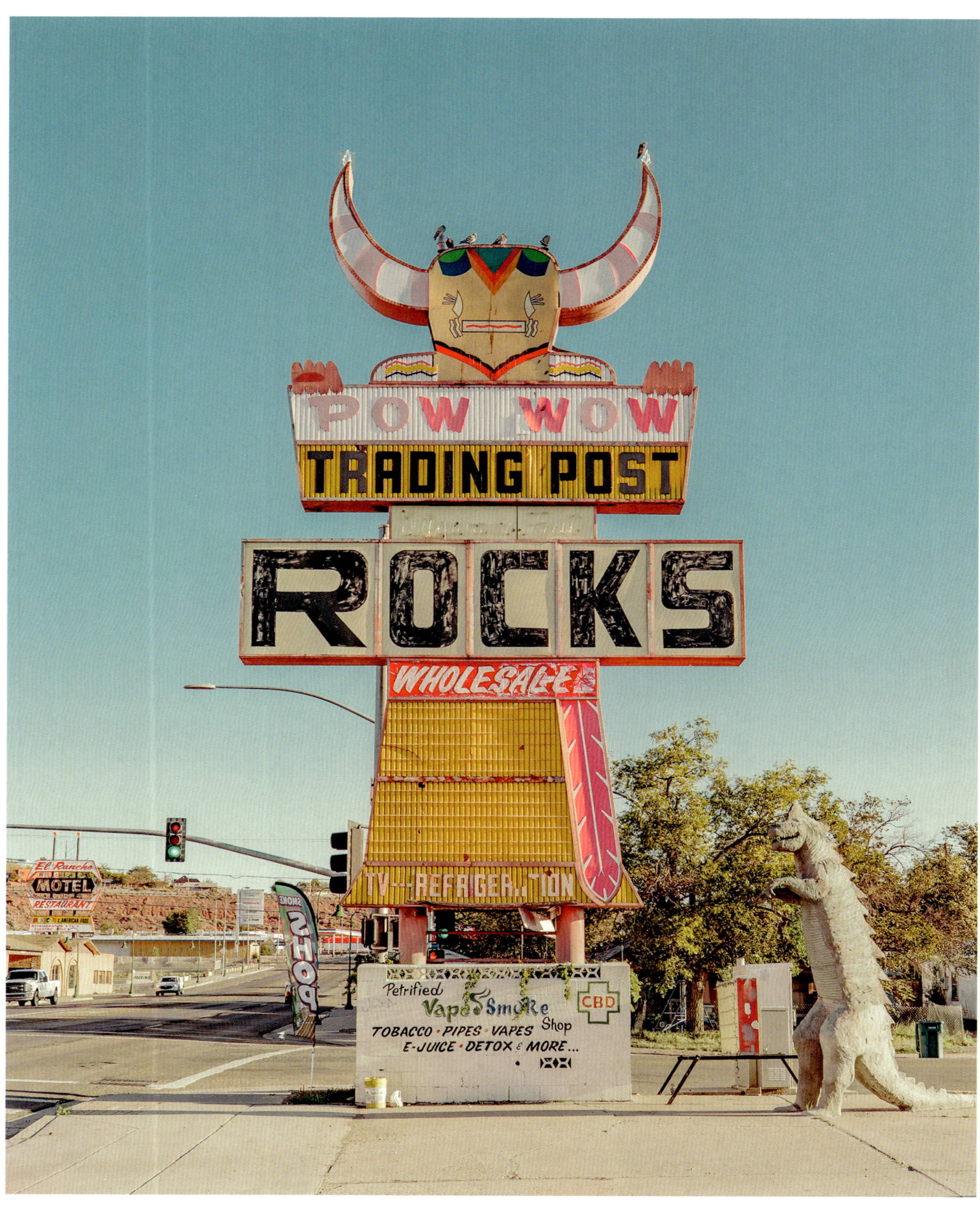

Pow Wow Trading Post • Holbrook, Arizona

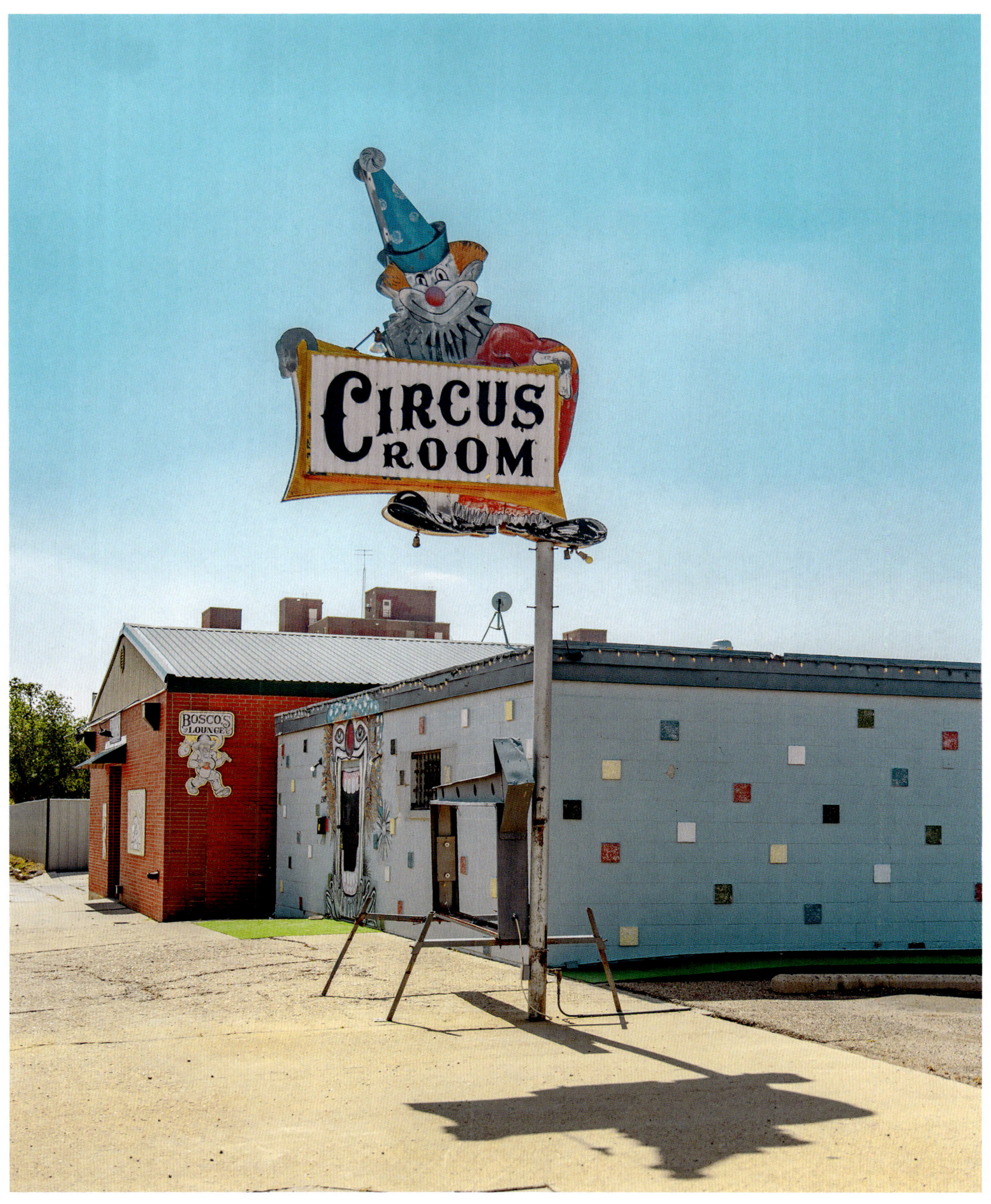

Circus Room • Amarillo, Texas

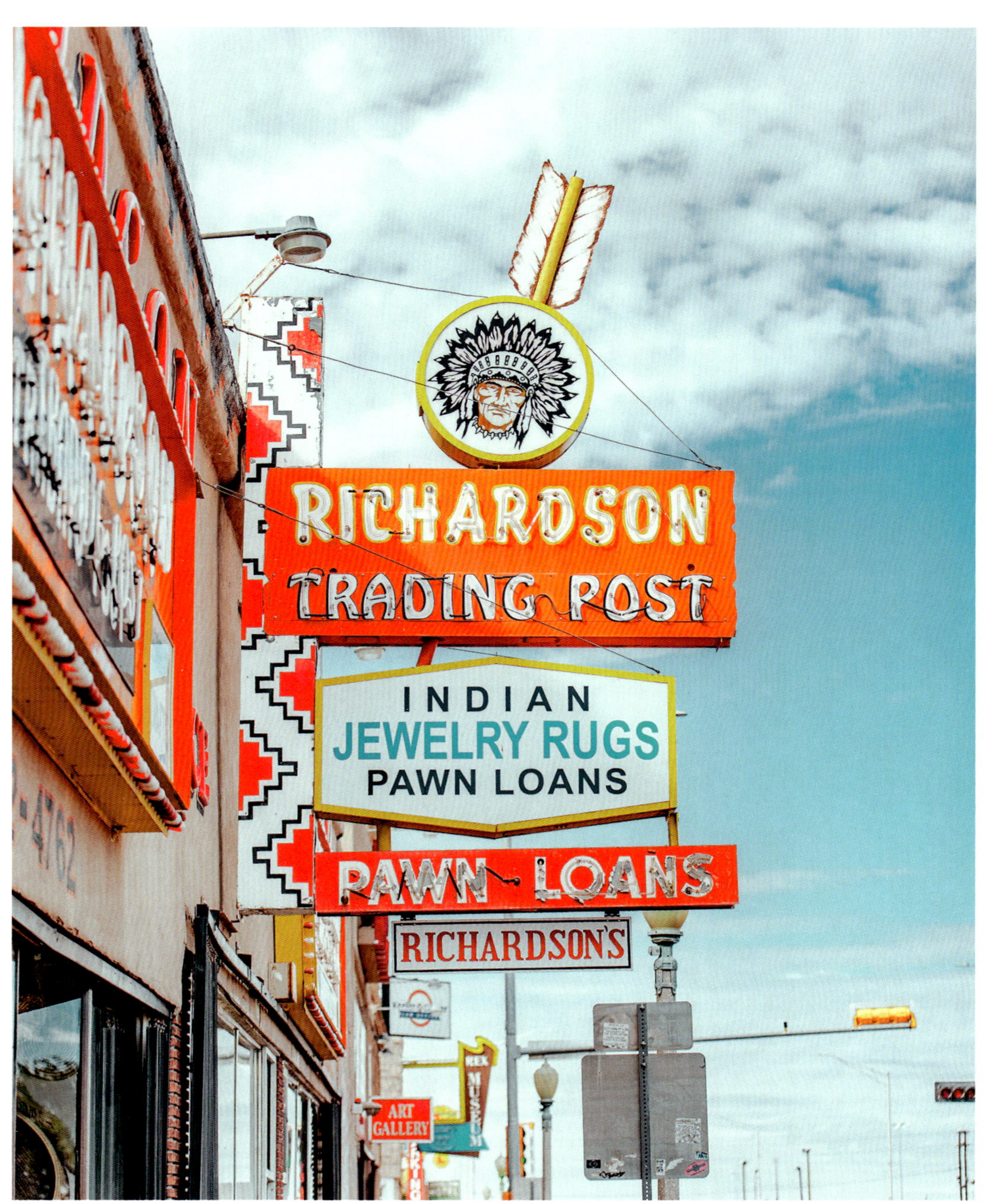

Richardson Trading Post • Gallup, New Mexico

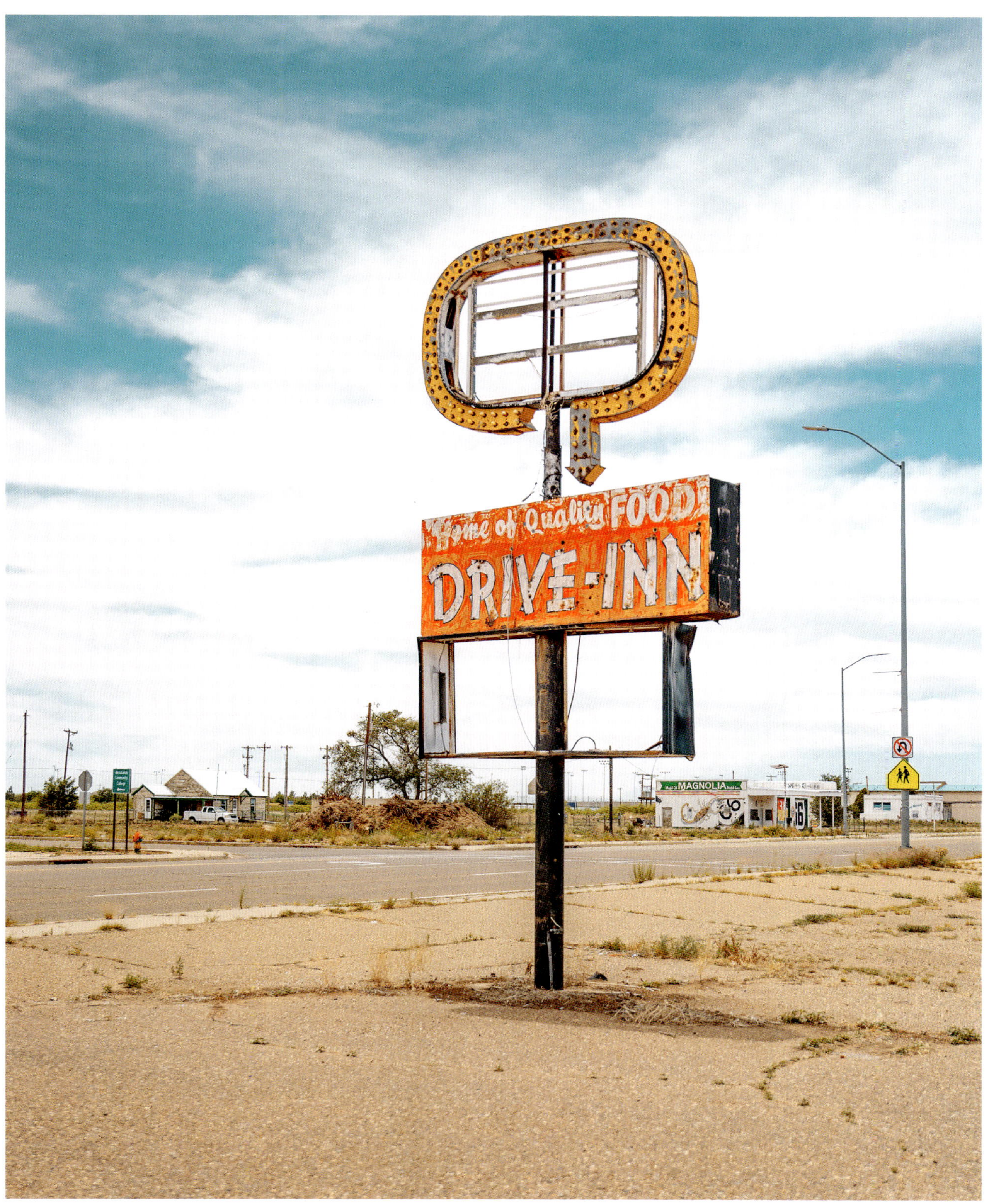

Abandoned Westerner Drive-Inn Sign • Tucumcari, New Mexico

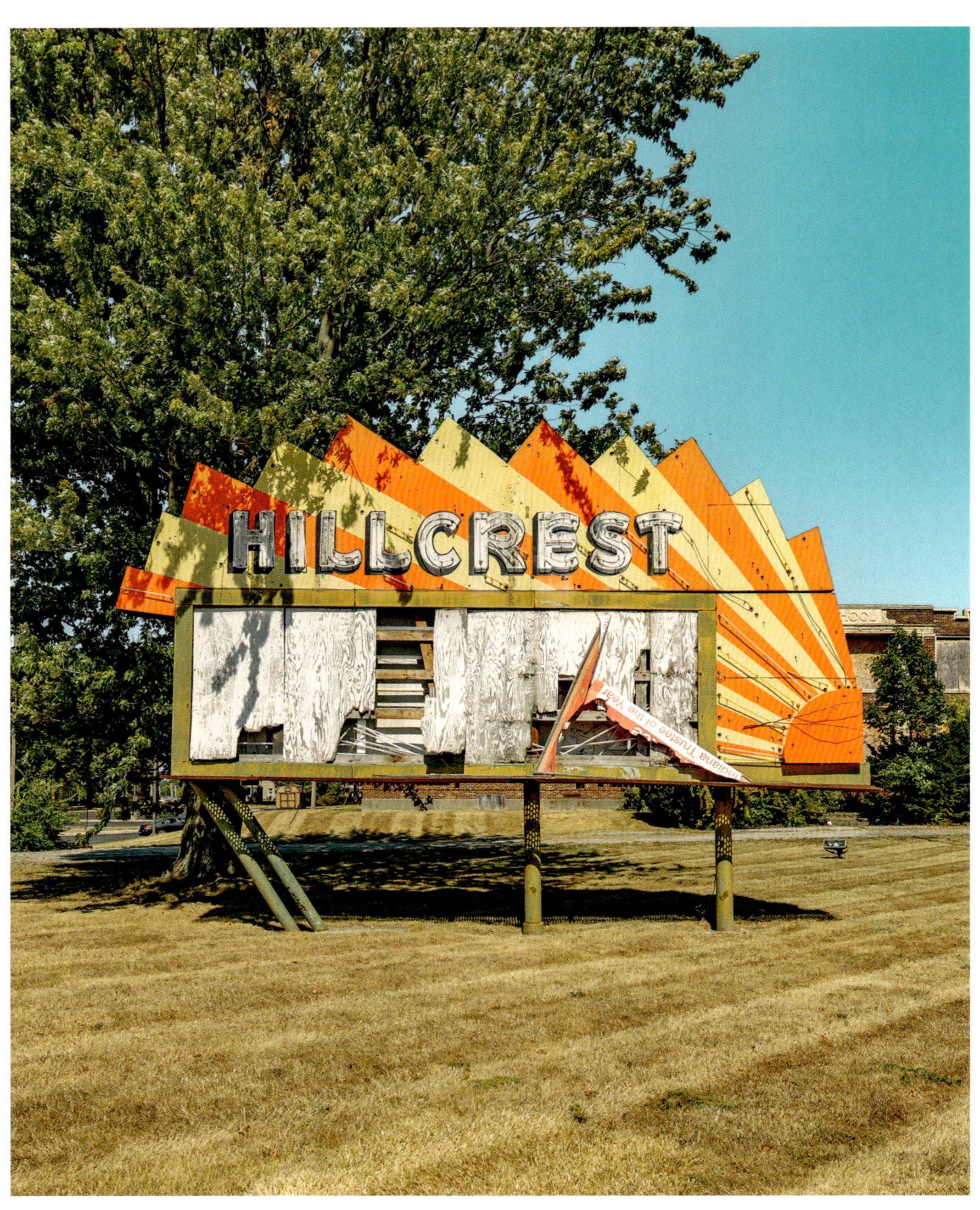

Abandoned Hillcrest Drive-In Theatre Sign • Fort Wayne, Indiana

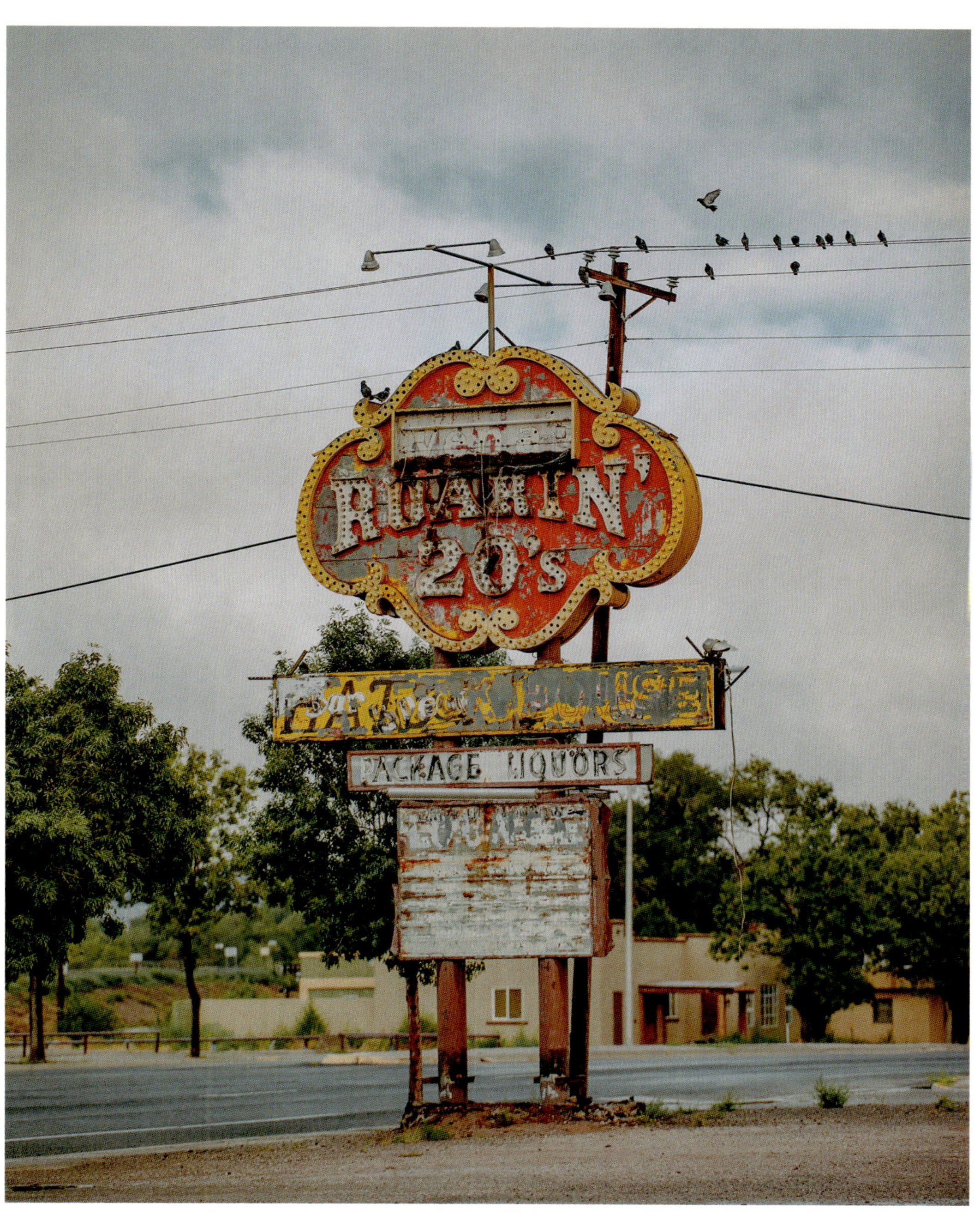

Abandoned Roarin' 20's Sign • Grants, New Mexico

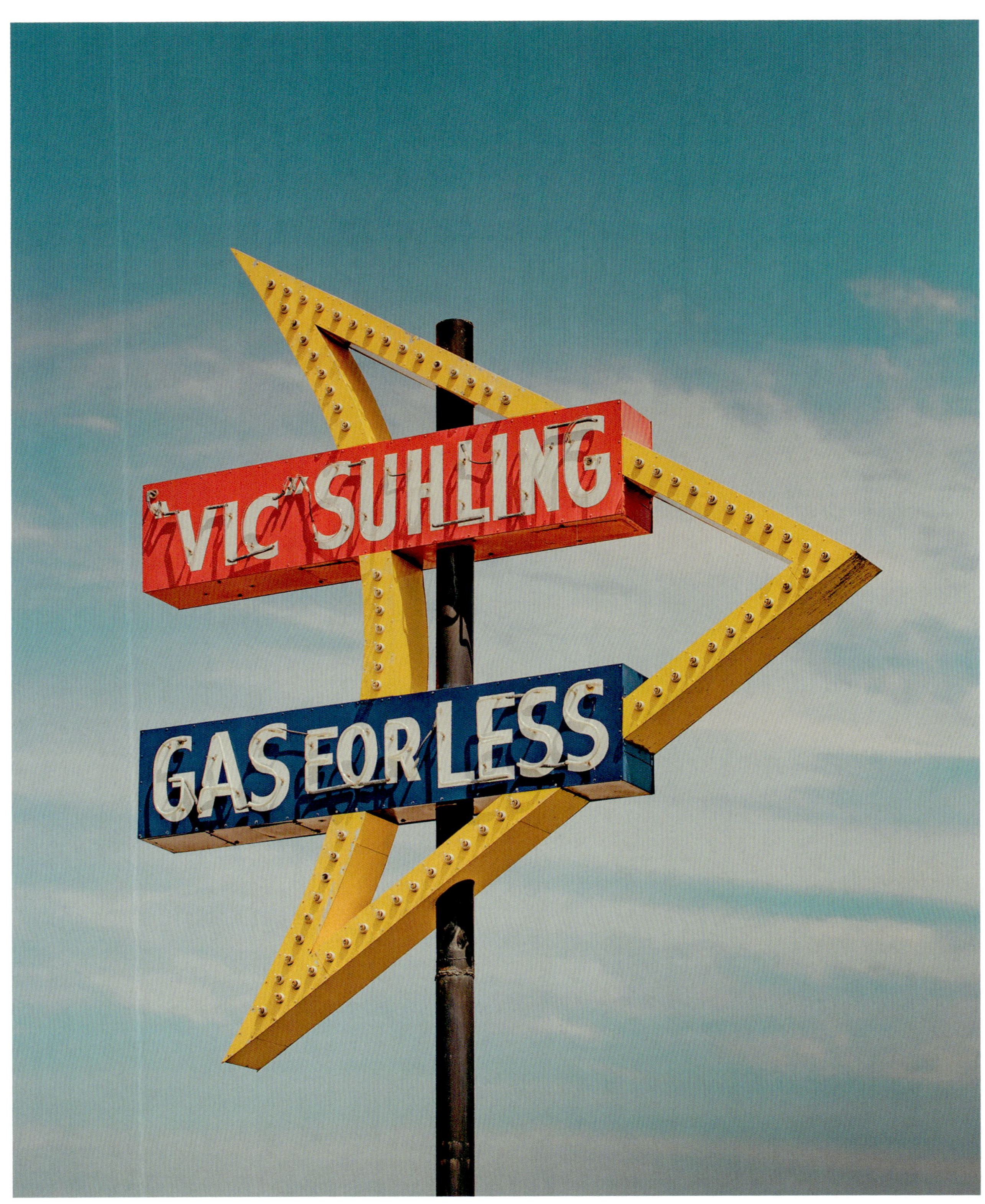

Vic Suhling's Gas Station • Litchfield, Illinois

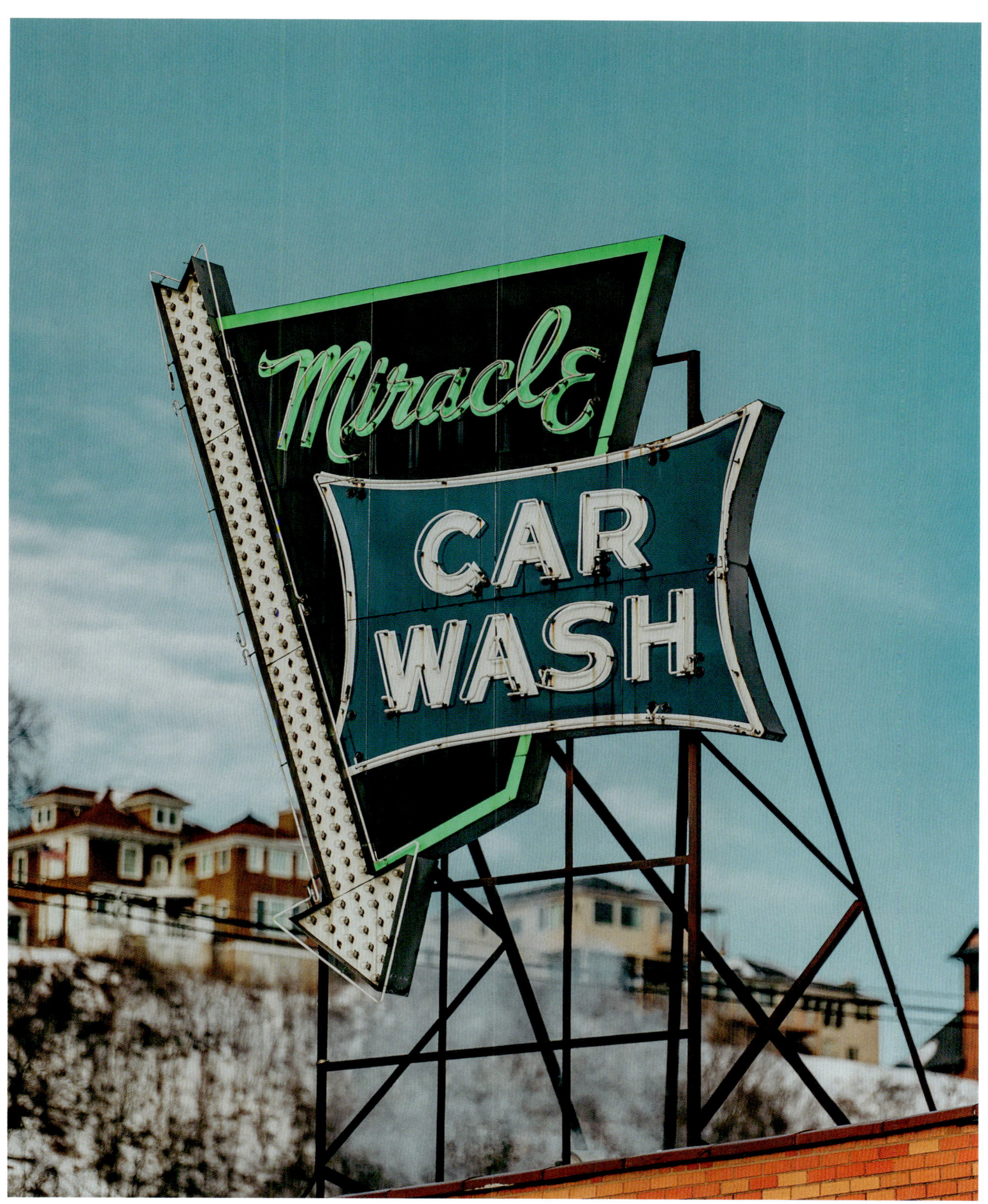

Miracle Car Wash • Dubuque, Iowa

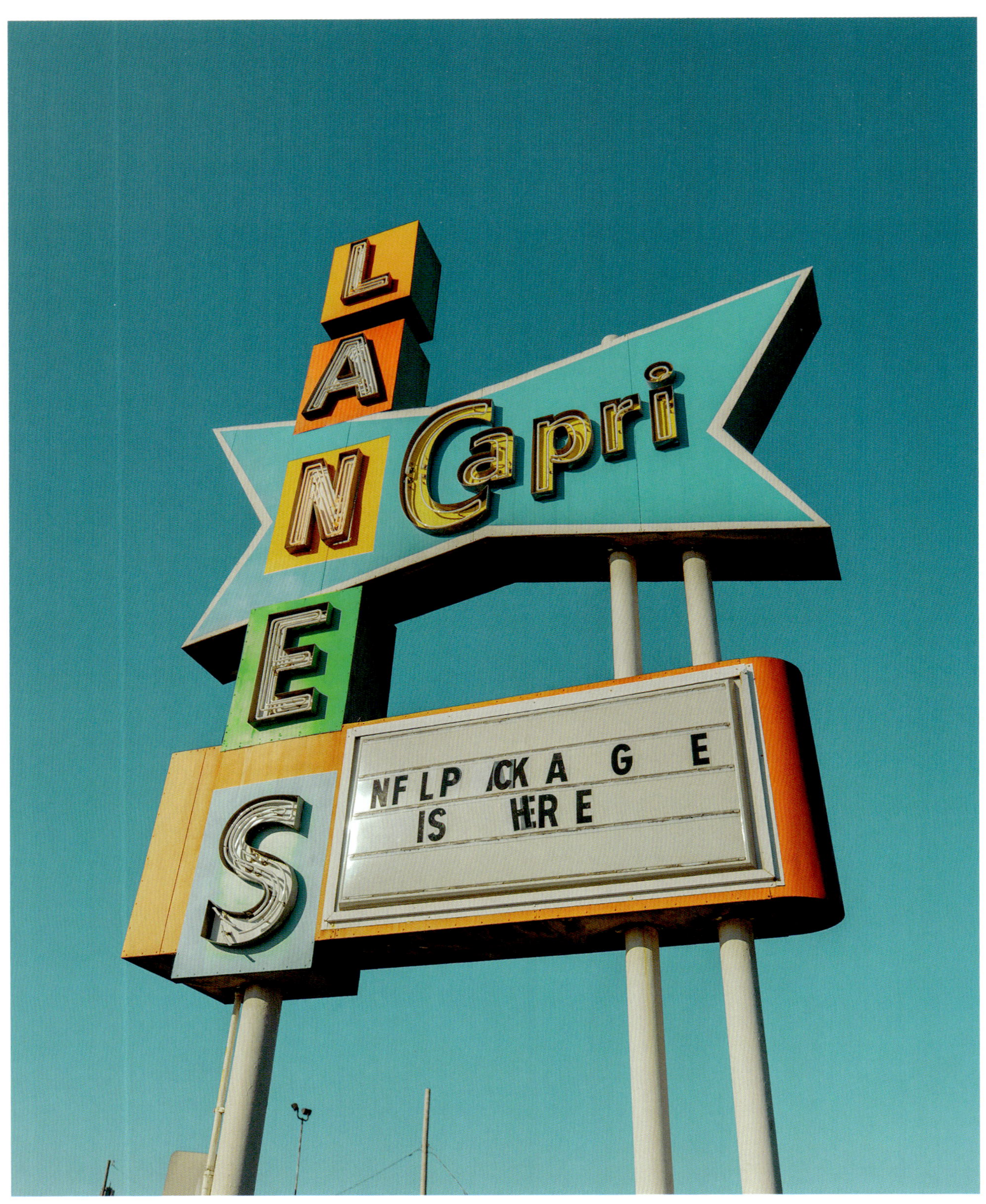

Capri Lanes • Dayton, Ohio

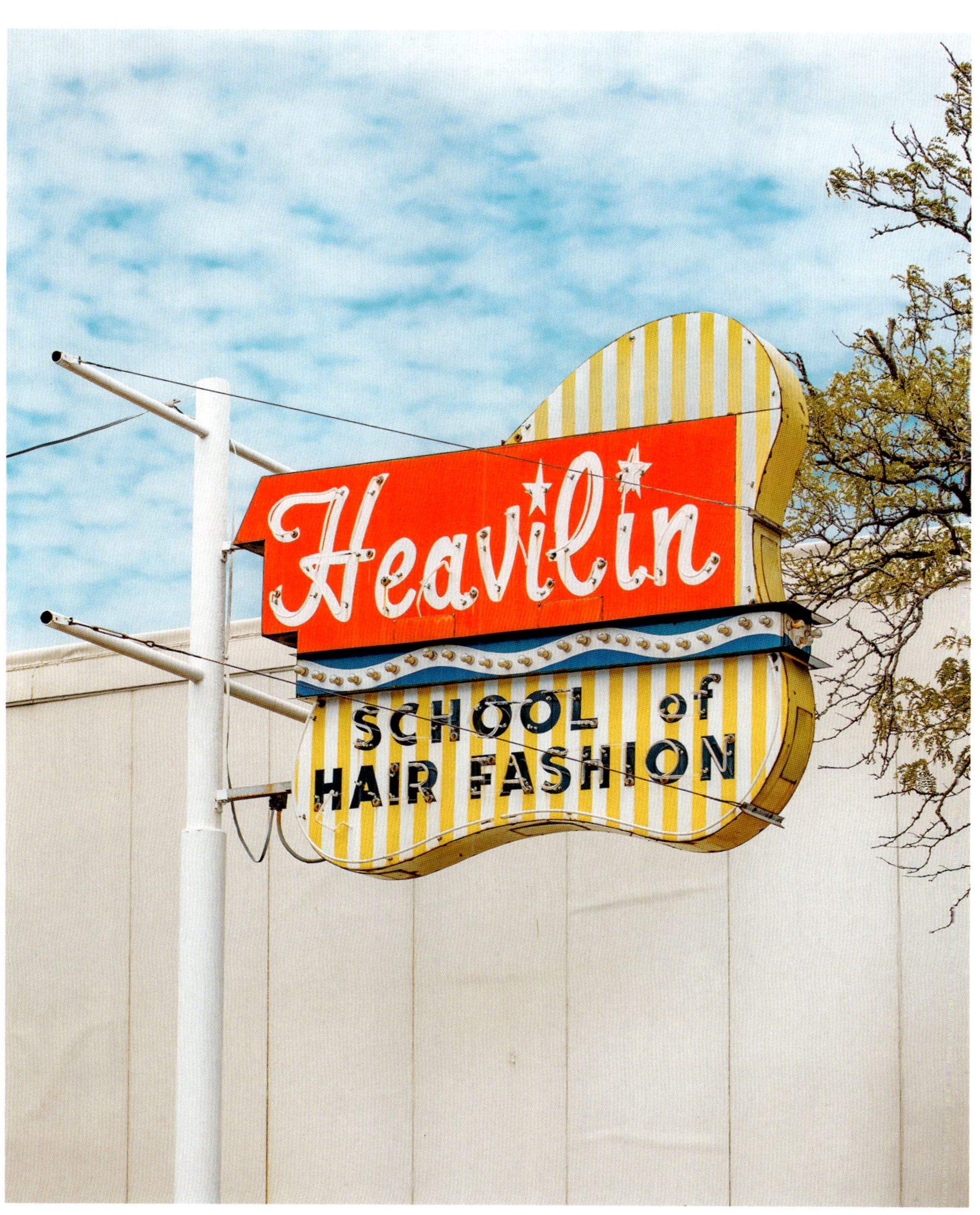

Heavilin School of Hair Fashion • Kansas City, Missouri

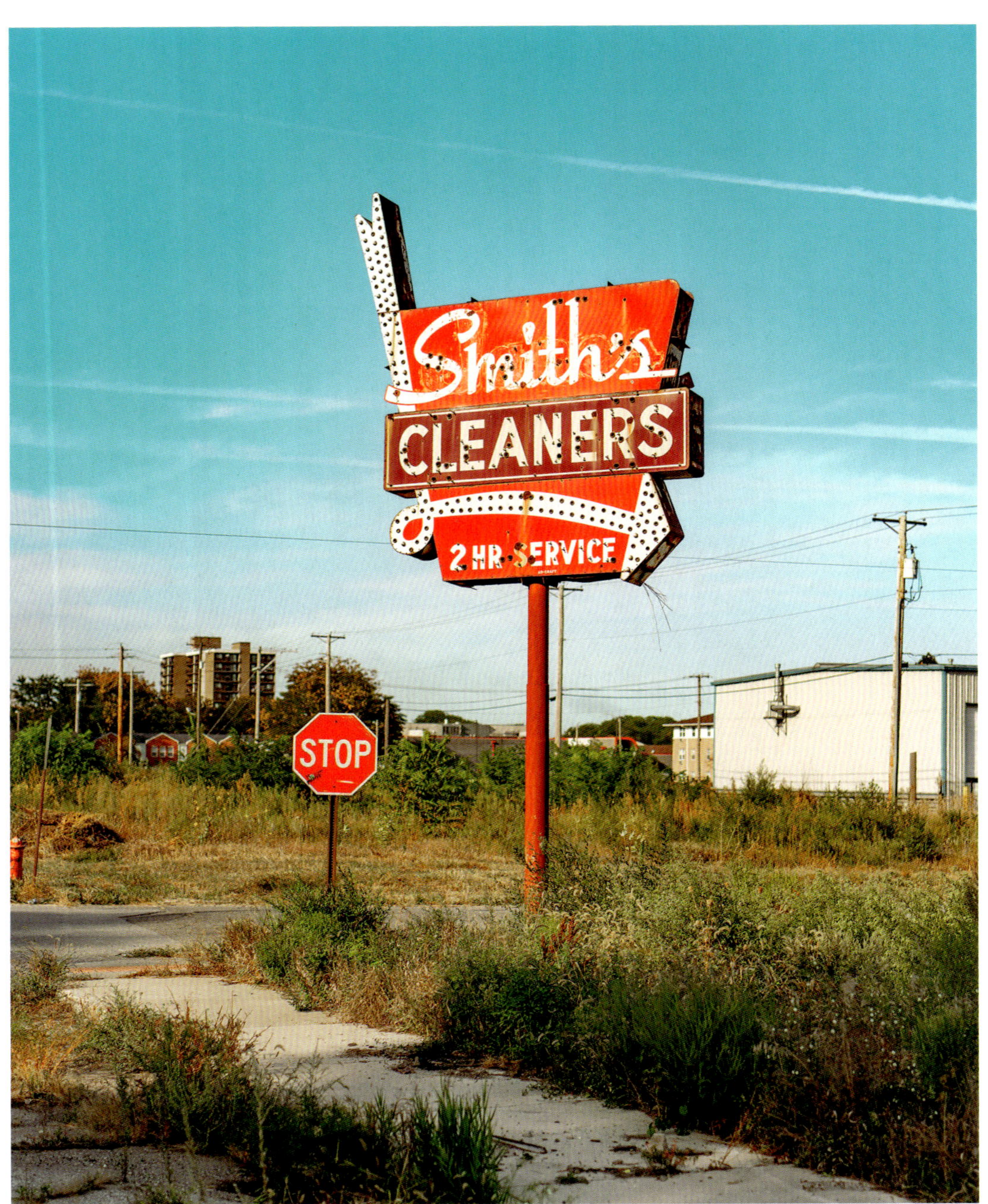

Abandoned Smith's Cleaners Sign • Gary, Indiana

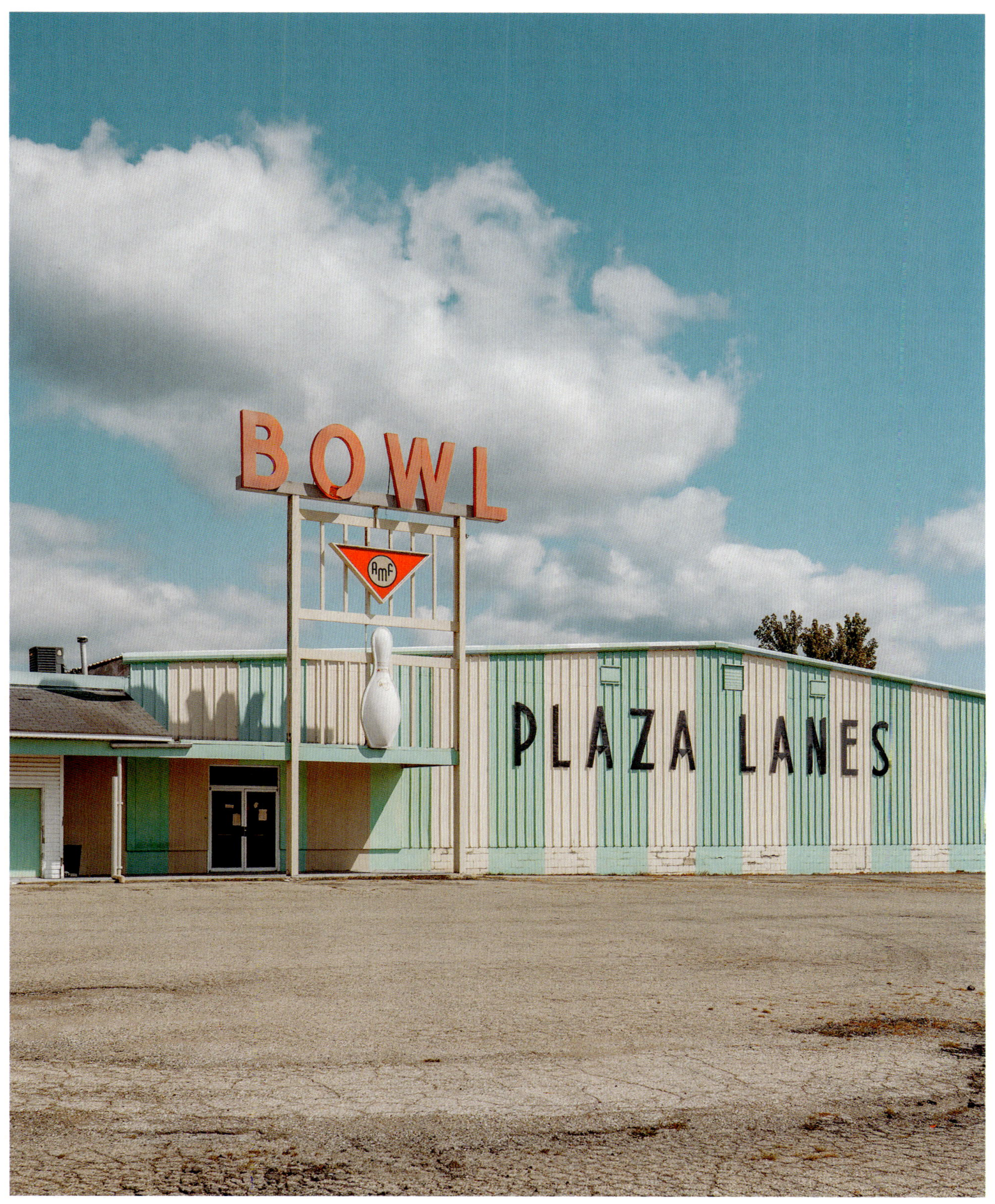

Plaza Lanes • Highland, Indiana

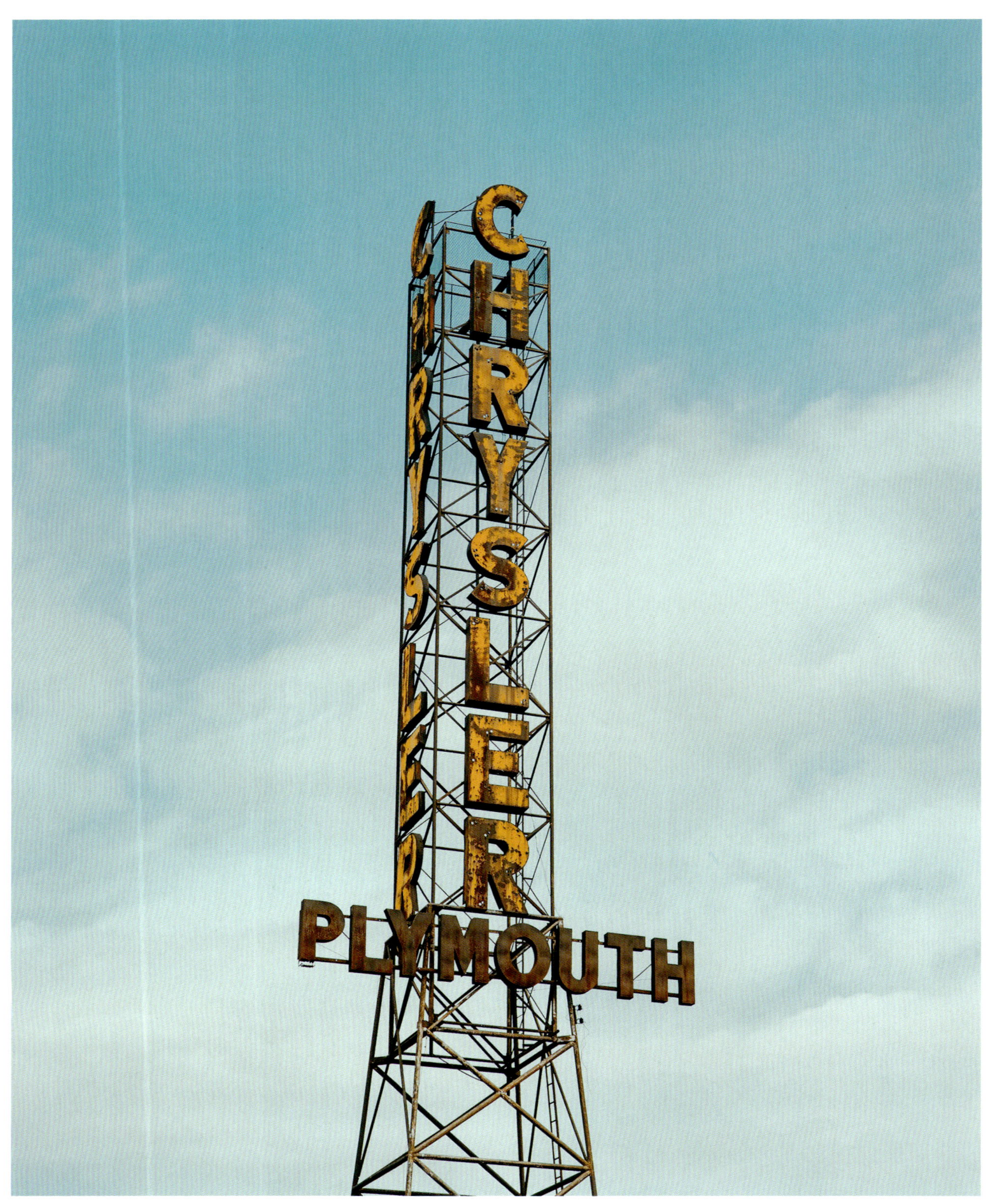

Chrysler Plymouth Tower • Bristow, Oklahoma

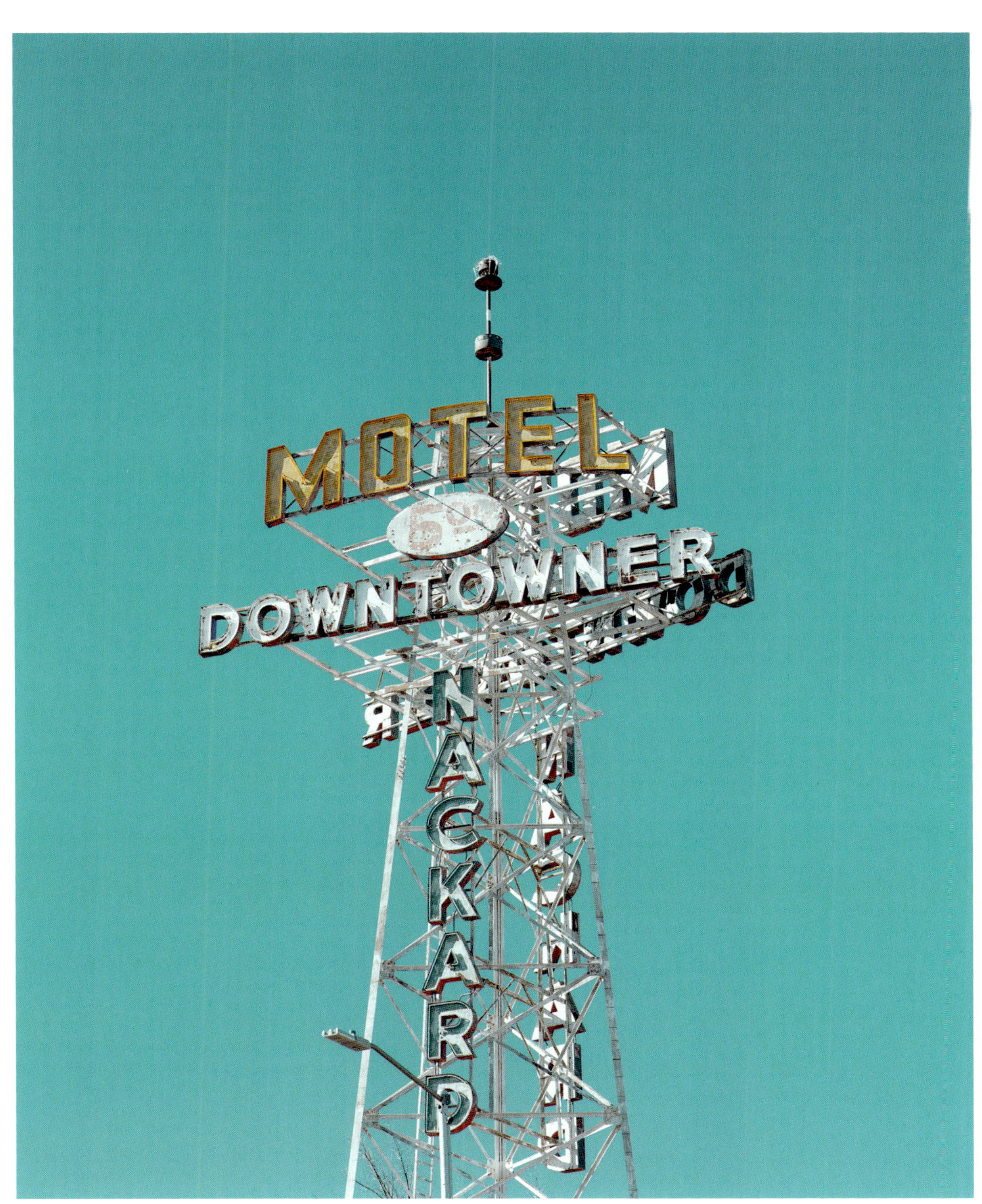

Downtowner Motel Tower • Flagstaff, Arizona

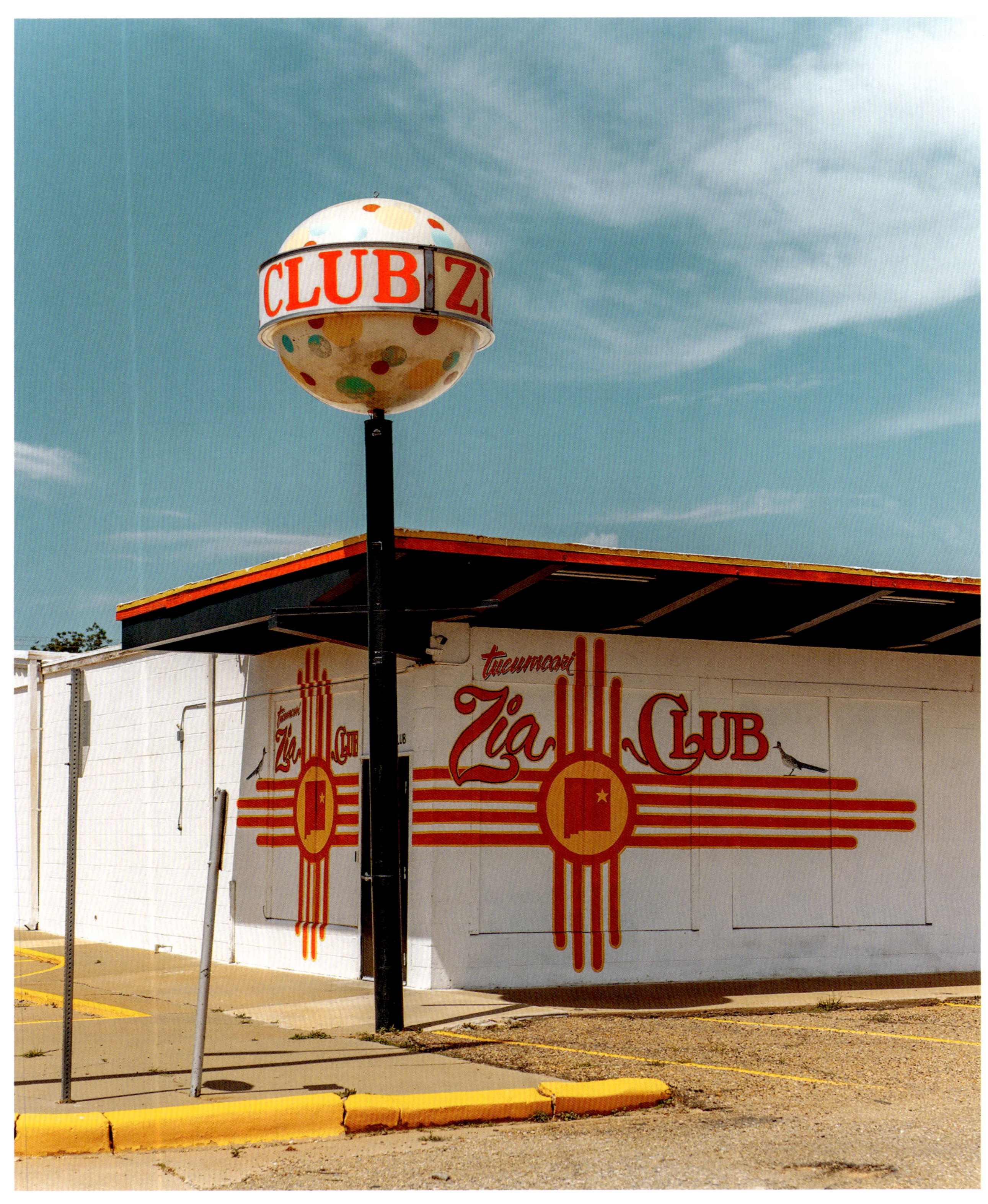

Zia Club • Tucumcari, New Mexico

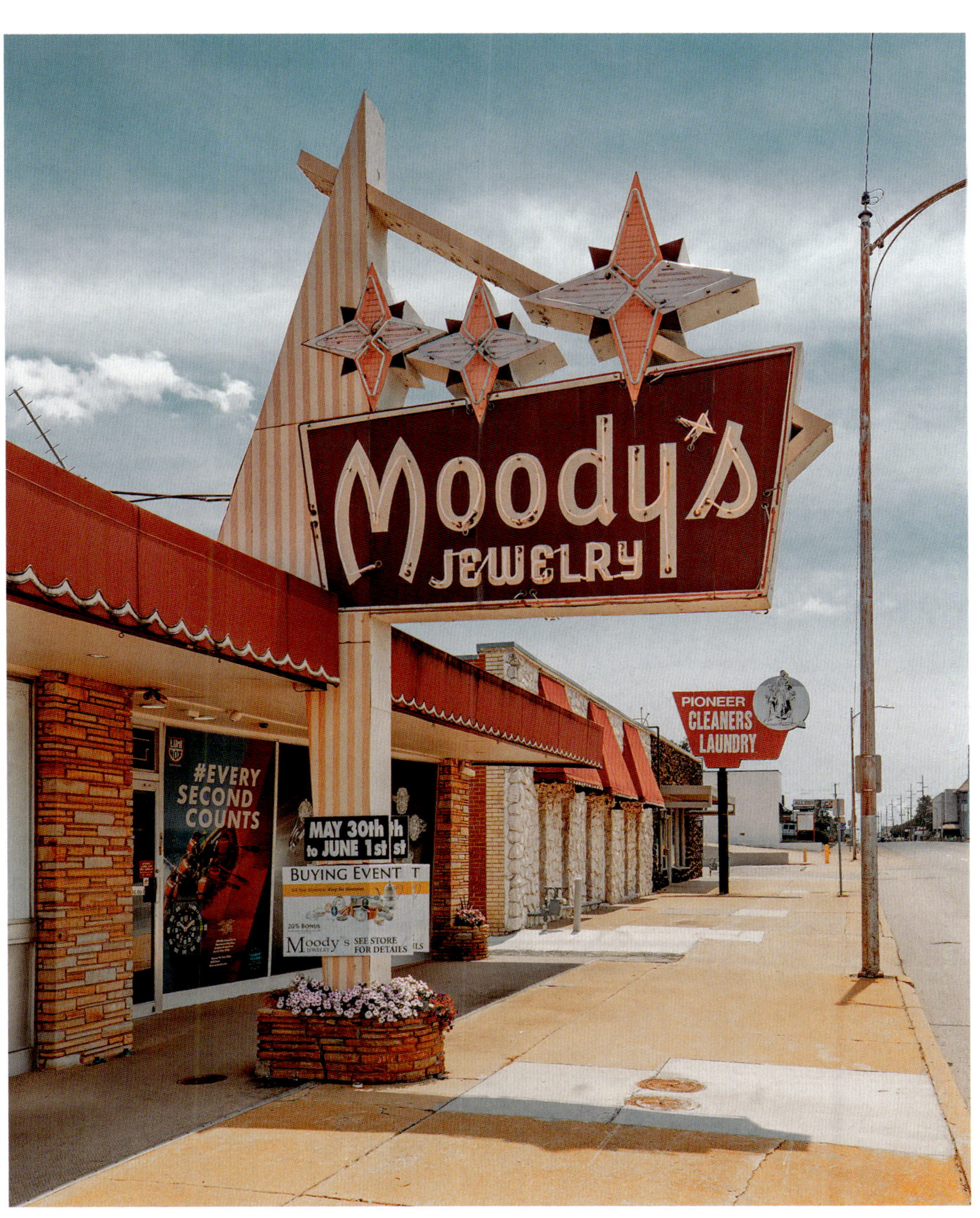

Moody's Jewelry • Tulsa, Oklahoma

THEATRES

The front of the Gem Theatre is the first photo I shot for this book back in June 2017, and also the first shot I snapped in Cairo, Illinois. Situated at the confluence of the Mississippi and Ohio Rivers, Cairo was once a bustling supply hub. But after years of flooding, it's now little more than a ghost town. I stepped out of the car, lined up the shot, and then heard an older man's voice shout, "You're too late!" He was referring to the theatre, which has been closed since the late '70s, as well as most of the town itself, which was largely desolate. He continued pointing in every direction, telling me what used to be where—like the chamber building with its missing front door, the neighboring structure with a dead Christmas wreath still hanging above it, and Commerce Street, which no longer had a single shop along the entire street.

With the rise of streaming and modern cinema, who knows how long any of these theaters will survive. Out of the 32 theatres in this book, 19 sit vacant, four are actively being restored, one has completely vanished (though its sign is being preserved and heading to a museum), and one is slated for demolition.

I really had no idea that when I framed up the photo of the Gem Theatre and the local man yelled out to me, that it would be the start of this whole book—it was the moment that set me down a path to document these historically vibrant places before they are completely gone.

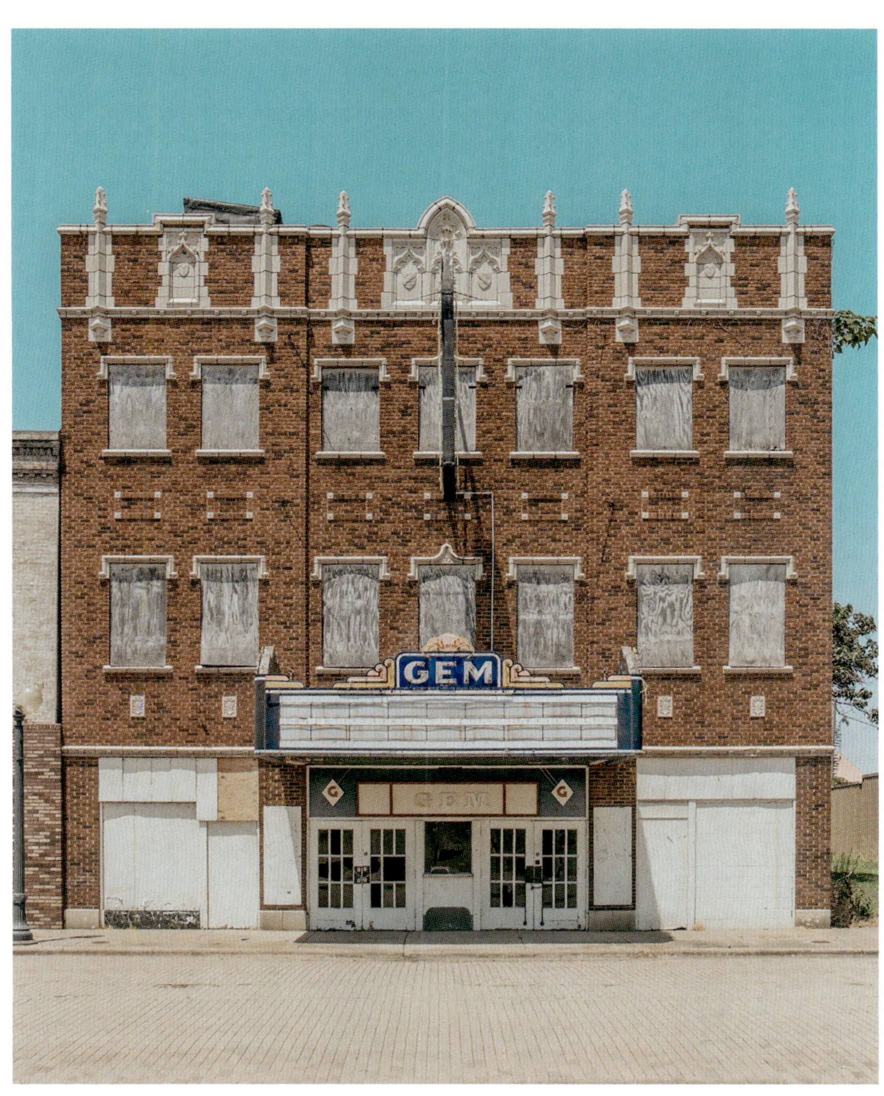

Gem Theatre • Cairo, Illinois

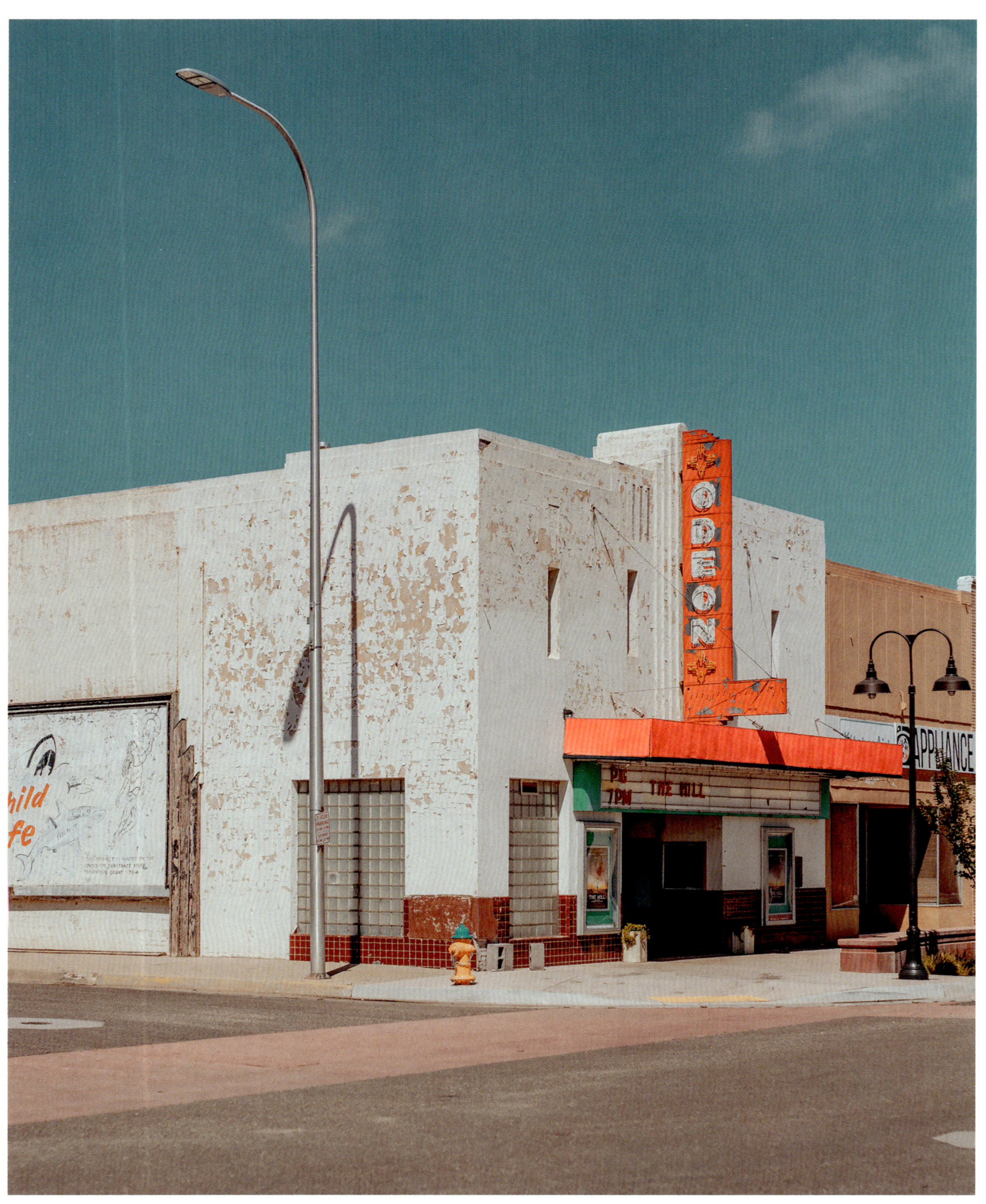

Odeon Theatre • Tucumcari, New Mexico

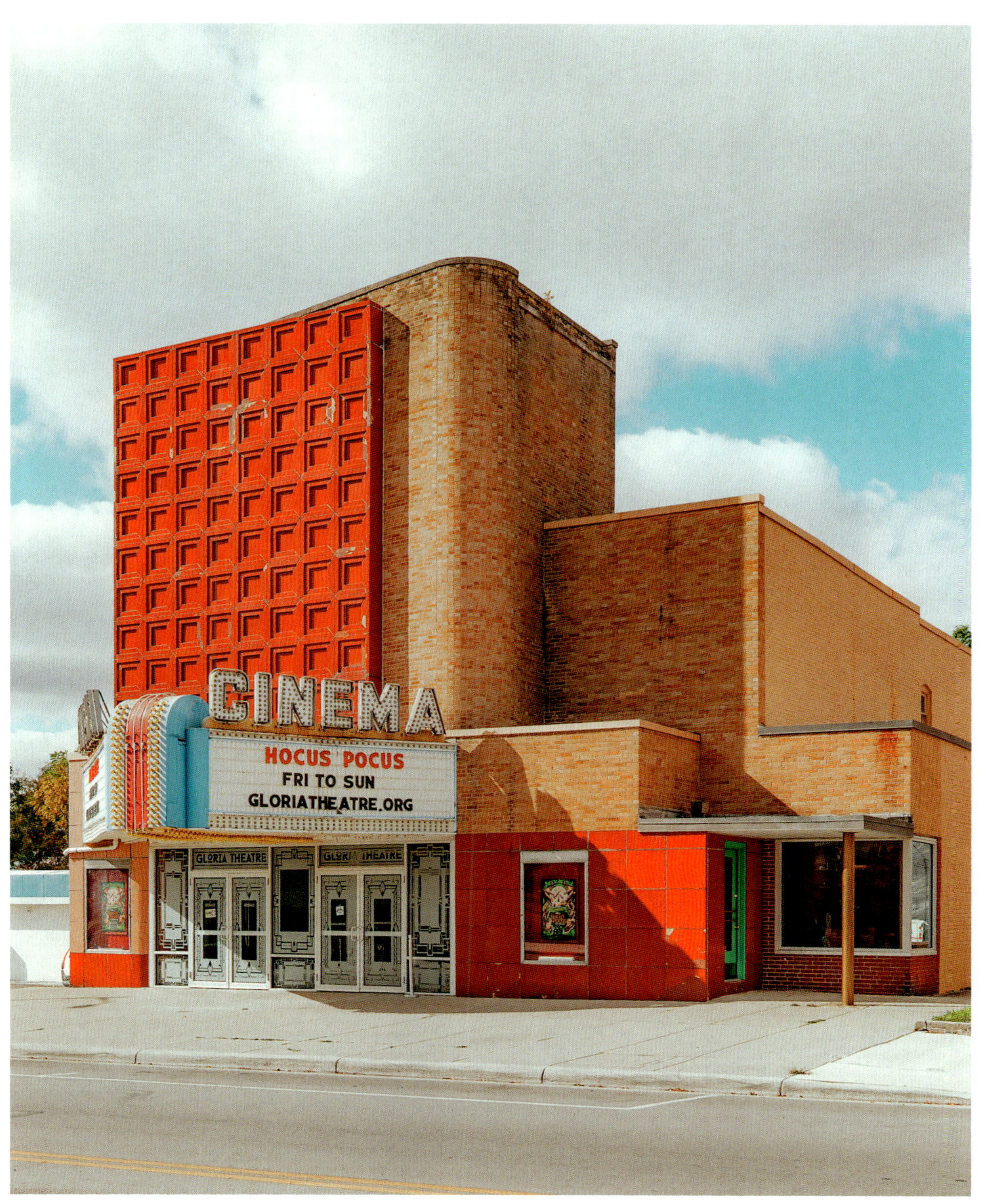

Gloria Theatre • Urbana, Ohio

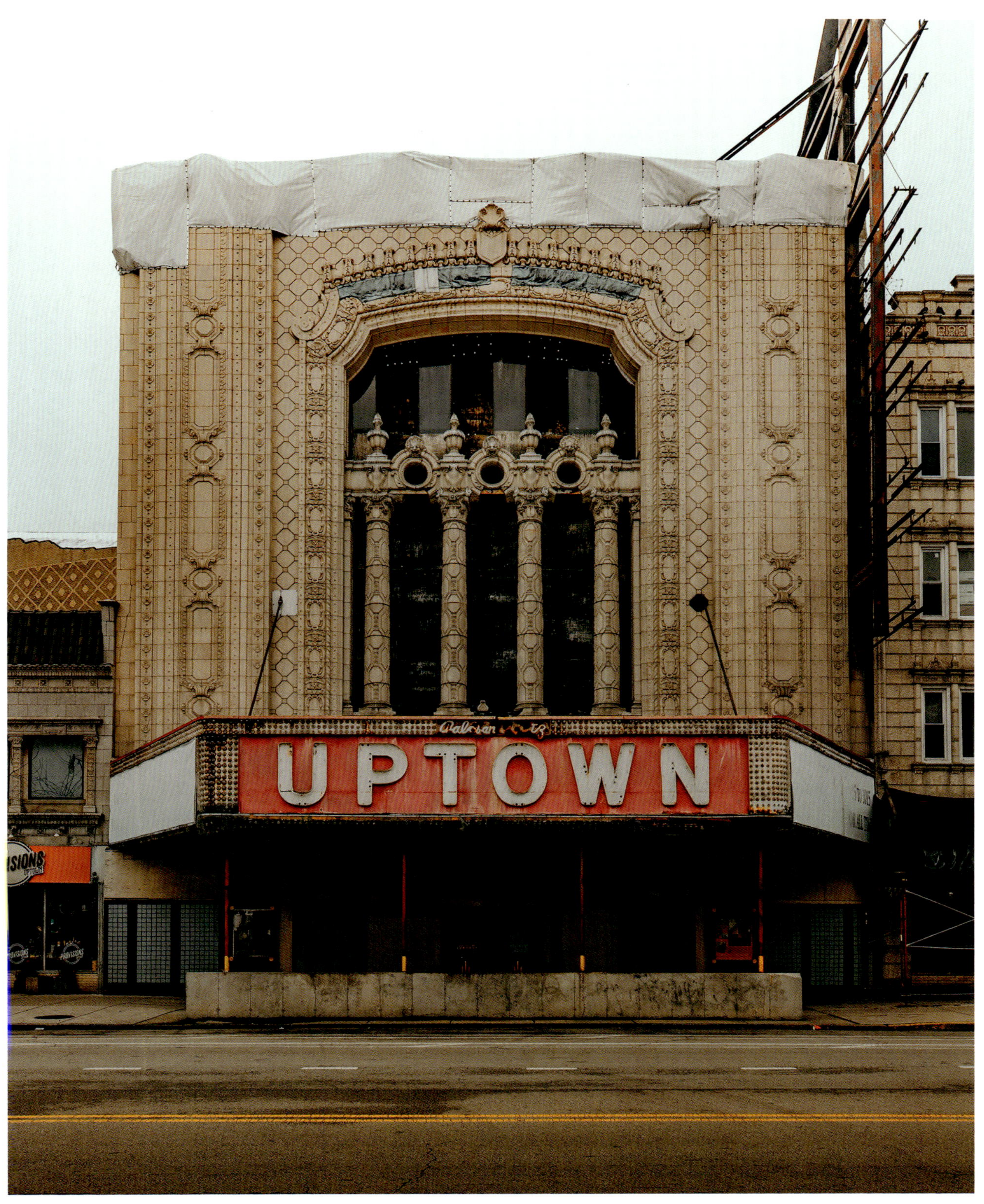

Uptown Theatre • Chicago, Illinois

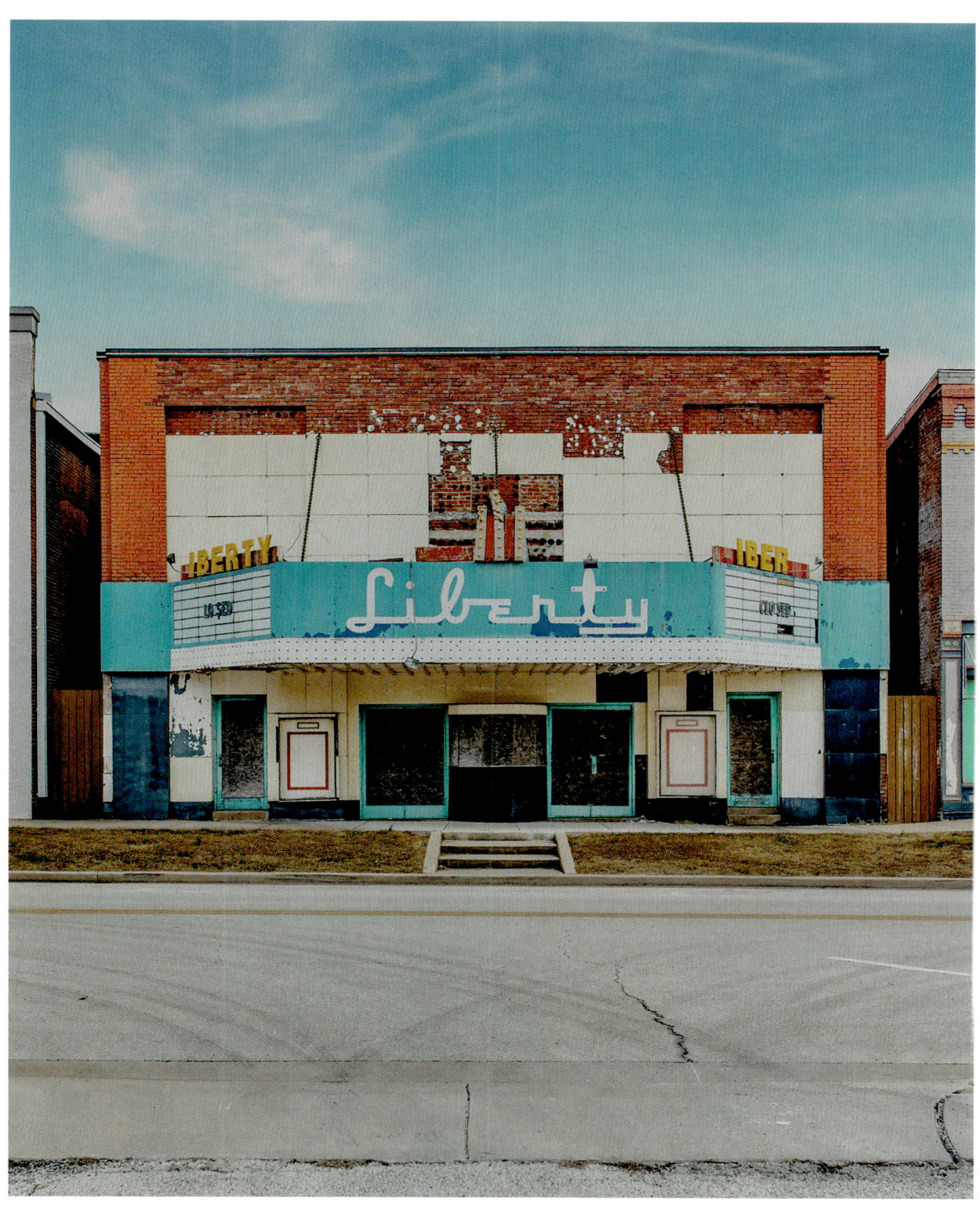

Liberty Theatre • Vandalia, Illinois

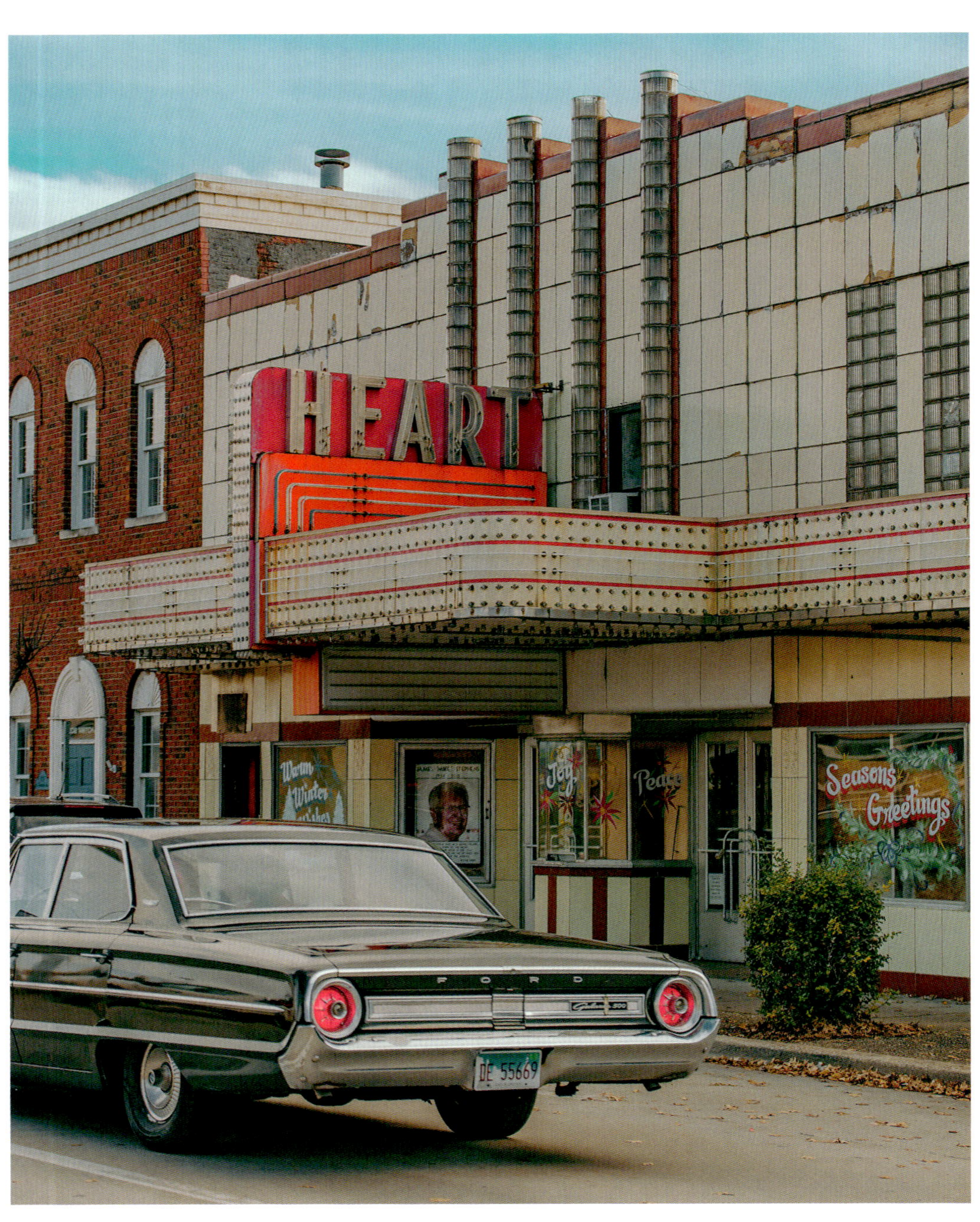

Heart Theatre • Effingham, Illinois

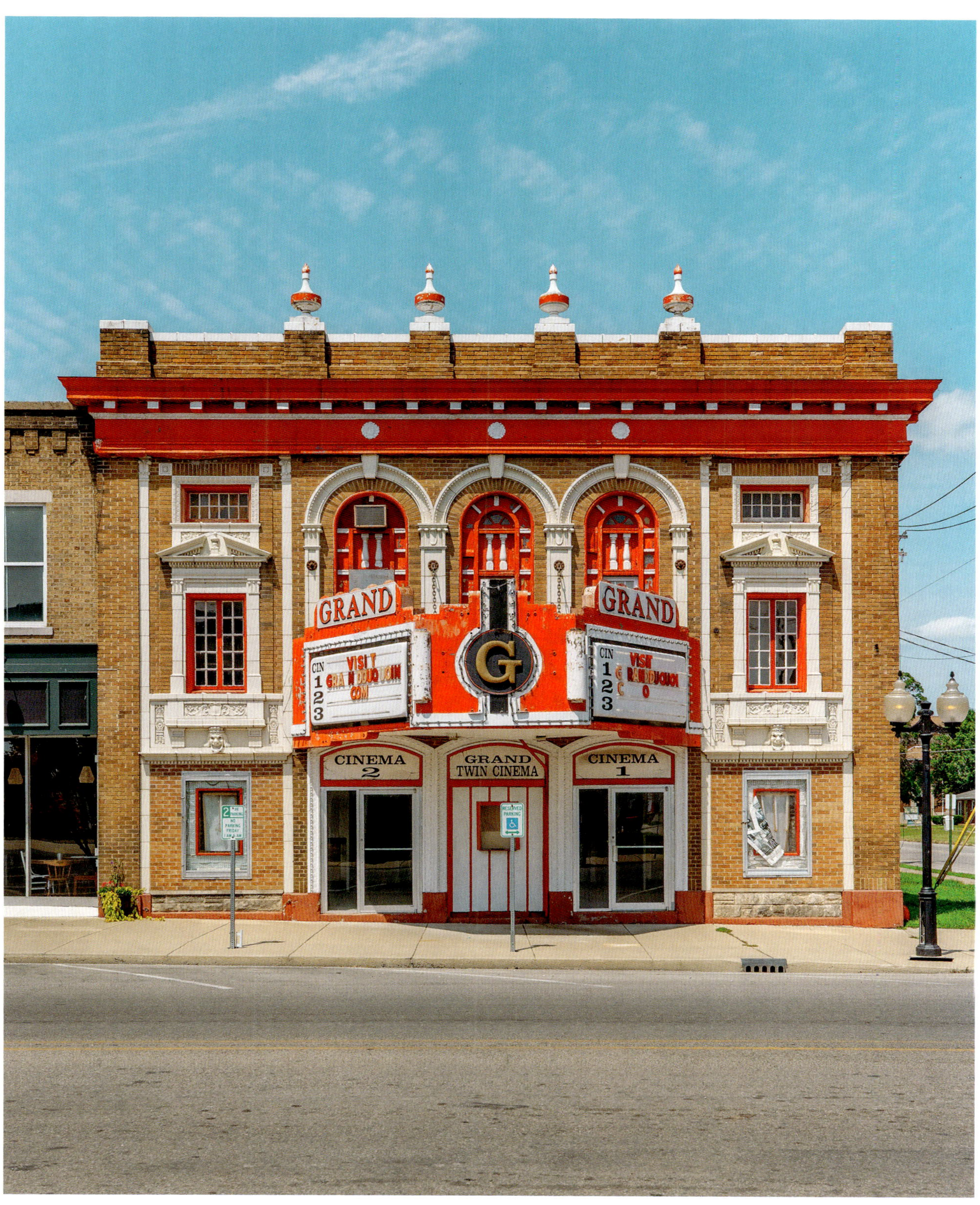

Grand Theatre • Du Quoin, Illinois

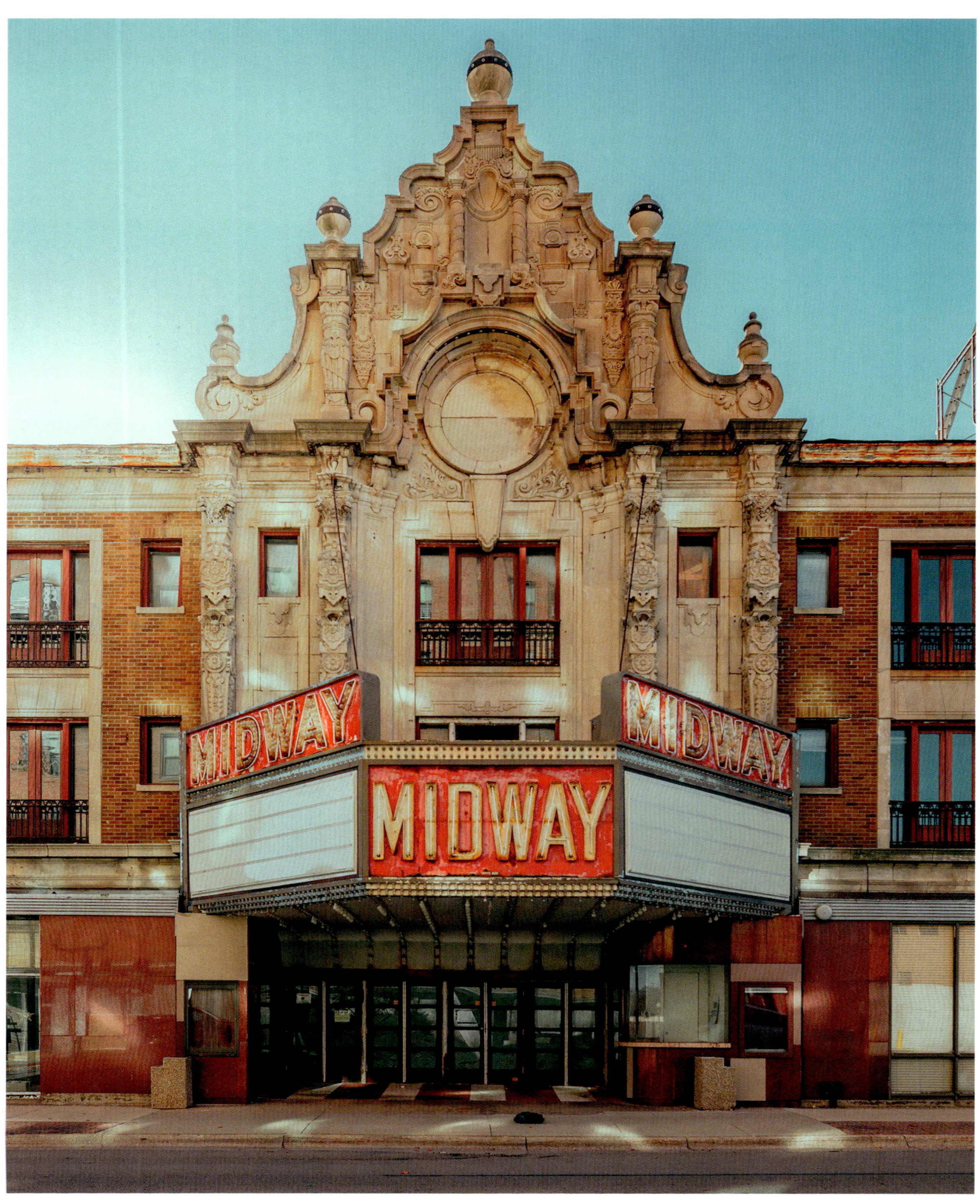

Midway Theatre • Rockford, Illinois

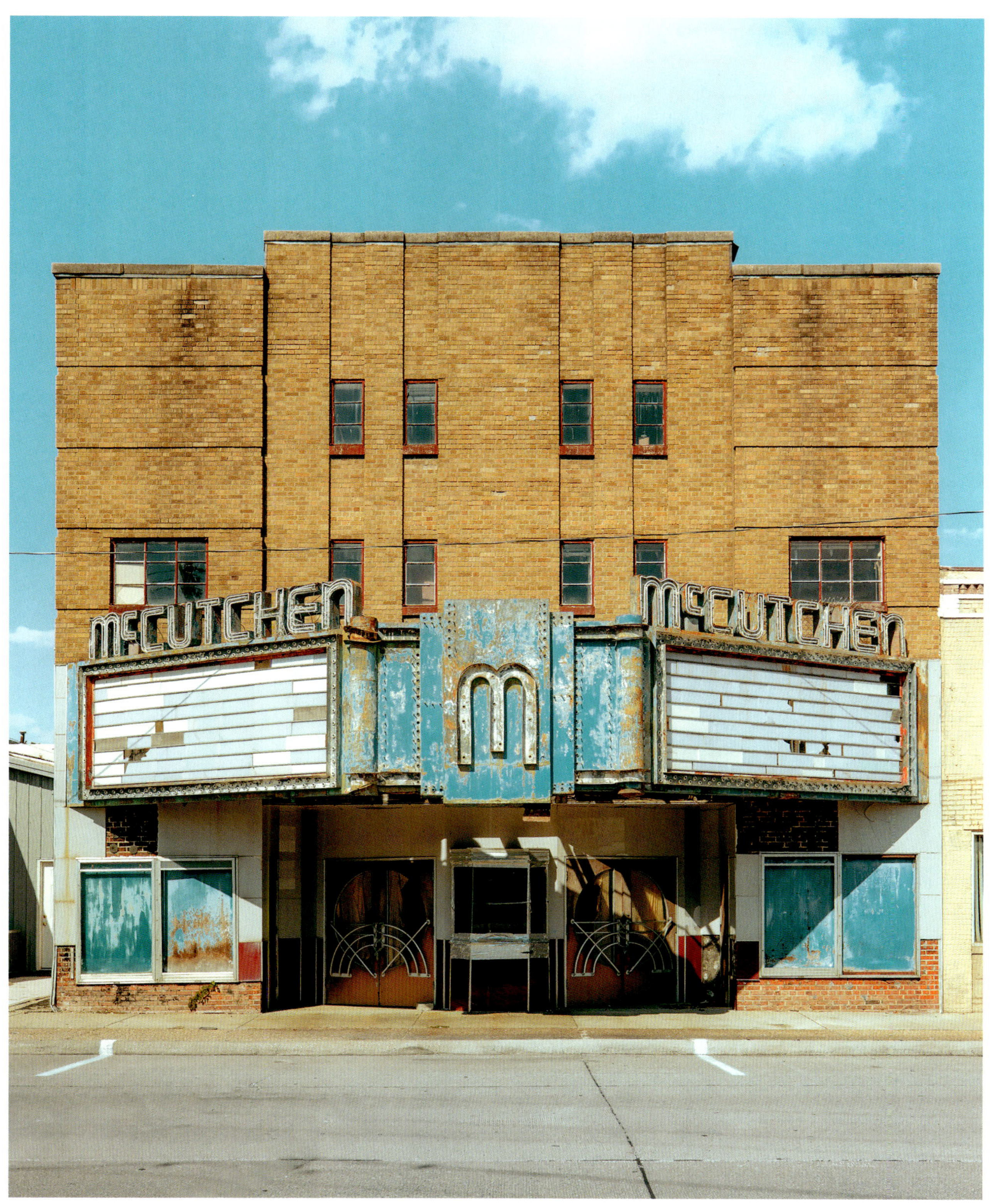

McCutchen Theatre • Charleston, Missouri

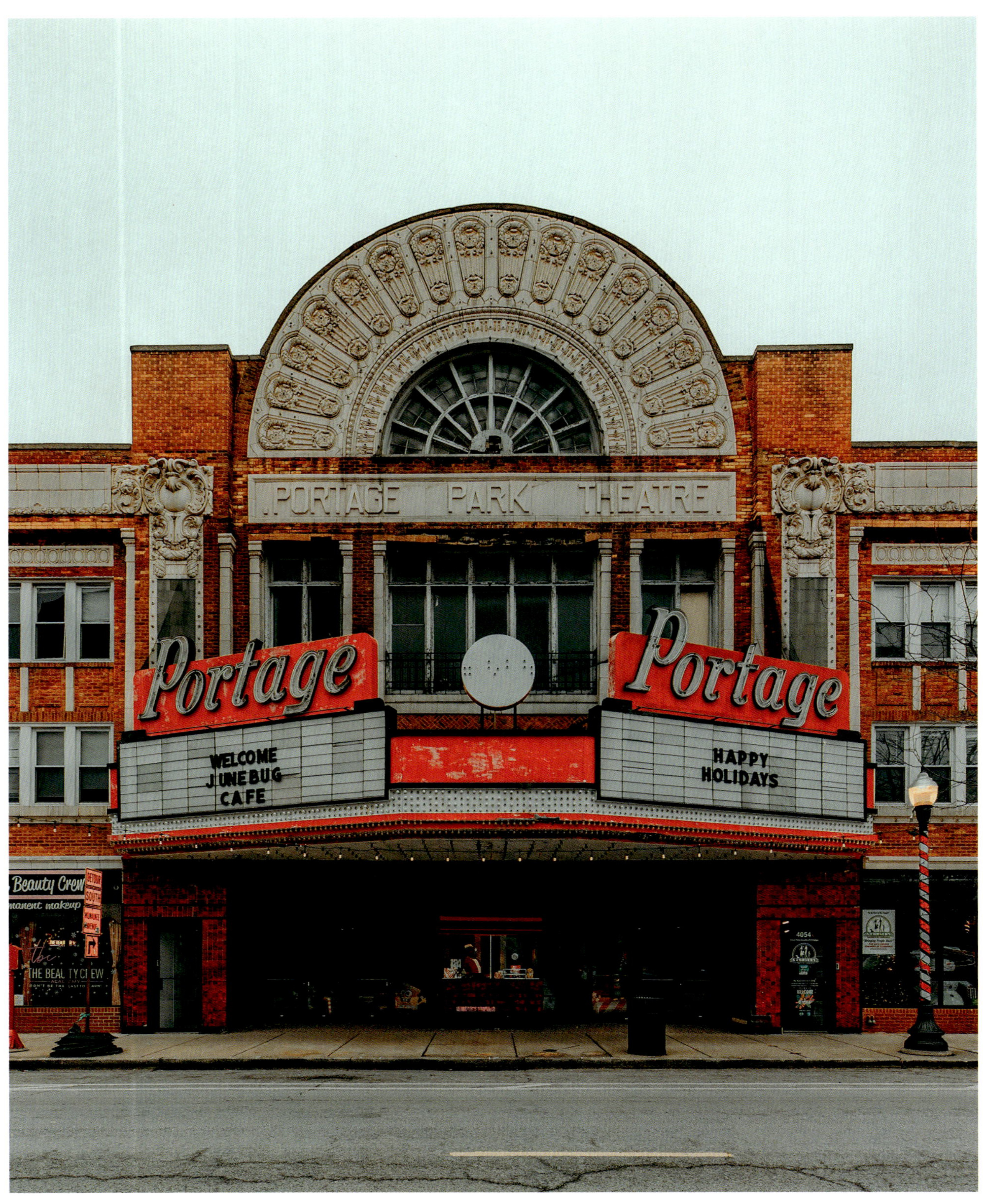

Portage Theatre • Chicago, Illinois

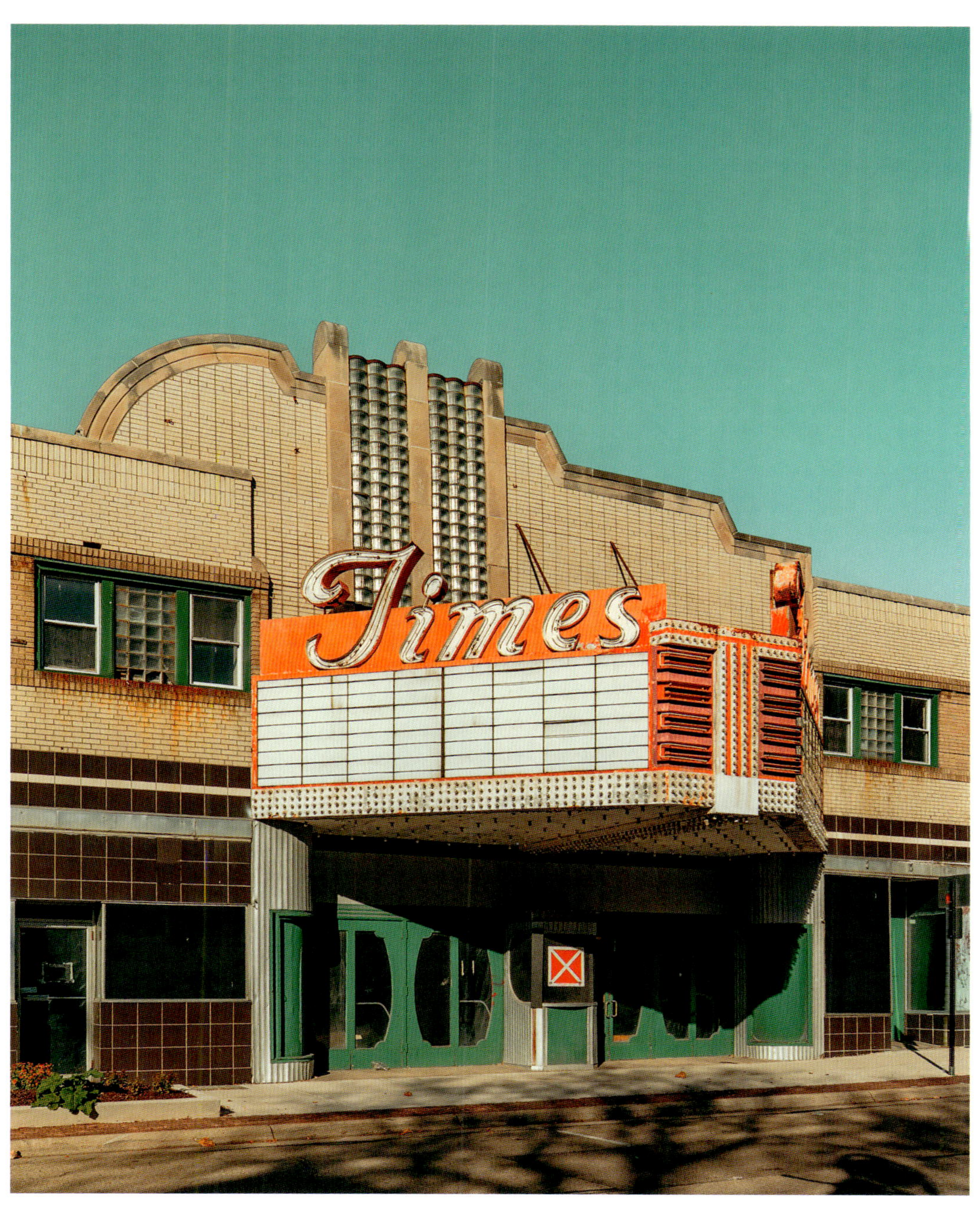

Times Theatre • Rockford, Illinois

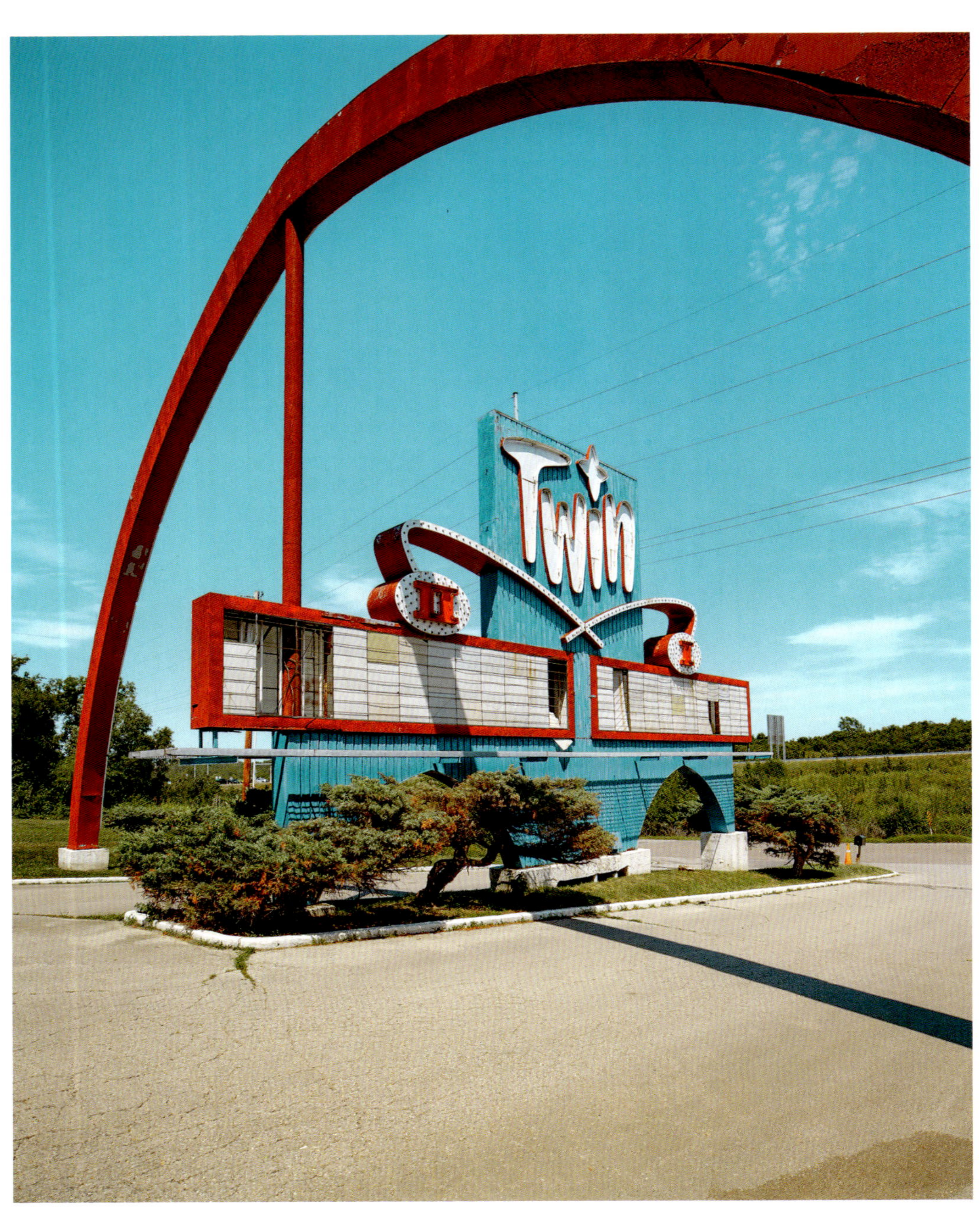

B&B Theatres Twin Drive-In • Independence, Missouri

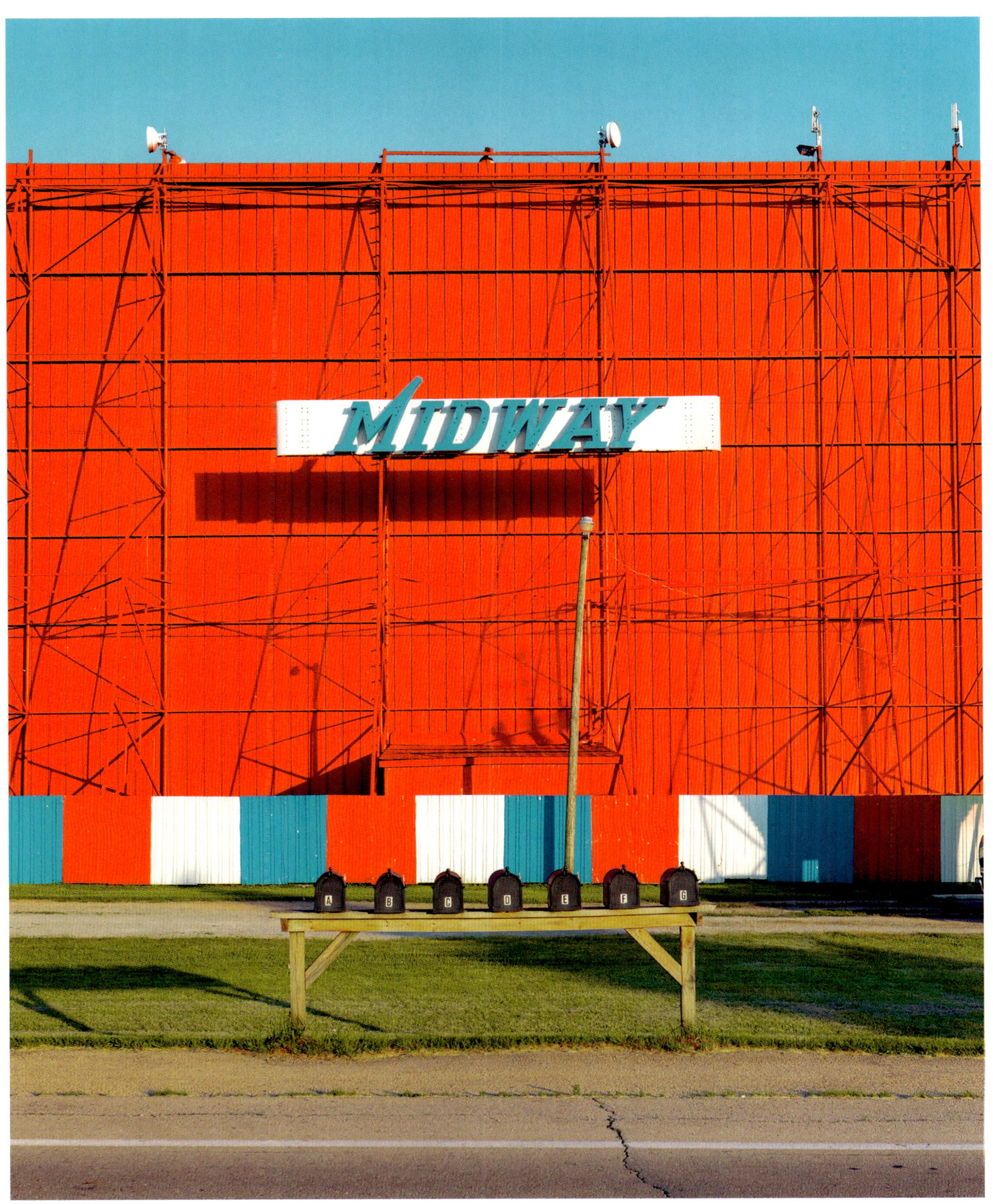

Midway Drive-In Theatre • Sterling, Illinois

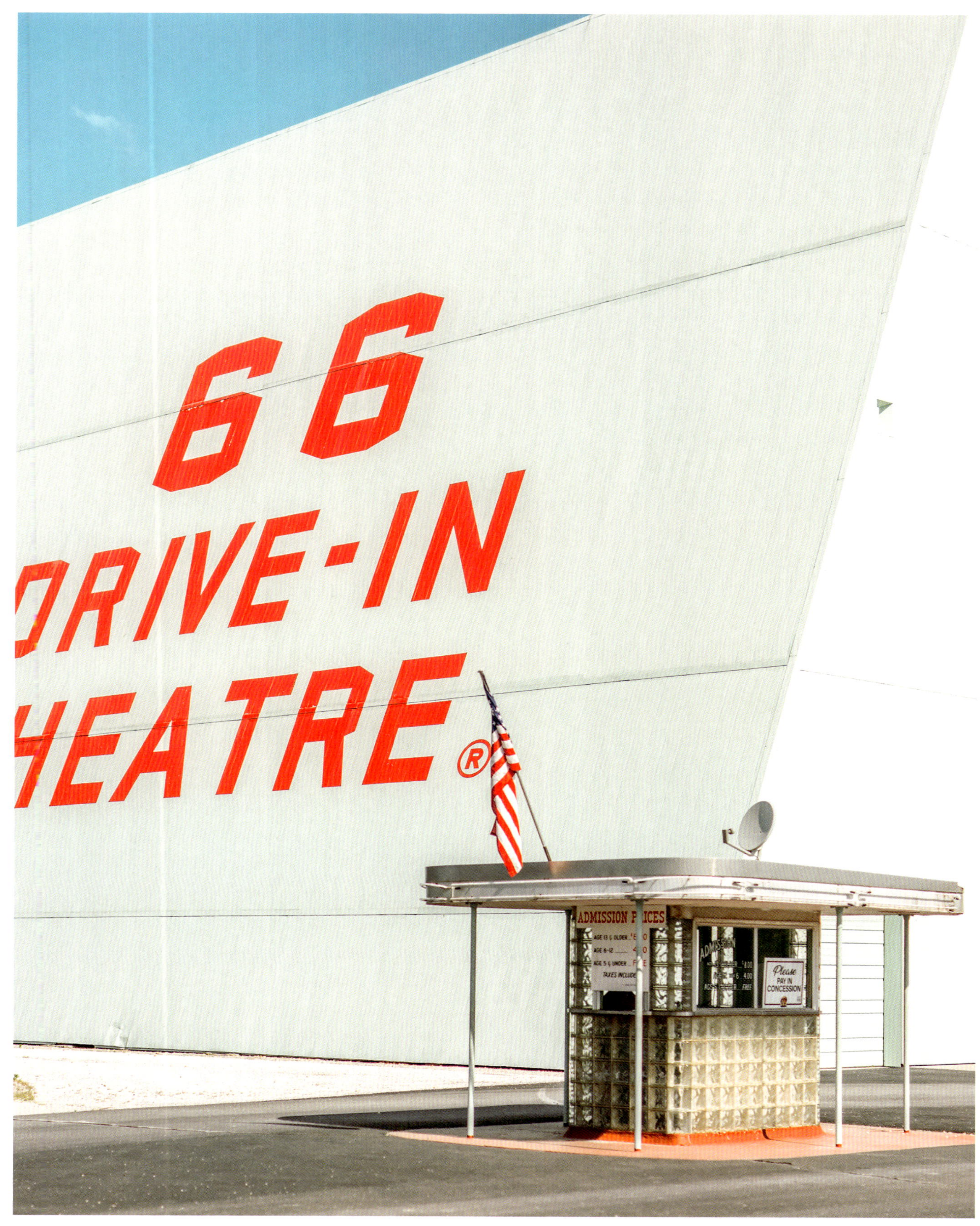
66
RIVE-IN
HEATRE
ADMISSION
AGE 13 & OLDER
AGE 6-12
AGE 5 & UNDER
TAXES INCLUDE
ADMISSION
Please
PAY IN
CONCESSION

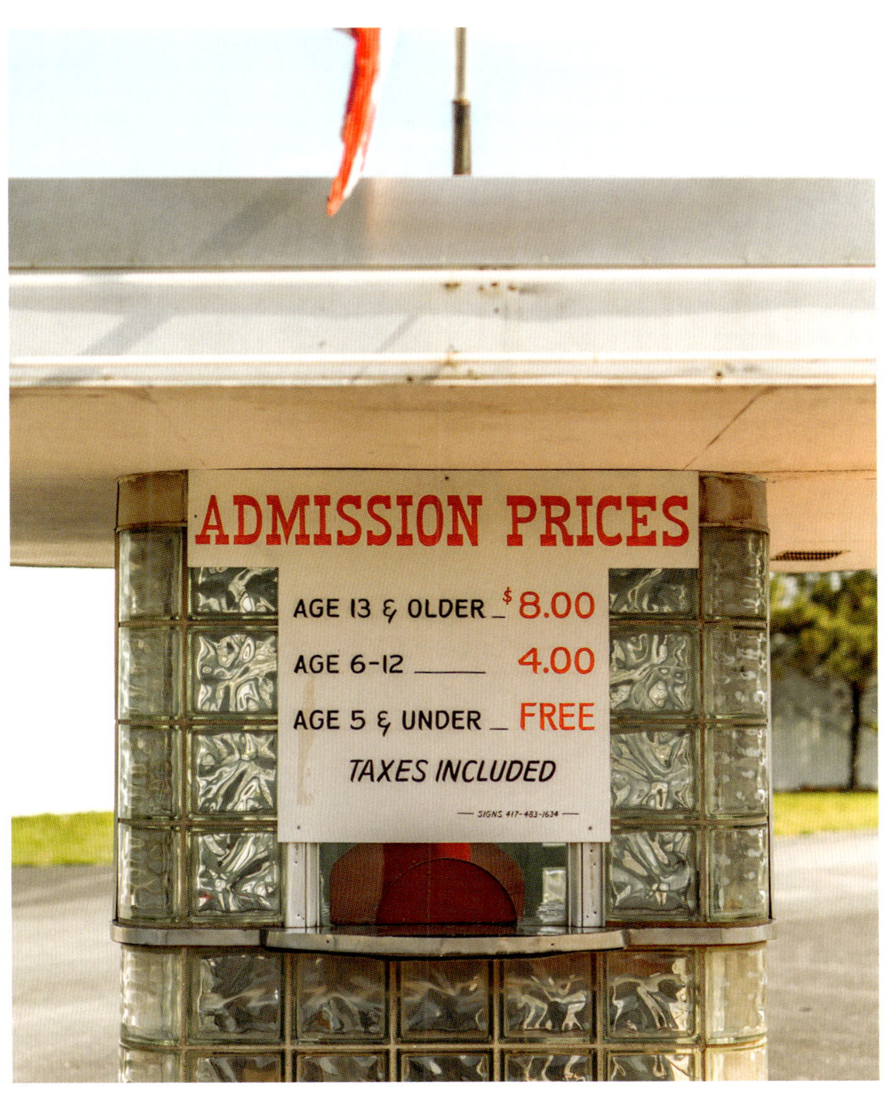

Route 66 Drive-In Theatre • Carthage, Missouri

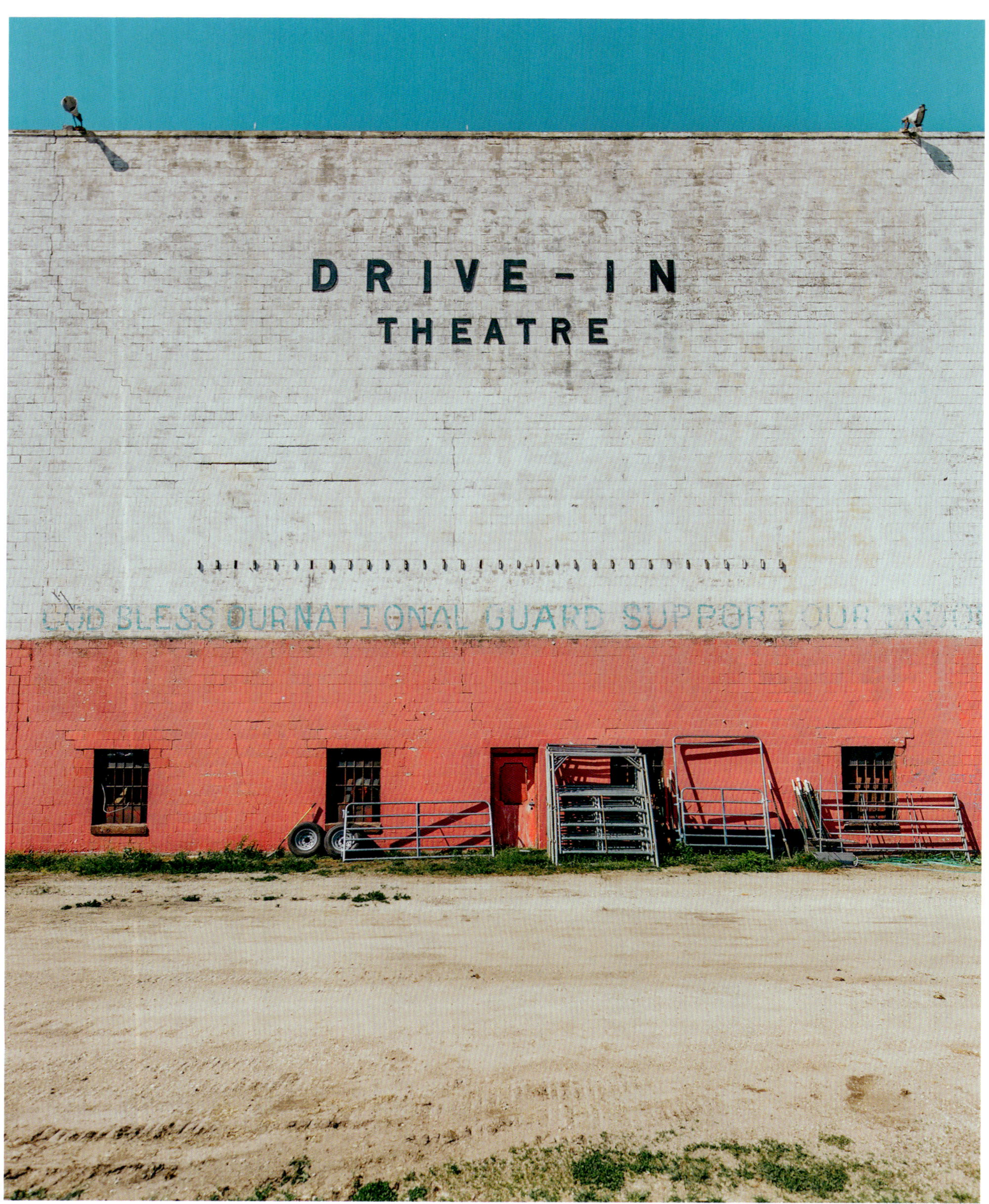

Blue Moonlight Drive-In Theatre • Galesburg, Illinois

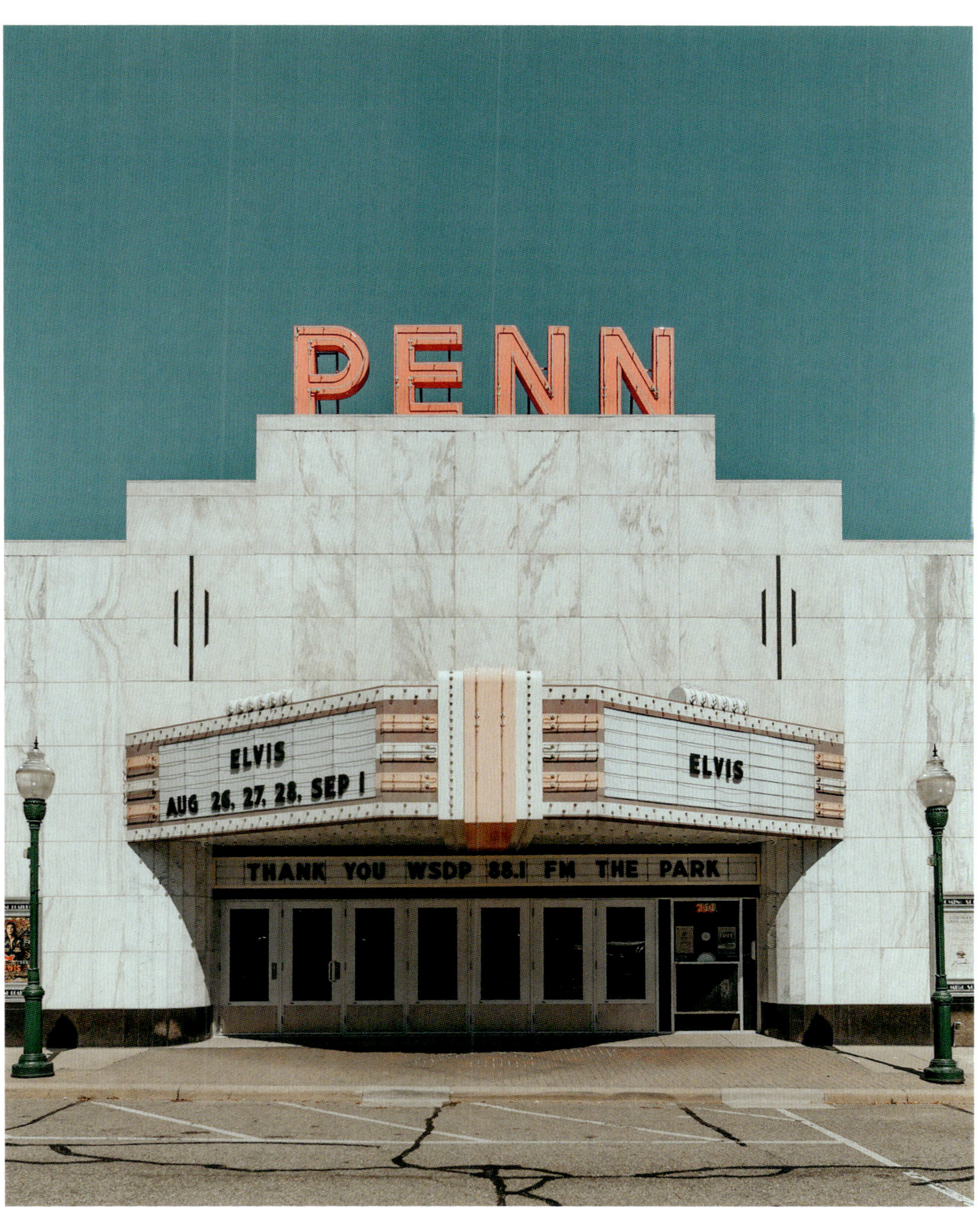

Penn Theatre • Plymouth, Michigan

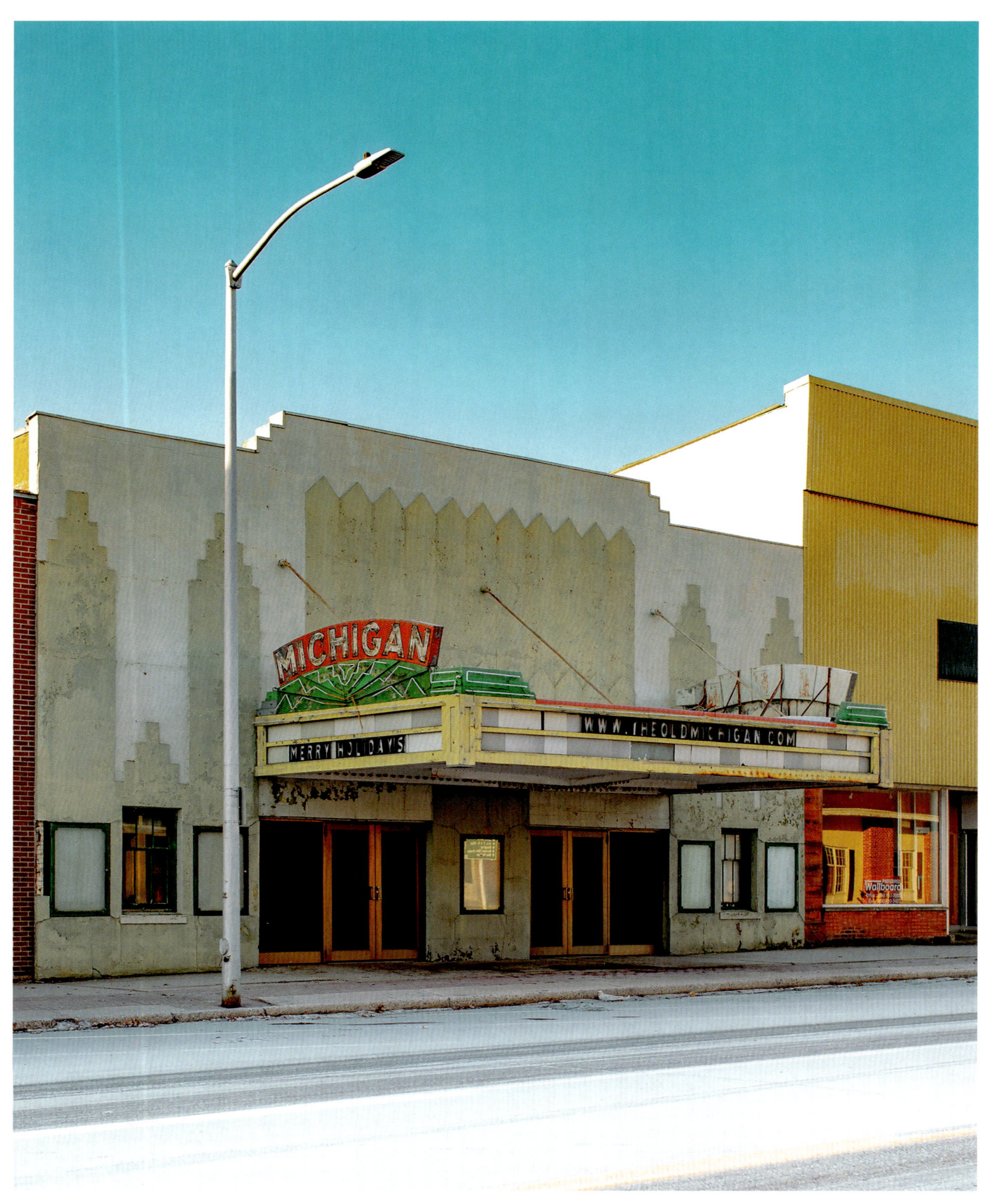

Old Michigan Theatre • Escanaba, Michigan

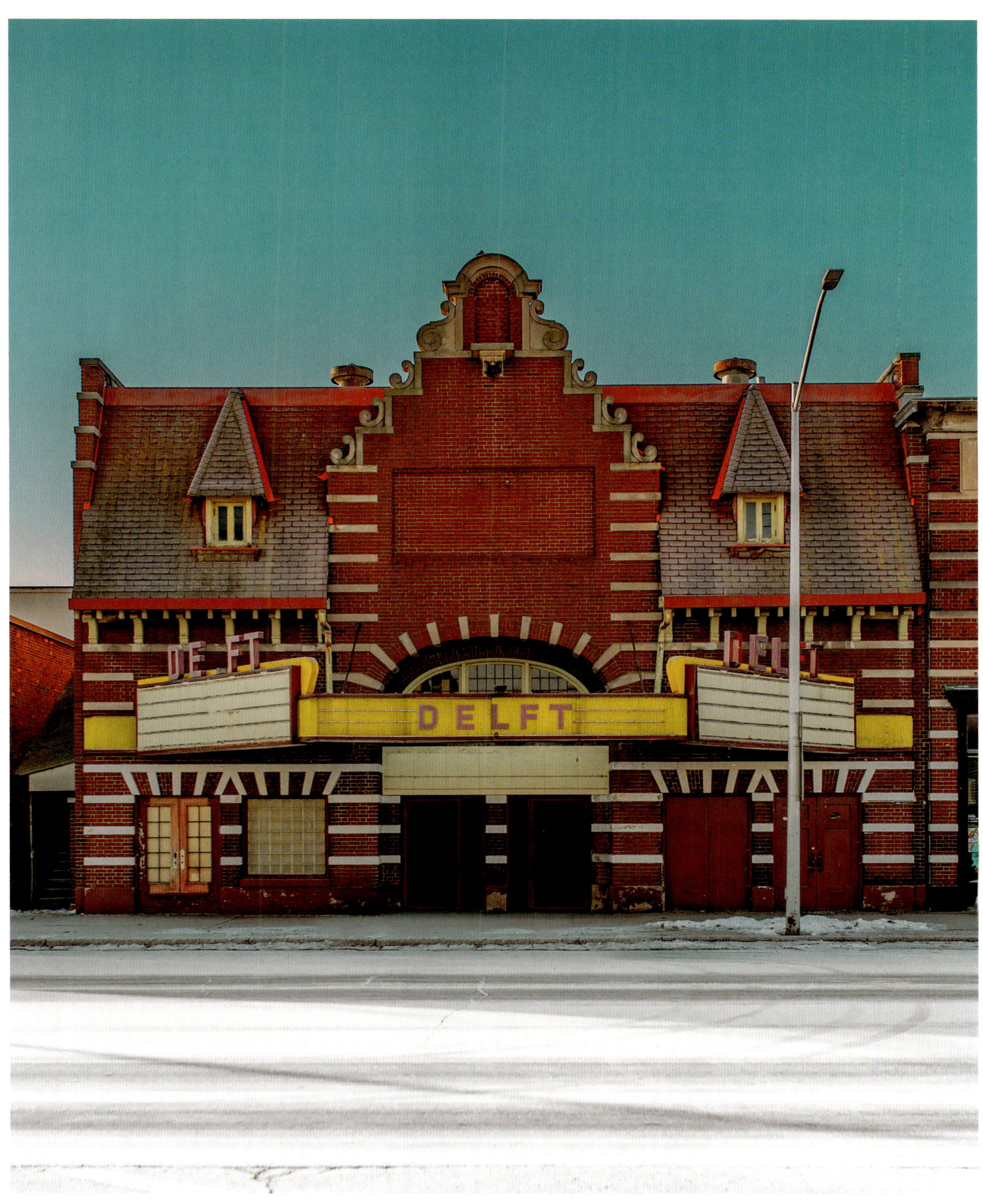

Delft Theatre • Escanaba, Michigan

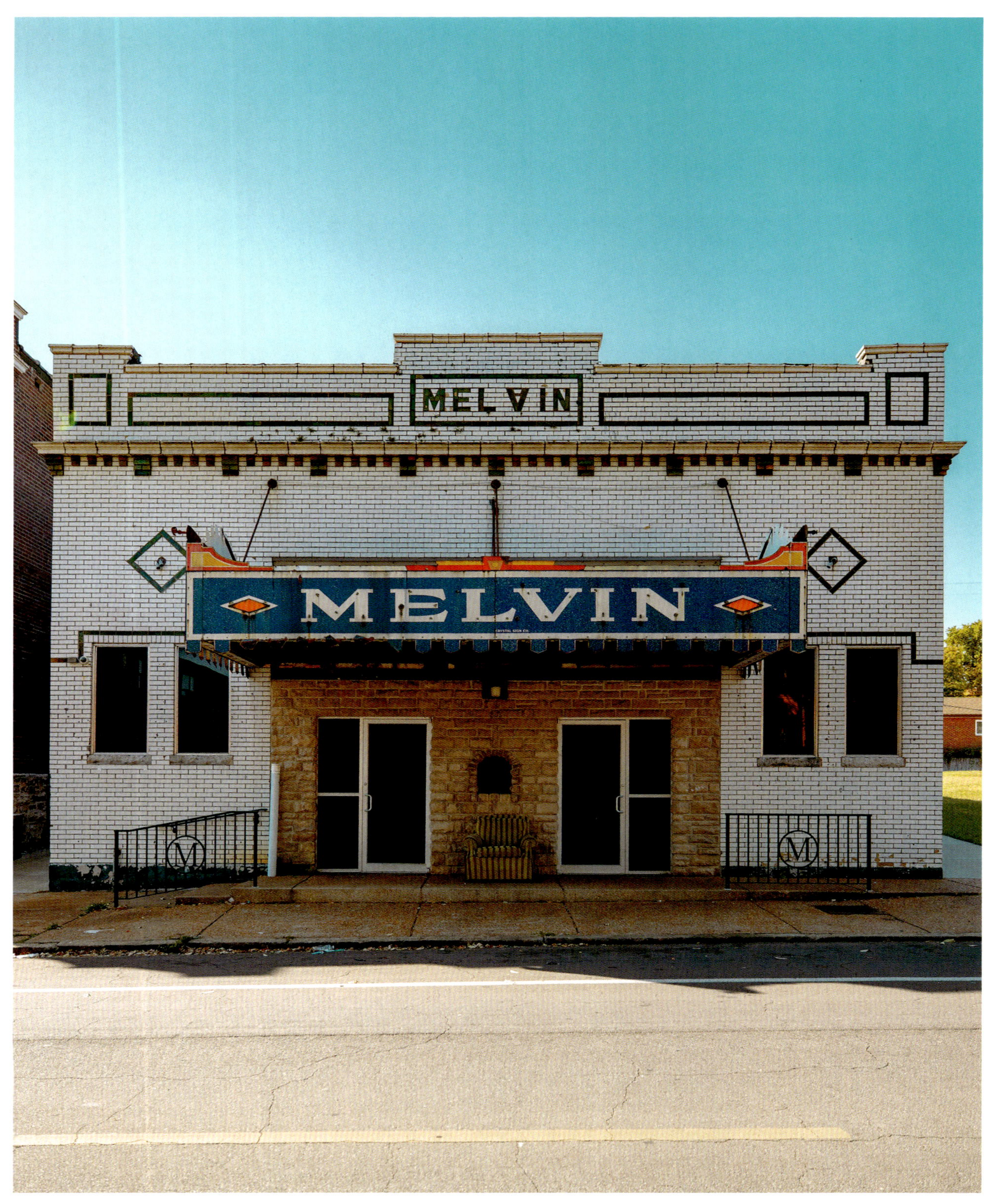

Melvin Theatre • St. Louis, Missouri

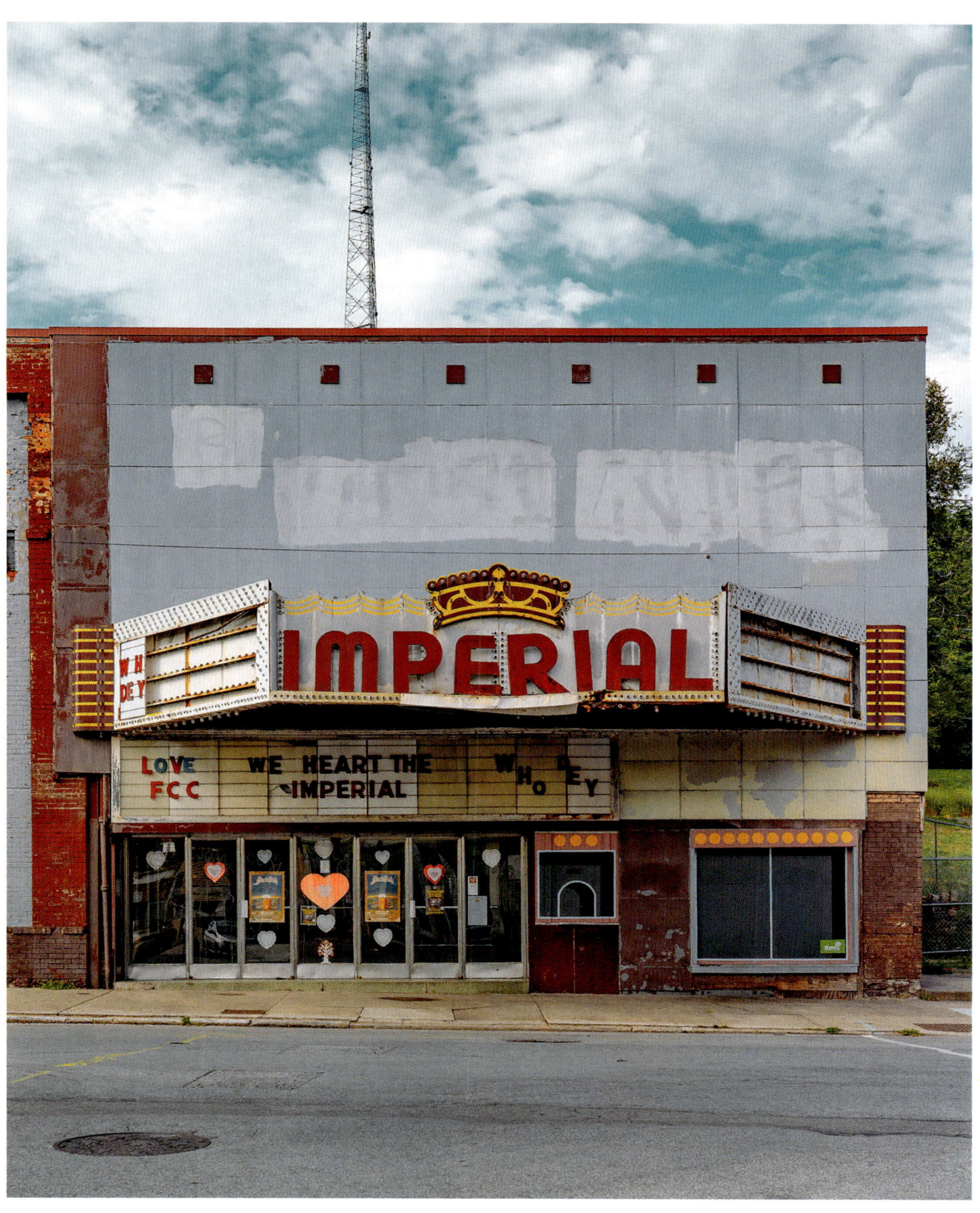

Imperial Theatre • Cincinnati, Ohio

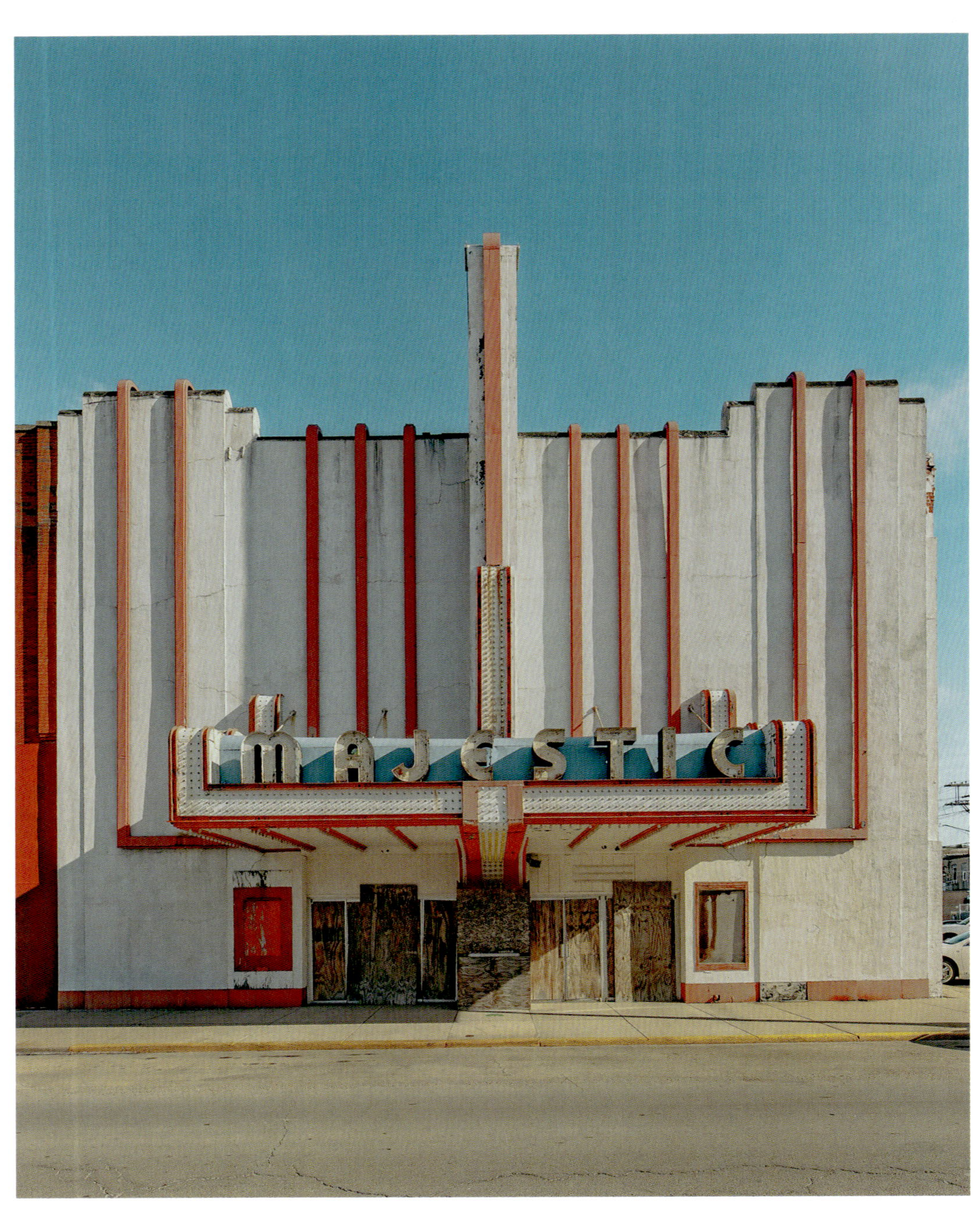

Majestic Theatre • Streator, Illinois

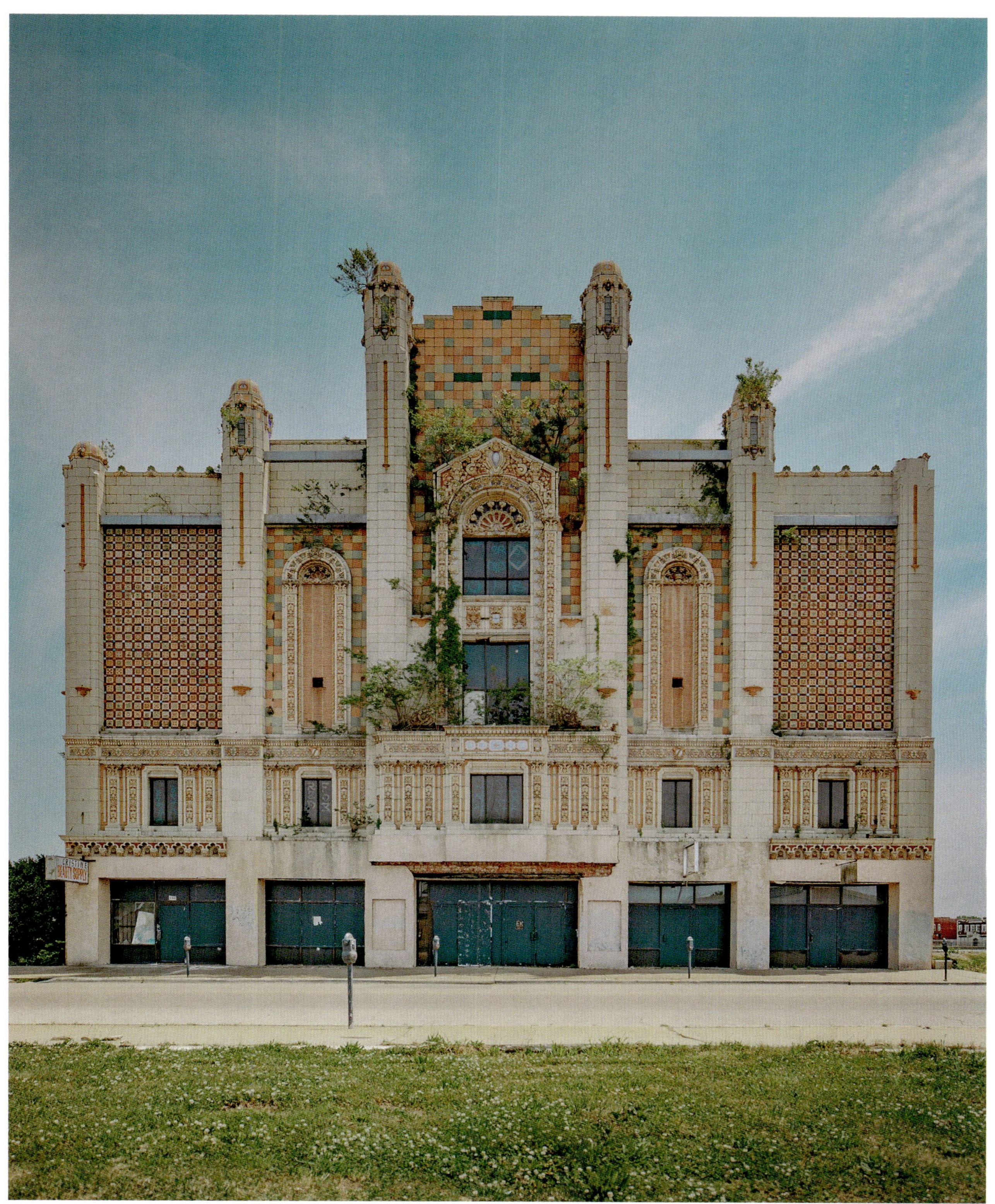

Majestic Theatre • East St. Louis, Illinois

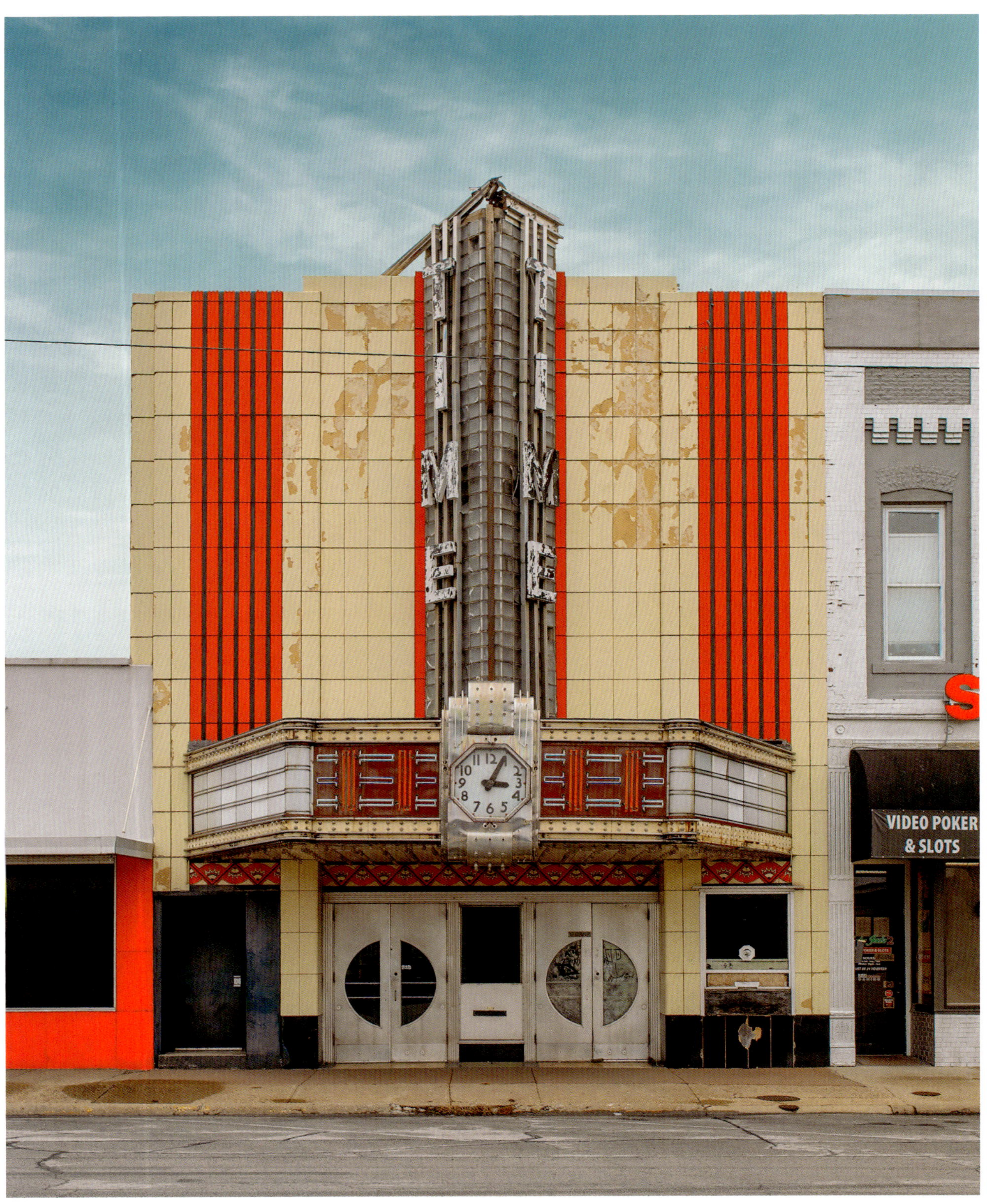

Time Theatre • Mattoon, Illinois

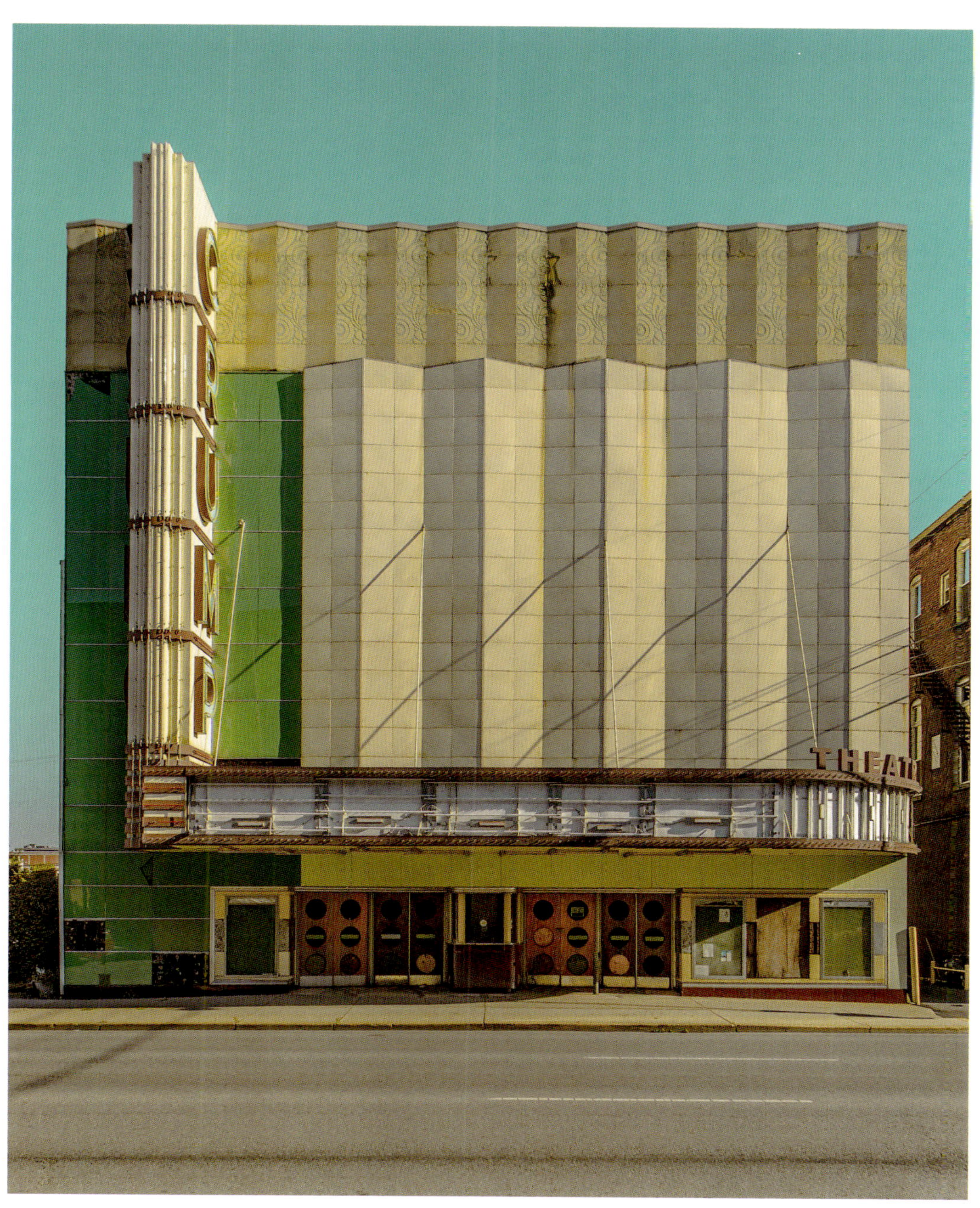

Crump Theatre • Columbus, Indiana

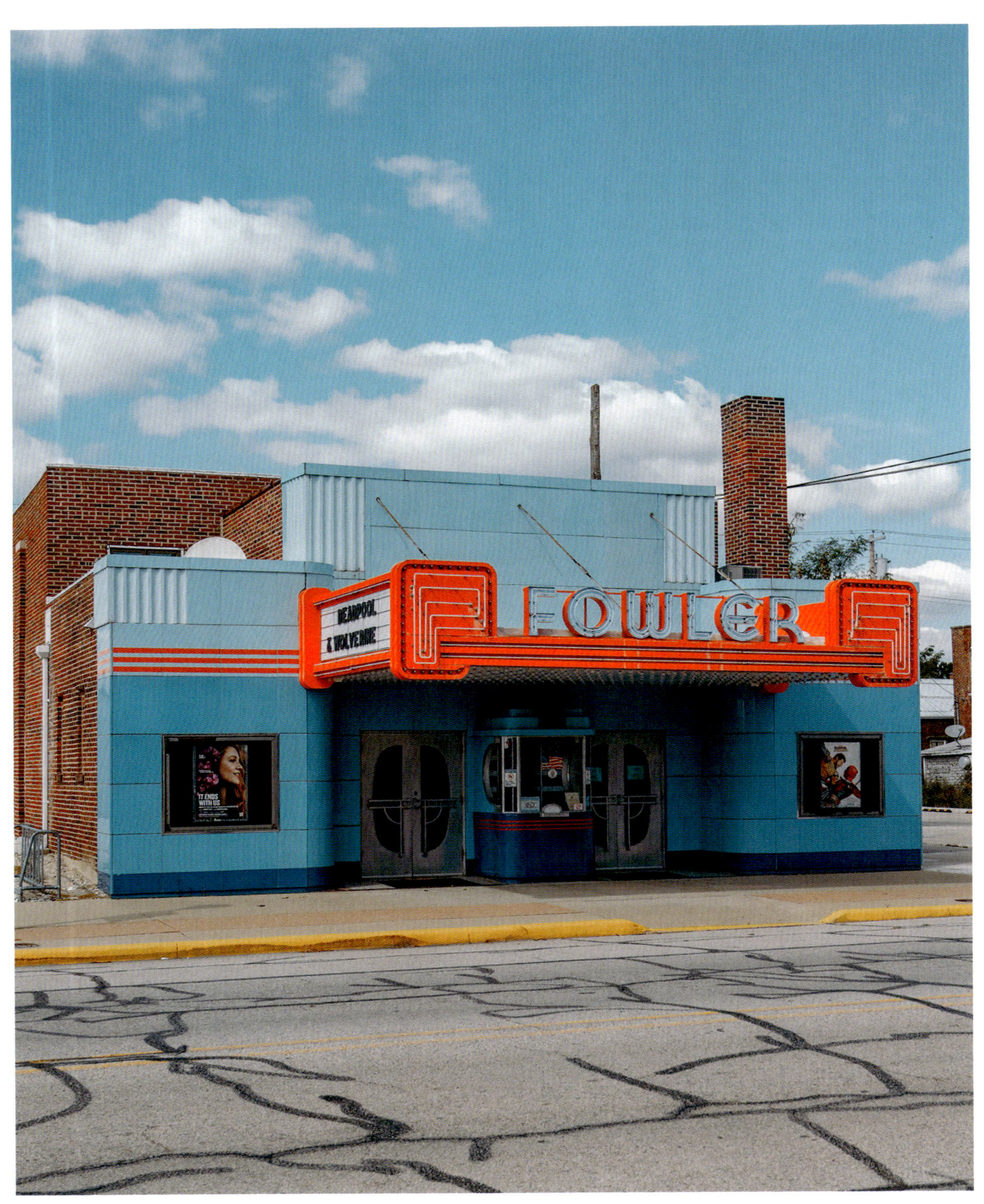

Fowler Theatre • Fowler, Indiana

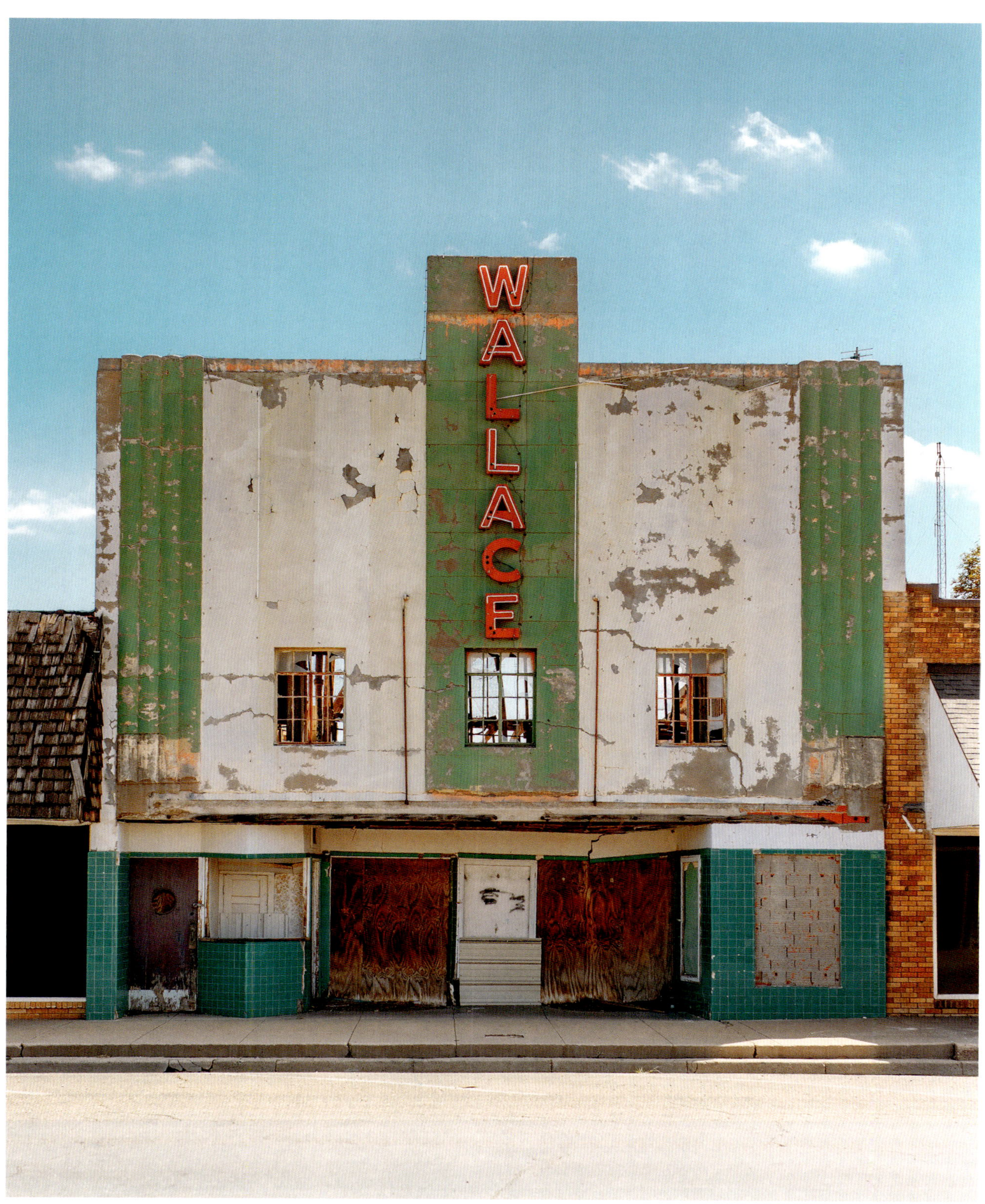

Wallace Theatre • Muleshoe, Texas

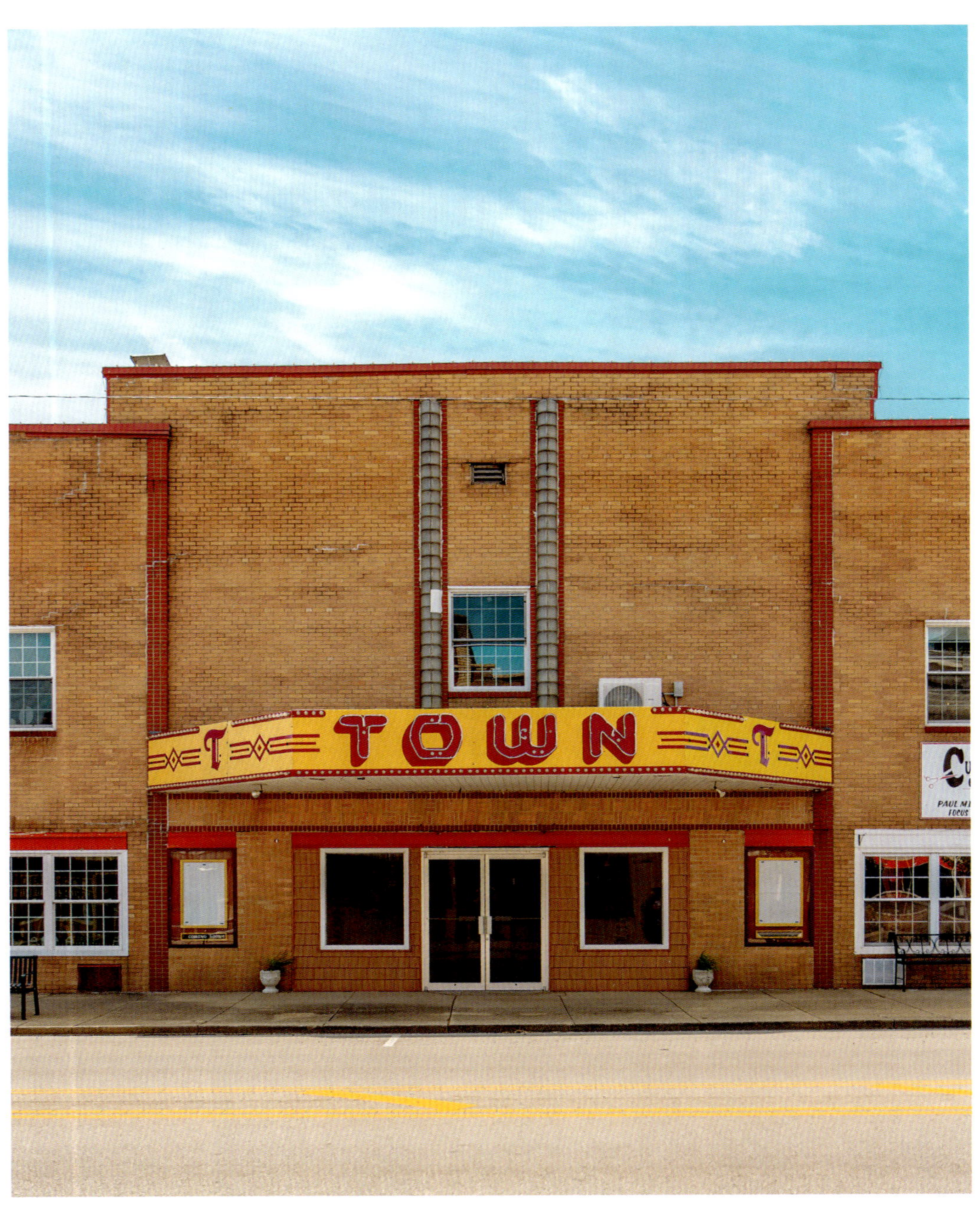

Town Theatre • Flora, Illinois

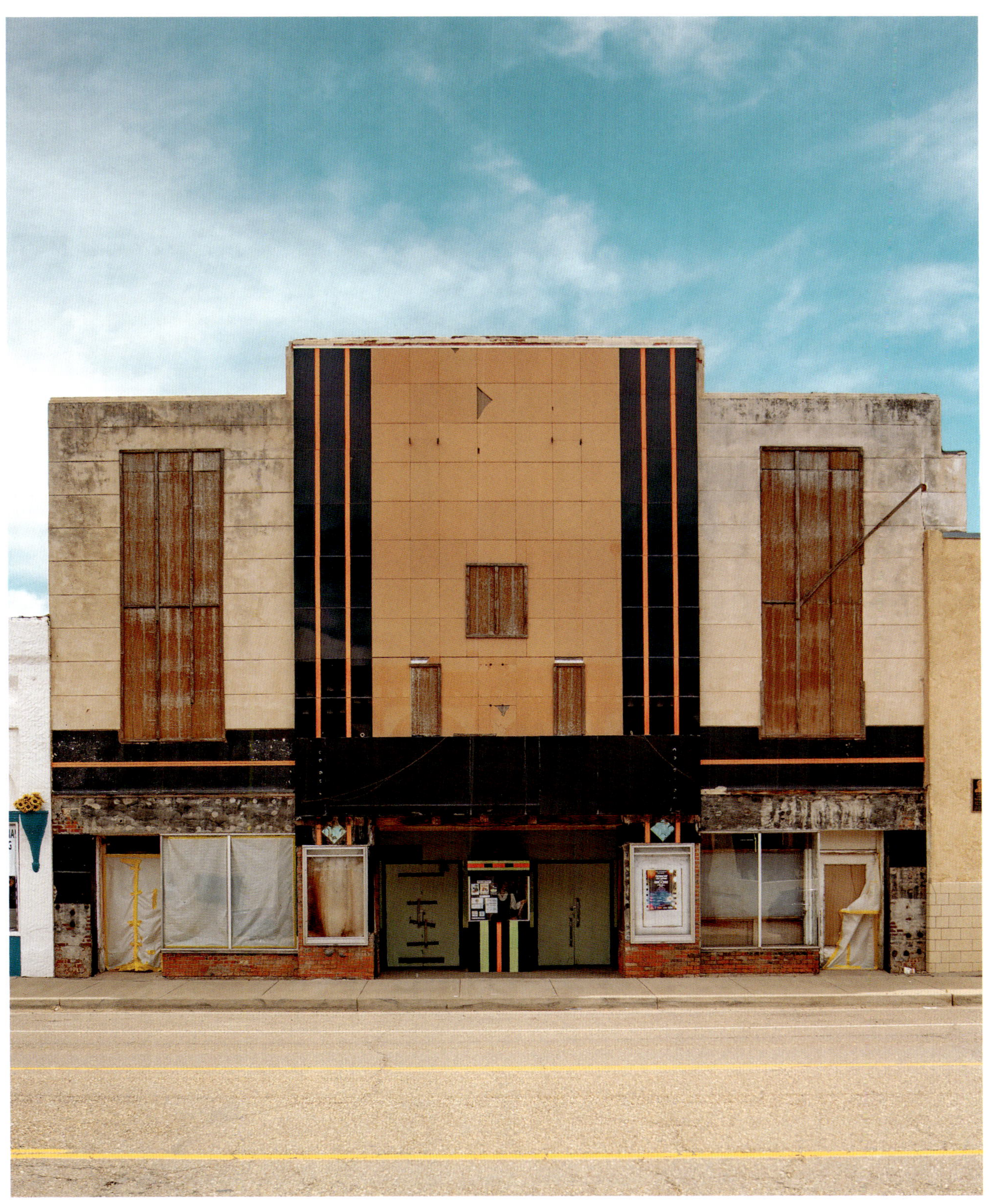

Princess Theatre • Tucumcari, New Mexico

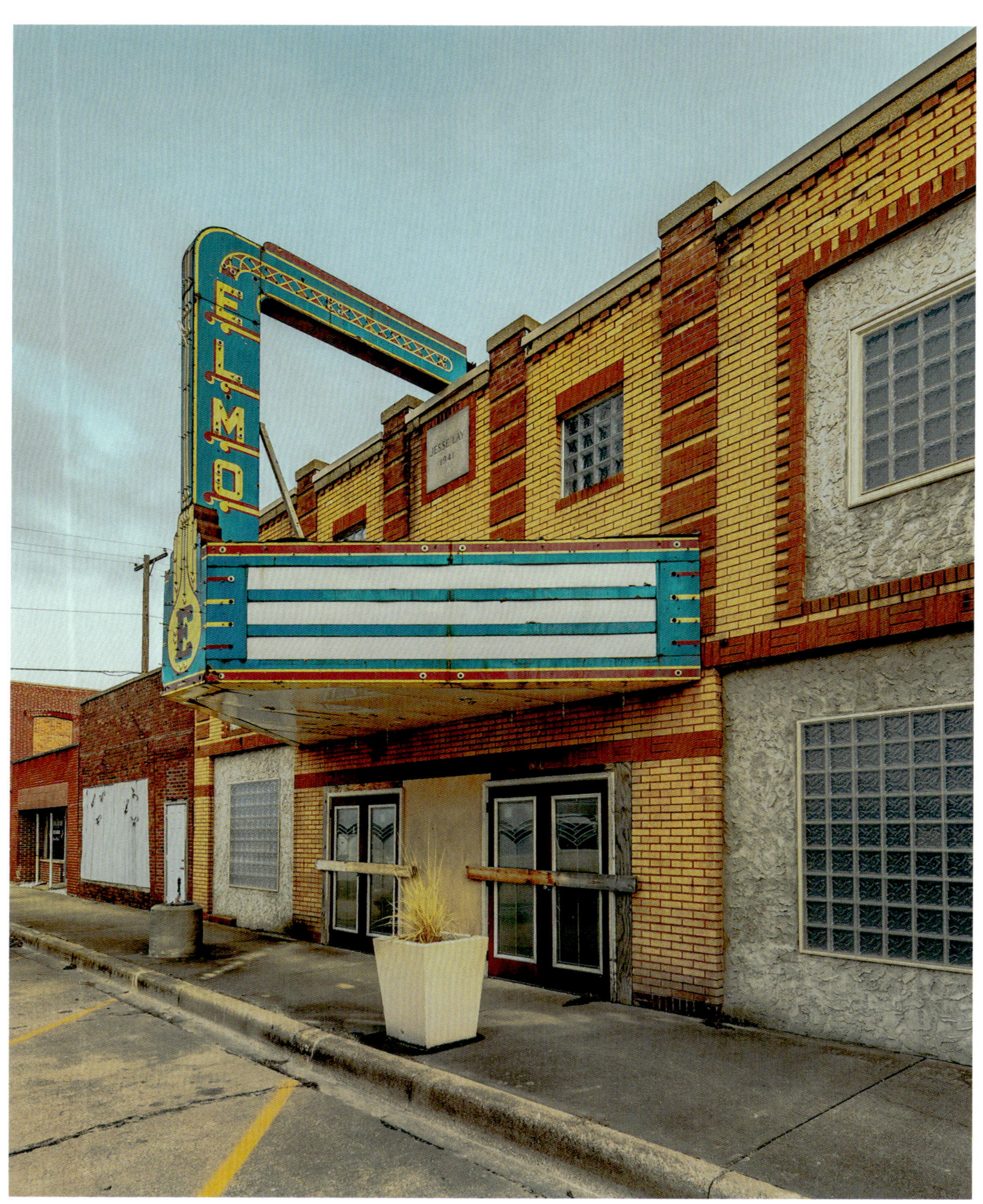

Elmo Theatre • St. Elmo, Illinois

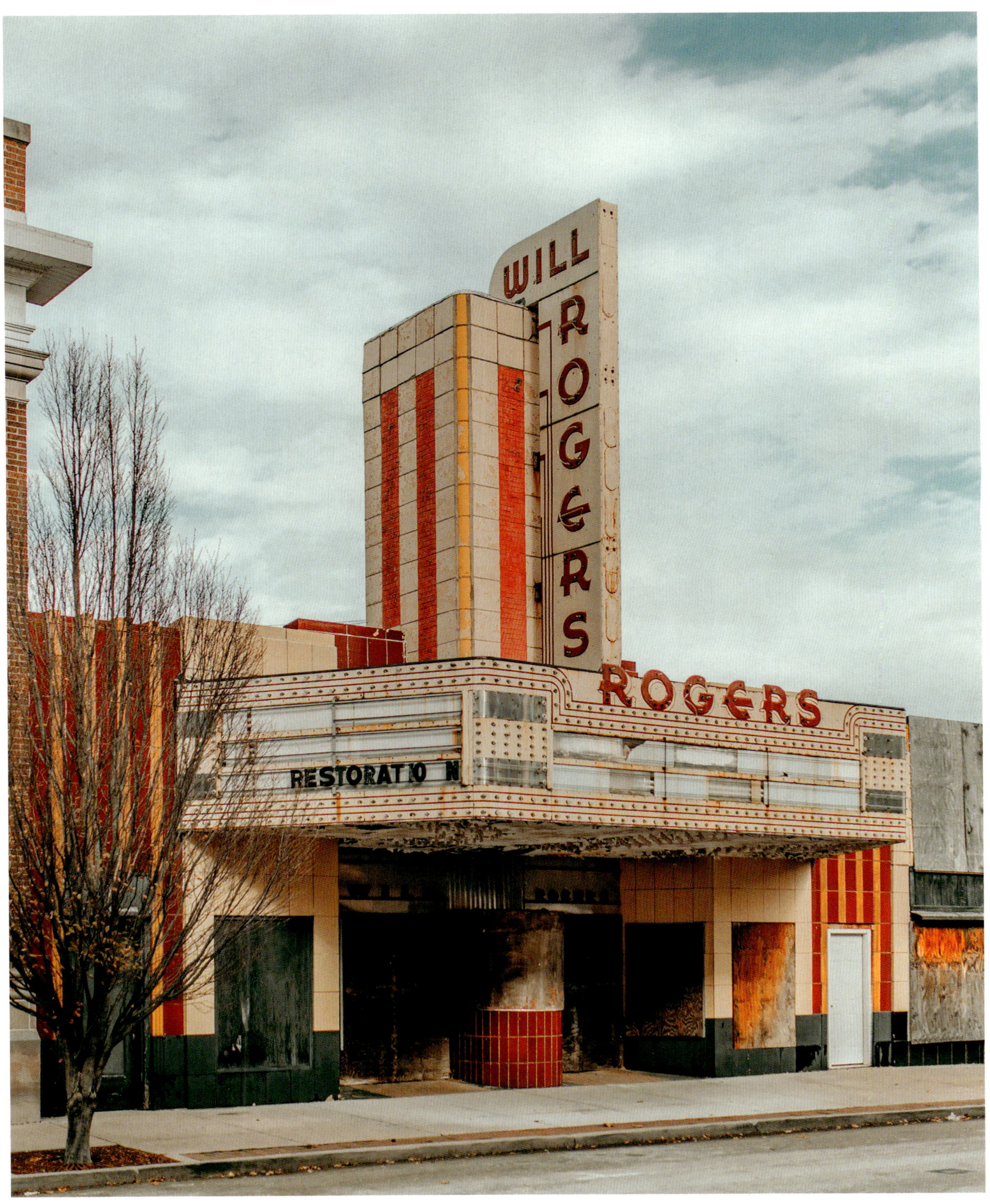

Will Rogers Theatre • Charleston, Illinois

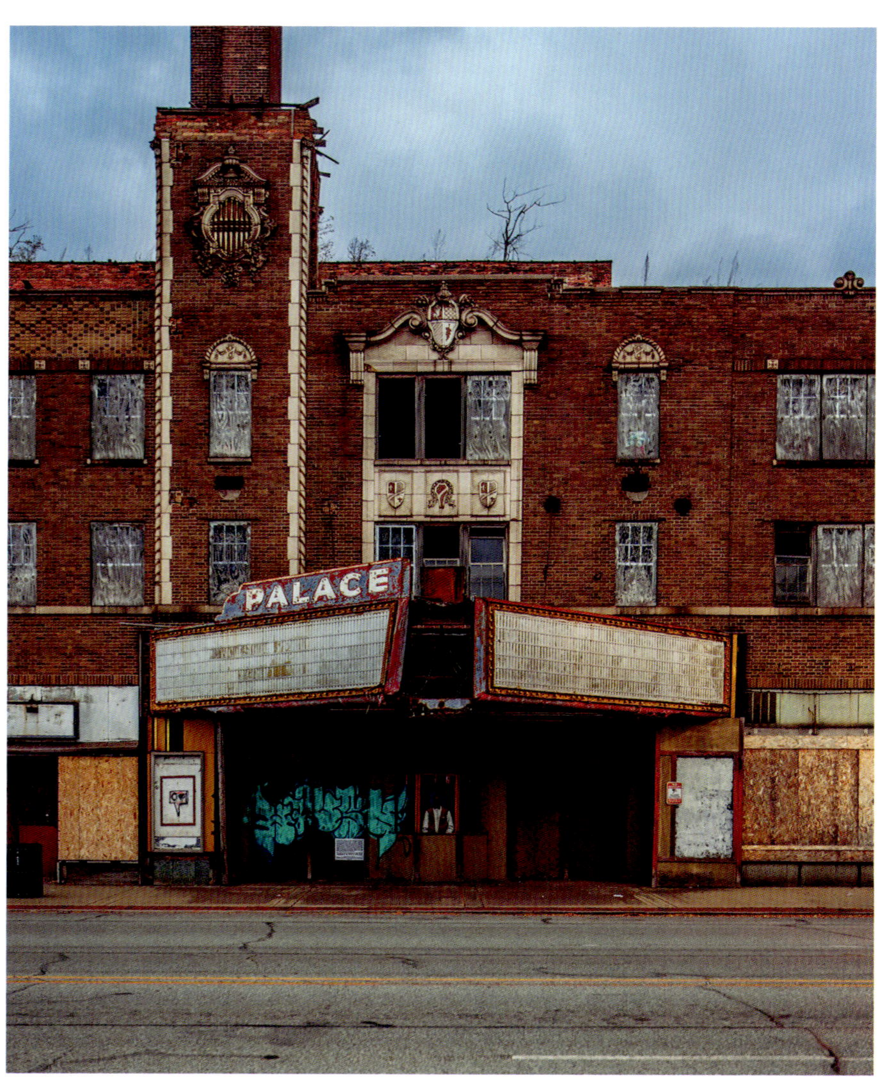

Palace Theatre • Gary, Indiana

BEN GEIER

Largely influenced by his Midwest upbringing, Ben Geier's pursuit of photography first began with a fascination for the abandoned, and since then he has focused on broadening his work to capture architecture, roadside attractions, and, his true passion, all things retro and Americana. His unmistakable aesthetic and color palette have breathed new life into faded old spaces. A multifaceted artist, he has spent over 20 years working for numerous design agencies, a quality which can be seen in his work.

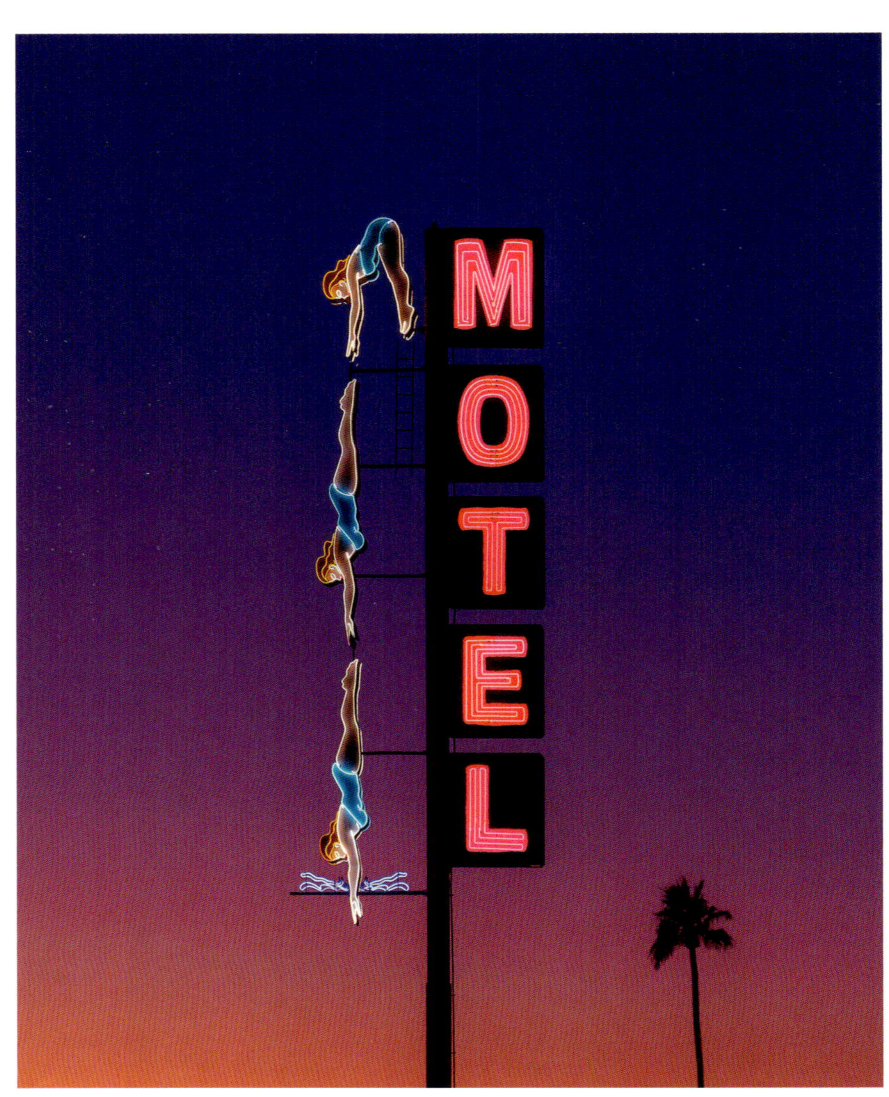

Starlite Motel • Mesa, Arizona

LCCN: 2025932264
ISBN: 978-1-951963-37-8

Trope Publishing Co.
Printed in China
First printing, 2025

Ben Geier's photographs are available
for purchase. For inquiries, go to trope.com
or email the gallery at info@trope.com

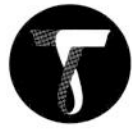

+ **INFORMATION:**
**For additional information
on our books and prints,
visit trope.com**

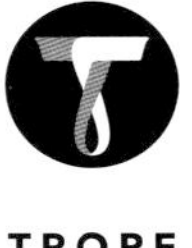

TROPE

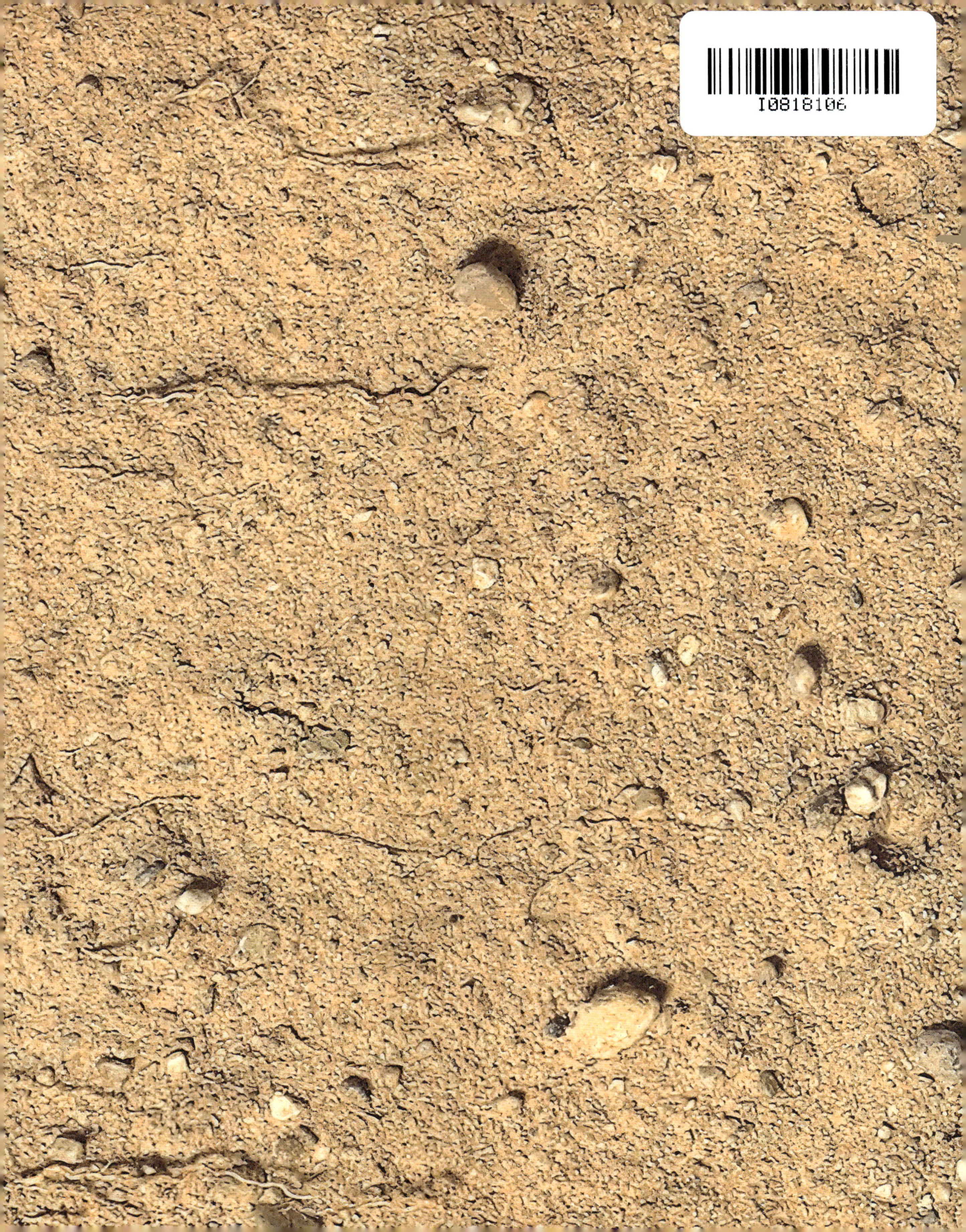
I0818106

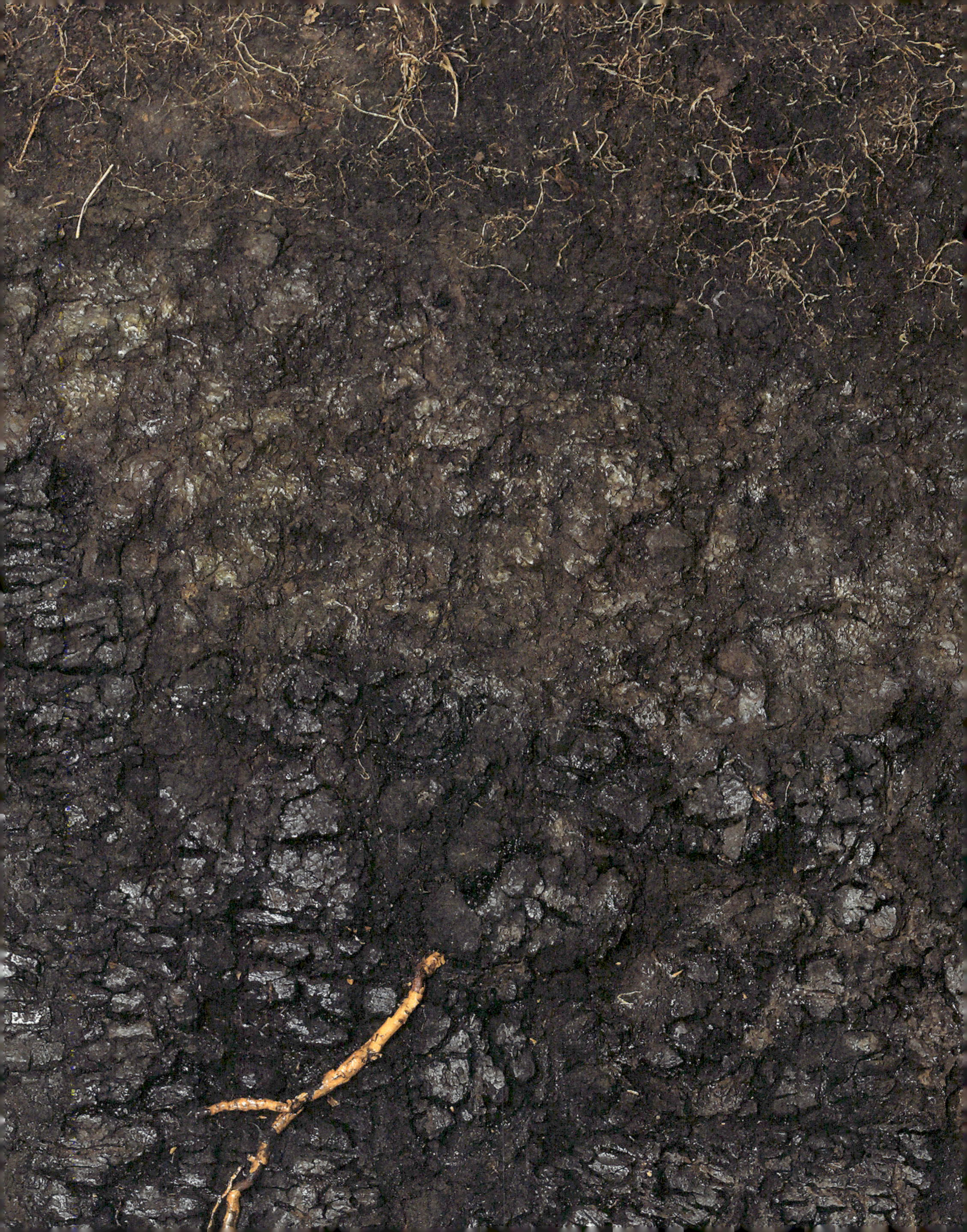

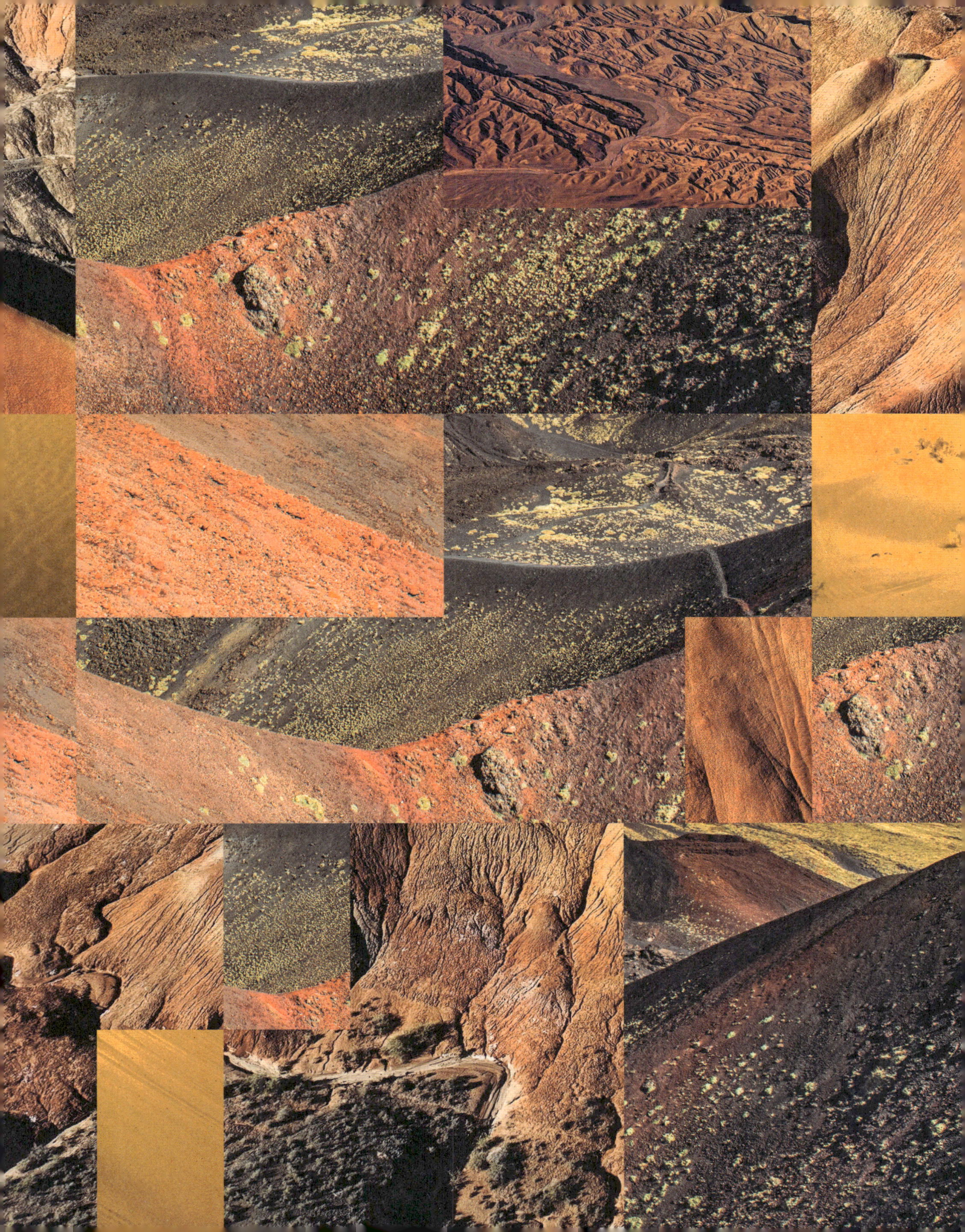

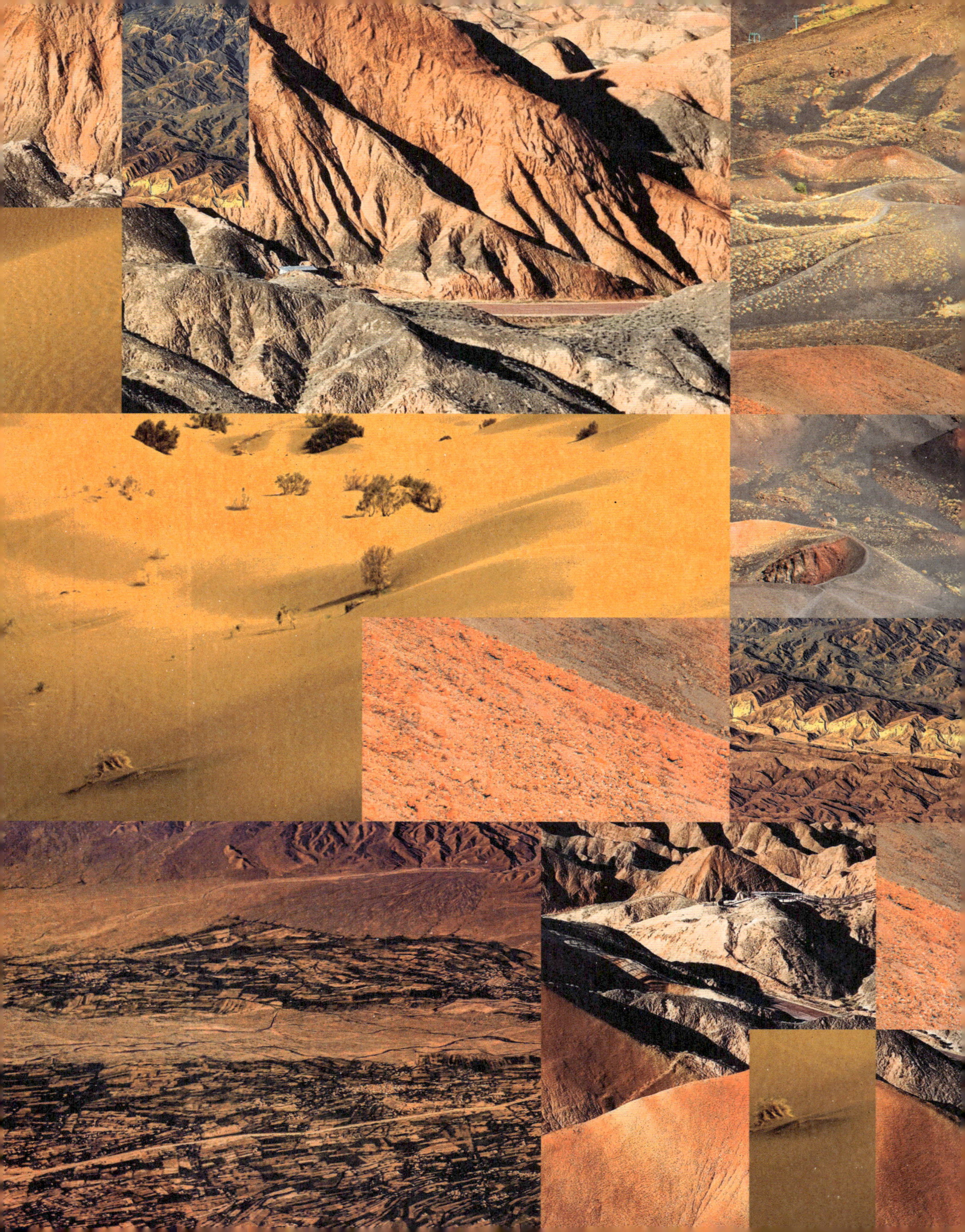

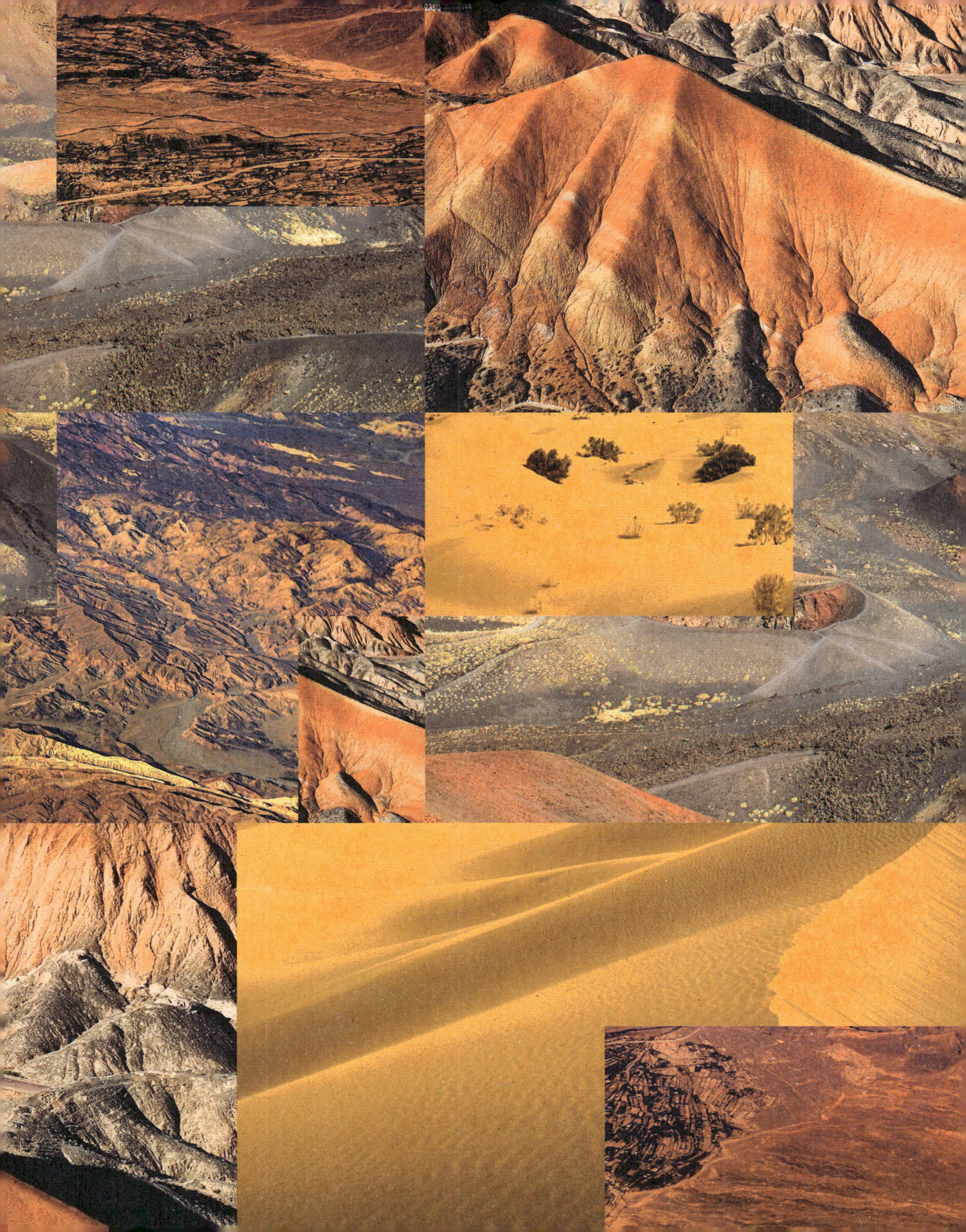

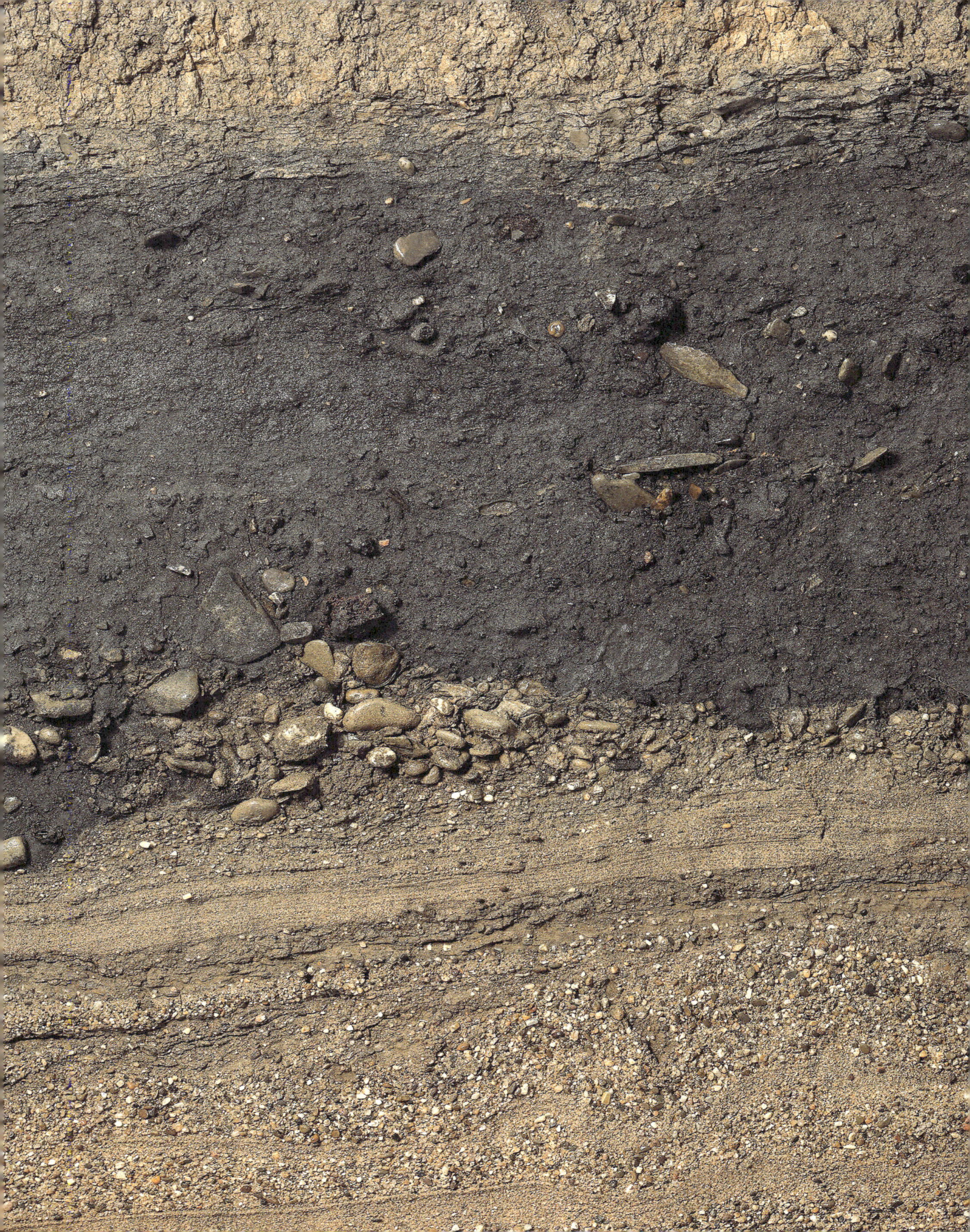

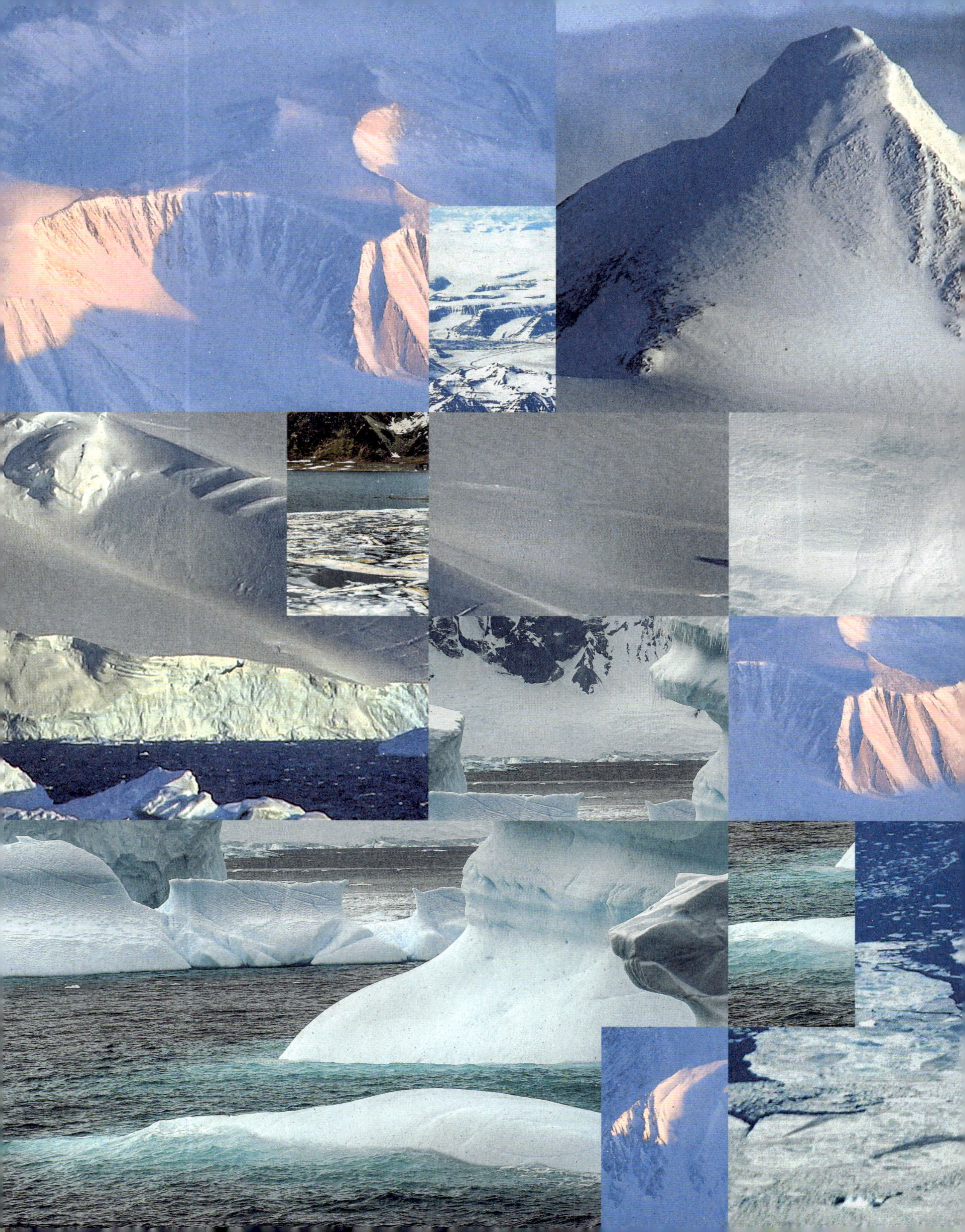

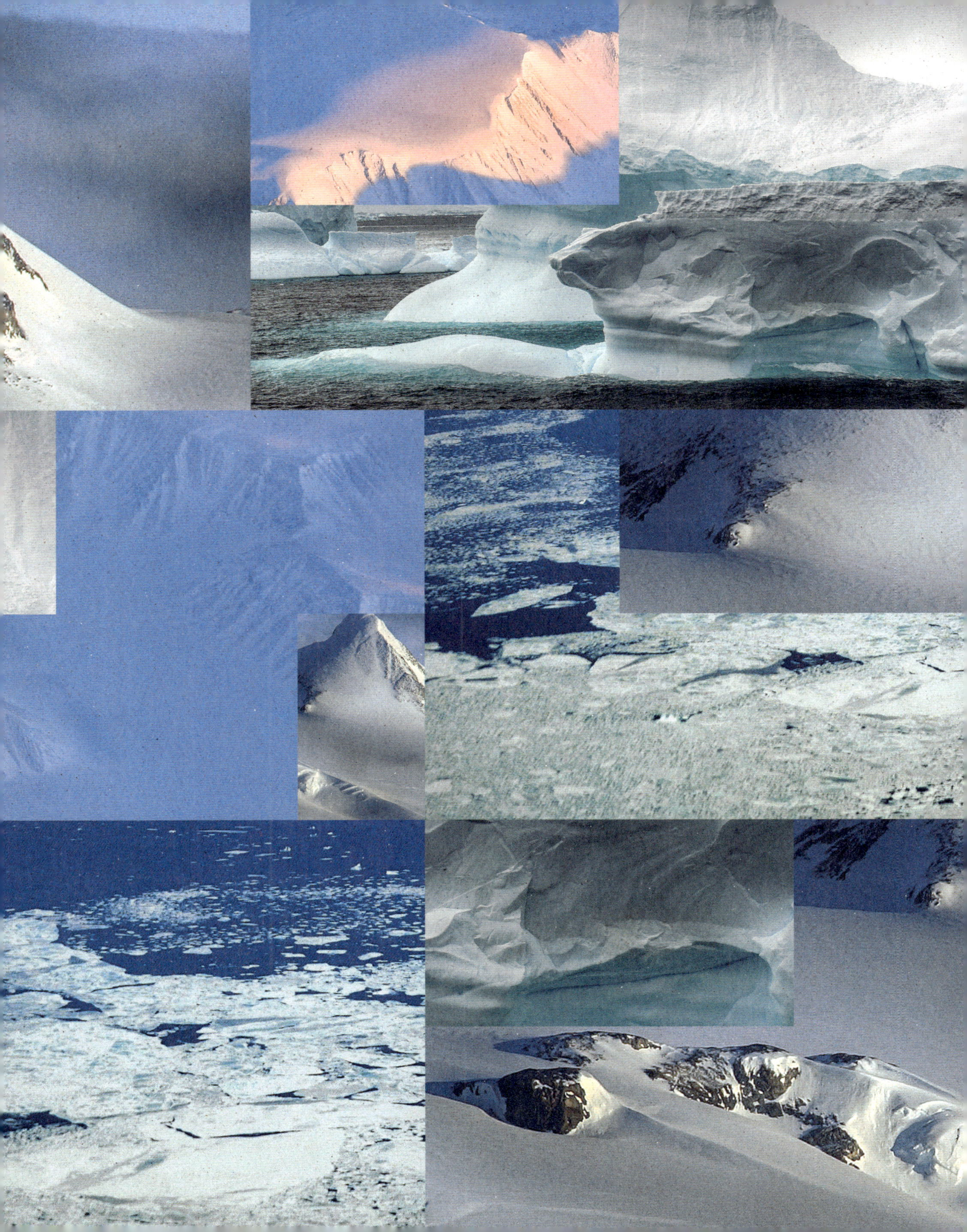

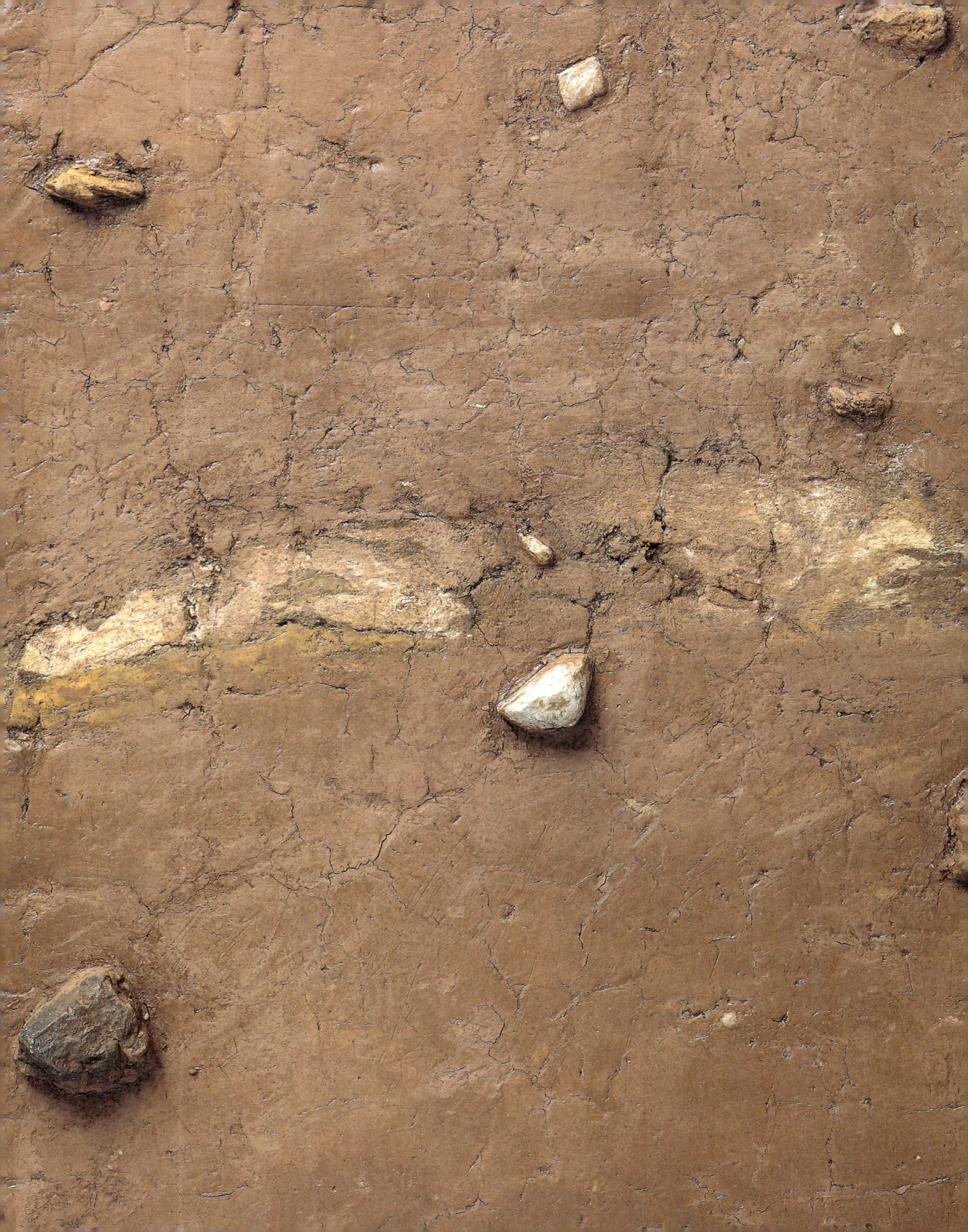

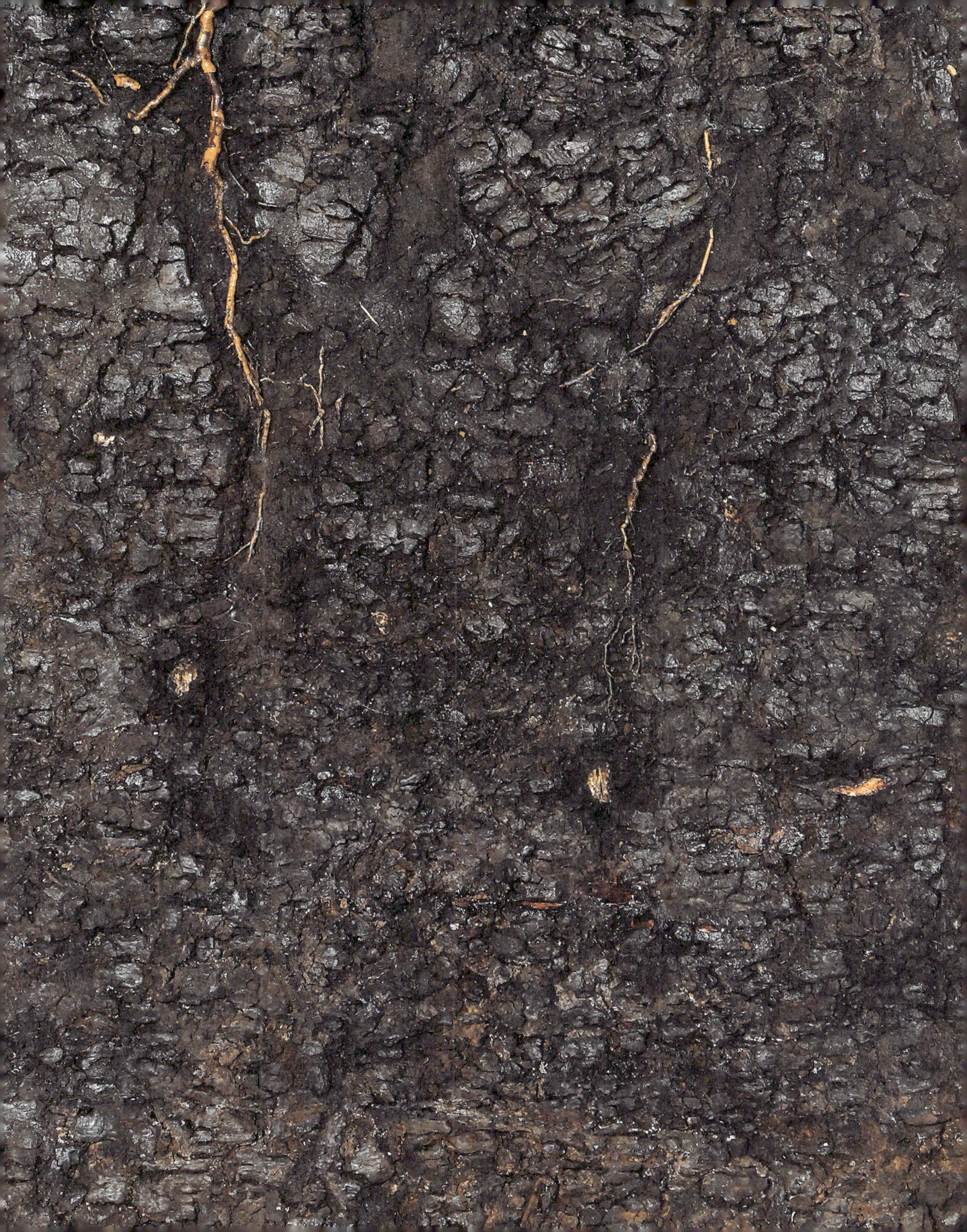

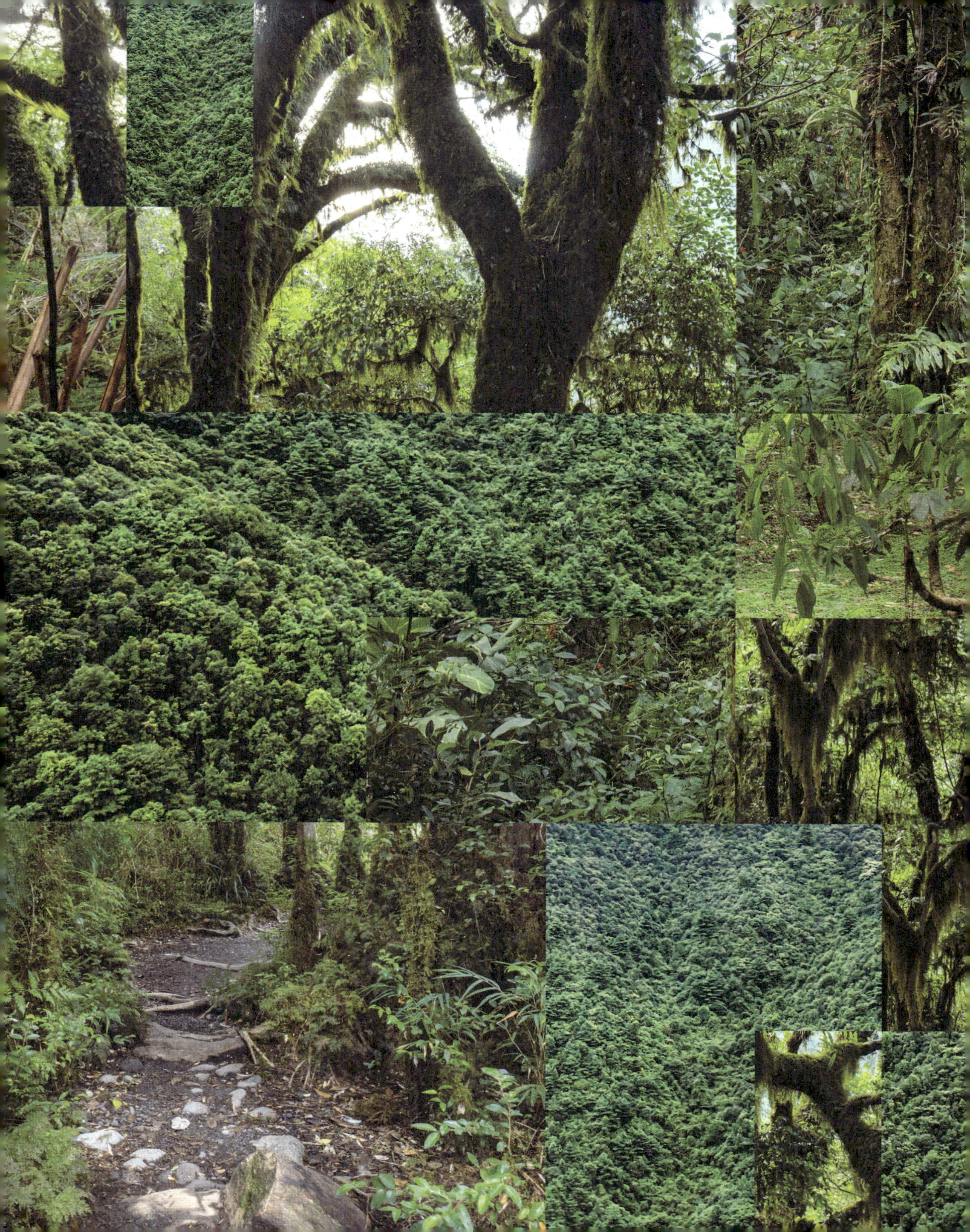

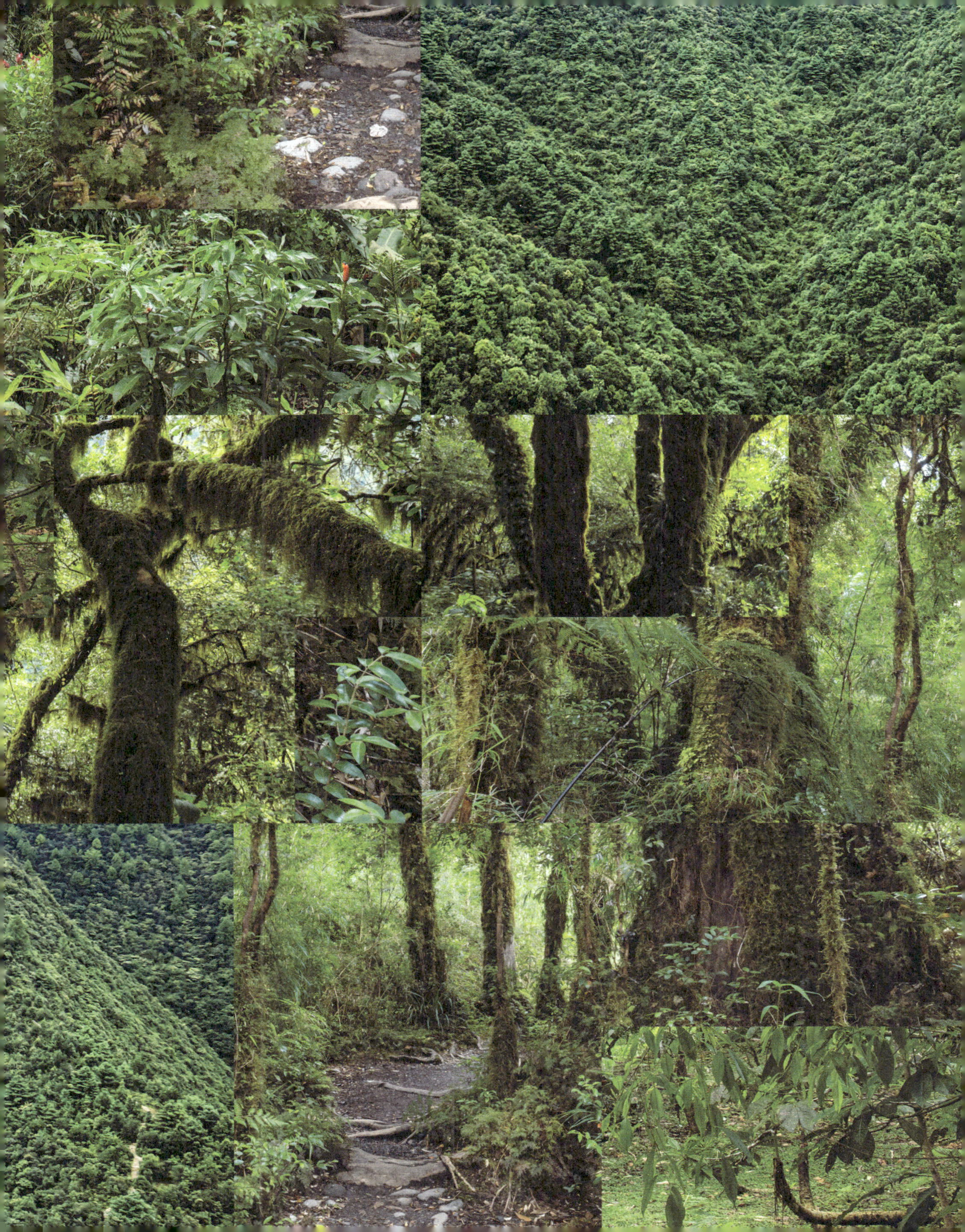

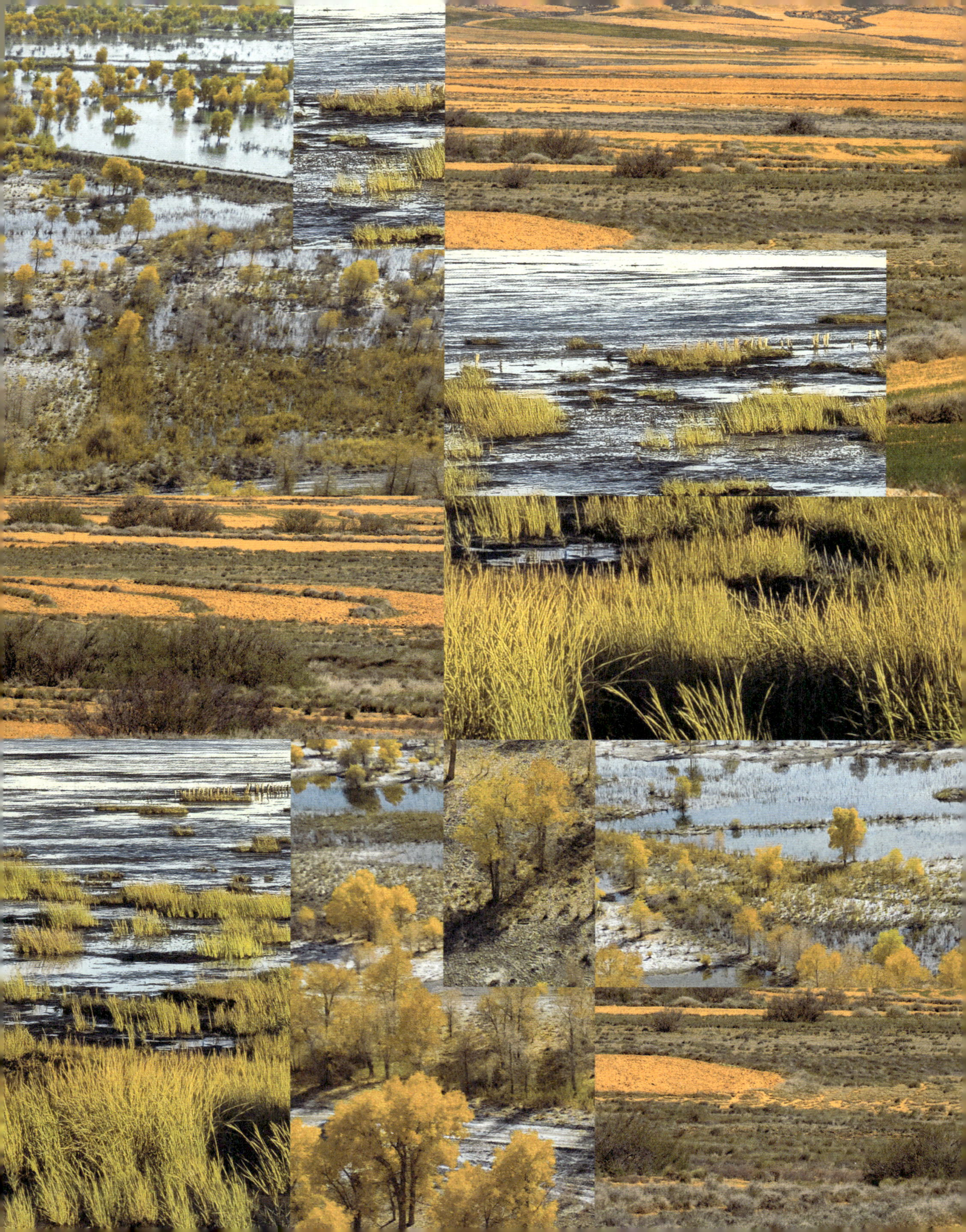

Save Land United for Land

BUNDESKUNSTHALLE
THEME YEAR SUSTAINABILITY 2025

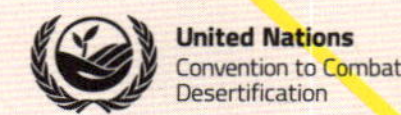

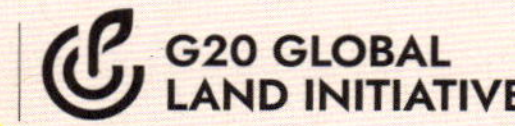

HIRMER

Save Land

Introduction 16

❶ Land is Life 46

❷ Cities – the Material World 90

United for Land

❸ Rural Land – the Big Harvest 132

❹ Natural Habitats – Nature's Core 178

❺ Take Action 214

Appendix 255

Patron's Welcome Message

Ibrahim Thiaw

Welcome to the *Save Land* exhibition and this accompanying book. *Save Land* is a journey of hope. This is a celebration of three decades of global efforts – notably through the UN Convention to Combat Desertification – to ensure land is kept healthy and productive. This is a moment to honour land as a vital source of life, not only as the soil we walk on.

Human beings are inherently connected to the land. Our lives and cultures have evolved on it, and we have built our homes and cities on it. The land nourishes us, providing the clothes we wear, the feed for our animals, and the medication we need.

The world cannot survive without healthy land. Twenty-five per cent of all medicines still have their origins in nature. What is more, 80 per cent of terrestrial species live in forests. Currently, healthy soils can store three times more carbon than the atmosphere, helping to combat climate change. Soil organic carbon needs to be both protected and increased as by 2050, 10 billion people will depend on this vital resource.

But we have broken our relationship to the land in the name of 'modernisation' and urbanisation. Our children and ourselves are no longer as connected to the land as our ancestors were. Our dependence on nature is no longer obvious, especially for the billions of people who live in cities.

Every second, we lose the equivalent area of the average smallholder farm or about four football pitches to land degradation, and the consequences of our unsustainable consumption for the health of the land remain remote and unaccounted for.

The *Save Land* exhibition explores our relationship with the land in urban, rural, and protected areas. The historical artifacts show us how we got here. Science clarifies where we are in relation to the past and where we are going. Technology helps us imagine different futures; what the world could look like if each of us took simple actions to restore degrading land. Social movements provide hope for taking efforts to a greater scale. And art can inspire us to take action.

Every action we take today to protect and restore our land counts. It is an opportunity to create jobs and lock away massive amounts of carbon back in the soil. It is an opportunity to turn dying ecosystems into thriving biodiversity havens and to reset our future on the path to sustainability.

This exhibition is designed to inform, entertain, and inspire. Come and explore, reflect, and enjoy the journey through *Save Land*. ✦

Ibrahim Thiaw
Patron, *Save Land* exhibition
Under-Secretary General of the United Nations and
Executive Secretary, UN Convention to Combat Desertification

Land Restoration, the Land of Opportunities – Word of Greeting

Muralee Thummarukudy

The health of our planet is inextricably linked to the health of its land. Human beings are a land-based species, who live and work mostly on land. But the health and productivity of this land are declining from natural and human-made sources.

Water and wind erosion, along with more frequent and recurrent droughts, are degrading the land even faster. Human activities, such as deforestation, unsustainable agriculture, increased urbanisation, and chemical pollution by industry all amplify the degradation.

Already, one fourth of all land on Earth, whether it is agricultural, forest, or rangeland, is degraded. Land degradation not only threatens our livelihoods, but also accelerates climate change. Climate change may in turn increase droughts, forest fires, and high-intensity rainfall, which degrade the land further, creating a vicious cycle.

And yet this gloomy scenario presents an opportunity. An opportunity to improve the quality and productivity of the land, both of which are economic activities with an existing market potential.

When land quality is improved, it increases agricultural outputs and the nutrient value of the produced crops. When wetlands are restored, they increase not just their productive functions, but their aesthetic value as well, which can be leveraged by marketing their tourism potential.

Reforestation not only increases biodiversity but also captures carbon dioxide, a greenhouse gas. Carbon capture is now monetised, if it is documented properly. The new Global Biodiversity Fund also has the potential to offer monetary credits for improving the status of biodiversity.

Young people around the world are becoming highly aware of land restoration as an opportunity of opportunities. With their digital fluency, problem-solving skills and passion for sustainability, they are developing groundbreaking technologies and business models. From drone-based monitoring and soil analysis to precision agriculture and carbon sequestration, the possibilities are endless.

Imagine creating a startup that uses artificial intelligence to optimise reforestation efforts or developing a mobile app that connects landowners with restoration experts. These are just a few examples of how young minds are transforming land restoration into profitable and impactful ventures.

Beyond entrepreneurship, land restoration offers a wide array of employment opportunities. Skills in ecology, agriculture, engineering, and technology are in high demand. Young professionals can contribute to creating a healthier planet while building fulfilling careers, for example, in established restoration companies, government agencies or non-profits. ▶

Moreover, land restoration is a catalyst for community development. By engaging local youth in restoration projects, they gain skills, knowledge, and opportunities. This not only helps to restore ecosystems but also builds social capital and strengthens rural economies.

The future of our planet depends on our ability to restore degraded lands. Young people have the power to turn this challenge into a triumph. By embracing land restoration as a field of innovation and opportunity, they have a pathway to create a sustainable, prosperous, and equitable world for generations to come.

For two years now, the Global Land Initiative has been working with the International Trade Center and other partners to identify and promote young people from around the world, who have shown leadership in establishing startups to support land restoration.

Our goal is to assist at least 10,000 young people in the coming ten years to establish such startups. In doing so, we hope to, at the same time, open up a 'restoration industry' in the global economy and promote millions of green jobs that young people need. Creating jobs for young people and healing Mother Earth is the ultimate win-win.

Land restoration is the land of opportunity. ✦

Muralee Thummarukudy
Director, G20 Global Initiative on Land, UNCCD

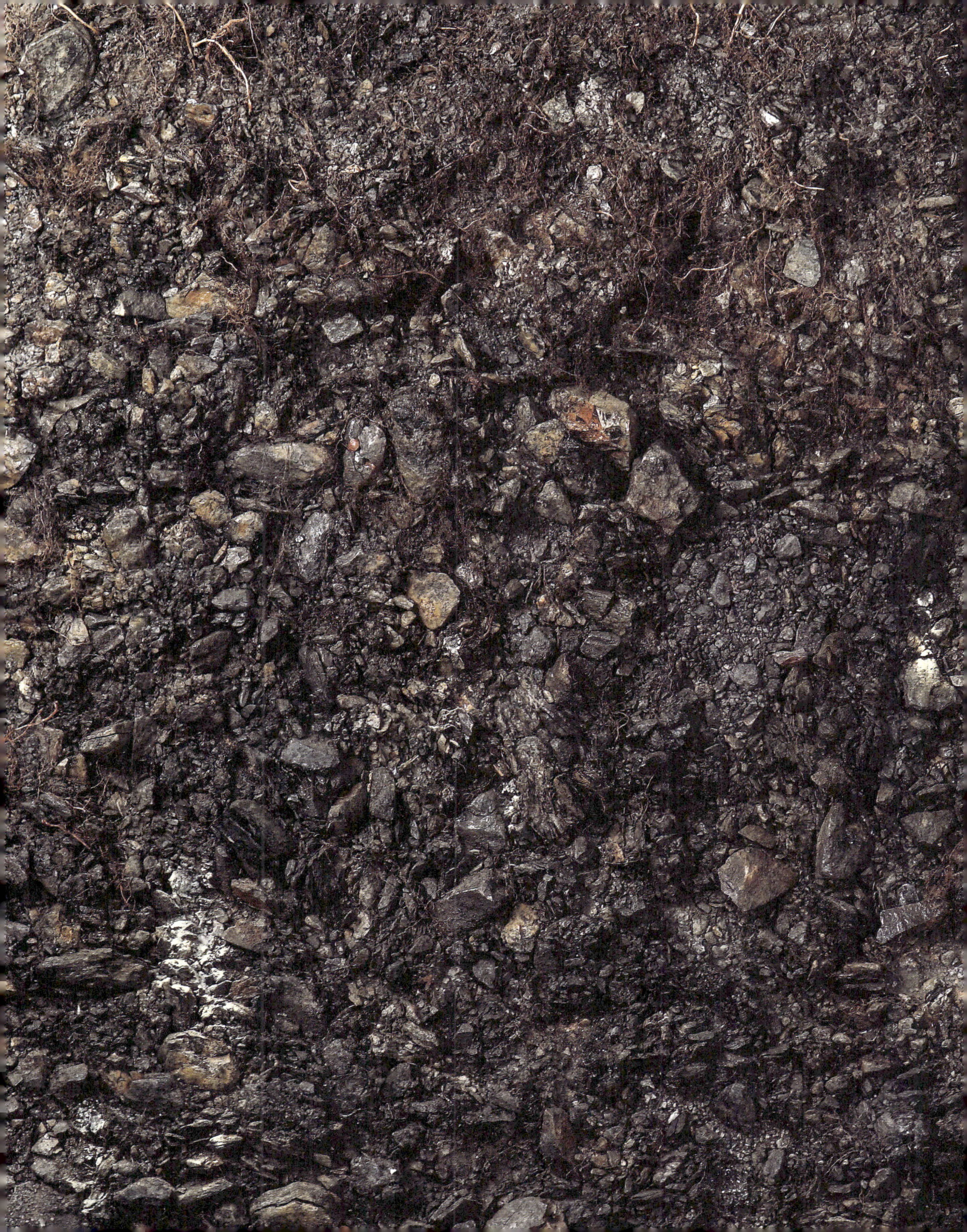

Preface

Eva Kraus

Land is an immensely important resource on Earth. That is why we are convinced that the revitalisation of our soils should mean something to everyone. Our goal is to create an exhibition that invites diverse groups of people to become curious about this topic, even if they may not yet know much about it. The exhibition is designed to be an immersive, emotionally transformative, and unforgettable experience. It aims to motivate our visitors to take long-term action in their daily lives and beyond to ensure that land remains a foundation of well-being on our planet and is treated as the treasure that it is.

With this mission statement, we embarked on a participatory creative process to develop the exhibition *Save Land. United for Land*. It was drafted during a Design Thinking Workshop as a prelude to a wonderful cooperation between the UNCCD-G20 Global Land Initiative and the Bundeskunsthalle, moderated by students from the University of Wuppertal. In this transdisciplinary exchange, we addressed a complex topic that concerns one of the most pressing challenges of our time – the ecological restoration of our land areas, as millions of hectares need to be revitalised in the coming decades. Would we be able to develop an adequate, insightful, and inspiring narrative in the context of an exhibition?

Healthy soil is an essential resource and the basis for all life on Earth. In addition to combating carbon dioxide emissions and the accelerated consequences of climate change, the protection and restoration of our soils is a task that concerns humanity as a whole in the face of our ailing planet. We need to prevent desertification and protect our soils – after all, they provide us with food, they maintain our ecosystems, and the most wonderful and diverse vegetation grows on them. We wanted to communicate our intensive examination of this major issue to a wide audience.

We therefore entered into a conversation with students, to create an exhibition that would appeal to young people in particular. We interviewed experts, launched a research phase, conducted field research, and initiated a series of workshops in a wonderfully experimental manner. This all happened in the run-up to our curatorial and scholarly development of the exhibition content. In a comprehensive presentation for a large feedback session, it became evident how these processual methods produced amazingly creative results. In the course of preparing for the exhibition, our team of curators worked with experts, designers, technicians, and consultants to translate complex knowledge into varied stories and develop many tools. The aim of the interdisciplinary collaboration was to implement as many immersive and didactically valuable design and communicative strategies as possible across the exhibition. A huge digital globe was developed to communicate facts and figures. A panoramic cinema was choreographed as a tribute to the beauty of our nature and its breathtaking landscapes. Interactive learning islands about major cities, cultivated lands, and untouched nature were developed and designed. 'Companions' were created to serve as animated guides through the exhibition. Numerous interviews were compiled from current land revitalisation practices around the world. All of this is intended to convey information, stimulate the senses, and impart knowledge in order to support the vital ecological concerns of global land restoration. Equally important are the many curated scientific materials. The artistic installations in particular deserve special mention, as they demonstrate once again the capacity of art to spark and engage us to communicate and fight for environmental protection. This is refreshingly implemented in the final exhibition area 'Take Action' – not least in order to inspire and encourage a young and diverse audience.

With *Save Land. United for Land*, we are realising another Art & Science exhibition that explores global issues and participates in relevant ongoing discourses. It is not only science and politics, but also artists and designers who are sharpening our attitude towards a more mindful use of our planet's finite resources. With this exhibition, we sought to make a contribution to a more sustainable way of life and set an example to combat our alienation from nature and the exploitation of our land. And finally, to sensitise our perception of one of the most vital foundations of life – our soil.

Thanks

On behalf of the management of the Bundeskunsthalle, we would like to thank the UNCCD, the Secretariat for the Implementation of the UN Convention to Combat Desertification, and its Executive Director Ibrahim Thiaw, for their generous partnership. We also thank the Director of the G20 Global Land Initiative, Muralee Thummarukudy, who had the idea to jointly develop such an exhibition project. Personally, I would like to thank Shen Xiaomeng, Vice Rector in Europe and Director of UNU-EHS, who facilitated the contact and encouraged us to work together on this important topic.

We would like to thank all the Master's students from the Faculty of Design & Art on the 'Strategic Product and Innovation Development' programme from the 2022/23 semesters at the University of Wuppertal and their supervisors, Professor Dr Martina Fineder-Hochmayr and Professor Dr Fabian Hemmert, for their stimulating collaboration. We would like to thank all the lenders and, in particular, the many artists for their works, which enabled us to direct alternative perspectives and inspiring associations to a scientifically complex topic.

Together with our exhibition curator Henriette Pleiger, the external curators and land experts Tony Simons and UNCCD colleague Wagaki Wischnewski curated the tour through the exhibition in a brilliant way. The three of them have succeeded in creating an impressive narrative that is both varied and stimulating – a big thank you for these illuminating results. We would like to thank the scientific advisory board, including the aforementioned professors from the University of Wuppertal, the Vice-Rector of the University of Bonn, Prof. Annette Scheersoi, and the ethnobotanist at the Royal Botanic Gardens, Kew, Prof. Mark Nesbitt. We are very grateful to the authors of this book for their contributions. Their texts provide fresh and important insights into the world of soil and its ecosystems.

This exhibition thrives on the many visually attractive and immersive experiences that have been created under the direction of dform and Andreas Pawlik with numerous colleagues in digital, interior, and graphic design. Our big thanks go to him, as well as to Fanny Arnold, Bernhard Poppe, Lara Nellißen, Matthäus Jandl, and the creative technicians Benjamin Pokropek and Leonard Pokropek from Bildwerk. Manuel Radde did a wonderful job designing the catalogue. We would like to thank Hirmer Verlag, Katja Durchholz, and our colleague Donatella Cacciola for the catalogue management.

We would further like to thank all of our colleagues at the Bundeskunsthalle, especially Henriette Pleiger, for her great talent in developing highly inspiring exhibitions in the field of Art & Science at the Bundeskunsthalle, our programme assistant Martin Hoffmann for his active support, and the helpful interns in this exhibition project: Dareen Syan, Rebekah Caesar, and Ronja Sturm.

We are extremely grateful to our entire team and all those involved in this highly successful project, which is the prelude to the theme of ecological transformation, which we at the Bundeskunsthalle intend to carry into the future with great commitment. ✦

Eva Kraus
Director, Bundeskunsthalle

Curatorial Introduction

Henriette Pleiger, Tony Simons,
Wagaki Wischnewski

Land is the crucial foundation for life on our planet. And our planet Earth is special as it is the only place that we are aware of that has life. It has a bimodal topography with a low-lying oceanic crust and a high-standing continental crust. Originally, our planet had an inert crust which was inorganic and devoid of life. Over billions of years, mixtures of sterile chemicals became reproducing single cells which in turn led to the tree giants of the plant kingdom, and the dinosaur and mammalian giants of the animal kingdom. And these living giants helped shape geological and biological processes that over time produced soil.

Healthy soil is the life-supporting link between the Earth's climate and biological diversity, and it provides a complex variety of different ecosystems that need to be preserved. However, as the foundation for agricultural and industrial use, land is at risk of devastating overuse, with half of humanity already affected by the negative impacts of land degradation. Land, in all its meanings for our lives, must be put back at the centre of our agenda in order to curb the economic and social overexploitation of our land resources.

The topic of land and soil is not confined to the natural sciences. It has shaped human social communities and cultures from the start around the globe and has ever since been a means and topic for artistic expression. From the epic landscape paintings and nature poetry in Chinese art to the classical landscape paintings in European art, from the American and British Land Art of the 1960s and 1970s to contemporary environmental artworks – land has not only been our habitat and provider of all we need to survive, but has also ever since had a tremendous aesthetic impression on us, evoking all sorts of emotions, from utter delight to deep fear. Land nurtures our intuition that art is not just artificial (human made) and that the great canvas of the Earth's crust is nature's expression to connect to our emotions and ideas.

But apart from its beauty, land is also 'historical through and through', as Theodor W. Adorno put it in his *Aesthetic Theory*. Human history has formed and degraded the land worldwide, especially since the industrial revolution around 1850. Today, at least 70 % of Earth's land has been altered by humans, a disaster that is yet to be recognised. Socially and economically, land has divided us in countless wars, but it also has an immensely unifying capacity.

This book accompanies the unique exhibition *Save Land: United for Land*, which in itself aims for a unifying approach regarding the globally urgent issue of land restoration. Today's global challenges, such as climate change or land restoration, call for a transdisciplinary approach in which all stakeholders in politics, business, academia, culture, and for society to join forces to support the agenda. Following this approach, our exhibition uses the perspectives of art, cultural history, and science to raise public awareness of this urgent issue. And to progress the narrative from land degradation to land restoration.

Of course, land is such a complex and comprehensive topic that it seems impossible to portray it in an exhibition space of 1500 square metres; this is only one hundredth of a billion of the total land on our planet. The topic of land is truly multidimensional in its natural and artificial shapes and forms, and in its social meanings and implications. We have structured the exhibition around five domains that correspond to this book's five chapters to make land's complexities understandable.

The first chapter, titled 'Land is Life', introduces a series of animated films (represented in this book as sequences of film stills), which speak of seven possible meanings of land. Land is the tectonic surface of Earth. Land is the source of life for plants when they transitioned to land from the oceans around 480 million years ago. Land is healthy soil. Land is a feeling of being rooted and grounded. Land is culture. Land is female in the majority of mythologies worldwide. Land is property. Similar to these definitions, the first chapter of this book explores the environmental, economic, social, and cultural meanings of land in four essays.

In the exhibition, a digital globe helps us to understand the state of land on Earth and the size, outcomes, and impact of the degraded areas, more specifically on three major habitats.

Firstly, the cities where currently 57 % of all people live on only 2 % of all habitable land. Secondly, the managed rural land areas used for agriculture and by industry. And thirdly, the almost natural areas globally and least untouched humans, which provide critical ecological services, including biodiversity and regulating the world's climate. A large panoramic cinema in the exhibition reminds us of the immense beauty and diversity of Earth's land ecosystems.

The following three exhibition rooms and book chapters, 'Cities – The Material World', 'Rural Land – The Big Harvest', and 'Natural Habitats – Nature's Core' combine exhibits from the natural sciences, cultural history, and contemporary art to understand the ecological problems and potentials of these three human-influenced environments. The exhibition not only enables a rational understanding of the importance of healthy soil for all of our lives, but also offers an immersive experience of the different habitats described above. Visitors will be able to tangibly experience the topic of land, for example, by walking over three large interactive floor projections allowing them to explore these environments with their feet.

Contemporary art will play a significant role in this exhibition, especially its potential to inspire, emotionalise, and deepen our thinking on these important issues. Far from a dark vision of the future, the exhibition presents an alternative, more hopeful narrative to inspire action for the common cause: to save land by halting, reducing, and reversing the loss of healthy and productive ecosystems.

Artists such as Julius von Bismarck, Stefanie Bühler, Julian Charrière, Agnes Denes, Ximena Garrido-Lecca, Alexandra Daisy Ginsberg, Nancy Graves, Jan Hostettler, Cao Fei, Richard Long, Grace Ndiritu, Claes Oldenburg, and Monika Sosnowska are represented in this exhibition. As the curatorial team, we thank them all for their outstanding contributions. We also thank all the wonderful lenders, experts, and co-workers who supported this exhibition project. Last but not least, we thank our institutions and leadership for entrusting us with the responsibility of curating this exhibition, which has been a wonderful journey of learning for all of us.

The fifth and last chapter both in the exhibition and in this book is a heartfelt, passionate and strong call to action. By introducing several projects of young people from around the globe, the 'Take Action' chapter aims to inspire both individual and communal first steps and future research as well as action for a land-friendlier life. We hope this exhibition motivates us to reflect critically on the impact of our lifestyles, make choices that offer long-term well-being and good health for us, our families and communities, and engage with others to protect land.

This project lives on at www.saveland.art. ✦

Henriette Pleiger, Tony Simons, Wagaki Wischnewski
Curators of the Exhibition

Interactive globe 'Land globally', 2024 © dform/Bildwerk, Vienna ▶

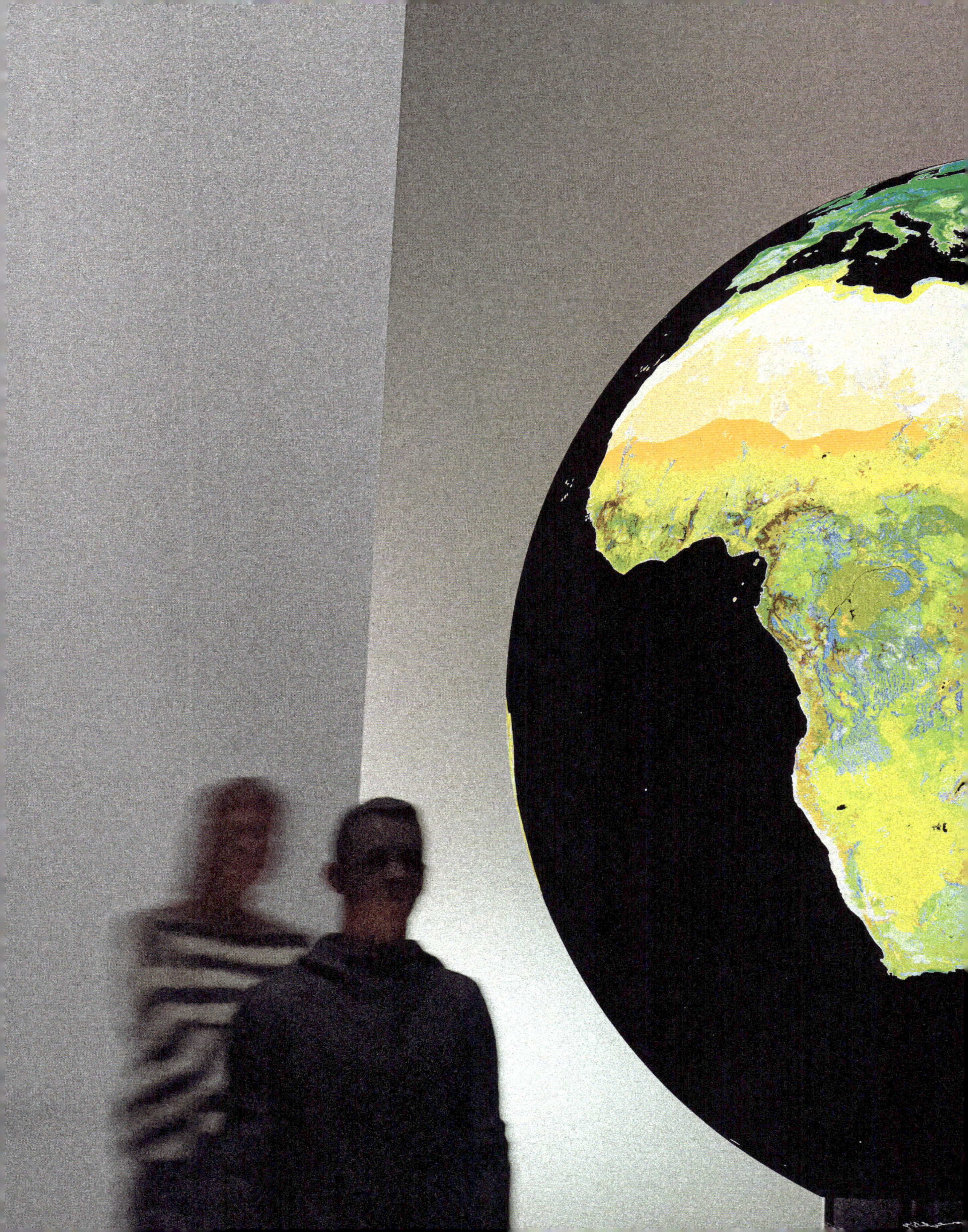

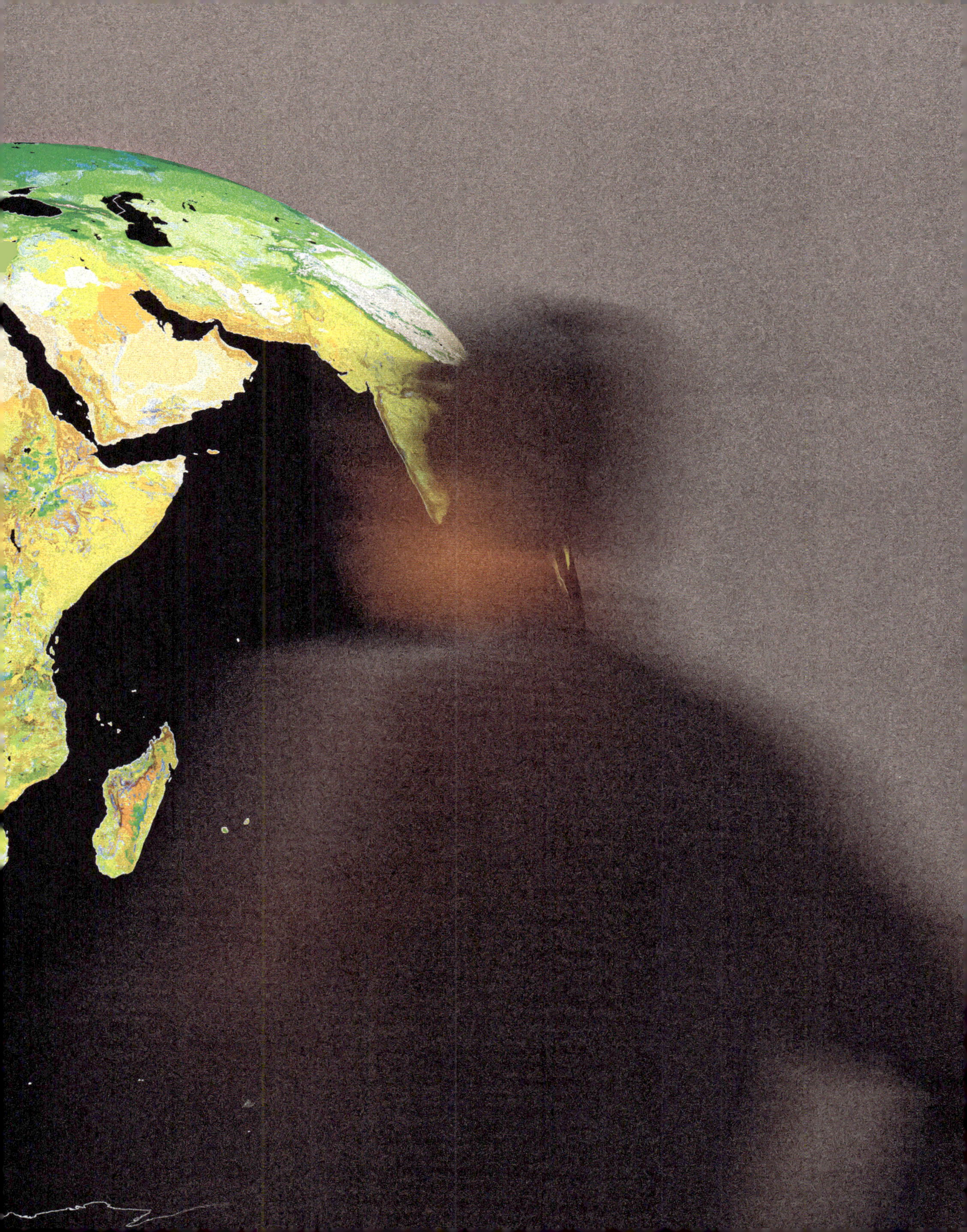

Land is ... the surface of Earth

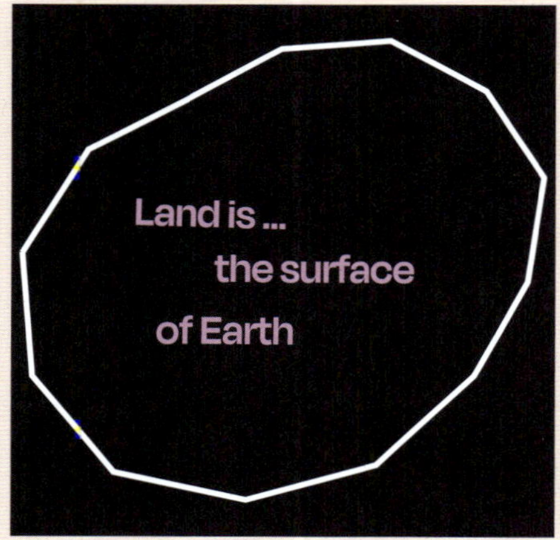

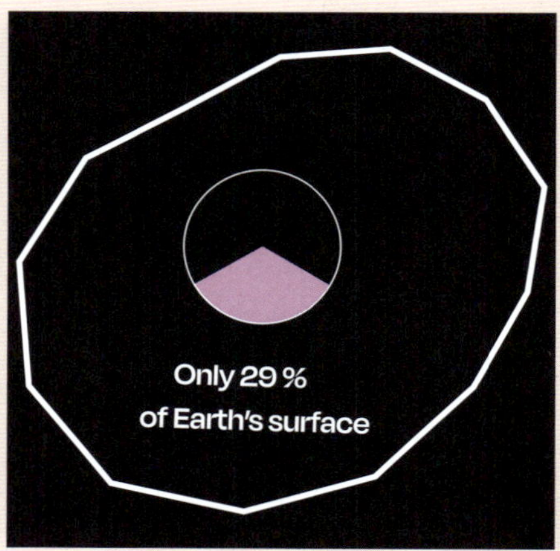

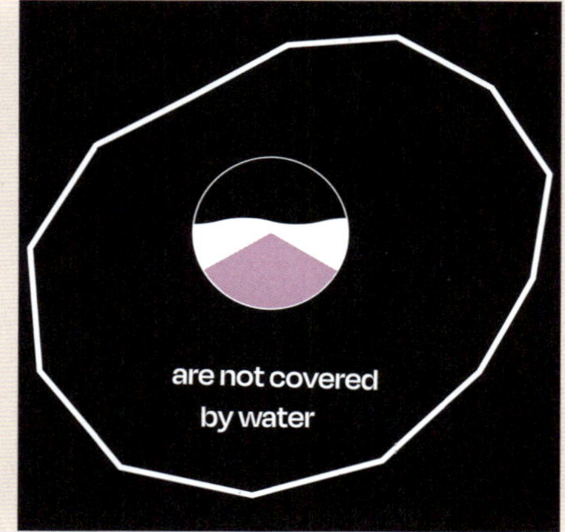

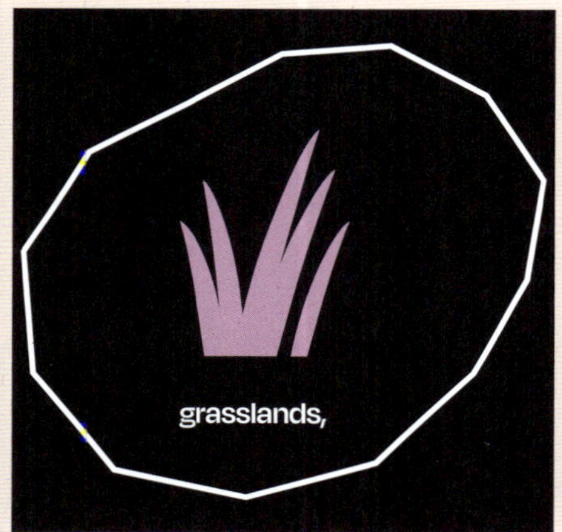

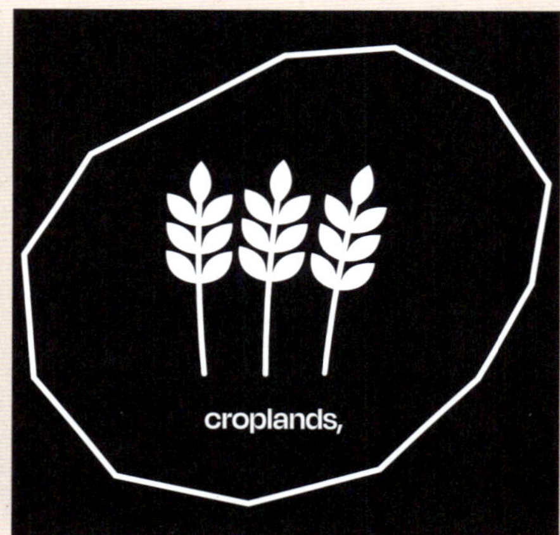

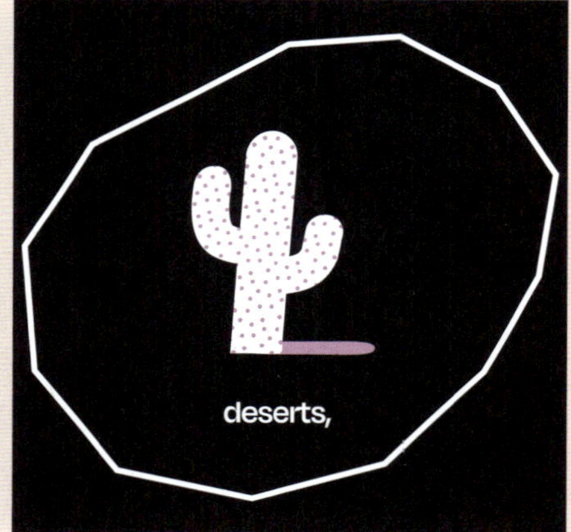

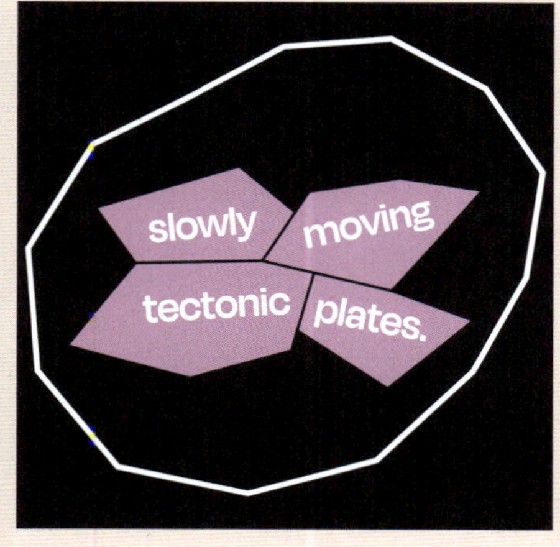

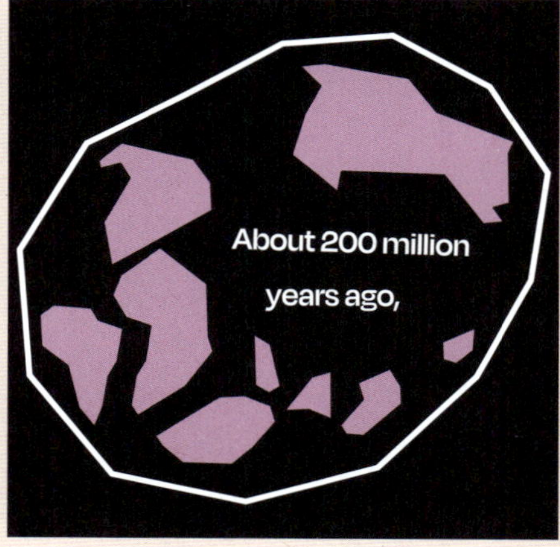

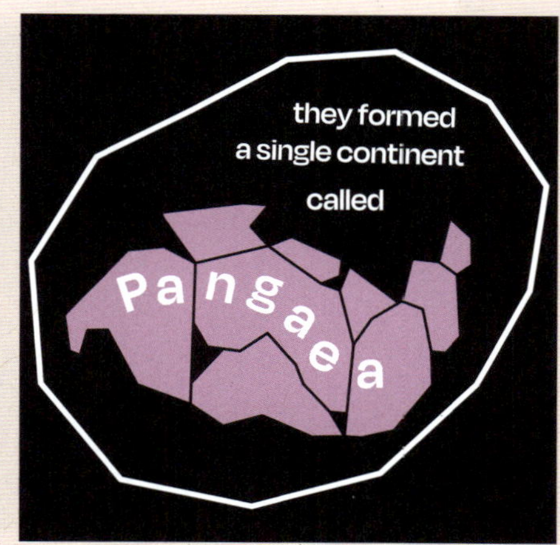

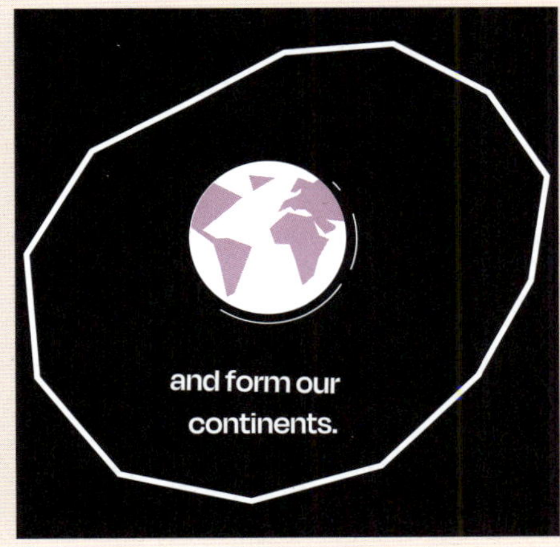
and form our
continents.

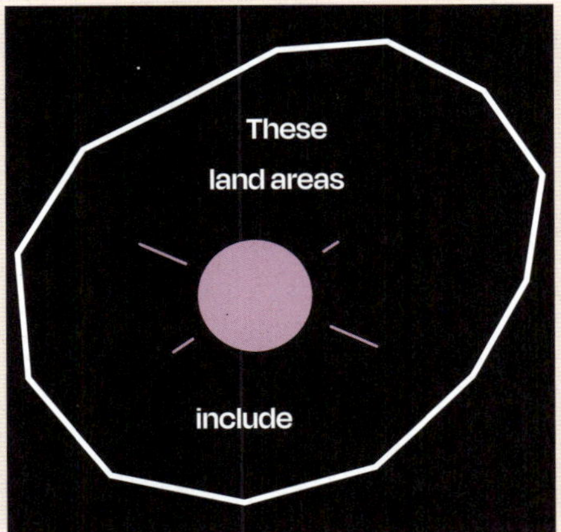
These
land areas
include

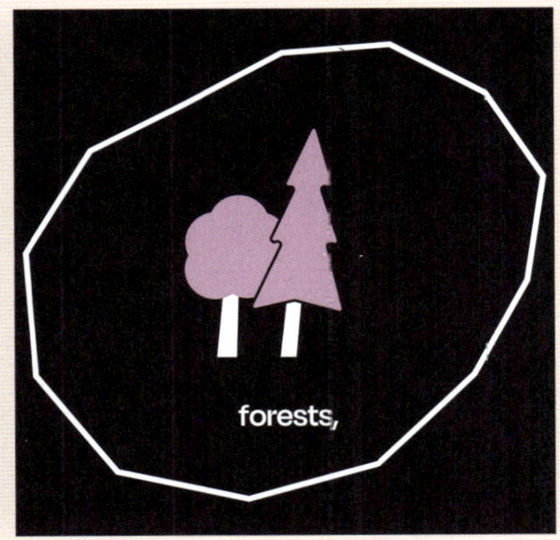
forests,

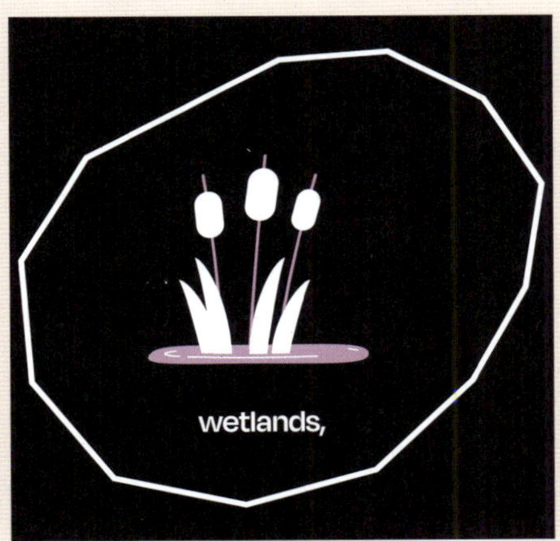
wetlands,

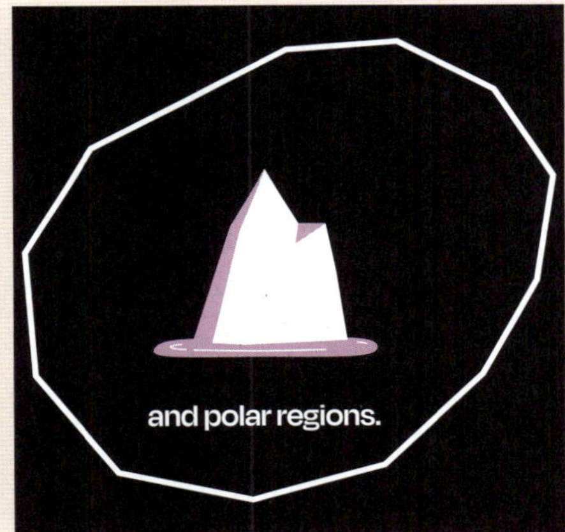
and polar regions.

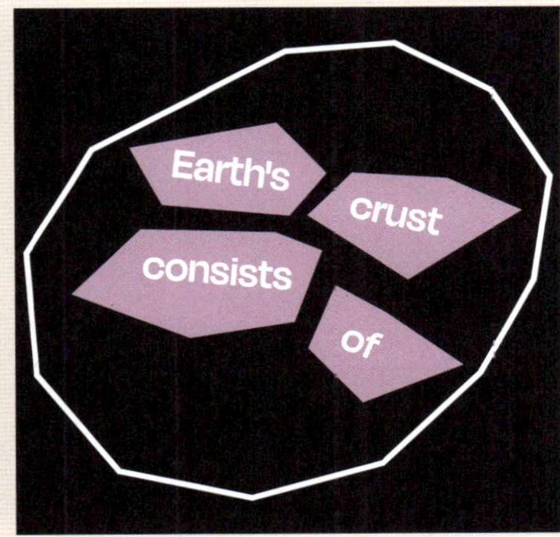
Earth's
crust
consists
of

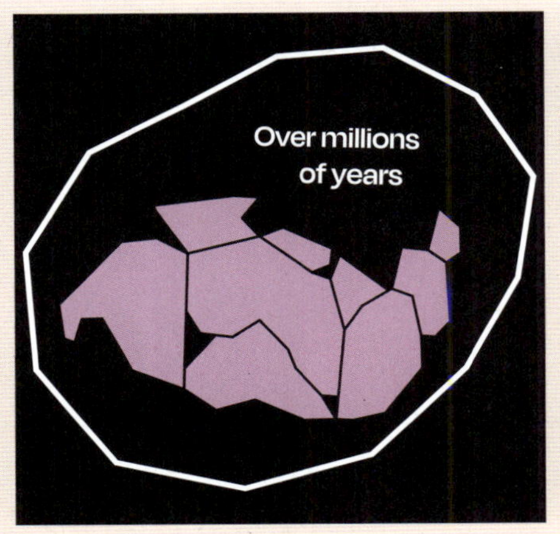
Over millions
of years

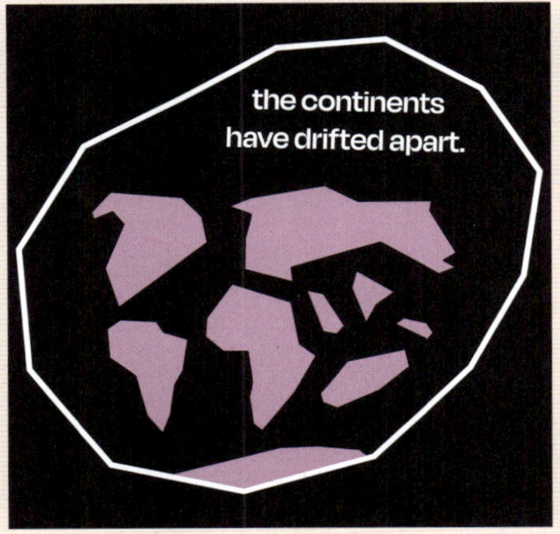
the continents
have drifted apart.

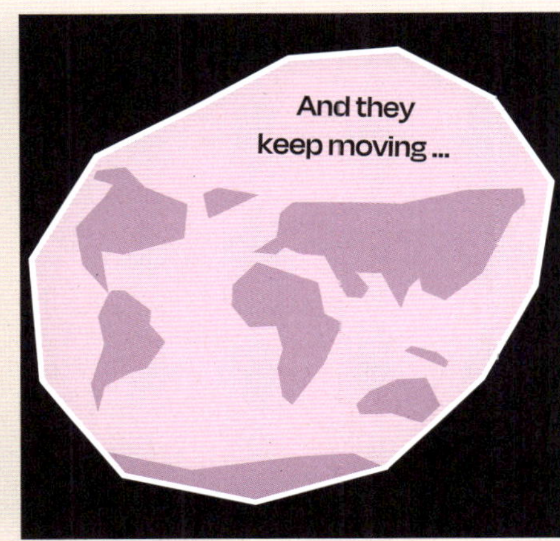
And they
keep moving ...

Land is ... life

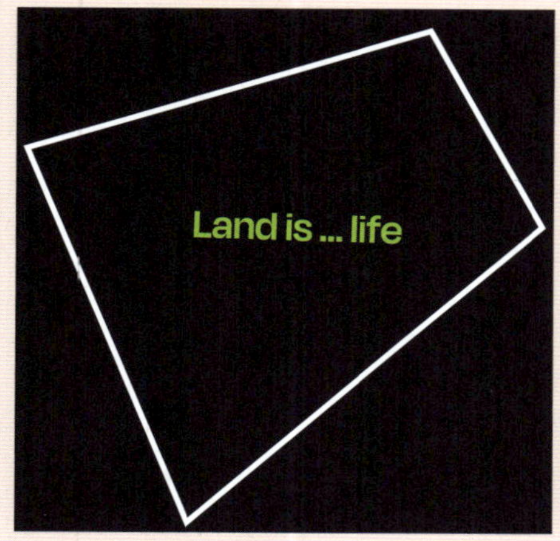
Land is ... life

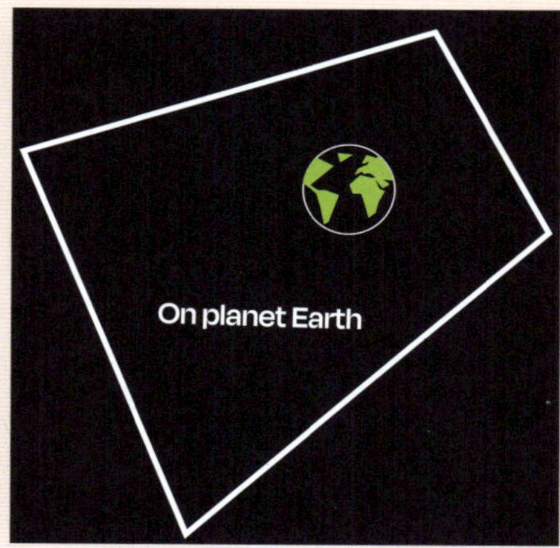
On planet Earth

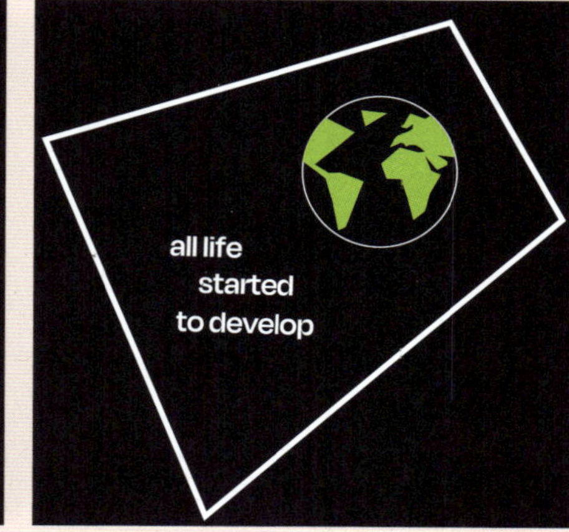
all life
started
to develop

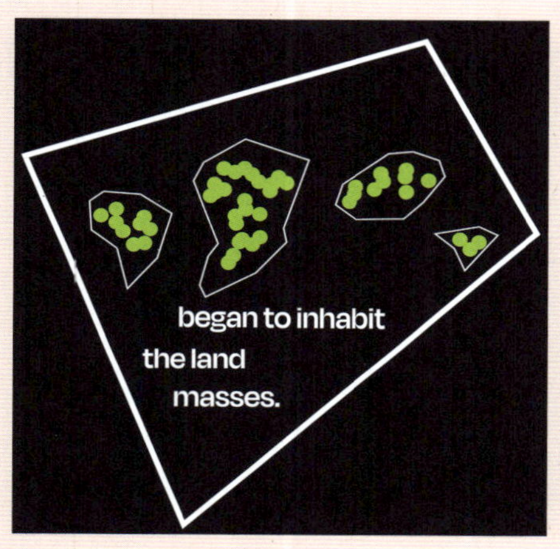
began to inhabit
the land
masses.

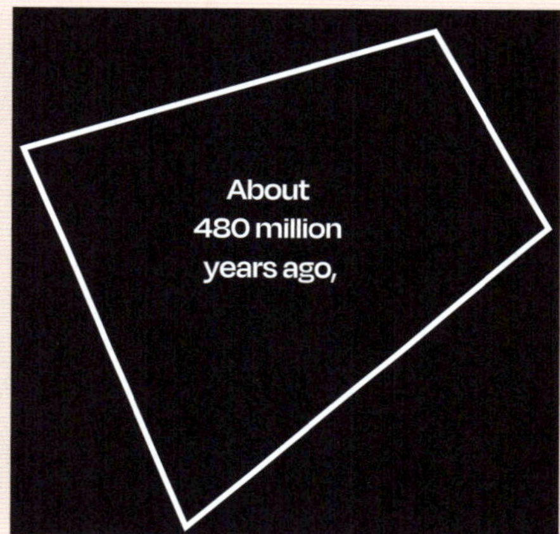
About
480 million
years ago,

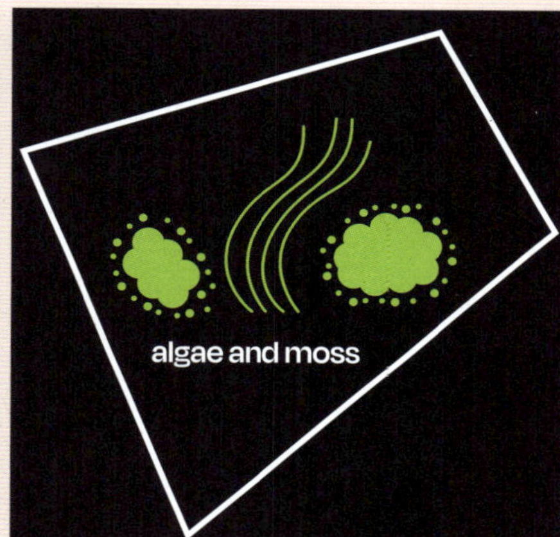
algae and moss

on the soil
they grow in,

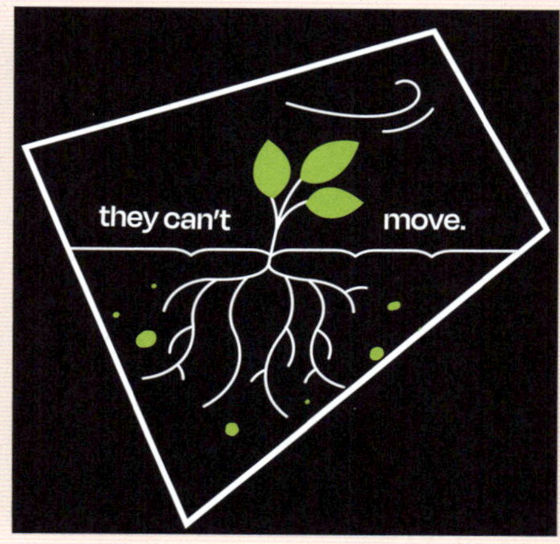
they can't
move.

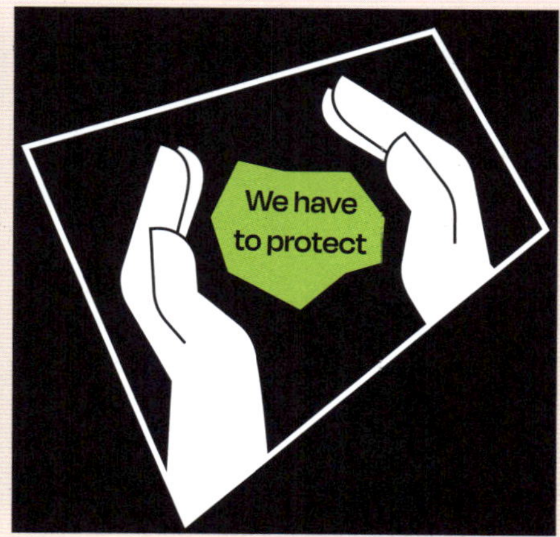
We have
to protect

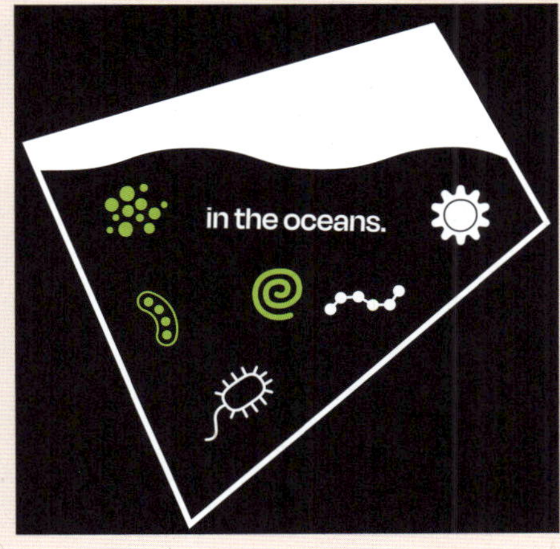
in the oceans.

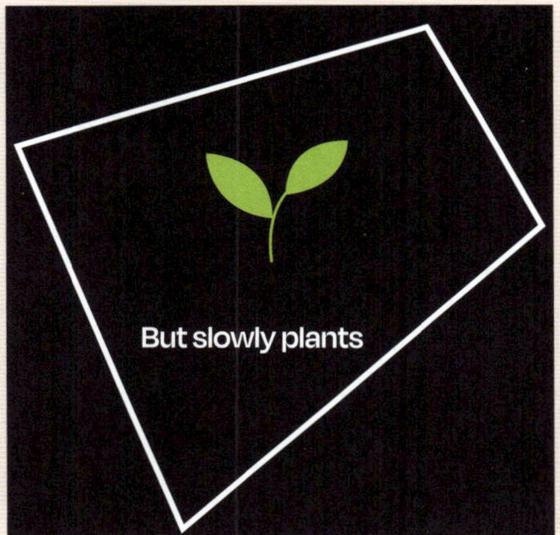
But slowly plants

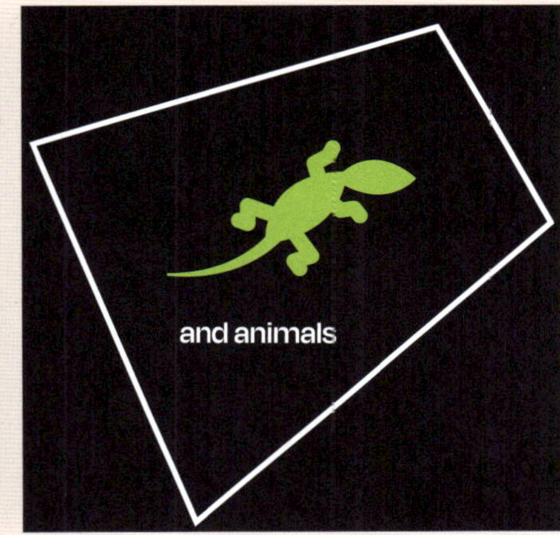
and animals

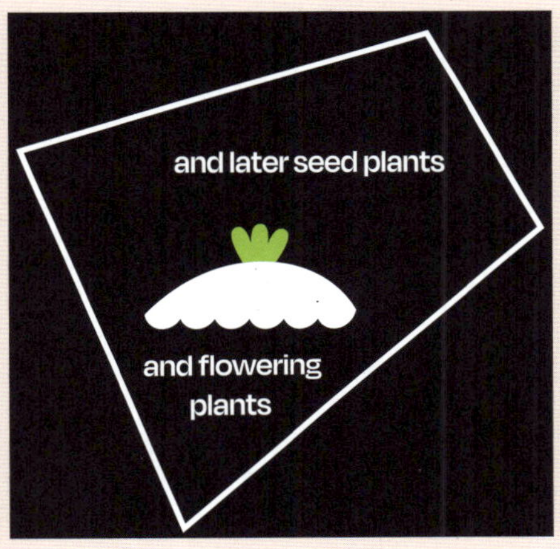
and later seed plants
and flowering
plants

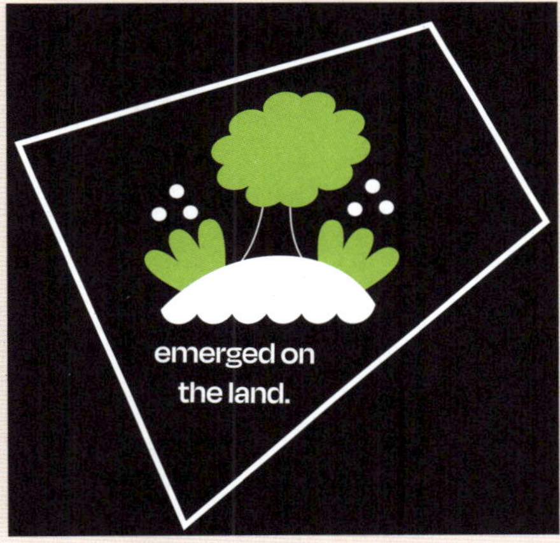
emerged on
the land.

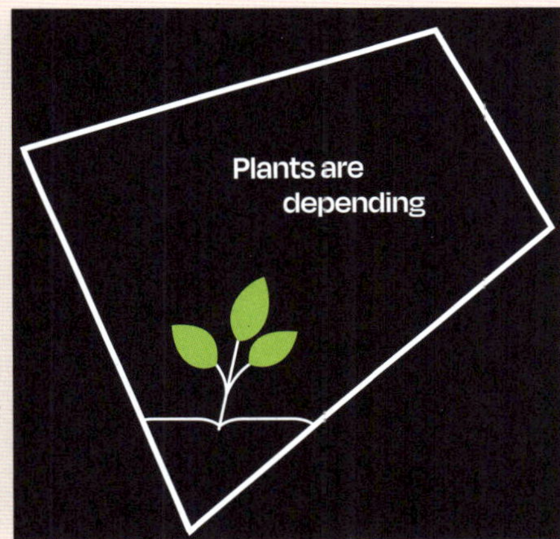
Plants are
depending

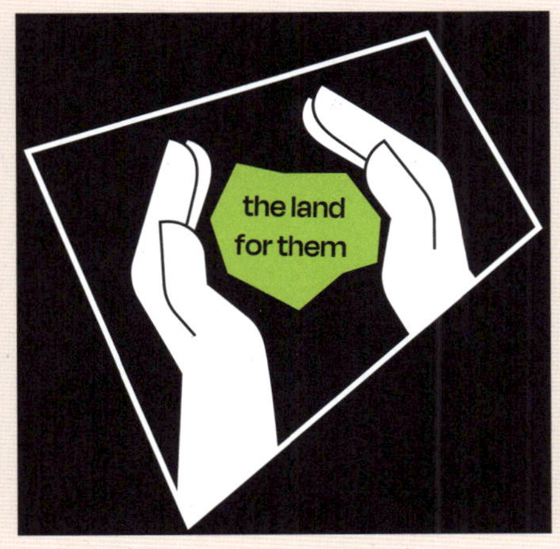
the land
for them

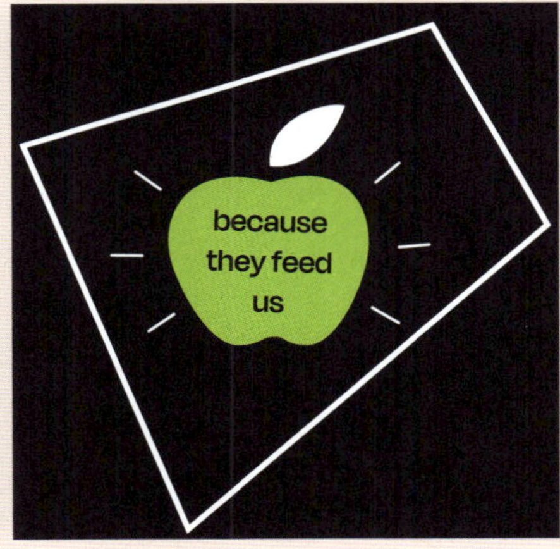
because
they feed
us

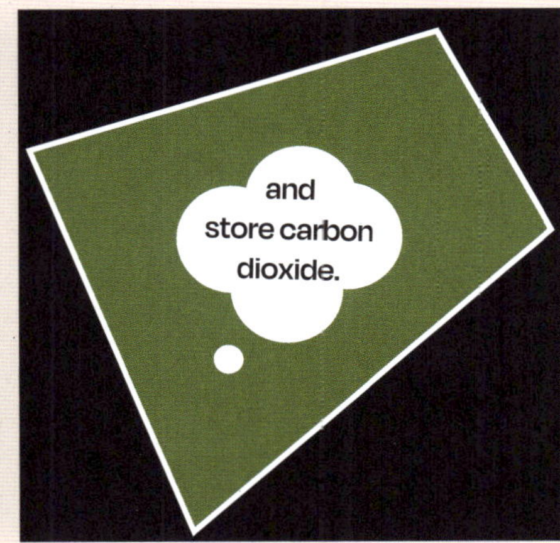
and
store carbon
dioxide.

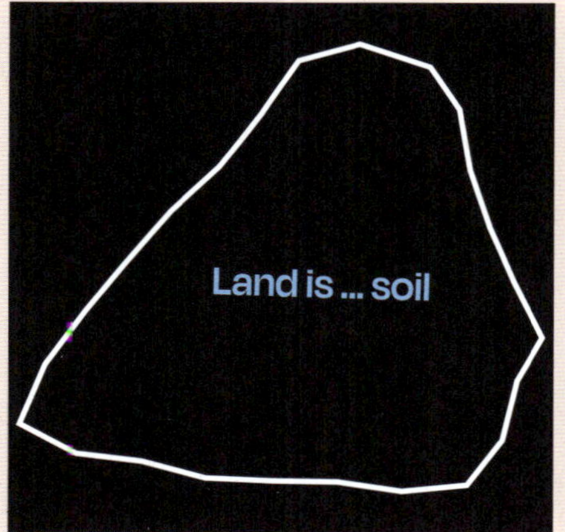
Land is ... soil

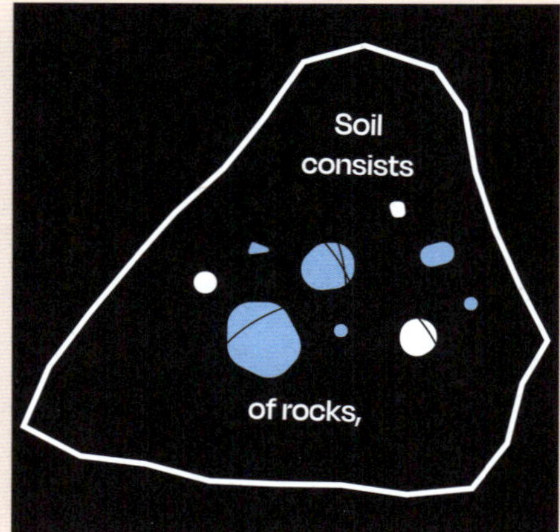
Soil
consists
of rocks,

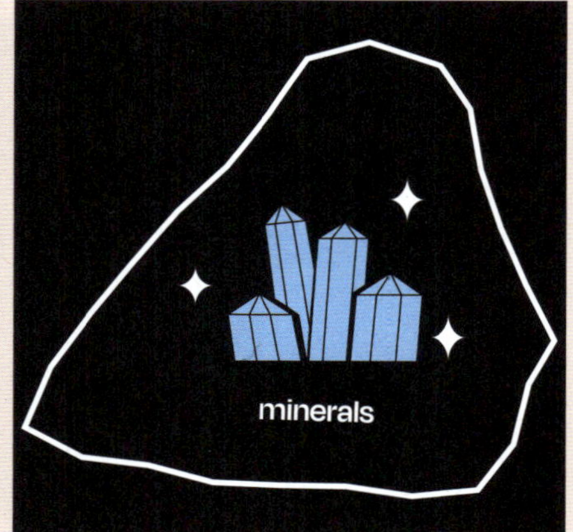
minerals

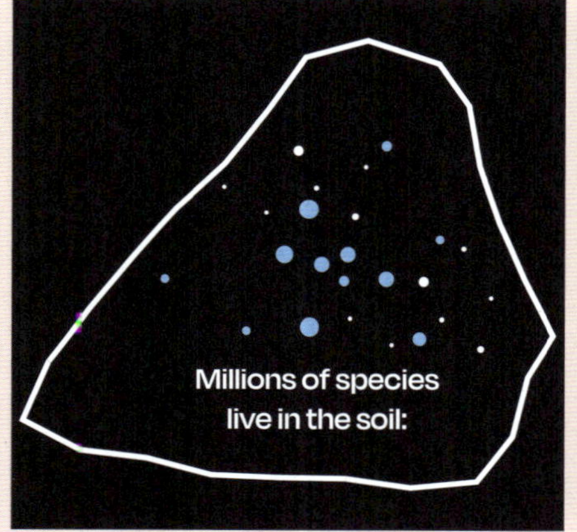
Millions of species
live in the soil:

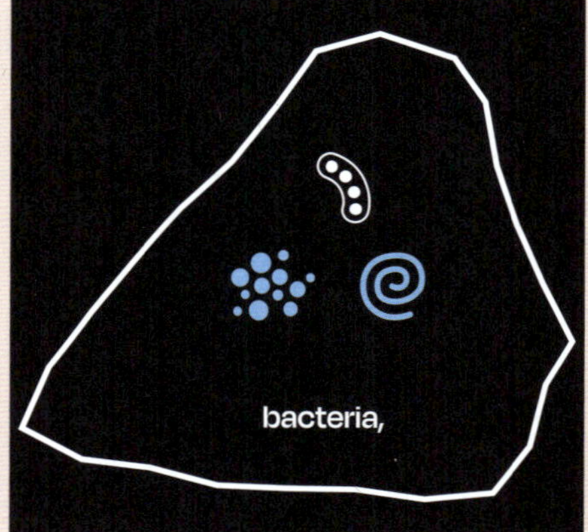
bacteria,

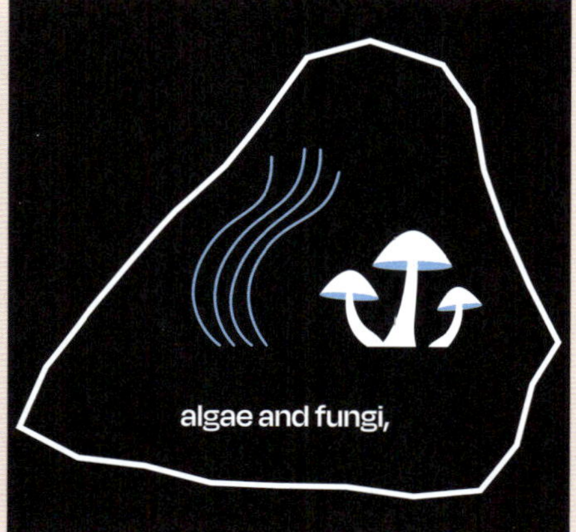
algae and fungi,

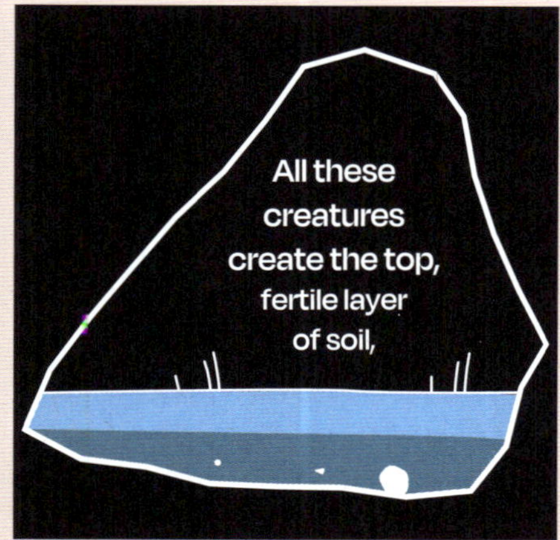
All these
creatures
create the top,
fertile layer
of soil,

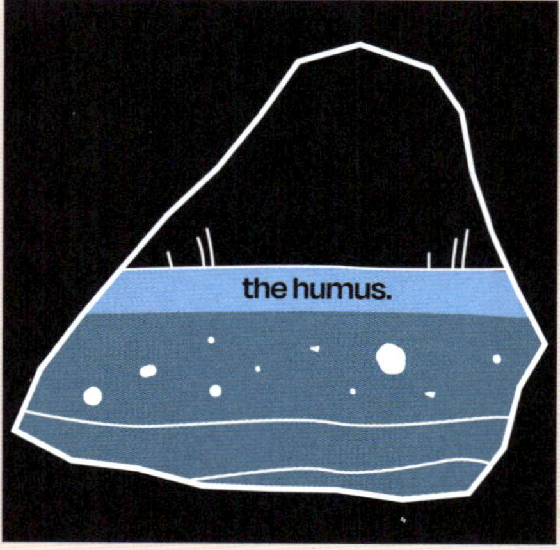
the humus.

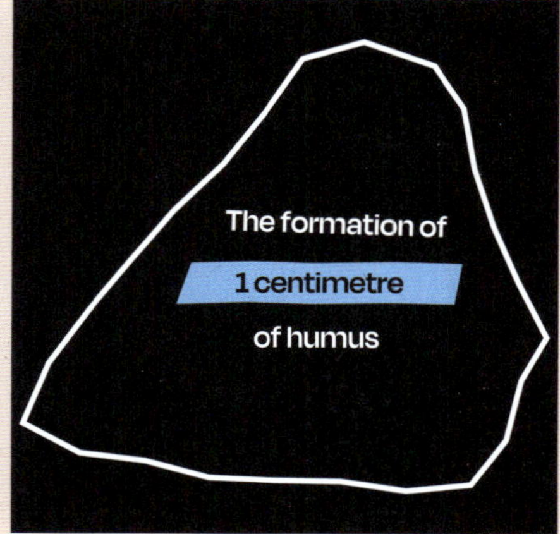
The formation of
1 centimetre
of humus

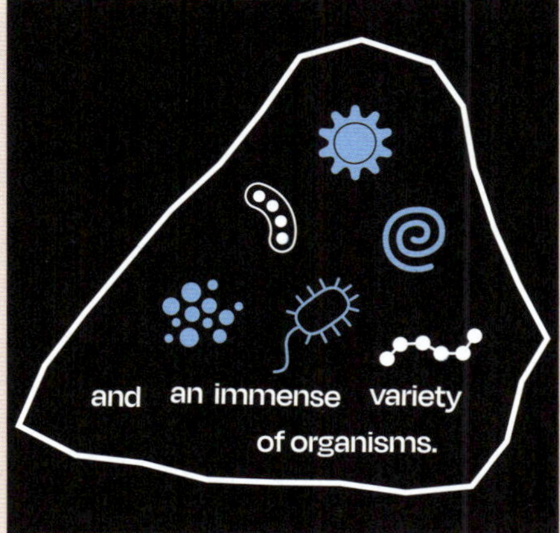
and an immense variety
of organisms.

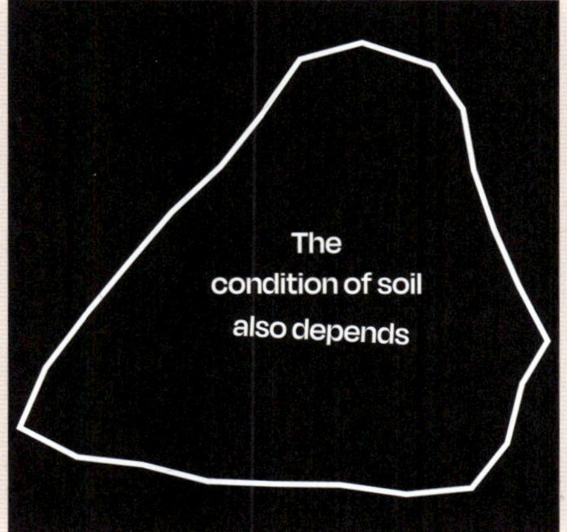
The
condition of soil
also depends

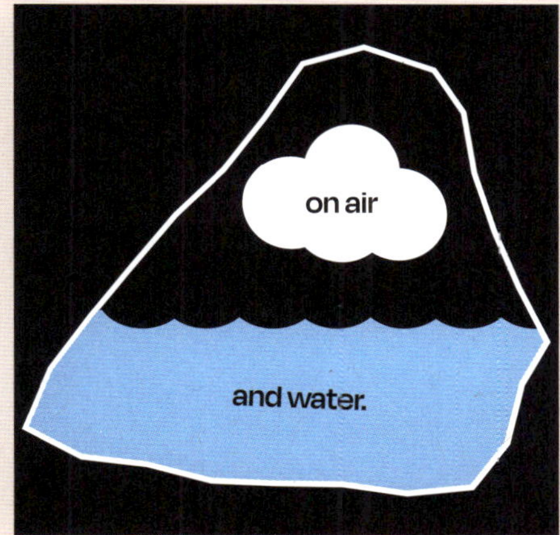
on air
and water.

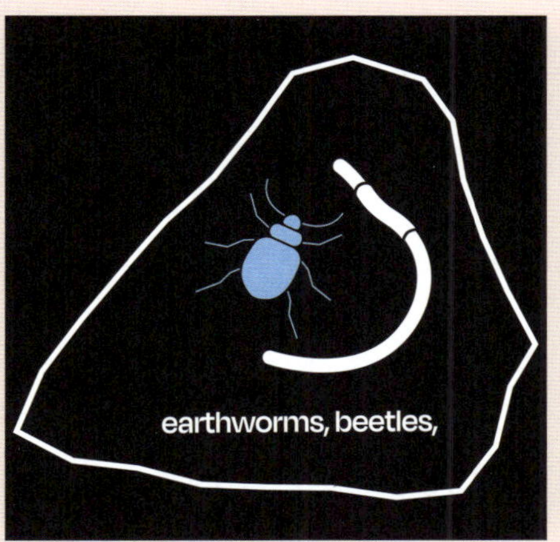
earthworms, beetles,

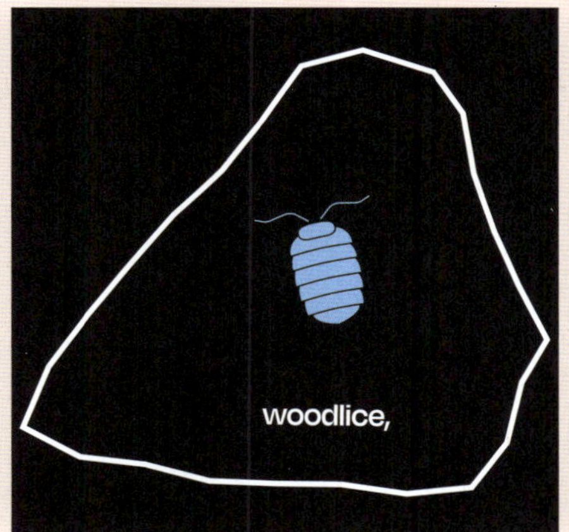
woodlice,

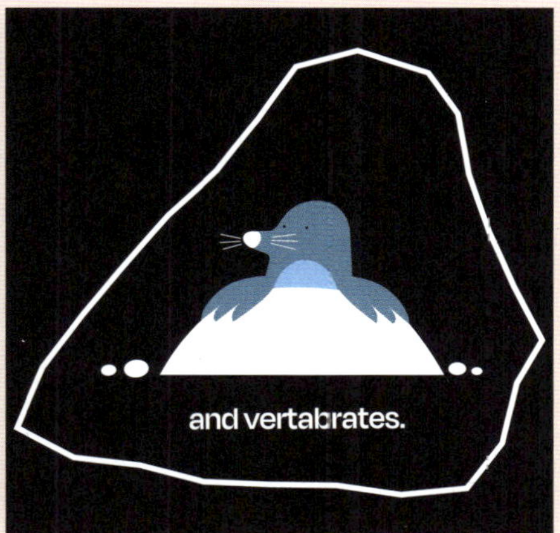
and vertabrates.

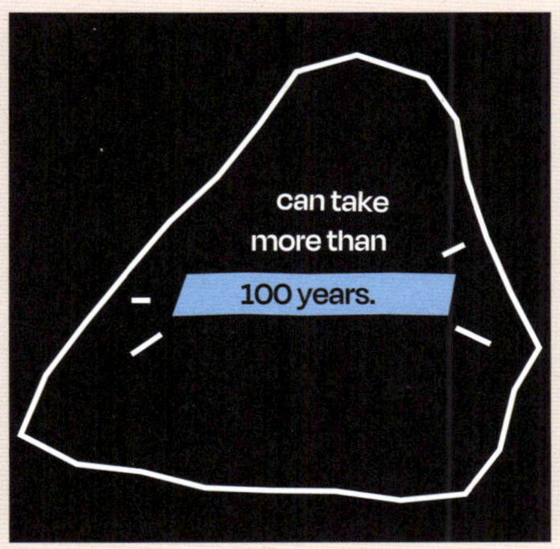
can take
more than
100 years.

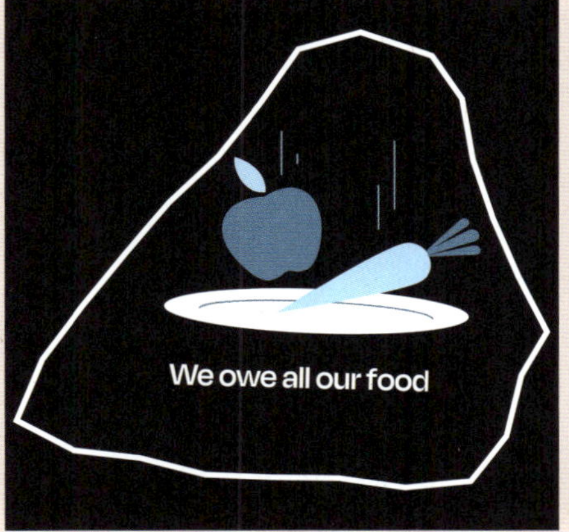
We owe all our food

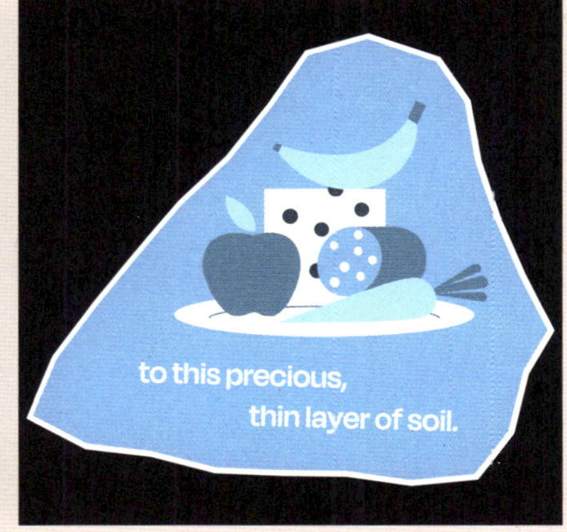
to this precious,
thin layer of soil.

Land is ... a feeling

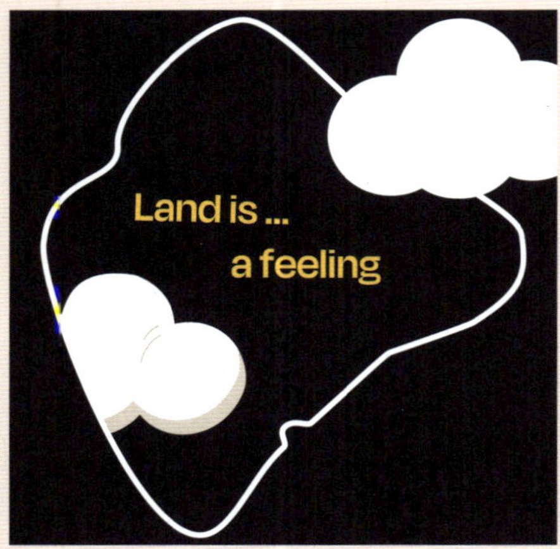

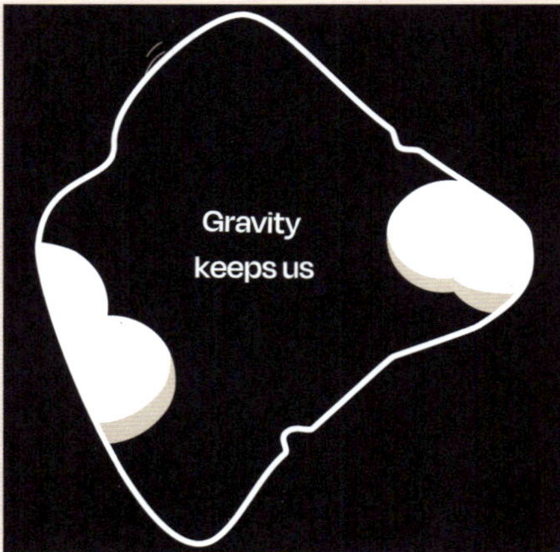

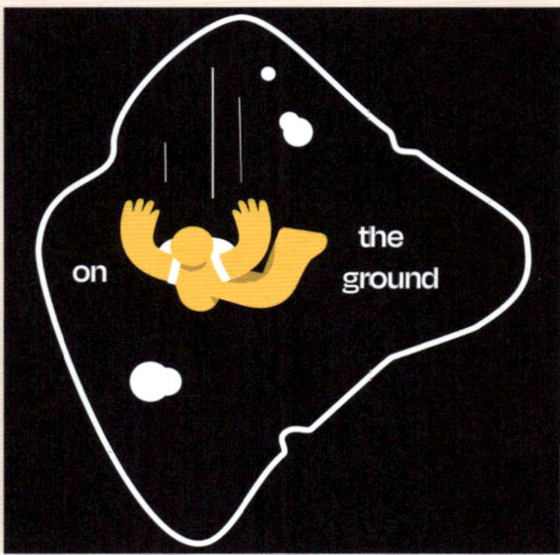

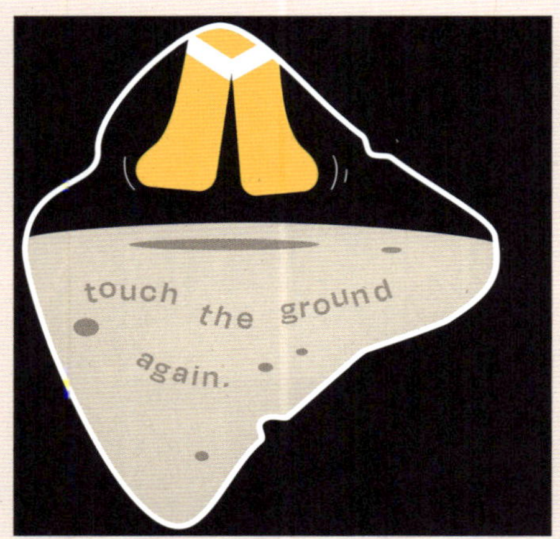

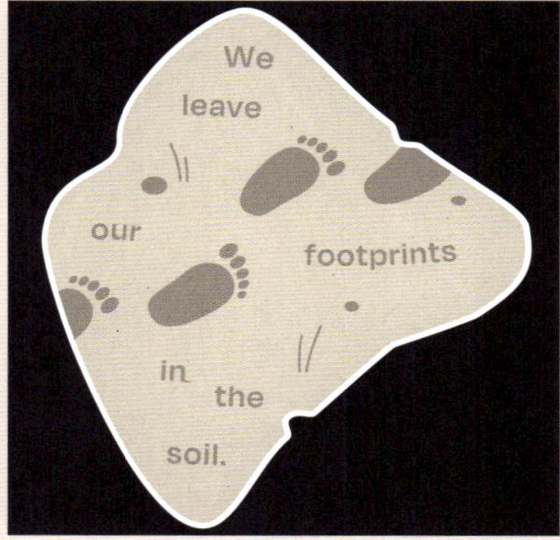

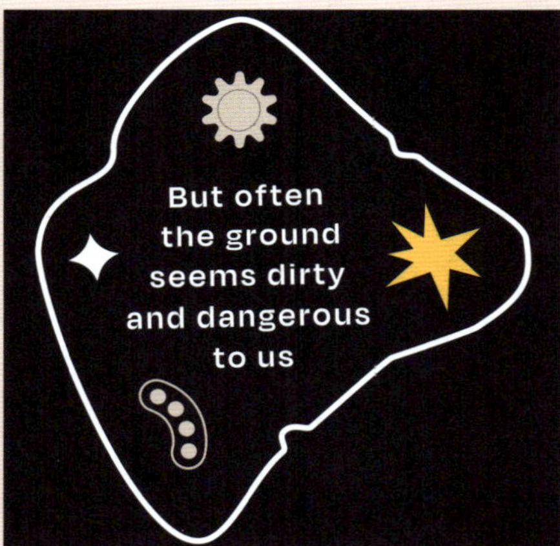

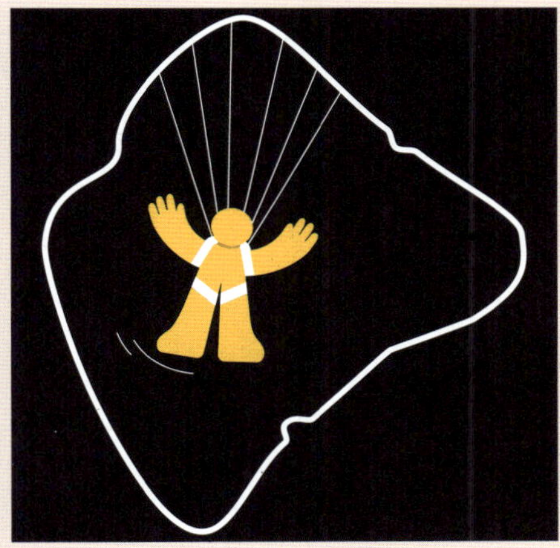

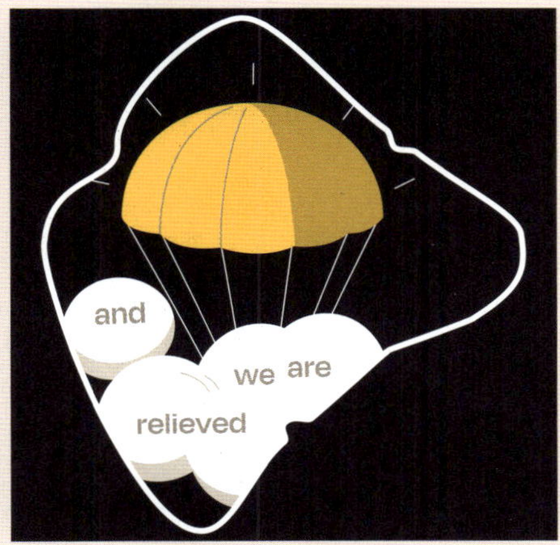
and
we are
relieved

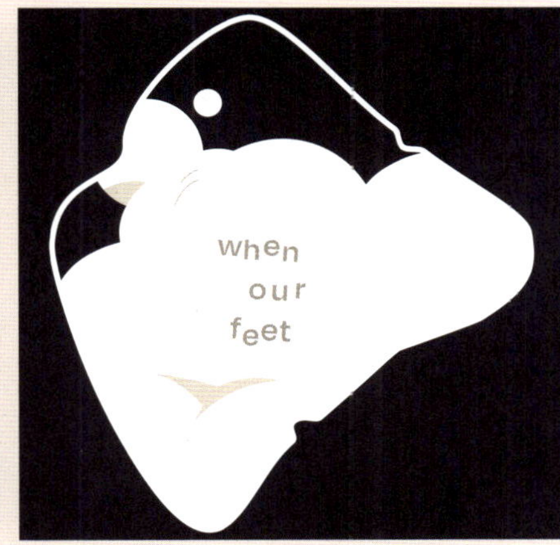
when
our
feet

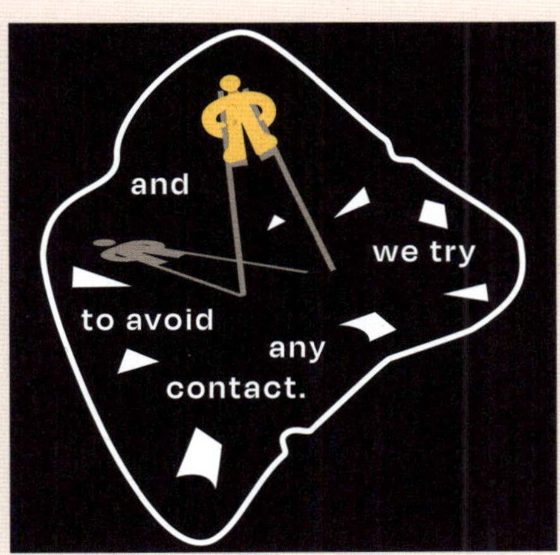
and
we try
to avoid
any
contact.

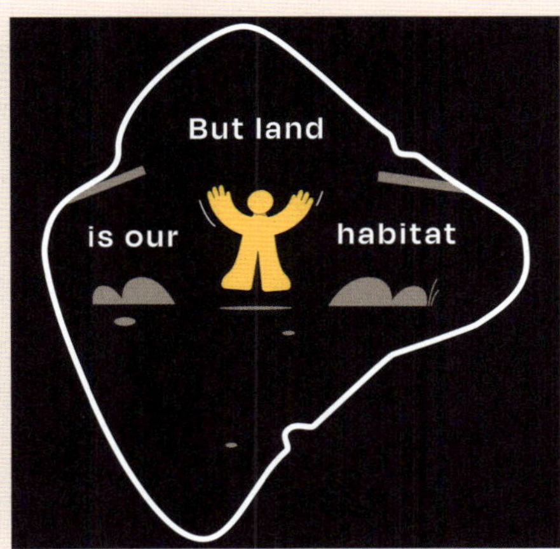
But land
is our
habitat

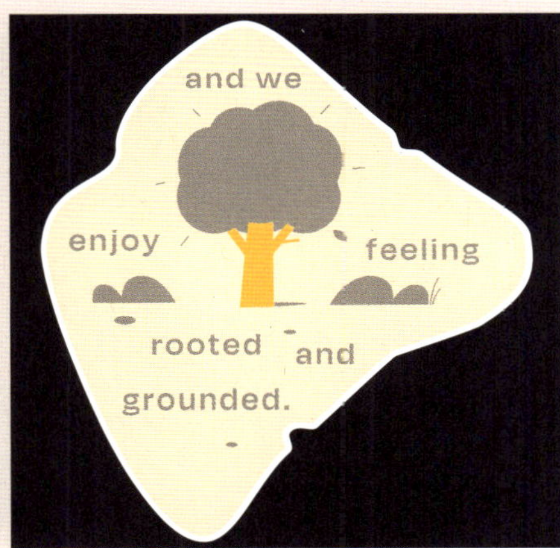
and we
enjoy
feeling
rooted
and
grounded.

Land is ... female

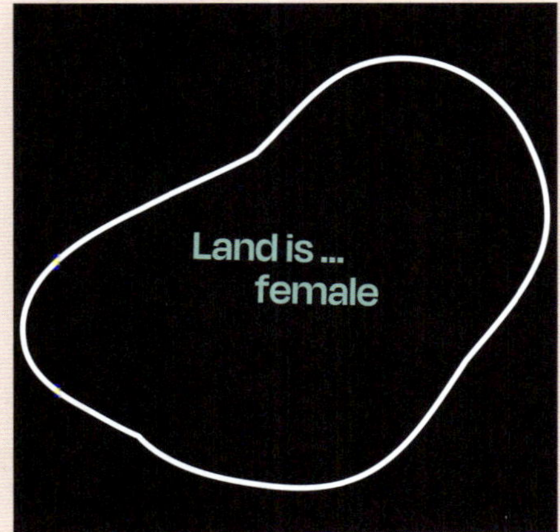

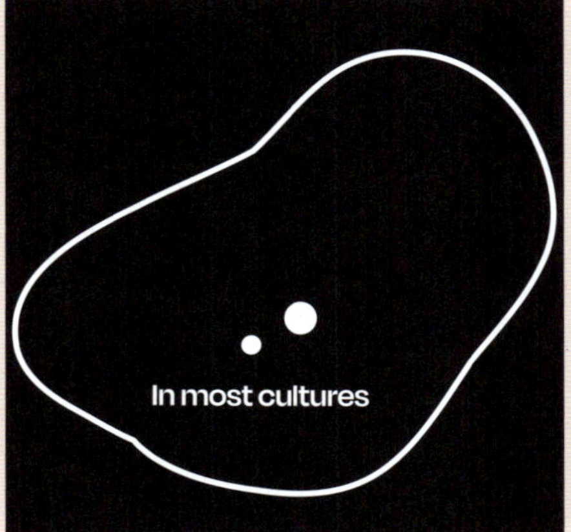

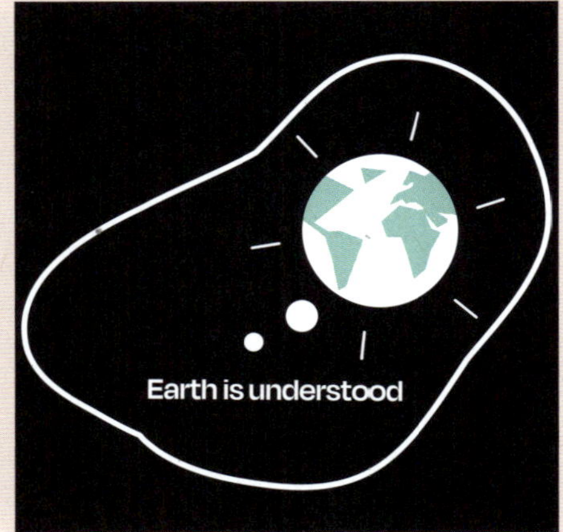

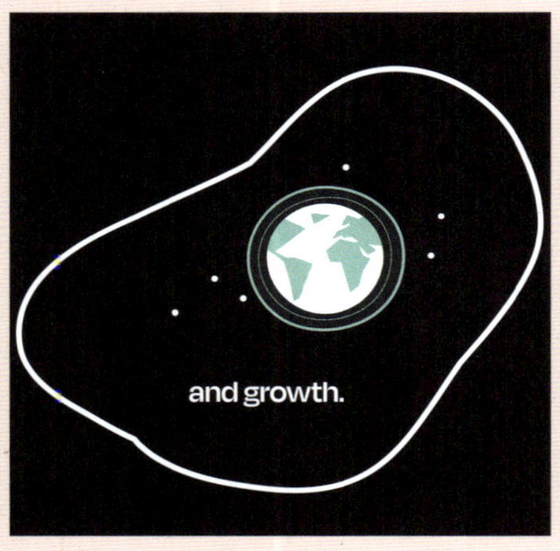

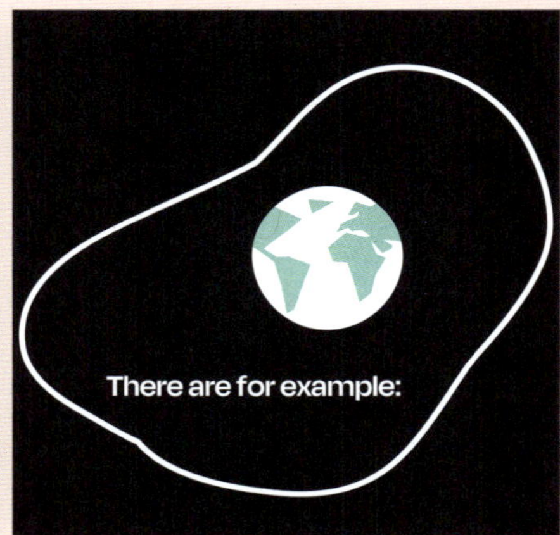

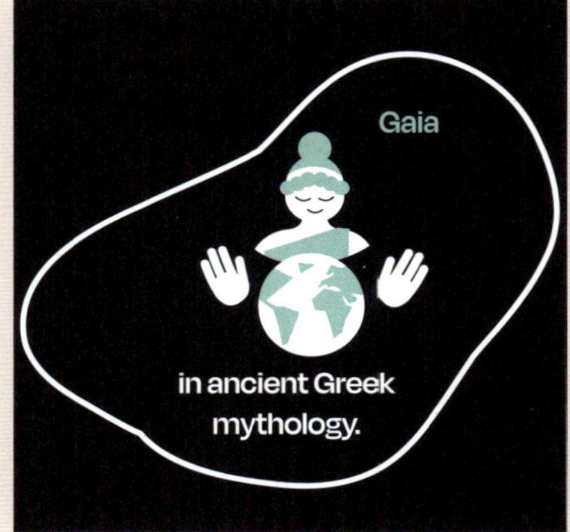

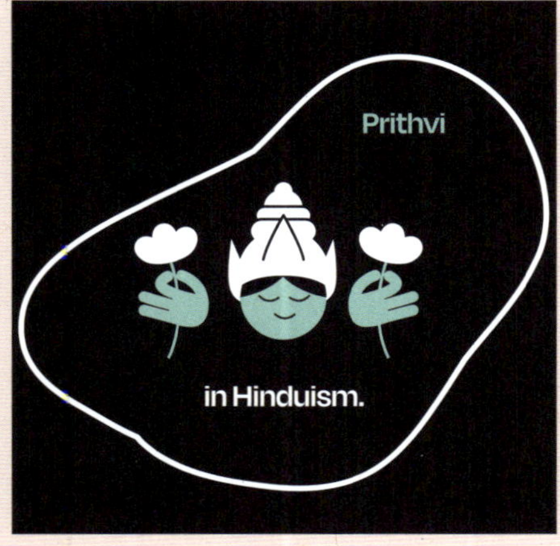

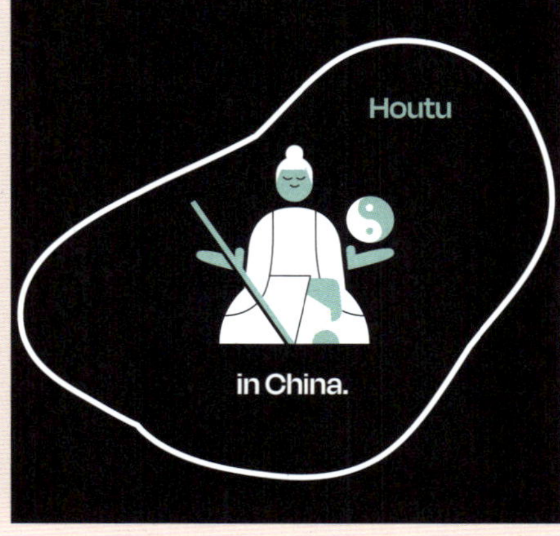

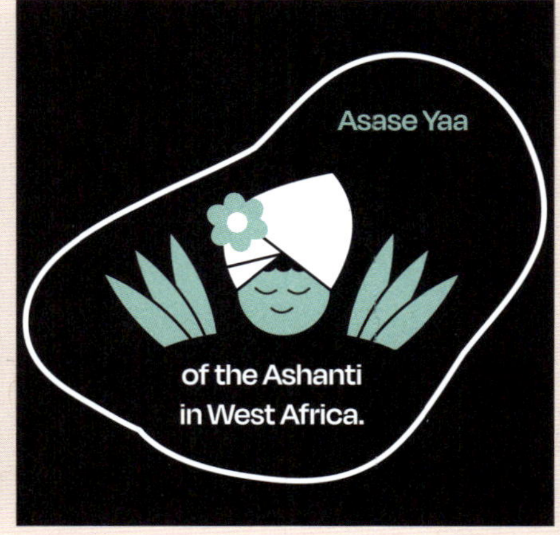

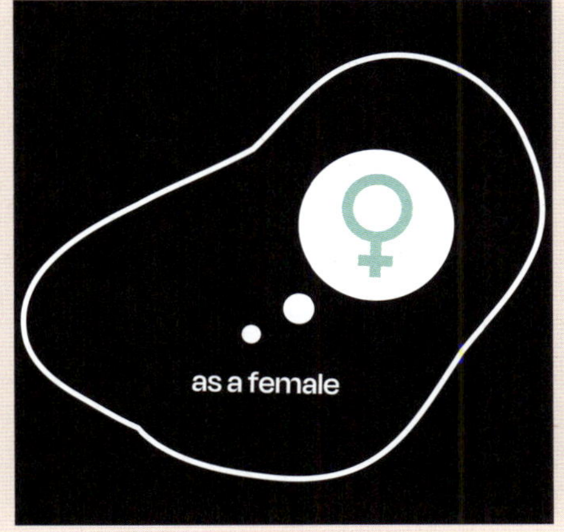
as a female

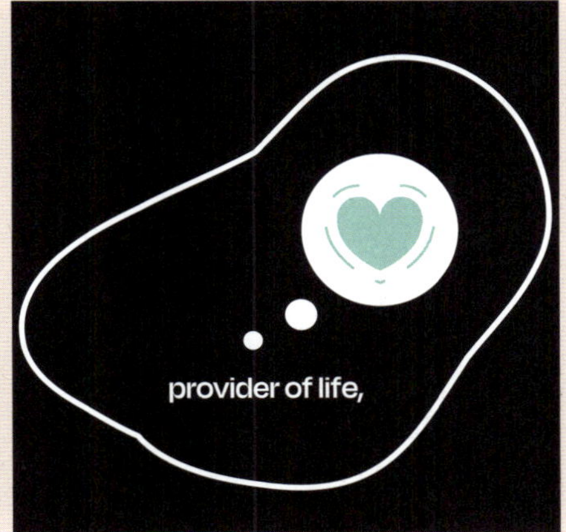
provider of life,

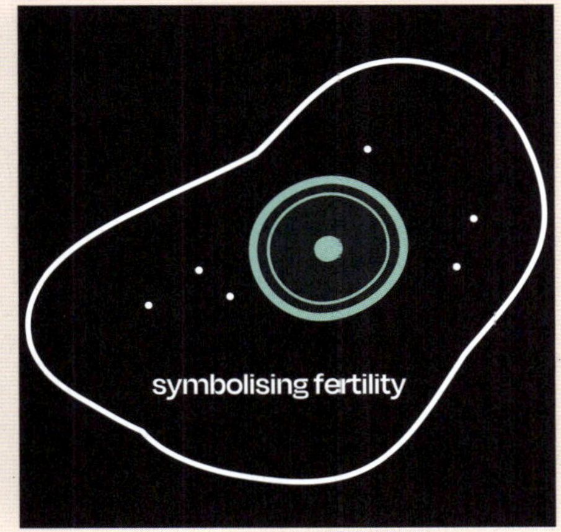
symbolising fertility

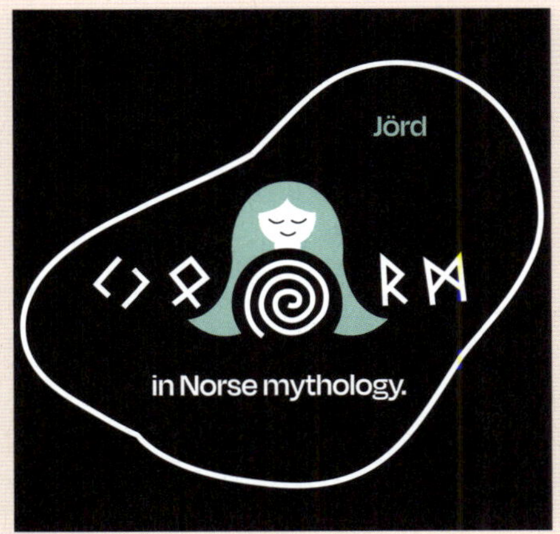
Jörd
in Norse mythology.

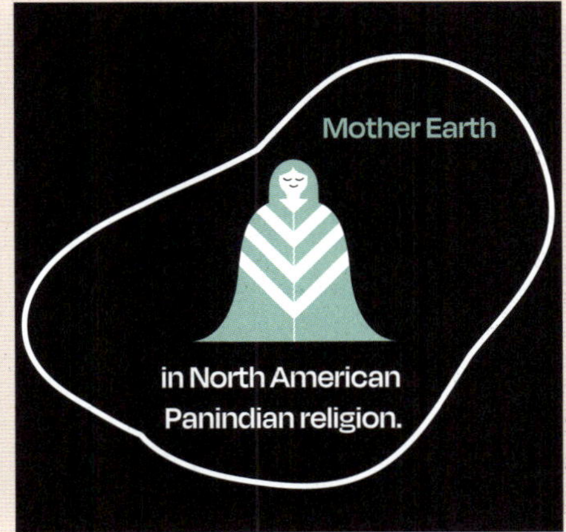
Mother Earth
in North American
Panindian religion.

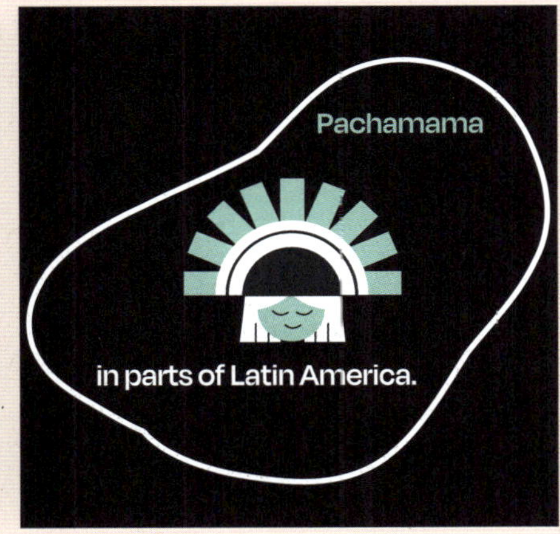
Pachamama
in parts of Latin America.

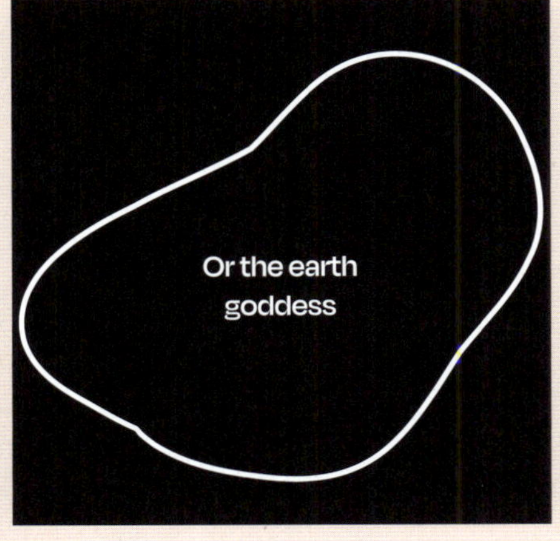
Or the earth
goddess

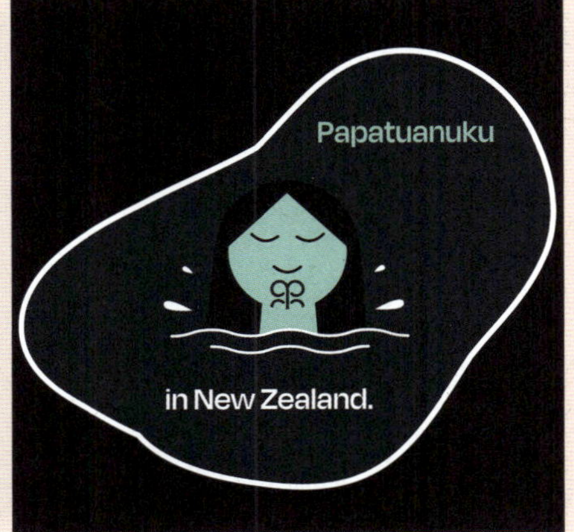
Papatuanuku
in New Zealand.

Land is ... culture

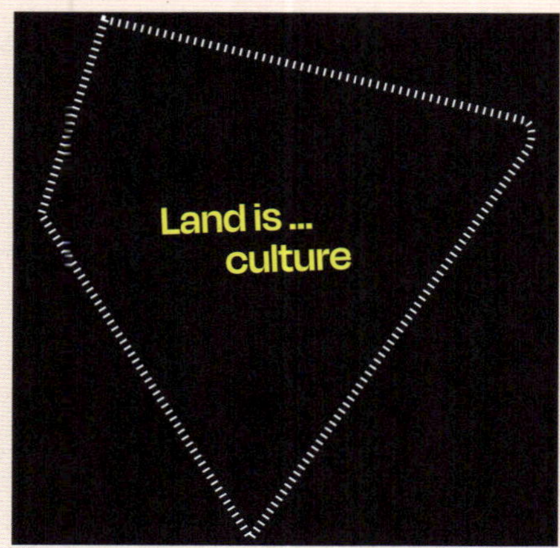

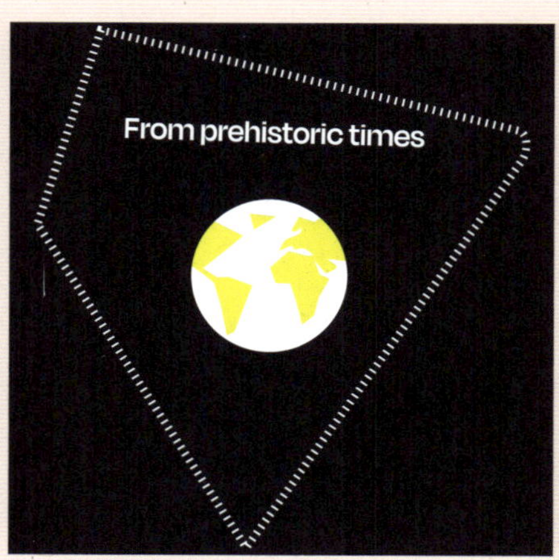

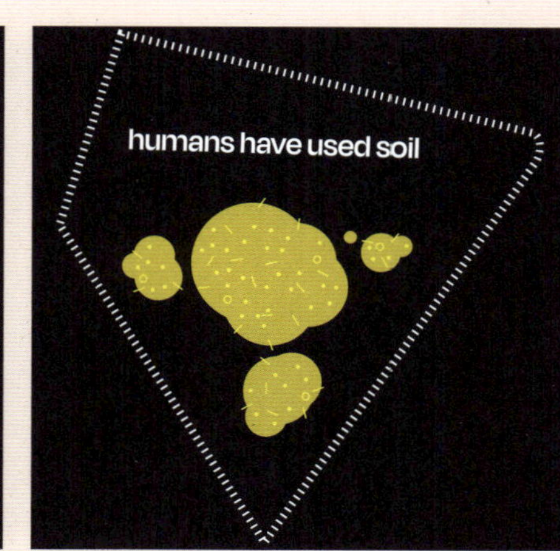

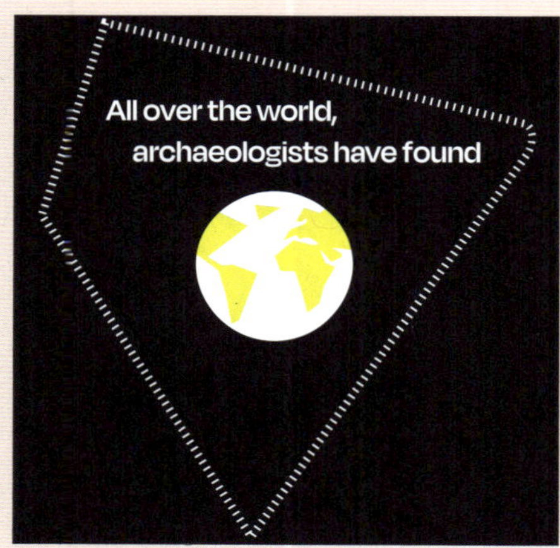

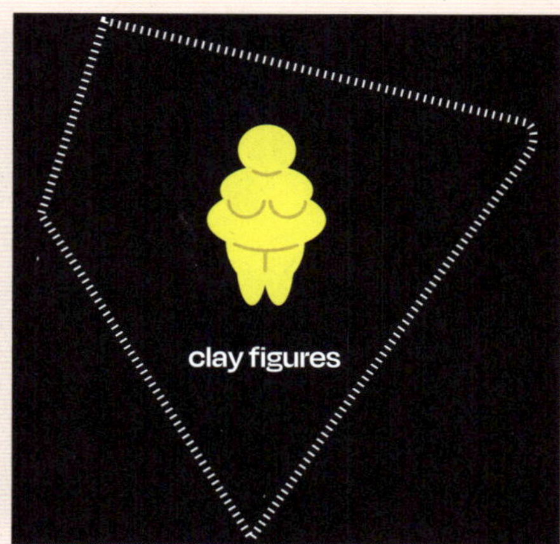

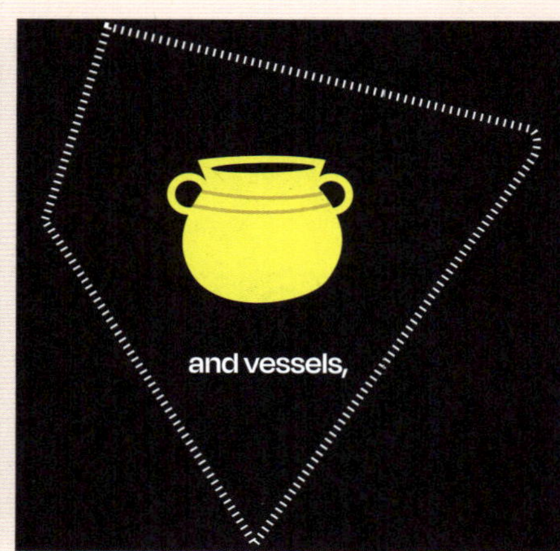

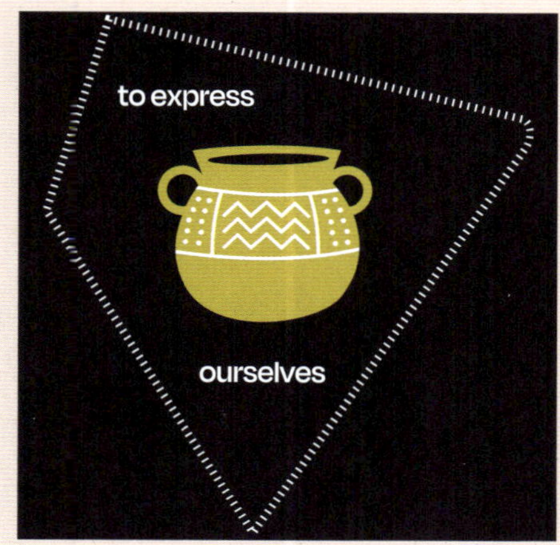

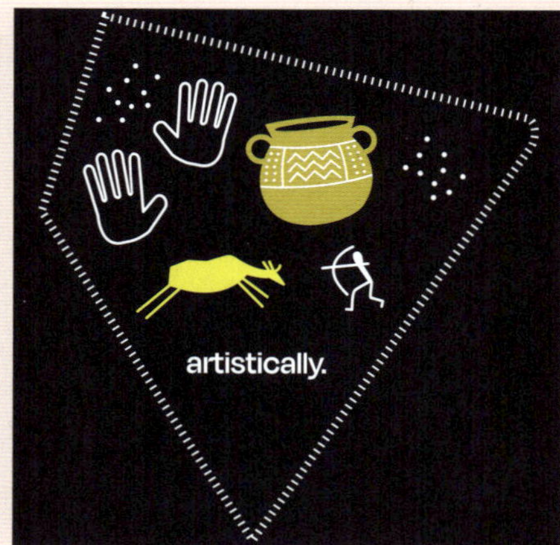

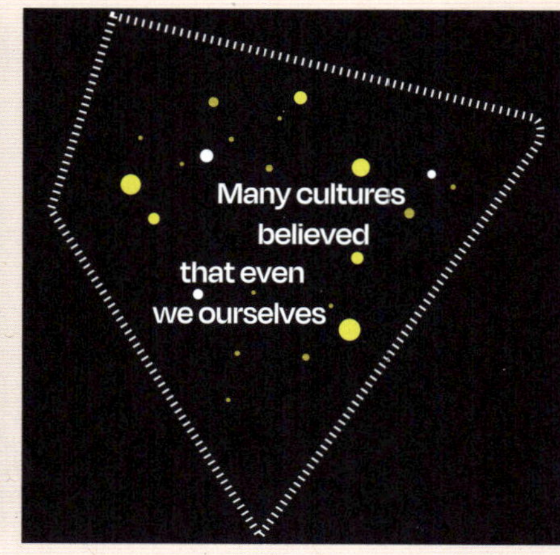

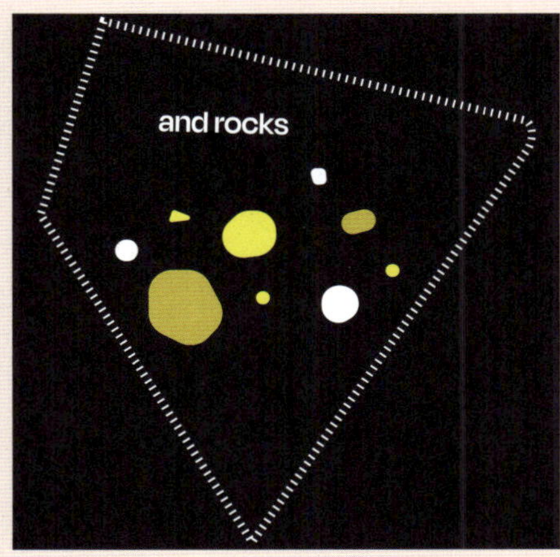
and rocks

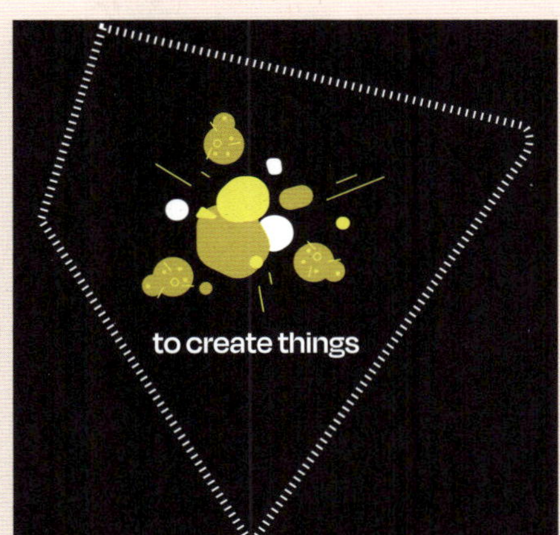
to create things

for their daily lives.

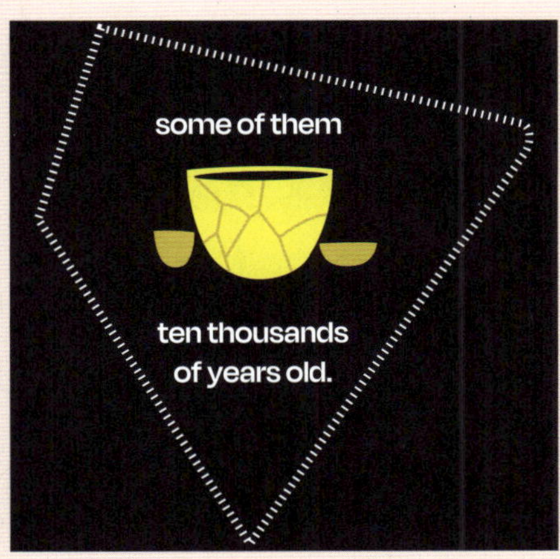
some of them
ten thousands
of years old.

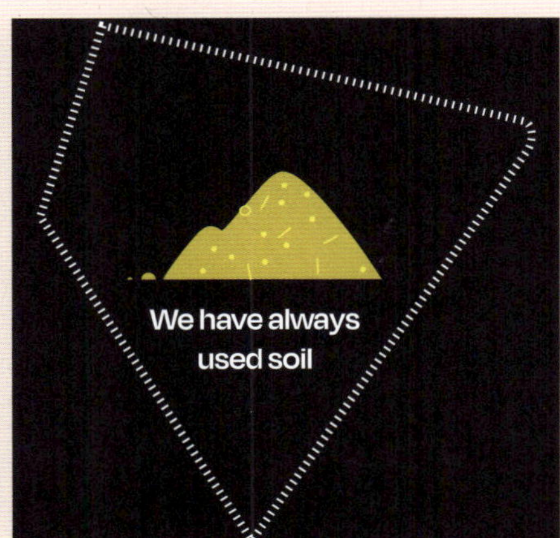
We have always
used soil

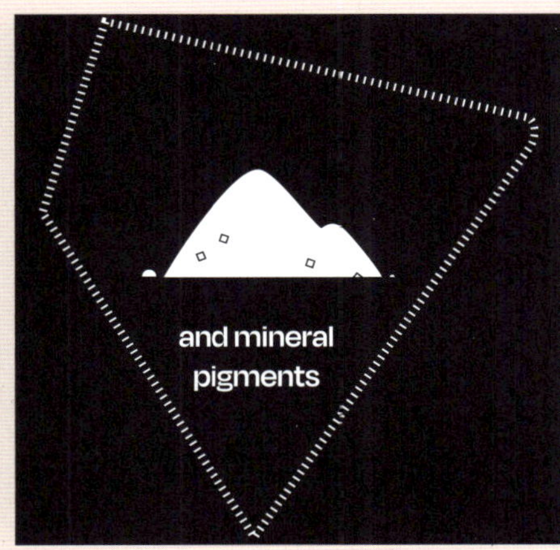
and mineral
pigments

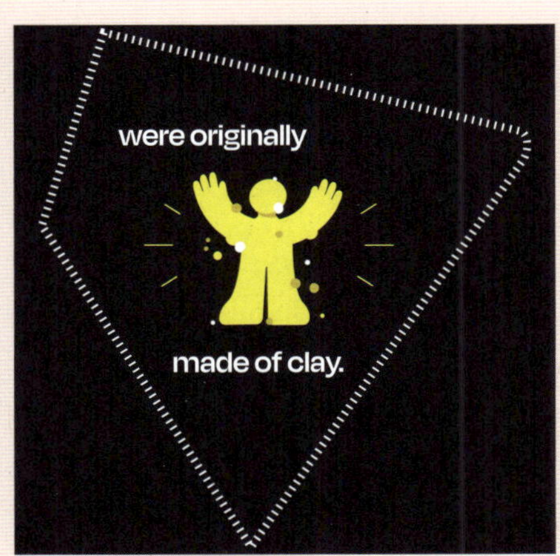
were originally
made of clay.

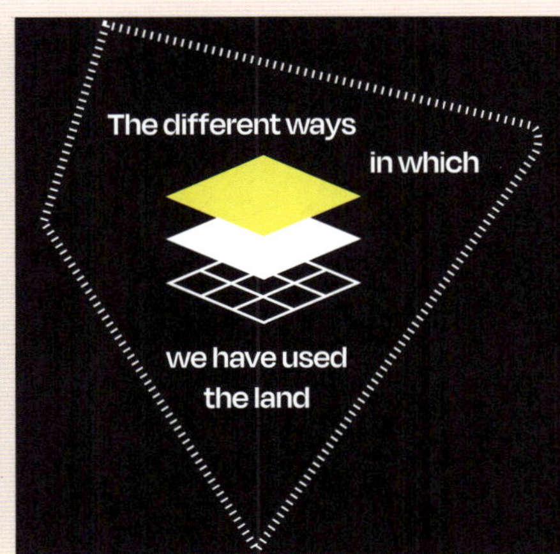
The different ways
in which
we have used
the land

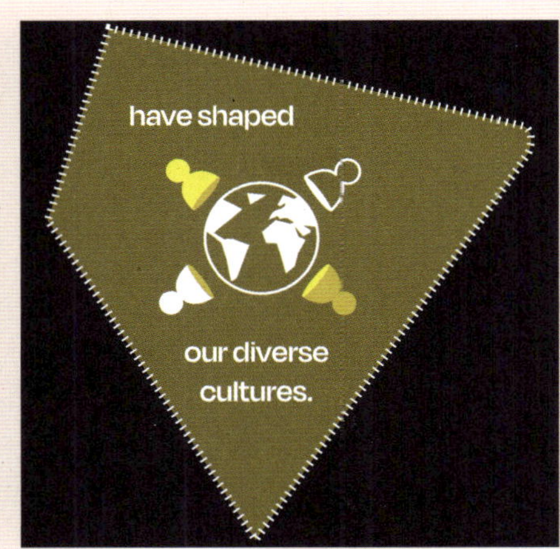
have shaped
our diverse
cultures.

Land is ... property

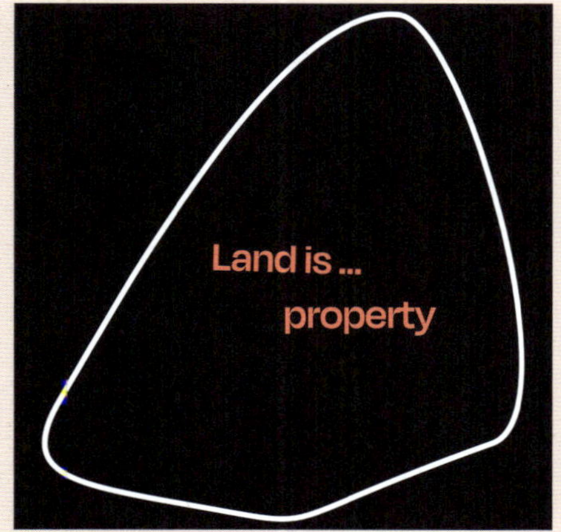

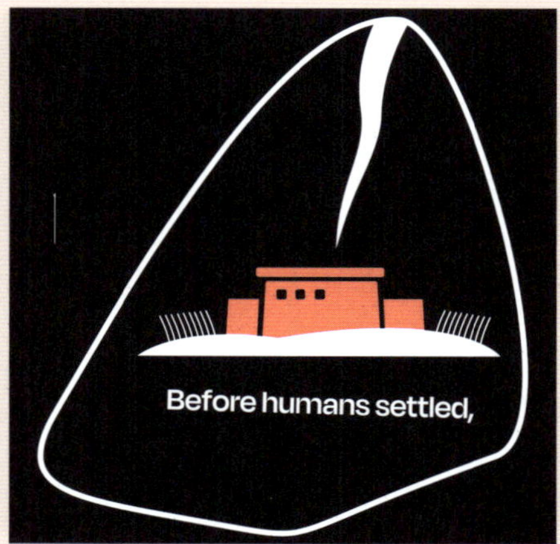

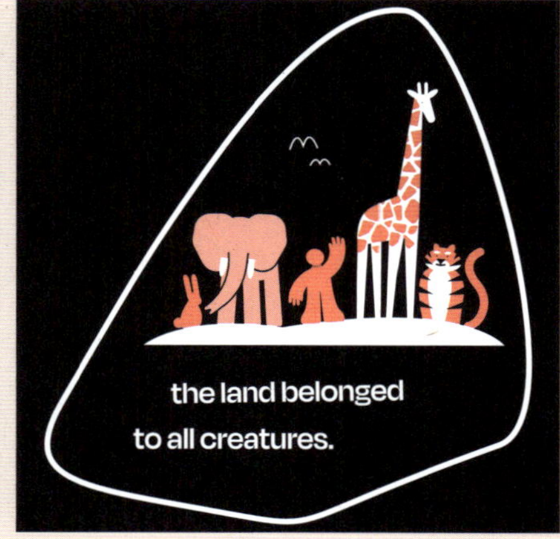

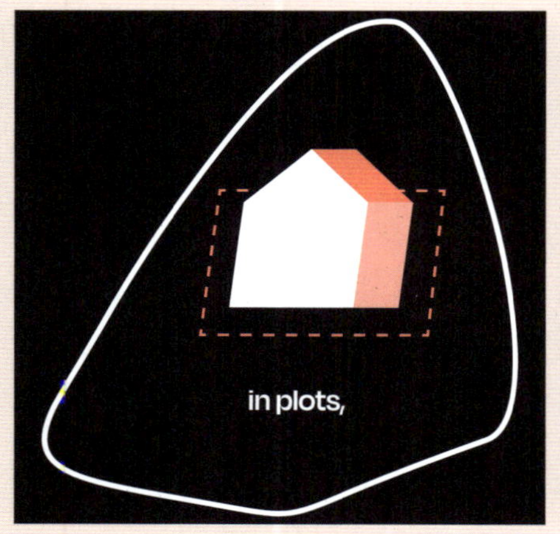

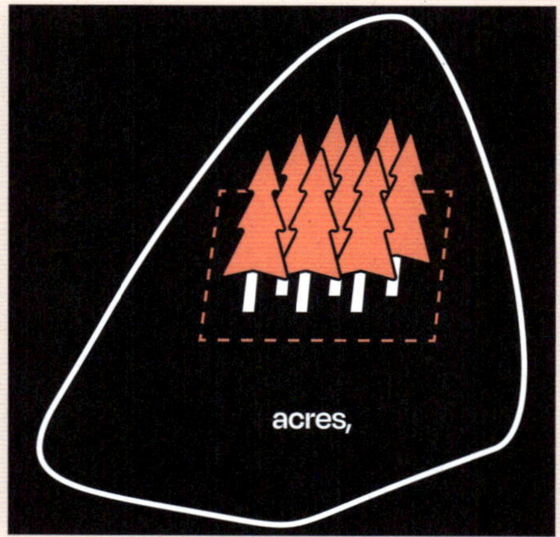

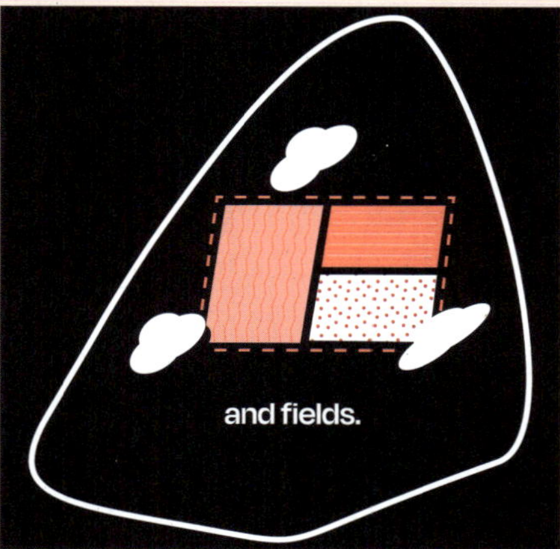

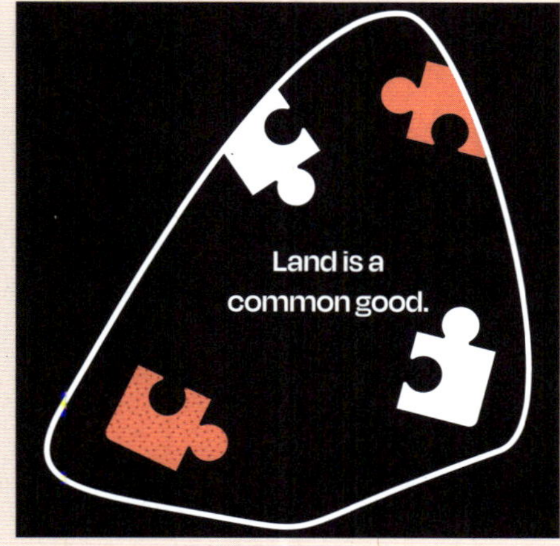

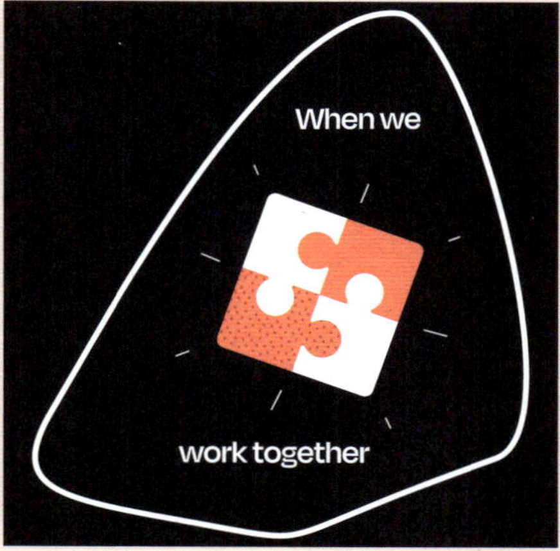

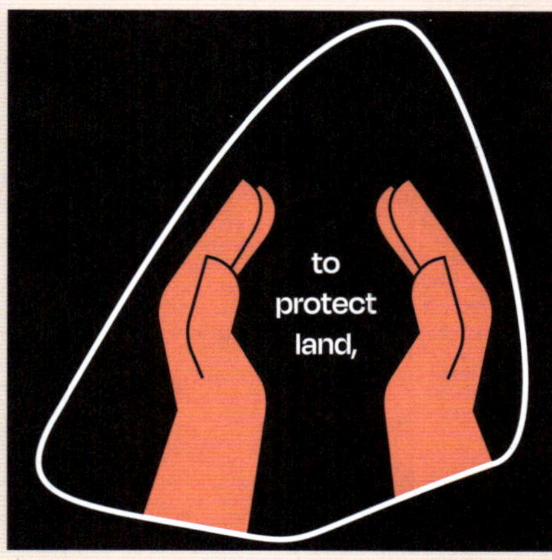

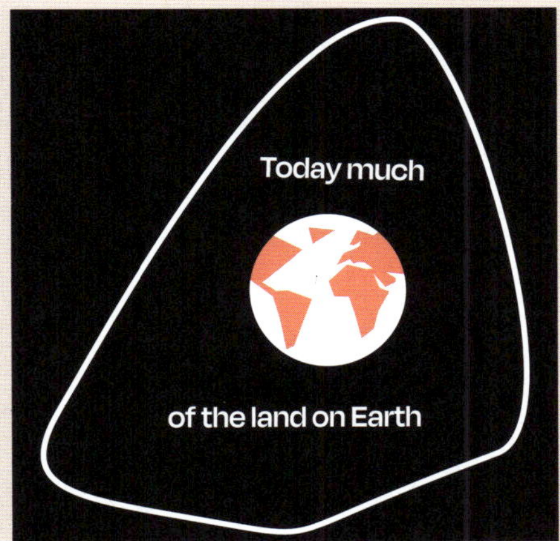
Today much
of the land on Earth

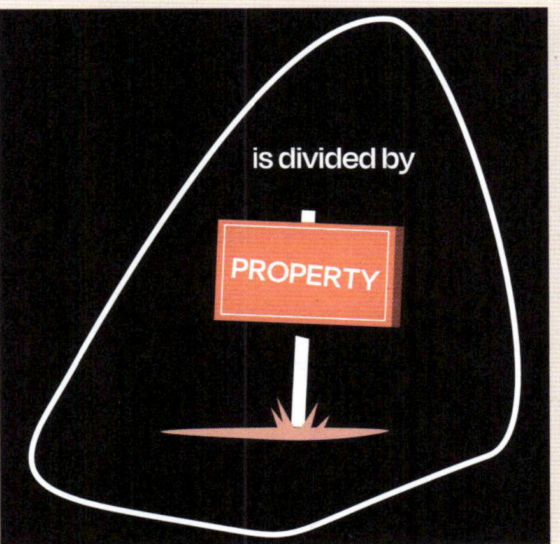
is divided by
PROPERTY

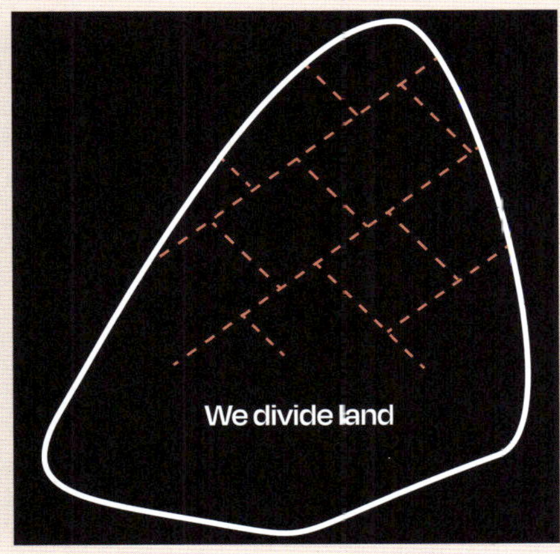
We divide land

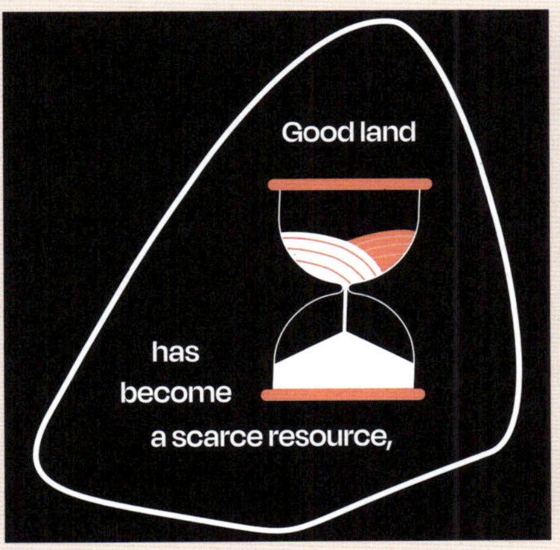
Good land
has
become
a scarce resource,

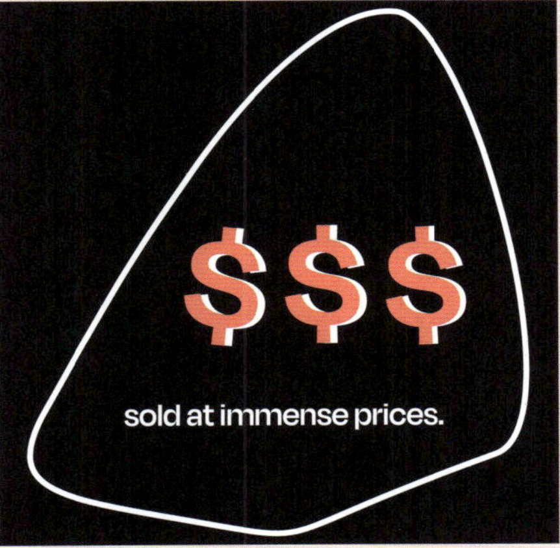
$$$
sold at immense prices.

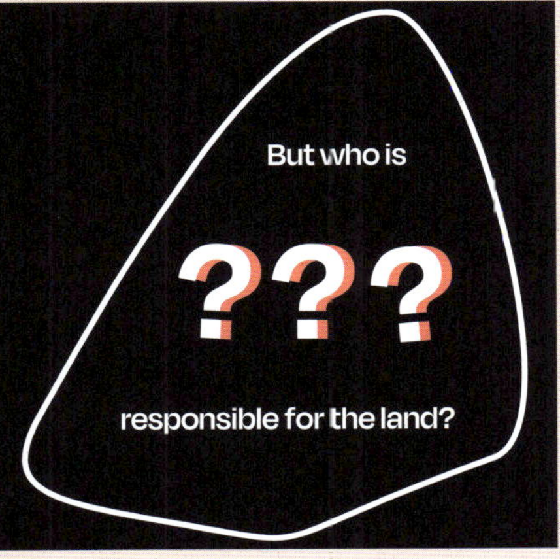
But who is
???
responsible for the land?

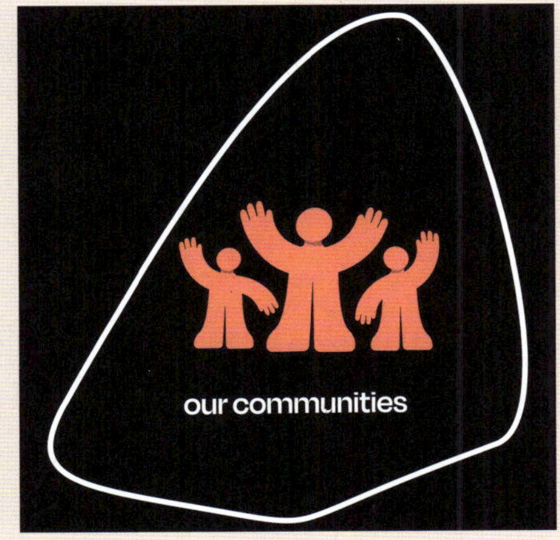
our communities

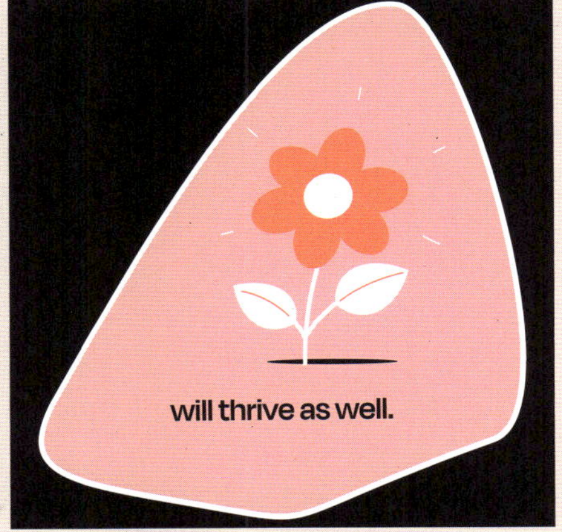
will thrive as well.

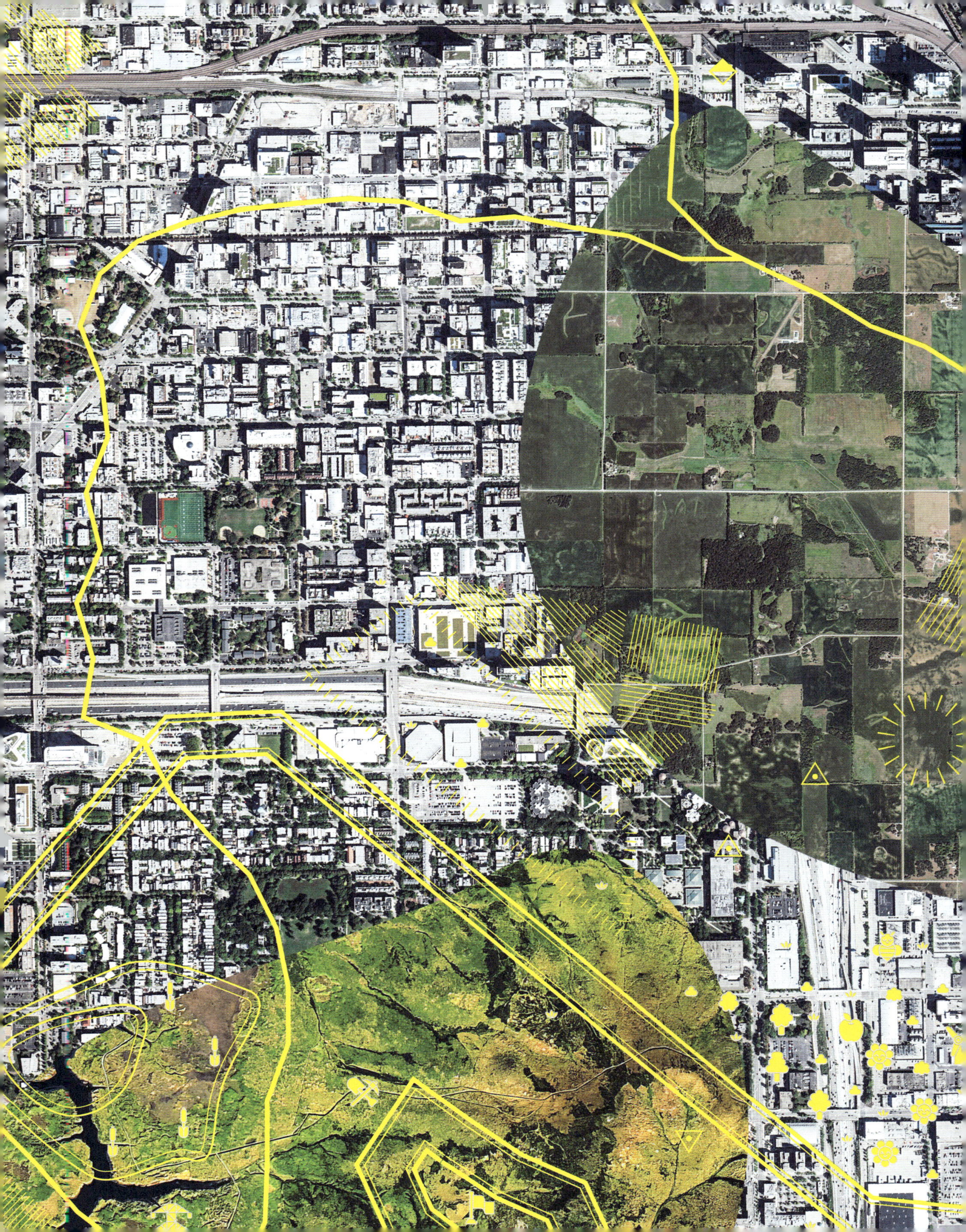

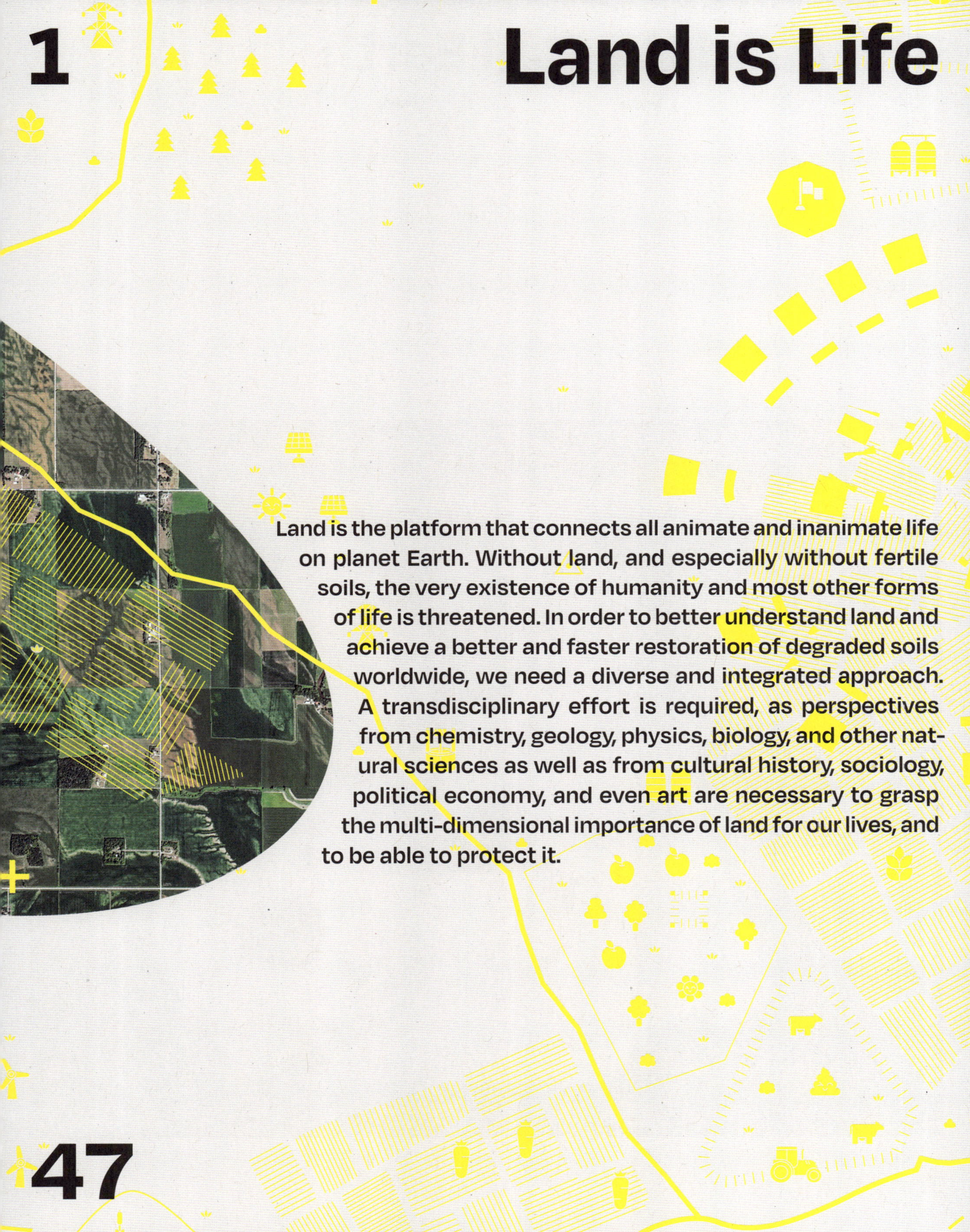

1 Land is Life

Land is the platform that connects all animate and inanimate life on planet Earth. Without land, and especially without fertile soils, the very existence of humanity and most other forms of life is threatened. In order to better understand land and achieve a better and faster restoration of degraded soils worldwide, we need a diverse and integrated approach. A transdisciplinary effort is required, as perspectives from chemistry, geology, physics, biology, and other natural sciences as well as from cultural history, sociology, political economy, and even art are necessary to grasp the multi-dimensional importance of land for our lives, and to be able to protect it.

The Land We Call Earth

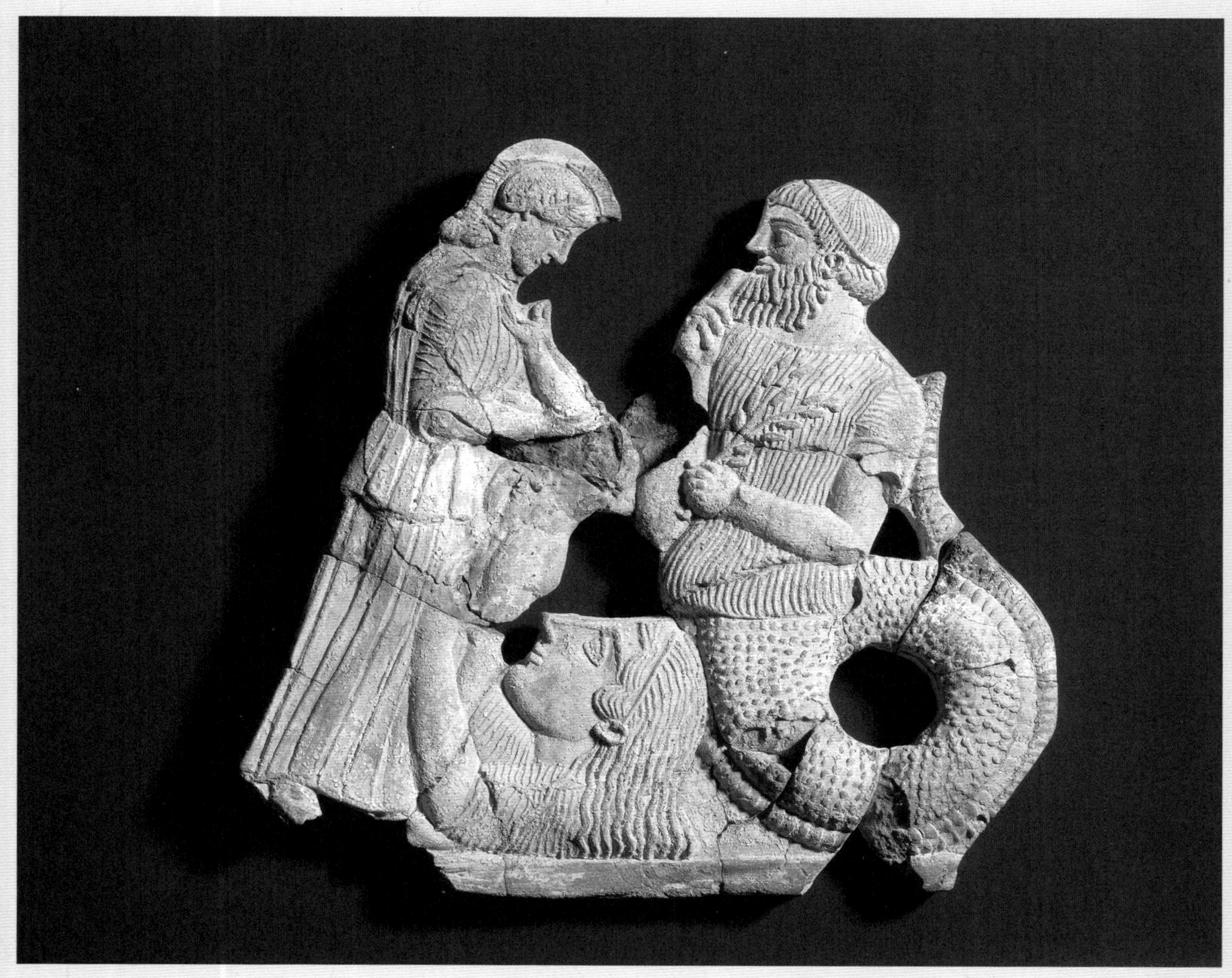

Tony Simons

Land is a somewhat fluid term we use to describe the Earth's crust. Four billion years ago – all of Earth's land had no surface water. Three billion years ago – 100 % of the land (51 billion hectares) was covered in water, and today approximately 71 % of all land is covered by water. There are currently 15 billion hectares of land above sea level under the management of 195 UN Member States. But countries also claim land under their Territorial Seas (up to 22 km from the shoreline) as well as land under their Exclusive Economic Zones (EEZ, up to 370 km from the coast). Amazingly, the combined total area of land under territorial seas (2.2 billion hectares), and under their EEZs (10.2 billion hectares) is almost the same (82 %) as the area of land above sea level.

The word 'land' has fascinating linguistic origins. In Western civilisations, it has Proto-Indo-European roots but occurs in various other constructions in all major written and spoken languages. Furthermore, the concept of Land or Earth as the provider or progenitor of life and resources is prominent in most cultures and spiritual affiliations, with terminologies including: Gaia (Greece), Jord (Norse), Asase Yaa (Ashanti), Akamu (Polynesia), Tonantzin (Aztecs), Hou Tu (China), Bhumi Devi (Hinduism), and other sacred references. The majority of these assign a female identity to land with only rare exceptions such as Geb (Ancient Egypt) who was referred to as Father Earth. Land is that multidimensional platform that connects all living and non-living things. Land literally is 'Life on Earth'.

So-called Melian relief: Athena, Kekrops, Gaia, c. 460 BC, Greece. The relief shows the birth of Erichthonios, the serpent-footed son of Hephaestus and Gaia. Gaia rises from the earth and entrusts her son to Athena. In Greek mythology, the primordial goddess Gaia represents the personified Earth. The so-called 'Gaia hypothesis', developed in the 1970s, is the assumption that the Earth is to be regarded as a living being that has always been self-sustaining and enables the life of all living beings.

Land as a Political Entity

More modern definitions and references of land, however, are dominated by geo-referencing and legal ownership. Land is equated to a geospatial plot with either natural or straight-line boundaries, or as a series of lat-longs on a title deed. Yet land also simultaneously encompasses multiple concepts of: land type; land resources; land use; land productivity; and land management. More recently, we have begun to classify land according to its state of health such as: ❶ intact/productive; ❷ degrading; and ❸ degraded. And most worrying for all societies is the burgeoning area of degrading and degraded land. To understand land more fully, and to catalyse better and faster restoration, we need to frame land in multiple and yet aligned ways. Land is that concoction of chemistry, geology, physics, biology, cultural sociology, and political economy. It is viewed by all as a tangible asset, but societies differ markedly in perspectives of ownership, valuations, inheritance, use rights, and historical legacies.

In recent times, land has been a point of contention in international fora and global politics. Whilst countries might quite readily agree to collective oversight of global issues such as depletion of the ozone layer, biological warfare, or preventing financial crises, when it comes to more sovereign issues there is more reluctance. As a territorial issue, land is as sovereign as it gets. With perhaps a few exceptions such as Antarctica, individual territories are seen as under the purview of national governments, and historically of their prior empires, kingdoms, and fiefdoms. Although Antarctica, at 1.42 billion hectares in area, makes up almost 10 % of all global land above sea level, it is the only continent without Indigenous populations of humans. This may explain why this space has been successfully managed under a 12 country treaty since 1959, and now has 54 country signatories covering over 80 % of the global human population.

Planet Earth and Outer Space

Another space that has been successfully managed multilaterally is space itself, or outer space. The 1967 Outer Space Treaty now signed by 138 countries governs the use and access of the Earth's moon and outer space. No country can claim domain over it, and space use is restricted to peaceful purposes only. Closer to home in the Earth's atmosphere there are six global treaties negotiated at United Nations level that lay out agreements to prevent conflicts in the atmosphere up to heights of 100,000 metres where the outer space of our solar system is deemed to begin.

The origin of the solar system, and the land on our planet Earth with all of the life it contains, is based on chemistry. The fundamental chemical foundation was then further shaped by physics. Around 4.6 billion years ago a huge cloud of gas and dust started spinning and collapsed in on itself. Roughly 99 % of this material condensed and through nuclear fusion of hydrogen, a powerful energy source and a strong gravitational force were created. And thus the sun was formed.

After formation of the sun, from the 1 % chemical leftovers of gas and dust, much smaller clusters formed under the laws of physics to create Earth and the other seven planets of the solar system. The sun was so hot that the nearest four planets, namely: Mercury, Venus, Earth, and Mars, could only survive so close to it as rock. Also in orbit around the sun, and outside the four rocky planets, are two ice giants (Neptune and Uranus), and two gas giants (Jupiter and Saturn). The size of our neighbouring planets in area ranges from 1/7th times the area of Earth (Mercury) to 120 times the area of Earth (Jupiter).

Let's Get Chemical

The chemistry of Earth, the sun, and all the other planets is identical and based on the periodic table of 92 naturally occurring elements. Elements are numbered 1 to 92 based on the number of protons in the nucleus, which reaches a maximum number of 92 protons as Uranium. However, our Earth is not just a homogenous chemical soup and has different compositions in the core, the crust, and the atmosphere. The five most common elements in the Earth's crust are: Oxygen (46.1 %), Silicon (28.2 %), Aluminium (8.2 %), Iron (5.6 %), and Calcium (4.2 %). And excluding water vapour, the most common elements in the Earth's atmosphere today are: Nitrogen (78 %), Oxygen (21 %), and Argon (1 %). But most worrying is the next largest gaseous compound of carbon dioxide which is close to 430 ppm and causing catastrophic global warming leading to even more pronounced land degradation.

At the beginning of Earth, some 4.7 billion years ago, there was only a molten core with lots of volcanic eruptions. Soon after there was a rocky crust on the outside, with no water, no life, and a toxic atmosphere. The Earth at that time was entirely land and no oceans or lakes, and of a similar total area as today, i.e. 510 million square kilometres (51 billion hectares). From 4.4 billion years ago, water started arriving on Earth as ice on asteroids and other space material that collided with our planet. So much water was carried in that about 3.2 billion years ago the latest research indicates the world was a 'water world' with all land submerged.

Currently, 29 % of the Earth's surface or 148 million square kilometres is terrestrial, or above sea level. If all the world's glaciers and icecaps melted sea level would rise 70 metres, we would have 10 % less terrestrial land area. Moreover, approximately 20 % of the world's people and infrastructure is below 70 metres altitude, and it would affect different countries and cultures in a highly asymmetric way, with low-lying small islands most disproportionately affected. Even if we only had a 10-metre sea level rise by 2100, the storm surges would be devastating for hundreds of millions of people.

A Breeding Ground for Biological Diversity

At some fortunate period in time, about 3.7 billion years ago, the Earth changed from a chemical make-up to a hybrid chemical-biological make-up. And that jump from chemistry to biology led to the wonderful explosion of life, including the emergence of our hominid ancestors around 6 million years ago. Modern humans evolved in Africa approximately 250,000 years ago and started expanding across the world from 90,000 years ago. That evolutionary journey from self-replicating chemicals to single-celled micro-organisms to higher plants and to animals continues today as we enter the Anthropocene with over 8.7 million species of plants, animals, archaea, and bacteria. Although the diversity and abundance of life on Earth has been interrupted dramatically with five mass extinctions in planetary history, the rate of extinctions due to human activities is reaching epic proportions (1,000 times the background extinction rate).

At one of the most pivotal worldwide events in human history, the United Nations Conference on Environment and Development (UNCED) in Rio in 1992, three topics were elevated to the apex for global focus. These three topics were climate change, biodiversity, and desertification which by 1994 had all been adopted at the highest level as UN Conventions. Whilst none of the three Conventions explicitly covered all global land issues, the fact that the word 'land' was in the top 30 words mentioned (based on word count) in the 600-page Rio Agenda 21 Declaration was hugely significant. Hence it seems perplexing that the word 'land' was not even in the top 100 words mentioned in 2000 for the Millennium Development Goals (MDGs) text, nor in 2015 for the Sustainable Development Goals (SDGs) Declaration. Moreover, out of the 169 SDG Targets only one explicitly references land (i.e. Target 15.3) and ascribes the monitoring lead to United Nations Convention to Combat Desertification (UNCCD).

Saving Land

To help better address the asymmetric treatment of land and its degradation challenges and restoration needs, in 2019 the G20 created the Global Land Initiative (GLI) and established a secretariat at the UNCCD HQ in Bonn, Germany. Hence in 2024, the world celebrates three decades of the adoption of UNCCD and fosters greater optimism to achieve the goals of halving degraded lands by 2040 through integrated approaches across jurisdictions, sectors, and institutions. And it seems fitting that we celebrate 30 years of UNCCD given the median period for a human generation around the world is 30 years. In the post-COVID world of greater scrutiny of the fitness-for-purpose and performance of the United Nations, there are repeated calls for greater innovation and more unconventional approaches. Fortunately for the world, with the renewed energy and focus on land that UNCCD and others have brought, it is apt to describe this progress as a truly UN Conventional and inter-generational approach.

Land is the platform that connects all living and non-living things. Without land and for that matter, productive land, humanity and most other life is highly threatened. Even with the advanced technological innovations of humans, we cannot survive merely on satellites orbiting a dead planet. ✦

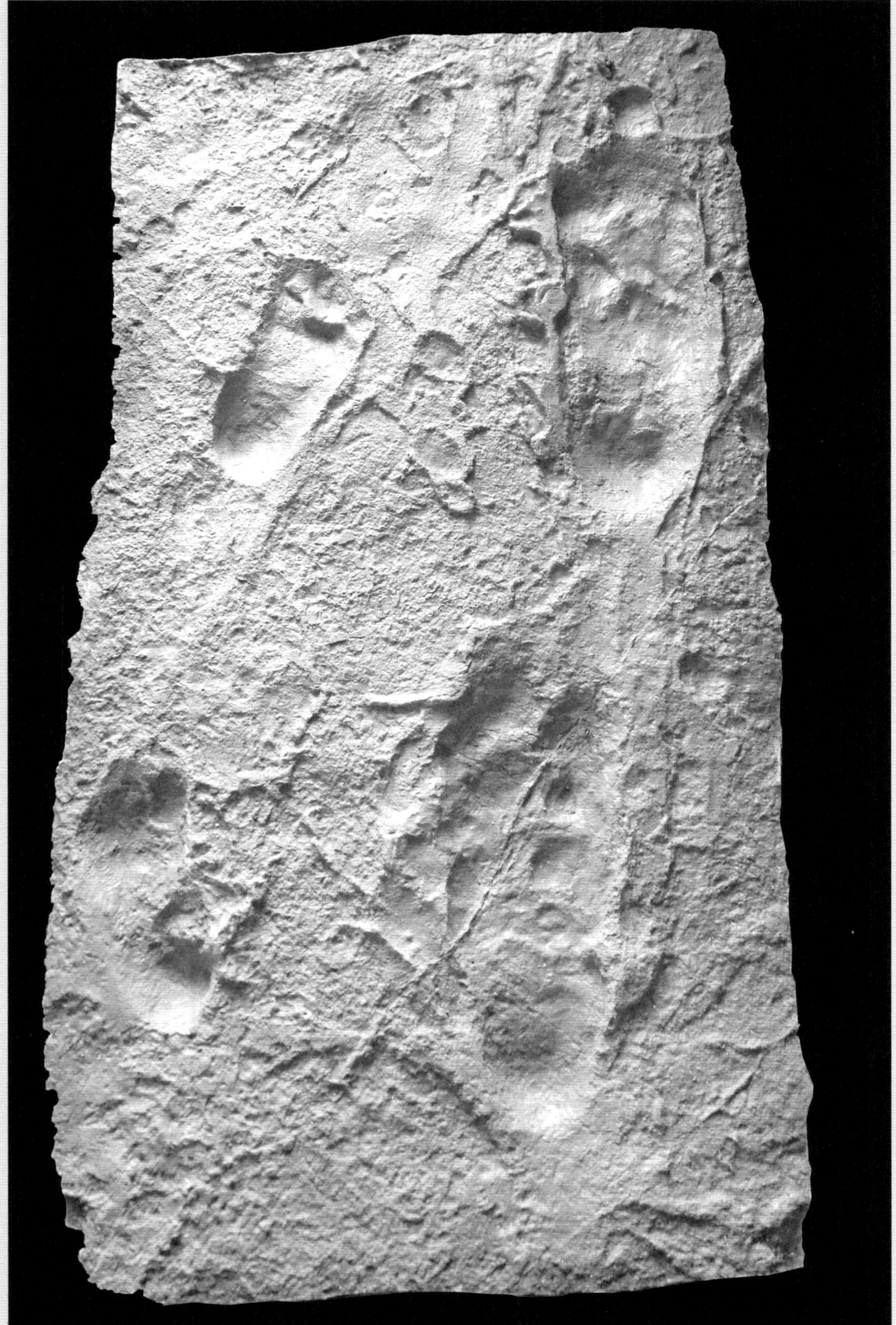

Footprints of *Australopithecus afarensis*, 3.6 million years old, Laetoli, Tanzania; cast: 1990/2000. The footprints, presumably left in the damp ash of an erupting volcano, prove that our ancestors walked upright millions of years ago. *Australopithecus afarensis* is a member of the great ape family. It was slightly larger than a chimpanzee and already walked on its hind legs.

Jan Hostettler, *Feet, over 3,000 km on foot, winter, spring and summer*, 2016/2019. Jan Hostettler cast an imprint of his feet in lead after walking from Basel to Istanbul in 2016. Walking, observing, and collecting is part of his artistic practice.

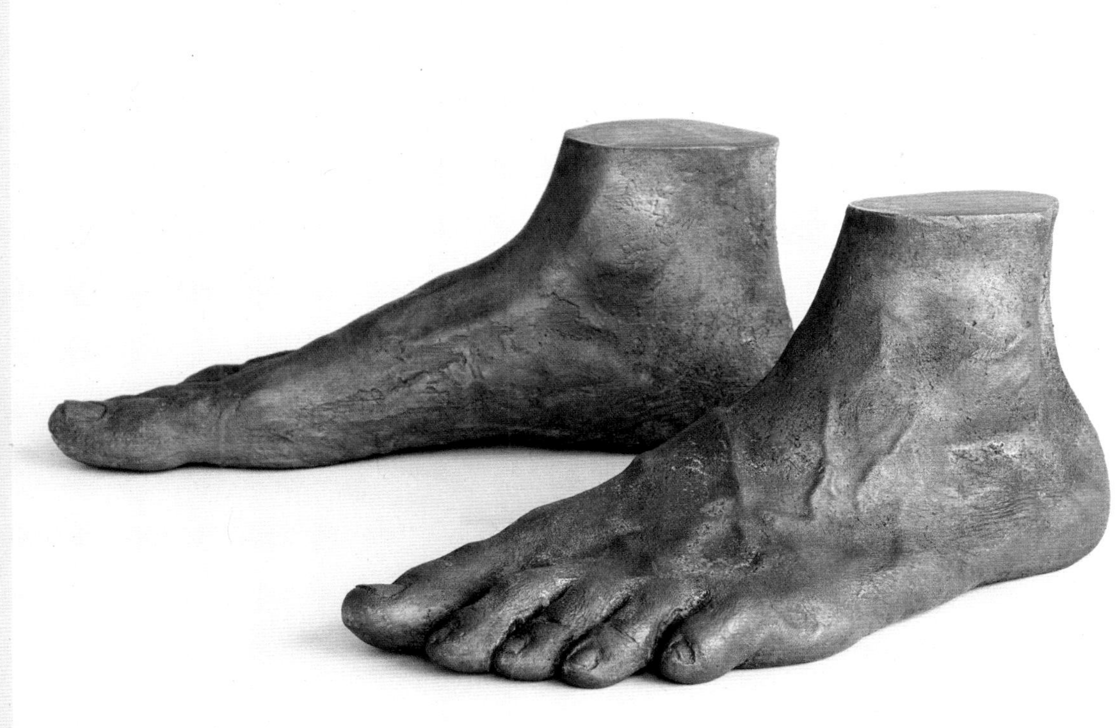

Historical haemoglobin preparation, late 19th century, Tübingen. Haemoglobin, the red blood pigment in humans, and chlorophyll, the leaf green necessary for photosynthesis, are chemically almost identical. The only difference is that chlorophyll has a magnesium molecule at the centre of its chemical structure, whereas haemoglobin has an iron molecule instead.

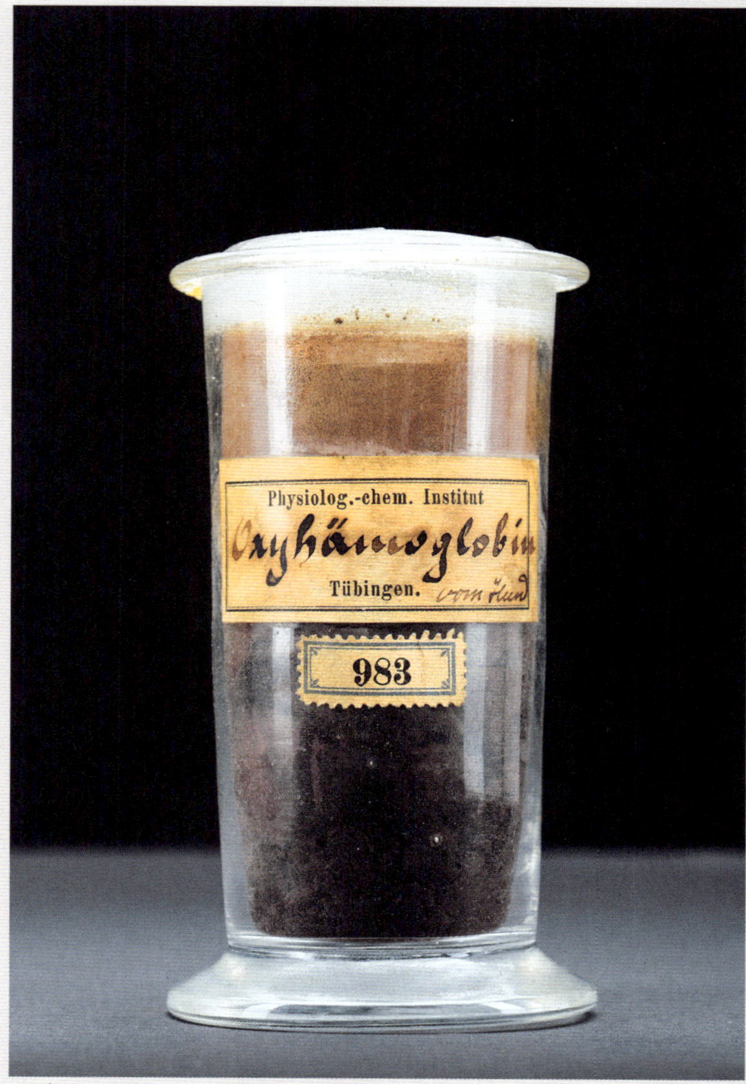

Dr. Scholl's Chlorophyll Foot Powder, 20th century, U.S.A. Due to its structural similarity to human haemoglobin, green chlorophyll attracted the interest of scientists at an early stage and many attest to its positive properties for the human organism. Chlorophyllin is a semi-synthetic chlorophyll that is produced by adding sodium and copper salts. It is used as a food colouring. Chlorophyllin is considered an antioxidant that can reduce the risk of cancer.

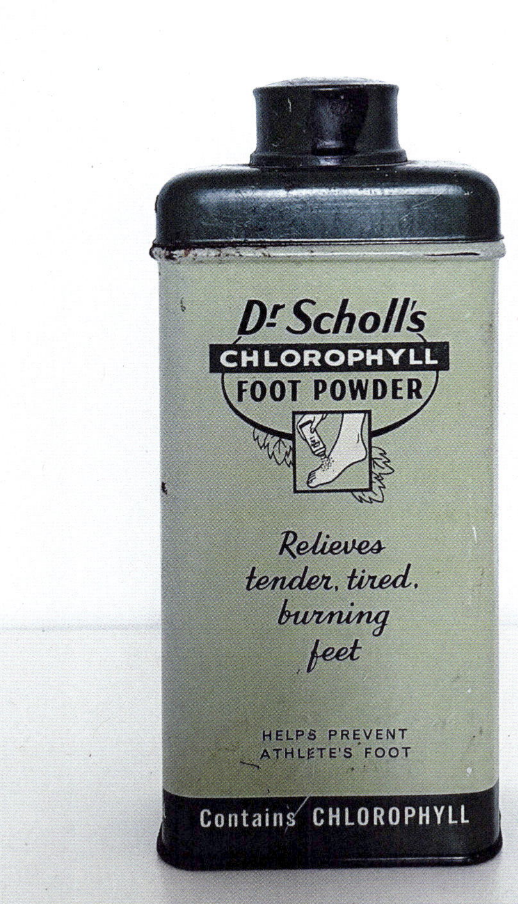

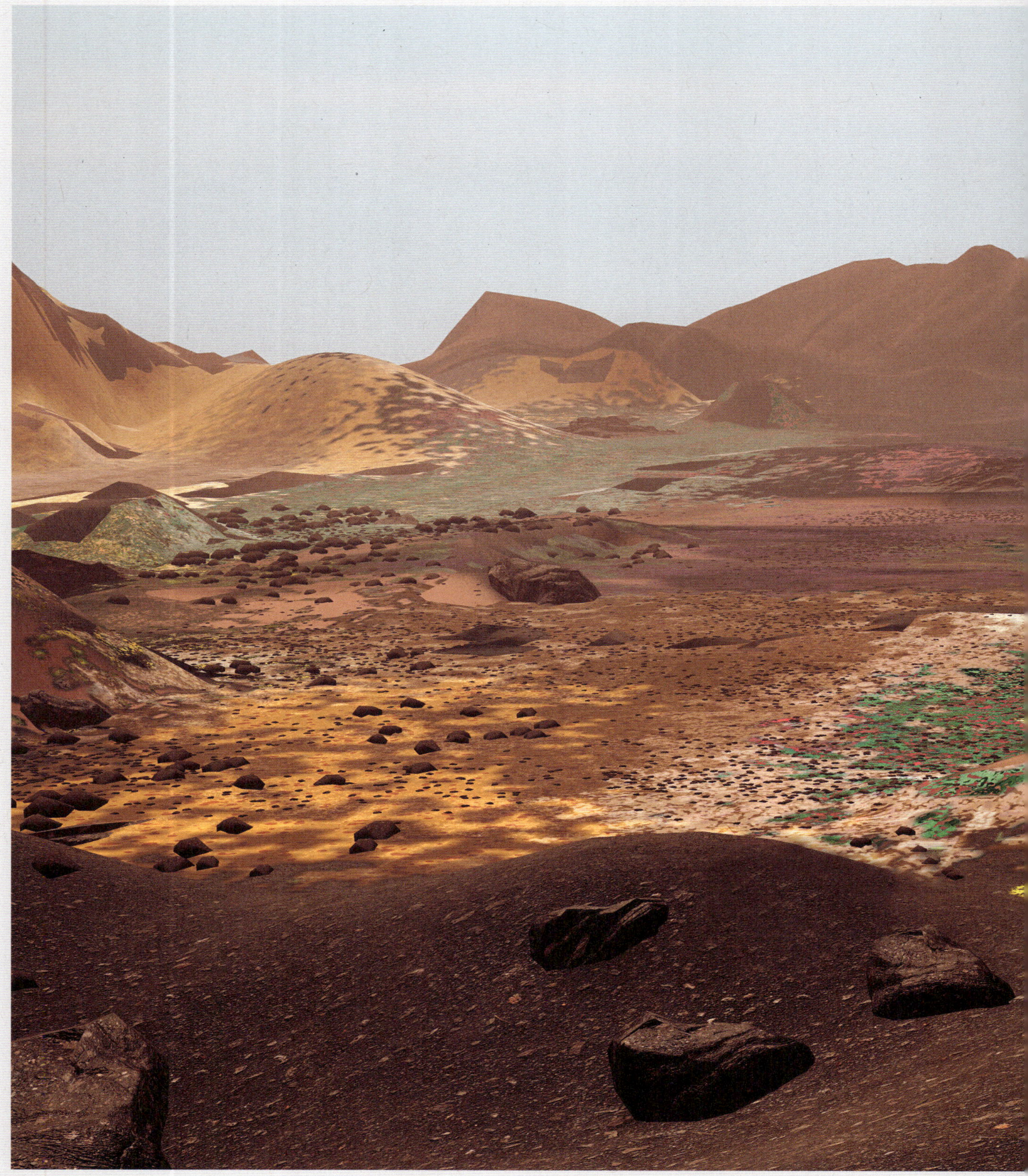

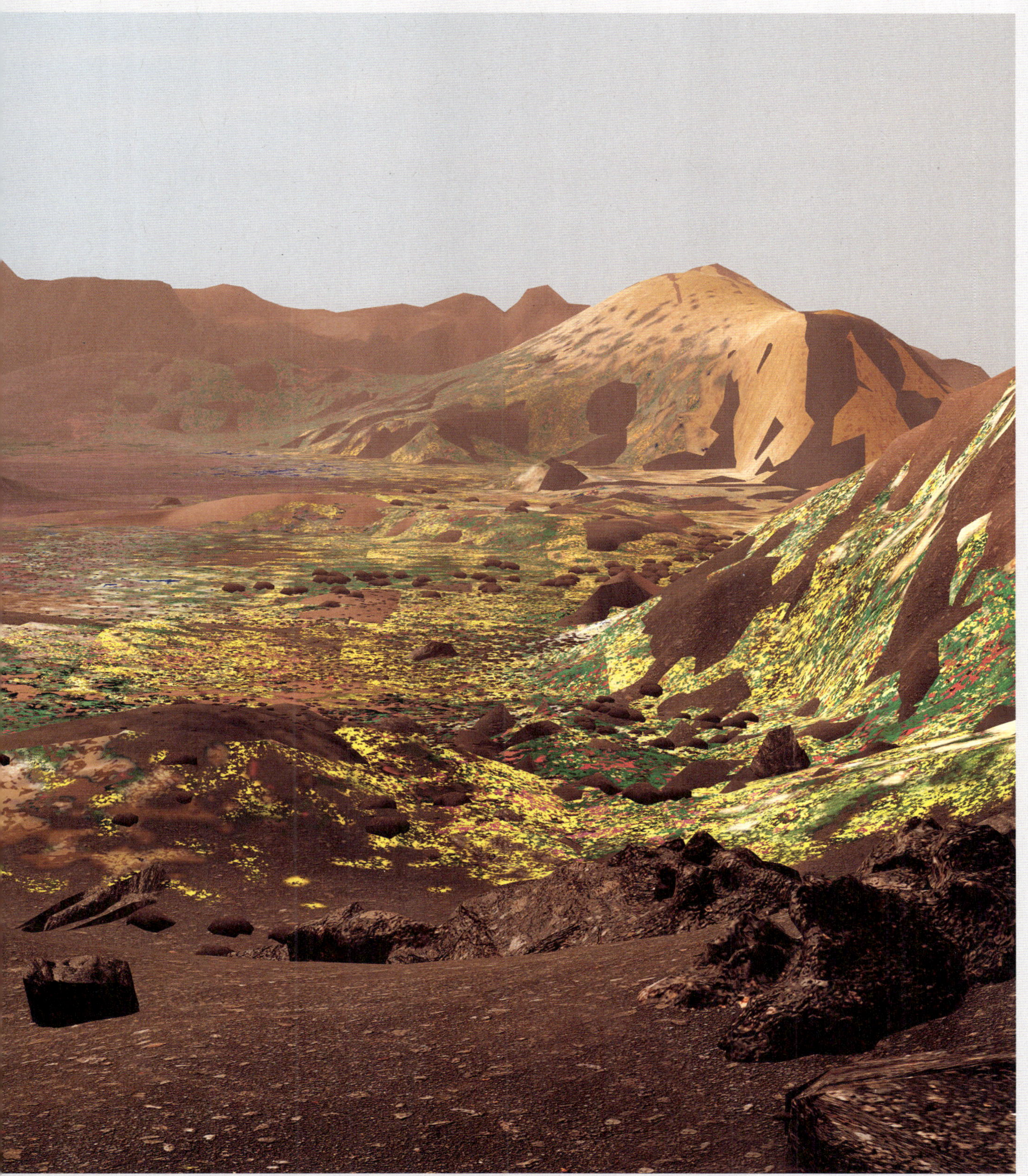

Alexandra Daisy Ginsberg, *The Wilding of Mars*, 2019, 12-channel video installation. We see Mars as just another planet to colonise. Could we instead imagine Mars being colonised only by plants that thrive without us? *The Wilding of Mars* simulates the growth of a planetary wilderness colonised by life forms from Earth. Several simulations run in parallel in the installation; an infinite number of possible worlds emerge, challenging the assumption that the outcome of space colonisation must be beneficial to humans. There are other paths that life could take.

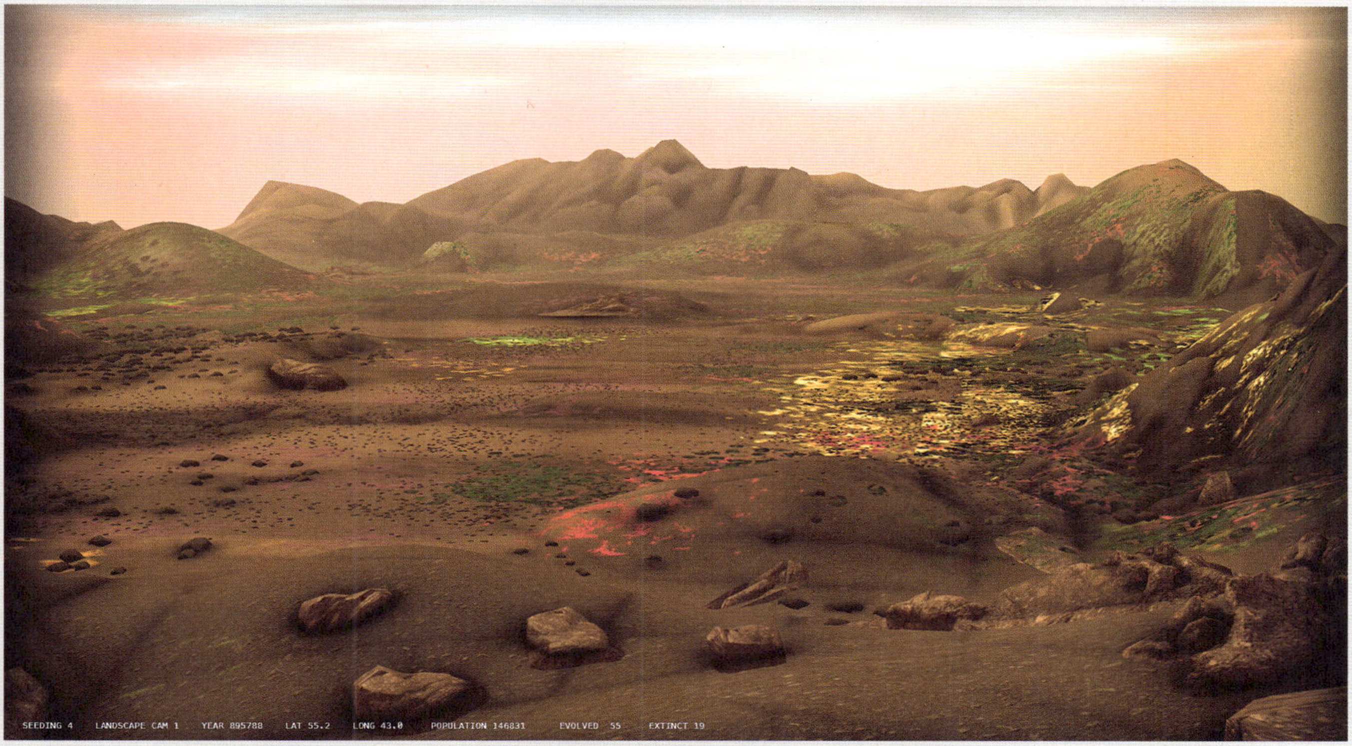

SEEDING 4 LANDSCAPE CAM 1 YEAR 895788 LAT 55.2 LONG 43.0 POPULATION 146831 EVOLVED 55 EXTINCT 19

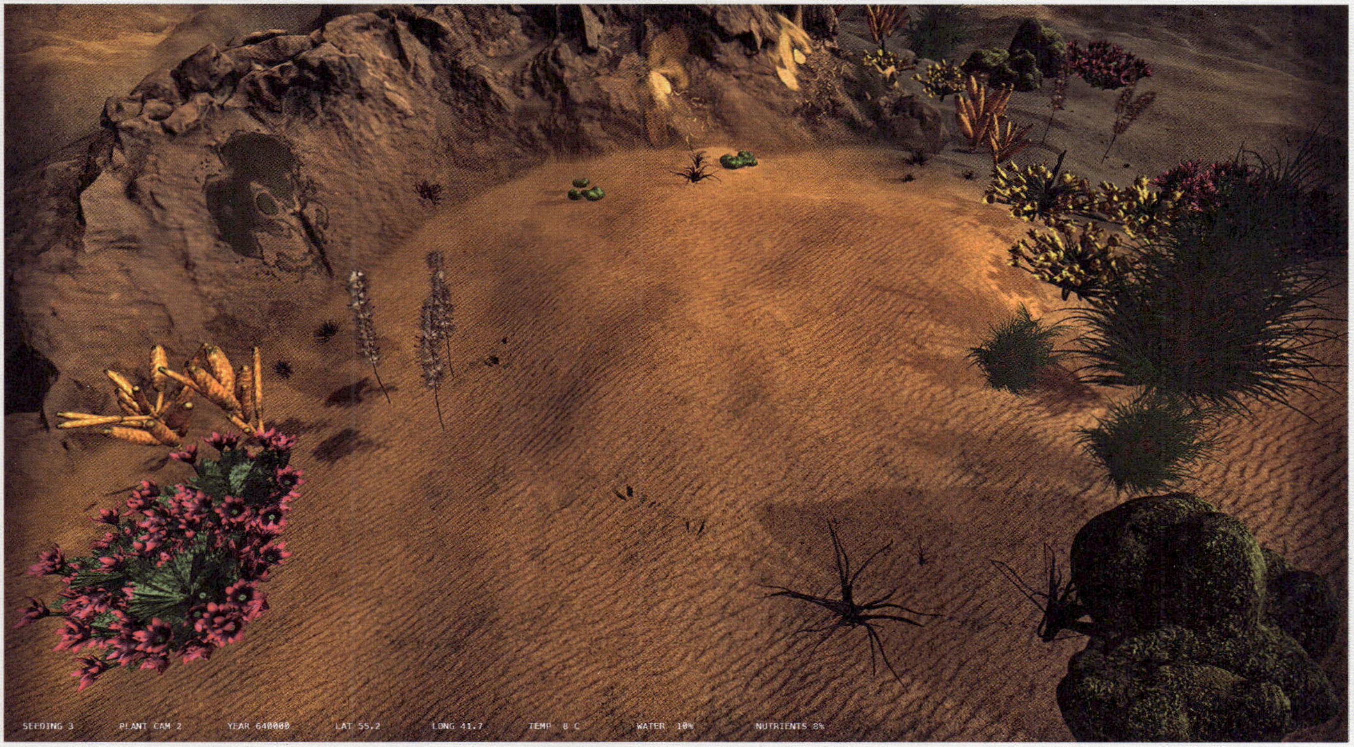

SEEDING 3 PLANT CAM 2 YEAR 640000 LAT 55.2 LONG 41.7 TEMP 8 C WATER 10% NUTRIENTS 8%

Nancy Graves, *Sabine D Region of the Moon, Lunar Orbiter Site 2 P-6, Southwestern Mare Tranquillitatis,* 1972. Using a specially developed dot painting technique, Graves painted the surface of the moon and Mars based on maps and photographic material from NASA. She also incorporated the distortions and image errors in her paintings, which were caused by the complicated process of transferring the photos from space to Earth.

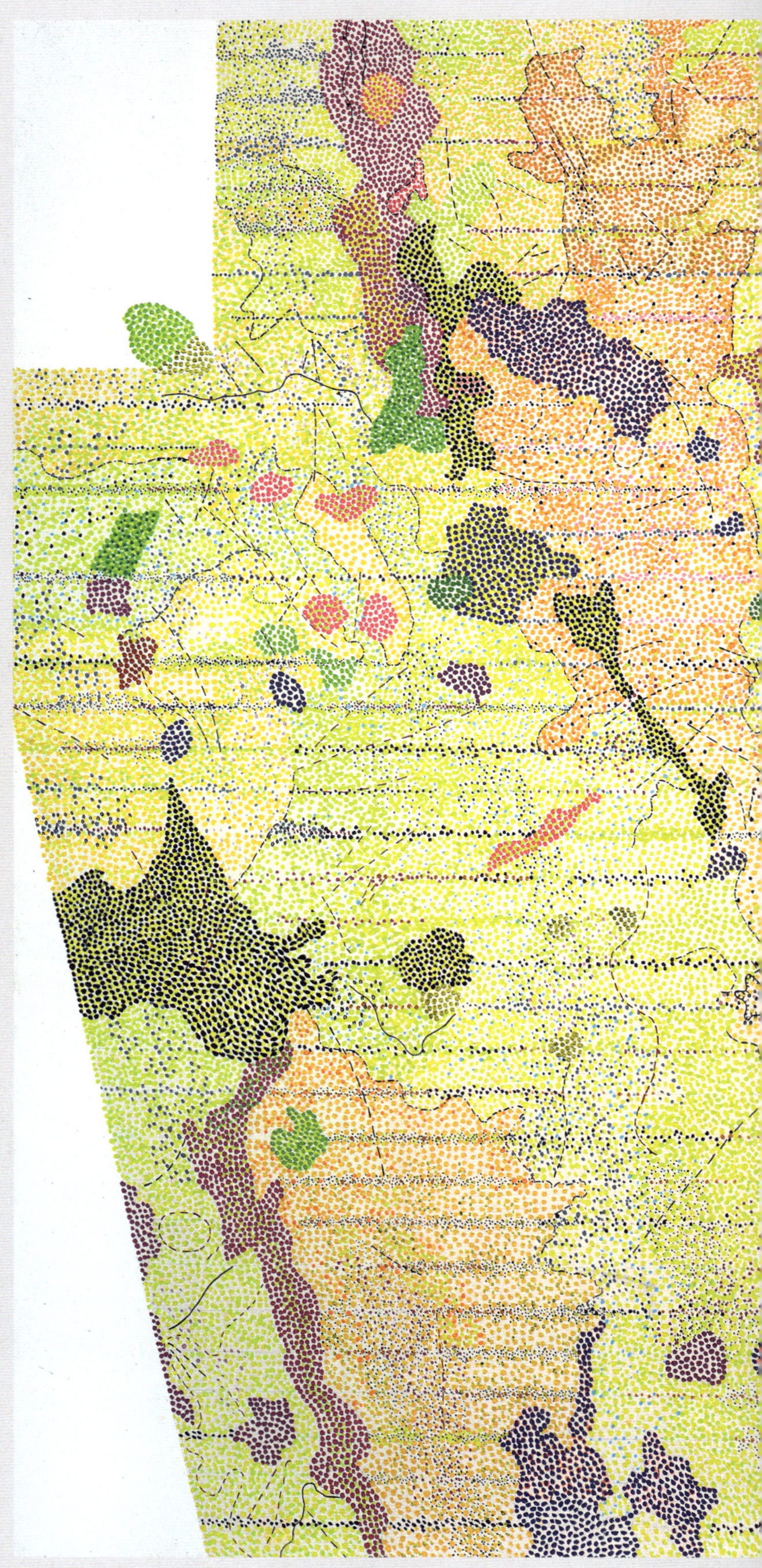

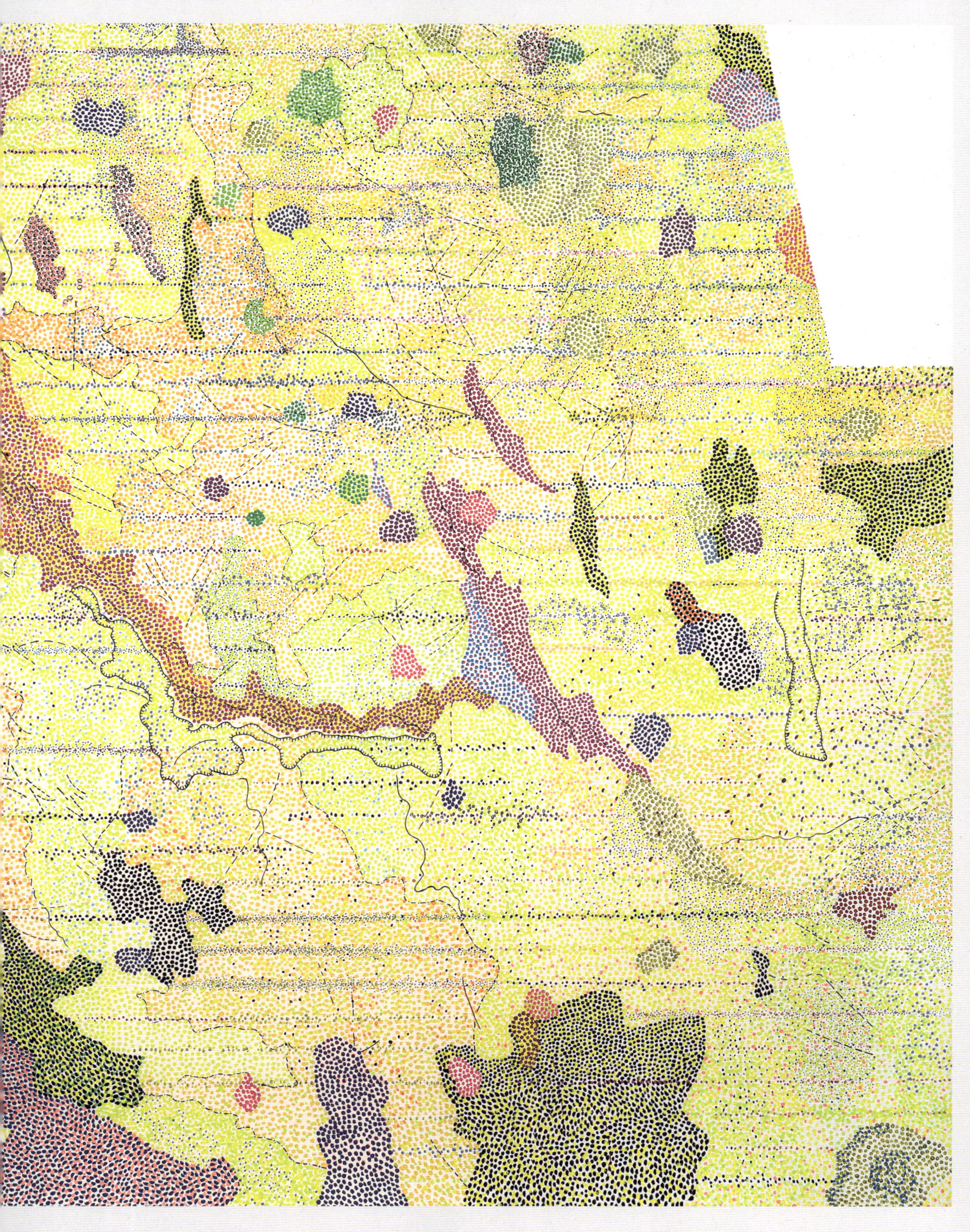

Land Values and Metrics

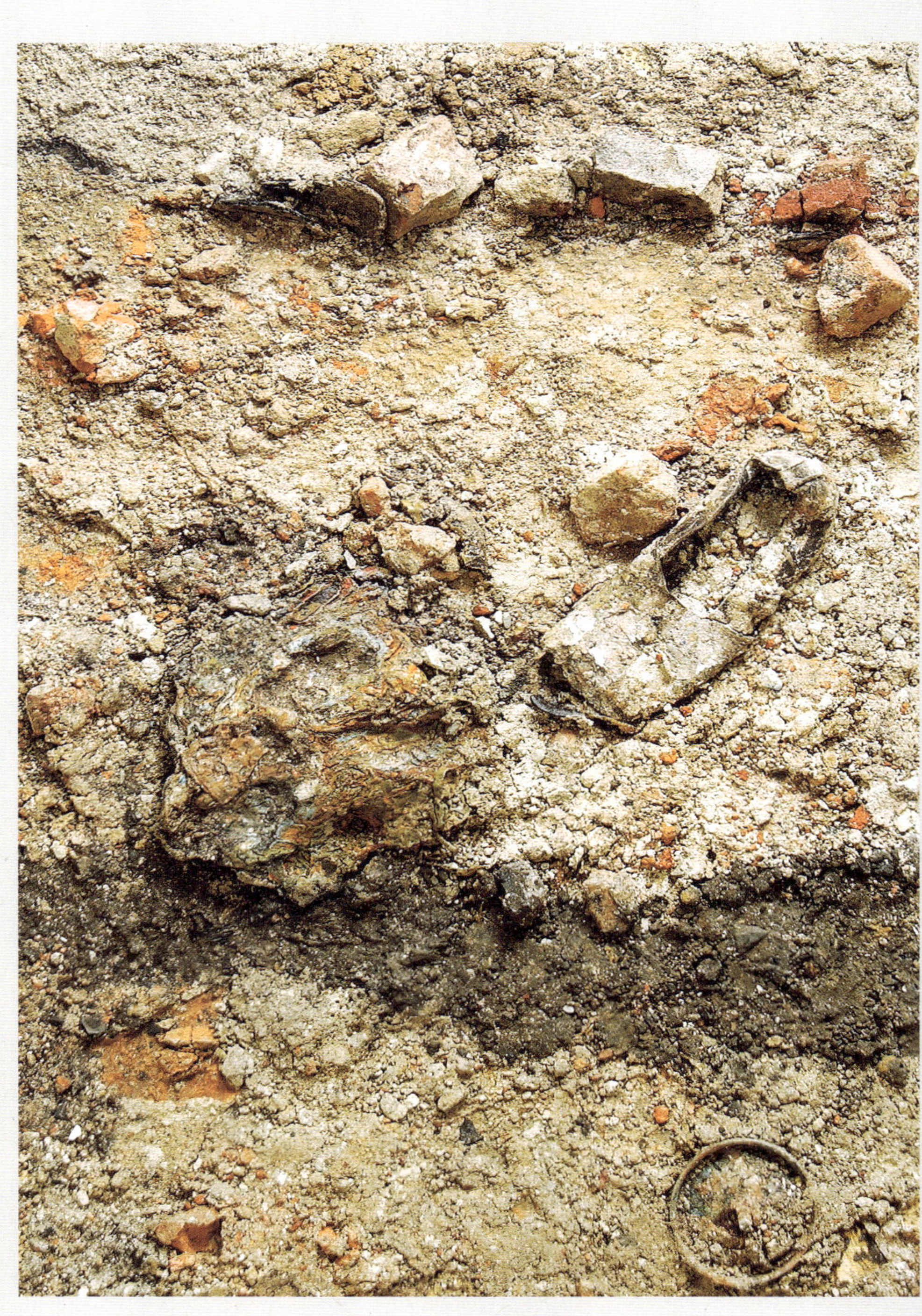

Tony Simons

Urban soil, soil-lacquer profile, Krefeld, Lower Rhine lowlands, Kempen clay plate. Urban soils are often artificially built up. They consist of both natural soil material and technogenic substrate such as building rubble, household waste, slag, and the like. The natural soils of Central Europe are around 12,000 years old.

Introduction

'Location, location, location' is the fundamental maxim of the real estate world. Typically, huge price premiums for property, whether commercial, residential, agricultural, or wilderness, are levied for highly desirable locations. At least such goes the logic for much of the global North where individual land ownership is legally and culturally the norm. That said, in the global North 'price' is what you pay, and it may not equate to what it should necessarily 'cost'. And 'value' is what you actually get or perceive you get. And it is these disconnects between price, cost, and value that explain much of the mismanagement and conflicts of land around the world.

At the other end of the land valuation spectrum, and more routinely associated with Indigenous communities are the concepts of either joint ownership or joint stewardship. And to a few cultures and communities the actual idea of land ownership whether individual or joint is an anathema. Whether derived from cultural norms or belief systems, the option that one individual has domain over one or more pieces of land is unfathomable.

Herein lies a difficulty for the global community as we try to tackle land degradation since there is much variance at the regional, national, and subnational levels when it comes to: ❶ systems of control over land; ❷ land use priorities; and ❸ accountability and responsibility for land-based goods and services. Firstly, land ownership/control might be vested in the state, municipalities, corporations, communities, or individuals. Secondly, few countries have functioning land use frameworks to be able to look at accurately prioritising land uses (urban infrastructure, residential, wetlands, agricultural, forest, amenity, wilderness, etc). And thirdly, land use is notorious in masking both negative and positive externalities and the associated free rider approach – the tragedy of the commons being a clear example.

The variance of land issues at the regional, national, subnational, and local levels mentioned above, however, is as much an opportunity as it is a difficulty. Areas of land that are contiguous and heterogenous provide greater abilities for resilience and coping with natural climate and biogeochemical change. However, viewing the issue through a single lens of economics is a huge problem. When it comes to land one size does not fit all.

Land Values and Valuations

Land valuations have been undertaken around the world for millennia in both urban and rural settings. The primary purpose of such valuations was for authorities (kingdoms, empires, feudal) to be able to tax land holdings under the assumption that those who held land also held the greatest wealth. The two main approaches were: ❶ a land value tax; or ❷ a buildings tax. The former was considered a progressive approach as it taxed wealthier people whereas the latter could make heavy burdens on often poor tenants.

There is no single agreed land valuation method and inherently all commonly used approaches are subjective. The main valuation techniques deployed include:

A Comparative market analysis – comparing similar properties nearby;
B Cost Approach – calculating cost of replacing or restoring the property;
C Income Approach – assessing the income generating potential of investment properties;
D Residual Method – looks at the present value of future benefits of the land;
E Capitalisation Method – examines net income and costs in commercial properties;
F Market Valuation – considers sales history of a specific property;
G Allocation Method – looks at relationship of value of land to all property components.

Importantly, from social and political viewpoints land values do not equate to land valuations. For several decades within the context of globalisation, policy makers have expressed strong interest in the environmental goods and services being associated with land value. Although historically these environmental goods and services were seen as largely public goods that were nonrivalrous and non-excludable in nature, a major shift came when they were perceived as a new growth sector (public and private), with dual purposes of: ❶ generating wealth and creating jobs; and ❷ transitioning economies towards more sustainable development.

During 2001–2005, the World Summit on Sustainable Development (WSSD) and the Millennium Ecosystem Assessment (MA) further elevated the recognition of ecosystems services in policy, management, and science institutions. For more than 20 years since the MA, ecosystem services have been mainly a lens for legislation, investment prospecting, and communicating the human dimensions of ecological change. Most of the standards, coding systems, developments, and research literature have focused predominantly on biophysical aspects and monetary valuations and only recently have the International Panel on Biodiversity and Ecosystem Services (IPBES) and others elevated the non-material values and benefits of its ecosystem services.

Human Impacts on Land Distribution and Values

Problems of land conquest, land ownership, land use conflicts, and land degradation are somewhat recent in human history and likely minimal before the start of cities and the advent of agriculture around 12,000 years ago. Human population size and local density would have been the original driving force for such problems. Archeological evidence from 80,000 years ago exists for individual clashes between *Homo sapiens* migrating out of Africa and encountering *Homo neanderthalensis* in Eurasia. However, many now believe the Neanderthals went extinct about 40,000 years ago not because of widespread conflict over land or resources but because they were outbred by a larger gene pool. The first recorded human war fought over land is reputed to be 4,700 years ago in Mesopotamia when the entire human population was only around 5 million persons in total.

Although the Anthropocene is not formally accepted as a geological epoch, for many decades it has been part of a common understanding that humans are shaping our planet in a way that will be reflected in future geological records. There is also no universally agreed starting point to the Anthropocene but many credit the 1940s and 1950s as the most common beginning following nuclear explosions and the so-called Great Acceleration. The Great Acceleration is that phenomenon related to dramatic increases in global population growth, unchecked pollution, and unsustainable exploitation of natural resources. Whatever the starting time of the Anthropocene, humanity's unchecked extraction, unsustainable use, and disregard for nature are based on two things: appreciation and prioritisation. We under-value and under-price land and nature, and we under-fund the management and protection of valuable natural assets. Humanity has privatised profits and socialised costs.

According to some estate agencies, the total value of the world's property in 2022 was almost 400 trillion dollars or four times Global GDP. Notwithstanding some likely COVID-related declines, this represented almost a 20 % rise over three years. This is not homogenous across land categories though and some data gaps exist. Notwithstanding such constraints, more than 75 % of the value in land and property is ascribed to residential property, whereas commercial property accounts for around 13 %, and agricultural land represents 11 % of value. Others cite much higher figures including the Yale University professor of astronomy, Michael Laughlin, who calculates the entire value of the Earth's land and resources at 5 quadrillion (i.e. 5×10^{15}) dollars.

Free market theory suggests that land and other assets would be allocated to increase total productivity. However, in practice many 'landholding' and 'landowning' actors have disproportionate influence and seek to control land to maximise their profit from tenants or subsidies from the state. Such behaviour then further exacerbates land concentration in the hands of a few in both the global North and the global South. For several decades the World Bank and others have monitored the concentration of land ownership in countries around the world. According to Eurostat, only 3.6 % of agricultural holdings in the European Union are greater than 100 hectares in size but disproportionately they cover more than half (52.5 %) the area of all agricultural land. And according to the International Panel of Experts on Sustainable Food Systems (IPES), globally 1 % of farms control 70 % of farmland with significant regional variations.

Reconciling Land Values and their Attributes

Halting and reversing land degradation is one of the most pressing challenges of our time – we need to transition heavily to delivering on restoring land in all ecosystems while monitoring closely and reporting widely on the trends in land degradation. Moreover, land restoration cannot be done in isolation of challenges to biodiversity loss and anthropogenic induced climate change. It is clear that there is not just a disconnect between price, cost, and value of land but a totally inadequate conceptualisation of value. With respect to land, whether urban, rural, or natural habitat settings, we generally under-value and under-support (financial and non-financial) land protection, land restoration, and prevention of land degradation.

Perhaps the most constraining circumstance we have when trying to value land is the consideration of not only economic values but also ecological values, socio-cultural values, intrinsic values, and service provisioning values. These are as applicable to rural land and land use as they are to urban geographies, and also in wilderness settings where economic value is typically equated only to the value of extracted resources.

To help achieve land restoration and to be able to incorporate both negative externalities and positive externalities in real, accurate, and workable land values and valuations, a framework is needed to combine all of these dimensions as well as simultaneously model them, undertake sensitivity analyses and examine trade-offs. Given the huge heterogeneity in land and local contexts of it, different parameters can be weighted differently but the main aim is to be able to look at synergies, trade-offs, and antagonisms. A framework is suggested in the table below which includes a typology of five main land value dimensions, namely:

A economic value;
B ecological value;
C socio-cultural value;
D ecosystem functions, goods and services provision value; and
E intrinsic value.

It may be easier to get broad agreement on the typology than to identify those few indicators with highest information value and which have a high co-variance to positive impact. It is suggested to prioritise such indicators and limit them to a maximum of two indicators per attribute.

It is becoming clear that we can no longer consider the value of land as space at a location, as conceptualised solely by urban rent theory. Rather, new ideas are needed considering the bundle of neighbourhood, environmental qualities, and local public goods that the land incorporates. Previously most land valuations have been done looking to the past whereas given the extent of land degradation that we have, and the need for urgent action, we globally need to be more forward looking and setting meaningful, achievable and binding goals. Learning from our errors with climate change and carbon emissions that we thought we could fix solely with Nationally Determined Contributions (NDCs), it is imperative that we combine important NDCs with Corporate and Individual Contributions (i.e. CDCs and IDCs) when it comes to land.

Land is that multi-dimensional platform that connects all living and non-living things. And if we value life then we need to value land much higher than we currently do. ✦

A Economic Value	B Ecological Value	C Socio-culture Values
The real and perceived asset values of the land, its earning potential and associated resources	The make-up, patterns, abundance and health of the living and non-living natural elements of the land	Spiritual and cultural benefits, use/ownership dimensions of land incl. resources present and extracted.
A1. Income	**B1. Diversity**	**C1. Identity**
A2. Infrastructure	**B2. Intactness**	**C2. Security/Justice**
A3. Market	**B3. Threats**	**C3. Living with Nature**
Indic. A1.1 Indic. A1.2	Indic. B1.1 Indic. B1.2	Indic. C1.1 Indic. C1.2
Indic. A2.1 Indic. A2.2	Indic. B2.1 Indic. B2.2	Indic. C2.1 Indic. C2.2
Indic. A3.1 Indic. A3.2	Indic. B3.1 Indic. B3.2	Indic. C3.1 Indic. C3.2

D Services Value	E Intrinsic Value
Provision of individual and bundled ecosystem goods/services to the land and off-site actors/locations	Extent, geo-location, local context, supply amenities/utilities, and any financial/legal encumbrances or conditions
D1. ES Function	**E1. Size**
D2. ES Goods	**E2. Proximities**
D3. ES Services	**E3. Resources**
Indic. D1.1 Indic. D1.2	Indic. E1.1 Indic. E1.2
Indic. D2.1 Indic. D2.2	Indic. E2.1 Indic. E2.2
Indic. D3.1 Indic. D3.2	Indic. E3.1 Indic. E3.2

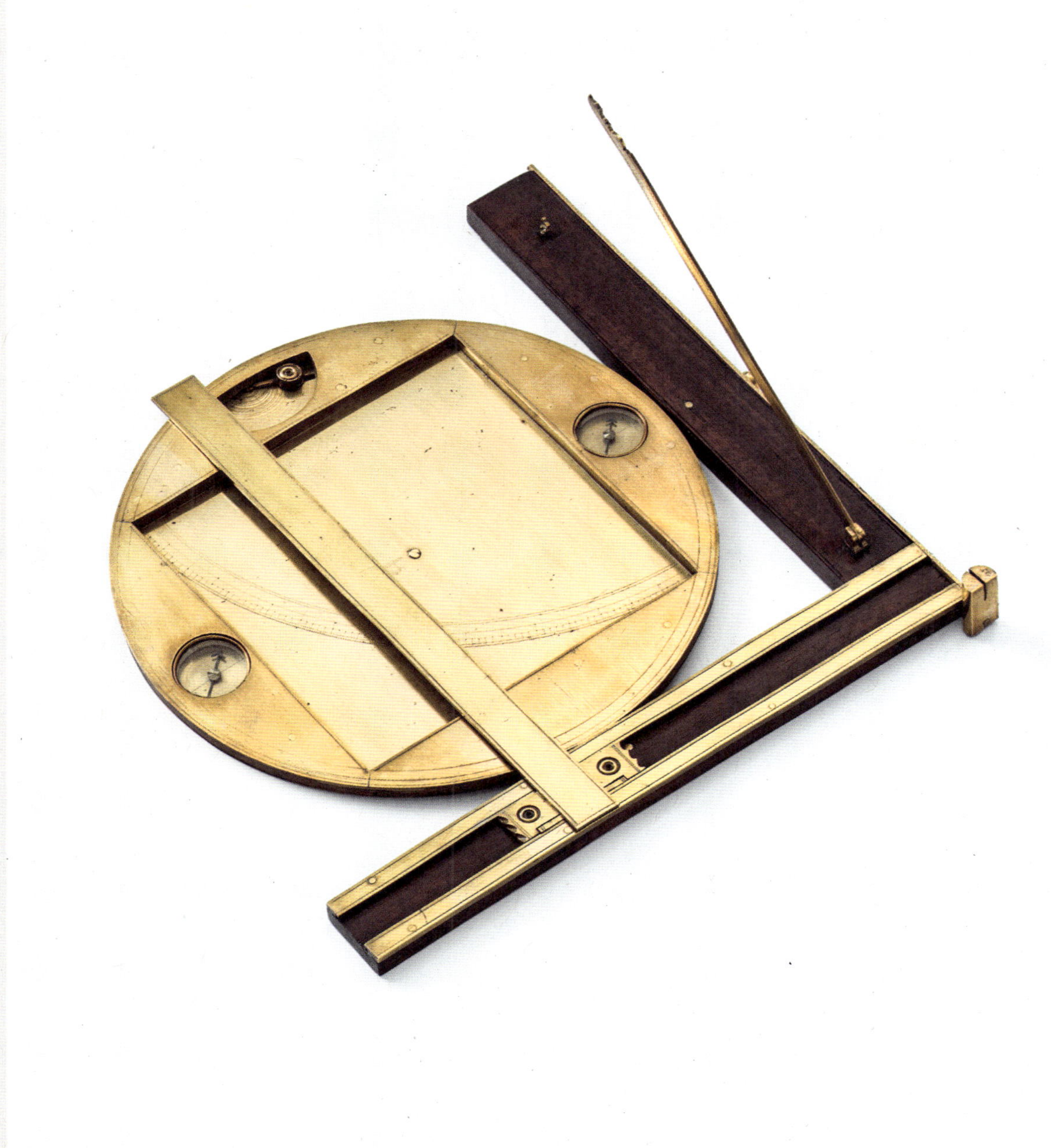

Athanasius Kircher (1602–1680), Pantometrum Kircherianum, 2nd half of the 17th century. The three precious measuring instruments from the Landesmuseum Württemberg, Stuttgart, date from the 17th century, when the demand for accurate maps increased. On the one hand, this meant maps for voyages of discovery and trade, but also increasingly the marking out of land and property boundaries and the localisation of mineral resources and timber deposits. The Pantometrum Kircherianum made it possible to calculate distances across the terrain.

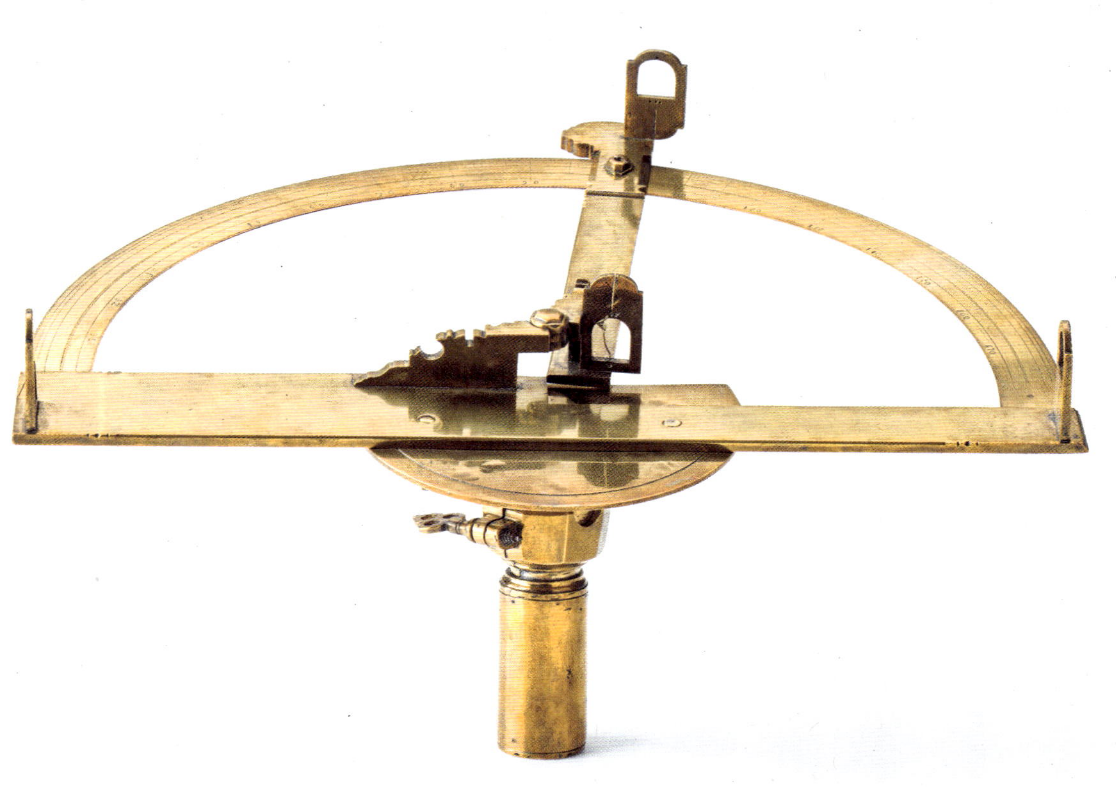

Half disc instrument (graphometer), 17th century. This graphometer consists of a semi-circular ring attached to a central bar. It has two sighting discs with a slit and a thread sight at both ends. The semi-circular ring has an angle scale from 0° to 180° in 1° increments. The angular distance between two points on a terrain can be measured with the aid of the sighting device and the scale.

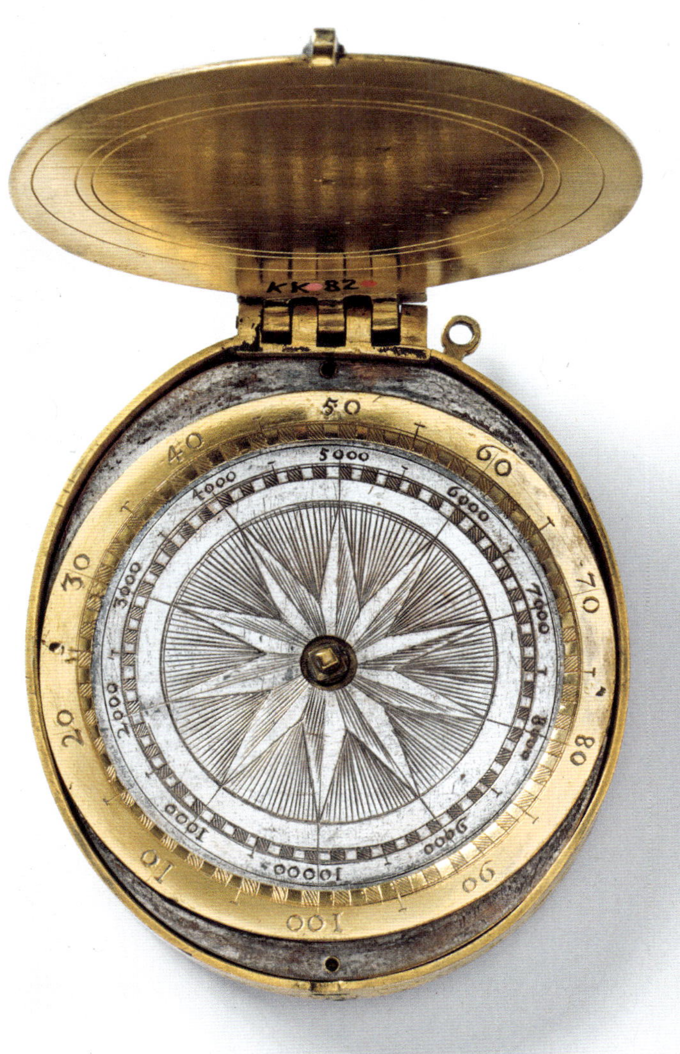

Pedometer in the shape of a pocket watch, 17th century. While pedometers are used by athletes today to monitor their performance, in the 17th century these instruments were innovative tools for measuring distances travelled. Once the average stride length had been set, the pedometer was attached to the subject's body with a tension connection to the leg. The knowledge gained about the actual distances that traders, country messengers, and travellers had to cover played an important role in the economic development of a region.

Richard Long, *Bluestone Circle*, 1978. The British artist Richard Long is one of the most prominent representatives of Land Art. Beginning in the 1960s, artists created ephemeral works in nature and documented them in photographs and maps or brought the materials from nature into galleries. A repeated work by Richard Long is the 'Stone Circle', which is composed of different types of stone to create various formations. These installations create a connection between landscape and people. The artwork shown here is from the collection of the Stedelijk Museum Amsterdam.

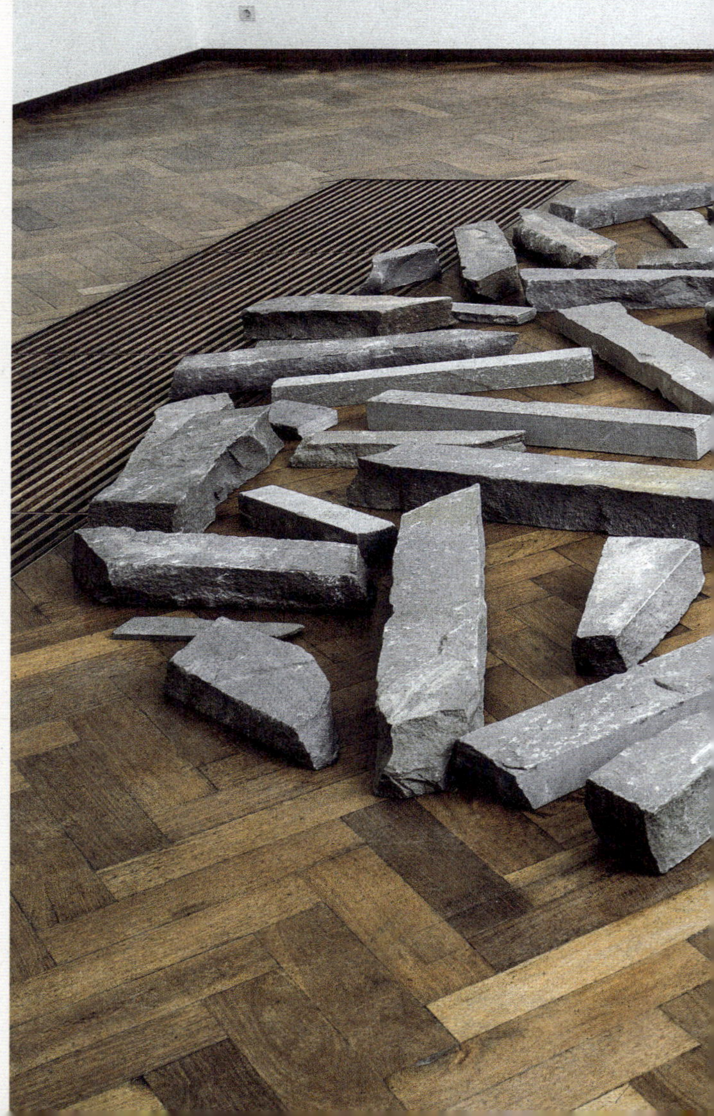

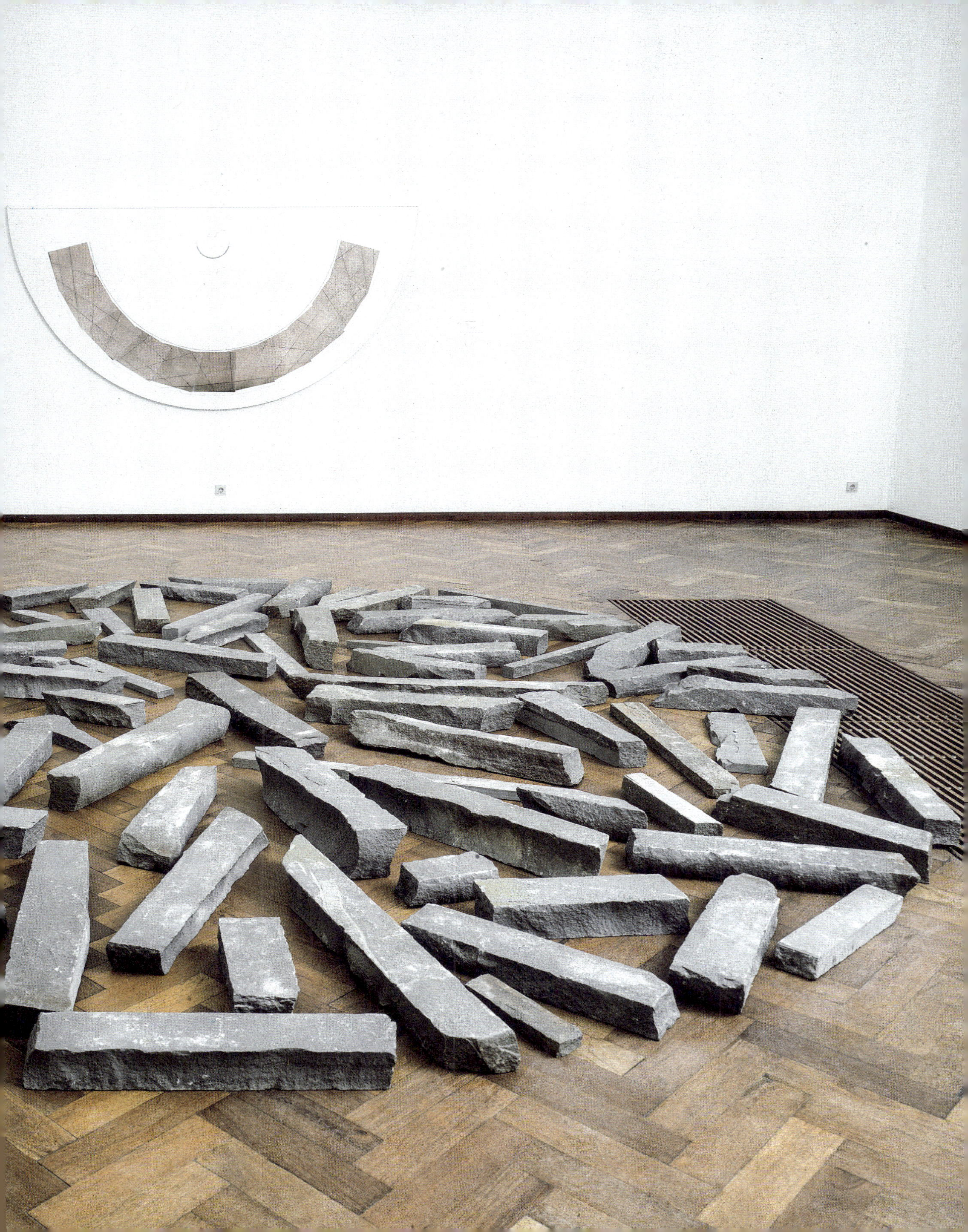

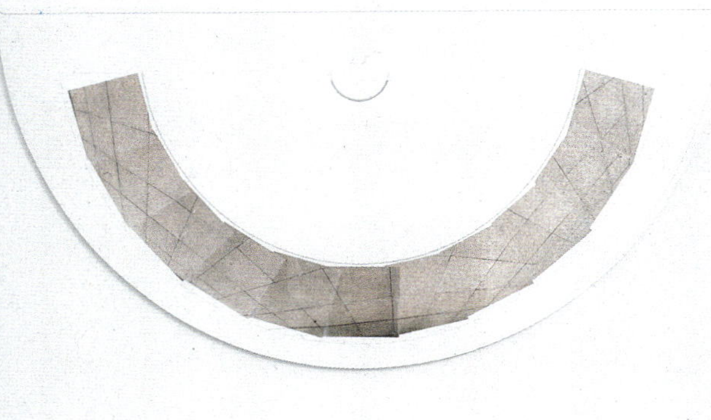

‘Even the Smallest Crumb of Soil is a World of its Own’

Susanne Wedlich

We and all life on the planet depend on the soil. If it works as an ecosystem, in short: if it is healthy. An encounter with the strange universe beneath our feet, its complex architecture, and uniquely diverse inhabitants.

On 14 February 1990, an iconic photograph was made. The Voyager 1 space probe was on its way into space and a good six billion kilometres away. One more time, it turned its view back for a series of photos: 'family portraits' of our solar system. One famous image continues to shape how we see ourselves to this day. It shows scattered rays of sunlight against a dark background – with a tiny pale blue dot. This pale blue dot is our home planet.

The planet shimmers blue because of the water that covers around two thirds of its surface. Nevertheless, we do not live on *Aqua* or *Ozeania*. Our planet is named after the ground beneath our feet: Earth.

Soil is an essential player in global cycles. It stores and purifies water. It recycles nutrients such as nitrogen, potassium, and phosphorus. It binds enormous amounts of carbon, which helps to combat the climate crisis. Its wealth of species is uniquely diverse. Last but not least, it enables plants to grow, without which we could not survive. More than 90 % of the world's food production depends on soil.

Tunnel Vision

Nevertheless, we know little of its complexity. We allow ourselves a kind of tunnel vision when it comes to the earth. Humans and their needs take centre stage. This reduces soil to its function and measures its quality purely in terms of yields. Fertilisers, insecticides, and heavy agricultural machinery are used without regard to losses – even if such activity damages the soil in the long term.

'It is not sufficient to investigate the effects of one pesticide in the soil if ten toxic substances are interacting there,' says soil scientist Matthias C. Rillig from the Free University of Berlin. 'We are lucky that the soil can withstand so much. You have to really make an effort to damage it so much that it no longer functions. It is highly resilient, but of course it has limits.'

Pale Blue Dot: Photo of the Earth taken by the Voyager 1 space probe, 14 February 1990.

There are probably no natural soils left in the world. All of them have been altered: depleted, over-fertilised, or contaminated with pollutants such as heavy metals, microplastics, and so-called forever chemicals.

Environmental Crises and Rising Demand

The climate crisis is now also affecting the soil with high temperatures and a disturbed water balance. This is accompanied by a dramatic loss of species, which certainly also impacts the soil – even if we can hardly estimate the extent. Everything is in flux and at the same time a growing global population needs to be fed in the future.

It is encouraging that the importance of soil for us and life on Earth is receiving increasing attention from scientists, politicians, and the public. It helps that modern soil science aims to decipher the ecosystem using new methods and approaches, at least as far as this is possible.

One thing is beyond question: we need the soil. It needs us. And time is running out. So what makes a good and healthy soil?

'Until now, soil has been considered good if crops thrive on it,' says Rillig. 'There is now a relatively new and broader concept of soil health in science, but it has yet to become established. We also look at criteria such as the absence of pollutants and a high level of biodiversity.'

A Finite Resource

The crust is the thin skin of our planet. This is where all the spheres overlap. The lithosphere provides rocks and minerals. Water comes from the hydrosphere and the atmosphere supplies air. A dead mixture that only comes to life with the help of another agent: the biosphere with inhabitants of the soil ranging from bacteria to mammals.

Almost like flour, salt, and water only become bread dough when yeast is added – and the ingredients become active.

The land can also be told in plain and prosaic figures. The surface of the planet measures just under 510 million square kilometres, 71 % of which is covered by water. Excluding deserts, forests, ice, and lakes, around a quarter of the Earth's surface is used for agriculture. However, a large proportion of this is pastureland.

Another figure: land is a finite and dwindling resource. Every year, an estimated ten million hectares of arable land or 24 billion tonnes of soil are lost worldwide.

But damage is often difficult or impossible to repair and losses can be irrecoverable. 'Good soil can be lost in a short space of time due to erosion and other disturbances,' says Rillig. 'It takes a very long time to rebuild it. For some types of soil, the process can take several thousand years.'

Mole. By burrowing in the soil, subterranean moles play a key role in soil formation. They contribute to the mixing and aeration of the humus-rich upper layer. Their loosening influence on the soil structure also encourages plant growth. Numerous other animals benefit from the burrows created by moles.

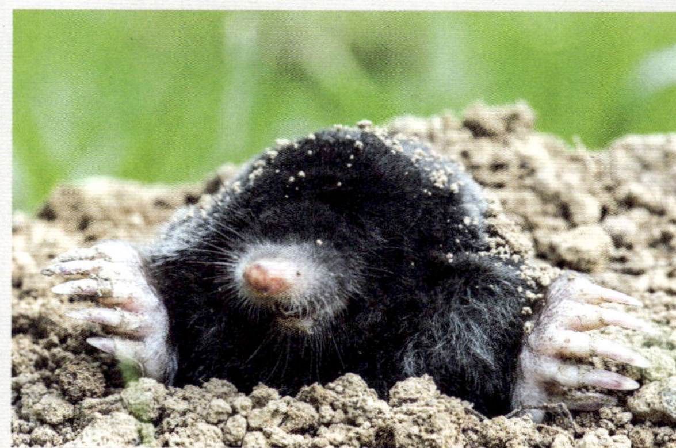

Woodlouse. Millions of animals and microorganisms live in the soil. If you were to collect and weigh all the living creatures from one hectare of farmland, you would arrive at a weight of up to 5 tonnes.

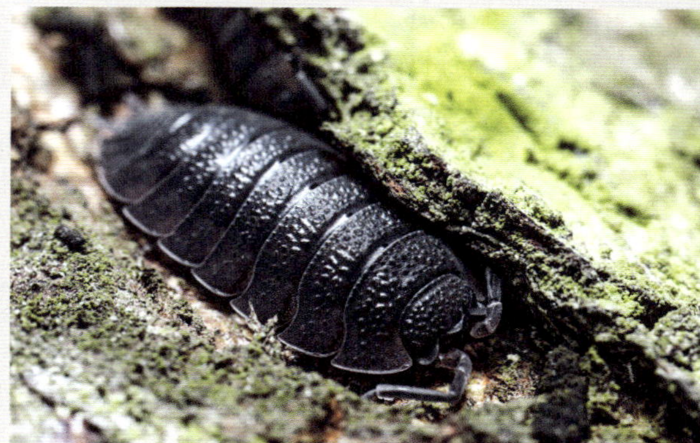

Between Sieve and Storage

This has something to do with the texture of soil. Soil is often thought about in layers, so-called horizons. Although there are no fixed boundaries here, the topsoil is enriched with a significant amount of organic material, while further down there is more mineral content.

Generally weathered and fragmented rock is the basis of any soil. Its fertility depends on many factors, including the type of rock and, crucially, the size of the particles. Gravel is too large-pored and sandy soils can allow water and nutrients to pass through so quickly that plants struggle to grow. Tiny clay particles, on the other hand, swell upon contact with water, but do not always readily release it to the vegetation.

Silt, with particle sizes between two and a good sixty micrometres, hits the golden mean. It binds water, but thirsty plants can still retrieve it. Almost all soils are mixtures, and clay soil can have a balanced and therefore fertile composition. It contains sand for good aeration and permeability, clay as a nutrient reservoir, and silt for water retention.

Living Architecture

But even a perfect mixture does not make a true soil. Its smallest functional units are aggregates of mineral particles: crumbs of earth that are as stable as possible. If they disintegrate, the soil cannot withstand erosion by rain, wind, and water. Precious topsoil is then lost. Flooding and landslides threaten us and our infrastructure. The water quality of rivers and other bodies of water can also suffer from the influx of soil particles.

'Soil is not a maximally dense mass, but is permeated by free spaces,' says Rillig. 'I imagine it as an incredibly multi-layered inner surface. Its structure is the stage on which life occurs in this ecosystem and works on the three-dimensional architecture of its own habitat.'

Land as a Multinational State

The cement for the necessary strong bond is provided by the edaphon – the totality of all the organisms that live on and in the soil. They creep, crawl, dig, tunnel, swim, burrow, or are otherwise involved in underground construction. But we only know a few of them. These include bacteria, amoebae, fungi, and other microorganisms, arthropods such as insects, mites, and springtails, as well as earthworms and related species and mammals such as moles.

According to a study from 2023, soil as a habitat could contain up to 59 % of the world's total species richness. With 430 million species, it also contains half of all bacteria and, with 5.6 million species, up to 90 % of fungi. Because not every single species can be tracked down, identified and counted, the actual numbers could be significantly lower – or possibly even higher. 'It's just an estimate,' says Rillig. 'But the study is very good and the order of magnitude is definitely astonishing.'

Another figure: a single gram of soil can contain an estimated one billion microbes.

Numbers alone are not decisive. The crucial thing is how soil functions in the ecosystem. Its inhabitants help to produce our food, recycle organic material, and could even provide new medical agents such as antibiotics. They also bind enormous amounts of carbon as organic matter. Soil is considered the largest carbon store in the world. However, all of this only works if diverse life is preserved in the soil and can hold the earth together.

Why Sticky Mucus Is So Important

An extreme habitat. It is dark, which is why many underground dwellers are colourless, translucent, and without eyes. It is silent because communication takes place via chemical signals and along gradients: away from deterrent and toxic substances and towards nutrients. It is damp or wet and progress is difficult.

This is one reason why plant roots have slimy tips that can penetrate the soil more easily. Much like earthworms, which are slippery thanks to their coating of mucus. Or the fungal threads that densely permeate good soil and also secrete mucilage. Bacteria and other microbes produce biofilms, a slimy matrix in which they live, co-operate, and are protected from environmental stress.

All this mucus and the dead mass of plants, animals, and other organisms are the essential glue for inorganic soil particles. Aggregates are formed via the sticky bond and are the cornerstone of the soil's complex three-dimensional architecture of crumbs and open pores.

A Delicate Balance

This system can collapse if the aggregates are broken down too much purely mechanically through ploughing. Or if the soil's inhabitants are disrupted or overstressed and disappear. Organic matter is then lost and the cycle of decomposition, recycling, and new life is interrupted. 'It's a vicious circle because the soil then becomes increasingly unstable and continues to degenerate,' says Rillig.

But too much life is no better. Rising temperatures could increase the number of active bacteria in the soil. If they release more greenhouse gases into the atmosphere, the soil itself may help fuel the climate crisis. A nightmare scenario that we can only prevent if we don't treat our soils like dirt, but rather as a precious heritage. Which we must first better understand.

'Soil is like another universe,' says Rillig. 'Even in a tiny volume, conditions can change radically from one corner to the next or even have the opposite effect. It's fascinating: every crumb of earth, no matter how small, is a world of its own.' ✦

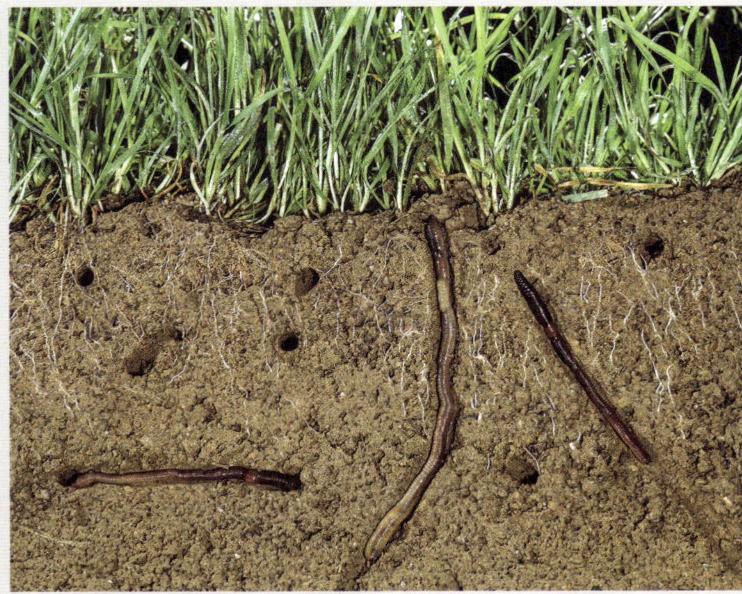

Earthworms. Earthworms play a particularly important role in the formation of humus. They mix the soil and loosen it by eating and excreting dead plant material.

Treposol (deep ploughed soil) of gleyed podzol from deep ploughed drifting sand over low terrace deposits, soil-lacquer profile, Paderborn. The sloping position of the former soil strata indicates that hardened areas in the soil were broken up by deep ploughing in order to expand the root space of the plants for better cultivation.

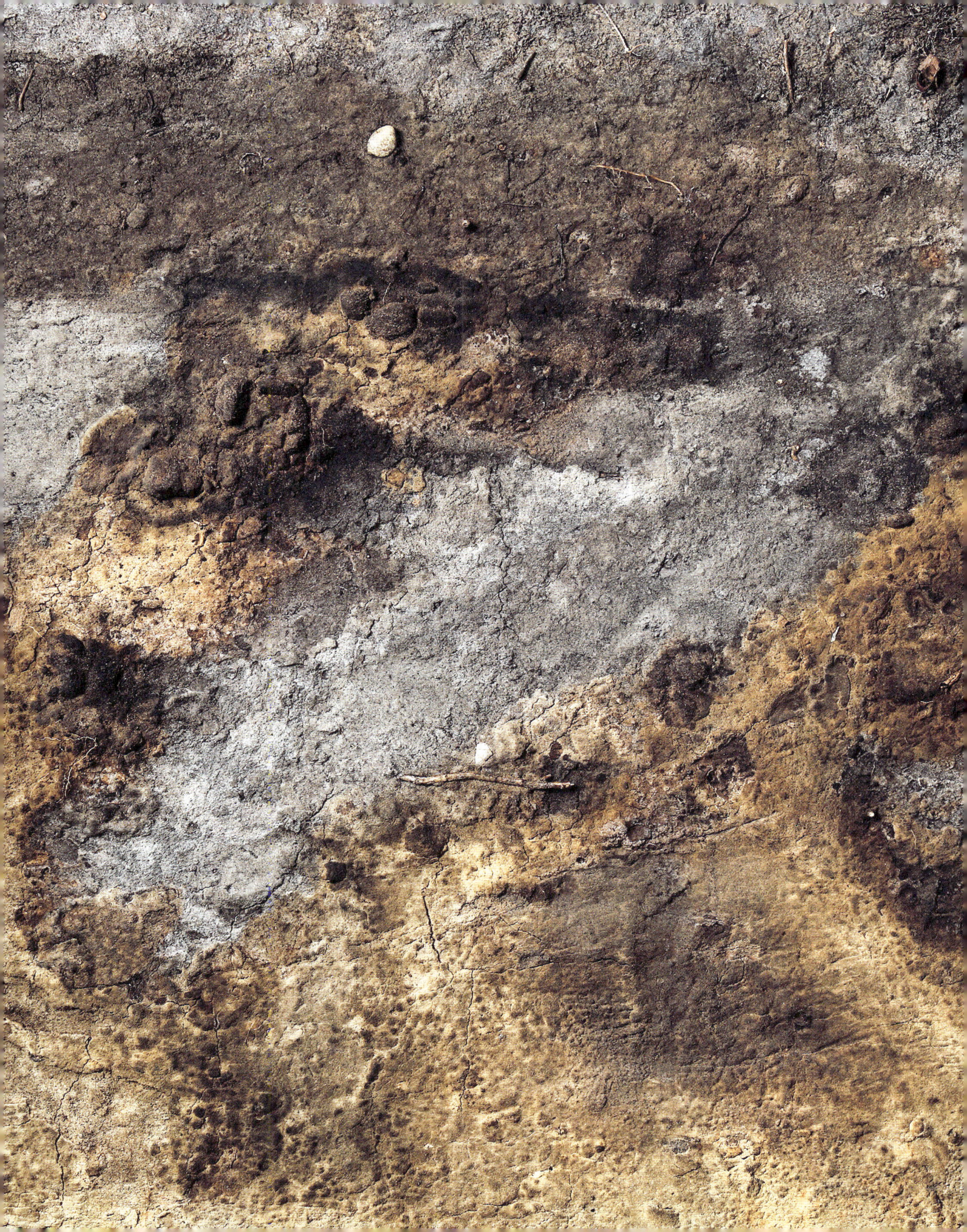

Sedan chair (doll's furniture), 2nd half of the 19th century. As well as transporting people with walking disabilities, sedan chairs were used around the world primarily as an elite means of transport that physically elevated its occupants above the common ground.

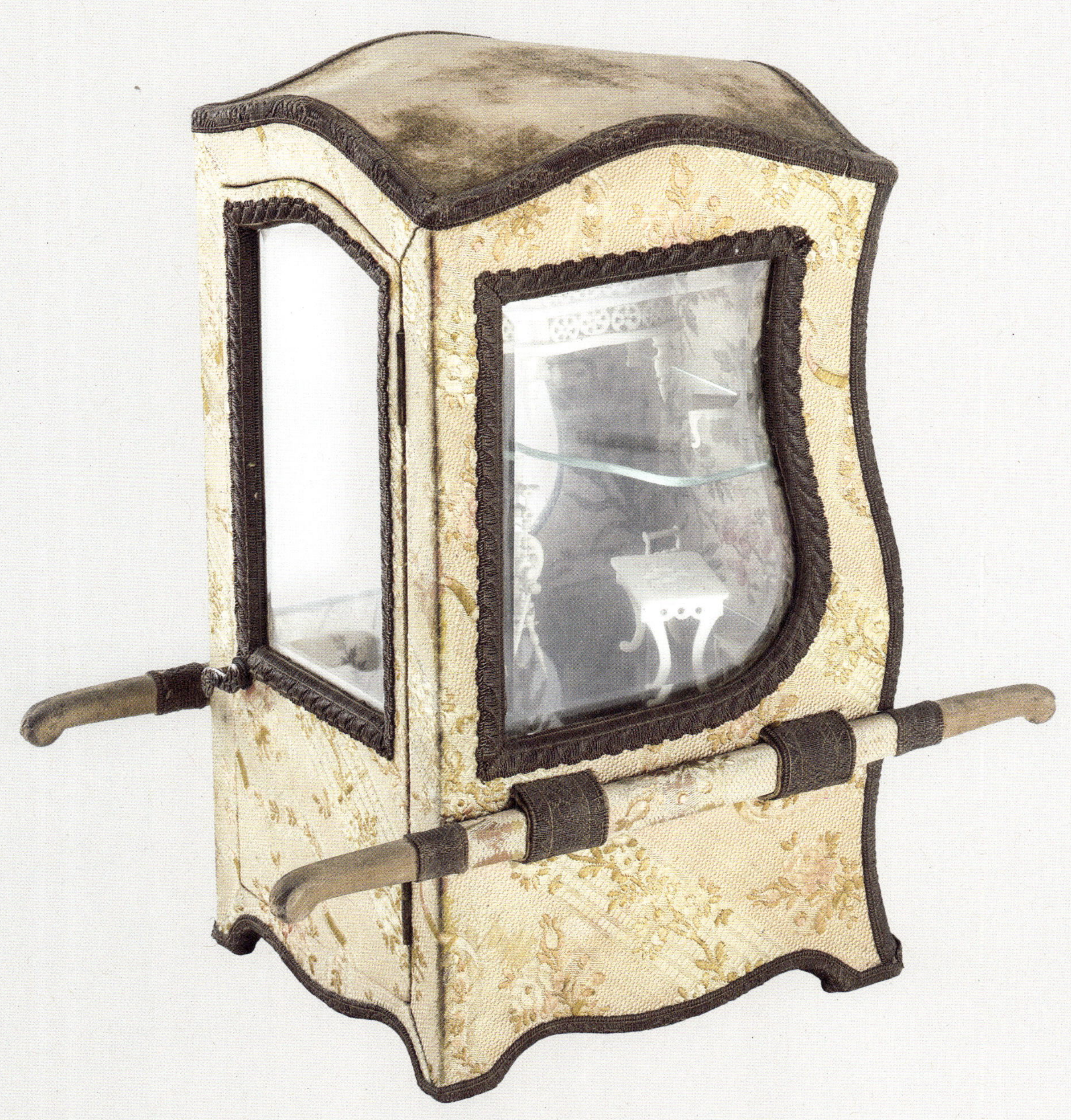

The Socio-Cultural Views of Land

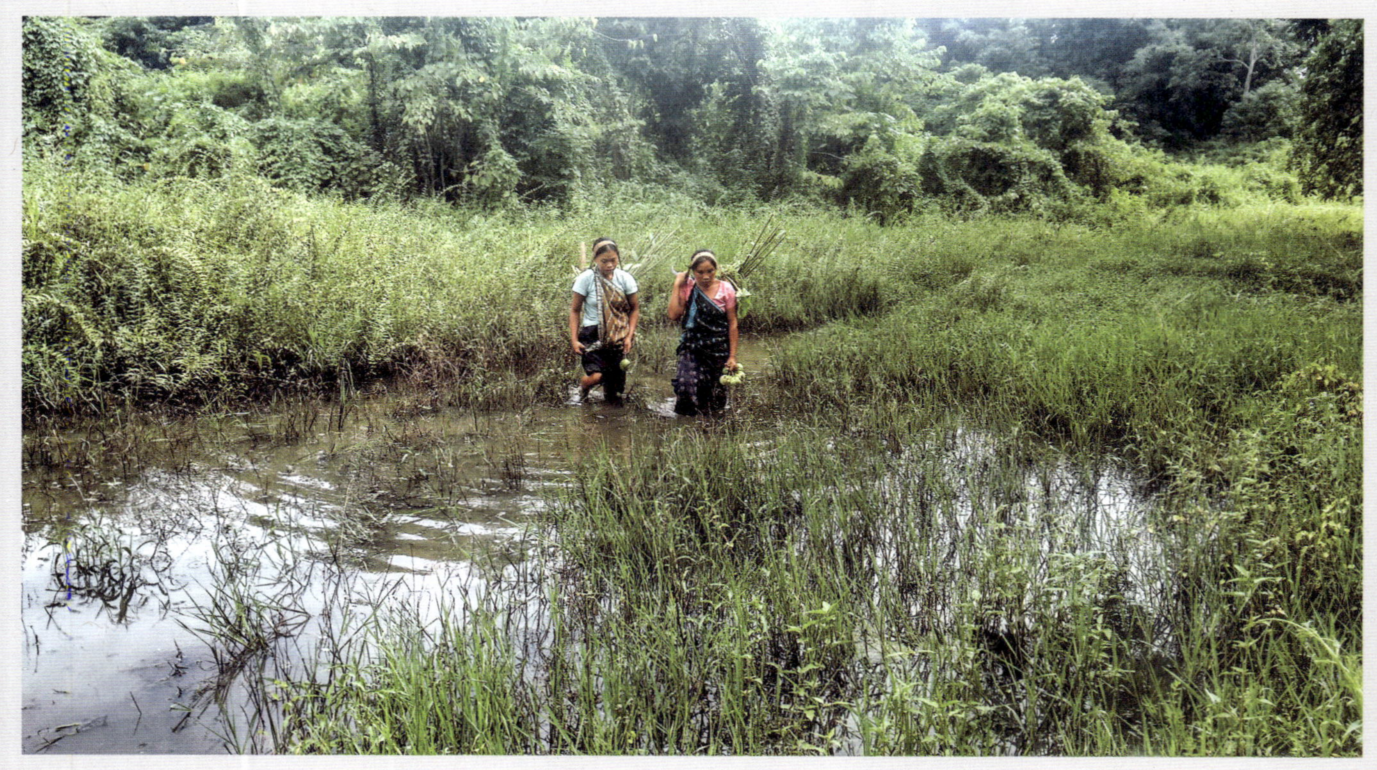

Purabi Bose

Mountains, hills, plateaus, plains, and all landforms are critical sources of life. Be it deserts, savannahs, wetlands, prairies, glaciers, forests, or agricultural land – they are inextricably linked to the identity of distinct social and cultural communities. For millennia, land and its natural resources have formed collective ancestral ties for people across the globe that shape their identities, languages, cultures, livelihoods, and social, emotional, and spiritual well-being.

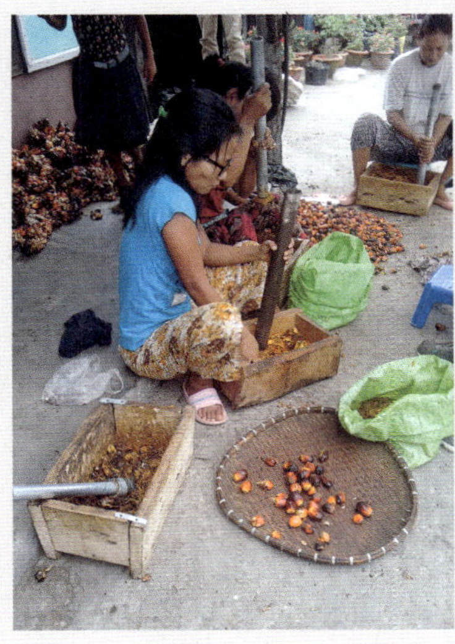

Women in Kolasib in the Indian state of Mizoram are pounding the fruit of the oil palm.

Unearthed: the Cultural Value of Land

'Āina' is the Hawaiian word for land meaning that which feeds; therefore, land should be treated with reverence and respect. 'Bhūmi' is the Sanskrit word for earth or land. In Nepal, 'Bhūmi Naach' is a folk dance to worship the Earth, a symbolic demonstration of the relationship between people and nature to highlight that without land there is no life. In South Asia, many communities in urban and rural areas perform 'Bhūmi Puja', an auspicious ceremony on a new land site to honour Mother Earth before constructing a house or any buildings. Many Indigenous people's cultures hold ceremonies emotionally connecting them to the land – from the unborn, the living, and the dead – and offerings of foraged edible wild food or the first harvest to land are a common practice. Ceremonies related to land bring people together giving them an identity rooted in the sacred sense of place, community bonding, preserving languages, and history. These cultures are visible in many communities through mural paintings on house walls depicting stories of their land, folk music and dance, and storytelling that promotes the narrative of land and its biodiversity as a living being.

Indigenous Karbi women, district Karbi Anglong, Assam, India.

The cultural value-based conservation of land, soil, and its natural resources enables us to understand the broader definition of land – one that is linked to being, identity, and citizenship. Cultures across the globe, encode shared norms, values, respects, and collective meaning of sustainable livelihoods using the land. However, culture is not static. Culture evolves with the changes in land use systems to adapt to new instrumental value systems. For example, in the Mizoram state of Northeast India, the cultural significance of land has shifted from 'land as life' to 'land as commodity'. Traditionally, Mizo and Lai Indigenous peoples have been practicing 'jhum' farming, swidden or shifting cultivation in mountainous terrain, a traditional agricultural process that plays a significant role in soil fertility and allows breathing time for the land to recover. In the past decade, oil palm plantations have replaced traditional jhum farming under the claim that jhum is an unsustainable practice for land use systems. This unintended impact of a new land-use policy leads to further commodification and social fragmentation of collective land management. One of the negative consequences on land is soil degradation, which impacts smallholders' ability to produce food from crops and agroforestry.

How do locals perceive their land-use change? One of the Indigenous women, echoing the sentiments of other locals, states: 'Earlier we worked in our community farm sharing a common culture – singing songs, preserving Indigenous fruit trees and heirloom seeds – it kept us healthy. Now I'm indoors all day alone in front of the fire, manually roasting the oil palm fruit to extract (artisanal) palm oil. Land use change changes the cultures of land users more so for women.' The significance of cultural value associated with land is manifold and difficult to put a price tag on. A community's shared sense of stewardship of the land and place-based knowledge of land users for land restoration and the well-being of millions, when lost, is permanent and irreplaceable.

Pastoralist of the Maldhari (with Kankrej cows) in Gujarat's Banni Grasslands Reserve, Western India.

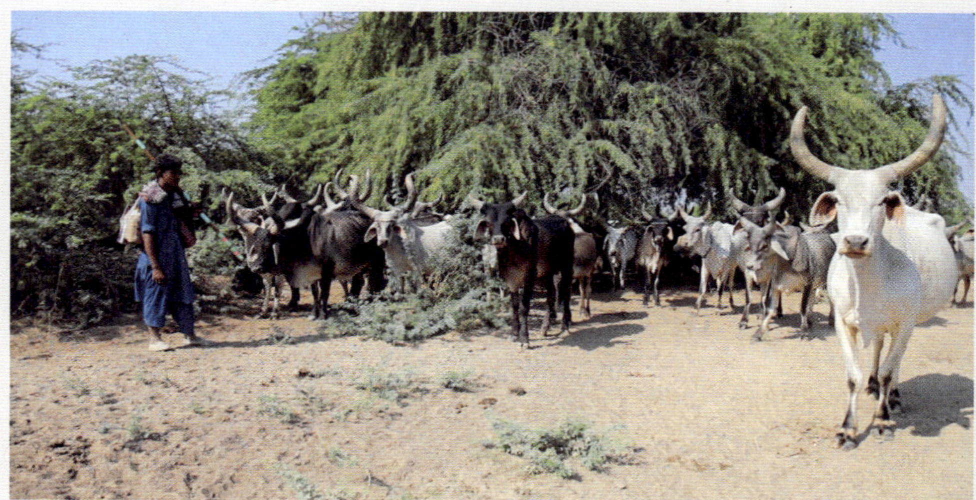

Governing Common Land

Globally, land has become a scarce resource and economically valuable commodity for trade. It is estimated that by 2050, half of the world's land that is 'sitting idle' will be converted into productive land. The Western colonial misconception of uncultivated land in the Global South as economically unproductive has left many highly productive range lands tagged as 'wasteland' or 'barren land' ignoring its inhabitants and rarest biodiversity. These so-called idle or wastelands are often grasslands, savannahs, woodlands, and pastoral or rangelands that are valuable commons.

Common land is the key source of livelihood for traditional communities such as pastoralists, and many continue to govern these commons protecting and preserving rich biodiversity. Common land is traditionally governed collectively. A unique feature is that commons are open to other commoners with entitlements such as to collect mushrooms, berries, and other wild food or have free access for their livestock to graze it. For many rural communities and Indigenous peoples, the land is more than a production, commodity, or individual ownership. It is this social responsibility to govern the land that brings hope for conserving the fragile common land from degradation.

Listening to the Guardians of Lands

Land distribution has been a historical structural problem in many countries. Appropriation of native lands, formal diversion of common lands towards more 'productive' use, and land grabs for industrial food production pose a livelihood challenge for many traditional communities. The traditional land curators, guardians, or stewards – who have been protecting the land for generations – are often ignored in land-use policy and decision-making. For example, the Sámi, a semi-nomadic reindeer herding community in Scandinavia, are navigating across vast pasture areas from mountain to coast. With the increasing demand for critical sub-soil mineral mining permits and sustainable 'green energy' windmills, they face threats of dispossession of their land and land-related livelihoods.

Likewise, semi-nomadic pastoralists in Asia and Africa have been land curators for over two hundred years. They use traditional knowledge for pastoral land management by following a pattern of land rotation that contributes to soil fertility, water regulation, pest and disease control, fire management, and biodiversity conservation. The Maldhari pastoralists of Western India and East Africa's Maasai pastoralists' knowledge of ancient rangeland is intertwined with their pastoralist identity in maintaining the natural ecosystems. To illustrate, an elder Maldhari pastoralist explains, 'Our elders have followed a culture of the land that has a quote in our language, it is *Asi Maitri Viyahu*, which means all living beings, wherever we are living, we are children of one parent. The migratory birds and wildlife in our rangeland have the same status of respect as our livestock. Everyone is equal in common land.'

Grounded Gender Parity

With land tenure reforms across the globe, many communities gained access to individual land holdings. The challenge with property rights to land – farmland or housing – is that they are handed over to heads of the households, often men, as defined by the states. Women own less than 10% of the world's land and those who legally own the land may not necessarily have the rights to access, manage, and make decisions. The underrepresentation of women continues to pose a challenge in land ownership and access to land continues to challenge because depriving them of land means denying them their full humanity. In places where women may have had strong traditional rights to land and forests they may find themselves without such rights when the land use system changes.

In the Central Indian state of Jharkhand, tribal women have been at the forefront as part of community forest land management despite challenges they face from policymakers denying their traditional rights. One of the Oraon tribal women leaders explains, 'Forestland is everything we have; it's our identity by birth. Our last names are linked to wildlife from our land – for example, Kerketta means Quail bird while Lakra means Tiger, Tigga means monkey, Xaxa means bird – that live in our forestland. How can we have our identity if we lose our land? Collectively, we women must conserve our land so that we can continue to collect wild edible food, which forms our safety nets and direct source of nutrition security.' These local examples of self-governance of land could reverse the global trend wherein industrial development threatens over half of Indigenous peoples' lands (approximately 22 million km^2) in about 60 countries. The direct negative impact of these land conversions and lack of land tenure is on the world's women and youths.

Building Land Equity in a Polarised World

Competition for land and natural resources is one of the major contributing factors to many armed conflicts and wars. The direct consequences are displacement, the destruction of local livelihoods, particularly for marginal groups including children, youths, and women, urban expansion, and biodiversity loss. Such conflicts have a long-lasting effect on land systems, and are therefore an important driver of rapid diversified land-use change. One of the 17 United Nations' Sustainable Development Goals (SDGs), SDG 15, is about 'Life on Land'. All the targets and indicators for the SDG 15 are ambitious, but social and cultural aspects of the land users remain understated. Yet, in a heterogenous world of culture, tradition, and diversity of Indigenous knowledge, achieving land equity requires a holistic understanding of interpretation of socio-cultural heritage. Global land management should be a priority in political decision-making, but even more in explicitly recognising the social and cultural values of traditional land users. Adding a social science lens to focus on how we relate with land systems in their entirety is what is required as a next step. To overcome a one-sided narrative of land science, which is often influenced by economic incentives, land systems need to be re-examined to foster the socio-cultural value of land, its users and stewards, and ecological well-being. ✦

Women's forest land, Jharkhand, Central India (Landing Together Films).

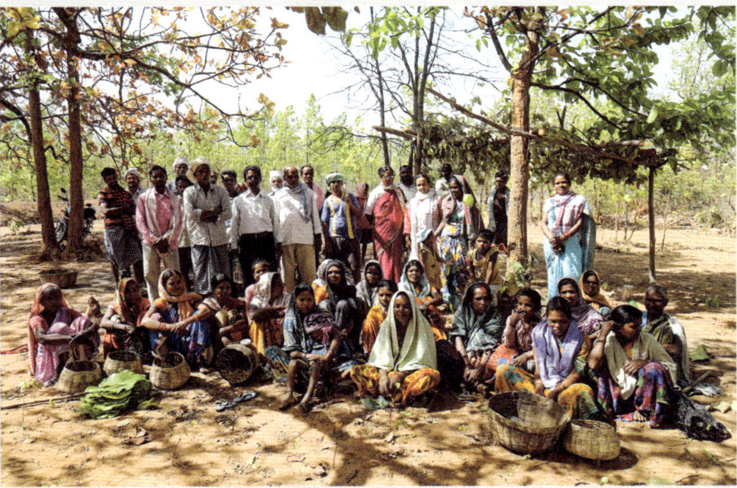

Grace Ndiritu, *Natural Disasters: No. 3 Tremor*, 2007, video, music by Michael Nyman. Grace Ndiritu is a British-Kenyan artist whose work encompasses performance, film, social activism, shamanism, and textile art. Similar to some of her photographic works, this 'hand-crafted' video tells a story of creation from the beginning of time.

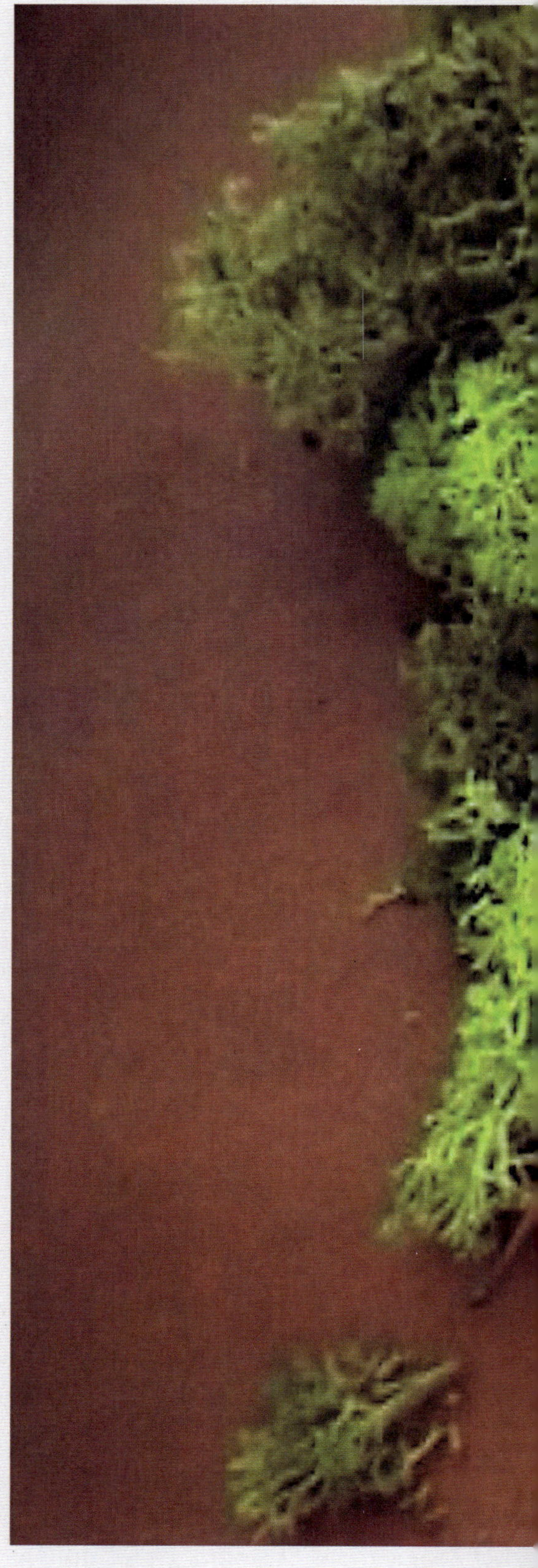

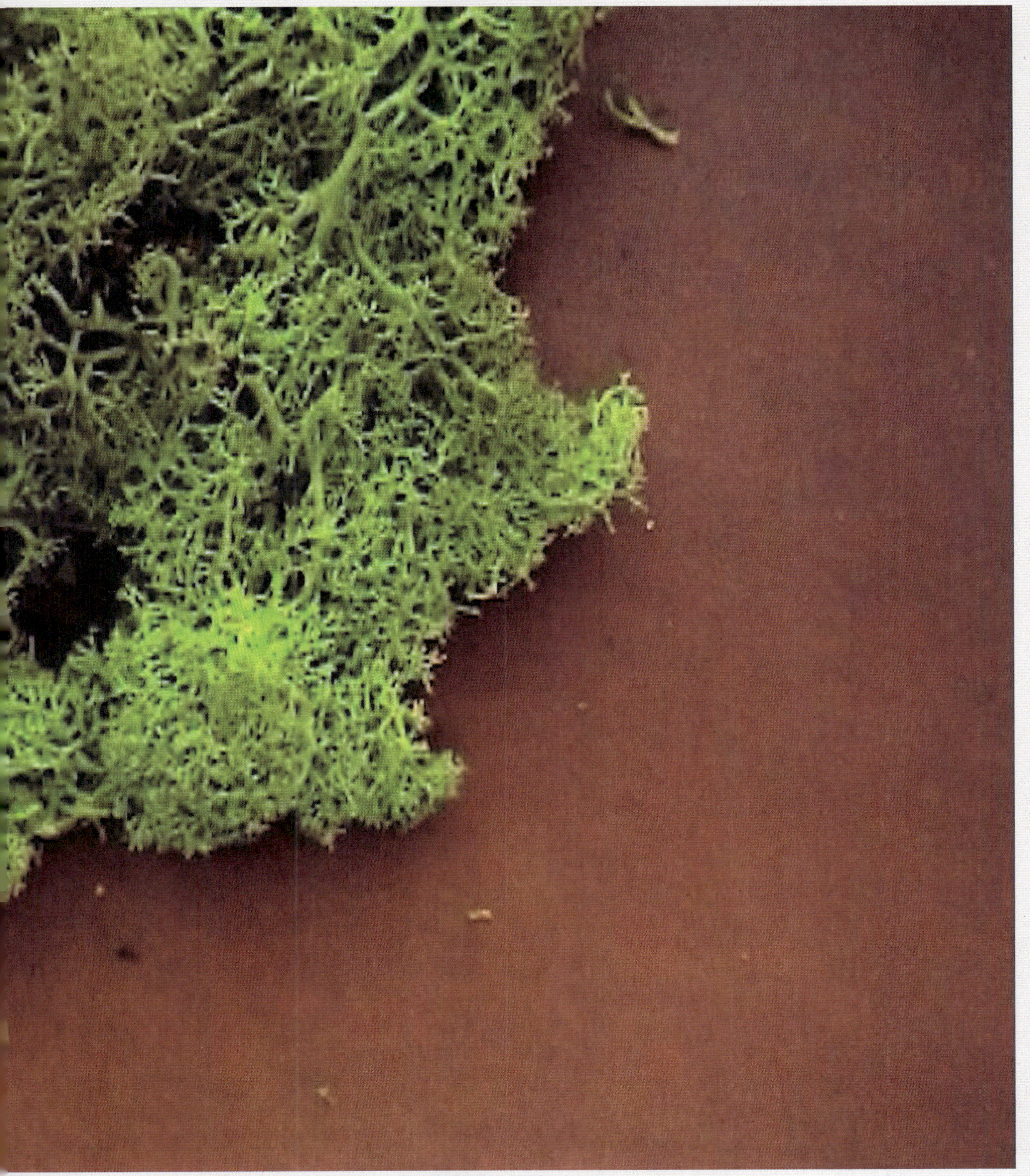

Interactive floor projection 'Cities', 2024 © dform/Bildwerk, Vienna ▶

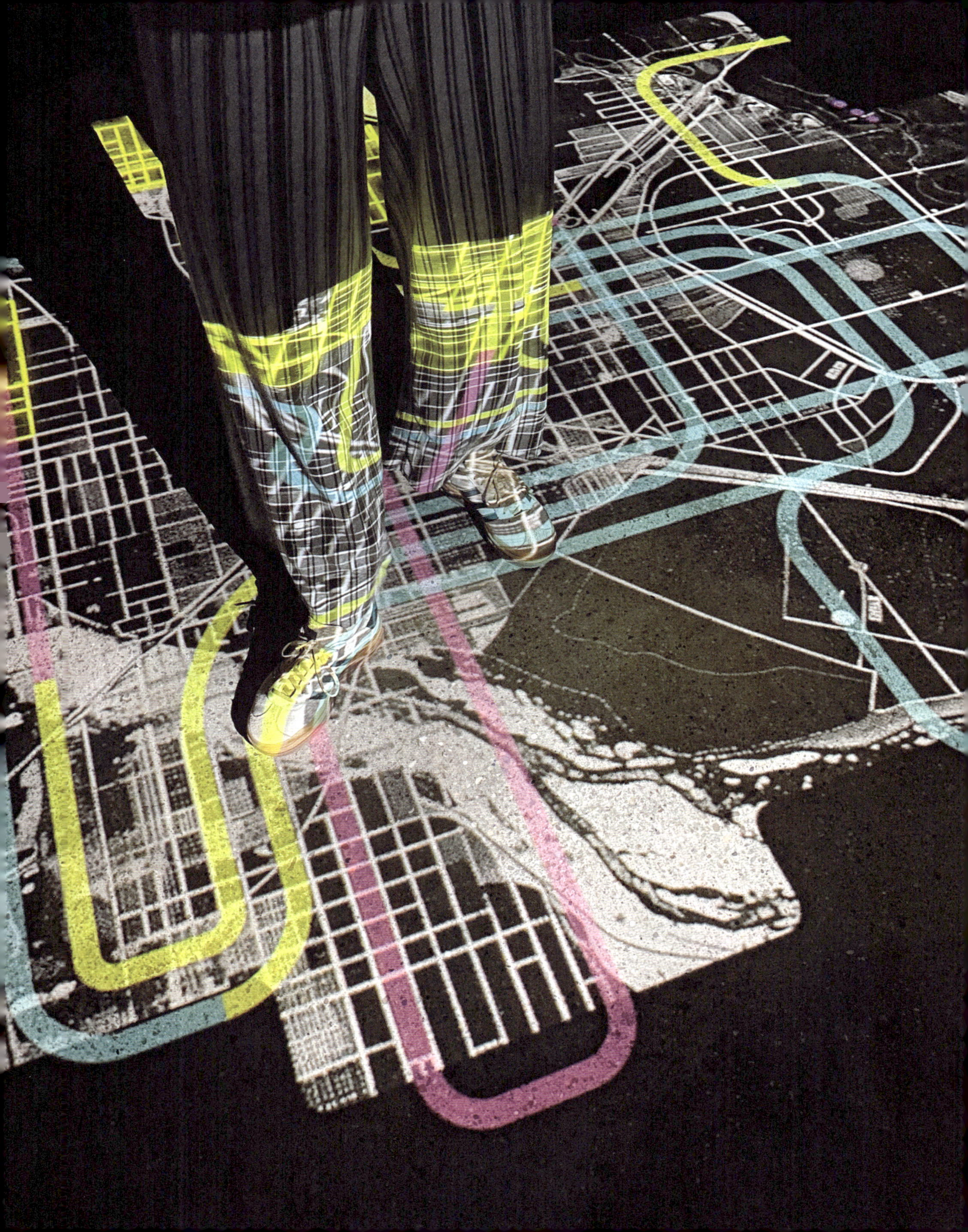

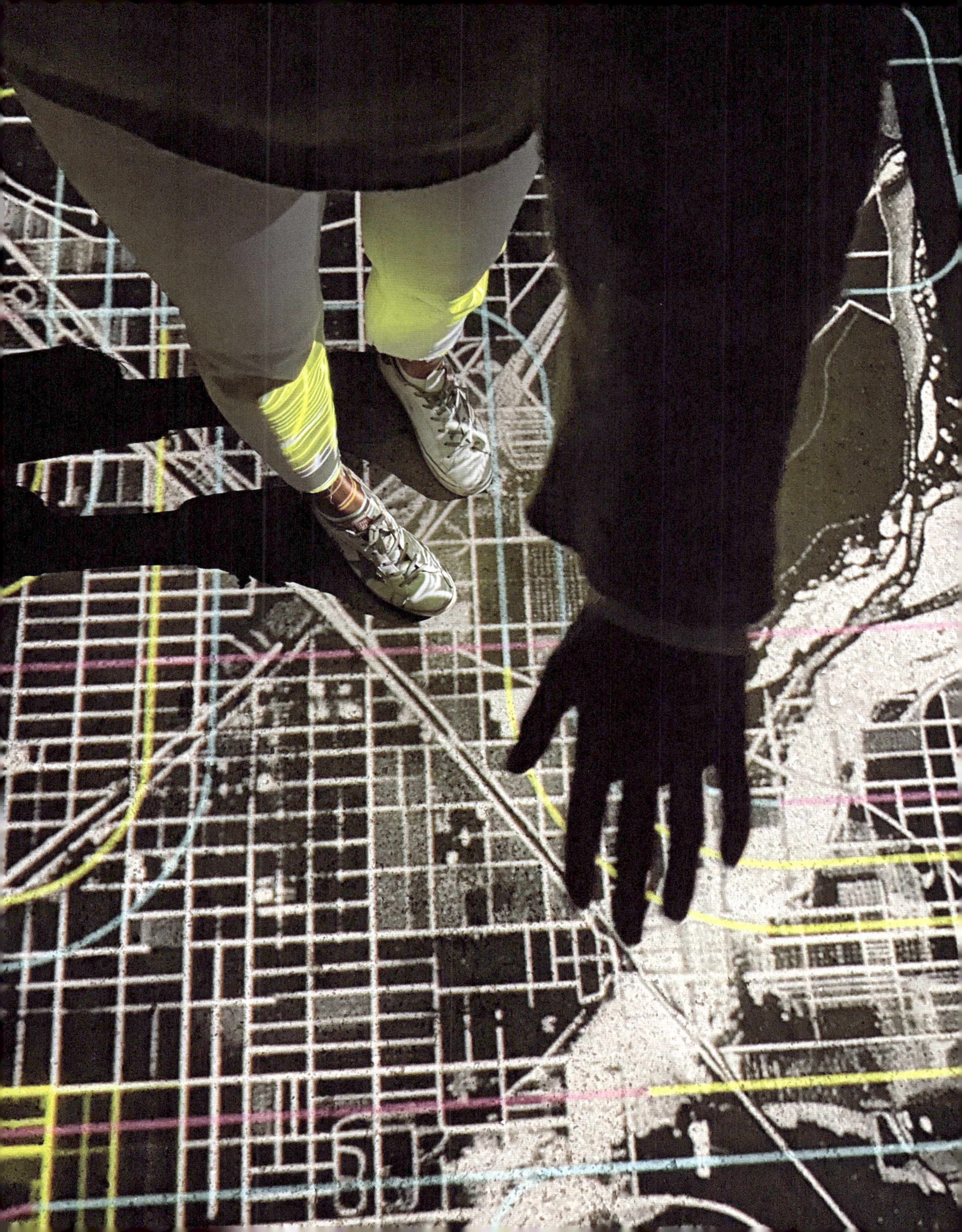

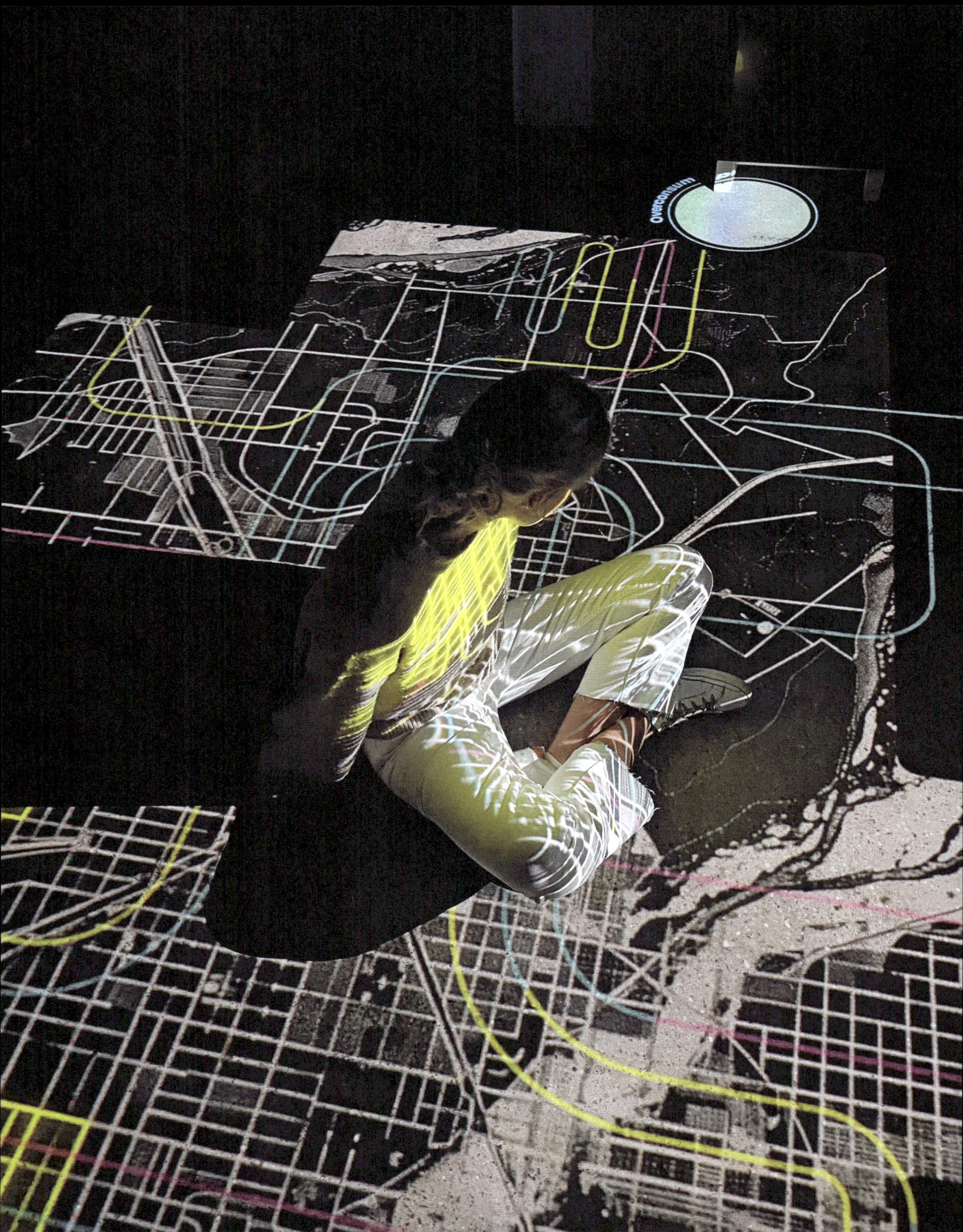
overconsum

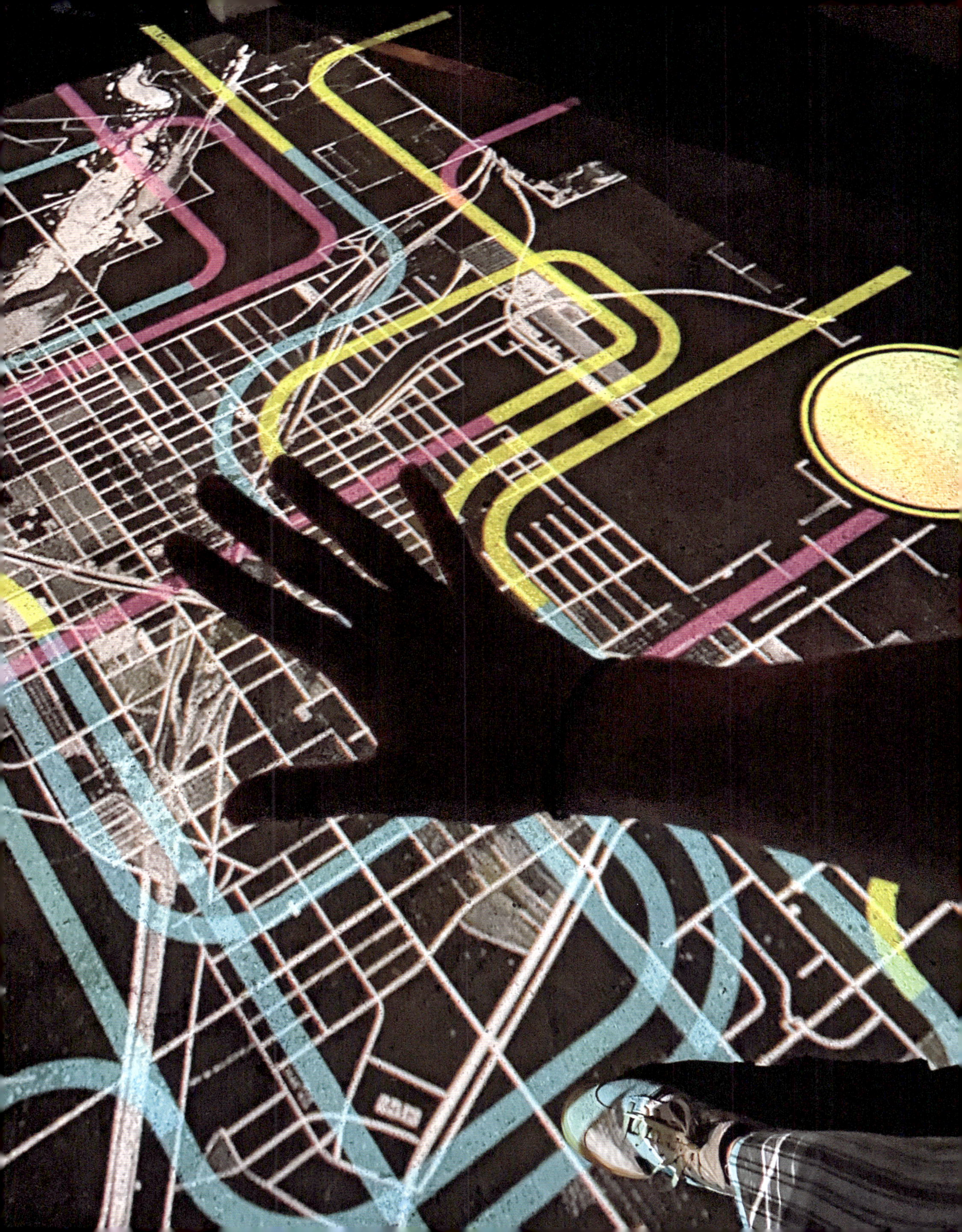

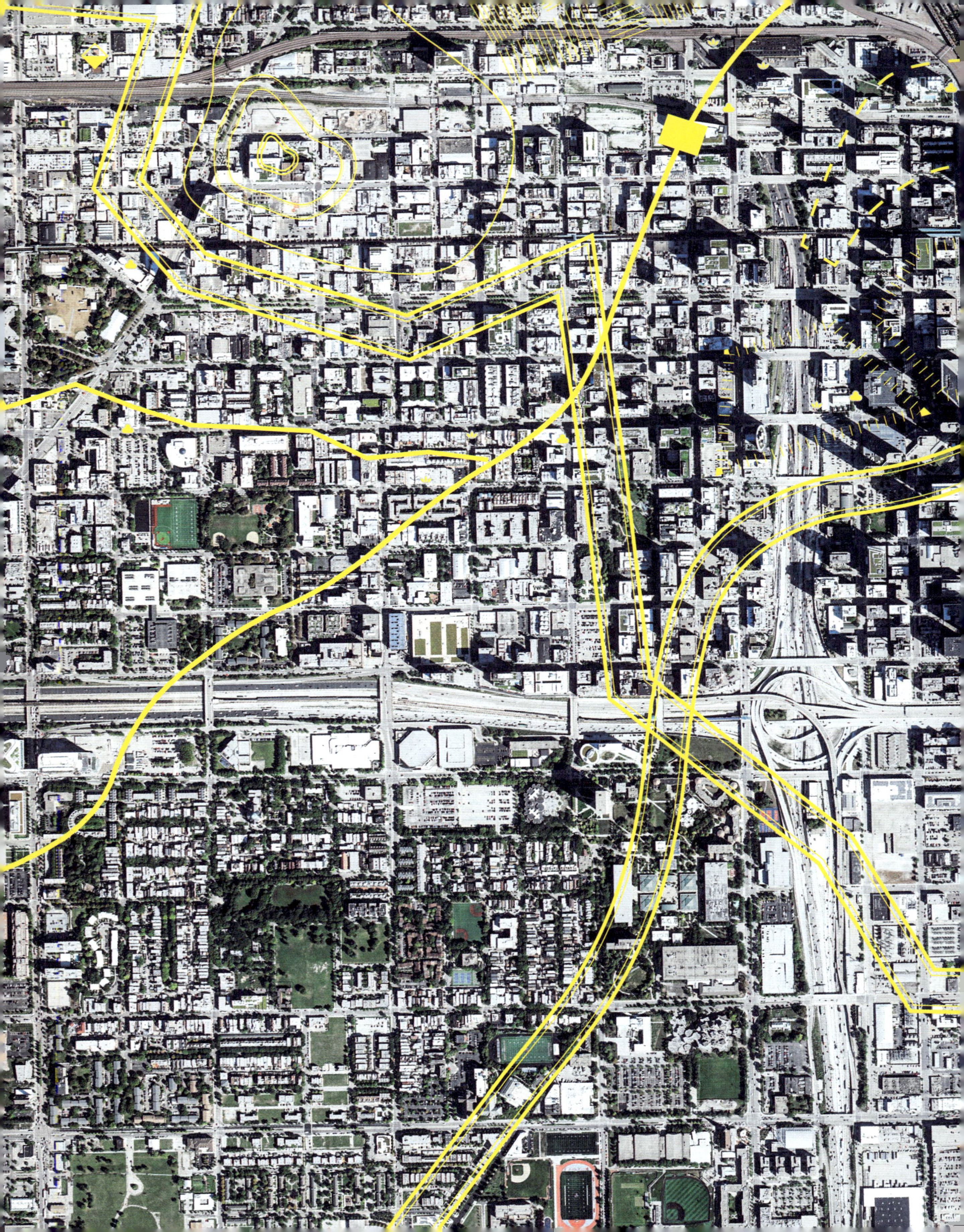

The Material World

The global population has grown from 1 billion in 1800 to 8.1 billion today, and keeps growing. Only 76 % of Earth's land is habitable, and more than half of the global population (57 %) shares just 2 % of land: cities. It is predicted that the urban share will increase in the coming decades as cities expand into and fragment rural areas.

By 2050 more than two thirds of the world's population will live in cities. Urban areas are responsible for about 78 % of all globally produced energy, and to grow, cities consume over 75 % of the planet's material resources from mines around the world. We have sealed over half a million square kilometres of land by building on and expanding urban areas. Buildings and parking lots as well as the construction of roads and other infrastructure renders the soil impermeable. Sealed soil loses its ability to capture carbon, regulate water availability, and serve as a healthy habitat for a host of organisms.

Urban Ecology

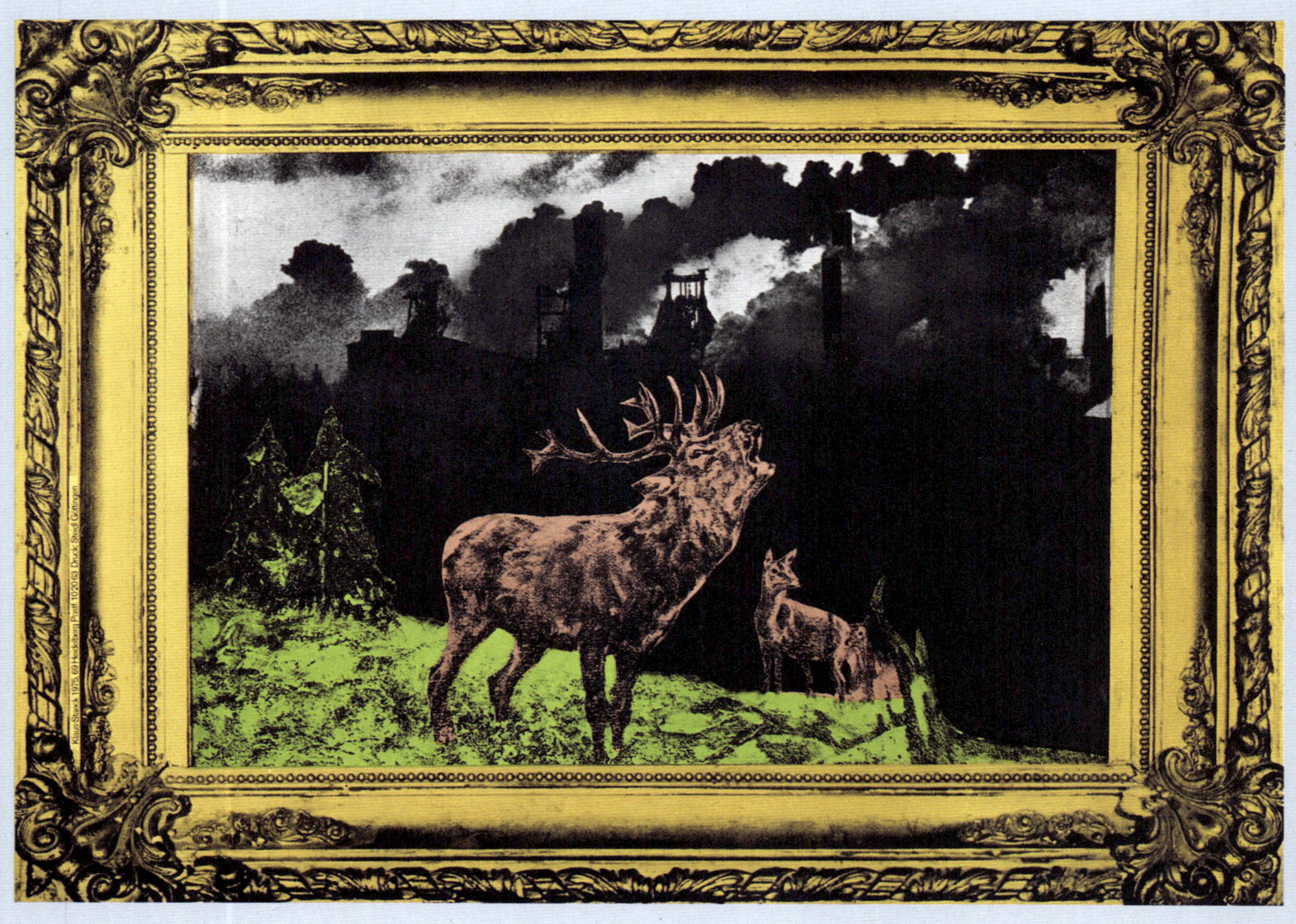

Florian Mayer

More than half of the world's population now lives in cities and urban centres. According to United Nations forecasts, this figure will rise to 60 % by 2030. Urbanisation is not only progressing globally; the majority of large cities in Germany are also continuing to grow. Today, 78 % of Germany's population live in cities and urbanised regions. Cities are not simply places where many people live, but also where the major challenges of our time converge: climate protection, adapting to climate change, maintaining and creating healthy living conditions, social justice, and the loss of biodiversity. However, conventional approaches to tackling these challenges are no longer suited to the complex demands of globalised cities. What is needed therefore is a fundamental and long-term change by means of an approach in which processes are interlinked and multifaceted: urban transformation.

Klaus Staeck, *Bellowing stag in front of an industrial chimney*, 1975, poster. The increased greening of our cities would not only support biodiversity, but would also have immense benefits for us: better air, more comfortable temperatures, cleaner water and a more attractive environment.

Sealing and Heat – The Consequences of Climate Change

What characterises cities as specific ecosystems? Where can the transformation begin? As ecosystems, cities are characterised by heavy building development, highly sealed surfaces, dense traffic, and a high level of human disturbance. Open spaces, fields, meadows, and forests are being built over every day for the continuing growth of cities and settlements as well as for transport areas. In Germany, this currently amounts to 52 hectares per day – land that can no longer provide important natural services for us humans. Under concreted and asphalted surfaces, ground and drinking water cannot be replenished, surface water runs off more quickly, increasing flash floods and flooding, concreted and asphalted surfaces become very hot and put a strain on health, and the loss of green spaces deprives people of recreational areas. Last but not least, the habitat of animals and plants is being lost. According to studies by the World Biodiversity Council, the expansion of urban areas and the associated changes in land use are considered to be one of the main drivers of biodiversity loss worldwide.

The effects of global climate change will also have a lasting impact on ecosystems, their water balance, and therefore land use in Germany. In cities, the effects of increased heatwaves and more frequent heavy rainfall are already being felt today and require mitigating measures, as recognised by the Intergovernmental Panel on Climate Change (IPCC) in 2021. In this respect, it is primarily the heat extremes that lead to summertime stress for people. Urban heat islands form in cities, which lead to higher air temperatures, especially at ground level. The extreme temperature differences between urban and rural areas can be up to 10 °C at night. The average number of hot days per year (> 30 °C) in Berlin has already doubled in the last 30 years to 11 days today, and up to 35 hot days per year are forecast for the end of the 21st century. Tropical nights, i.e. nights in which the temperature does not fall below 20 °C, have particularly negative consequences for health. A significant increase is also forecast for these. Simultaneously, as a result of climate change, dry periods such as those in 2018/2019 will increase on the one hand and heavy rainfall will become more frequent on the other.

Combating Environmental Stress with Urban Greening

For this reason, climate adaptation strategies for cities are increasingly focusing on green and open spaces as well as trees. Large green spaces have demonstrable cooling effects, while numerous smaller, scattered open spaces are important for their bioclimatic impact because they are easier for people to reach in their neighbourhoods and form cool oases on hot days. Corridors from the surrounding countryside into the city that are kept free of buildings, such as the 'green fingers' in Osnabrück, bring fresh and cool air into the city at night. Street trees reduce the overheating of pavements through the shade they cast and cool through the evaporation of water. The greening of roofs and façades reduces the heating of buildings. This also requires a rethinking of urban water management: it is important to store water, buffer rapid runoff, and not channel it into the sewage system as quickly as possible. By unsealing asphalted surfaces, retaining water on green roofs, using infiltration troughs, and renaturalising watercourses and floodplains, more water can be kept in the city. Like a sponge, the city must therefore be able to temporarily retain water and slowly release it again ('sponge city').

Health problems resulting from environmental factors are unevenly distributed in Germany, particularly in cities. Many studies show that low-income people tend to be more exposed to negative environmental influences. They are more frequently affected by traffic-related health hazards such as noise and air pollutants and have less access to urban green spaces, i.e. they have fewer opportunities for exercise and recreation. Avoiding and reducing the spatial concentration of health-related environmental pollution caused by traffic, noise, etc., and ensuring equitable access to green and open spaces can therefore make a significant contribution to greater environmental justice in urban areas. The World Health Organisation (WHO) has also called for all residents of cities to have access to public parks within walking distance of their homes.

Developing Urban Nature

One of the main reasons for the diversity of species in urban areas is the variety of habitats, from river meadows, forests, gardens, and parks to different building structures, including detached houses and industrial premises. The better a city is greened, the higher the proportion of native species and species with special habitat requirements. In addition, green spaces whose use has not changed over many decades are rich in species, such as historic parks or cemeteries with old trees. The networking of different habitats, e.g. along watercourses, railway lines, and green corridors, facilitates the spread of animal and plant species. Last but not least, special site characteristics such as urban wastelands, which are favoured by warmth-loving species like lizards, are also important.

Some cities in Germany have now started to organise the maintenance of their green spaces in a nature-oriented way, for example by converting lawns into flowering meadows, actively promoting insect diversity, and thus also promoting and developing urban nature. This demonstrably increases the biodiversity of parks and green spaces and allows people to experience nature more intensely in their immediate neighborhoods.

Approaches for Green Transformation

Awareness of the services that nature provides in cities has increased, also as a result of international strategies and their national implementation. These services are just as important for life in the city as water, sewage, roads, etc. Urban development is therefore increasingly focusing on the development of these green infrastructures.

A green infrastructure is made up of a network of near-natural and designed areas and elements in cities that are planned and maintained in such a way that they collectively offer high quality in terms of usability, biodiversity, and aesthetic appeal and provide a wide range of ecosystem services. The transformative character of the concept is primarily due to the fact that green infrastructure is strategically and participatively conceived in the planning and development of cities. In terms of socially, economically, and ecologically sustainable urban development, the aforementioned challenges can be tackled with the help of a biodiversity-orientated green infrastructure.

Opportunities to experience nature in urban nature close to neighbourhoods can make an important contribution to both human health and social cohesion. Urban nature, with its value for people, thus plays an essential role in the provision of services of public interest and is therefore an integral part of transformative change in cities.

Nature-based Solutions as Part of Urban Transformation

Due to the high-density usage demands in urban areas, the challenges outlined here require solutions that give equal consideration to climate protection, adaptation, and biodiversity. Nature-based solutions can make a significant contribution here.

What are nature-based solutions? The approach was first presented by the International Union for Conservation of Nature (IUCN) at the COP15 climate conference in 2009. These are solutions inspired and supported by nature that are cost-effective while providing environmental, social, and economic benefits and increasing resilience. They are designed to benefit biodiversity and support the provision of a range of ecosystem services.

Such solutions should be systematically incorporated into urban planning in order to give nature more space in our cities and at the same time improve the quality of life for residents. Nature-based solutions are to be understood as so-called 'no-regret options', i.e. measures that are low-risk and definitely create added value for society. They can only be labelled as such if they simultaneously contribute to human well-being and biodiversity. In addition, nature-based solutions must preserve biological and cultural diversity and the ability of ecosystems to develop.

All over the world, long-established techniques and traditions are being utilised that incorporate nature in the shaping of life and the land. One example is agro-agriculture, where the planting of trees has a positive influence on the water balance and the growth of crops. A modern adaptation of this form of utilisation for the city are urban forest gardens, such as those currently being implemented in Berlin. A forest garden consists of predominantly edible plants that partially overlap in several layers of vegetation. These layers consist of fruit and nut trees, berry bushes, vegetables and herbs that can be grown and harvested together over the long term. In this way, a permanent forest-like cultivation system develops in which organic gardening is practised.

The Bottom Line

Cities around the world and in Germany are facing major challenges. When weighing up the various demands and interests, it is vital for sustainable cities to maintain and expand their green infrastructure. This is the only way to achieve the necessary green transformation of cities for the people who inhabit them. ✦

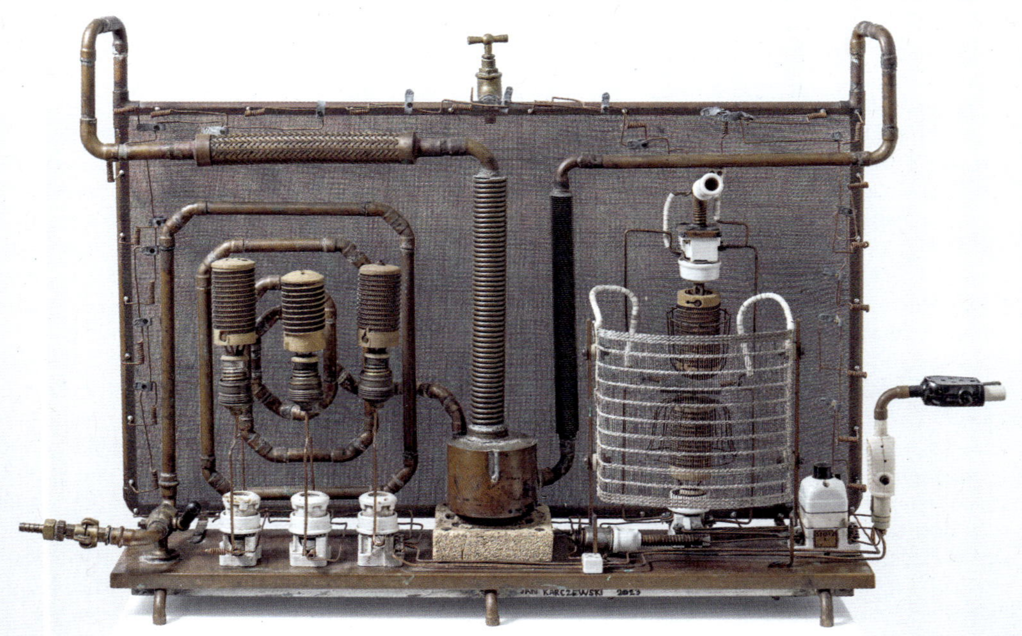

Jan Karczewski, *Heat pump*, 2023. This heat pump runs particularly quietly without a compressor and independently of geothermal energy, and adjusts to the ambient temperature when switched off. Whether it can halt global warming as hoped remains to be seen.

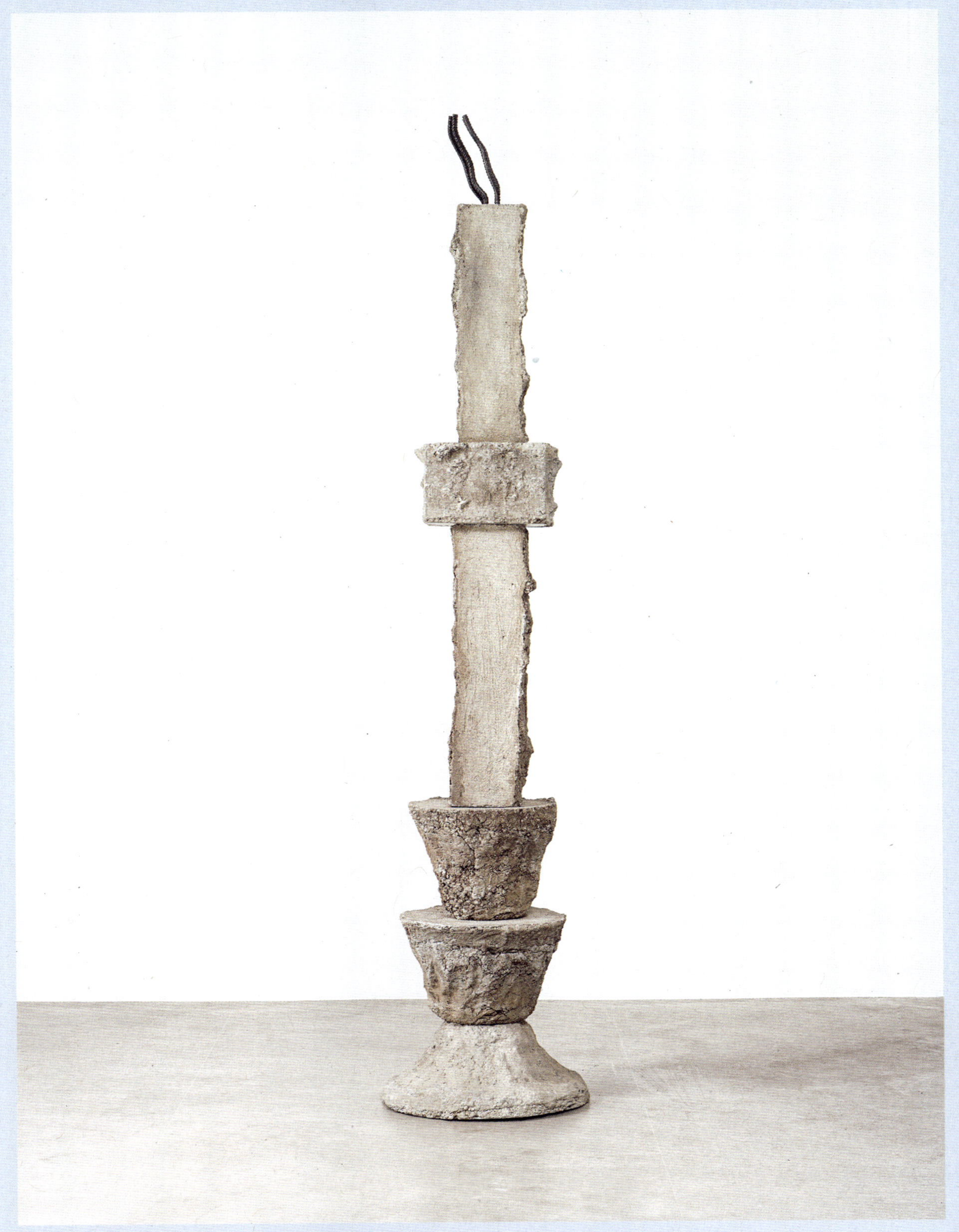

Monika Sosnowska, *Pillar*, 2018.

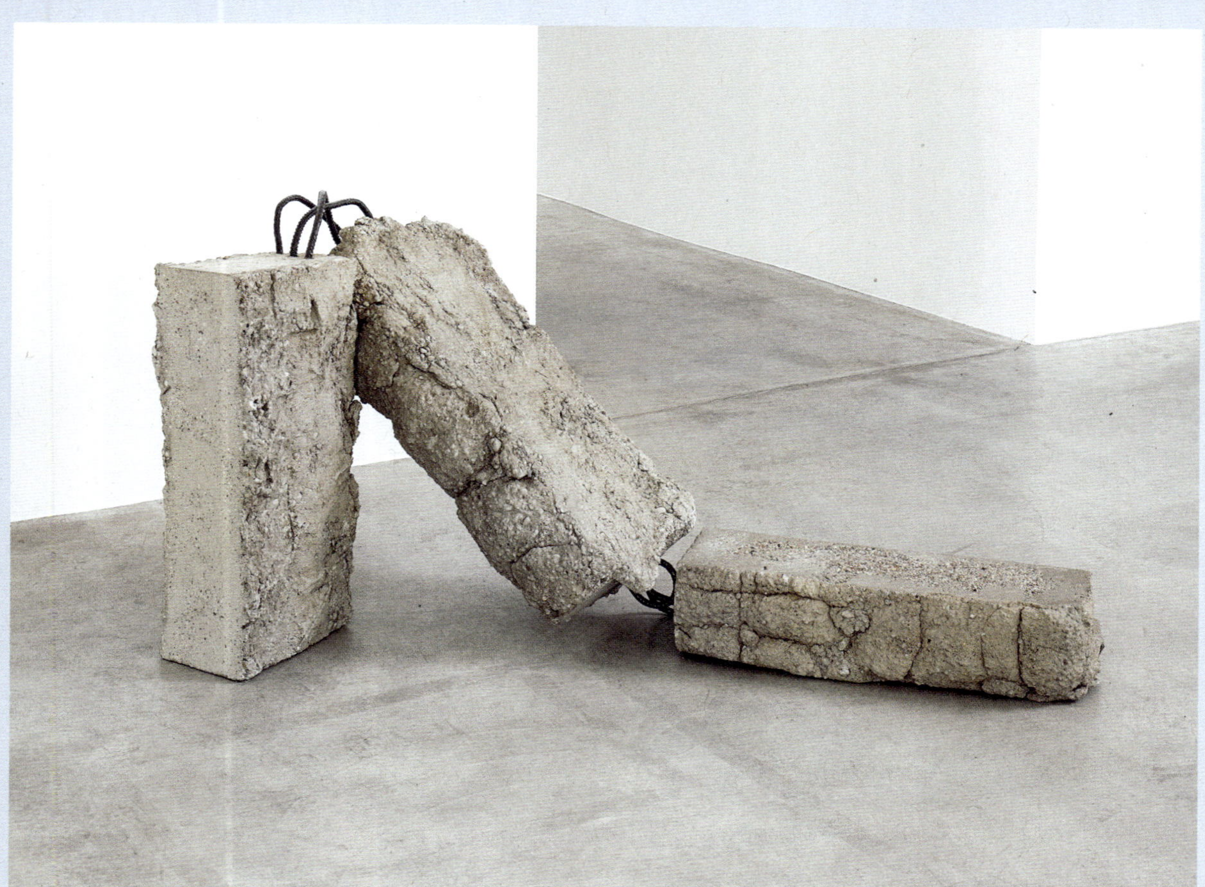

Monika Sosnowska, *Pillar*, 2018.
The Polish sculptor Monika Sosnowska is known for her architectural installations. The artist is particularly interested in provisional and makeshift urban architecture that speaks of social change. The works *Pillars* and *Pots* were inspired by a trip to Bangladesh and her observations there.

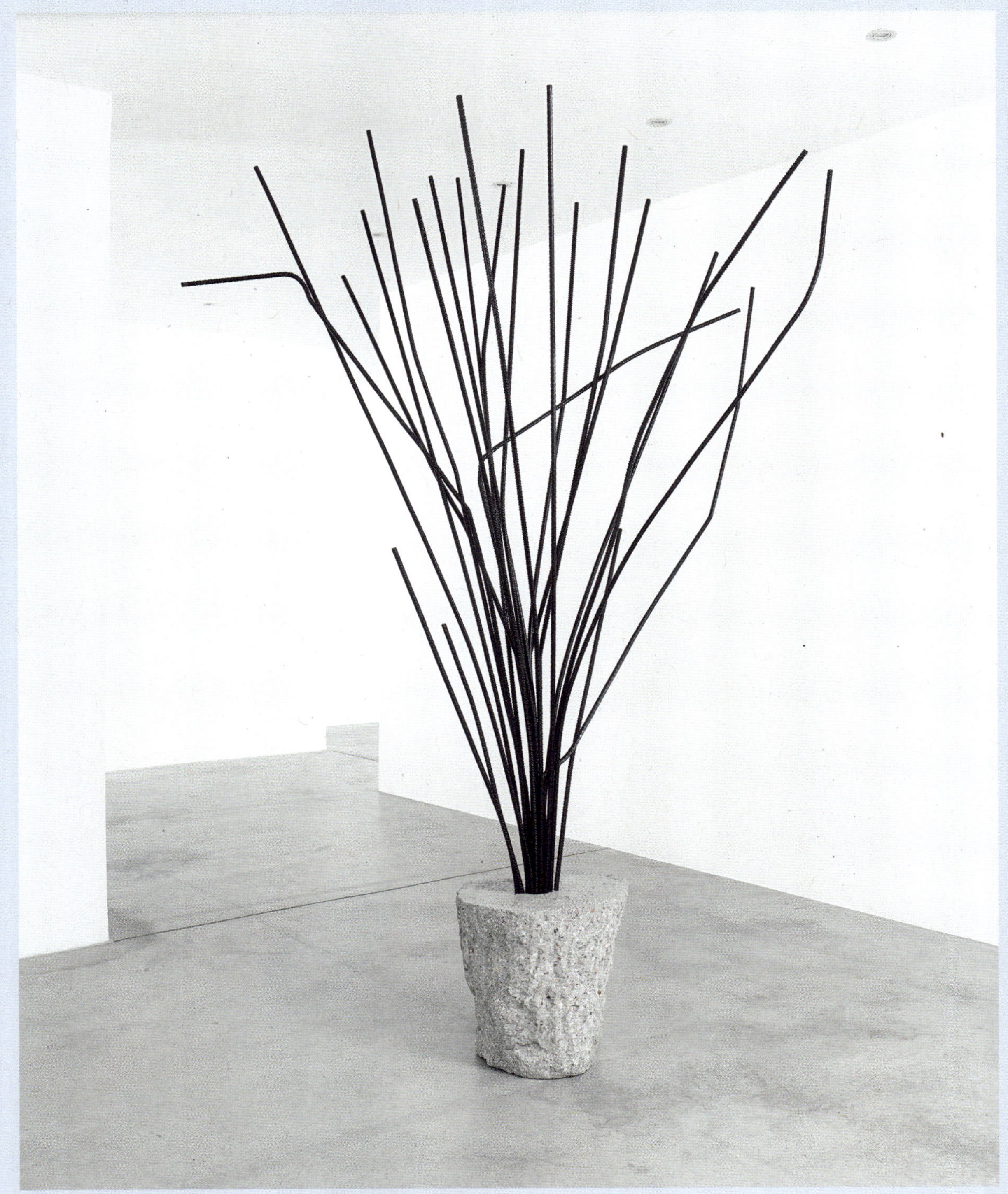

Monika Sosnowska, *Pot*, 2018.

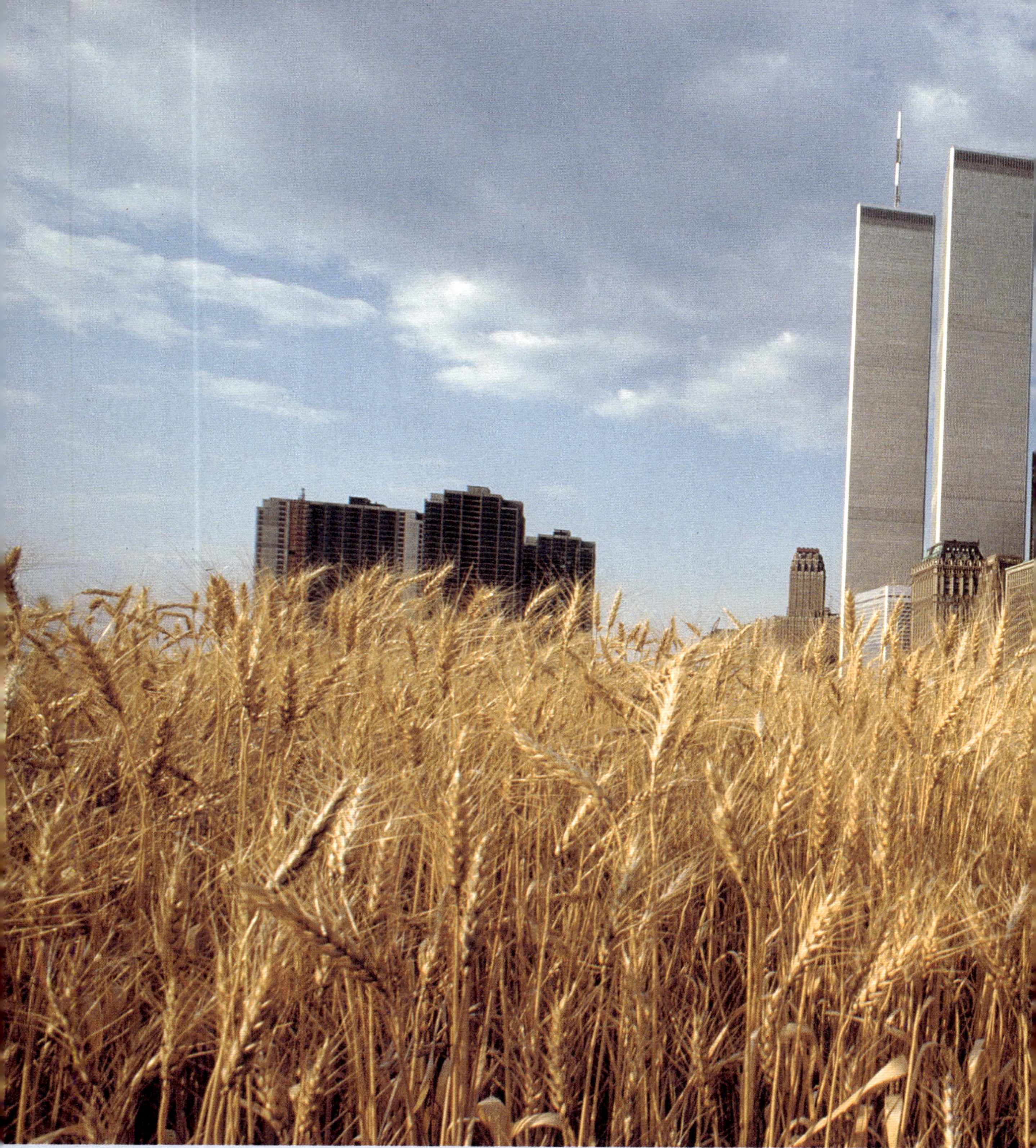

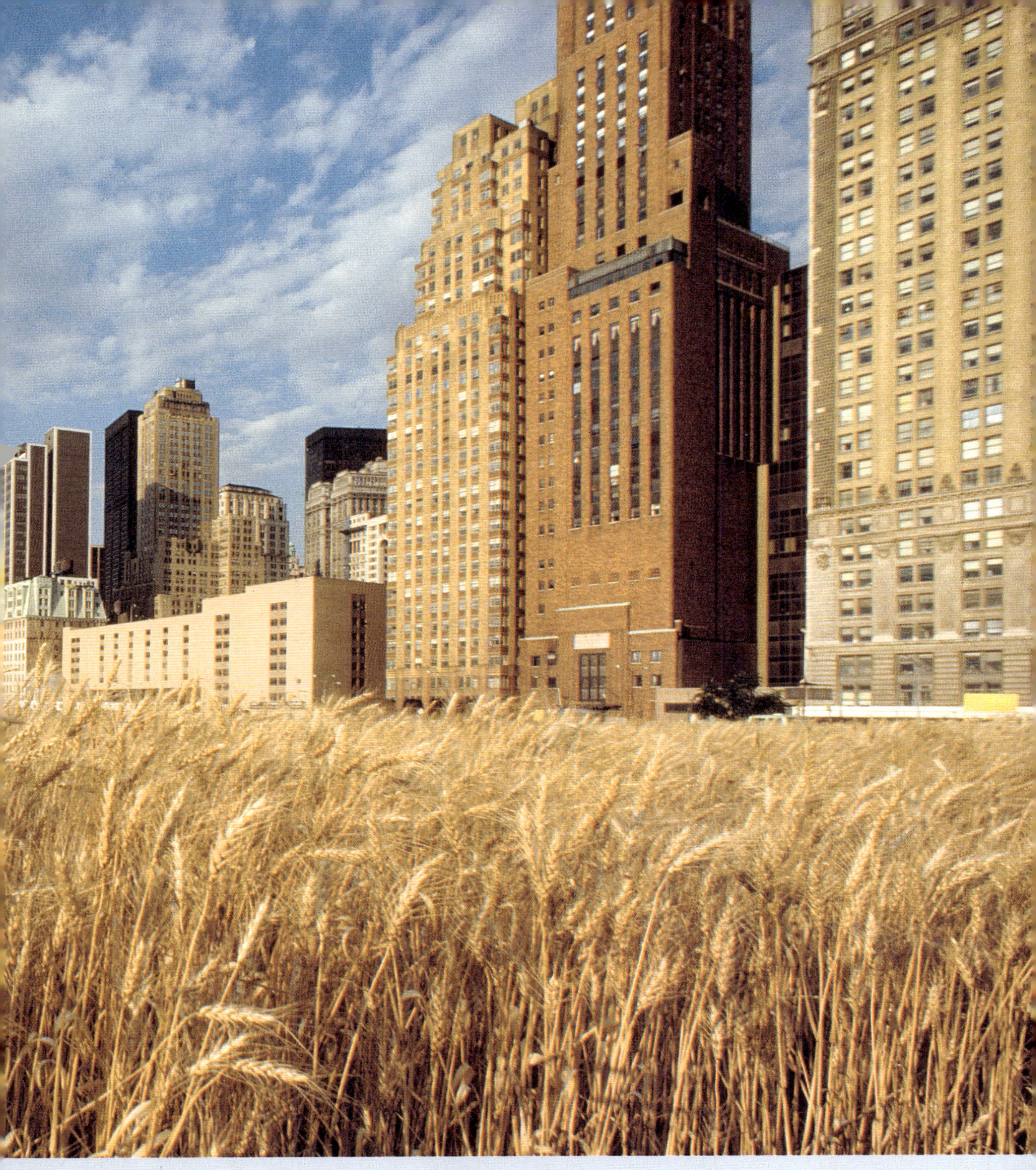

Agnes Denes, *Wheatfield – A Confrontation*, 1980s, video. On 1 May 1982, conceptual artist Agnes Denes planted a 2.2-acre wheatfield on the empty Battery Park landfill in Manhattan. Even back then this piece of land was valued at 4.5 billion US dollars. Denes, two assistants, and rotating volunteers maintained the field for four months. They harvested the wheat on 16 August 1982 and distributed it across 28 cities around the world. This work was intended as an act of protest to highlight the paradoxes between the urban and rural worlds.

The Miracle of Miyawaki Forests

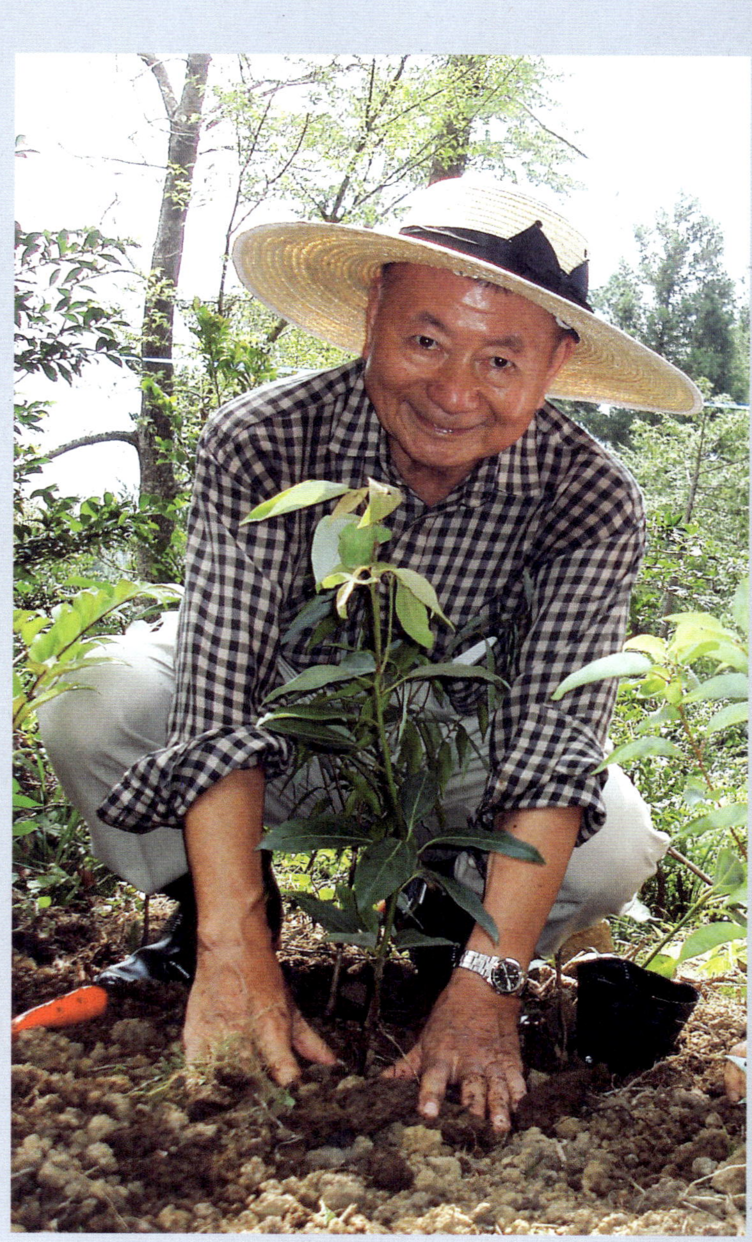

Kazue Fujiwara

For Akira Miyawaki, the 1960s were a time of nature conservation. After returning from Germany in 1964, he spread the strict nature-conservation philosophy he had learned from German Professor Reinhold Tüxen throughout Japan. Miyawaki's forest creation involves ❶ using seedlings of stable natural-forest species in the target land; ❷ preparing the soil environment of the planned planting site as much as possible (improving drainage and adding fertiliser); ❸ dense, mixed, random planting to promote growth through competition using different growth strategies of tree species; ❹ mulching with rice straw, fallen leaves, or bark, etc. to retain soil moisture, prevent soil erosion, promote the development of soil fauna and soil development; and ❺ planting trees together with local children and residents as environmental education and real experiments.

The Beginnings

The history of Miyawaki Forests began in 1970, with the release of the US Environmental White Paper and Professor Miyawaki's desire to restore the nature that had been destroyed by the remodeling of the Japanese archipelago in the 1960s. In 1969, when he drew a schematic diagram of natural forest regeneration based on a basic survey of vegetation around power plants, he produced a diagram for planting pioneer species, *Robinia pseudoacacia*, and planting seedlings of natural forest species underneath. In 1970, the Environment Office of Nippon Steel Corporation consulted him about greening the vast vacant land of the Oita Steel Works. At that time, Professor Miyawaki, with the natural forest restoration along the autobahn in Niedersachsen (Lower Saxony) in mind, proposed sowing acorns and plant seedlings to restore the natural forest. Before restoring the natural forest, Miyawaki and his team visited Nippon Steel Corporation locations all over Japan, surveyed the original natural vegetation of the land, and submitted a report on the potential natural vegetation at the steelworks. During that time, he advocated acorn ecology, in which acorns are sown and thinned out to restore nature. It is a famous story that, among the seedlings used at the Nagoya Steel Works, a *Persea thunbergii* seedling (canopy tree species) was mistaken for a *Neolitsea sericea* seedling (understorey tree species). The person in charge insisted that the *Persea thunbergii* brought by the landscaper was a *Neolitsea sericea*, and Professor Miyawaki was furious, saying, 'Who do you believe, me or the landscaper?'

Akira Miyawaki (1928–2021) was a Japanese university lecturer and plant sociologist.

Landscapers and Locals Working Together

The landscaping contractor sent his future son-in-law to his laboratory as an apprentice to learn the basics of vegetation research. When he returned to the company after six months of apprenticeship, he suggested that the method of growing seedlings in pots, as used in the United States, and planting them was less maintenance-intensive and produced faster-growing trees than acorn ecology. Since then, acorns have been collected in various places and pot seedlings have been produced. In the 1970s, many companies, including Nippon Steel Corporation, Honda Motor Co., and power plants across Japan, started creating forests under Professor Miyawaki's guidance. The method was for the landscaping companies to plant the seedlings.

From 1984 to 1986, under the leadership of the Kanagawa Prefecture Governor at the time, Kazuji Nagasu, and Professor Miyawaki, 10,000 trees were planted under the black-pine plantations on the Shonan coast with 10,000 local people, including students, and in another action 30,000 trees were planted under black-pine plantations with 30,000 local people. Before these the Miyawaki Laboratory was consulted about the coastal black-pine forests being damaged by sea breezes and growing extremely poorly. After three years of experimental planting, the black pines began to grow vigorously after being protected from the wind by the dense Miyawaki planting in front of them and the seedlings planted under the black pines. This was the beginning of planting with the participation of local people including high-school students. Unfortunately, in 2022 and 2023, the tips of the evergreen broad-leaved trees planted under the pines were being cut, using tax money, by uninformed staff in the name of management that prioritises pine trees.

Others Get on Board in Japan and Beyond

In the 1990s, Mitsubishi Corporation, which was criticised around the world for environmental destruction due to the destruction of tropical forests, established a global environment office and asked Professor Miyawaki to provide guidance on the restoration of tropical forests in Borneo. At the same time, AEON Co., Ltd. asked overseas shopping centres to create forests. AEON also began the nationwide method of gathering local people and working together with the company to plant trees when constructing domestic shopping centers.

In the 2000s, the Ministry of Land, Infrastructure, Transport and Tourism, Kyushu Electric Power, Matsuo Copper Mine, and Non-Profit Organisations (NPO) created by citizen activity, which advocated securing a sustainable environment as a millennium goal, began creating Miyawaki forests in various places. In 2001, Hideo Yamada, president of Yamada Bee Farm Co., Ltd., met with Professor Miyawaki and began tree-planting activities on company premises in Japan as well as in China and Nepal, as a good environment for bees, consistent with the human environment. In 2006, Hioki Electric also began field surveys to identify the natural forests in Kenya, and forest restoration in Kenya continued until 2018. In 2006 and 2007, more companies became active in tree planting, including Sango since 2006, Toyota and Toyoda Gosei since 2008. In 2007, a Shinto shrine forest was created by the Miyawaki method at the Sagami branch of Izumo Taisha Shrine in Hadano City (Kanagawa), where 1,700 people planted trees together with Professor Miyawaki.

Further, various municipalities and companies have been planting trees together with local residents in various regions. In the wake of the Great East Japan Earthquake in 2011, Professor Miyawaki launched the Great Forest Wall Project, which utilises rubble from the earthquake as a way to create forests for life that can reduce the power of tsunamis. With former Prime Minister Hosokawa Morihiro as Chairman and Professor Miyawaki as Vice Chairman, they built a Great Forest Wall in Tohoku. The project has now been renamed the Chinju-no-Mori Project, and the Public Interest Incorporated Foundation is creating forests to protect lives all over the country.

Miyawaki's Legacy

In 2015, after Professor Miyawaki collapsed due to a cerebral infarction, the planting by each company was halted, as they had completed the intended number of trees planted. NPOs such as the Chinju-no-Mori Project, Hokkaido Millennium Forest Project, Creation of Natural Forests for Life 2020, and the Association for Fostering a Green Globe continue to promote forestation in Japan. Overseas, Yamada Bee Farm continues forestation in Nepal and China. Since 2014/2015, forestation under the guidance of Afforest (India) has become popular around the world and many people were trained to become Miyawaki forestation instructors. It will be groundbreaking that people who have created Miyawaki forests around the world will gather at Yokohama National University, where Professor Miyawaki had worked, on October 10 and 11, 2024, sponsored by the G20 Global Land Initiative (United Nations) and the Chinju-no-Mori Project. If the natural forest restoration that is the foundation of Miyawaki forestation can become part of saving the global environment, it will be the culmination of the forestation that Professor Miyawaki started.

Parks are places that continue to be managed at a cost but are open and have no shady interiors. In contrast, Miyawaki-style forests, managed for three years after planting, create closed spaces where the forest continues to develop through its own regulation. By not requiring management, such as thinning or top cutting, the forest protects the local environment. We hope that planting will continue, in order to save the global environment and protect people's lives, and that Miyawaki's correct natural forest restoration will continue. Continuation of Miyawaki forests for millennia, until the next ice age, will fix more carbon dioxide as more trees are planted, restore biodiversity, and create a forest in the hearts of the participants. ✦

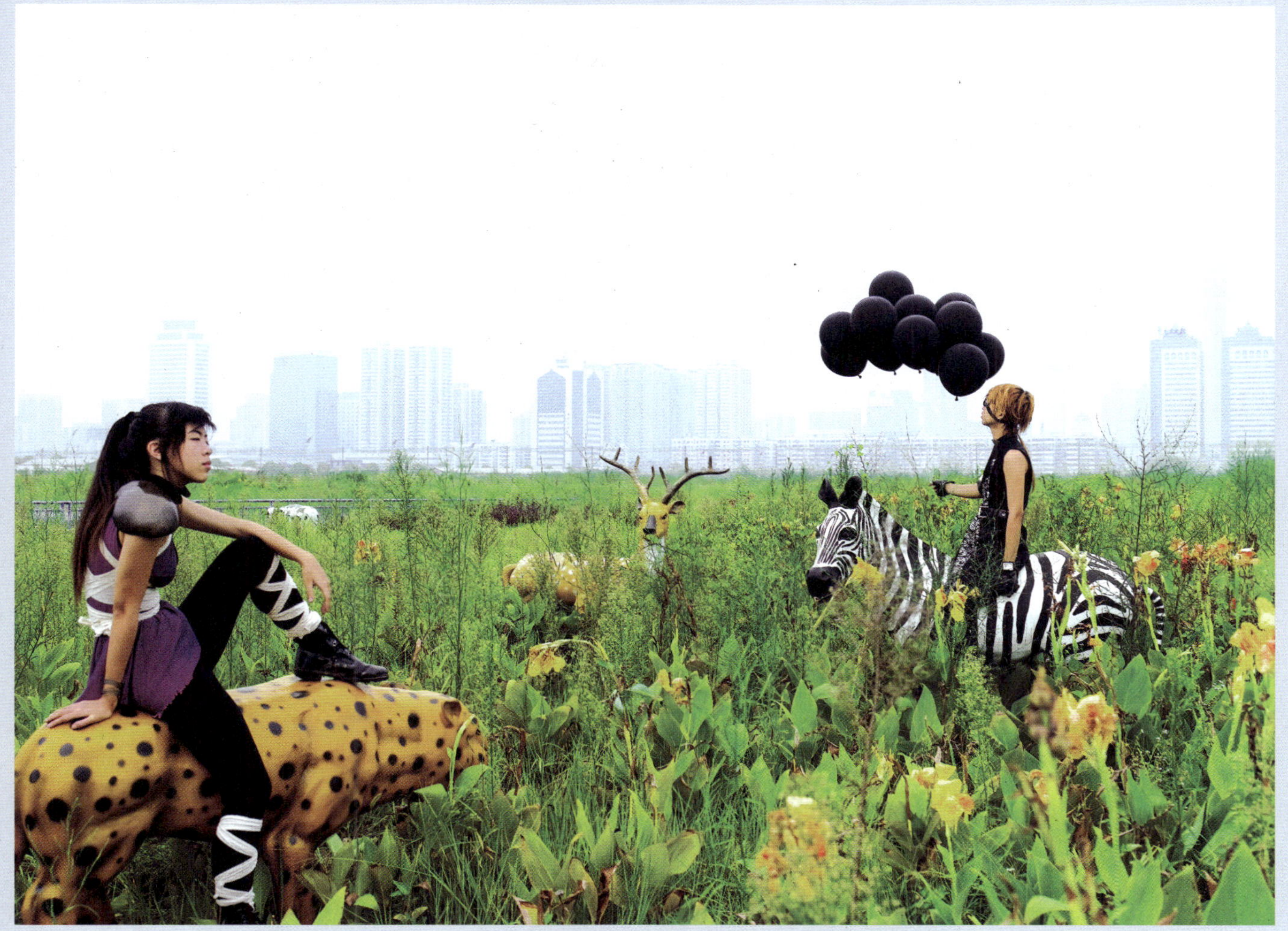

Cao Fei, *A Mirage* (from the *Cosplayers* series), 2004.

Cao Fei, *Deep Breathing* (from the *Cosplayers* series), 2004. Cao Fei's visionary artworks oscilate between artistic invention and social documentation and contain a surreal beauty. The teenagers in this early photo series, for instance, are dressed in the colourful costumes of Japanese manga warriors. They roam urban and suburban landscapes during the day, only to spend their evenings in the cramped confines of their families' small apartments. They are the protagonists of China's first youth subculture mediated by the Internet, and their daydream-like role-playing in large cities seems an understandable reaction to the unforeseeable upheavals of the society in which they live.

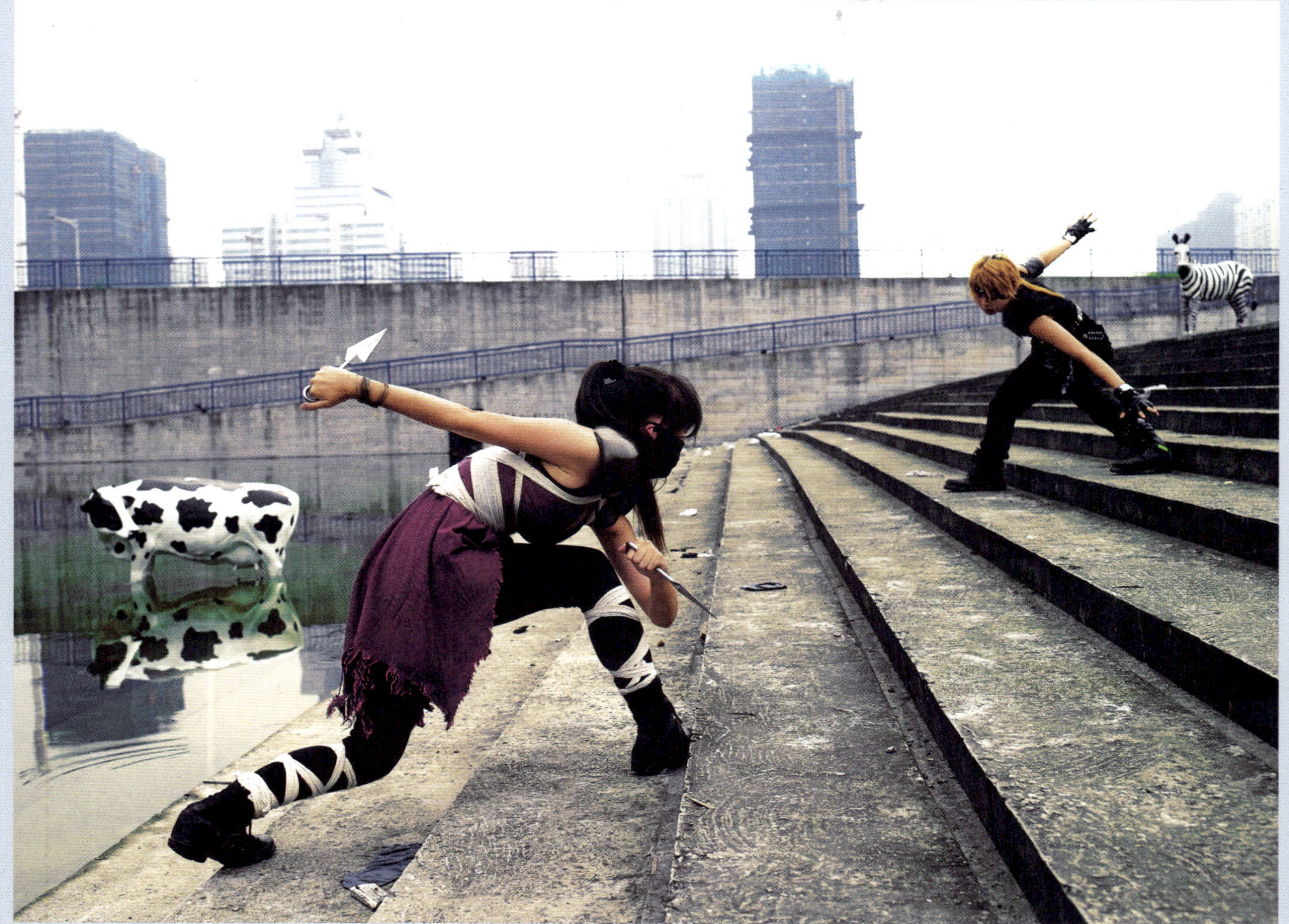

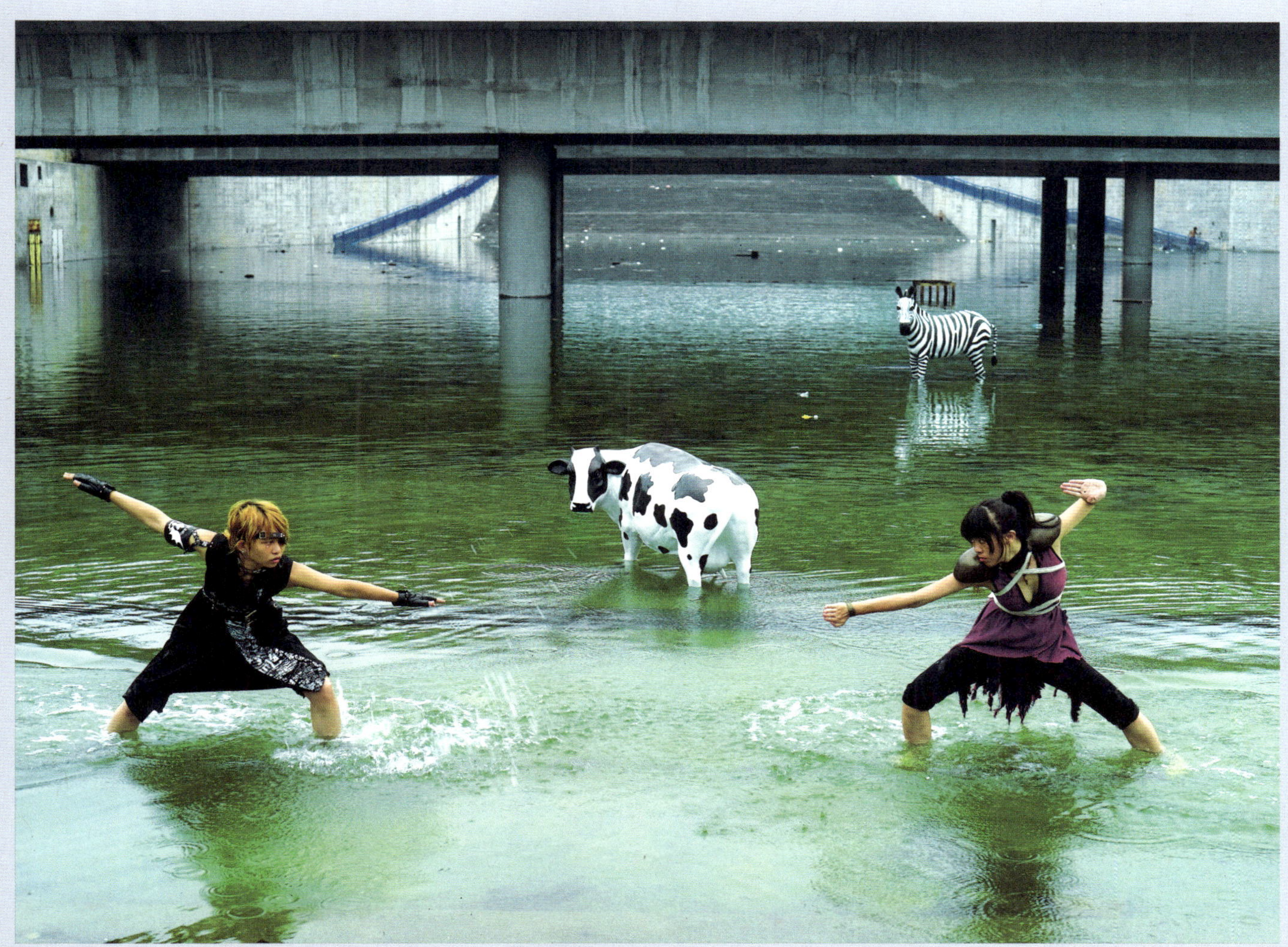

Cao Fei, *Tussle* (from the *Cosplayers* series), 2004.

A Call to Innovative Philanthropy

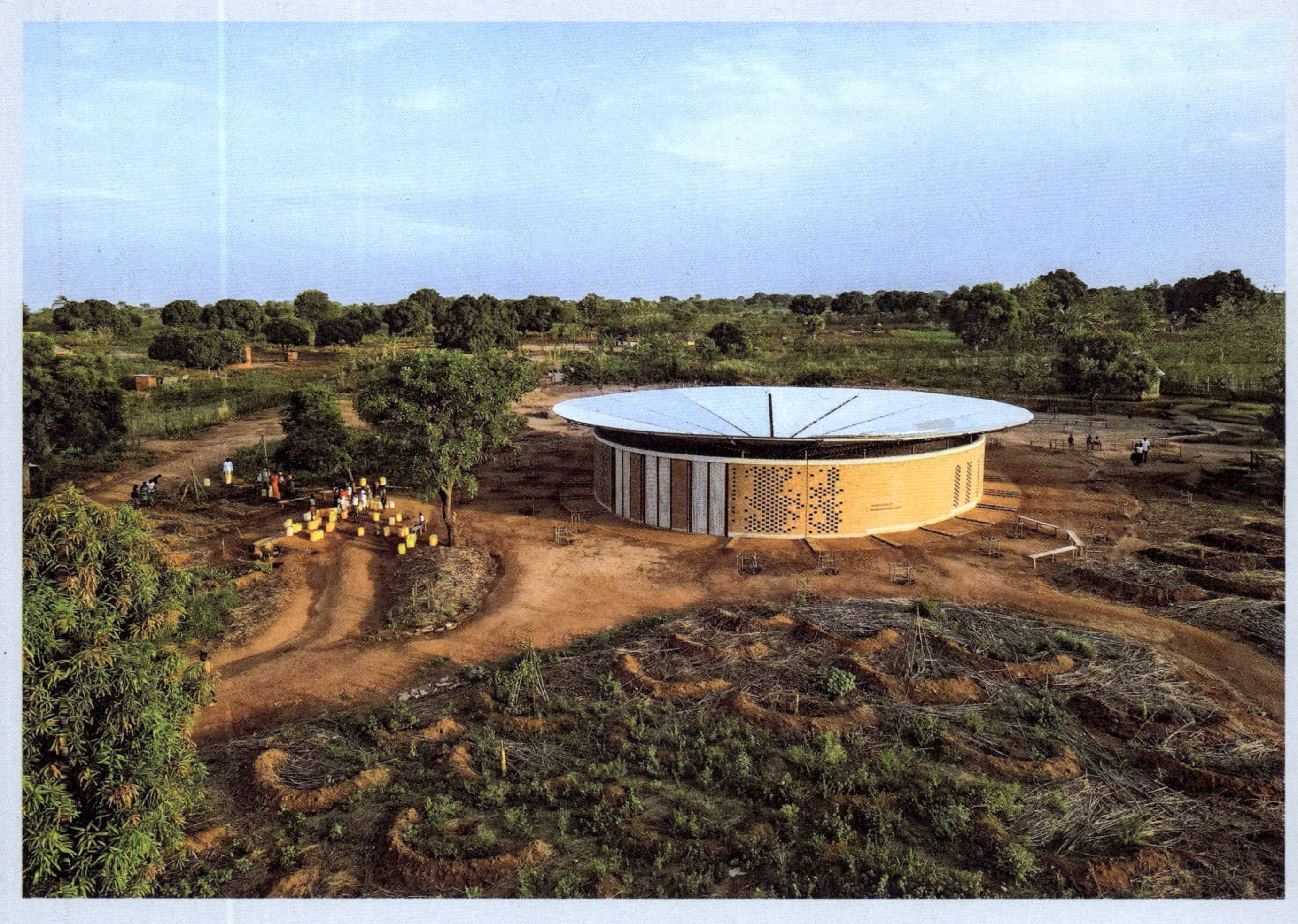

Nachson Mimran, Brian Harris &
To.org Creative Activists

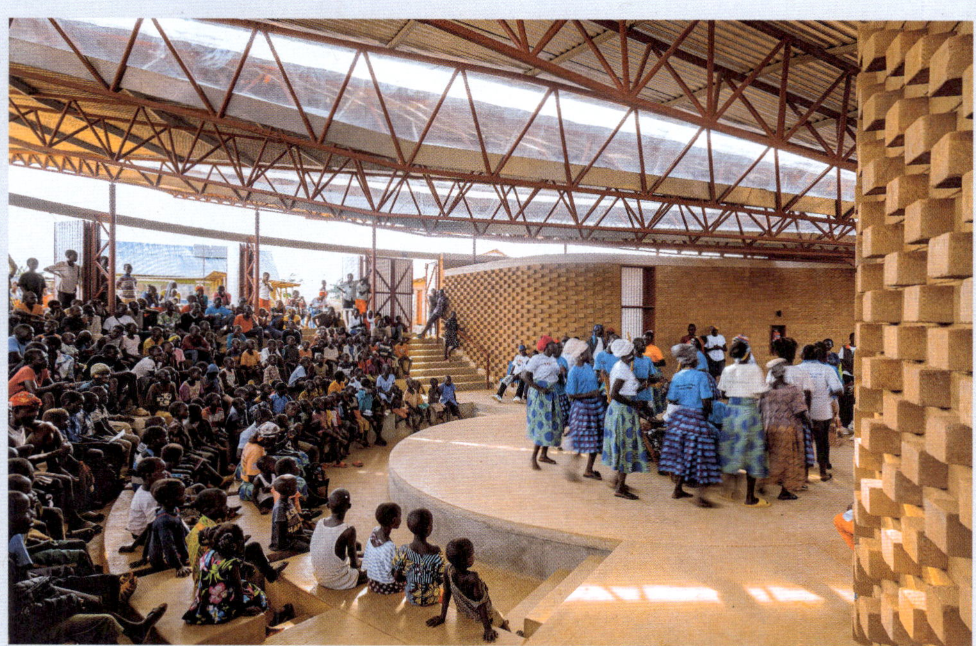

Bidi Bidi Performing Arts Centre, Uganda. Designed by Hassell Studios.

The Intersection of Climate Migration and Urbanisation in Africa

Africa stands at a pivotal juncture, where the forces of climate change and rapid urbanisation are profoundly reshaping the continent's landscape. As the world grapples with the escalating impacts of climate volatility, Africa emerges as both a battleground and a beacon of hope. With its cities growing at unprecedented rates and its lands becoming increasingly uninhabitable due to climate extremes, the need for innovative solutions has never been more urgent.

Climate Migration: Africa's Growing Challenge

Globally, one in two climate migrants is in Africa, and the continent is projected to see a staggering increase in this figure over the coming decades. By 2050, sub-Saharan Africa alone is predicted to have 86 million climate migrants. This migration is not just a movement of people; it represents a seismic shift in the human geography of the continent. The displacement of millions will place immense pressure on cities and the land, demanding a radical rethinking of urban planning, infrastructure, and resource management.

The world's ten fastest-growing cities are all in Africa, and by 2050, the urban population of the continent is expected to reach 900 million. This urban boom is both a symptom and a cause of the challenges Africa faces. As rural areas become less viable due to climate impacts, people are flocking to cities in search of better opportunities. Yet, these urban areas are often ill-equipped to handle such rapid growth, leading to the proliferation of informal settlements where basic services are scarce, and vulnerability is high.

Harnessing Technology to Predict and Prepare

In response to these challenges, To.org Foundation has partnered with AlphaGeo, the leading AI-powered geospatial predictive analytics platform, to create 'Africa at Risk', an interactive StoryMap that demonstrates the flow of human migration and projects population growth driven by climate volatility across Africa's 54 nations. This collaboration is a testament to the power of innovative technology in addressing some of the most pressing issues of our time.

Using complex data sets that span demographics, urbanisation patterns, transportation networks, and climate modelling, forced migration across the African continent until 2050 is systematically anticipated. The findings are stark: annual cross-border migration is expected to rise to more than 10 million people per year by 2050. Additionally, by 2040, Africa will be home to a dozen cities with more than ten million people each. This macro perspective has allowed To.org Foundation to strategically plan its philanthropic project pipeline, proactively preparing for the increased influx of migrants to major cities, as well as to informal and refugee settlements.

Urbanisation: The Strain on Land and Resources

The rapid urbanisation of Africa brings with it a host of challenges related to land use and infrastructure. Cities like Lagos, currently home to 15 million people, are projected to swell to 32 million by 2050. This explosive growth will strain existing infrastructure to its breaking point, exacerbating issues such as housing shortages, traffic congestion, and inadequate public services.

But urbanisation is not just about numbers; it's about the transformation of land and its implications for its inhabitants. As cities expand, they consume vast tracts of land, often encroaching on agricultural areas and natural habitats. This land transformation can lead to conflicts over resources, displacement of communities, and the destruction of ecosystems.

To.org Foundation and like-minded partners recognise these challenges and are committed to addressing them through innovative projects that aim to create sustainable and resilient urban environments. One such project is the Bidi Bidi Performing Arts Centre, located in Africa's largest refugee settlement in Uganda. This interdisciplinary project illustrates the potential to transform the lived experience in refugee settlements by providing creative infrastructure that prioritises expression, trauma reduction, and youth development. Since its inauguration in December 2023, the centre has become a thriving hub where youth gather to create, share music and dance traditions, and build community.

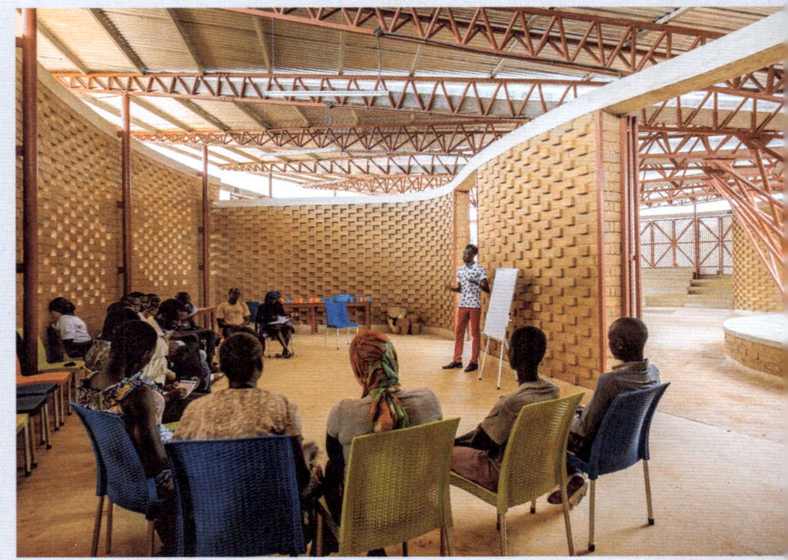

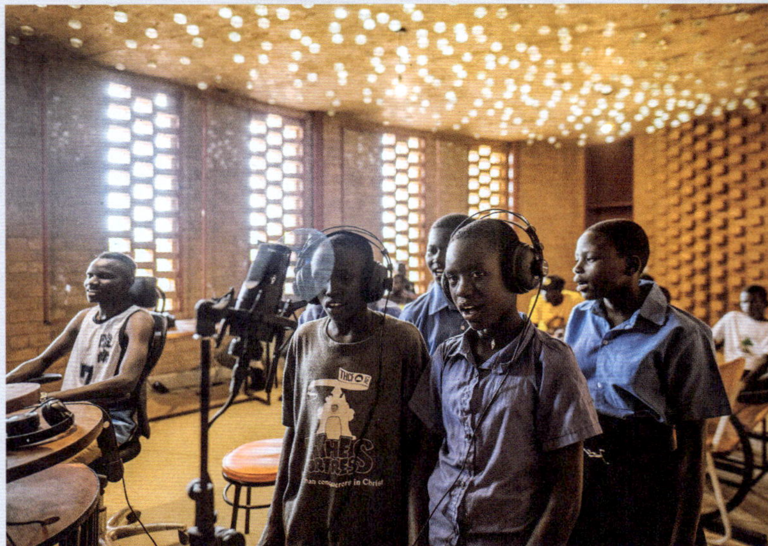

Bidi Bidi Performing Arts Centre, Uganda. Designed by Hassell Studios.

Innovative Philanthropy: Building Resilience

Key to the success of projects such as this is the combination of venture capital, philanthropy, and the creative space that drive meaningful change. By collaborating with leaders in cutting-edge technology, non-profit organisations are creating new humanitarian models that address the root causes of climate migration and urbanisation.

One of the key strategies is developing sustainable infrastructure in vulnerable areas. For example, in addition to the Bidi Bidi Performing Arts Centre, another major project is being planned in the Kakuma refugee settlement in Kenya. These initiatives are part of To.org Foundation's broader refugee empowerment grant thesis, which aims to support grassroots organisations and social enterprises that are making a tangible impact on the ground.

Through past collaborations, To.org Foundation has also explored innovative solutions to environmental challenges. For instance, the organisation has worked with designers and additive manufacturing experts to transform plastic waste into a construction material. This approach not only helps to eradicate plastic waste but also provides a sustainable alternative for building infrastructure in rapidly growing urban areas. The Pavilion and The Throne are two proof-of-concept projects that demonstrate the potential of this approach. Both structures were designed and built using computational techniques and 3D printing, allowing for customisation to match local climatic conditions.

As Africa continues to urbanise at an unprecedented rate, the need for innovative, sustainable solutions to land use and infrastructure challenges becomes ever more critical. The work of To.org and its partners represents a forward-thinking approach to addressing these challenges. By leveraging technology, creative thinking, and strategic philanthropy, it is possible to build a more resilient future for Africa's rapidly growing urban populations.

In this context, the role of creative activism becomes crucial. This ethos aims to inspire and challenge those who use creativity to disrupt and provoke naughty industries and act responsibly. The aim is to treat waste plastic not as a byproduct to be discarded but as an inexhaustible resource. By advocating for the adoption of circular economy practices, To.org Foundation seeks to transform how these industries approach material use, reducing pollution and reversing the damaging impact of climate change that they have contributed to. By rethinking waste and embracing the principles of a circular economy, there is an opportunity to not only mitigate the negative impacts of industrial activities but also to create new, sustainable pathways for development.

This approach aligns perfectly with To.org's broader mission of 'tikkun olam'– healing the world. Collaborations across sectors, encouraging a shift in mindset, are paving the way for a future where creativity and responsibility go hand in hand. Projects such as the Bidi Bidi Performing Arts Centre or the transformation of plastic waste into construction materials, exemplify how innovative philanthropy can drive meaningful change.

As we look to the future, it is clear that the intersection of climate change, urbanisation, and corporate responsibility will define the challenges and opportunities of the coming decades. The actions we take today – whether in the form of new technologies, creative collaborations, or shifts in industry practices – will shape the world we leave for future generations.

The story of land and urbanisation in Africa is still being written, and the narrative is one of both immense challenge and incredible potential. It is a story that calls for bold, innovative thinking and collective action. Through our collective efforts, there is hope that Africa's urban future can be one of opportunity, sustainability, and resilience – a future where the land is not just a resource to be exploited, but a shared heritage to be preserved and nurtured for generations to come. ✦

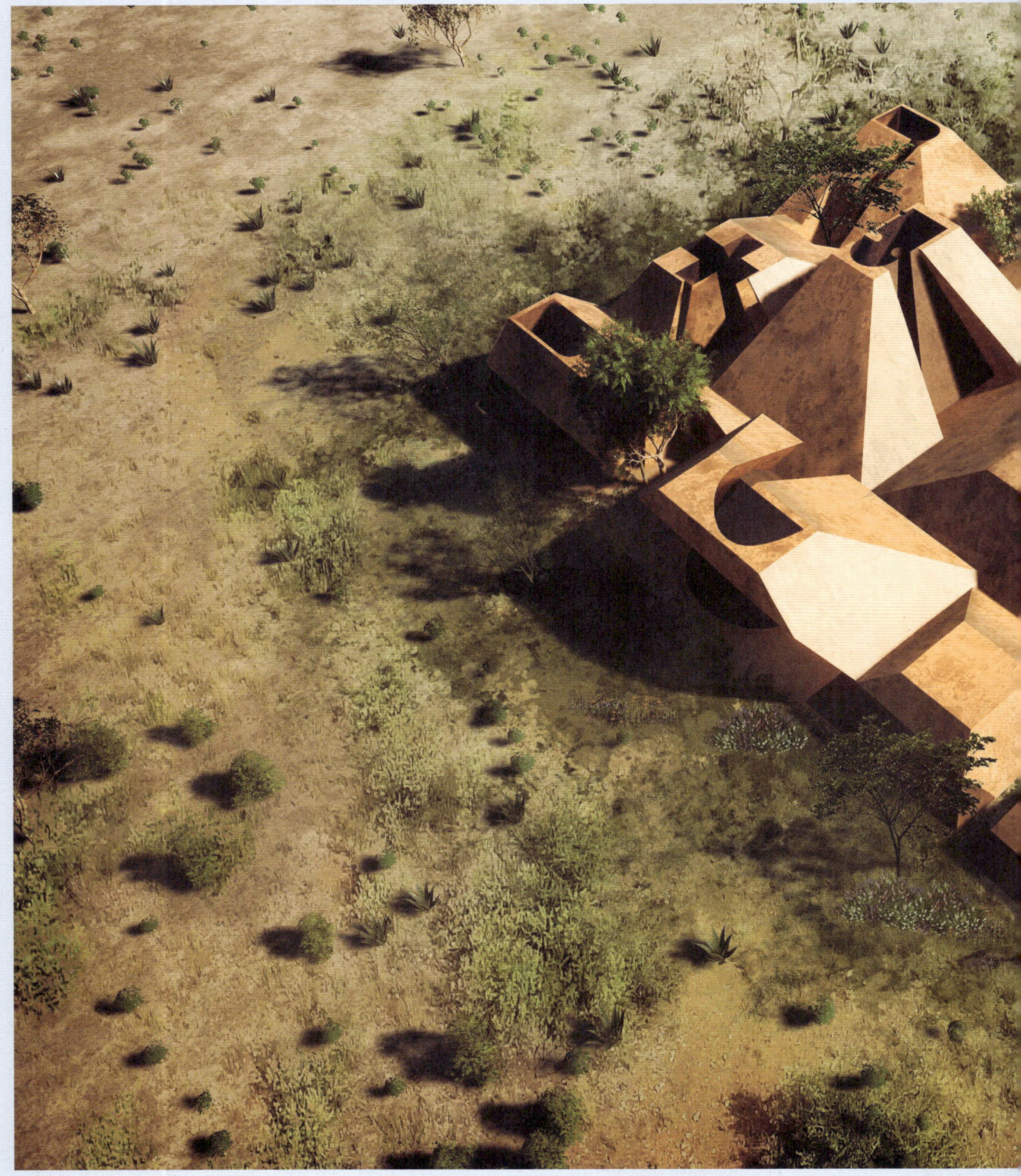

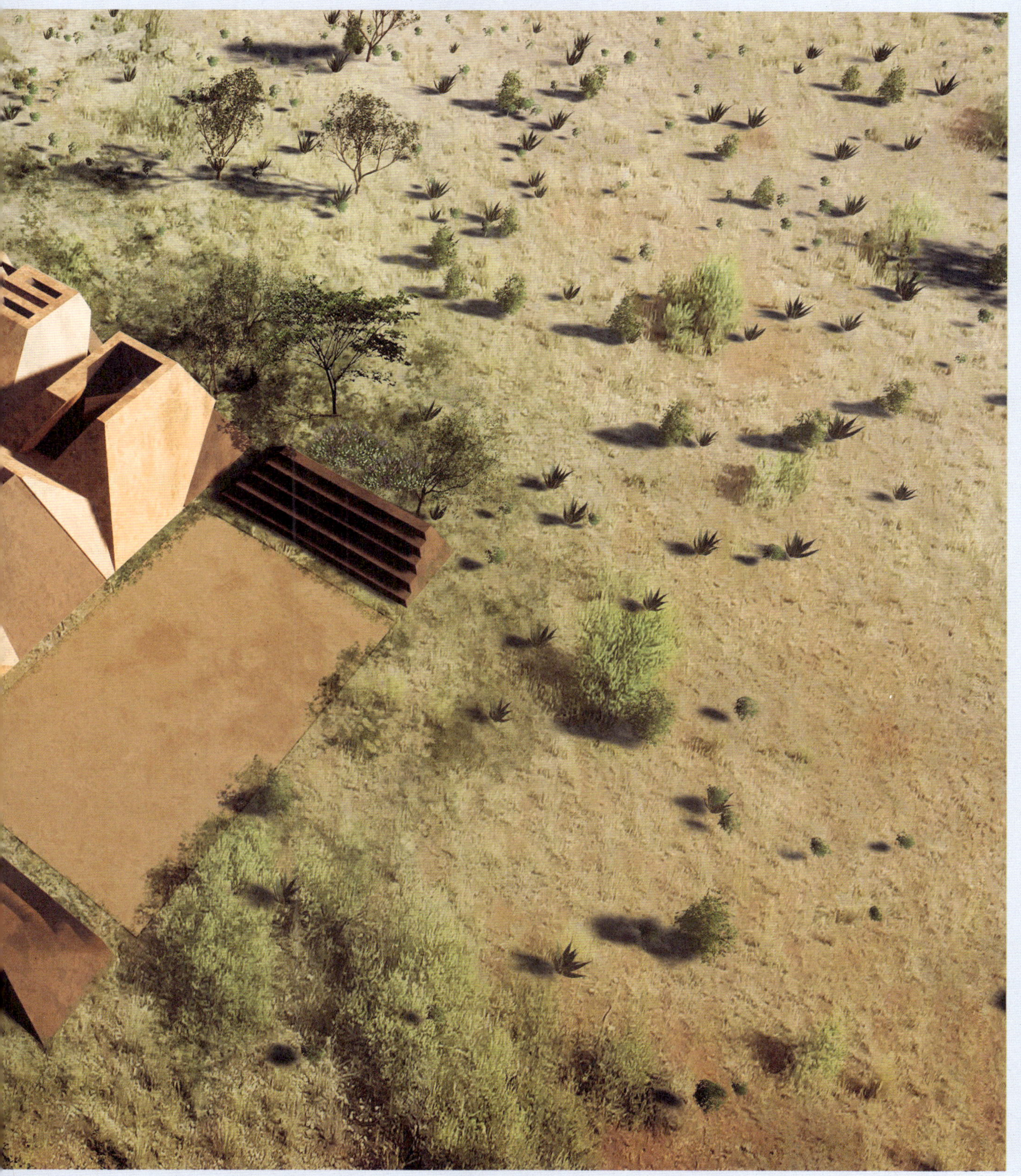

Regenerate Kakuma refugee settlement, Kenya. Designed by Counterspace by Sumayya Vally.

The Throne – innovative use of recycled medical waste to produce a mobile toilet.

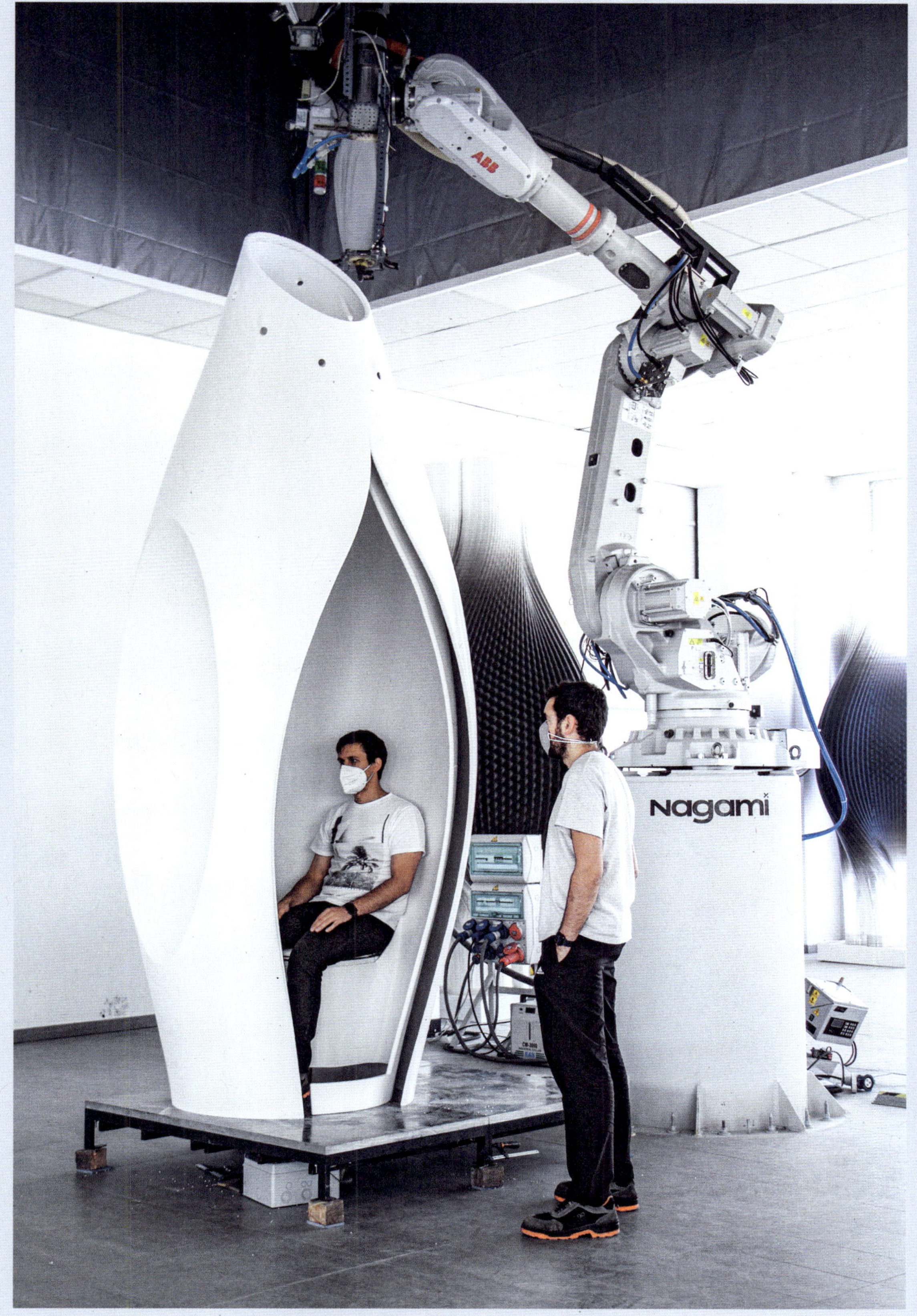
ABB
Nagami

Urban Geography and Sustainable City Land Management

Moustapha Cisse and Tony Simons

Introduction

The Earth and its associated land have existed for around 4.7 billion years, whereas modern humans have been present only a small fraction of that time at around 250,000 years. Cities are an even more recent addition to land on Earth, having emerged 9,400 years ago. If we equated Earth's existence from the beginning until now to a single calendar year, then humans came on the scene around 11:33 pm on December 31st, and, even more recent, cities arose at around one minute to midnight (11:59 pm) on December 31st.

Cities and their emergence, geolocation, and growth are highly correlated to human population increases and strategic positioning. They were a neolithic creation that arose when food surpluses were produced from agriculture away from historic 'hunter-gatherer' practices. Interestingly, more than half of all cities above 1 million are located on the coast, and two-thirds of cities above 2.5 million inhabitants are at coastal sites. Coastal locations were chosen historically for a number of reasons including: ease of transport, security, health, food supply, and access to a hinterland. More than 60 % of all city dwellers live in a coastal city. With looming sea level rise due to man-made climate change, the need to better manage the land of coastal urban settings is particularly pressing.

UNESCO recognises 1,199 World Heritage Sites covering 480 million hectares (3 % land above sea level). Of the 1,199 sites, 933 properties (78 %) are classified as being of high 'cultural' significance, and these are nearly all located in current or past city environments. Only 227 sites (19 %) are classified of having high 'natural' significance and the vast majority of these lie in natural habitats (19 %). The remainder of 39 sites are classified as 'mixed' with both cultural and natural significance. This situation perhaps highlights that as a global community we prioritise human endeavours above natural wonder. We seemingly marvel at a stone structure created by our ancestors some 4,000 years ago but are apparently less interested in the stone formed 4 billion years ago and its weathering to create soils and ingredients for life.

To most urban authorities the concepts of land degradation and restoration equate to the infrastructure and services dimension of land and less so to the biophysical make-up, land health, and intrinsic productivity. This view however might be outdated as in 2018 it is estimated that between 5 to 10 % of the global production of legumes, vegetables, and tubers was done in urban settings. And if cereals, tree crops, and oilseeds are added, then between 15 to 20 % of global food is produced in urban and peri-urban environments. These figures may have likely moved upwards also as a result of stay-in-place measures endured during the COVID-19 pandemic from March 2020 to May 2022.

Poverty is rooted in inequality and in inequity, where inequality refers to the *uneven* distribution of resources and opportunities, and inequity refers to the *unfair* distribution of resources and opportunities. Since land resources are most expensive in cities it is not surprising that inequality and inequity of land use and rights are most pronounced in cities. Poverty is not just a financial state but one that involves just as much issues of self-esteem and self-determination, as well as social, spiritual, and cultural dimensions.

City Classifications

Although most people might feel they know what an urban setting looks like, countries vary considerably in how they define urban areas due to the multiplicity of local contexts. Unfortunately, this makes comparison of urbanisation patterns across countries difficult. Most countries use a minimum population size to define an urban area, but this can be hugely discrepant. In China, the minimum threshold for urban categorisation is 100,000 inhabitants whereas in Denmark it is only 200 persons. There might be a 300-fold difference in total population between China and Denmark and so here a similarly scaled ratio for urban congregation could be argued for. But then how does that explain India, which in 2023 surpassed China as the most populus nation, and which has an urban definition of above 5,000 inhabitants?

Heterogenity in urban definitions in turn affects attempts to disaggregate other parameters in a clear binary urban/rural way, including things such as eligibility for financial support and poverty. In some countries, areas are eligible for fiscal transfers if they are classified as rural hence there may be reluctance to be re-categorised, or authorities may hesitate if they are unable to meet statutory requirements such as provision of health clinics or police stations if it was reclassified as urban. The World Bank recently took up the issue and rather than follow a single metric they now promote the use of a new measure called '*Degree of Urbanisation*'. This combines population numbers and population density to simplify analyses and be transparent, and to make it independent of additional services and infrastructure. One key reason for the change is to prevent the circular argument in some countries where urban is defined as having access to water and electricity. Sustainable Development Goal (SDG) 7 tracks this indicator and the World Bank reports the latest rates of electrification as 97 % in urban areas worldwide and 84 % in rural areas.

The *Degree of Urbanisation* identifies three types of settlements:

A Cities, which have a population of at least 50,000 inhabitants in contiguous dense grid cells (>1,500 inhabitants per km²).

B Towns and semi-dense areas, which have a population of at least 5,000 inhabitants in contiguous grid cells with a density of at least 300 inhabitants per km².

C Rural areas, which consist mostly of low-density grid cells (<300 inhabitants per km²).

Of course, individual countries may decide to add additional criteria, but the *Degree of Urbanisation* allows direct comparisons with the past and future for a given location as well as at a given time for different locations. This urban definition may also not be accepted by all for things like refugee camps which are intended to be temporary but sometimes end up lasting for decades with semi-permanent shelters and service facilities. According to UNHCR, approx. 78 % of refugees live in cities, and many in substandard living conditions.

Land Degradation in Cities

Few datasets are collected and limited analyses are undertaken for land degradation in cities, however, this does not mean degradation is not happening there. The greatest degradation driver on land health and land functioning in cities is the sealing of land. In one study undertaken by the European Environment Agency of 622 cities (so called functional urban areas) in Europe-27 and UK between 2012 and 2018 there was a rural land grab of 360,000 ha and a new sealing of soil of 150,000 ha. The reduced carbon sequestration by vegetation on the 150,000 ha alone was a staggering 4.2 million tonnes. Land sealing though not only affects carbon sequestration but also hydrology, biodiversity and ecosystem functioning. It also creates heat islands.

Against a population increase of 3.1 % in the 622 cities during the 6-year study period introduced above, there were also per capita increases in mineral extraction, dumping sites, and construction. Encouragingly though per capita use of land over the 6 years decreased to 418 m² per capita from a 2012 baseline of 423 m² per capita. Currently, there are no legally binding policy targets in relation to land take and soil sealing at the EU level. However, the new EU Soil Strategy for 2030 calls on Member States to set 'land take' targets for 2030, with the aim of reaching 'land take neutrality' by 2050.

The EU also seem by default to have defined land degradation in urban areas to include inefficient use of land. The EU now have a land class called 'discontinuous urban fabric' which refers to urban structures and transport networks associated with vegetated areas and bare surfaces that occupy significant area in a discontinuous spatial pattern. The impermeable features like buildings, roads, and artificially surfaced areas range from 30 to 80 % land coverage. Low land use efficiency means that few people use a lot of artificial area and hence the amount of artificial area per capita is high. High land use efficiency means that small amounts of artificial area are used by many inhabitants. This is only possible when buildings have several storeys and the built infrastructure, in particular the road network and public transport, are frequented by many people.

It is encouraging that the EU-27 plus UK are taking land degradation and the flip side land restoration seriously, however it is not truly representative of the global situation. Currently, the EU only accounts for 2.8 % of land above sea level, and only 5.5 % of the global population.

The situation in Africa contrasts sharply with that in Europe. Firstly, although there is a parallel organ to the European Union, the African Union, it is less active so far in setting harmonised policies across African countries given higher perceived social and economic needs. Secondly, little data and few analyses are undertaken of land degradation or restoration in African cities. Thirdly, in sub-Saharan Africa most countries are monocentric with most urban dwellers in a single city unlike the polycentric European situation. These features raise some concern when, amongst the few studies that have been undertaken, they show that urban sprawl in Africa is more pronounced than in the global North.

Encouragingly, new initiatives such as the creation of the African Institute of Mathematical Sciences (AIMS) is addressing some of this imbalance. Here AIMS are equipping Africa's youth with critical, independent thinking and problem-solving skills to tackle global, national, and regional challenges. Climate Science and machine intelligence are among the top specialisations being taught.

Land Restoration Opportunities in Cities

Even though only 2 % of land area is occupied by cities, it is home to nearly 60 % of humanity. In terms of land restoration opportunities and preventing further land degradation the urban segment of the human population is perhaps the most significant. And it can do this in direct ways in city environments and indirect ways in adjacent rural settings and natural habitats.

Direct ways for the average city person to exploit opportunities would be with actions such as:

A engaging with a cross-section of actors to better understand, share, and prioritise actions needed;
B advocacy for policy, behavioural, and fiscal change;
C individual decision-making on choices and consequences of restorative and preventative actions;
D revegetating the urban environment and other urban renewal options; and
E elevating land health as an individual, household, and intergenerational issue.

Simple things like reducing waste, recycling to avoid contamination, using public transport, planting shade trees, and installing green roofs can collectively make large positive impacts.

Indirect ways include reducing the footprint of the city on the rural and natural habitat settings. Cities are not self-sufficient and largely rely on non-city areas for the provision of food, energy, water, labour, and materials. Specific actions might include being more conscious of water use and efficiency, choice of building materials, switching to renewable energies, sourcing food more locally, and helping build a circular bioeconomy.

Perhaps most impactfully everyone needs to realise they can be engaged in land restoration and in preventing land degradation. It is about a change in mindsets. We can all do something about it. We can all be more conscious of it. We can set personal, household, and community targets and feel accountable to them.

The advances in Earth Observation, Artificial Intelligence, and Machine Learning can help assess land, target areas for interventions, explore and reduce inequities, and monitor progress. Technology alone will not halt land degradation, nor will it restore degraded areas, but it will be an incredible ally moving forward. ✦

Liam Young, *Planet City*, 2021, video. Centuries of human expansion and extraction, colonisation and globalisation have shaped every part of our planet. This has changed our atmosphere and caused dramatic threats to biodiversity. In his radically utopian work *Planet City*, Liam Young proposes that humans should retreat to a single, hyper-dense city housing ten billion people. The whole global population could live in a giant, self-sufficient city occupying a fraction of Earth's surface, freeing the rest of the planet for rewilding and regeneration.

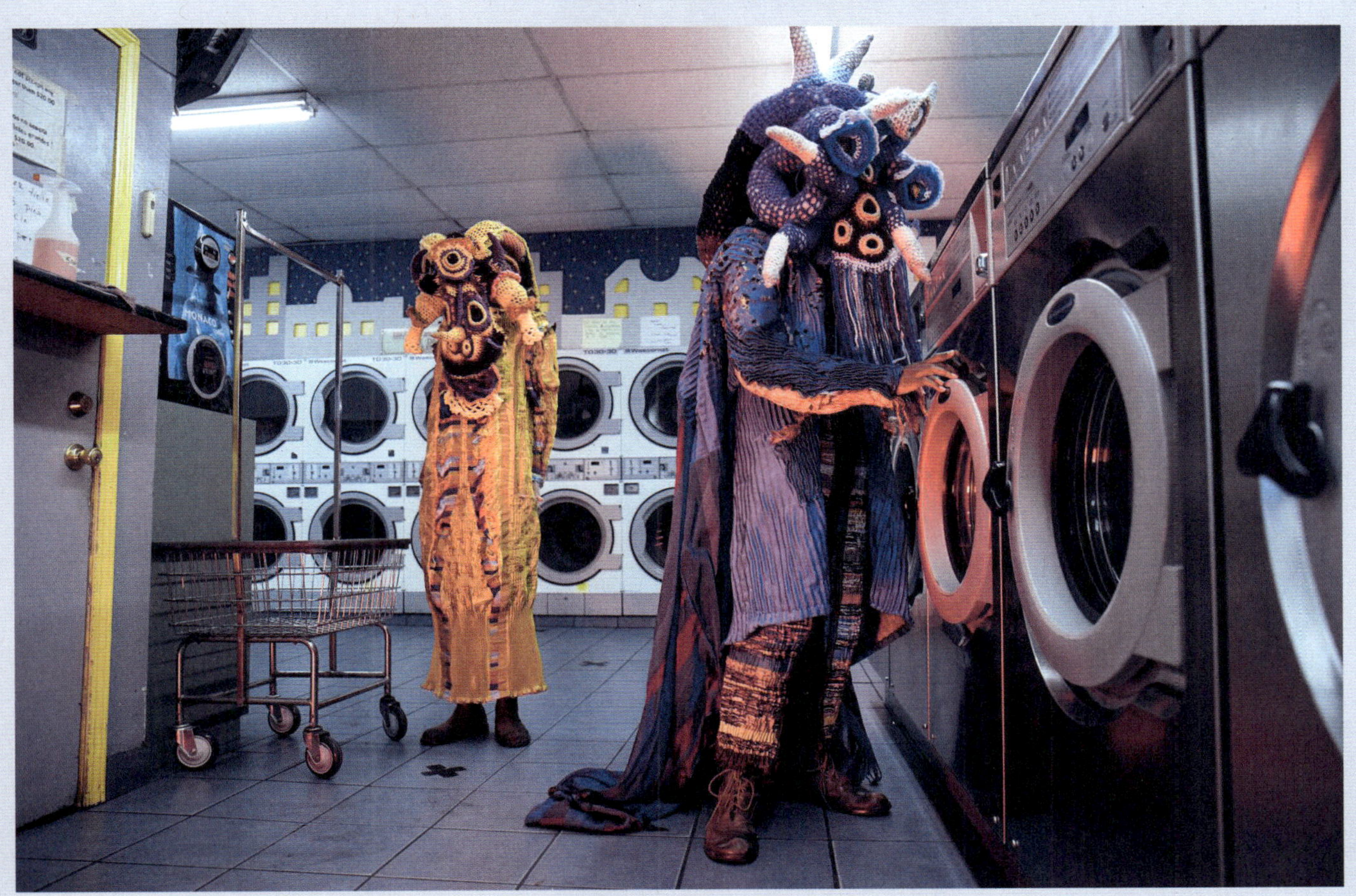

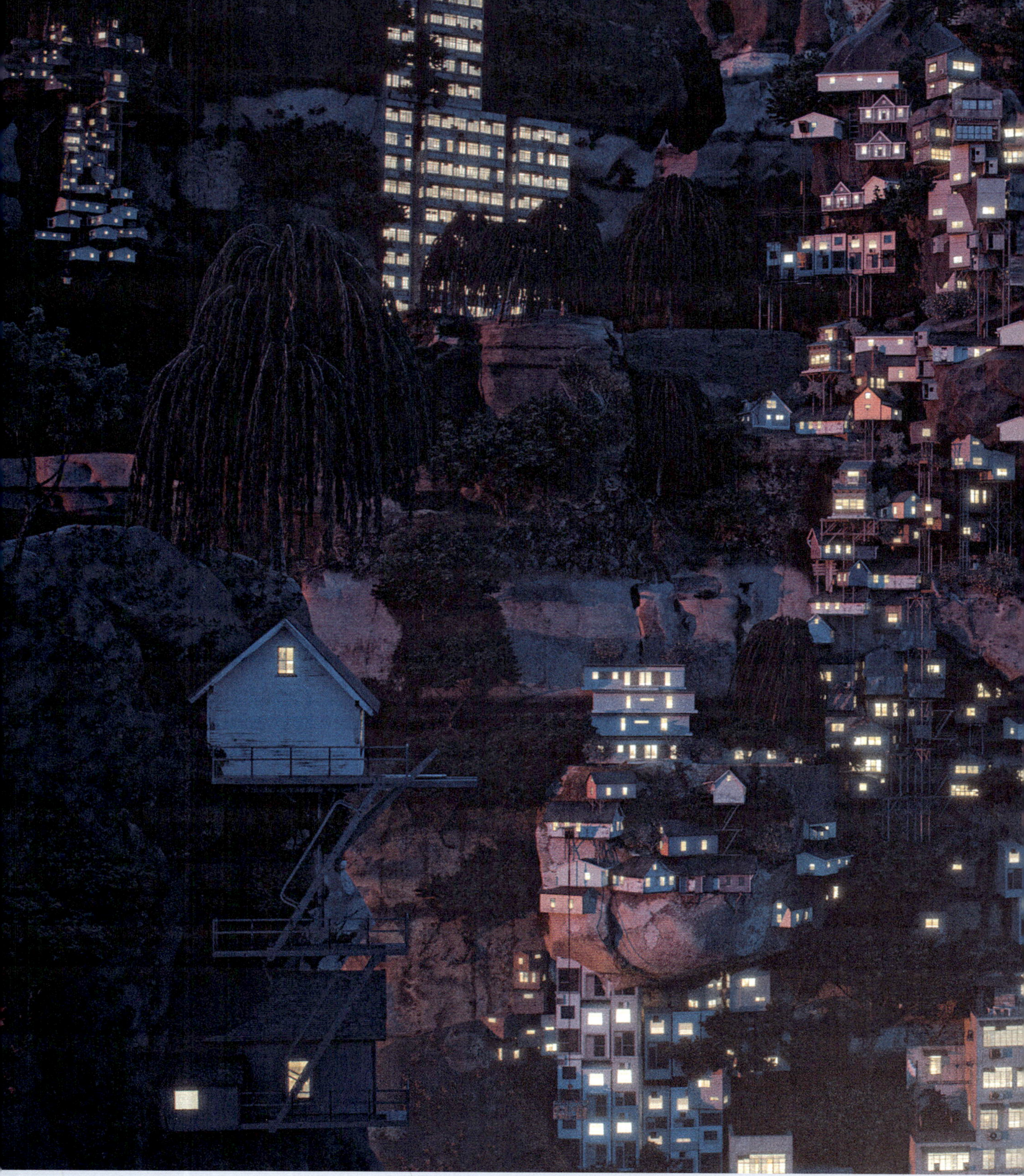

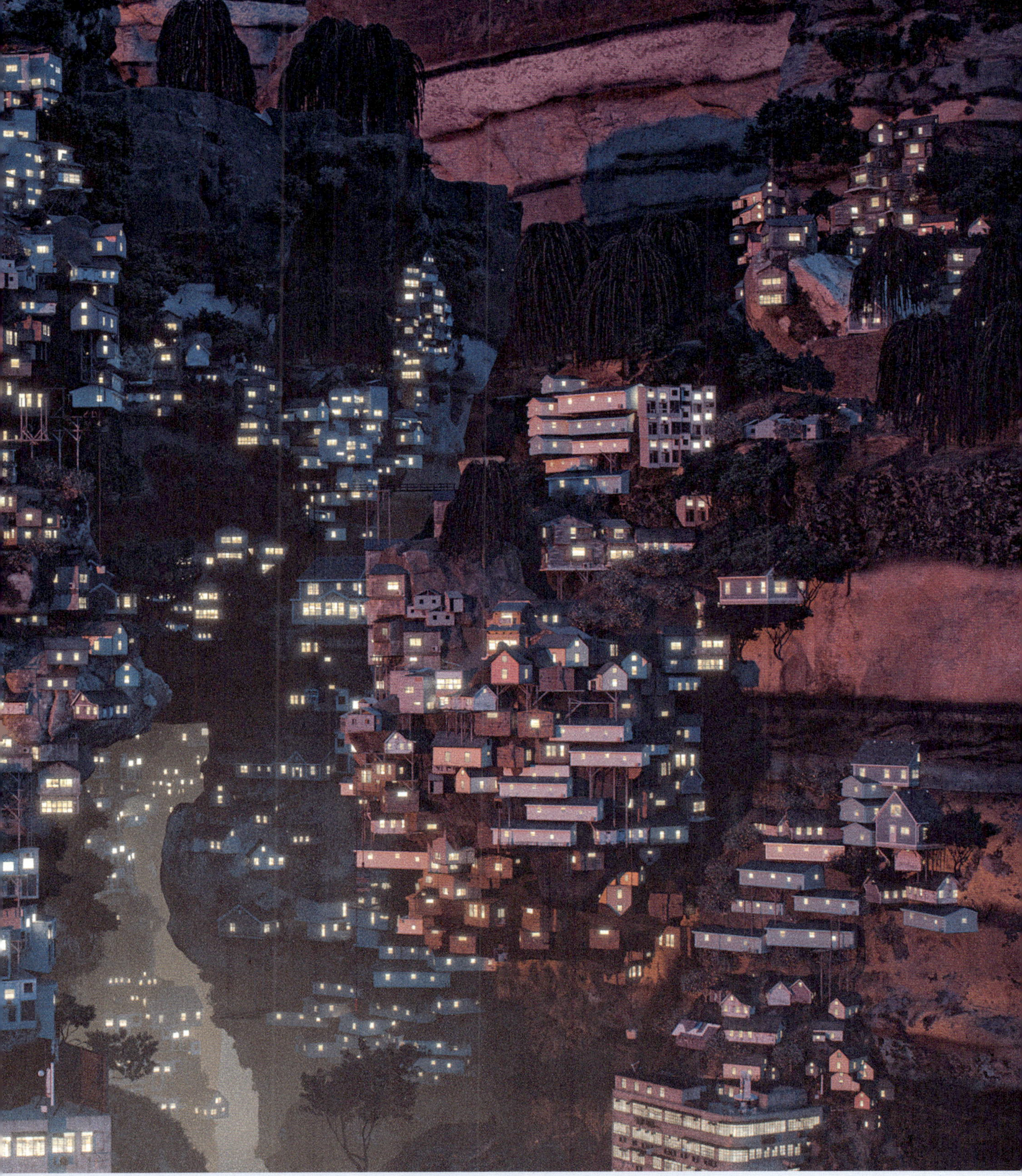

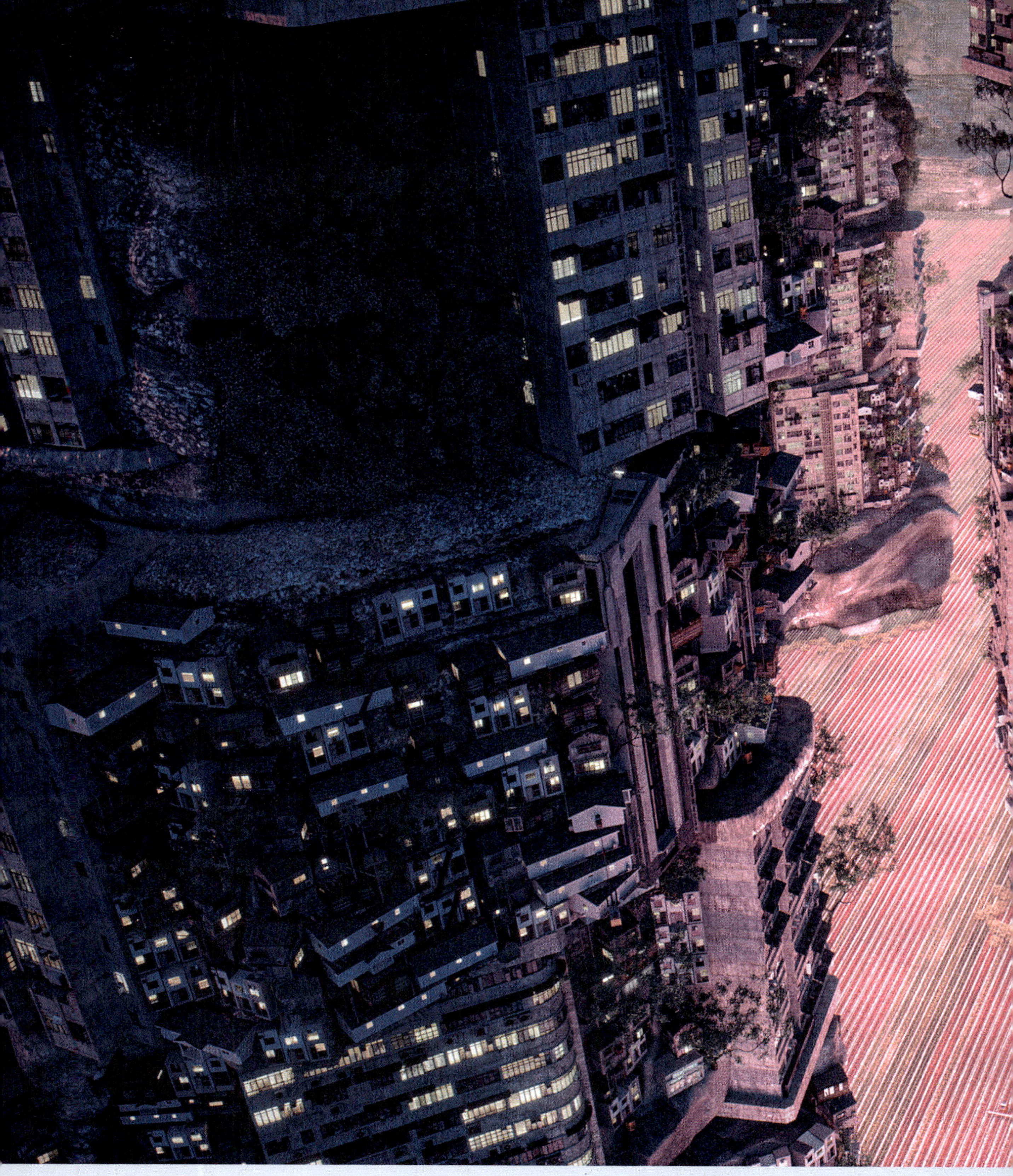

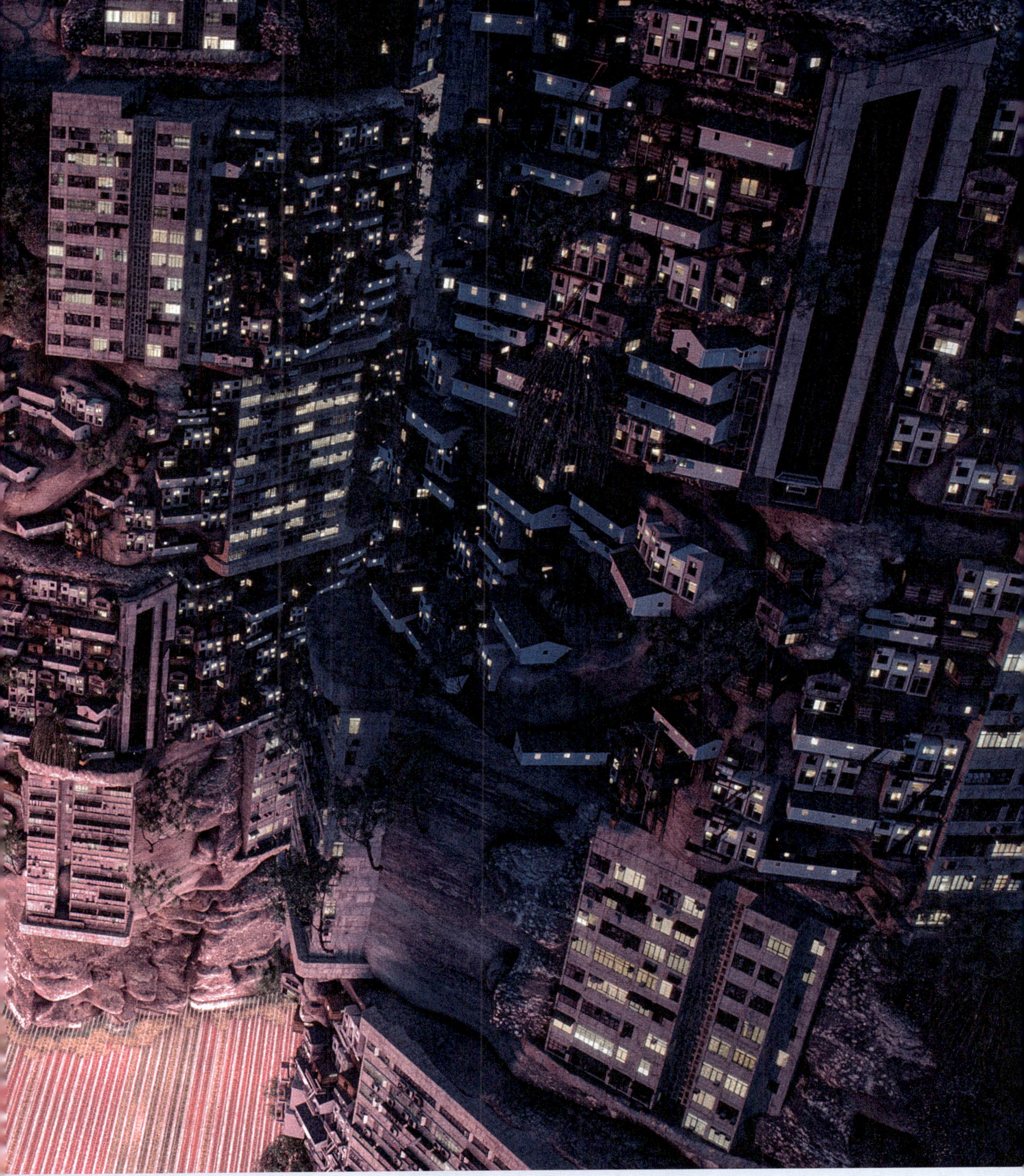

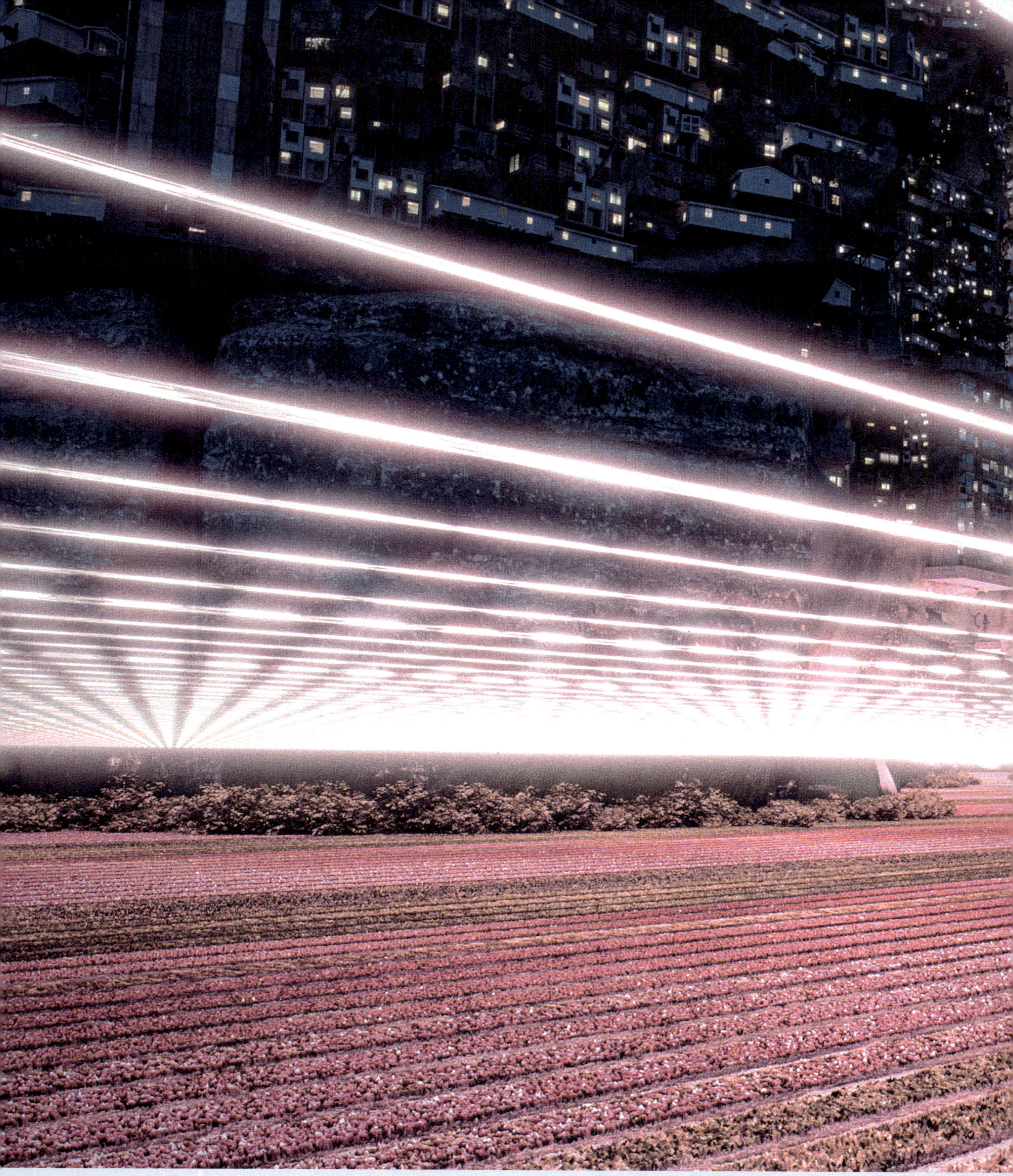

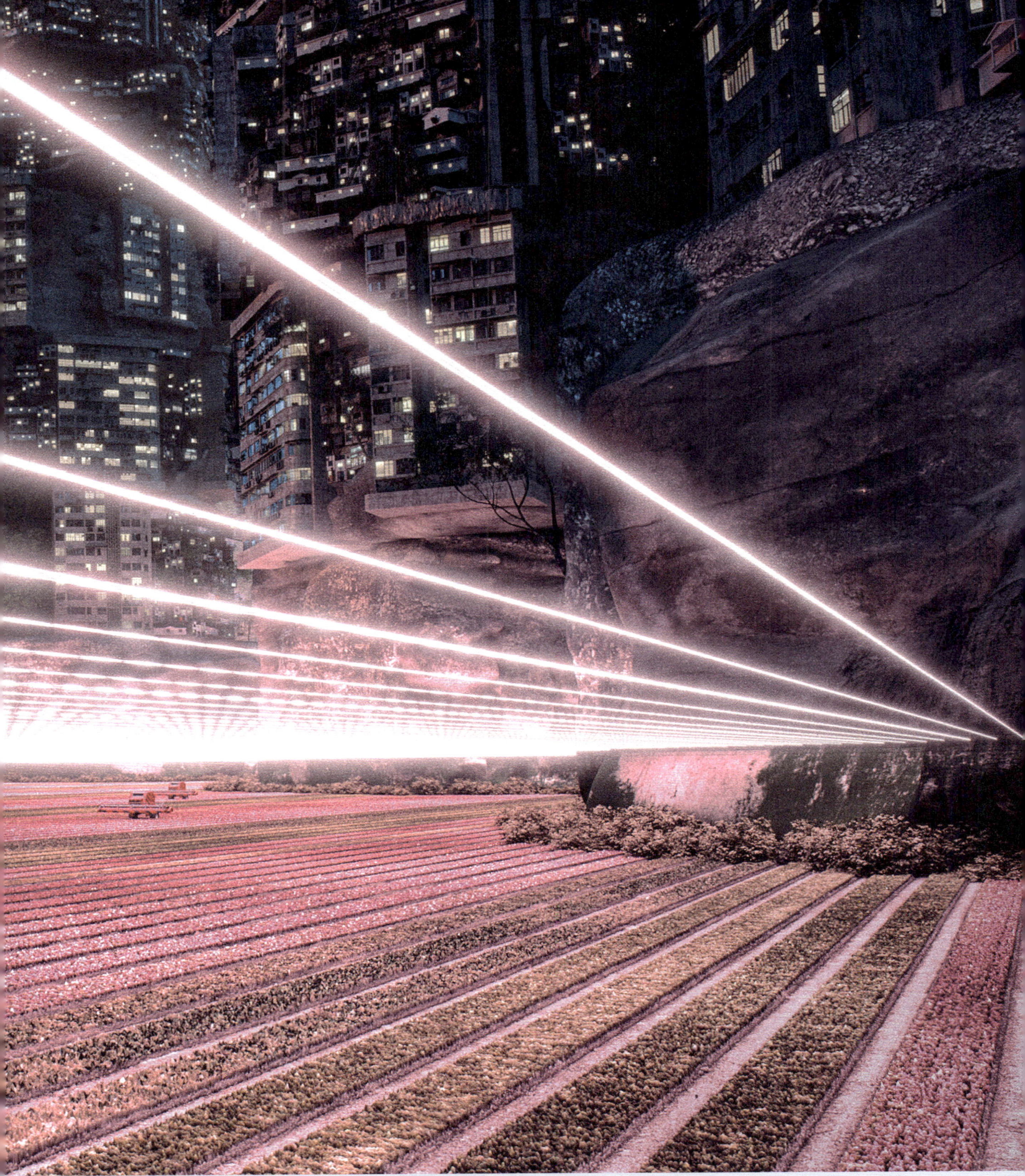

Interactive floor projection 'Rural Lands', 2024 © dform/Bildwerk, Vienna ▶

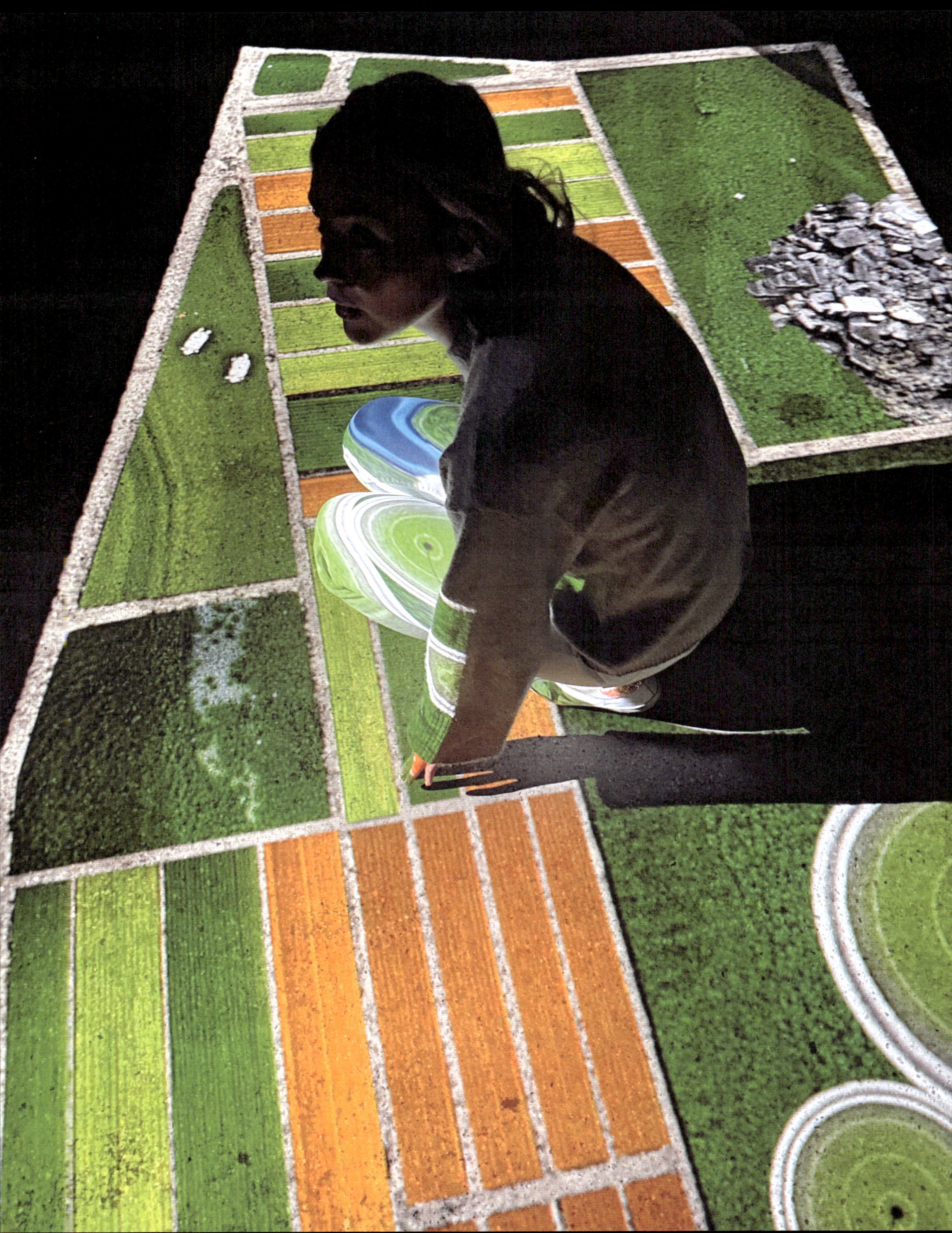

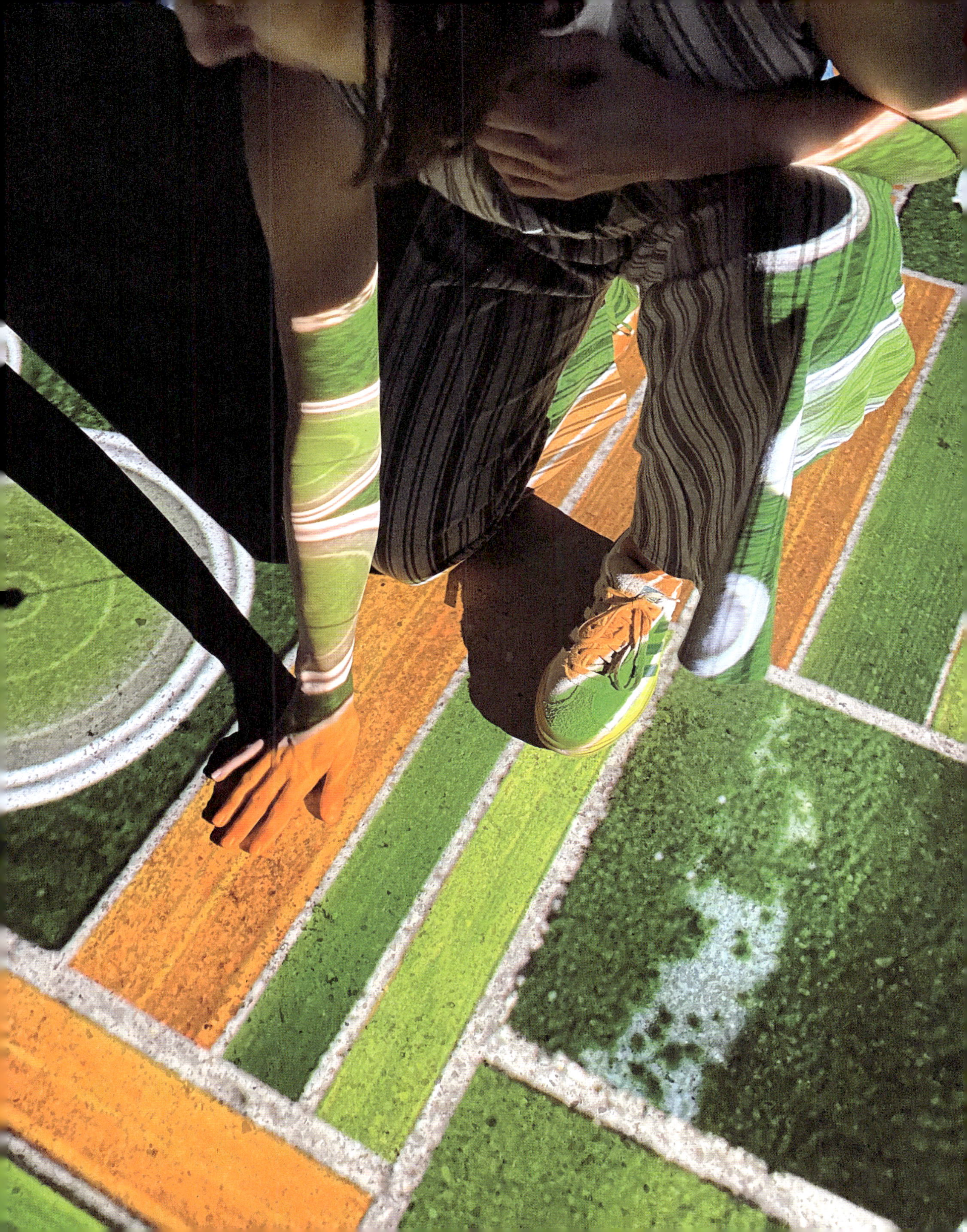

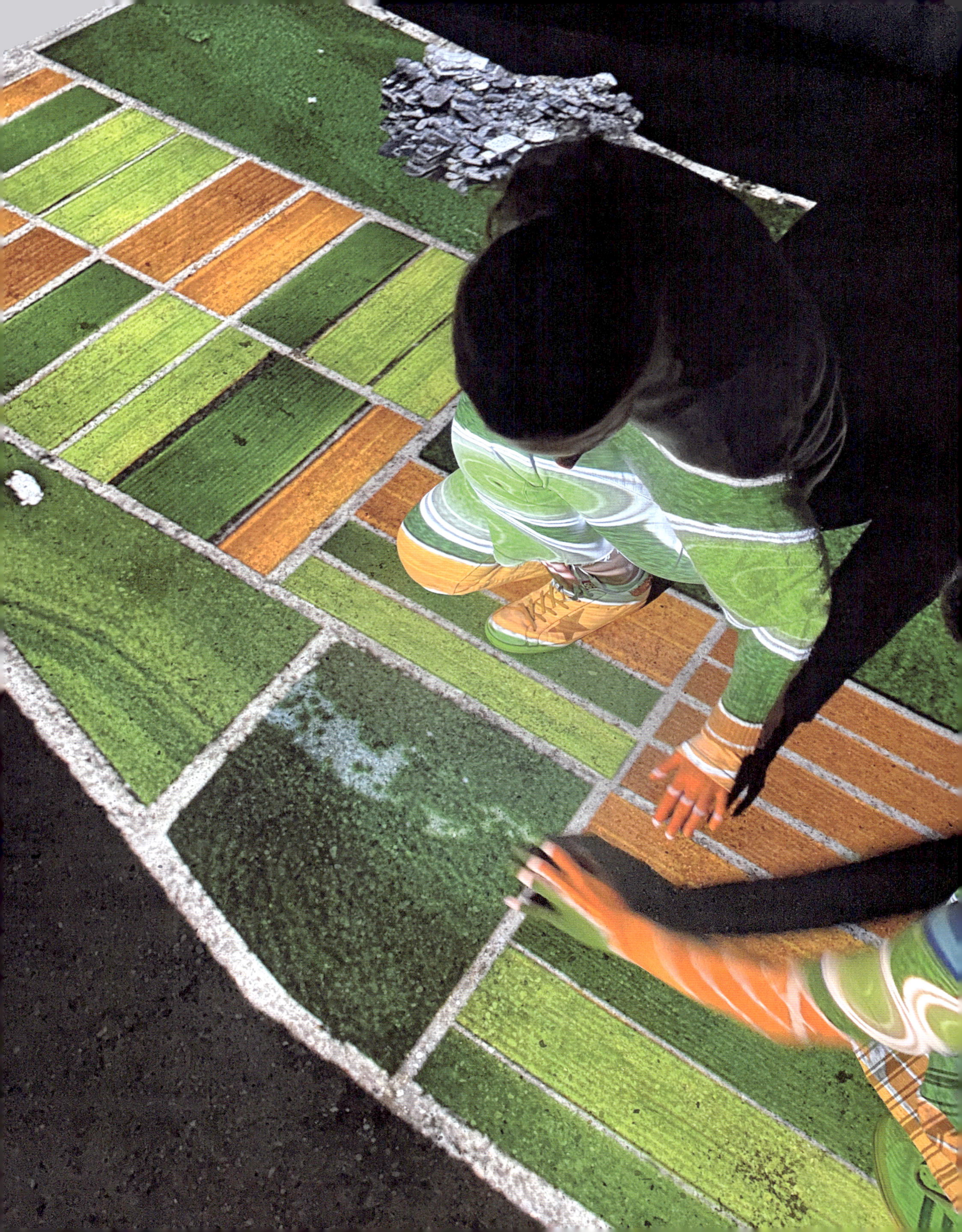

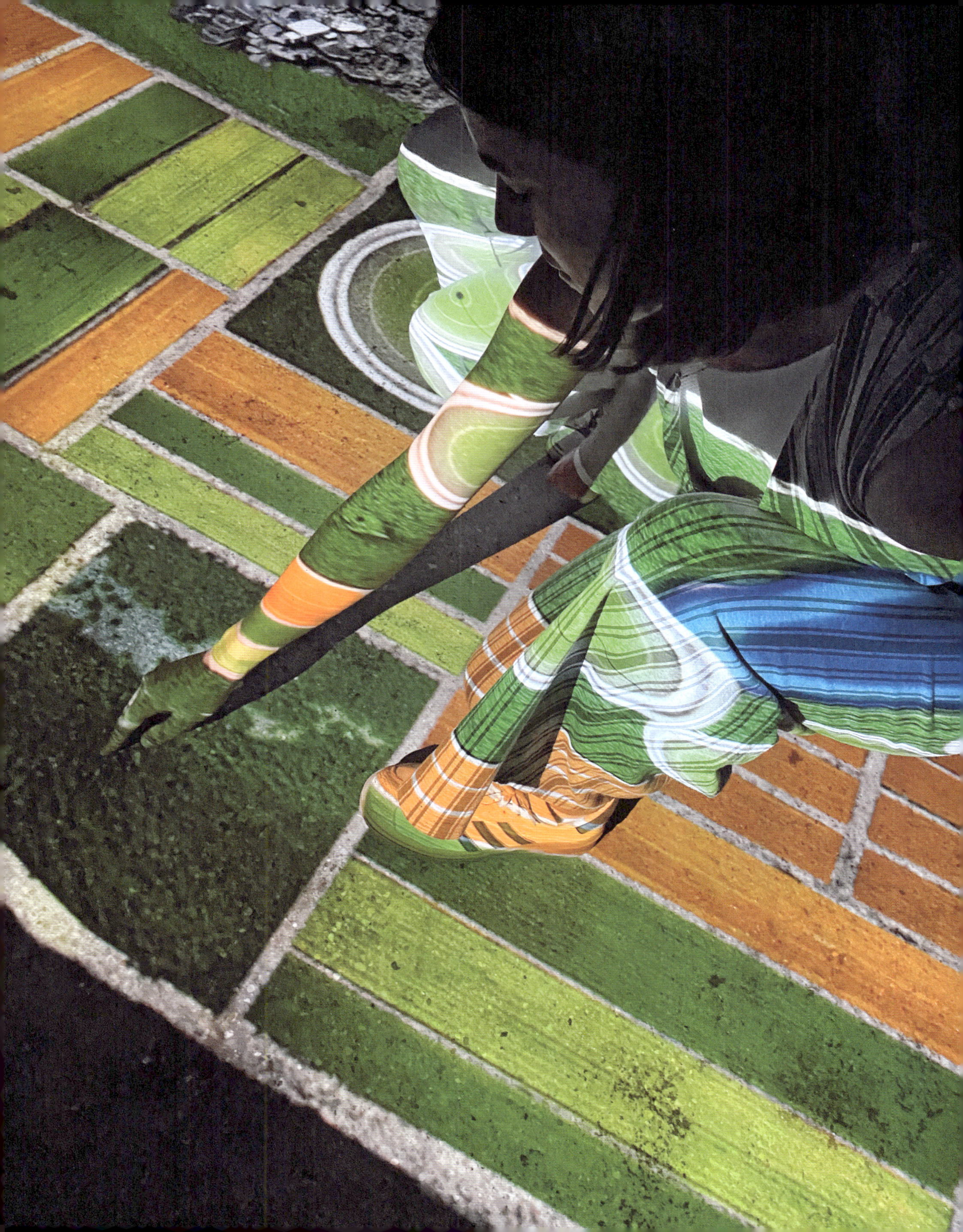

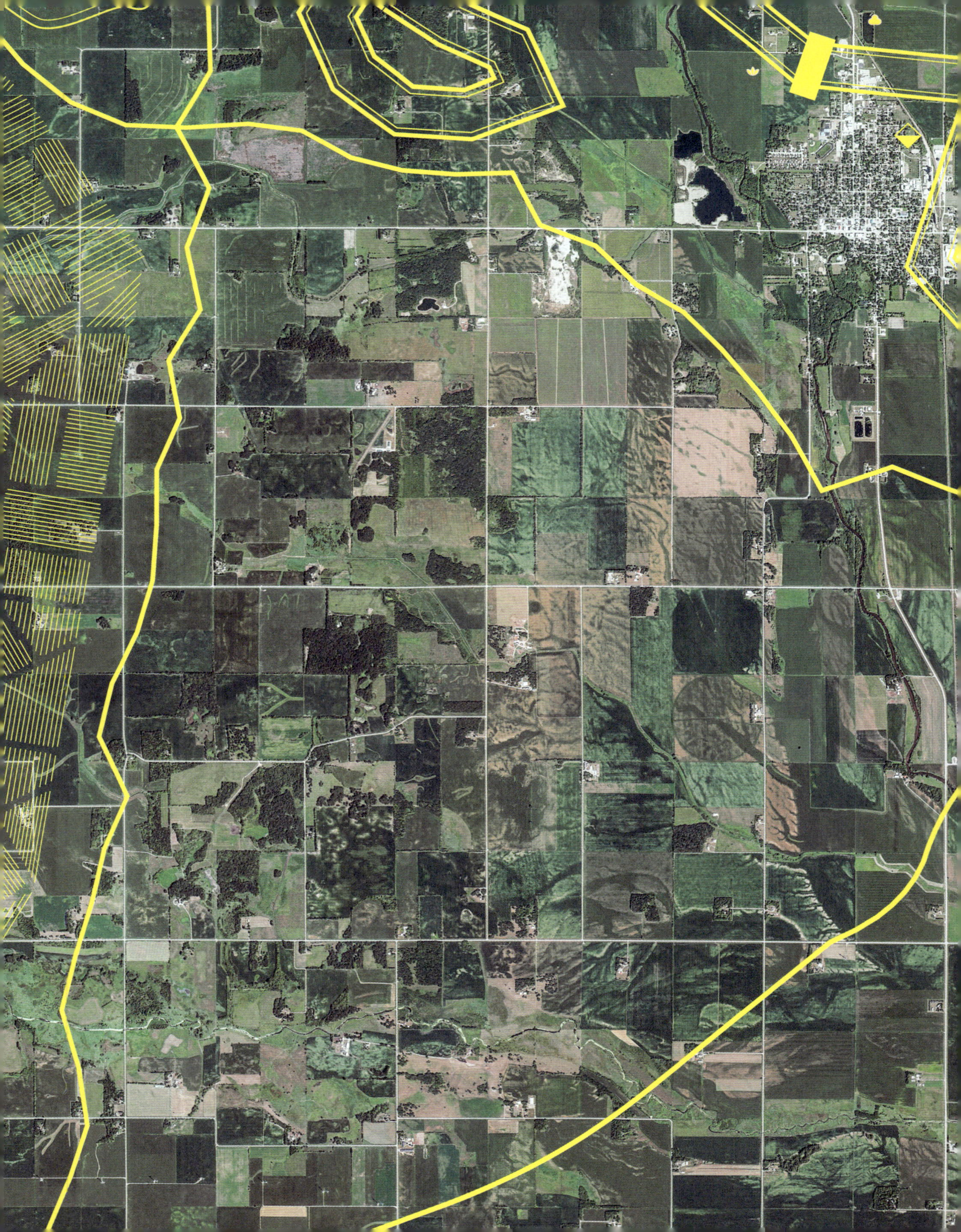

The Big Harvest

Food requires agricultural land for cultivation. This amounts to an average of 2,250 m² per capita annually. More than half is needed for livestock feed production and only 39 % for the cultivation of plant-based foods for human consumption, yet animal products provide only 18 % and plant products 82 % of the world's calories. Agriculture now occupies up to 40 % of the world's land area, of which 50 % is used for growing food, 38 % for feed production, and 12 % for non-food crops. Most of this is grown in the Global South. Globally, food production is responsible for 80 % of deforestation, 70 % of freshwater consumption, 29 % of greenhouse gas emissions, and is the single greatest cause of biodiversity loss. Modern agriculture, with its monocultures and extensive use of chemicals, leads us to use up the land and is responsible for half of all degraded land. Between 2015 and 2019, an area of healthy and productive land twice the size of Greenland was degraded each year, affecting global food and water security.

Strategies for Economically, Socially, and Ecologically Sustainable Agriculture

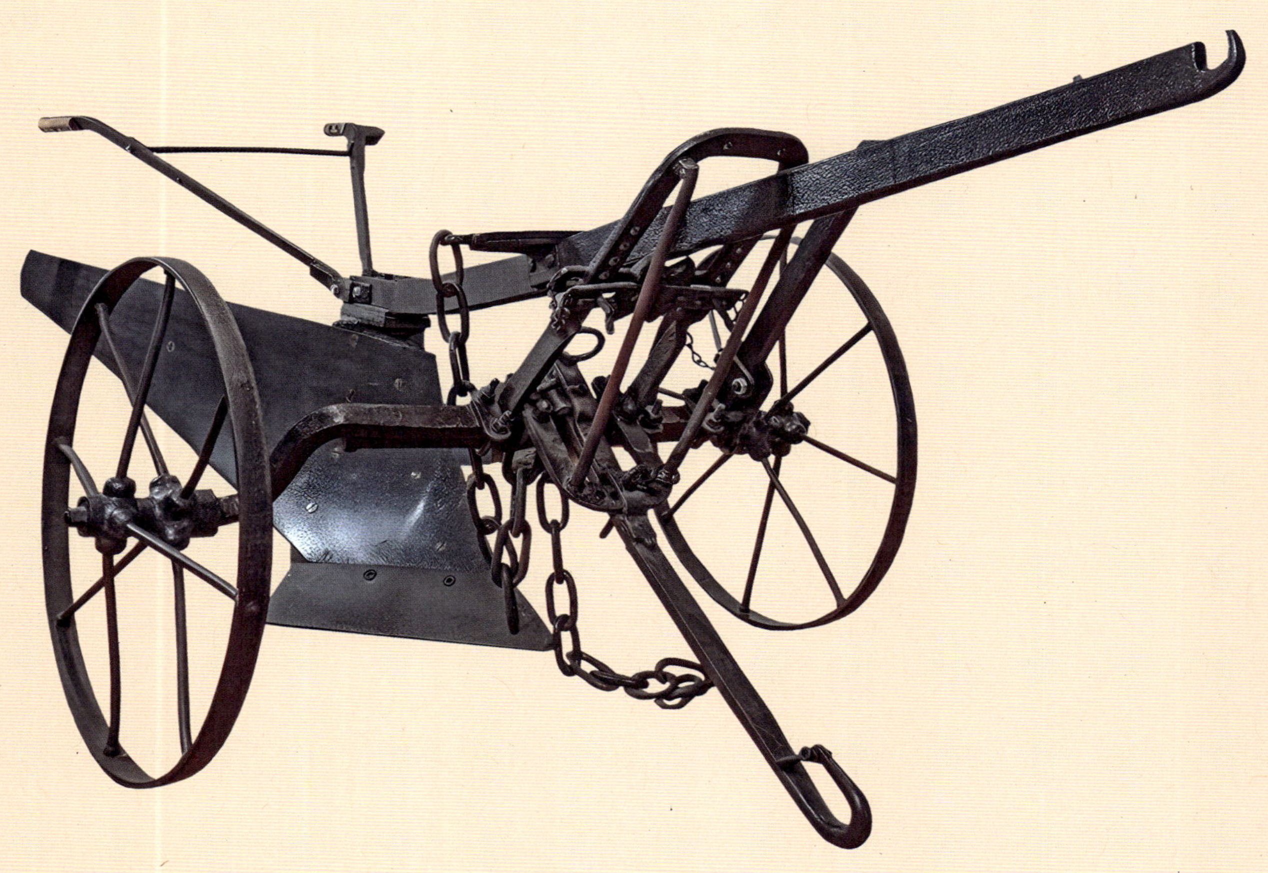

Eike Lüdeling

Agriculture has been the backbone of human civilisation for at least 12,000 years. Without agriculture, there would be no dense human settlements like villages, towns, and cities, and our planet would only be able to support a few million people rather than the more than 8 billion who live on Earth today. Only since people started to grow crops and raise livestock have they been able to produce enough energy – calories – to engage in the complex activities that shape our modern world. It is for this reason that producing more and more calories has long been the main goal of agricultural production.

The greatest boost to our ability to produce energy-rich food came from the so-called 'Green Revolution', which started shaping the face of global agriculture around the middle of the 20th century. A series of scientific discoveries, including synthetic fertilisers, a wide palette of agrochemicals, and new crop and animal breeding techniques, enabled farmers to drastically increase their calorie production. Mechanisation, irrigation, and land consolidation efforts also contributed to the rise of the highly labour- and cost-efficient agricultural systems that characterise most agricultural regions today.

The tremendous productivity gains of the Green Revolution, along with improvements in our ability to transport food to where it is needed – even in times of local food shortages – have largely put an end to the long string of famines that haunted human societies until only a few decades ago. Hunger still persists where people cannot access food because of poverty or local conflicts, but the overall amount of food energy produced by the world's farms is easily sufficient to feed all people on our planet.

Sustainability Challenges in Agriculture

Today's agricultural systems excel at producing calories, but this productivity has not come for free. Excessive use of fertilisers and pesticides has caused problems for human health and the environment. Intensive practices have led to widespread land degradation, with large areas experiencing declining fertility due to topsoil erosion, salinity, and other issues. Simplified agricultural landscapes offer little habitat for wildlife. These and other unintended impacts of modern agriculture have led to widespread doubts about the sustainability of our food production system.

In addition to being environmentally benign, a sustainable agricultural system must work economically and socially for all involved. Modern agriculture faces many challenges in these areas. In Germany, nearly three-quarters of farms had to close down between 1975 and 2023 alone, and over half of the remaining farms no longer rely on farming as the main income source. According to the World Bank, about 78 % of the world's poorest people find themselves in poverty despite being employed in agriculture, often enduring harsh working conditions, unstable employment, and fragile social safety nets.

Despite an unprecedented abundance of food calories, 2.4 billion people were moderately or severely food insecure in 2022, and about a third of them faced hunger, according to estimates by the Food and Agriculture Organization of the United Nations (FAO). Yet staple foods are already being produced so cheaply that the farmers growing the crops can barely make a living. At the same time, about 2.5 billion people were overweight in 2022, with almost 900 million considered obese. A striking feature of our food system is that only about a fifth of the world's agricultural land is used to produce food for direct consumption by humans. Most of the remainder is used to feed livestock, fuelling the production of cheap animal products, which are widely consumed in quantities considered detrimental to human health.

All these developments have led many to conclude that we need to reconsider the way we produce food. We need to take a much broader view of the various impacts of agricultural production, considering environmental, social, and economic dimensions.

Historic ripper plough, 1875. The plough is one of the oldest and most important agricultural implements. This special plough from the Germersheim Road Museum was used to tear up road surfacing, i.e. to unseal land.

Beyond Calorie Production

Today, we still expect agriculture to produce food and fibre to sustain our lives, but we have also come to realise that agricultural land use systems, which cover about 45 % of the habitable land on our planet, must fulfil other functions as well. These so-called ecosystem services include regulation of landscape-level water flows, preservation of soil fertility, habitat for natural plants and animals, and various functions related to climate change adaptation and mitigation. Agricultural systems also hold cultural and spiritual significance to many people, and attractive agricultural landscapes can have considerable aesthetic and recreational value.

The Sustainable Development Goals (SDGs), proclaimed by the United Nations in 2015, provide a comprehensive framework for evaluating the sustainability of human actions, including our agricultural endeavours. The SDGs still clearly stress food production as an important goal, most notably in their call to end hunger (SDG 2). Yet they also emphasise poverty reduction (SDG 1), good health and well-being (SDG 3), gender equality (SDG 5), clean water (SDG 6), decent work and economic growth (SDG 8). They stress the need to reduce inequalities (SDG 10), take climate action (SDG 13), and preserve life on land (SDG 15). All these goals are clearly related to agriculture, but it seems obvious that past approaches to agricultural development have not been very effective at addressing many of them.

Making Agriculture More Sustainable

Concerns about the sustainability of modern agricultural practices are longstanding, and farmers and researchers have made numerous attempts to address them. *Organic Agriculture* aims to eliminate dependence on external inputs, reduce negative environmental impacts, lower health risks from chemicals, and enhance animal welfare. *Fair Trade* ensures equitable trade relationships for producers in developing countries, aiming to reduce poverty and hardship among farmers and labourers. *Community-Supported Agriculture* (CSA) recognises that sustaining local agricultural livelihoods and preserving attractive rural landscapes require active support by local consumers.

Many attempts to make agricultural systems more resilient and sustainable draw inspiration from natural ecosystems. In *Conservation Agriculture*, or *Minimum-Tillage Agriculture*, farmers reduce soil disturbance, achieving erosion control and carbon sequestration without significantly reducing yields. Integrating trees into agricultural landscapes through *Agroforestry* enhances ecosystem services. Trees on farms provide income, reduce wind speed, enhance water and nutrient cycling, sequester carbon, and offer habitat for wildlife. Adding trees to pastures can improve animal welfare by providing shade and shelter.

Regenerative Agriculture takes the concept of sustainability one step further by not only preserving but actively enhancing ecosystem functions, ideally restoring the functionality of the pre-agricultural ecosystem. This approach focuses on restoring soil health through minimum tillage and accumulation of biomass. It often involves integrating trees in strategic landscape positions where they are particularly effective in controlling erosion and regulating water flows.

Scaling Up Sustainable Approaches

There is no longer a shortage of farmers who have managed to make their farms more sustainable – environmentally, economically, and socially. Many other farmers have become inspired by such pioneers, and in some cases, sustainability-oriented approaches to agriculture have turned into global movements. Yet given the major sustainability challenges global agriculture faces, it is easy to feel that progress is happening too slowly. Can we speed up the process?

Many changes that make farms more sustainable also raise farmers' incomes. For instance, integrating fruit or timber trees into agricultural fields adds an additional source of income that may make a farm more profitable. In other cases, however, farmers may rely on public support to implement changes that benefit the public. How to make appropriate support available to farms that make investments or take risks to help society achieve its sustainability goals is a question we need urgent answers to.

For a large-scale transformation towards more sustainable global agriculture, we still have a lot to learn about what keeps farmers from changing their ways. We need to understand what ingredients or mechanisms are currently missing. Do farmers need training and advice on how to implement new practices? Do they have access to planting materials of sufficient quality to implement agroforestry or other innovations? Are there legal obstacles to certain innovations? Do we need new insurance schemes that allow farmers to take risks in trying new practices? Do we need new marketing mechanisms for sustainably produced – but possibly more expensive – products? How can the investments in farm machinery that are needed for many practices be supported?

On the path towards sustainable agriculture, many questions remain unanswered. Yet awareness of the need for change is spreading rapidly, and attempts to create an enabling environment for sustainable solutions are becoming increasingly noticeable, also in the political arena. Most importantly, farmers in many places are getting more and more creative in finding solutions to sustainability challenges, and they are not shy about telling their stories.

As we strive for sustainable agriculture, the growing awareness, political support, and innovative spirit of farmers worldwide offer hope and inspiration, indicating that a collaborative and determined effort can lead to meaningful and lasting change. ✦

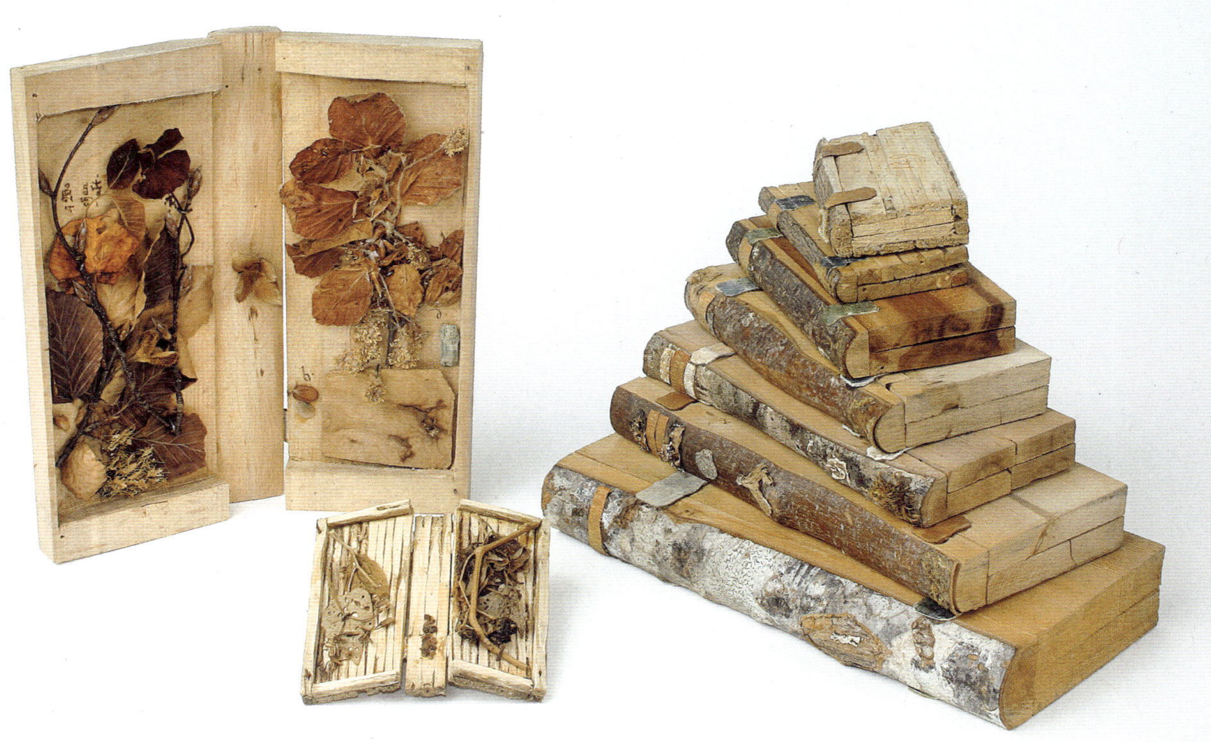

Candid Huber, historical xylotheque, late 18th century. Candid Huber (1747–1813) was a Benedictine monk and forest botanist. He produced several unique wood libraries to be sold to monasteries or royal houses. The collections each comprised around 150 sample books of wood with associated leaves, flowers, fruits, lichens, and mosses as well as insects. The collection, kept at the Institute for Wood Research at the Technical University of Munich, contains woody plants that have become rare in Germany, such as the hawthorn, the slippery elm, and the checker tree. It is testimony to a past diversity of species.

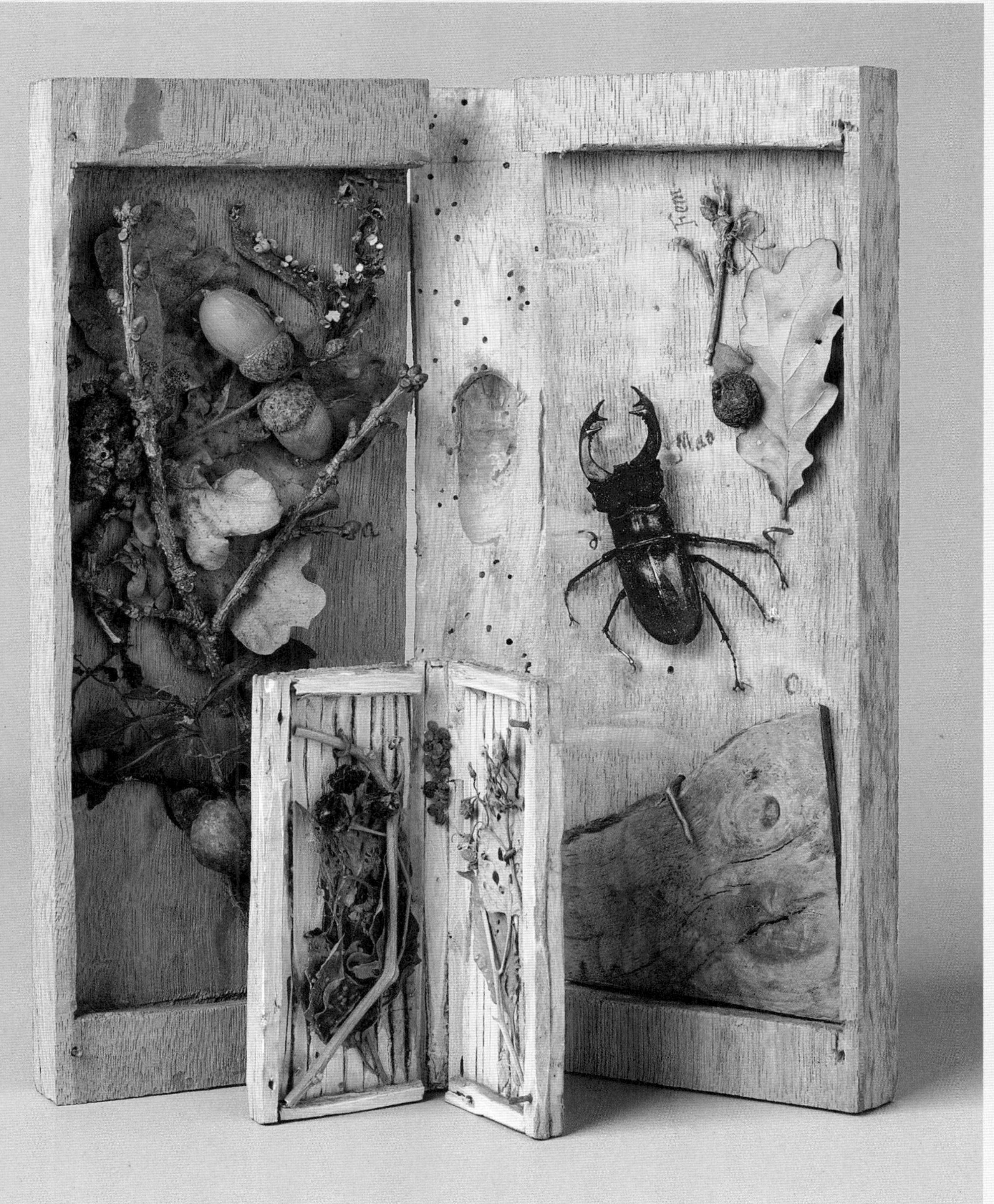

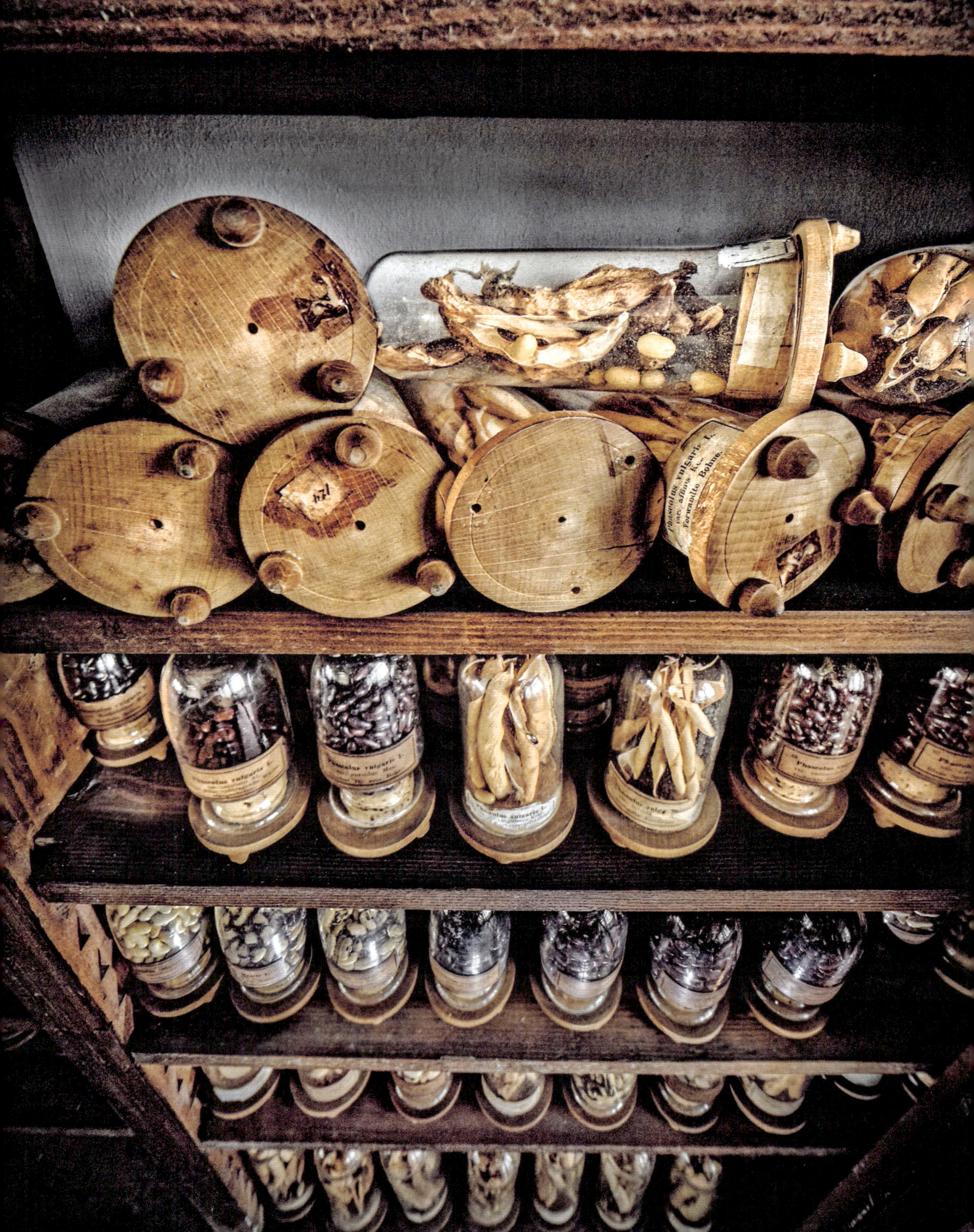
Phaseolus vulgaris L.
var. affinis K.
Verwandte Bohne.

Friedrich August Körnicke, Crop Collection, Botanical Gardens of the University of Bonn. Friedrich A. Körnicke (1828–1908) was a botanist from Bonn who focused primarily on agriculture. In his experimental garden he researched crops in particular and published a famous 'Handbuch des Getreidebaues' (Handbook of Cereal Cultivation). He collected his specimens in countless glass cylinders. The collection was exhibited and honoured at the World Exhibition in Vienna in 1873. It contains, for example, rare original forms of small spelt and amelcorn as well as an astonishing variety of pulses.

Model of a corn of wheat, University of Jena. Among the crops, maize, wheat, and rice make the largest contribution to feeding the world's population.

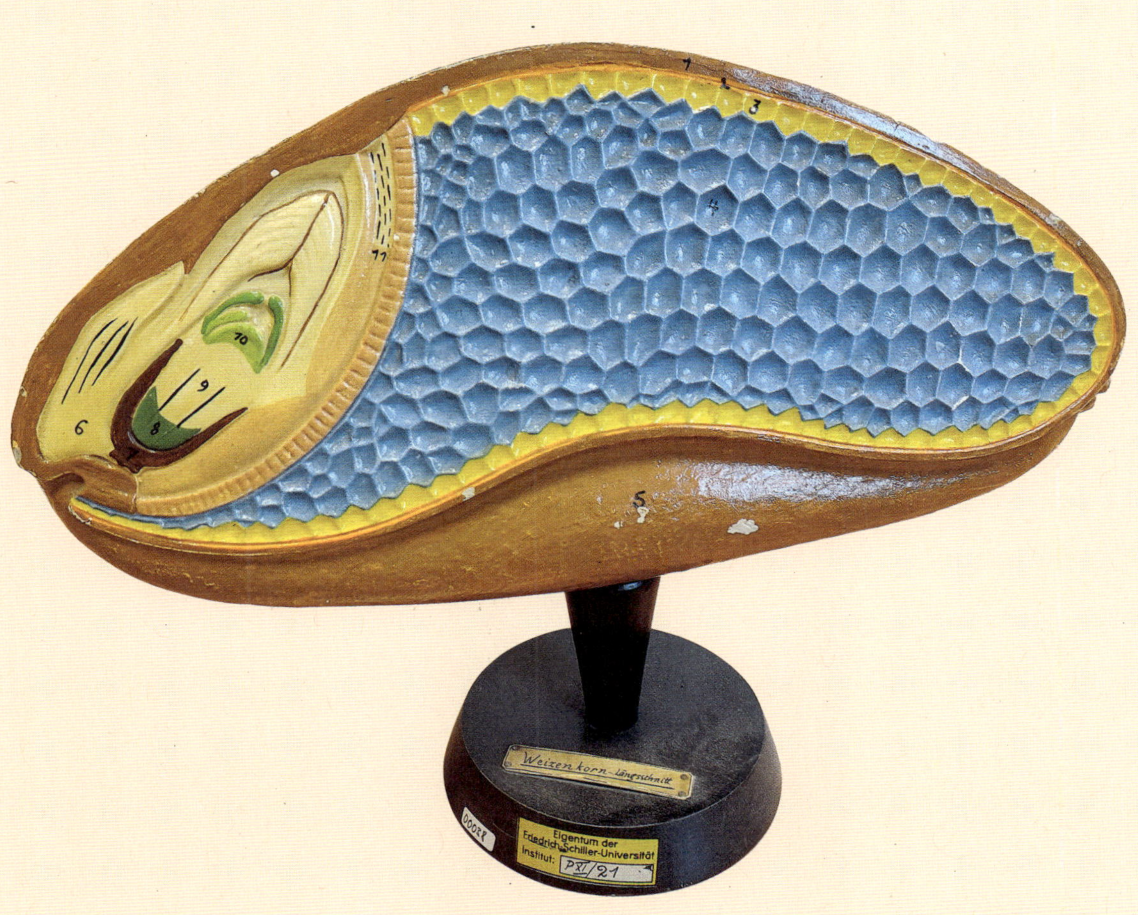

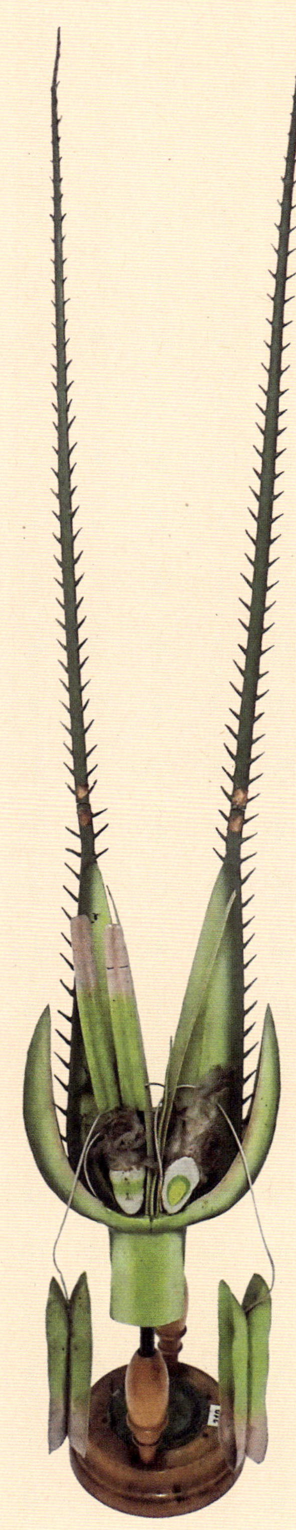

Rye model, University of Greifswald. According to the Food and Agriculture Organization (FAO), 13,143,055 tonnes of rye were harvested from around 4 million hectares of land worldwide in 2022.

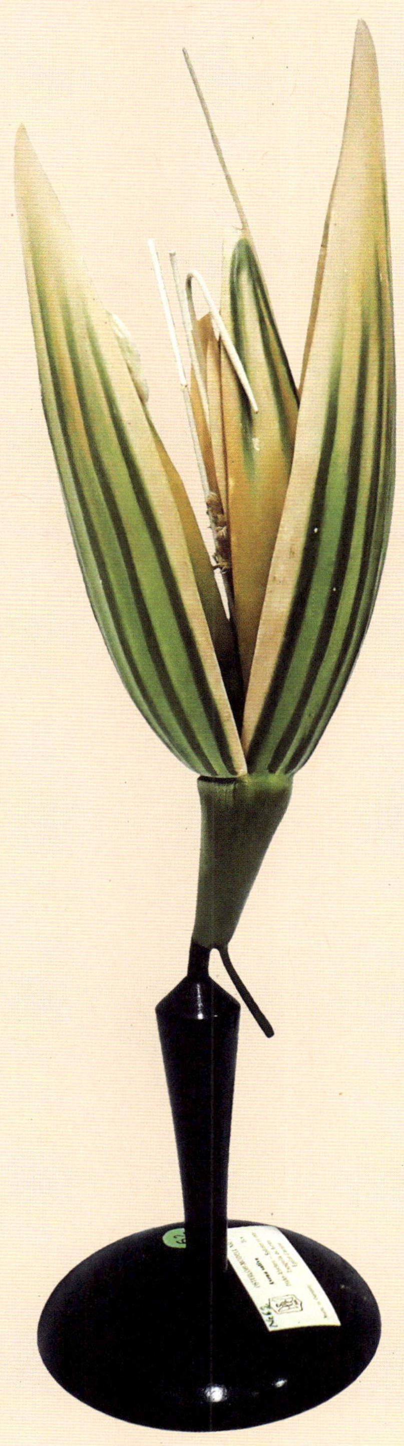

Barley model, University of Greifswald. Barley originated in the Near East and the eastern Balkans. The oldest evidence of barley utilisation dates back to 15,000 BC.

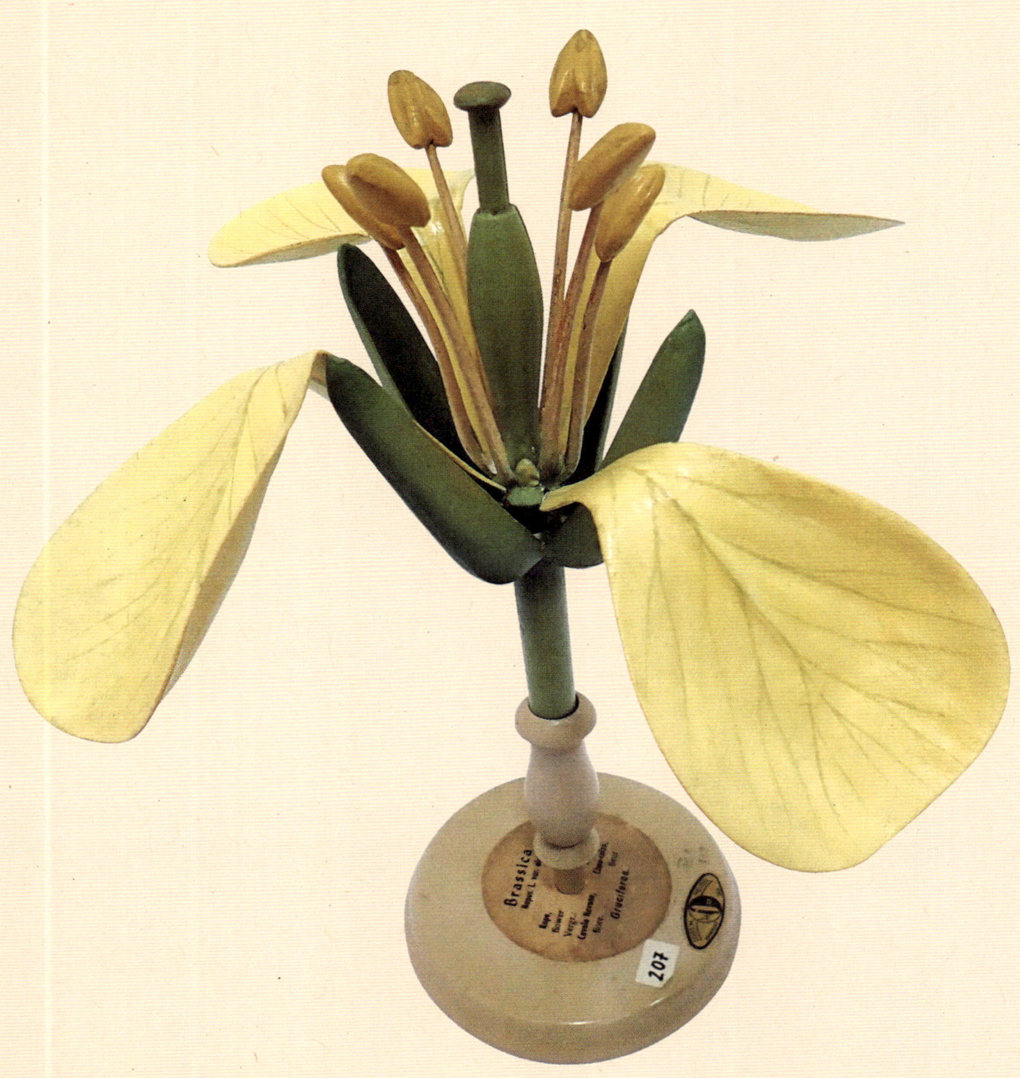

Model of rapeseed flowering, University of Greifswald. Since the 1990s, rapeseed has been the oilseed with the second highest share of the global market after soya. Rapeseed oil is used as a culinary oil and animal feed, but also as a biofuel. It is also used in the chemical and pharmaceutical industries.

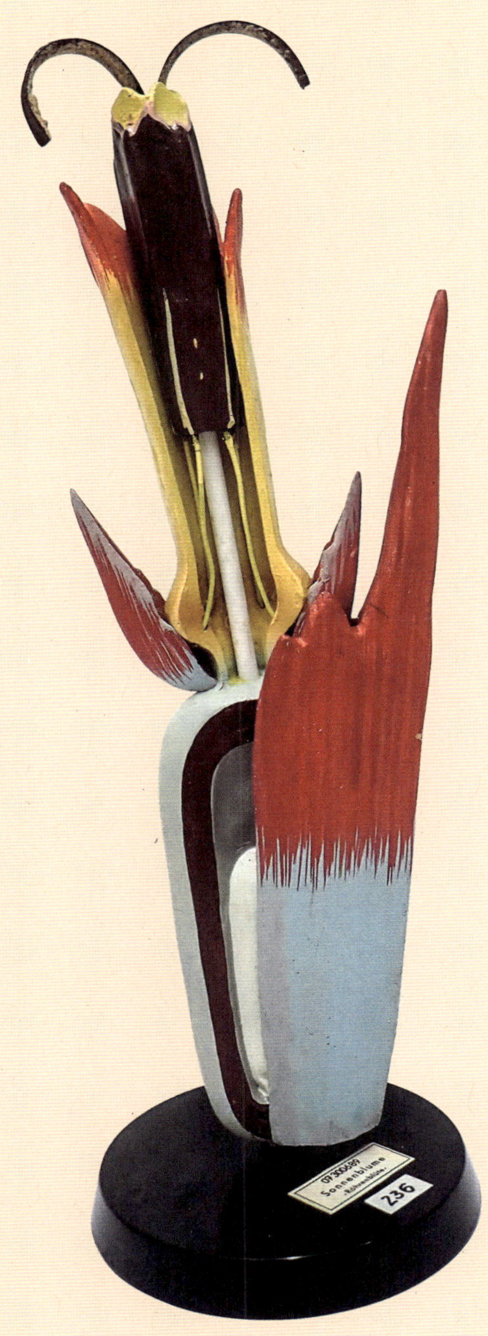

Model tubular bloom of the sunflower, University of Greifswald. Sunflowers were cultivated on 29.5 million hectares worldwide in 2021. This makes sunflowers the oil plant with the third largest area under cultivation globally, after soya beans and rapeseed, and ahead of oil palms and olive trees.

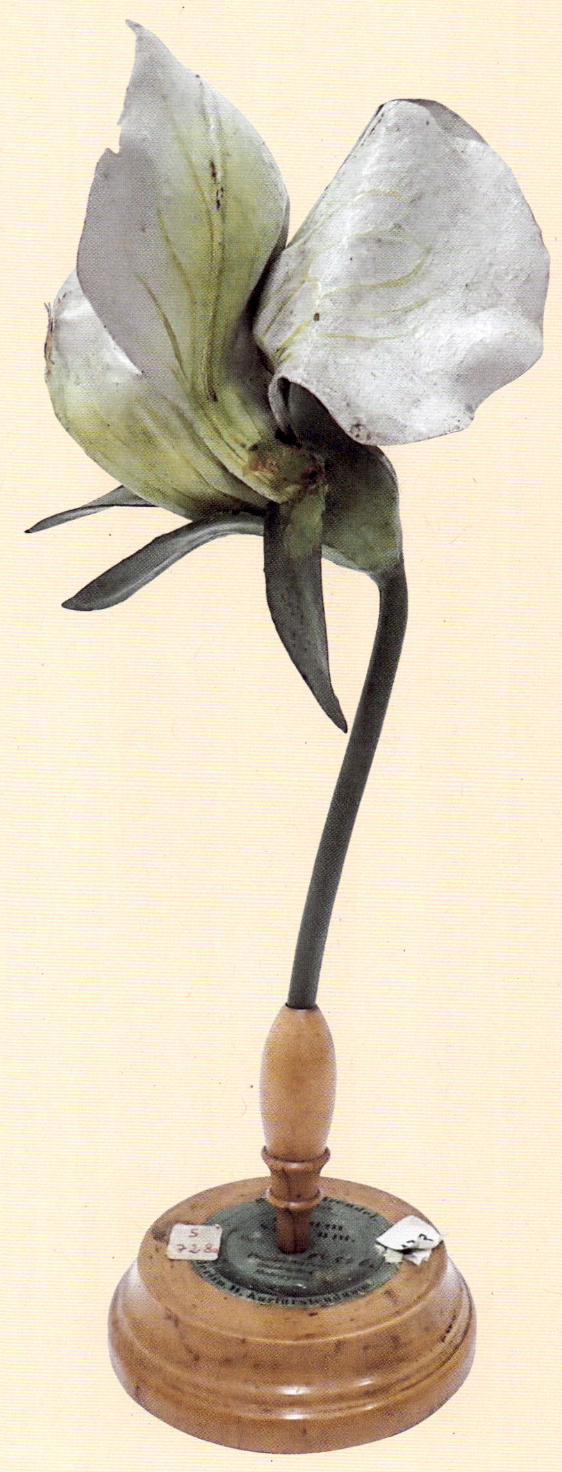

Pea model, University of Greifswald. There are more than 18,000 varieties of legumes. They enrich biodiversity and crop rotation for soil improvement through their ability to absorb nitrogen from the air.

Ximena Garrido-Lecca, *Inflorescence – Seedings*, 2022–2024. The Peruvian artist, living in Mexico City, writes about her artwork: 'Corn is one of the most important crops in the current global economy. It's used to produce more than 4,000 industrial products, such as pills, cosmetics, adhesives, oil, flour, fructose sweetener, chewing gum, and ethanol.

Historically, its origins as a plant native to the Americas have been overlooked. It held a central position in pre-Columbian mythology and was a significant source of nourishment, enabling the birth of civilisation in the Americas. Considered the origin of humanity by the Maya and Aztecs, its cultivation has shaped all aspects of life, from social environments to the notion of time.

In many agricultural civilisations in the Americas and Europe, threshing floors were sacred spaces used as platforms for ceremonies and rituals and were thus central to the community. Before industrialisation, threshing was mainly related to communal work and involved a series of harvesting rituals and festivals that united a community in one gathering place. Corn threshing by hand is still practiced in many rural areas in the Americas, where the communal act of harvesting remains a significant part of social organisation. In many Mesoamerican rituals still practiced today, participants will form a semicircle, delimiting the space with corn stalks, and make offerings to the corn while playing music and performing dances in gratitude. They also still perform divination with corn grains as well as elaborate different corn drinks that have been used in ceremonies since ancestral times in Peru and Mexico.

The installation *Inflorescence – Seedings* recreates a threshing floor where cultural transmissions and exchanges with natural elements can take place, restoring ancient forms of communication between humans and nature. The reactivation of corn harvesting rituals and ancient threshing techniques reflects on the radical reshaping of our relationship to the natural world following industrial revolutions, social paradigm shifts, and the current configuration of the information age. It also exposes Meso and South American mythologies and knowledge, emphasising the origins of corn, the crop's multilayered meanings to ancient societies, the modernising of its harvesting, and its current exploitation by capitalism. This exploitation, particularly in the form of genetically modified maize (in the USA, 90 % of the cultivated crops are GM), has a significant negative impact on the environment, public health, and Indigenous agricultural communities, sparking concerns and urgent discussions.' ▶

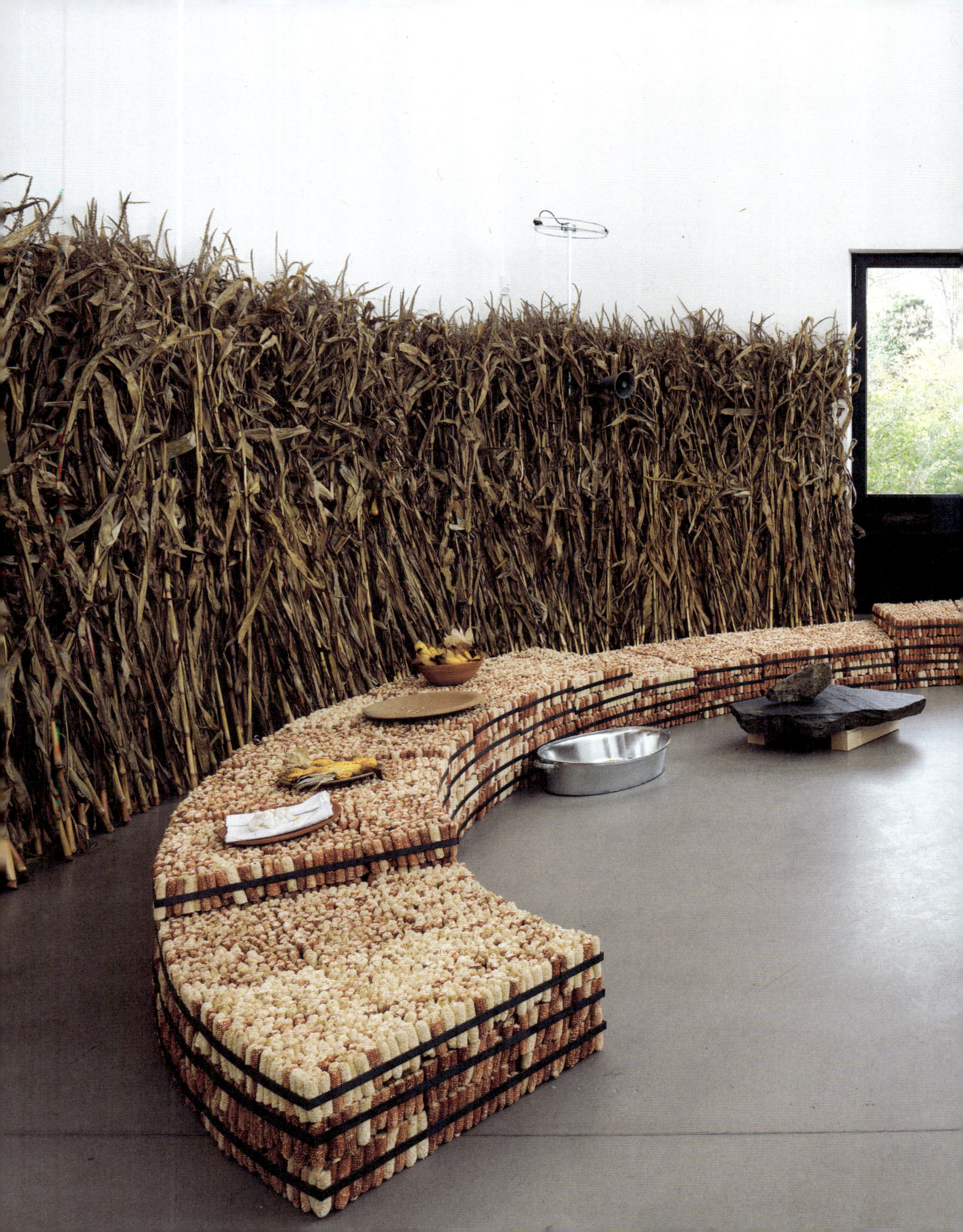

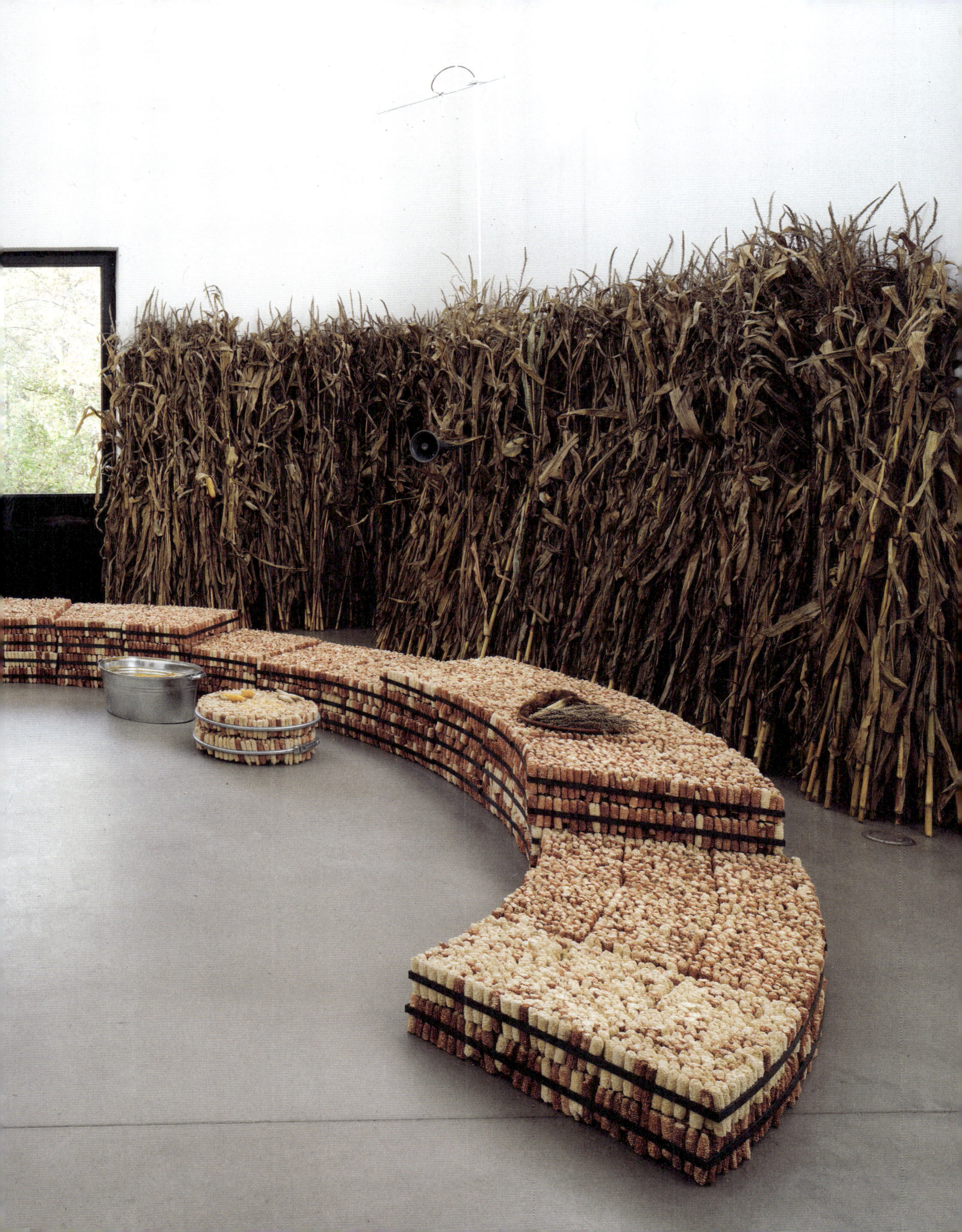

Stele of the maize god, Epi-Olmec/Isthmic style, 100 BC–250 AD, unknown provenance in the region from the Mexican Gulf coast to the Pacific coast and the highlands of Guatemala. The stele made of igneous rock preserved in the Rautenstrauch-Joest-Museum shows an ancient, bearded maize god in whose costume rulers could sometimes be depicted. The three-leafed element of his headband symbolises maize as an emblem of power. The cultivation of maize played a central role in pre-Columbian mythology and characterised all aspects of life for thousands of years.

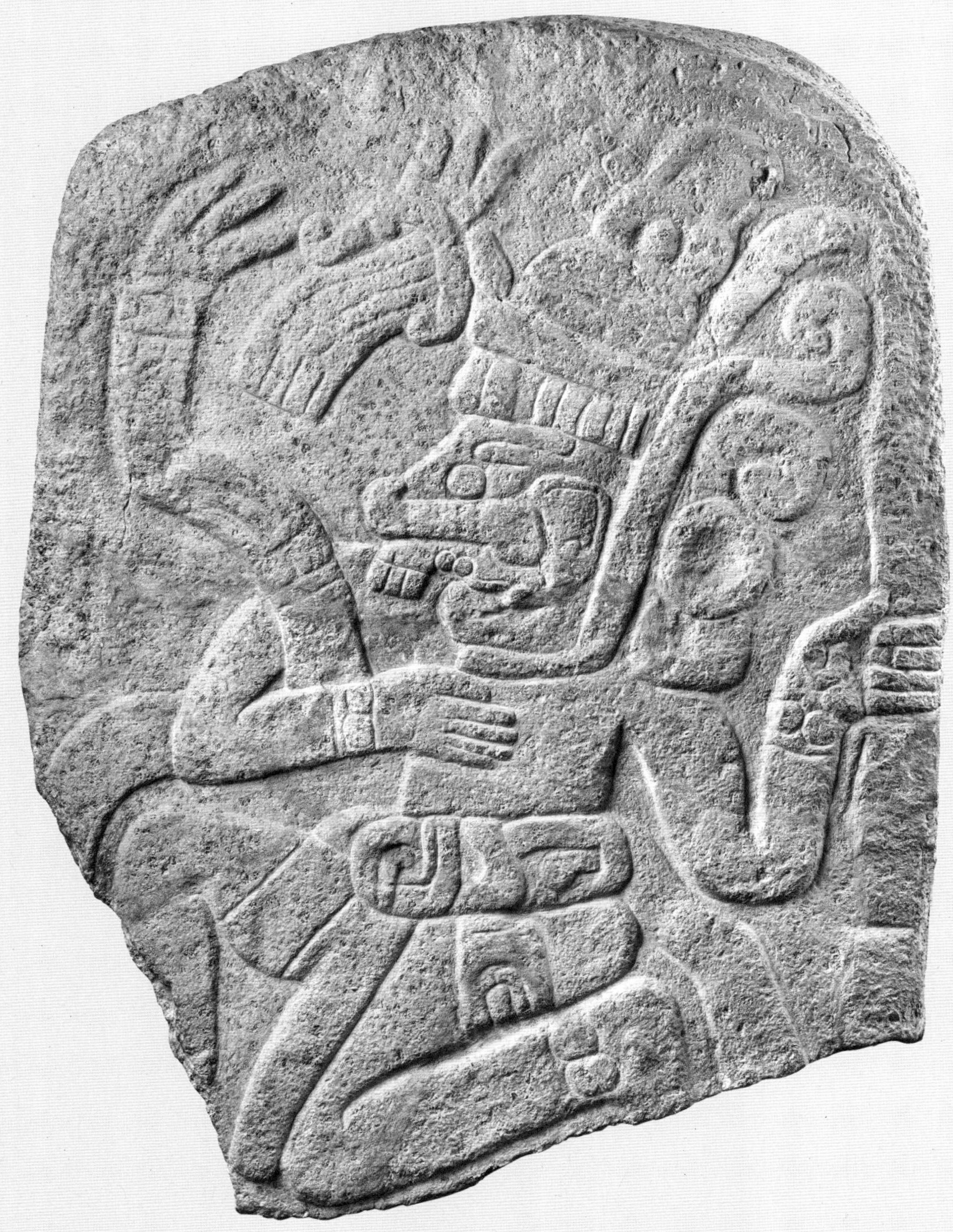

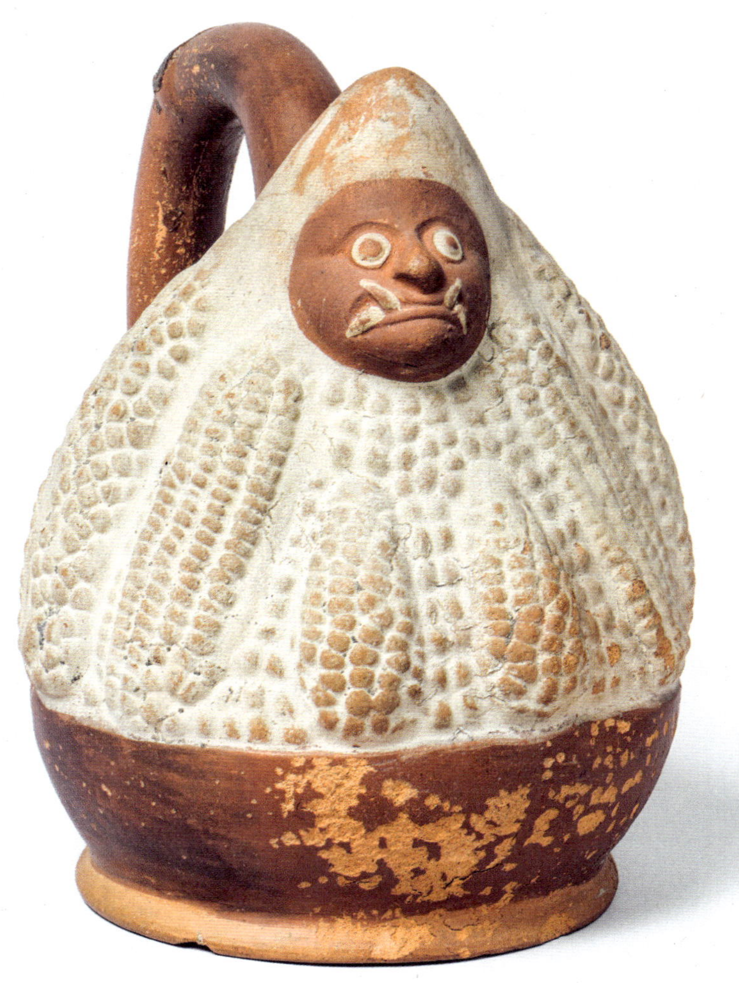

Vessel in the shape of a maize creature, 450–750, Moche culture, Chimbote. The red clay vessel preserved in the Rautenstrauch-Joest-Museum is a variation of the anthropomorphic Proto-Chimú pottery. The vessel is decorated with corn cobs, with a face with four fangs protruding from the upper section. The interpretation varies greatly: it could depict a supernatural being, a person with a specialised ritual role, or a creation story of a figure born from maize.

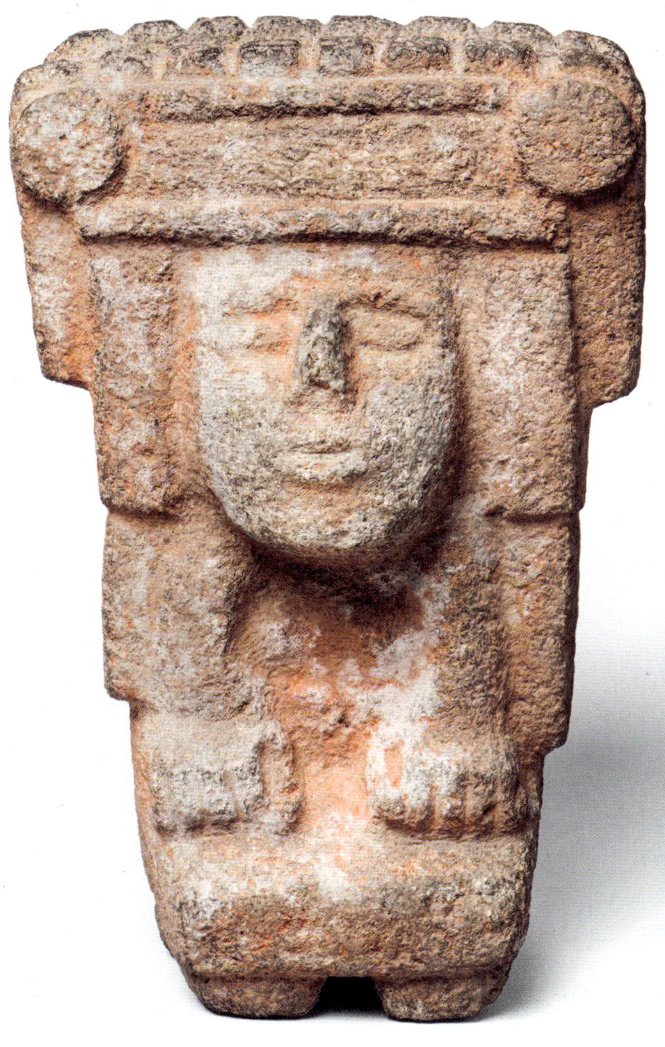

Aztec corn goddess, 14th–16th century, Mexico. The Aztecs were farmers. In Mexico's tropical climate, they were able to cultivate maize, beans, pumpkins, amaranth, chia, agaves, and cacti, among other things. In addition to terraced cultivation in hilly areas, they utilised the fertile swampy soil in the lowlands. In Tenochtitlán, almost every house had a field (chinampa) for its own use, but the larger the city grew, the more food had to be brought into the urban centre. The largest chinampas were located in Xochimilco at the southern end of Lake Texcoco, where agriculture is still practised in this way today.

Global Livestock Farming and its Multi-Layered Consequences for Land Degradation

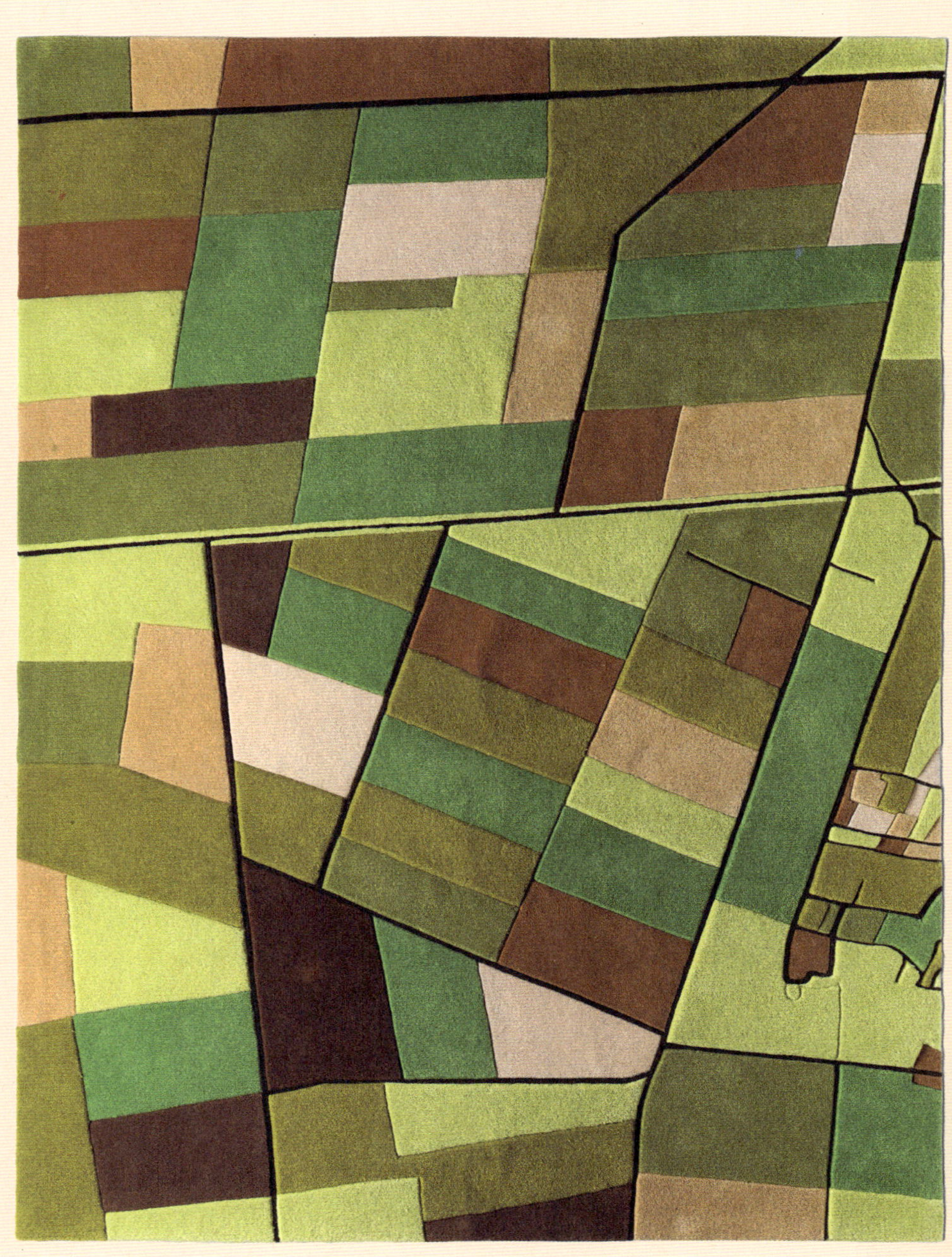

Reinhard Geßl

Humans have been farming and raising animals for thousands of years to facilitate the use of meat, milk, eggs, wool, hides, and labour. For a long time, grasslands were only put to use by shepherds or small farmers, who kept the land open with their manageable herds of cattle, sheep, or goats and obtained valuable animal protein in the form of milk and meat, as well as the animals' labour and hides.

With the start of the Green Revolution in the mid-1960s, the way we treat the land and the animals in our care changed radically. Today, almost 70 billion farm animals live on our planet, often in very large numbers. Every hour, 7.8 million animals are slaughtered in order to process the 360 million tonnes of carcasses into meat and meat by-products. The average person on Earth consumes 45 kilos of meat each year. The World Agriculture Report assumes that the demand for meat will continue to rise, primarily because the emerging countries will move closer to the 'Western diet' of North America and Europe with its burgers, steaks, and schnitzels.

More and More Meat and Milk

Global meat production has more than quadrupled in the last 50 years, and there is no end in sight. The Food and Agriculture Organization of the United Nations (FAO) expects meat production to increase to 455 million tonnes by 2050, with an exponential increase in global poultry production in particular. The FAO also forecasts further growth in global milk production, based on the current annual production of 950 million tonnes.

Florian Pucher, *Landcarpet Europe*, 2007: The carpet from the collection of the Museum of European Cultures in Berlin bears witness to the mosaic-like fragmentation of our landscapes.

Domesticated animals are animals that only exist in the world because we humans have an interest in utilising them. Modern farm animals are specifically bred high-performance animals that must be fed according to their enormous genetic potential. In the past, farm animals were mostly fed with the by-products of human consumption, but today cattle, pigs, and poultry are fed an optimised mix of high-quality cereals and pulses, augmented with nutrient supplements. Farm animals therefore mainly eat arable crops that could be directly used for human consumption.

Animal Feed Instead of Human Food

Almost half of the grain grown worldwide now ends up in the stomachs of animals. Of the global soya harvest – more than two thirds comes from Brazil and the USA – as much as 80 % is earmarked specifically for livestock feed. Experts assume that this trend will continue in the coming years, with the demand for grain as animal fodder likely to increase sharply due to the continued growth in meat consumption. This means that more and more arable land will be needed to grow food for animals instead of food for humans. The further expansion of industrial livestock farming is therefore likely to jeopardise a key Sustainable Development Goal (SDG 2) of the United Nations: ending hunger, achieving food security and better nutrition, and promoting sustainable agriculture.

Livestock is the largest user of land today. Around 26 % of the world's land area, i.e. around 3.5 billion hectares, consists of permanent meadows, pastures, and rangelands, most of which are used for grazing livestock. In addition, a third of the world's arable land, i.e. half a billion hectares, is used for the production of energy- and protein-rich animal feed. Livestock farming uses a considerable proportion of the almost 200 million tonnes of nitrogen, phosphate, and potash fertilisers that are applied annually to fertilise the crops grown for fodder. Further, the expansion of pasture and arable land to feed livestock continues to be one of the most important driving forces behind changes in land use and deforestation.

While in many places overgrazing can lead to soil degradation, in other cases the problem is undergrazing. Both lead to a loss of biodiversity, a deterioration of ecosystems, and decreased productivity of fertile land.

Food and Its Role in Climate Change

Globally, food production, i.e. agriculture and nutrition, is responsible for up to 30 % of climate change. Direct emissions from livestock farming include methane emissions (CH_4) from ruminants (especially cattle) as well as nitrous oxide (N_2O) and methane emissions from manure. Indirect greenhouse gas emissions, especially N_2O and carbon dioxide (CO_2), are caused by regional feed cultivation, but also in international areas, including former tropical forest and savannah regions. Intensive, land-independent animal husbandry, the production and use of mineral nitrogen fertilisers, and changes in land use – i.e. the conversion of grassland or (tropical) forest into arable land, for example to grow animal feed such as soya – release large quantities of CO_2 bound in the soil, thus causing both soil degradation and additional greenhouse gas emissions.

The 120 million tonnes of nitrogen fertiliser alone that are produced each year worldwide using the energy-intensive Haber-Bosch process for fertilising (fodder) plants release almost 800 million tonnes of CO_2. The easily water-soluble compounds applied in turn interfere with organic soil processes such that humus loss, soil erosion, and changes in land use are accelerated, thus causing additional greenhouse gas emissions.

Water Scarcity and Erosion

Agriculture consumes around 70 % of the world's available freshwater resources. Around 30 % of global agricultural water consumption is attributed to livestock farming. Three forms of water are taken into account in a complete water balance: 'Blue water' is surface and groundwater that is used directly for watering animals, but also for the production of mineral fertilisers. 'Green water' is evaporated by plants and from the soil. 'Grey water' refers to the amount of water needed to 'dilute' pollutants (e.g. nitrate, phosphates, pesticides, pharmaceuticals) introduced into the water to levels below the limits that apply to drinking water. In intensive forms of farming, this can amount to several thousand litres of water per kilo of meat. In addition to the general shortage of water, the environmentally friendly management of the large quantities of animal excrement and the minimisation of excess nutrients from feed production are therefore major challenges.

In the last 40 years, around a third of the world's fertile arable land has been lost through erosion. And even though soil erosion is an important natural process, it is seriously exacerbated by human activities: more than 24 billion tonnes of soil are lost worldwide every year through erosion – that is around 3 tonnes of fertile soil per inhabitant – which subsequently leads to the silting of water bodies or is responsible for the release of fertilisers and pollutants such as phosphorus, nitrogen, or pesticides into ground and surface waters.

What to Do About Desertification?

With the rapid population growth of the twentieth century, more and more people needed food – and therefore more land for agriculture and livestock farming. The parallel increase in the industrialisation of livestock farming led to the following causes of erosion: loose soils due to overuse with insufficient time for regeneration, loose soils due to overgrazing, lack of water in the fields and pastures and, as a result, salinisation of those areas, deforestation for changing land use, e.g. (fodder) soya cultivation in rainforest areas. Often a rain shower or a strong wind is enough to irretrievably wash or blow away a layer of fertile soil that has developed over several thousand years. Progressive desertification causes the loss of ecosystem services through land resources, e.g. for food production, nutrient cycles, and water filtration, or for the climate due to the importance of soils as carbon sinks. As part of the carbon cycle, livestock farming is both a sink and a risk factor.

The Global Land Outlook (GLO), the flagship publication of the United Nations Convention to Combat Desertification (UNCCD), warns that the exploitation of the Earth's natural reserves has doubled in the last 30 years and that a third of the world's soils are already severely degraded. Agriculture and livestock farming, which take up a third of the global land area, are mainly responsible for this. Modern agriculture, with its intensive livestock farming, monocultures, genetically modified crops, and the systematic use of mineral fertilisers and pesticides is not compatible with long-term sustainability. The majority of cultivated and natural ecosystems are suffering from degradation. This affects 20 % of arable land, 16 % of forests, 19 % of grasslands and 27 % of pasturelands.

There Are Alternatives

Currently, 1.3 billion people live in areas with degraded agricultural land. The report calls for a paradigm shift and a move away from intensive production, high-emission processing and transport systems, and wasteful, meat-intensive food chains. On the production side, instead of intensive farming, a management of land resources that brings benefits for society, the environment, and the economy must be promoted. Agricultural production should no longer be measured solely in terms of yield per hectare, but should include nutritional value and – previously externalised – values such as cost to the environment and society along with the benefits for a healthy landscape.

The report highlights that it is already possible today to grow food without excessive environmental costs, both through adaptations of conventional systems and through alternative modes of production like organic farming, where yields are getting closer and closer to those in more intensive systems. Organic farming avoids many of the drivers of soil degradation and its effects by avoiding synthetic chemical fertilisers and pesticides and by rearing livestock in a species-appropriate and land-bound manner as part of a broad ecological system. On the consumer side, a switch to a predominantly plant-based diet is necessary.

The authors of the UN report are optimistic that with these changes and improved land use, there will be sufficient fertile land in the long term to meet the demand for food, feed, and energy. ✦

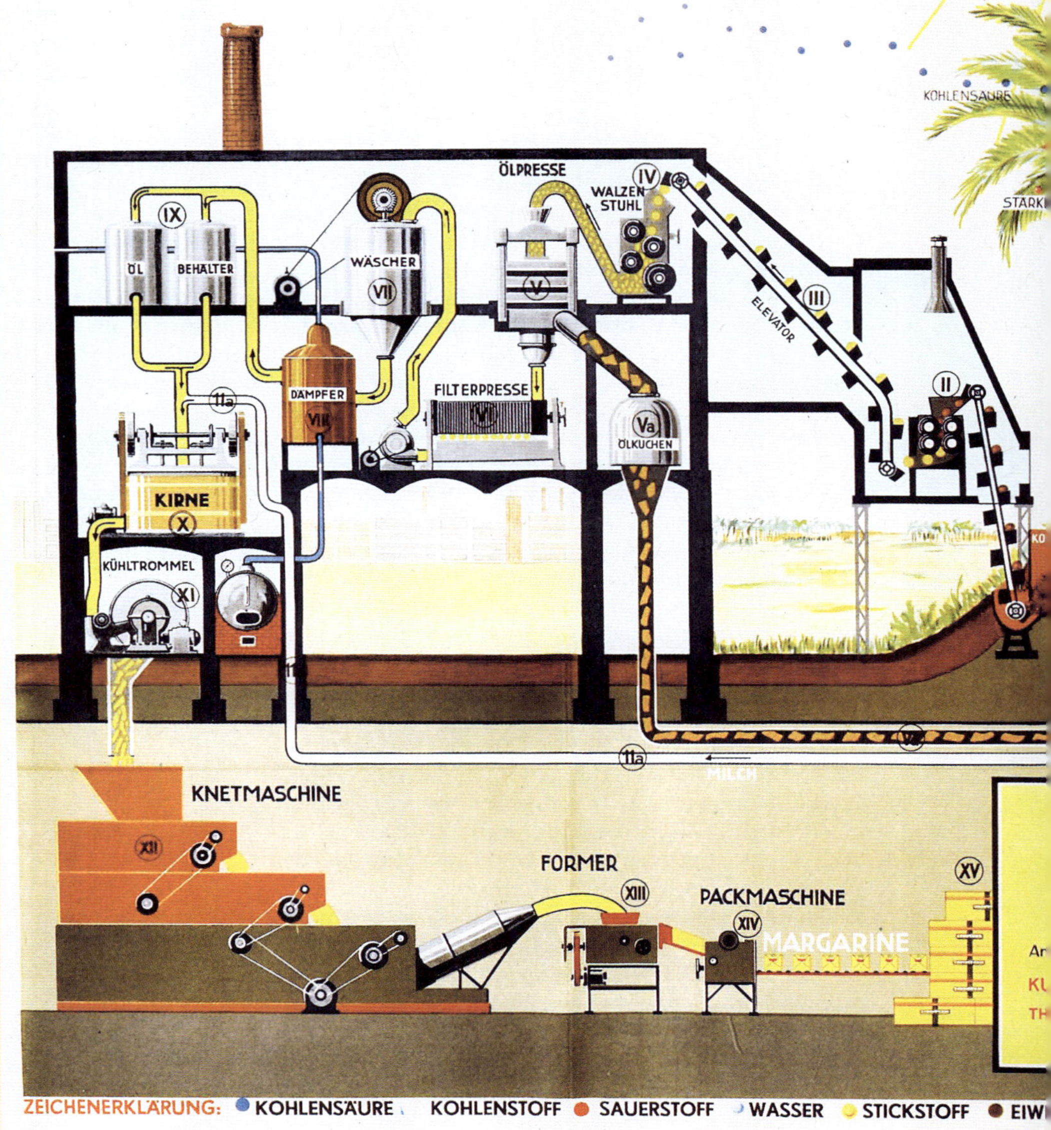
VON DER PFLANZE
AUF GERADEM WEGE
DURCH DIE MASCHINE
KOHLENSÄURE
ÖLPRESSE
WALZEN STUHL
ÖL
BEHÄLTER
WÄSCHER
ELEVATOR
DÄMPFER
FILTERPRESSE
ÖLKUCHEN
KIRNE
KÜHLTROMMEL
MILCH
KNETMASCHINE
FORMER
PACKMASCHINE
MARGARINE
ZEICHENERKLÄRUNG:
KOHLENSÄURE
KOHLENSTOFF
SAUERSTOFF
WASSER
STICKSTOFF

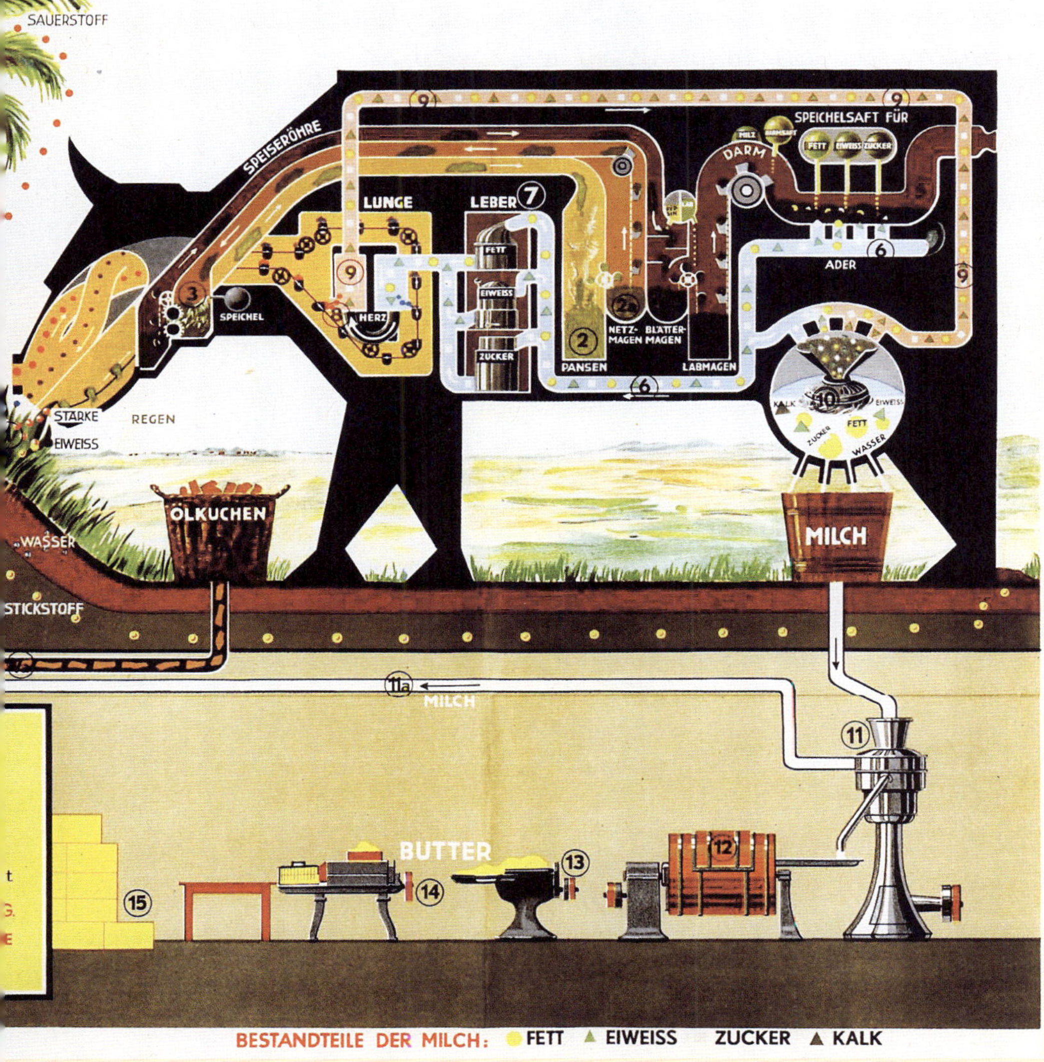

Kunerol works, Thea Margarine Poster: *From Plant to Fat Nutrient*, a. 1930. The poster advertises margarine, which is produced as vegetable fat 'from the plant, straight through the machine', whereas butter still has to be produced 'on a detour through the animal'. The cow is also depicted as a kind of machine for producing milk.

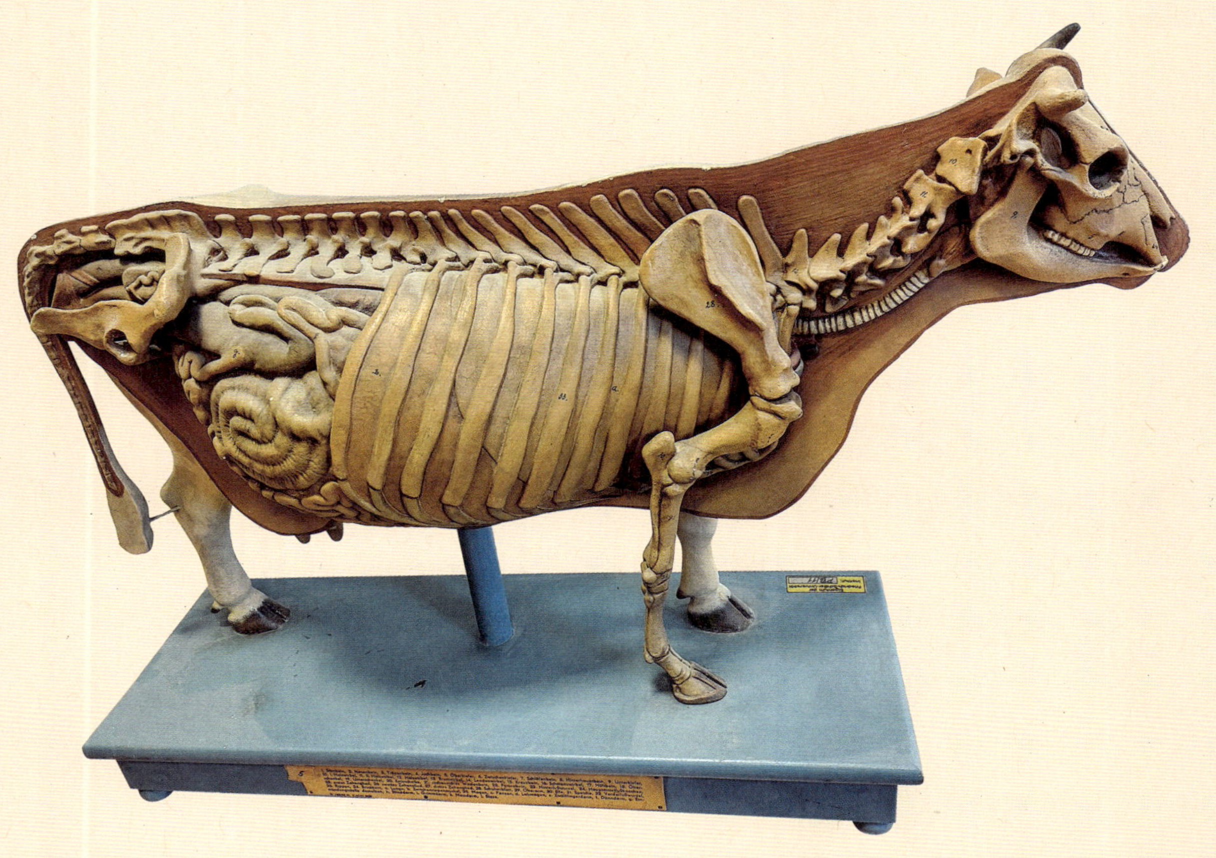

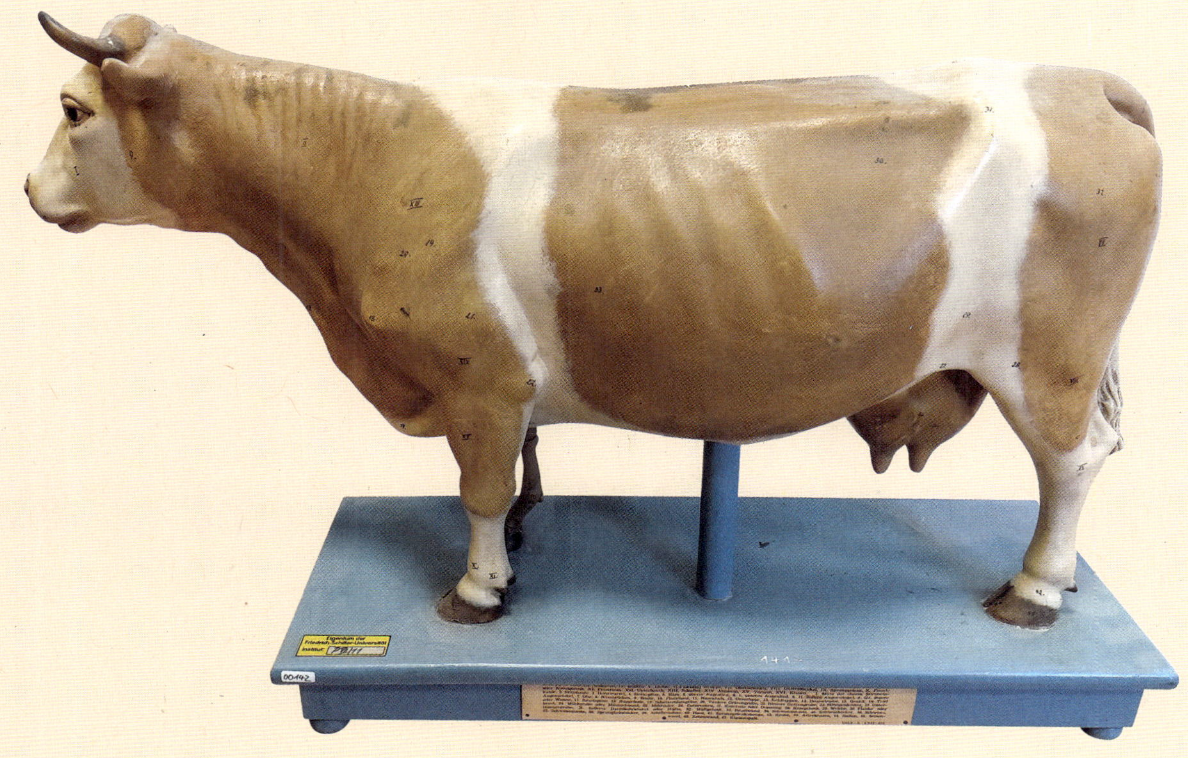

Anatomical model of a cow, front and back. The model comes from the collection of the Biology Didactics Department at the University of Jena.

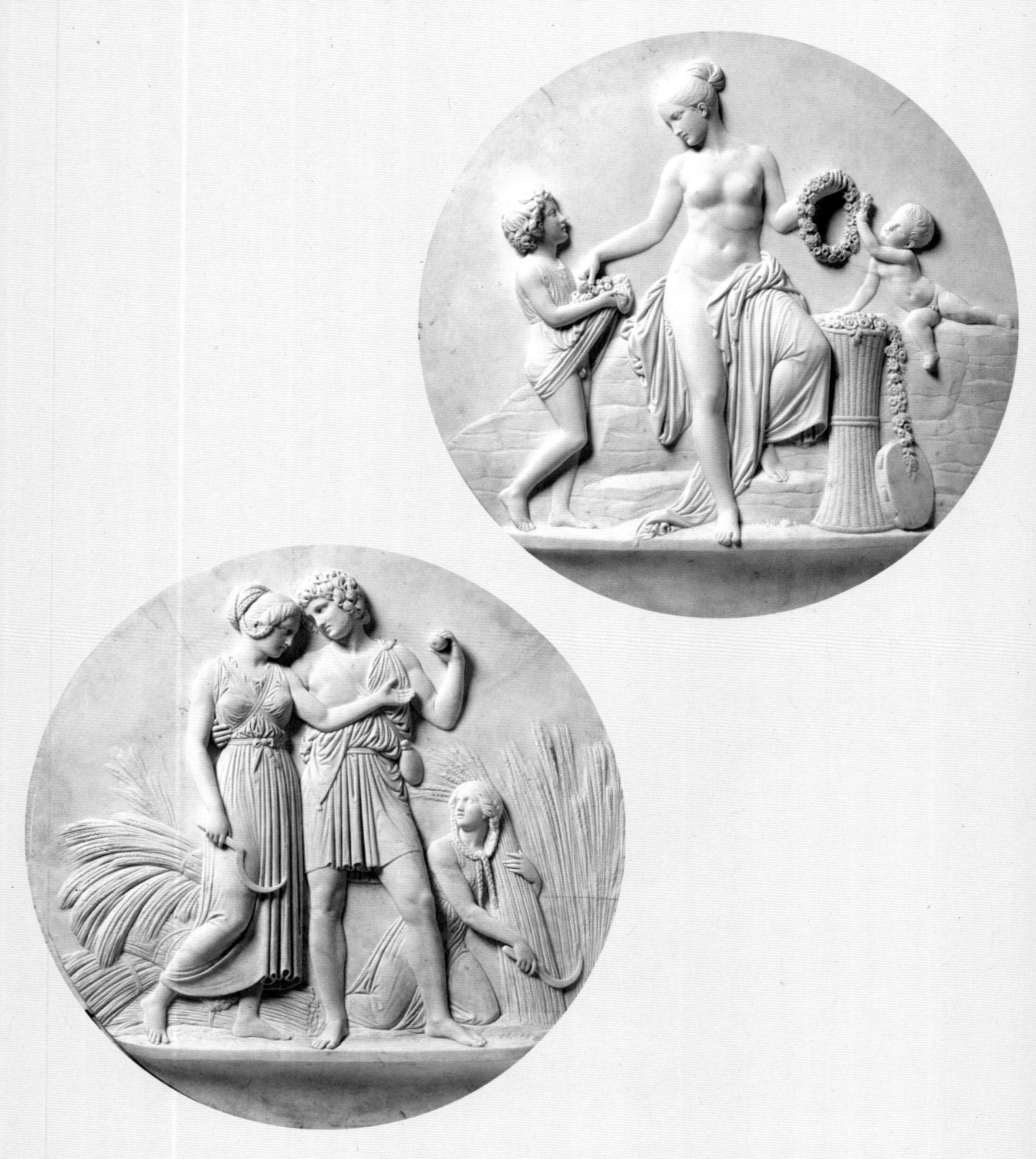

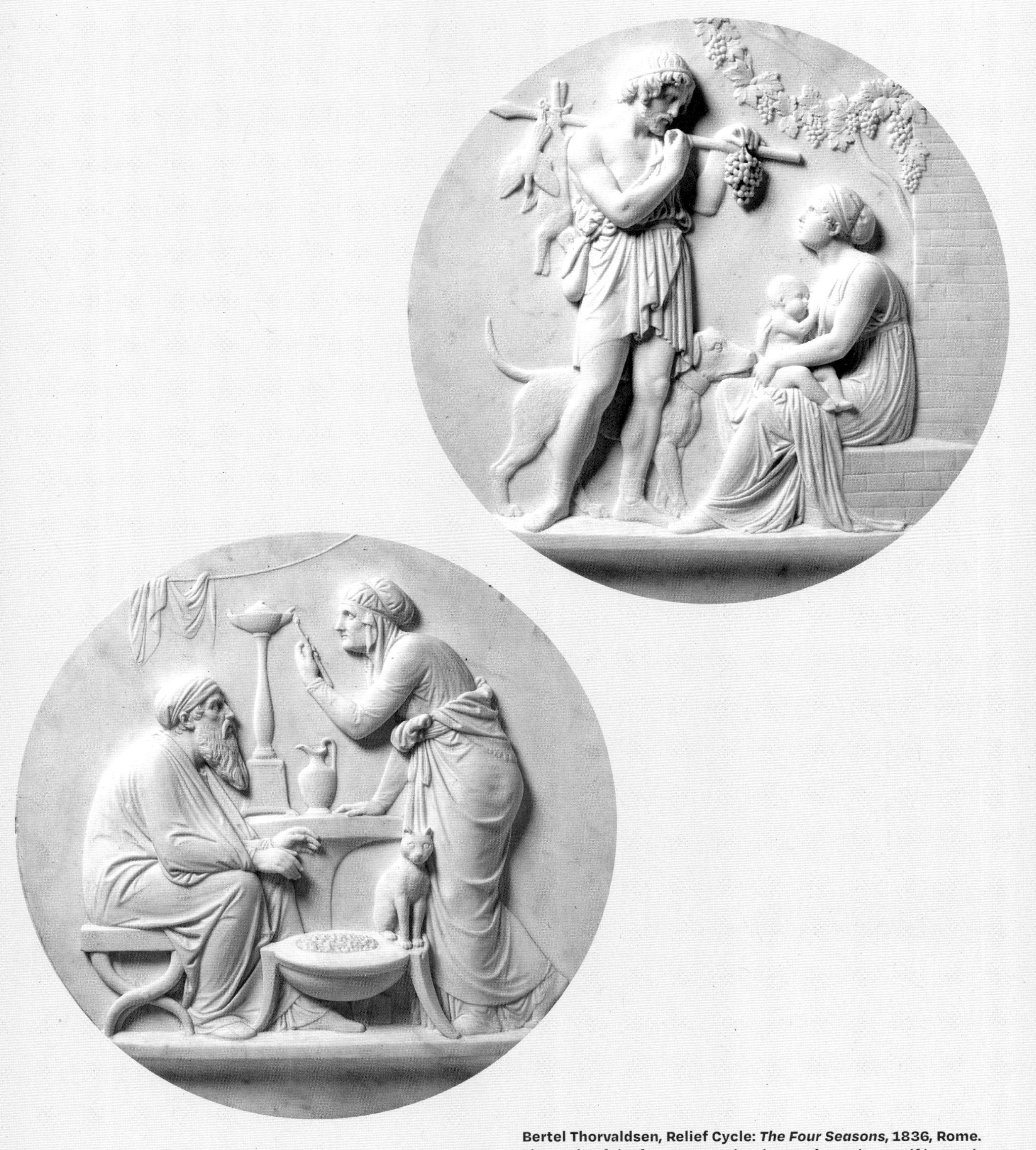

Bertel Thorvaldsen, Relief Cycle: *The Four Seasons*, 1836, Rome. The cycle of the four seasons has been a favourite motif in art since antiquity. Bertel Thorvaldsen (1770–1844) depicted spring as a girl twining a wreath, summer as a couple in love during the harvest, autumn as a family sitting under ripe grapes, and winter as an elderly couple in the warm refuge of their home. The marble reliefs kept in the Württemberg State Museum also bear witness to the existential importance of the seasons in agriculture. Today, man-made climate change is leading to a shift in the seasons in many parts of the world.

Women in Artisanal Small-Scale Mining and Land Restoration

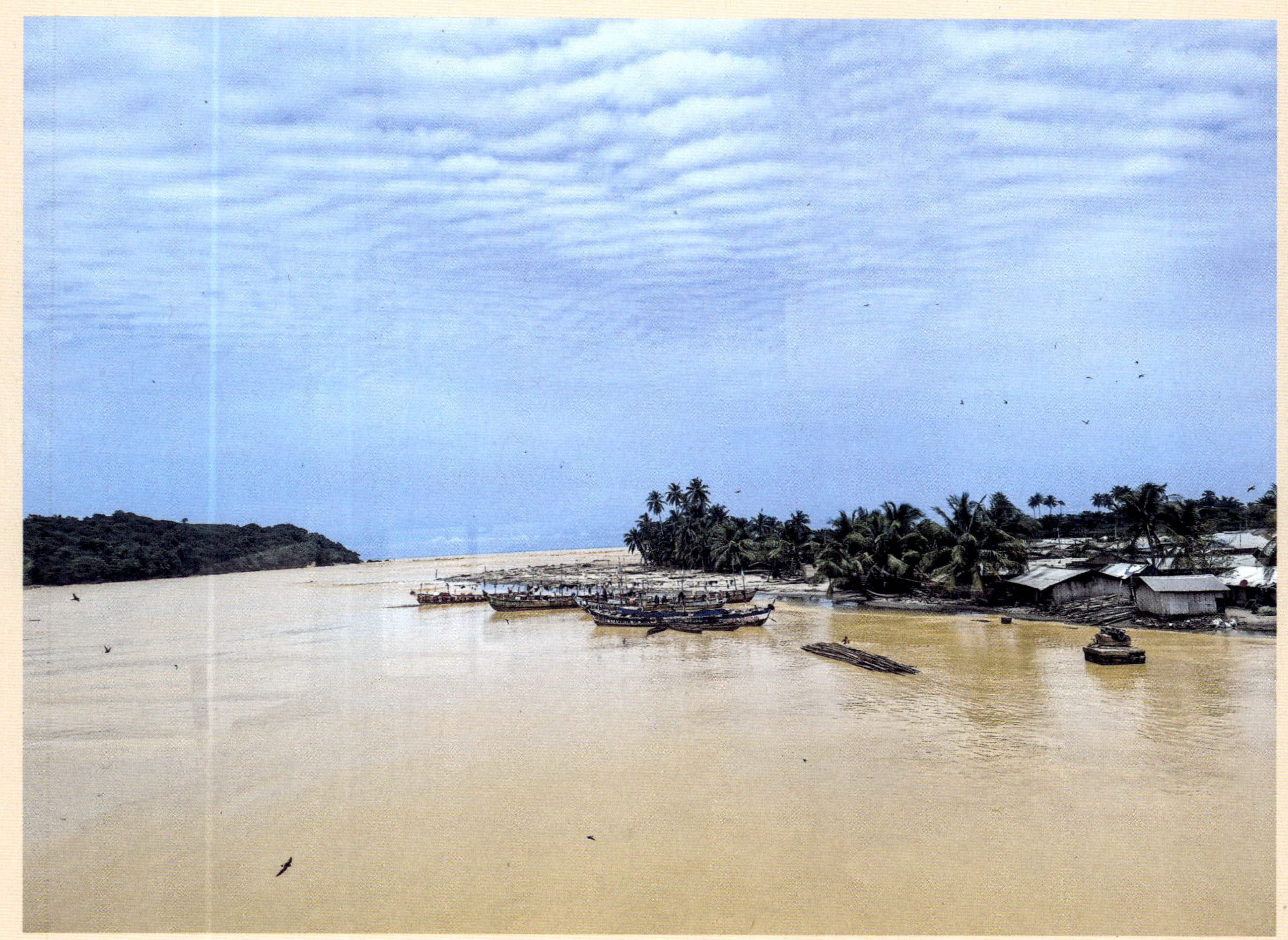

Iyenemi Ibimina Kakulu

Artisanal and Small-Scale Mining (ASM) and Environmental Degradation

Men and women practice artisanal and unregulated small-scale mining in several countries. Besides the obvious economic benefits and poverty reduction, artisanal and small-scale mining (ASM) can result in a chain of negative environmental consequences with the impact felt beyond the geographical and spatial boundaries of these active artisanal mining areas. Often, local communities, villages, towns, and cities that are within proximity to active ASM locations – or even those that are remote – can be victims as they grapple with and suffer from these negative impacts of ASM operations, particularly the destruction of natural habitats and ecosystems.

Various methods may be used by ASM operations in extracting precious metals. These methods can also contribute directly to land degradation, pollution, and other forms of environmental degradation based on how they are applied and whether due diligence is observed to reduce the impact. In the case of alluvial mining for example, which is practiced by ASM operators in several parts of Africa, mercury and other chemicals are used to extract the gold and other precious metals. While mercury use in ASM can be monitored and controlled within the formal and heavily regulated corporate mining industry, this is not the case with ASM operators who sometimes operate under the radar of enforcement agencies and sometimes in criminal contexts.

ASM operators usually work within limited or no regulatory frameworks for their operations. This situation is exacerbated by these operators having poor access to finance to fund responsible mining. Sometimes supervision by the responsible regulatory agencies is reduced due to the clandestine way ASM takes place. So, there is a lack of clearly defined standard operating procedures, which makes it difficult for activities to be properly monitored and controlled.

The Ankobra River as it empties into the Gulf of Guinea in the northeastern part of the tropical Atlantic Ocean.

Not only does ASM pose a serious health hazard to those who are engaged in the practice, and to their unborn children, but it also leads to ecosystem degradation. Alluvial ASM results in the contamination of adjacent lands, air pollution, and the pollution of nearby creeks, rivers, larger receiving seas and oceans as well as in the loss of livelihoods of fisherfolk, including women.

Poverty, Unemployment and Artisanal Mining

It is quite common for women to engage in both unregulated artisanal mining and regulated small-scale mining, as a means of employment and income generation to enable them to sustain their livelihoods and those of their families. Economic empowerment is one of the key drivers behind women's engagement in different forms of employment, including mining. The need to be empowered economically, and the benefit of financial independence are key motivators for women to engage in these extremely labour-intensive and dangerous activities. The anticipated wages in the face of extreme poverty that hits women disproportionately, and the high unemployment rate coupled with the anticipated reward of precious metals, make ASM an option for women in mineral-rich countries. Their goal however is to cater for themselves and their families and to give them a better life.

Unfortunately, the environmental footprints of ASM are huge, as several habitats and ecosystems are continually being destroyed, which in turn affects people. Across some mineral-rich countries in Africa, the Caribbean, Latin America and around the globe, the quest for precious metals has led to a steady rise in ASM operations in the last decades. Women continue to be part of this ever-expanding workforce taking on opportunities where they are directly involved or service the mining industry.

Often artisanal refiners use labour-intensive and often non-mechanised methods in their operations as they typically possess limited technical knowledge, and little or no knowledge of geology or engineering. While ASM operators may be aware of some of the environmental and health challenges associated with their activities, poverty and unemployment override the need to pay attention to these glaring environmental consequences and the potential for land degradation.

Women in Artisanal and Small-Scale Post-Mining Restoration

Women in ASM should have an obligation to ensure that mining operations are done responsibly, and that the negative social, health and environmental impacts are kept to a barest minimum, in order to enable mined areas to be used alternatively following post-mining restoration. In fact, this is an opportunity for women to be part of a growing body of advocates for land and ecosystem restoration and the rehabilitation of landscapes that have been destroyed through mining. Following discussions with women in mining related fields, female traditional leaders, women's land rights policy advocates and land professionals, it is safe to assume that with the right platforms and technical capability, women in ASM can promote restoration. There are several reasons why women should consider and develop an interest in the restoration of terrestrial habitats post-mining. Following decades of women's exclusion from formal rights to land ownership, and the commitment under the sustainable development goals (SDGs) to ensure their equitable access to land rights, restoration of abandoned mines could signal a new opportunity for ownership.

As the world comes to terms with an increased understanding about the impacts of gender stereotyping, which consistently excluded women from certain occupations, including artisanal and small-scale mining, it has become clear, with the number of women currently working in this area, that the narrative has changed. To satisfy their desire to combat poverty and need for financial independence, women currently engage in several entrepreneurial and artisanal roles previously undertaken by men. Women can therefore leverage on their active involvement in the mining industry, by transforming the negative impacts of ASM into positive impacts through post-ASM land and ecosystem restoration. This can be done by channelling some of the energy currently fuelling ASM operations resulting in ecosystem degradation, into ASM Restoration.

To do this, however, the proficiency of women who are currently in ASM would need to be enhanced, particularly in the area of environmental awareness and the consequences uncontrolled and unregulated ASM has on the environment and life on the land. Their increased capacity to understand the interconnectedness of environmental media, such as that between ASM and biodiversity loss, and its impact on their immediate local community, at national, regional, and global scales, can be a starting point for their engagement in post-ASM restoration.

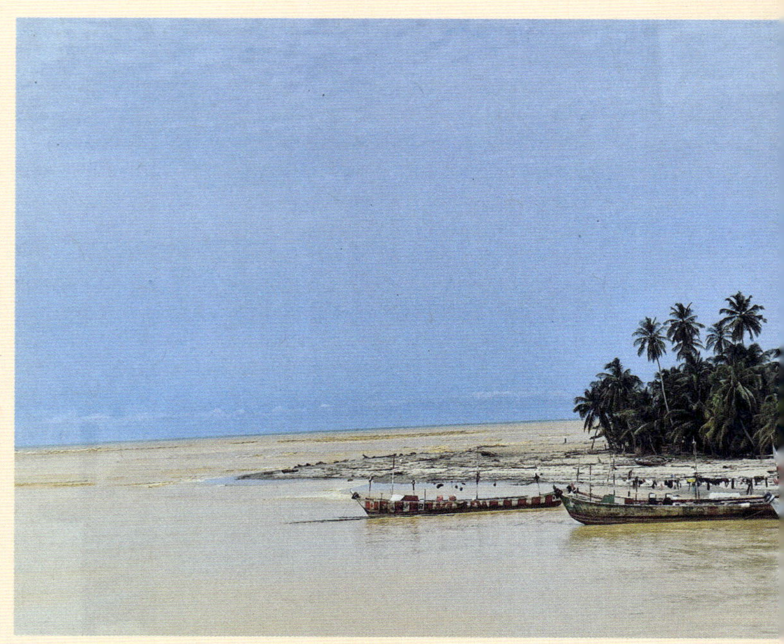

The Ankobra River as it empties into the Gulf of Guinea in the northeastern part of the tropical Atlantic Ocean.

Artisanal mining, though relatively uncontrolled and minimally regulated in several countries, does not justify the absence of organised and coordinated efforts at post-artisanal mining land restoration. The global land stock continues to decline, and this threatens the very existence of life on land as we know it. While concerted efforts must continue to be made for responsible artisanal mining, strategies for holding ASM operators accountable for post-ASM restoration should continually be explored.

As nations make commitments to restore degraded lands through nationally determined contributions, an organised post-artisanal mining land restoration regimen can form a major component in the achievement of such national land restoration pledges. It will open new employment and economic empowerment opportunities for people, particularly women. Women in traditional leadership at local community level can be instrumental to championing the cause for post-artisanal mining land restoration at the community level, by promoting the long-term sustainability benefits and encouraging community ownership and participation in them.

Similarly, small-scale mining operations, which are usually obtained through a more formal licensing process, and are better regulated than artisanal mining, also leave in their trail environmental consequences that can be traceable to licence holders. Sometimes, small-scale mining licence holders abandon their concessions, and these are then taken over by artisanal miners who mine for residual precious metals. Post-Small-Scale mining restoration can be promoted through capacity building and advocacy. Small-scale miners should be familiarised with the environmental, social, and health consequences of their actions particularly as the use of more mechanised approaches leaves behind an equally significant footprint when it comes to land degradation.

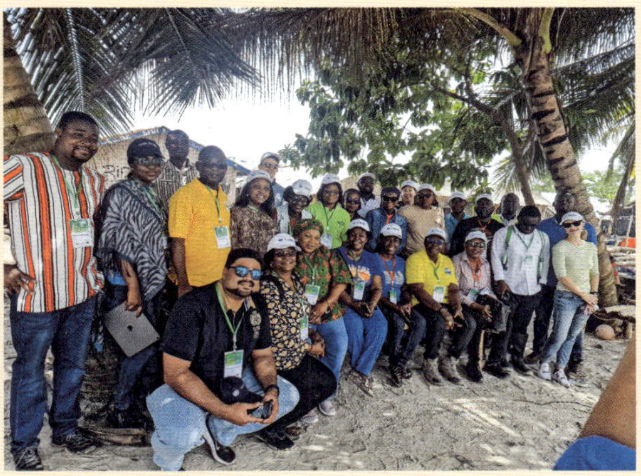

Participants from 10 Countries at the G20 GLI Roundtable on Gender in Post-Mining Land Restoration during a site visit to the mouth of the Ankobra River in the Gulf of Guinea.

Conclusion

The image on the left was taken at the estuary of the Ankobra River at the Gulf of Guinea, where it enters the northeastern part of the tropical Atlantic Ocean. The women here have lost their livelihoods due to heavy siltation and chemical contamination with heavy metals caused by uncontrolled and unregulated ASM operations and improper practices of regulated miners in the area, including women. While concerted efforts are undertaken to bring women out of poverty and into financial independence, this should not come at a cost to other women equally in search of similar livelihood aspirations. It is therefore necessary that women in mining related positions and other community leadership roles, including advocacy, come together to fix this menace. Working as organised groups, they can leverage on available funding mechanisms nationally and globally, to undertake post-ASM operations. The time to act is now, as we move towards halting and reversing land and ecosystem degradation because of artisanal and small-scale mining. ✦

Julian Charrière, *Pure Waste*, 2022, video projection on Japan paper, 5:30 minutes. Set in North Greenland, the film documents a material reversal that questions the conventional geological mining process. The artwork begins with several shots that capture the atmospheric quiet of the Arctic. Slowly entering the frame, a human hand opens to reveal five diamonds which are then tossed into a glacier mill. For this film, Charrière took part in a scientific expedition by Swiss scientists. Using a carbon capture process developed by ETH Zurich, they extracted CO_2 molecules from the air, thus literally mining the sky. The collected carbon dioxide was then enriched with the CO_2-rich exhalations of people from across the world and transformed into synthetic diamonds. The gesture of returning these diamonds, mined from the sky, to nature becomes an act of reconciliation. There is hope that we may one day close the destructive cycles so haplessly begun. ▶

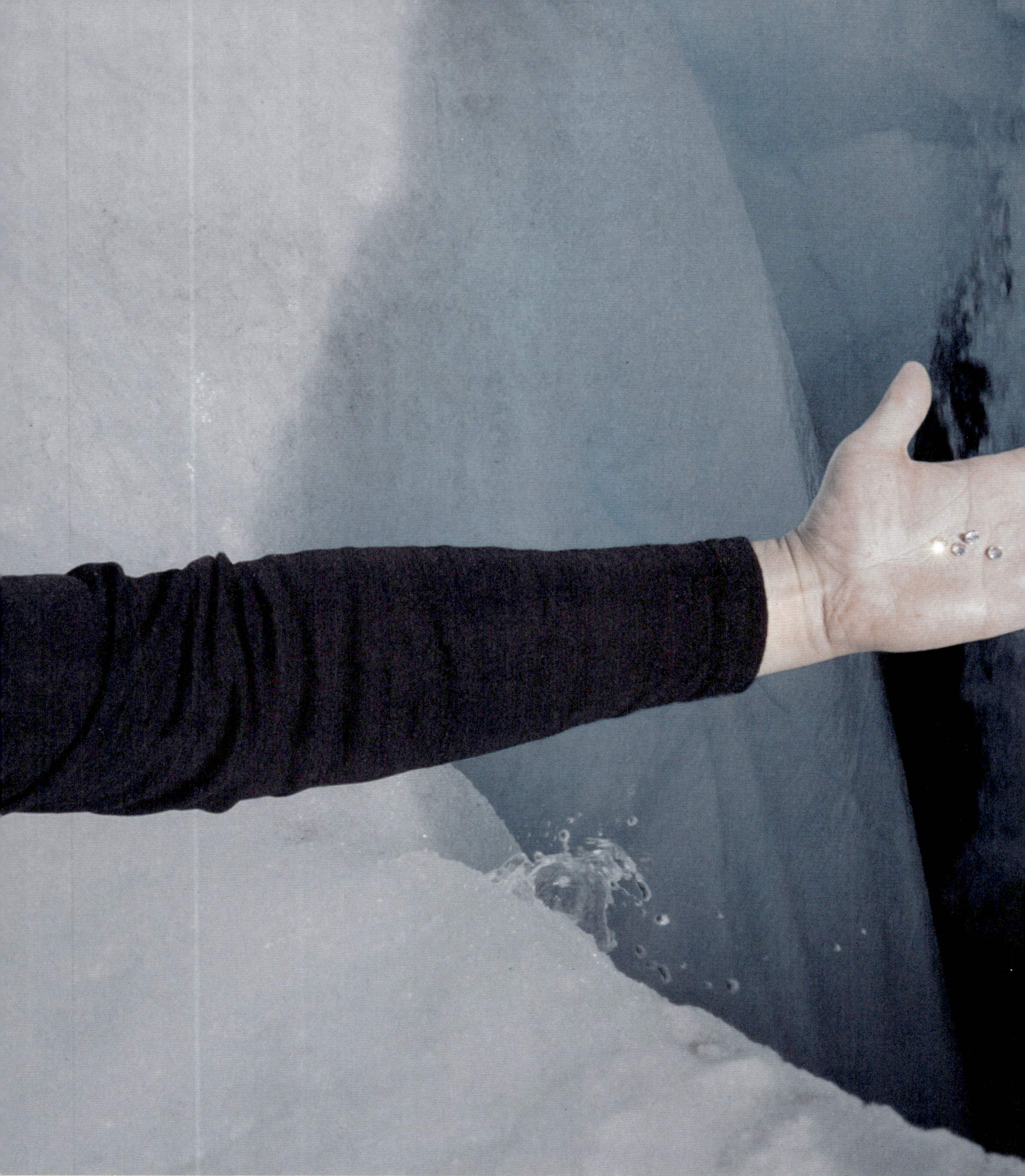

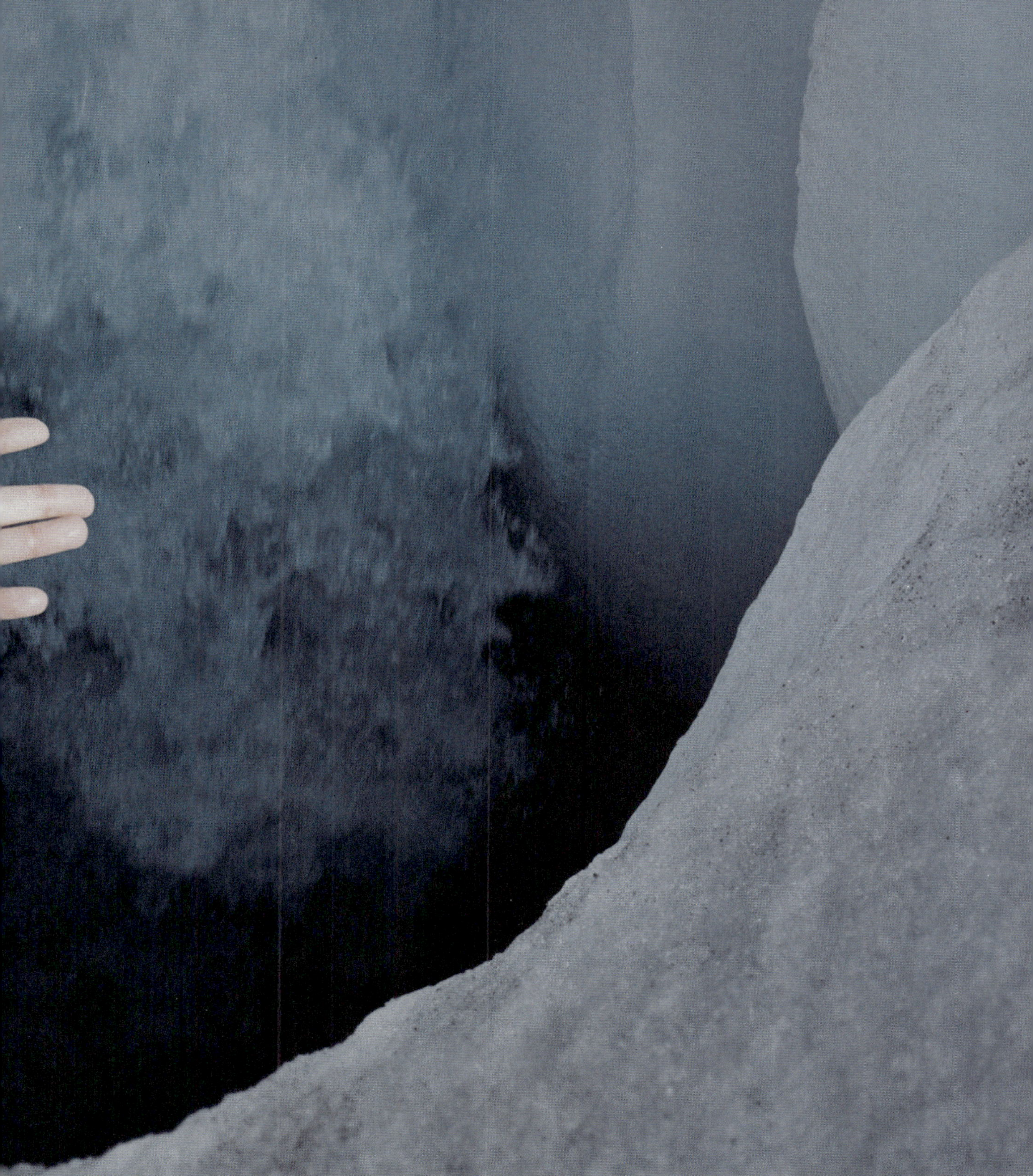

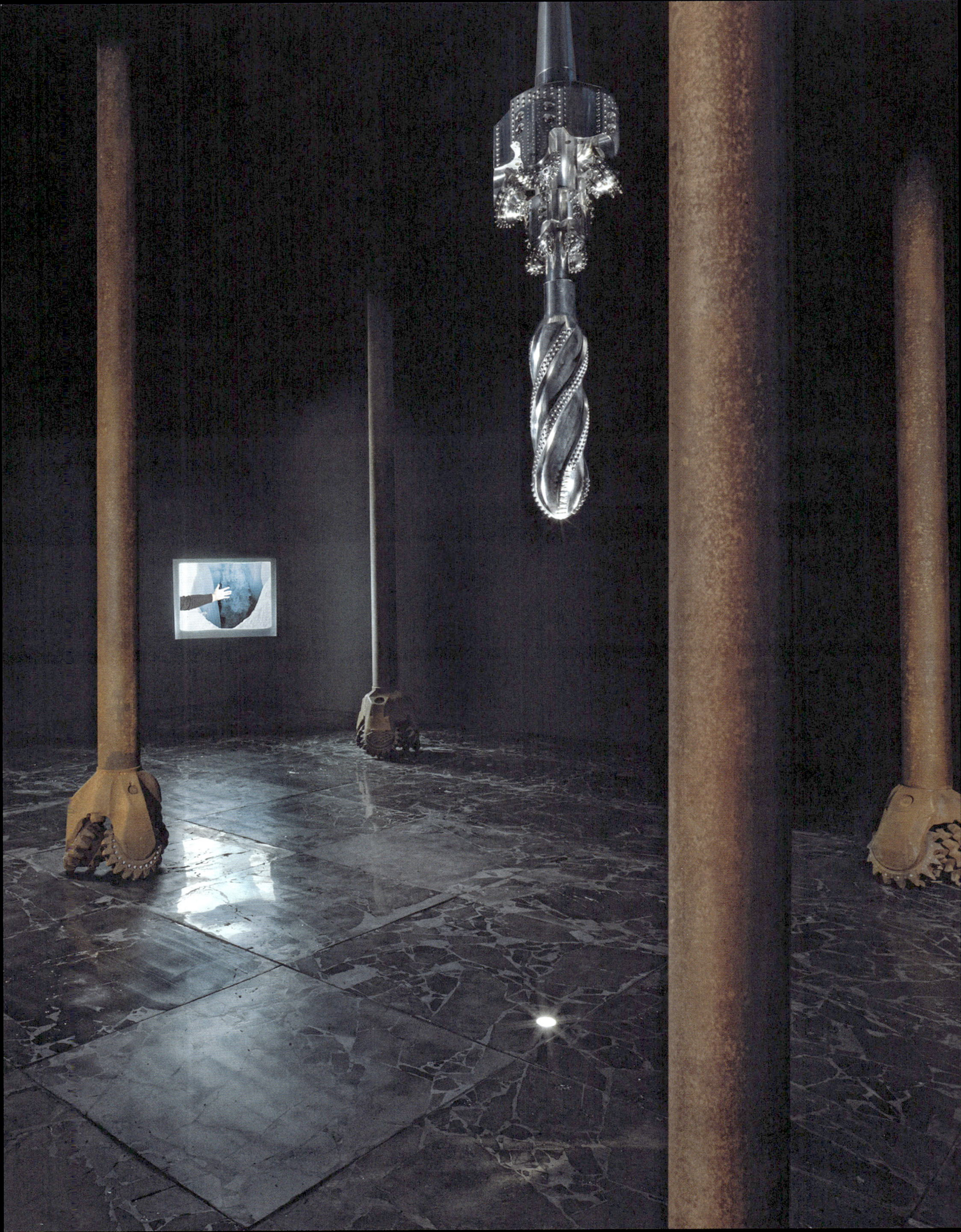

Julian Charrière, *Touching the Void*, 2021. In this art installation, a shiny new oil well drill hangs above the visitors' heads like the sword of Damocles. As a figure for drilling through layers of earth and sky, fossil fuels and atmospheric carbon, Charrière warns that carbon capture and storage techniques may also be developed merely in the service of insatiable greed. New technologies may be used to turn the tides toward a more sustainable use of energy or to perpetuate the catastrophe of business as usual.

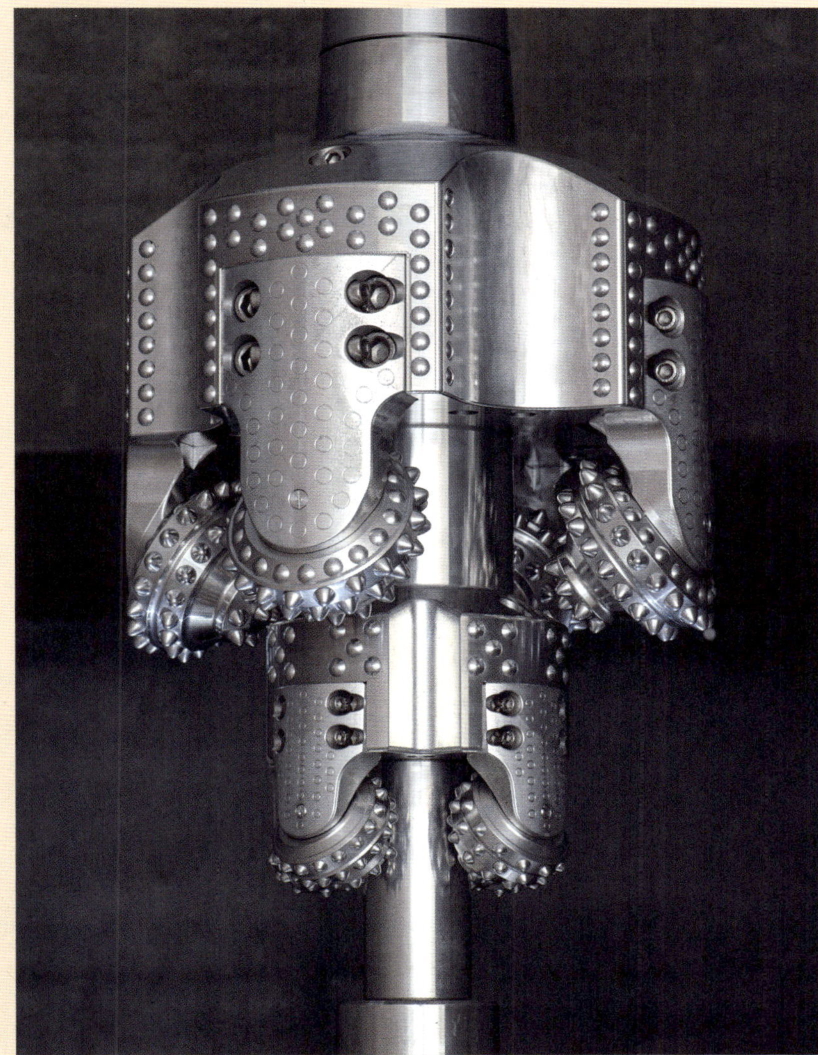

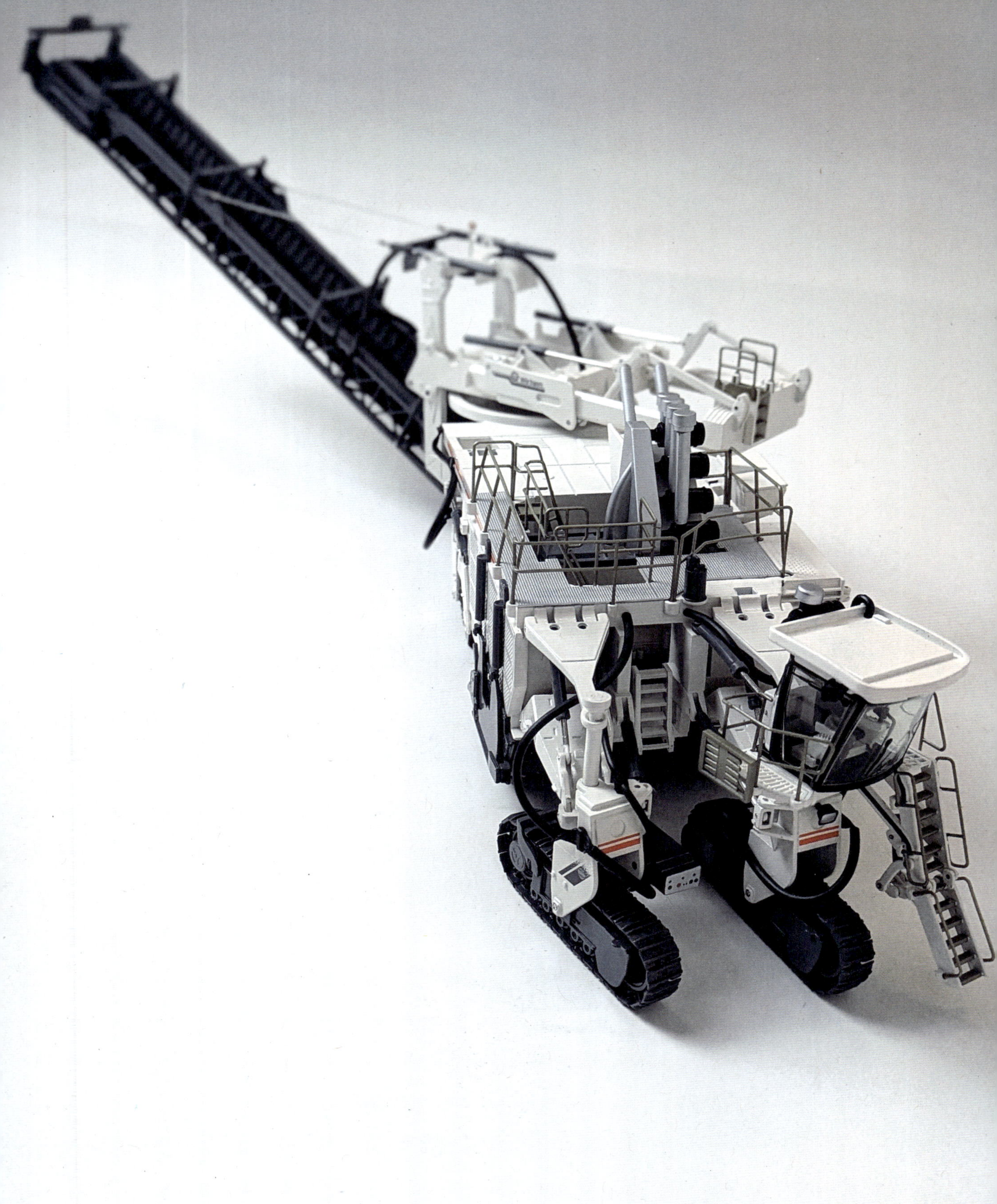

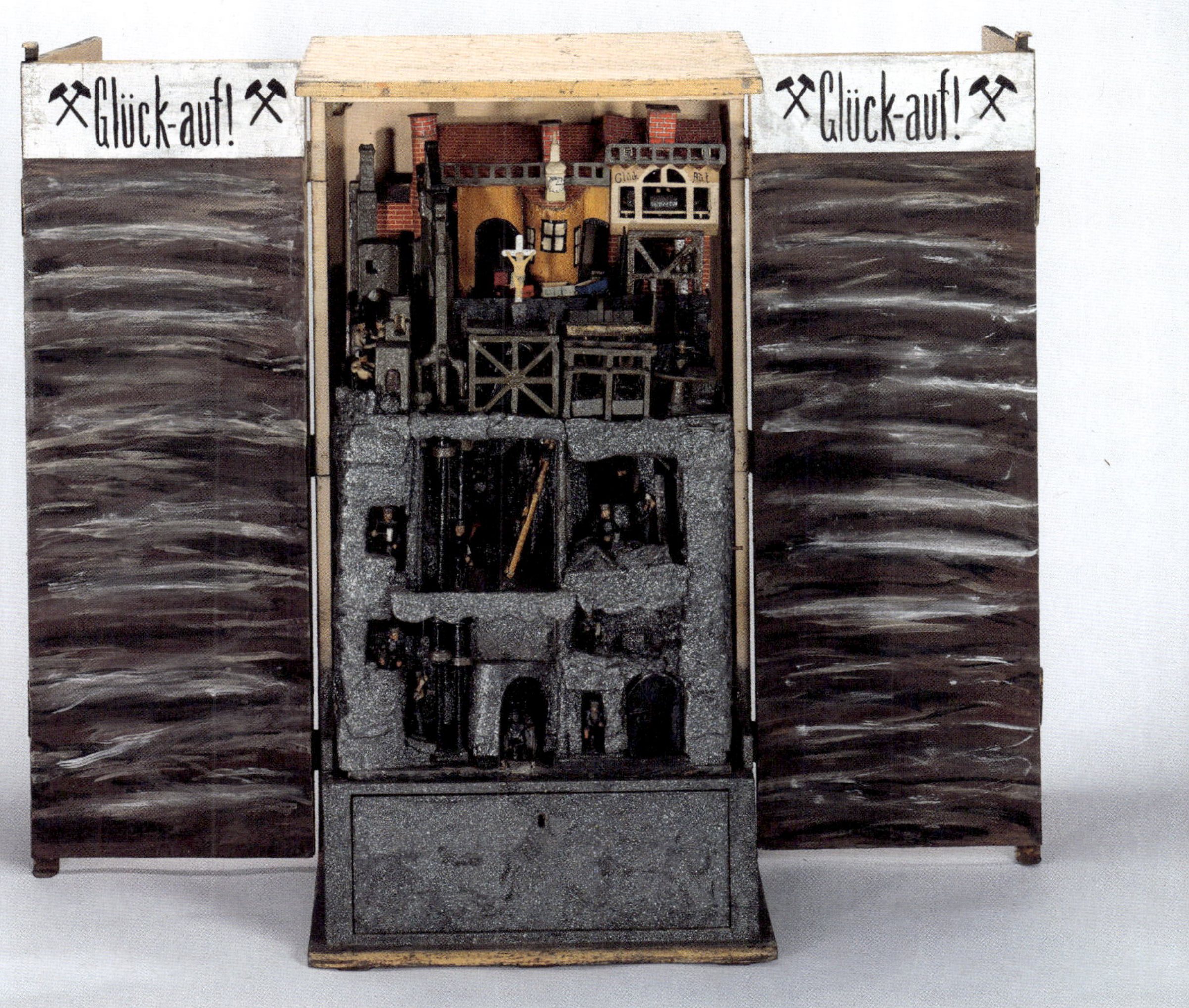

Wirtgen Group, Surface Miner 4200 SM, model. Raw materials for fossil energy (lignite), construction minerals (sands, gravels, stones) and mineral-industrial raw materials (salts, refractory clays) are extracted in open-cast mining. The extraction of raw materials in open-cast mines is accompanied by drastic destruction of soils and landscapes. The water balance and water quality can be permanently impaired. In some cases, entire villages are relocated for the operation of an open-cast mine. The renaturalisation or recultivation of the areas can take decades.

Portable model of a mine, ca. 1860/70, probably Saxony. The display mine, which is kept in the Museum of European Cultures in Berlin, consists of a back box that can be set up and opened. Inside, a mechanically movable underground mine is set up with successive work processes, including the chiming of bells and the man engine. The inscription reads: 'Good luck. Deep underground'.

Interactive floor projection 'Natural Habitats', 2024
© dform/Bildwerk, Vienna ▶

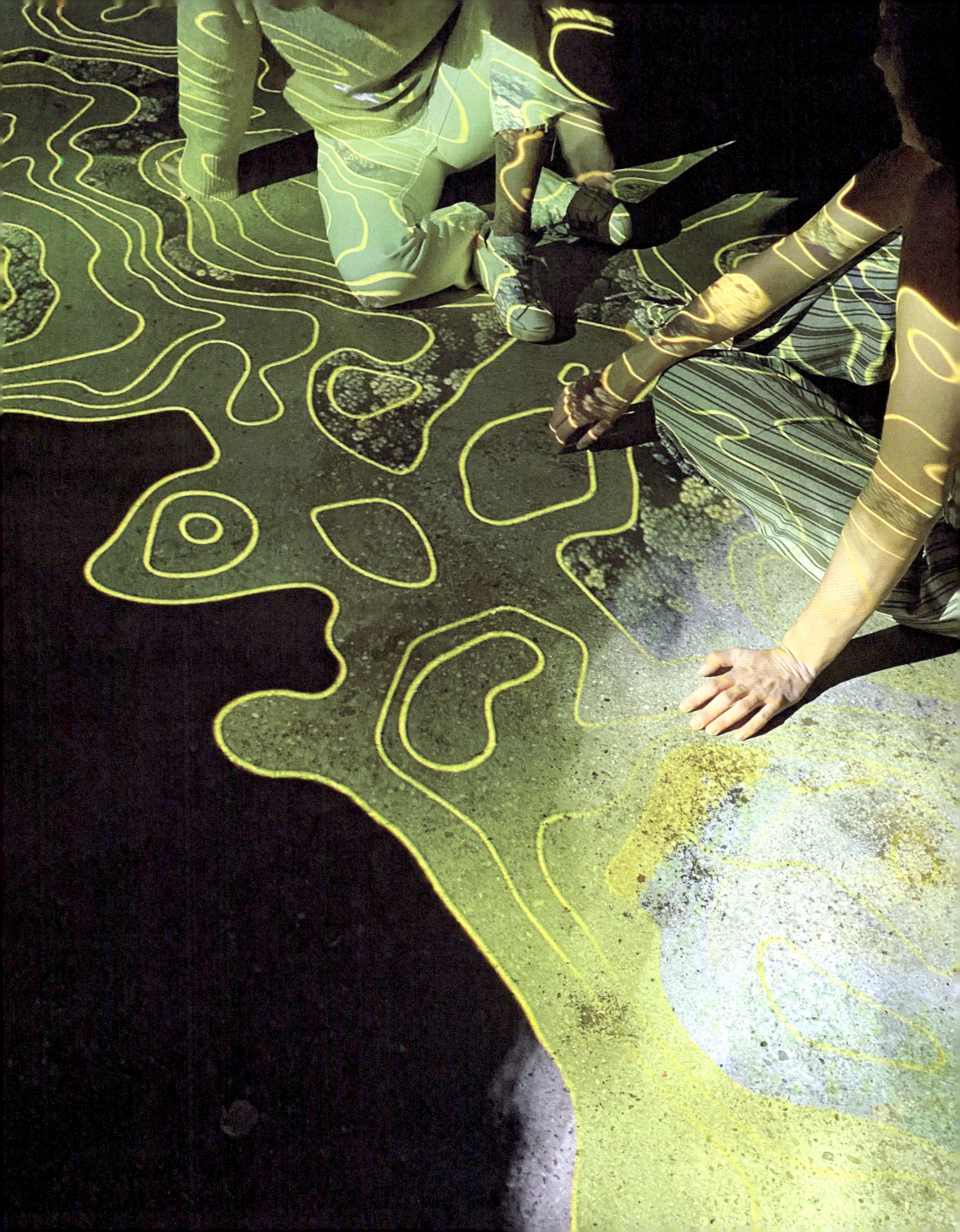

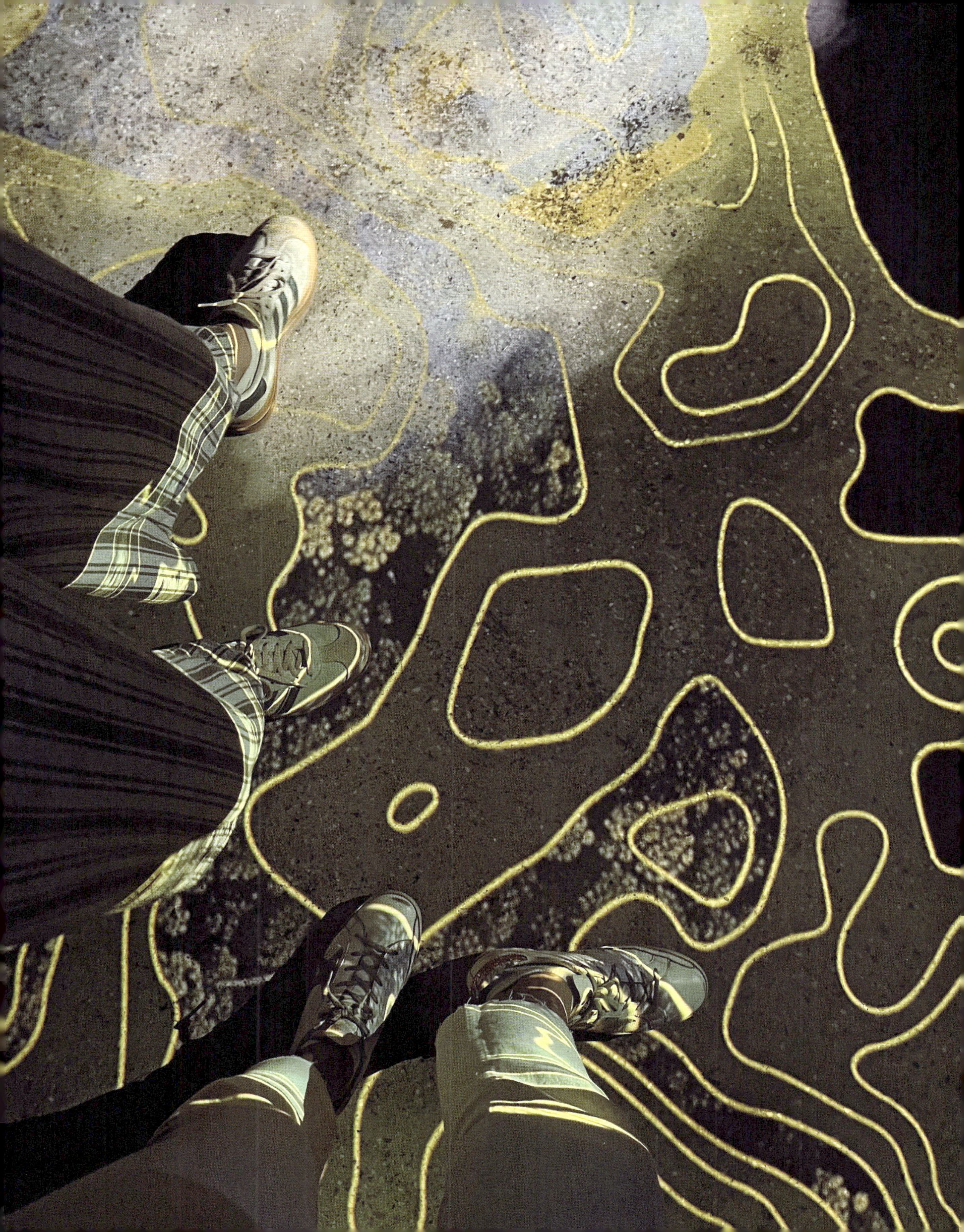

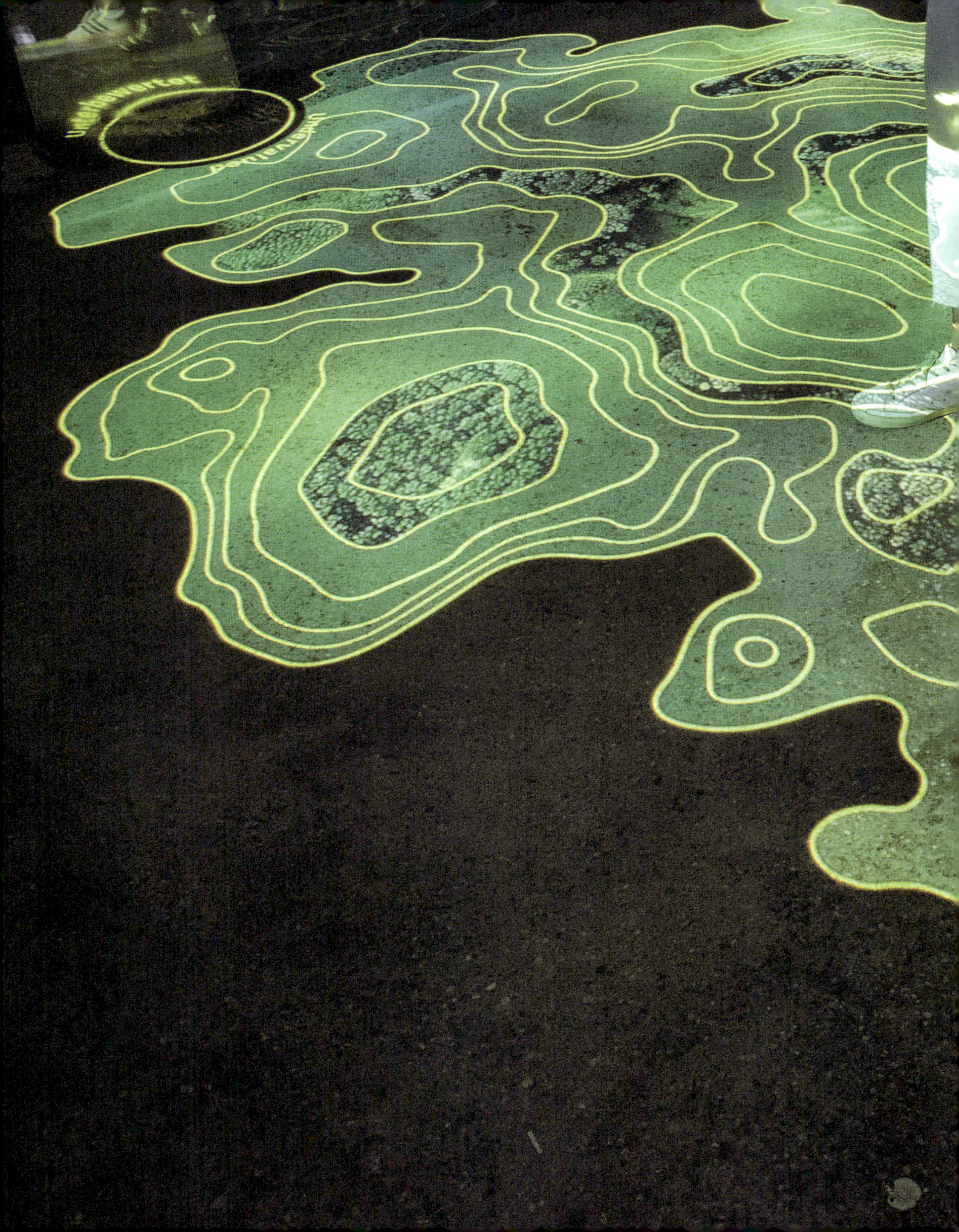
Unterbewertet
Undervalued

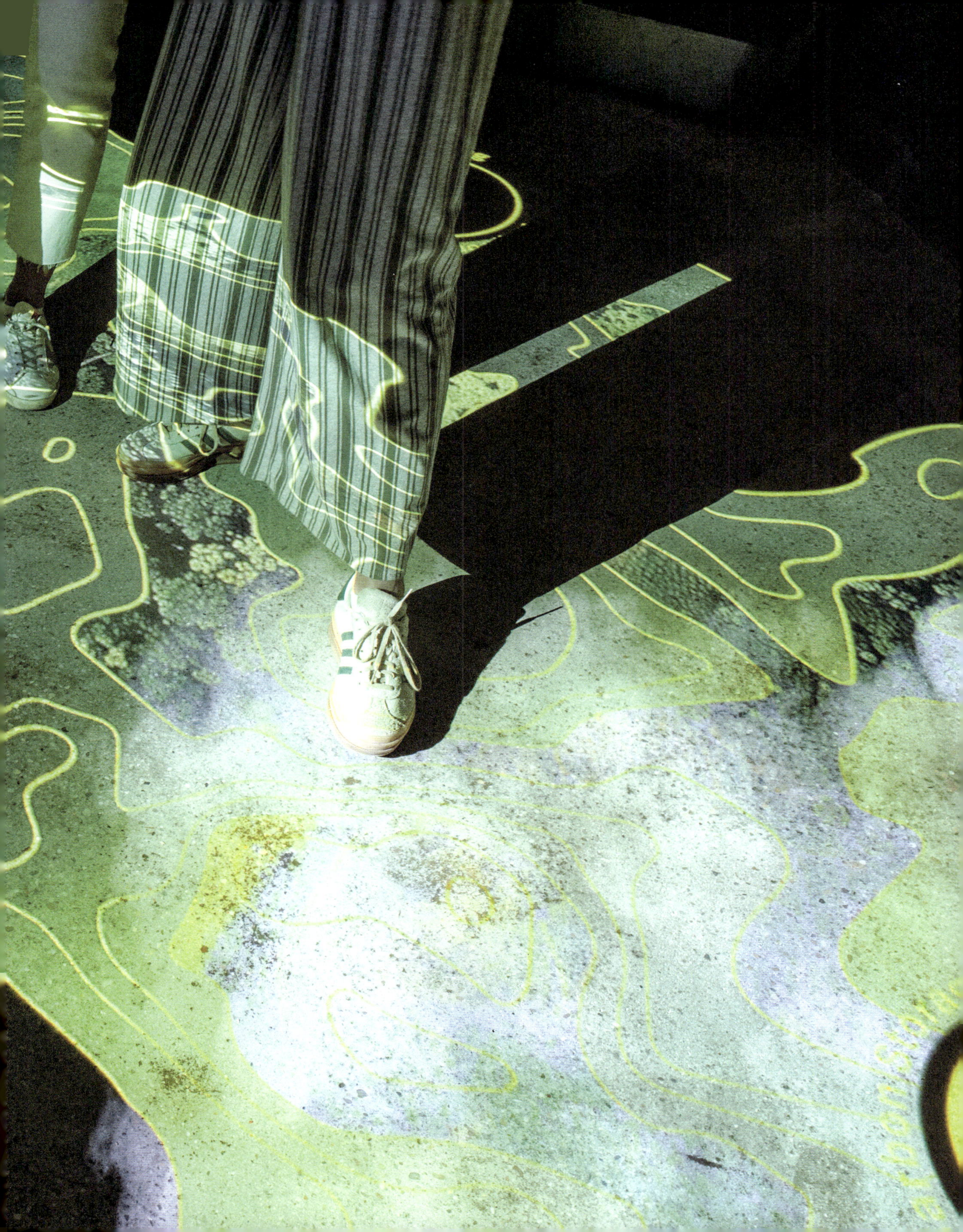

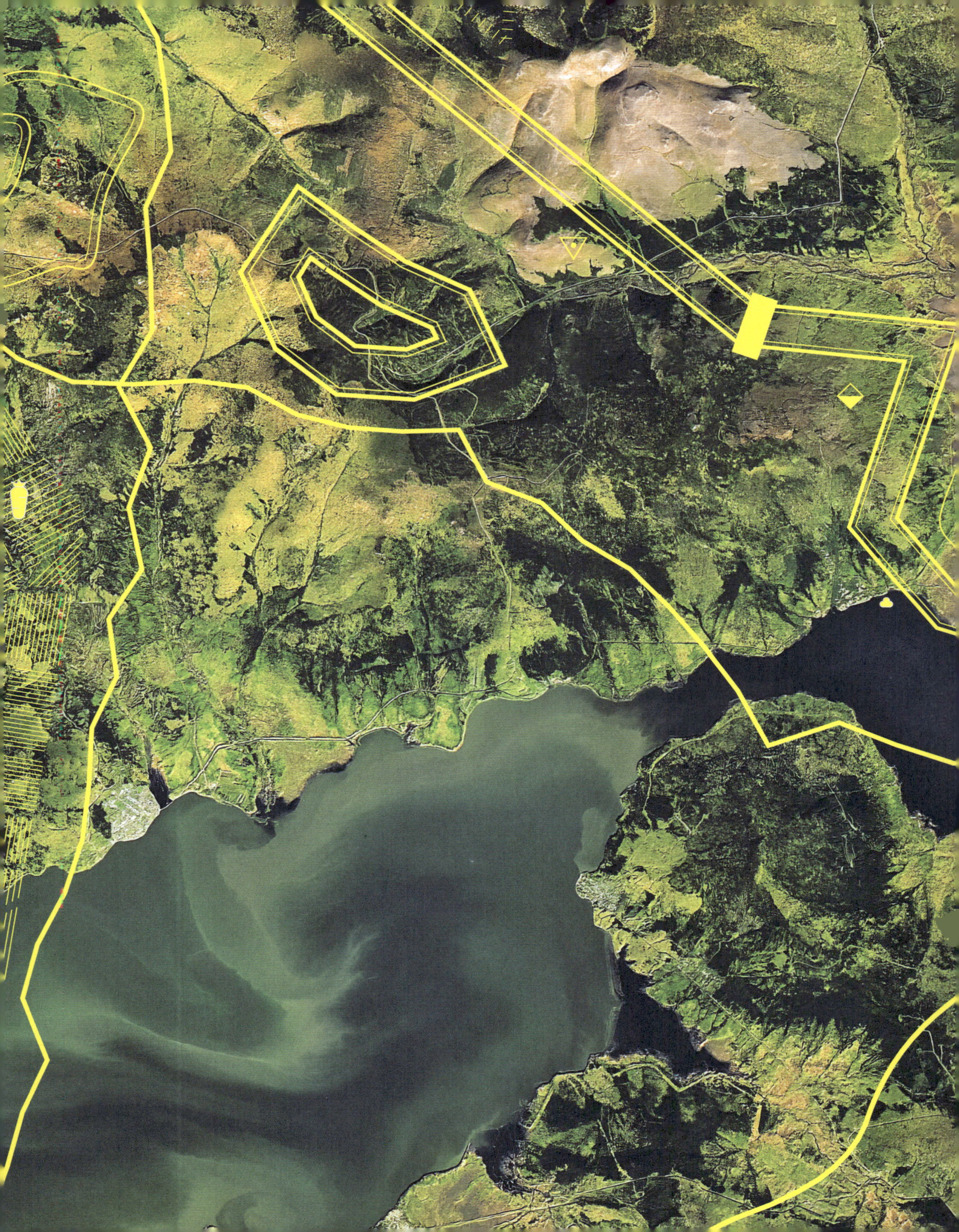

Nature's Core

Just 23 % of the planet's habitable surface can still be classified as 'wilderness' and has not been altered by human activity. Most of this is located in just 5 countries: Canada, Alaska, Brazil, Botswana, and Australia. Between 70 and 75 % of ice-free land ecosystems have been converted for human use. As a result, many areas are endangered and at high risk for desertification and biodiversity loss. Yet only 14.7 % of the world's habitable land is protected. We are destroying natural areas, especially forests and grasslands, at an increasingly alarming rate. Deforestation for agricultural expansion, urbanisation, and logging is taking place worldwide, most of it in the tropics. Every minute, 10,400 trees are felled. The destruction of natural habitats and their biodiversity impairs their ecological functionality and stability. However, it also affects us humans in many ways, as the increase in carbon emissions and the threats to fresh water and soil affect us all.

What is Our Natural Heritage?

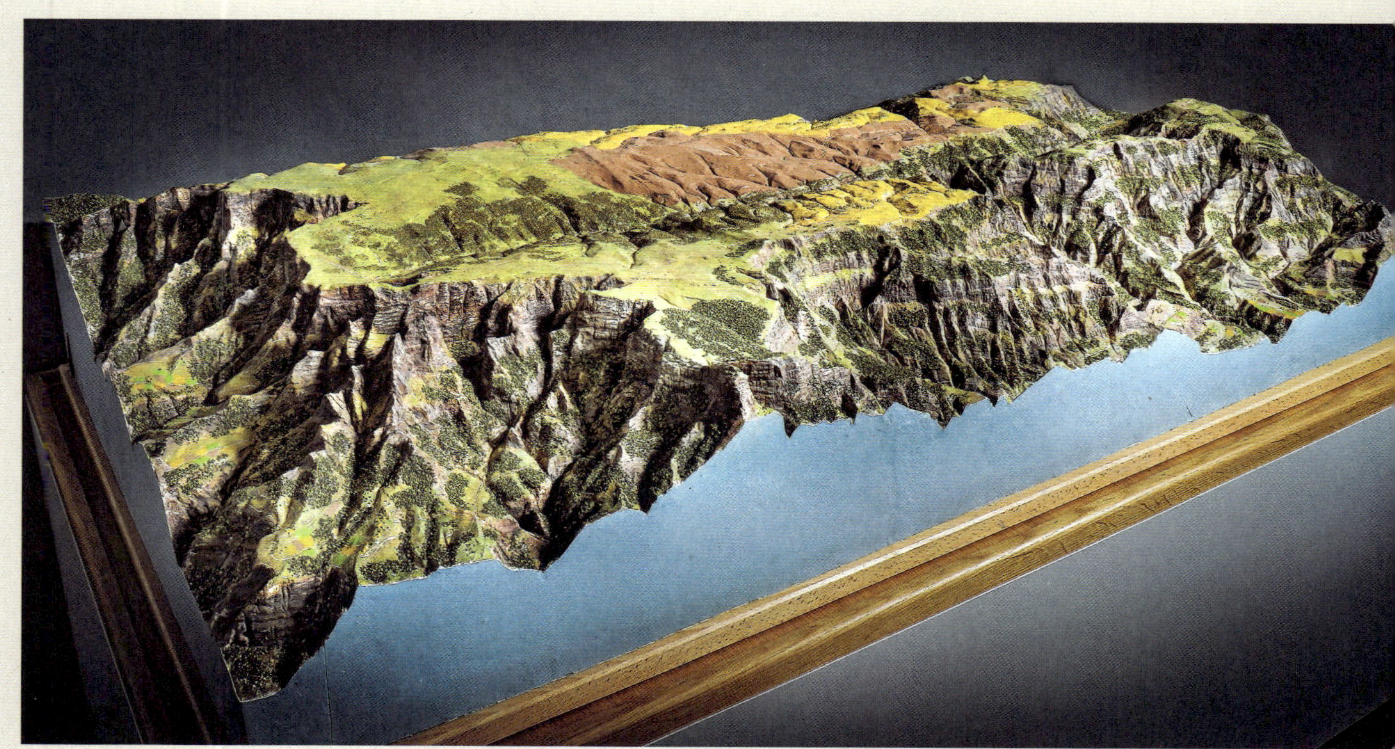

Eva Flinkerbusch

Humans as Part of Nature

Our planet is shaped by imposing mountain ranges as well as magnificent rainforests, vast grasslands, deserts, rivers, and oceans. All these unique habitats are inhabited by millions and millions of creatures. We ourselves are a part of them: a biological species in a biological environment. We have emerged from nature and are completely dependent on it. Insects pollinate our crops, soils filter our water, and plants produce the oxygen we need to live, to name just a few of these so-called ecosystem services that we have freely utilised since time immemorial. Our natural heritage is the Earth's biodiversity. How did it come about that we now have to protect this heritage from ourselves? How has humankind changed the natural environment to such an extent?

Revolutions in Human History and their Impact

Let's start at the very beginning – with a few highlights. Between around 9500 and 8300 BC, the first revolution in human history that had a major impact on natural habitats took place: the Neolithic Revolution. Rapidly accelerated social and cultural change occurred during this time. Many of the people who had previously been organised in hunter-gatherer societies became sedentary and began to cultivate crops and keep livestock. From this point onwards, people laboriously wrested the cultivated landscape from unspoilt nature. Wild nature was tamed and moulded for human purposes for thousands of years. Resources appeared to be endless, wild animals were fought or tamed. Humans made themselves the crown of creation.

Around 10,000 years later, the second great revolution in human history occurred: industrialisation. The use of machines and chemicals changed land use with striking consequences for nature. Small parcelled fields were enlarged and standardised, hedges and copses disappeared from the landscape. In addition to natural habitats, historically evolved, structurally and species-rich cultural landscapes slowly disappeared. Industrialisation also marked the beginning of global warming. Humans began to influence the planet's entire system on a global scale.

Model of the Simien National Park, Ethiopia (1:10,000), 2009. The model created by Tony Mair for the Technical University of Dresden shows the 179 km² Simien National Park in northern Ethiopia, which is characterised by its biodiversity. The green mountain landscape was one of the first regions in the world to be declared a UNESCO World Heritage Site in 1978. Between 1996 and 2017, however, the national park was placed on the World Heritage in Danger list. The main reason for this is the ongoing tension between protecting the environment and safeguarding the livelihoods of the population. 80 % of the more than 80 million Ethiopians live in the highlands and are dependent on agricultural yields.

Impoverished Nature

The loss of biodiversity, our natural heritage, has been progressing dramatically worldwide for many years now. Nature is becoming increasingly impoverished. Permanently unused areas in which ecosystems can develop naturally without direct human influence have now largely disappeared worldwide. This also jeopardises and destroys our own livelihoods.

While our ancestors did not for a long time realise the extent to which nature could be exploited, and the limitations of our home planet, we now possess certain facts on the basis of which action must be taken. Rachel Carson's book *Silent Spring*, published in 1962, is often cited as a starting point for the global environmental movement. In it, the American biologist sharply criticises the use of pesticides in industrialised agriculture and establishes a clear link between their use and the demise of a once rich animal and plant world. In the years that followed, further studies were published internationally and international programmes and efforts to protect and sustainably use the natural world were launched and developed for the first time.

First Programmes to Protect Nature and the Environment

The Man and Biosphere Programme was founded by UNESCO in 1970. Under this programme, UNESCO recognises biosphere reserves worldwide. The aim of the UNESCO biosphere reserves is to promote and model a balanced relationship between man and the biosphere. Today, there are 748 biosphere reserves in 134 countries worldwide. 17 of these are located in Germany, such as the Schaalsee in Mecklenburg-Western Pomerania or the Spreewald in Brandenburg.

The national park concept was also promoted internationally. The first national park in Germany, for example, was founded in 1970: The Bavarian Forest National Park. The history of national parks begins around 100 years earlier, in the nineteenth century in the United States. The world's first national park, Yellowstone National Park, was established there in 1872 to preserve the outstanding beauty of this natural landscape for all people. Numerous national park designations followed all over the world.

The UNESCO World Heritage Convention was also established in 1972, and has become one of the most successful international protection instruments for natural and cultural heritage worldwide. World Heritage Sites are testaments to unique natural landscapes of outstanding universal value. These sites are not only significant for national or local communities, but for humanity as a whole. Since the first listings in 1978, around 230 natural World Heritage Sites worldwide have been added to the UNESCO World Heritage List. The sites include extraordinary natural areas and ecosystems, such as the Wadden Sea in Denmark, Germany, and the Netherlands or ancient and primeval beech forests in the Carpathians and other parts of Europe. The World Heritage Convention has been signed by 195 countries and is based on a global social agreement.

Moving into the Future Together

The Brundland Report entitled *Our Common Future*, published in 1987, is regarded as the beginning of the global discourse on sustainability and sustainable development. The work of the World Commission on Environment and Development established the model for sustainable, environmentally compatible global development that is still in use today. Its publication was followed in 1989 by the convening of the United Nations Conference on Environment and Development, which took place in Rio de Janeiro in 1992. This was the first time that environmental issues were discussed in a global context.

One result of this 'Earth Summit' was the Convention on Biological Diversity (CBD). It is a global, internationally binding agreement on the protection and sustainable use of living nature and relates to the diversity of animal and plant species as well as diversity within species and the richness of ecosystems. The CBD is supported by 196 member states, including Germany, but also by the European Union. The member states have set themselves the goal of protecting and preserving the diversity of life on Earth and organising its sustainable use in such a way that as many people as possible can live from it today and in the future. The international community has recognised that the problem is highly complex and cannot be solved by isolated nature conservation activities, but rather requires global cooperation.

High Time to Take Action

More than 30 years have passed since then and the red lists of endangered species and biotopes are getting longer and longer, land encroachment is progressing unhindered, agriculture is becoming increasingly monotonous and intensive, and the world more polluted. Rachel Carson's book *Silent Spring* is unfortunately more relevant than ever. Long-term observations by volunteer entomologists from the Entomologists' Association in Krefeld, for example, have documented drastic declines in insect populations in Germany. The results were published in a highly regarded study in 2017. Alongside pandemics, wars and, last but not least, climate change, the ongoing mass extinctions in nature are among the greatest threats that humanity has imposed upon itself. In the World Economic Forum's Global Risks Report 2022, the loss of biodiversity was categorised as the third biggest threat that humanity will face in the next ten years. Losing so much of the Earth's biodiversity means not only destroying our natural heritage, but also jeopardising the stability of our planet today and for all future generations.

We do not have a knowledge deficit, but an implementation deficit. We need to recognise the realities we face as a human species – currently 8 billion and rising – and act accordingly. There are plenty of ideas for this. For example, the late American biologist E.O. Wilson and a new generation of scientists, ecologists, and conservationists have come to the conclusion that we need to reserve about half of the Earth's land and sea areas for nature in order to preserve a sufficient number of species and habitats and thus also humanity. The aim is to protect half of the land and oceans in order to create sufficient habitat to reverse the species extinction crisis and ensure the long-term health of our planet.

New Global Targets

In line with this, new global targets for the protection of biodiversity by 2030 have been in place since December 2022: With the adoption of the CBD's new global framework for biodiversity, around 200 countries agreed in Montreal, Canada, to protect at least 30 % of the world's land and marine areas by 2030, halve the use of pesticides, and spend more money on biodiversity conservation. All 196 signatory states to the CBD, including Germany, now have a duty to implement the resolutions and adapt their national strategies for the protection and sustainable use of biodiversity.

All these studies, conventions, programmes, and not least the commitment of many individuals around the world show that humanity has recognised and understood how valuable and vital our natural heritage is. The Earth is our home. If we do not manage to protect what remains of nature, we are in danger of destroying the basis of our existence completely. We should never jeopardise our natural heritage – even if only out of self-interest. ✦

Stefanie Bühler, *Primeval Forest*, 2006. Sculptor Stefanie Bühler created this primeval forest from polyurethane foam, among other materials. What initially looks like a diorama from a natural history museum also resembles a theatre backdrop. Bühler deliberately works with shifts in scale to emphasise the artificiality of the object.

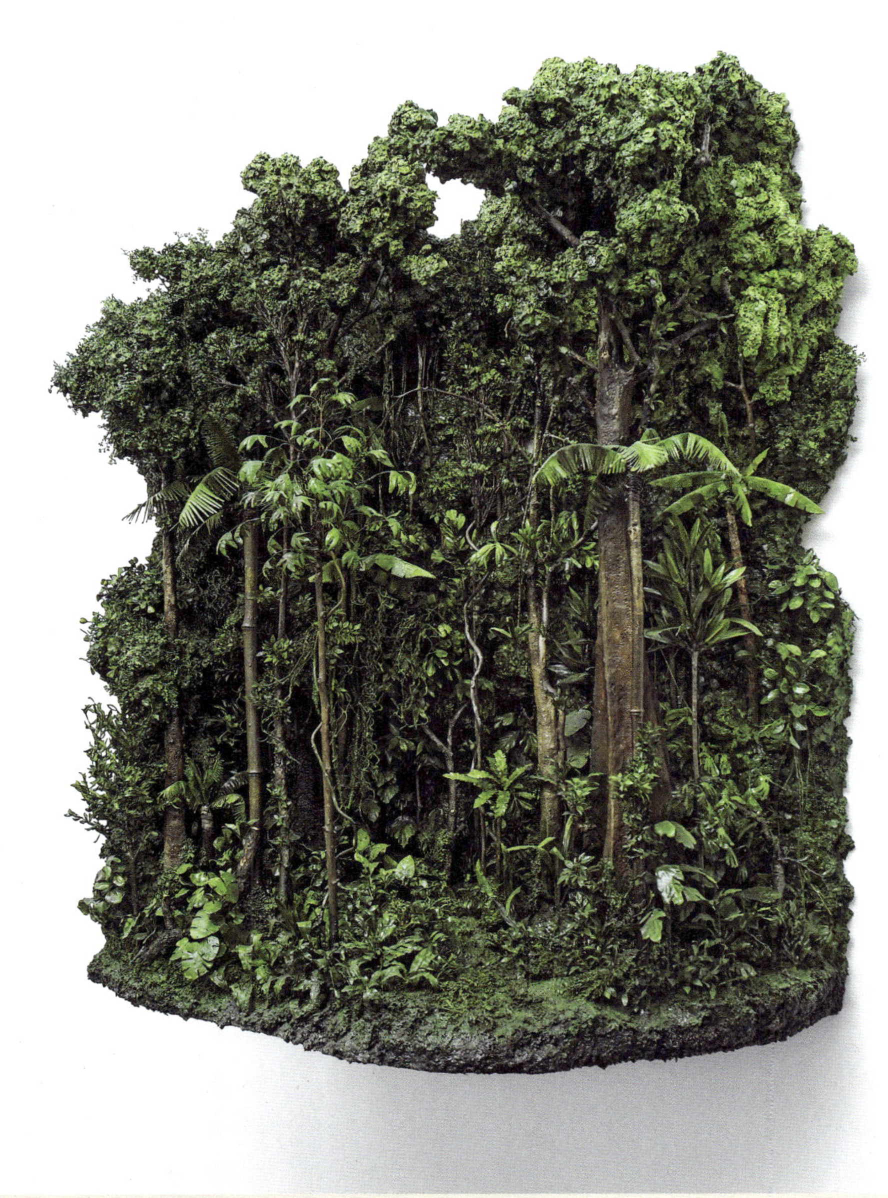

★ **Key Terms**

Biological diversity encompasses the diversity of ecosystems (communities, habitats, and landscapes), species diversity and genetic diversity within species.

UNESCO biosphere reserves serve the large-scale protection of natural and cultural landscapes. Biosphere reserves are also used to test nature-friendly ways of living and farming.

National parks are protected areas in which nature is allowed to unfold largely undisturbed and remain as pristine as possible. The primary aim of national parks is to allow nature to be nature.

UNESCO World Heritage Sites are testimonies to past cultures, material traces of encounters and exchanges, artistic masterpieces, and unique natural landscapes. What they have in common is their extraordinary universal value.

The Value of Nature for Climate Action

Model of carbon dioxide (CO_2) in solid form as dry ice, 2nd half of the 20th century, Humboldt University, Berlin. Carbon dioxide (CO_2) is a chemical compound of carbon and oxygen. CO_2 is a non-flammable, acidic, and colourless gas. In solid form as dry ice, it is used as a coolant. CO_2 is an elementary component of the global carbon cycle, a natural component of the air and a significant greenhouse gas in the Earth's atmosphere. Around 100 million tonnes of carbon dioxide are emitted into the atmosphere every day as a result of human activity (as of 2020), and the trend is rising. This increase intensifies the greenhouse effect and leads to global warming.

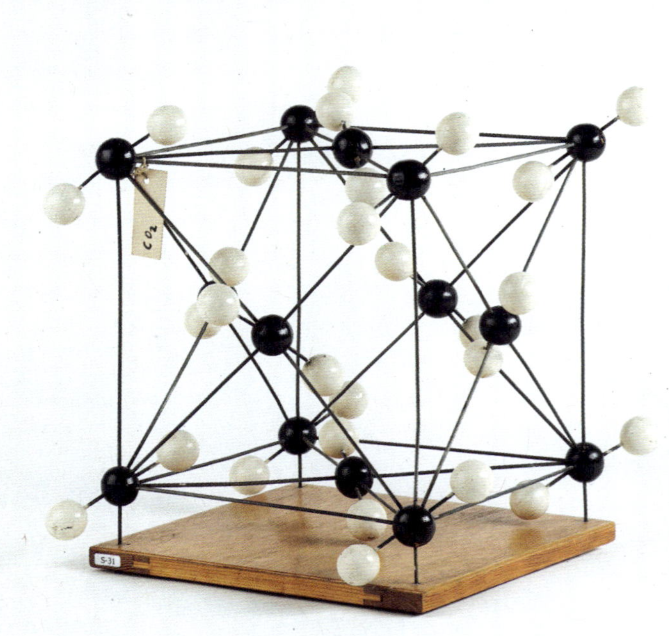

Angela Churie Kallhauge

Climate change, a complex and pressing global challenge, is wreaking havoc on our planet. From shifting seasons disrupting delicate ecosystems to the increased vulnerability of countless species, the impacts are far-reaching and profound. Yet, within this crisis lies an extraordinary opportunity: nature itself is a key to mitigating climate change.

Our planet's natural systems – forests, soils, and oceans – are carbon sinks, capable of absorbing and storing vast amounts of carbon dioxide from the atmosphere. This natural process has helped regulate our climate for millennia. However, human activities such as deforestation, unsustainable agriculture, and coastal development have compromised these vital nature-based solutions, diminishing their ability to perform this critical function.

The potential of nature-based solutions to combat climate change is undeniable: Studies indicate that protecting and restoring natural ecosystems could provide 37% of the emissions reductions needed by 2030 to achieve the targets of the Paris Agreement, according to the World Bank. Nature-based solutions often prove more cost-effective than technological alternatives, while also supporting communities and livelihoods.

Natural Ways of Storing Carbon

To put the scale of the opportunity into perspective, we need only look at our forests, oceans and farmlands. Forests currently cover approximately 31% of the Earth's land area and sequester billions of tons of carbon dioxide each year. Nearly half of Earth's carbon stored on land is found in our forests, according to NASA. At the same time, they provide critical habitat for biodiversity, help avoid erosion, keep temperatures cooler, and provide economic benefits to local communities.

Climate-smart agriculture is another example that enables farmers to retain more carbon in their fields as they produce crops. Currently, cropland takes up 10% of our planet's land, and global food systems are responsible for one-third of all emissions. But it doesn't have to be that way: Soil is a significant carbon reservoir that, when managed effectively, can store carbon for extended periods. And we can do this with practices that enable farmers and smallholder producers to grow more nutritious food to feed communities.

Deforestation – a Manmade Crisis

Despite these immense opportunities, investment in nature-based climate solutions is still far below what is needed. In fact, investment in nature-based solutions needs to almost triple to reach climate targets by 2030.

To fully understand the heart of this crisis, we need to deeply understand the rapid loss of tropical forests. We know that 95% of global deforestation occurs in the tropics. These vital ecosystems, teeming with biodiversity, absorb vast quantities of carbon dioxide.

Unfortunately, deforestation rates remain alarmingly high, driven 'commodity-driven deforestation' – cutting down forests to grow crops such as soy, palm oil, and cocoa, raising livestock on pasture, and mining operations. The consequences are devastating, not only for the climate but also for the millions of people who depend on these forests for their livelihoods and cultural heritage.

The loss of tropical forests exacerbates climate change in several ways. Firstly, it releases stored carbon into the atmosphere, contributing to global warming. The process of cutting and burning trees adds as much greenhouse gas to the atmosphere as all the cars and trucks in the world combined.

Secondly, it reduces the Earth's capacity to absorb future carbon emissions. Large-scale deforestation, habitat degradation, and climate change effects are already causing a decline in the Amazon rainforest's ability to absorb massive amounts of carbon, according to NASA researchers.

Thirdly, it disrupts rainfall patterns, leading to droughts and floods. This creates challenges for farmers and food systems, stresses water supply, and harms nature, as well as the communities that depend on them.

What Can Be Done?

To address this crisis, a multifaceted approach is essential. Protecting existing forests through effective governance and law enforcement is paramount. Additionally, investing in sustainable land-use practices, such as agroforestry and sustainable agriculture, can help reduce deforestation while providing livelihoods for local communities. Restoring degraded forest lands is another crucial strategy, as it can sequester carbon and enhance biodiversity.

As we know, there is no magic wand solution to climate change – but halting deforestation is one of the most powerful actions we can take. The Intergovernmental Panel on Climate Change notes that 'reduced deforestation in tropical regions has the highest total mitigation potential' of all land, ocean, food and water interventions.

Luckily, we have the knowledge, will, and resources to protect tropical forests. Now we need to mobilise a tool to drive action that protects tropical forests: High-integrity tropical forest carbon credits.

The knowledge and experience needed to protect tropical forests is held by Indigenous Peoples and local communities, who are often the best stewards of their forests. Indigenous territories – legally recognised or not – encompass 80 % of the world's biodiversity and hold nearly a fifth of the world's forest carbon. Their traditional knowledge and practices offer invaluable insights into sustainable forest management. Satellite data shows that the worlds healthiest forests are those legally managed by Indigenous Peoples.

However, in addition to the issue of Indigenous land rights being disrespected or denied, less than one percent of climate and biodiversity funding goes directly to Indigenous Peoples. Indigenous Peoples and local communities are not being compensated or resources for their vital conservation work.

Unlocking the Full Potential of Nature

The resources can come from engaging the private sector. More than half of the world's 2,000 largest companies have set net-zero targets and need credible tools to deliver on these commitments. Forest carbon credits provide the obvious bridge between corporate demand for emissions reductions and nature's need for finance.

By purchasing high quality credits – and investing in future supply through advance purchase agreements – companies can play an active role in the shift towards higher integrity, deliver on their climate and nature goals and support Indigenous communities who are protecting vital ecosystems. These purchases could make a significant contribution to providing the 130 billion dollars a year needed to end deforestation.

While the challenges are immense, there is also cause for hope. Growing global awareness of the climate crisis has led to a surge in interest and investment in nature-based solutions. Governments, businesses, and individuals are increasingly recognising the importance of protecting and restoring our planet's natural capital.

Ultimately, there is no pathway to net-zero emissions without nature. By embracing nature-based solutions, we can not only mitigate climate change but also create a more resilient, sustainable, and equitable future for all. It is time to invest in our planet's health and unlock the full potential of nature as our climate's greatest ally. ✦

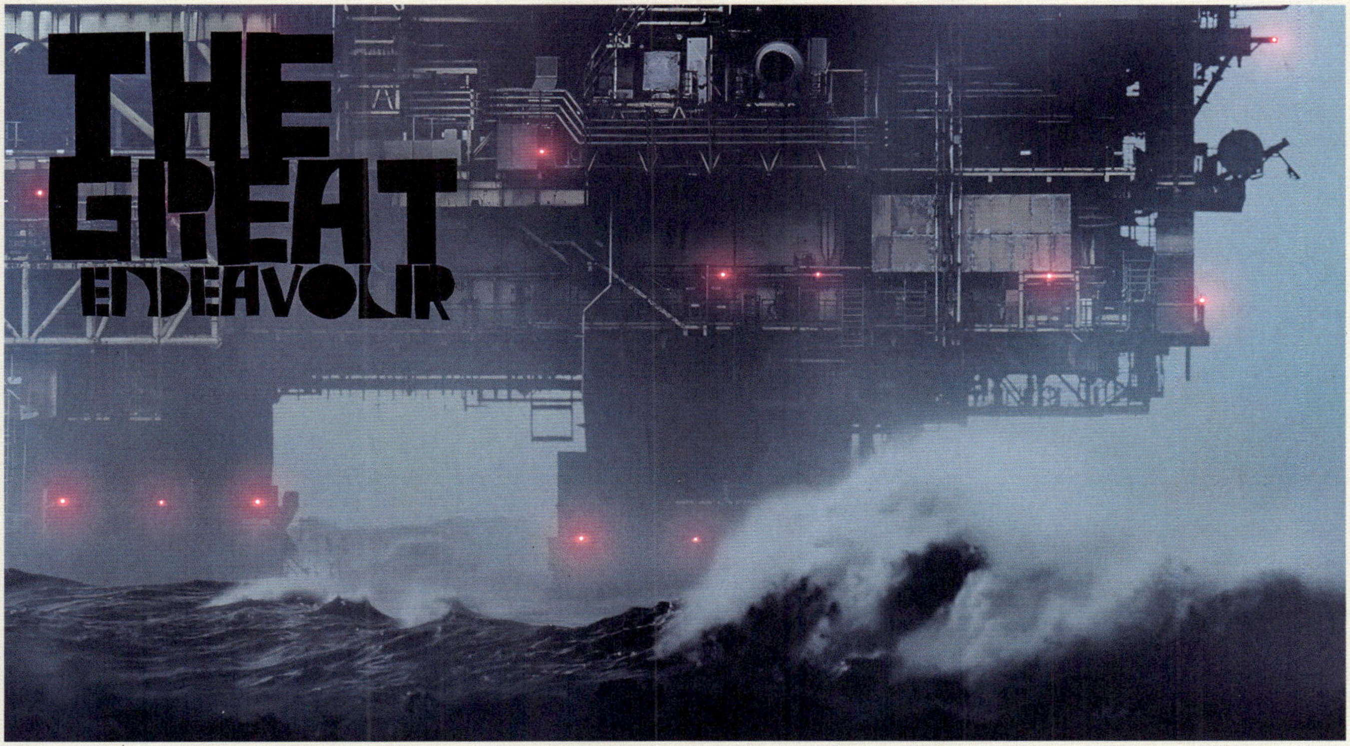

THE GREAT ENDEAVOUR

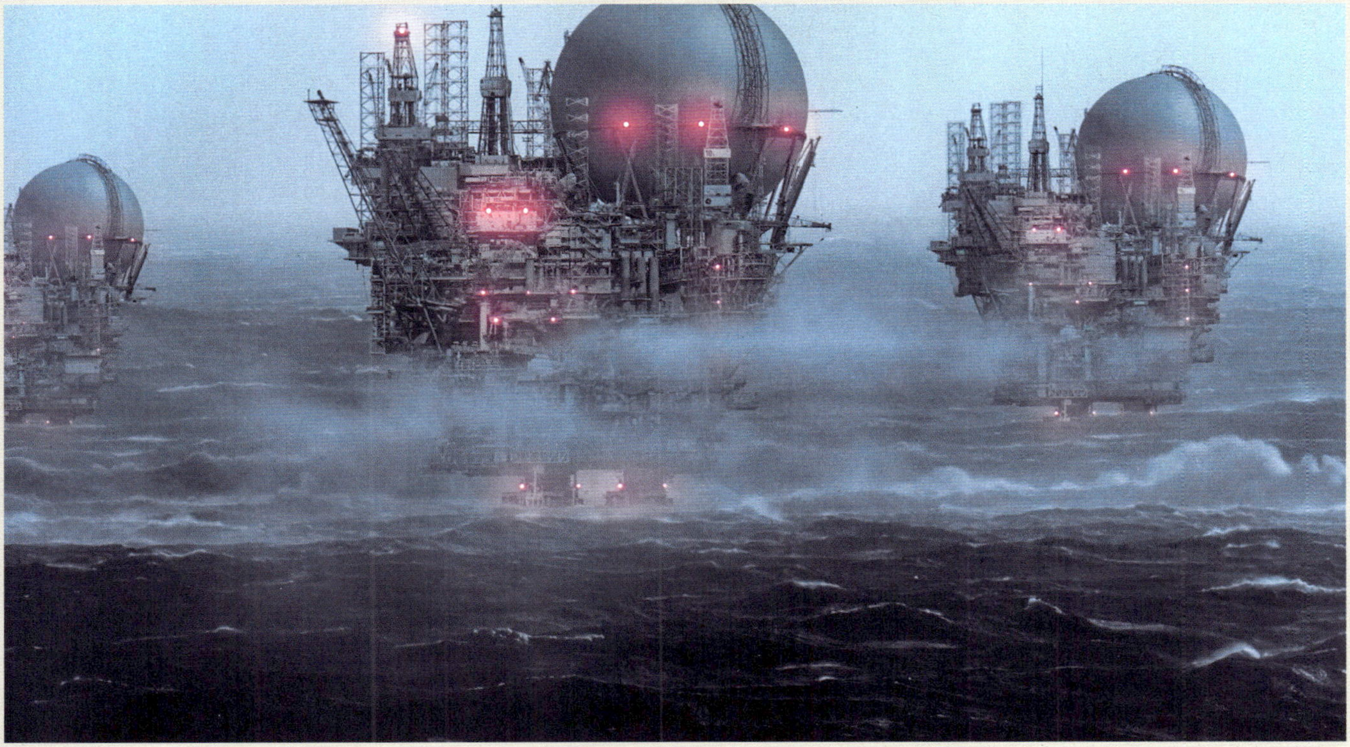

Liam Young, *The Great Endeavor*, 2023, video. Current climate targets cannot be reached by slashing future emissions alone. The capacity to remove existing carbon dioxide from the atmosphere and store it underground at gigatonne scales must be developed. The 'great endeavour' to capture all this carbon will involve the construction of the largest engineering project in human history, and the development of a new infrastructure equivalent in size to that of the entire global fossil fuel industry. *The Great Endeavor* approaches this challenge with a radical optimism that captures the design, construction, and drama of what it might look like to build this imaginary infrastructure.

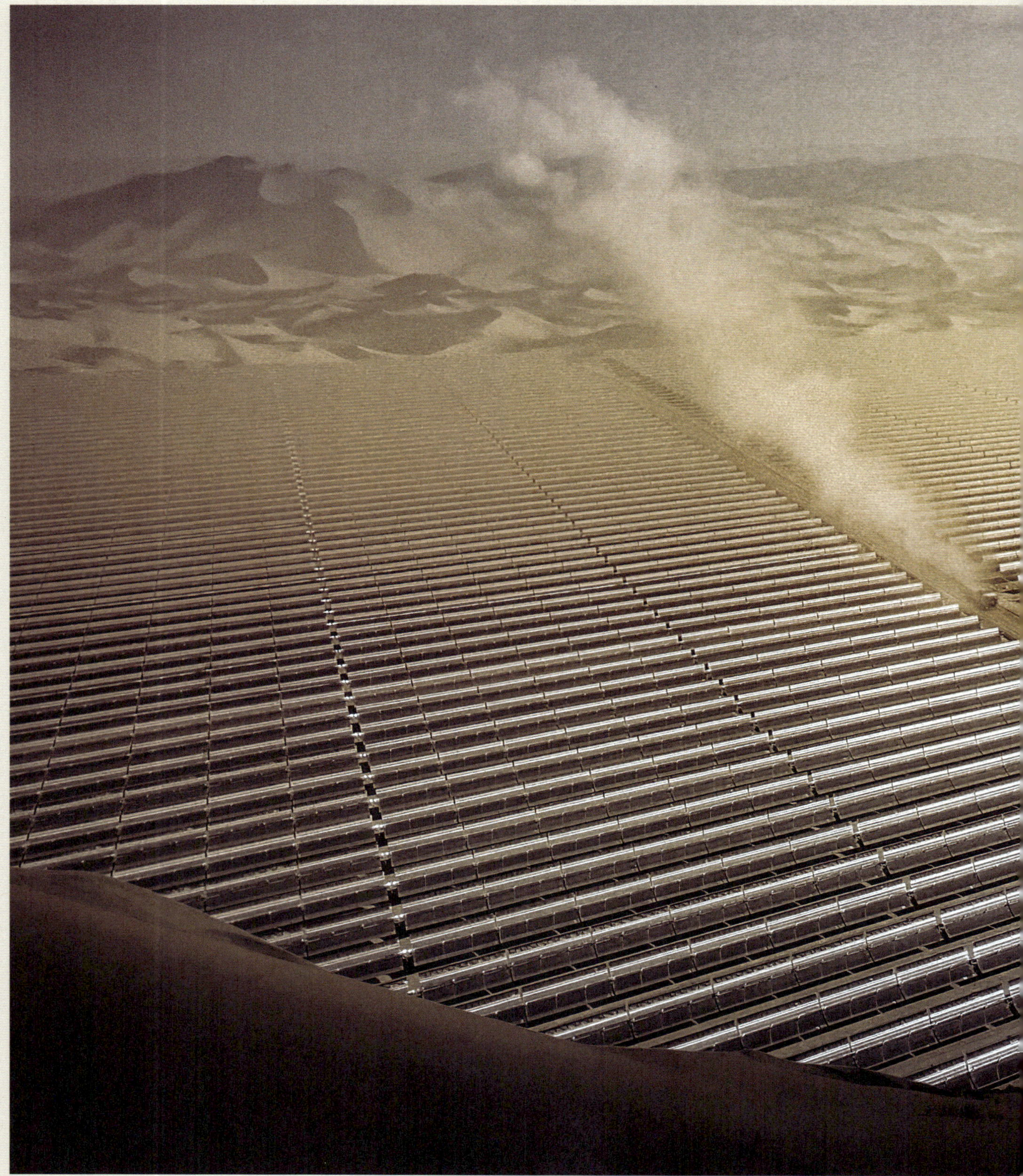

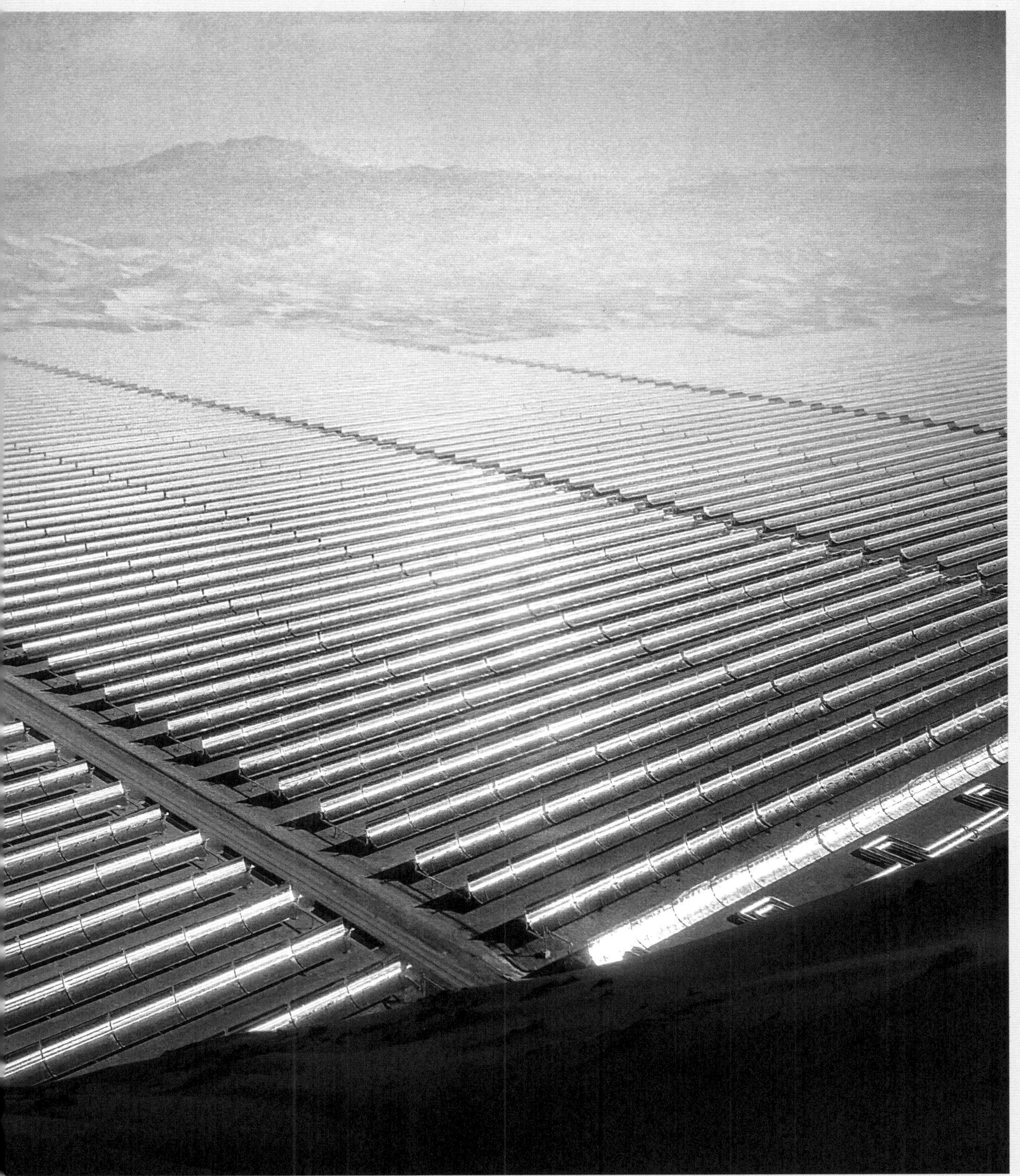

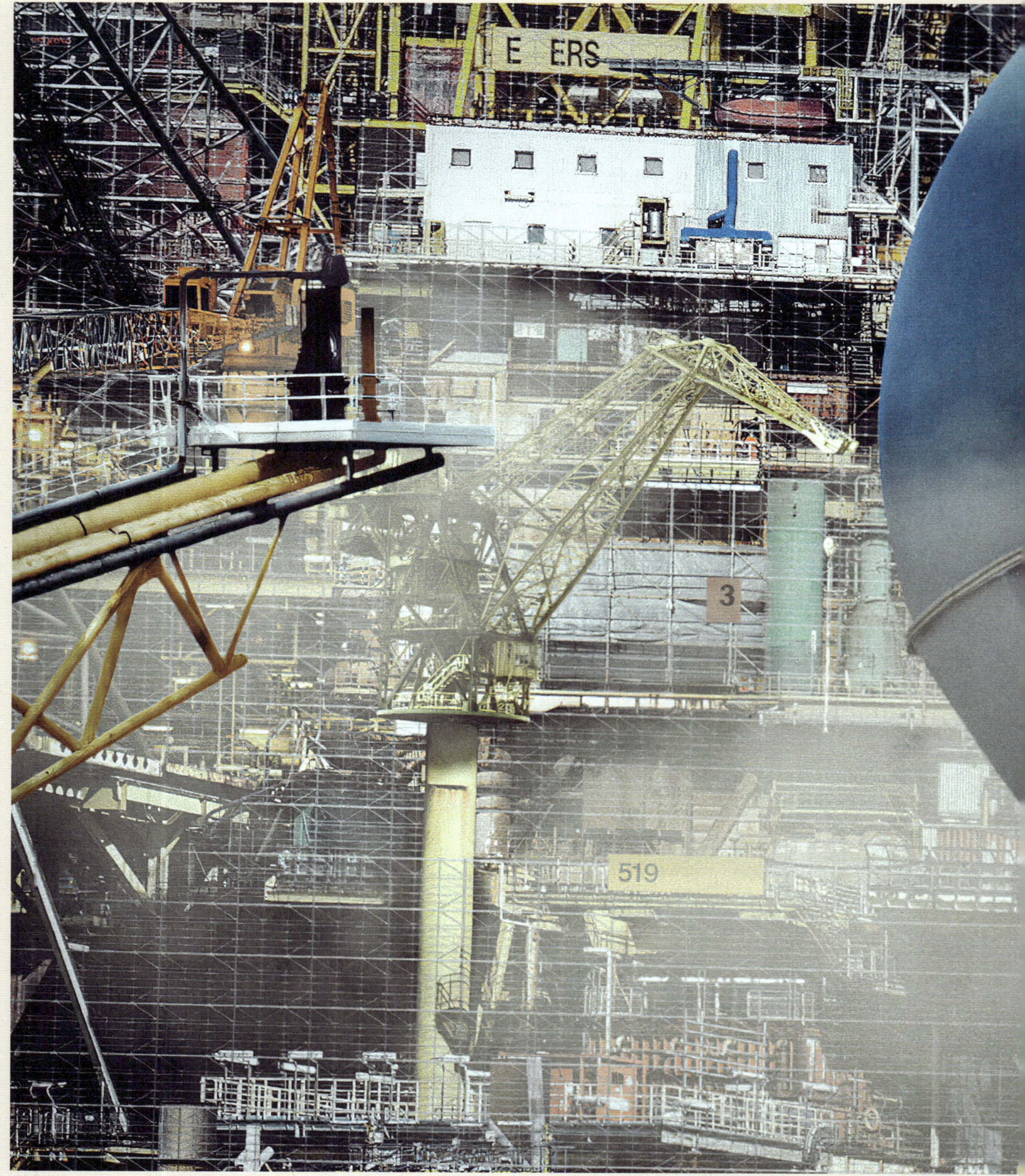
E ERS
3
519

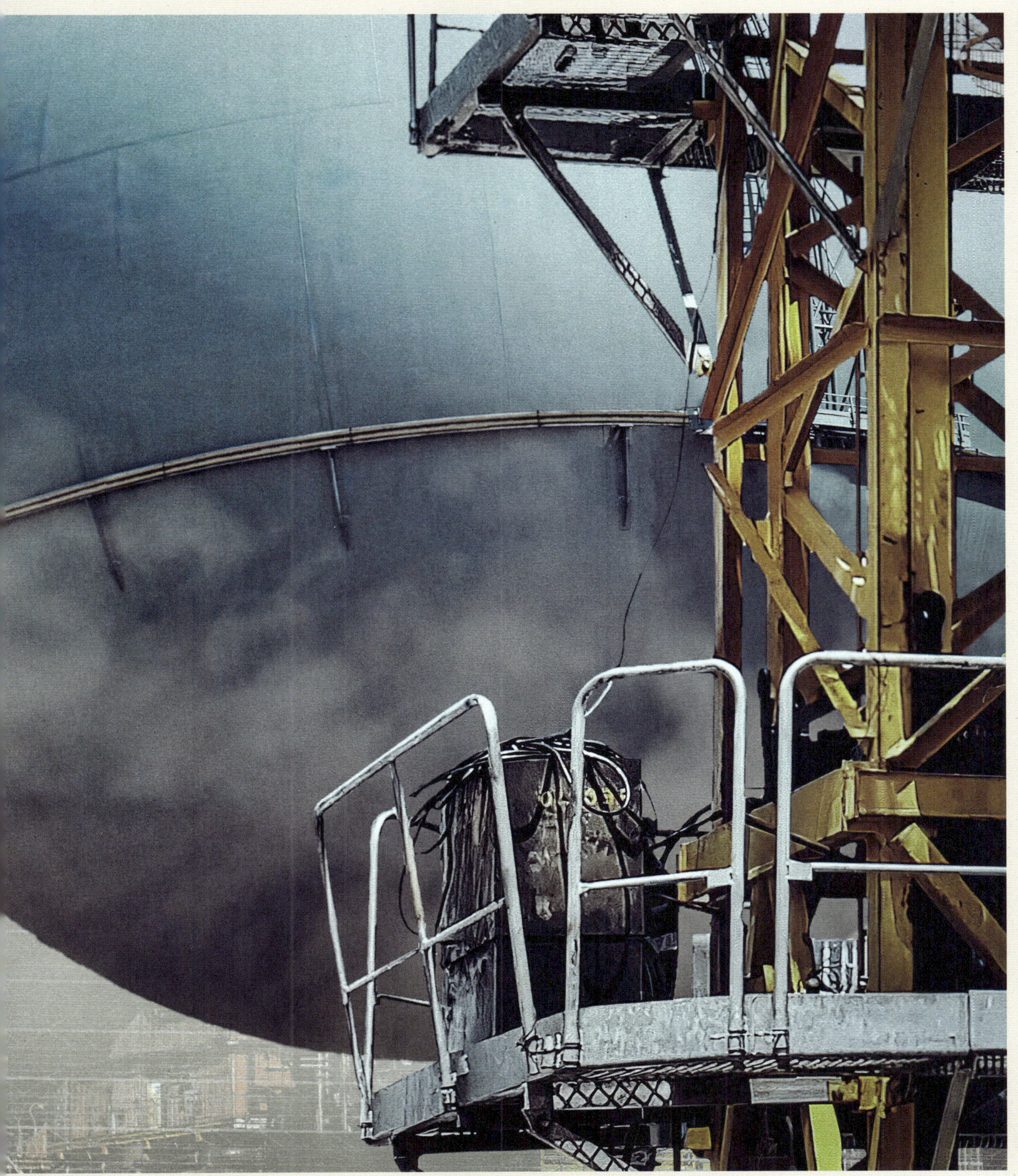

Forest Stewardship – The Long Journey to Sustainability

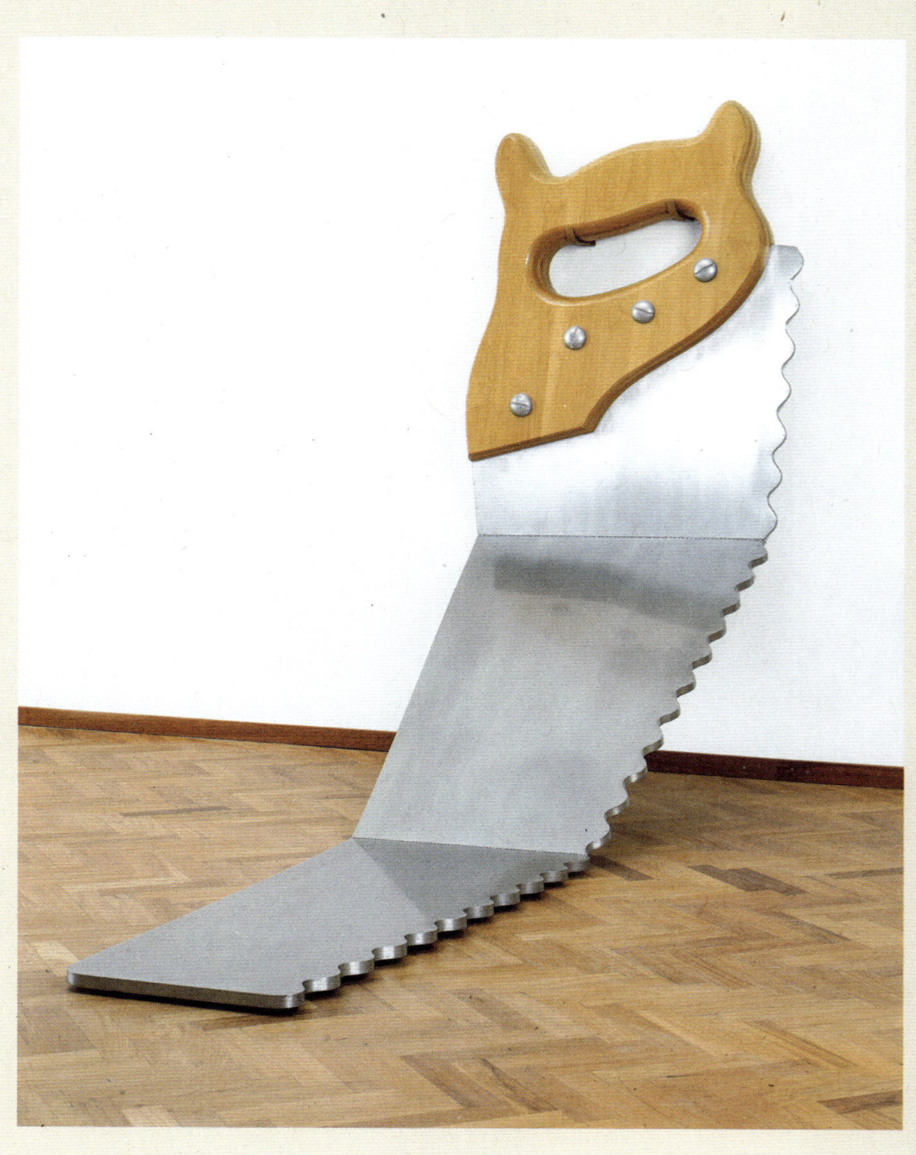

Peter Minang

Forests are one of the world's largest terrestrial ecosystems and amongst the most valuable in terms of supporting life on earth. In 2020, forests occupied about 4 billion hectares (over 10 million acres), representing about 31 % of the Earth's total land area. According to the Millennium Ecosystem Assessment's report in 2005, forests provide valuable life support systems including provision of food, fibre and fuel, as well as biodiversity. They also provide climate, air and water regulating services, pollination, and flood and disease control functions that are critical for the well-being of the planet. It is reported that about 1.3 billion people (about 25 % of the global human population) directly depend on forests for food and nutrition, energy and fibre. Despite the critical importance of forest ecosystems, forest area has been declining over the past century. Today we are losing about the size of eleven football (soccer) fields of forest per minute, according to the World Resources Institute (WRI), amounting to about 4 million hectares every year. Hence, the need for forest stewardship. Forest stewardship refers to the diligent and purposeful management of forest resources in ways that enable conservation of biodiversity and ecosystem functions, and contributions to and synergy with economic, social and cultural development.

Claes Oldenburg, *Saw (Hard Version II)*, 1971. Oldenburg's *Saw* from the collection of the Stedelijk Museum, Amsterdam, looks like a saw but diverges enough to provoke and even disturb the viewer. Oldenburg's version of the object is much larger, even monumental, and rendered unusable. The function shifts from utilitarian to aesthetic. Oldenburg's questioning of commerce and art, of functional and artistic value, epitomises the guiding ideas of Pop Art.

As the global population and per capita income continue to grow, more agricultural land would be needed to grow food, provide energy and fibre for material needs as well as infrastructural development such as roads and housing. These are often provided at the expense of forested lands. Poaching, illegal harvesting, and trade in animal and plant-based materials such as ivory and medicinal substances from forest ecosystems have grown worldwide. Rapid urbanisation has also influenced the dynamic relationship between humans and forest ecosystems through increased demand for timber and energy such as charcoal or wood-based fuels for cooking and heating. These threats to forests are real and growing, therefore, managing these threats at local, sub-national, national, and global level would be very important components of any successful forest stewardship.

Different Forms of Forest Stewardship

Given the tremendous importance of forests to life on Earth and the sustained decline in both the quantity and quality of forest ecosystems over time, forest stewardship has also been evolving in order to face and manage the dynamic threats to forests outlined above. That has meant trying many forms of forest stewardship including mainly, protected area management, community-based forest management, and joint forest management.

Protected Area Management approaches entail designating rich forest areas within specific geographies under legal protection and management for purposes of conserving and enhancing the ecosystem and the services and values associated with the forests. It is widely practised across most countries and covers about 18 % (about 700 million ha) of the world's forest lands according to the Food and Agricultural Organization of the United Nations (FAO) report of 2020 on the state of the world's forest. The United Nations Convention on Biodiversity (UNCBD) targets putting at least 30 % of all valuable ecosystems under protected area management as part of the Sustainable Development Goals, which provides a global legal framework for the protected area management approach.

This global framework goes alongside another global treaty for the protection of endangered plants and animals from the threats of international trade known as CITES. Lists of endangered species under CITES and the Red List of the International Union for Conservation of Nature guide the selection, prioritisation, and enforcement of protected areas and species management. Protected areas can take many forms: national parks, conservation areas, and game reserves. National parks tend to be areas of high biodiversity value and largely under government management while conservation areas and game reserves tend to target specific species or function, and can be under government, private or community management.

Community-Based Forest Management approaches represent stewardship of forests that is community-led or community-based. Here, communities play a significant role in forest and land use decision-making based on shared norms, rules, and interests. It tends to be based around community organisations, participation of local people, and negotiated spaces where stakeholder interests are explicitly considered and community benefits are prioritised, and largely accommodated. Forms of community-based forest management will differ based on local, social, and political context. In some countries, Indigenous peoples' rights are fully recognised, and they fully govern forests and lands under their territories. While in other countries, the degree of devolution of management rights, decision-making, and benefits varies as specified by law. According to the Rights and Resources Institute (RRI) report on rights to land and territories, about 26 % of Indigenous peoples' land and territories have full recognition and management rights. Other studies have highlighted growth in areas under community management worldwide.

Joint Forest Management approaches represent instances where attempts have been made at bringing both the protected area and community-based approaches together in order to take advantage of the positives from each of the approaches. While the protected area approach is very strongly grounded in law and enjoys government support, it has tended to exclude community interests and, therefore, generate conflicts with communities. Joint forest management embraces community-led approaches through legal arrangements that bring governments, communities, and sometimes the private sector together in the stewardship of forests. The forms and rules might vary from place to place.

What Is Needed in the Future

Overall, these various forms of forest stewardship and their evolution seek to make forests simultaneously work for biodiversity and ecosystems services and contribute to economic and social development as recommended in the sustainable development goals. While these approaches have so far seen some success in conserving and enhancing some forests, there is still a long way to go in terms of stemming loss in forest quantity and quality.

In order to contribute to sustainable forest management and enhance the contributions of forests to sustainable development, all of these forms of forest stewardship would have to try and promote and adopt a number of principles and practices that help foster progress towards sustainability including:

- maintaining and enhancing ecological diversity and functions,
- inclusion and participation,
- prioritising and recognising tenure and rights,
- enhancing contributions to local economy and development, and
- compliance with laws and norms

Maintaining and enhancing ecological diversity and functions: Keeping the highest value forests standing and enabling the provision of the ecological services desired requires the deployment of the best knowledge and science available. In a world where we continue to lose forests and also the quality continues to degrade, prioritising the restoration of forests is also an important objective. That is why the international and regional initiatives in support of forest restoration have grown over the years, namely the Bonn Challenge, The New York Declaration on Forests, African Forest Landscape Restoration Initiative (AFR100) and the Initiative 20X20 in Latin America.

Inclusion and participation: Including all stakeholders and interests in the management of forests is key to the governance of forests if conflicts are to be avoided. Governments, communities, private sector, and civil society are all key in the process. Many partnership models have been tried including public-private-partnerships that enable balancing diverse and conflicting interests.

Prioritising and recognising tenure and rights: Indigenous and local people are often custodians of valuable knowledge relating to forests as well as traditional rules and norms that have kept forests for generations. Therefore, they need to be fully considered in forest stewardship. Bringing these into decision-making should be prioritised, otherwise an important piece is missing. Their benefits should also be prioritised.

Enhancing contributions to local economy and development: As about 1.3 billion people depend directly on forests for the provision of food, fibre and fuel, and also other global commodity value chains such as wood depend on forests, it is important to consider balancing demands for these commodities and forest health in the stewardship of forests. Failure to consider these is likely to lead to over-exploitation and continued loss of forests. Several value addition approaches, landscape plantation and agroforestry for wood, and other viable approaches have been deployed with success, and can be scaled up to meet the demand. Success would require incentives, green enterprise, and innovation ecosystems in forest stewardship.

Compliance with laws and norms: Compliance with laws, regulations and norms at local, national, and international levels is imperative for achieving sustainable forest management. Requirements exist around planning, monitoring, reporting, and certification that guide, incentivise, and regulate the management of forests. Adhering strictly to these would help progress towards sustainable forest stewardship.

Saving forested lands on Earth needs dynamic, efficient, effective and equitable forest stewardship. The approaches and experiences in good forest stewardship exist as well as the knowledge. We would however need significant doses of political goodwill, partnerships, and investments to scale up the best practices and principles of forest stewardship. The growing awareness and advocacy for this and the recent rise in multilateralism on environment, forest and land issues offers real hope. ✦

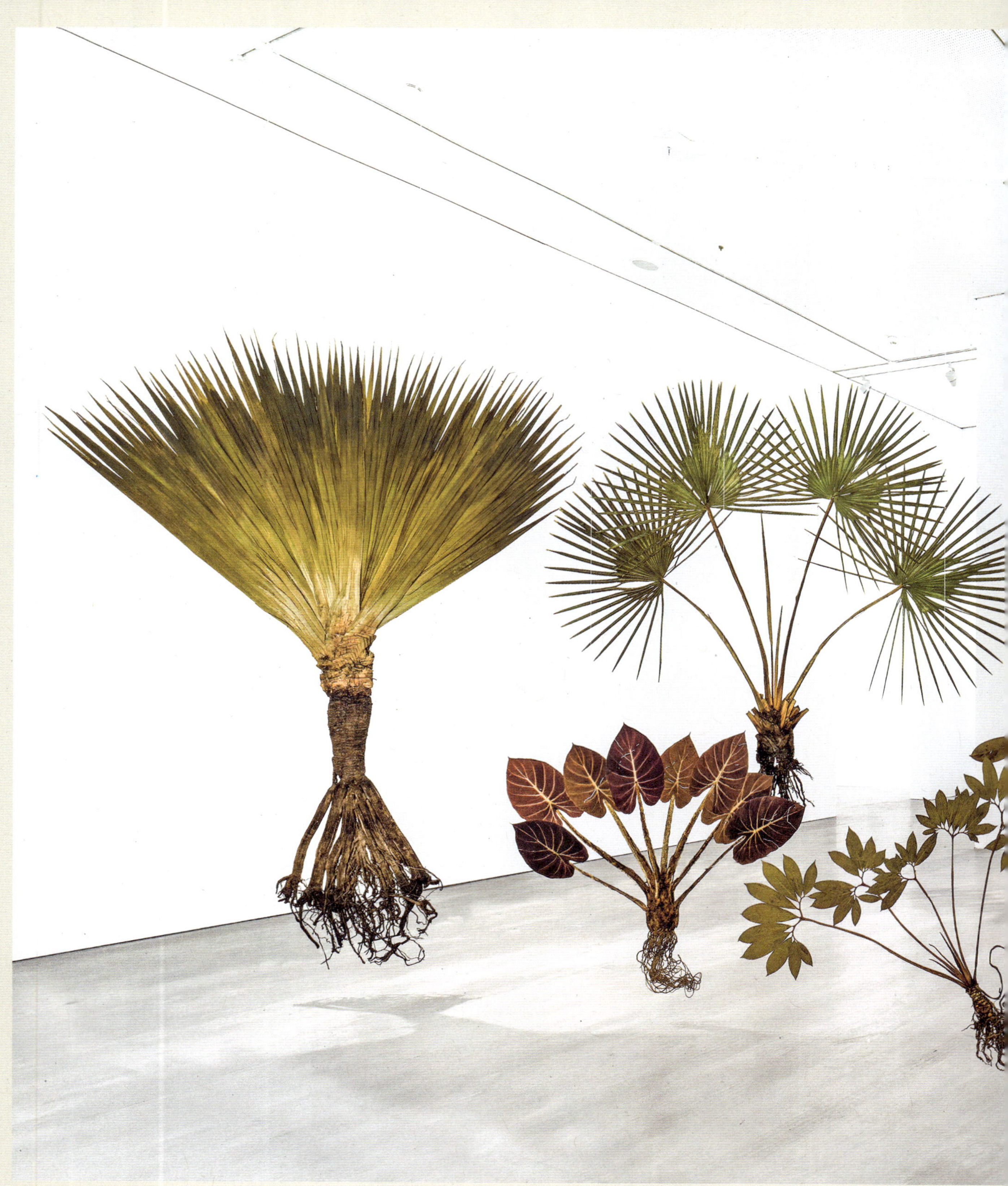

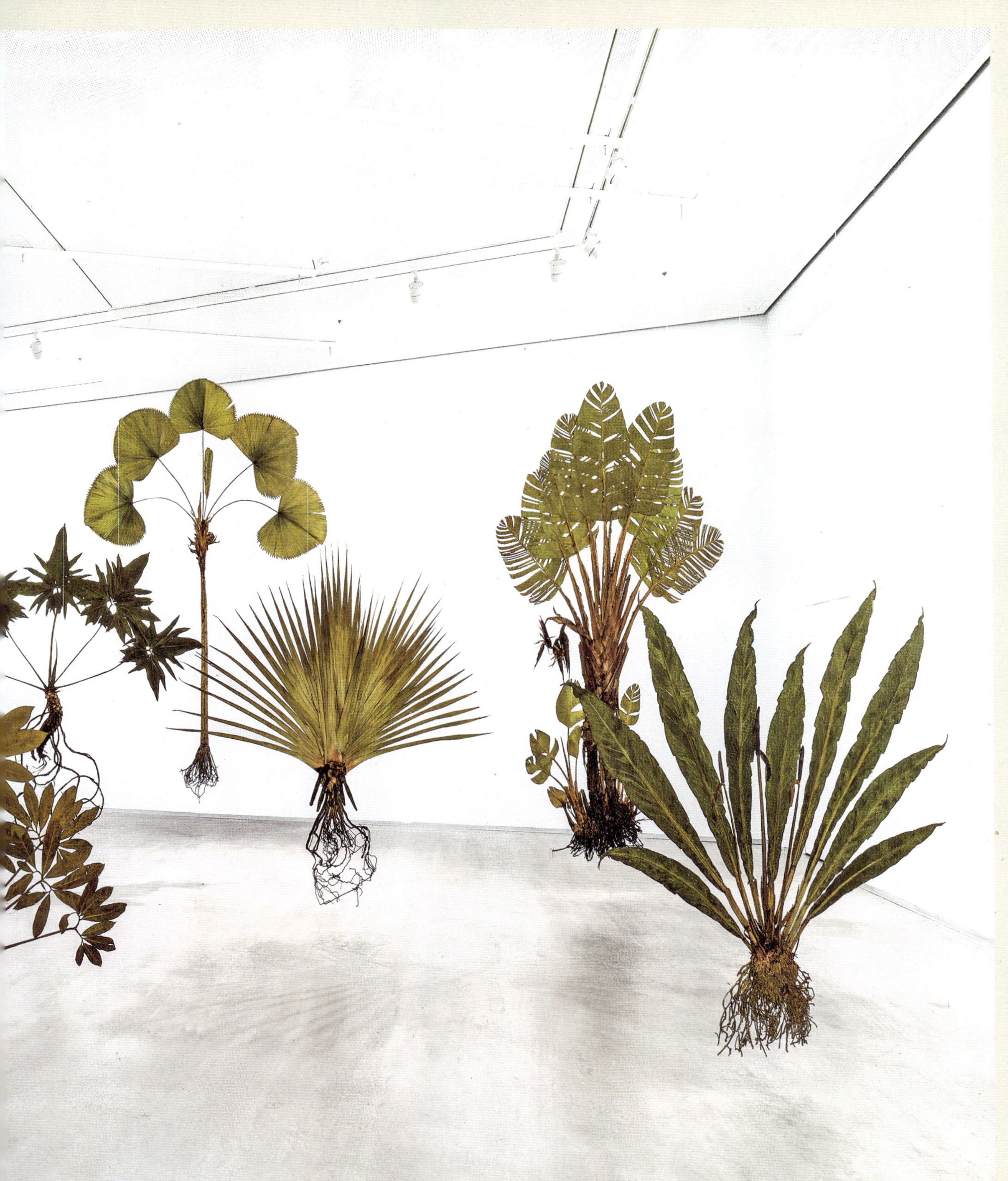

Julius von Bismarck, *I like the flowers*, 2023. This installation shows large 'exotic' plants, pressed as if for an herbarium and delicately suspended in space. The plants presented here are not, however, mere images of floral beauty. They also allude to the brutality inherent in the Western conception of nature. The violence of the works' production becomes impossible to ignore. The plants were boiled and then robbed of their third dimension with the aid of a 50-tonne hydraulic press and press oven, and finally attached to a thin stainless-steel plate. The series consists exclusively of species not native to central Europe. They often still bear the names given to them by their European 'discoverers' instead of their native names, testifying to the ongoing process of the Global North's appropriation of nature.

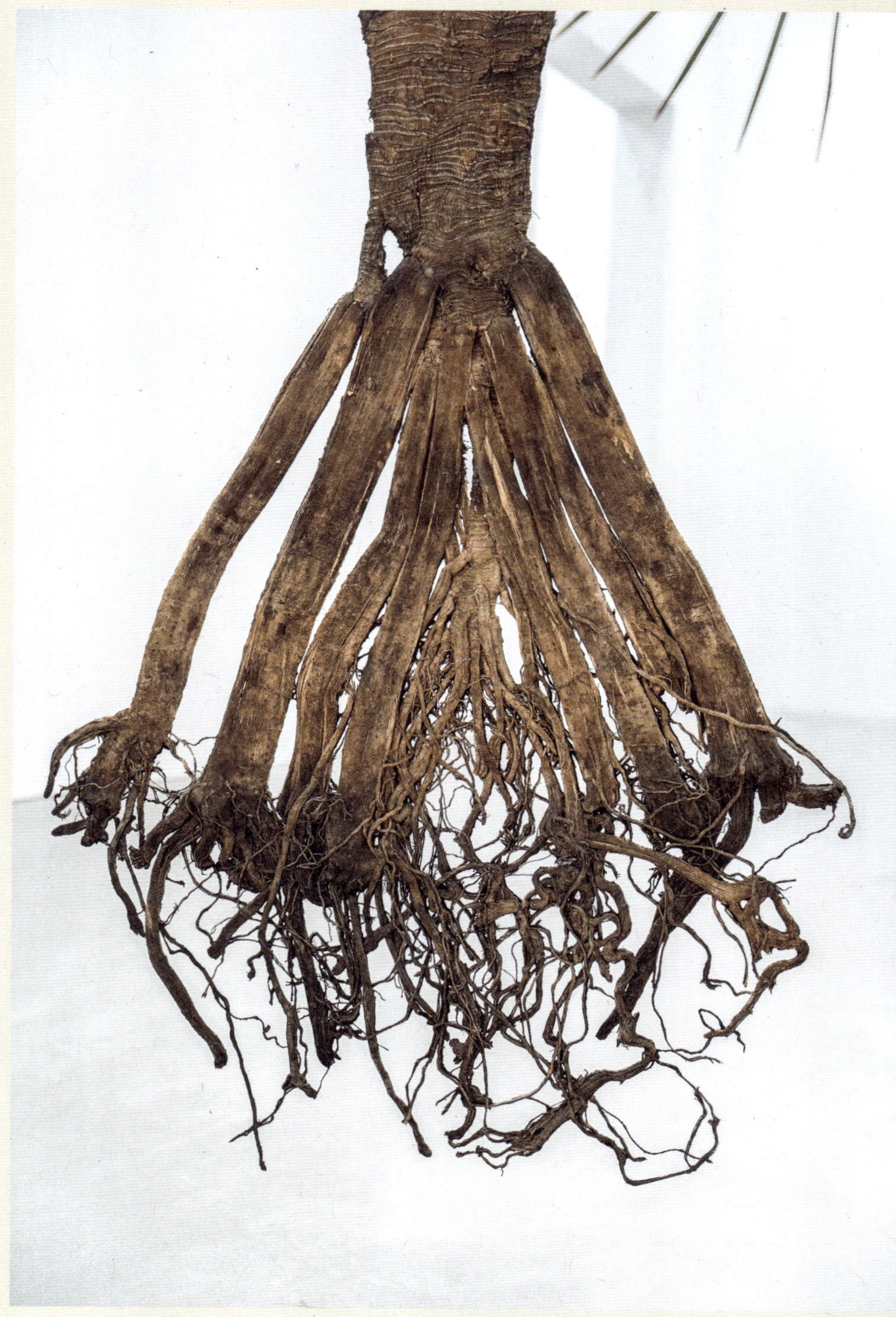

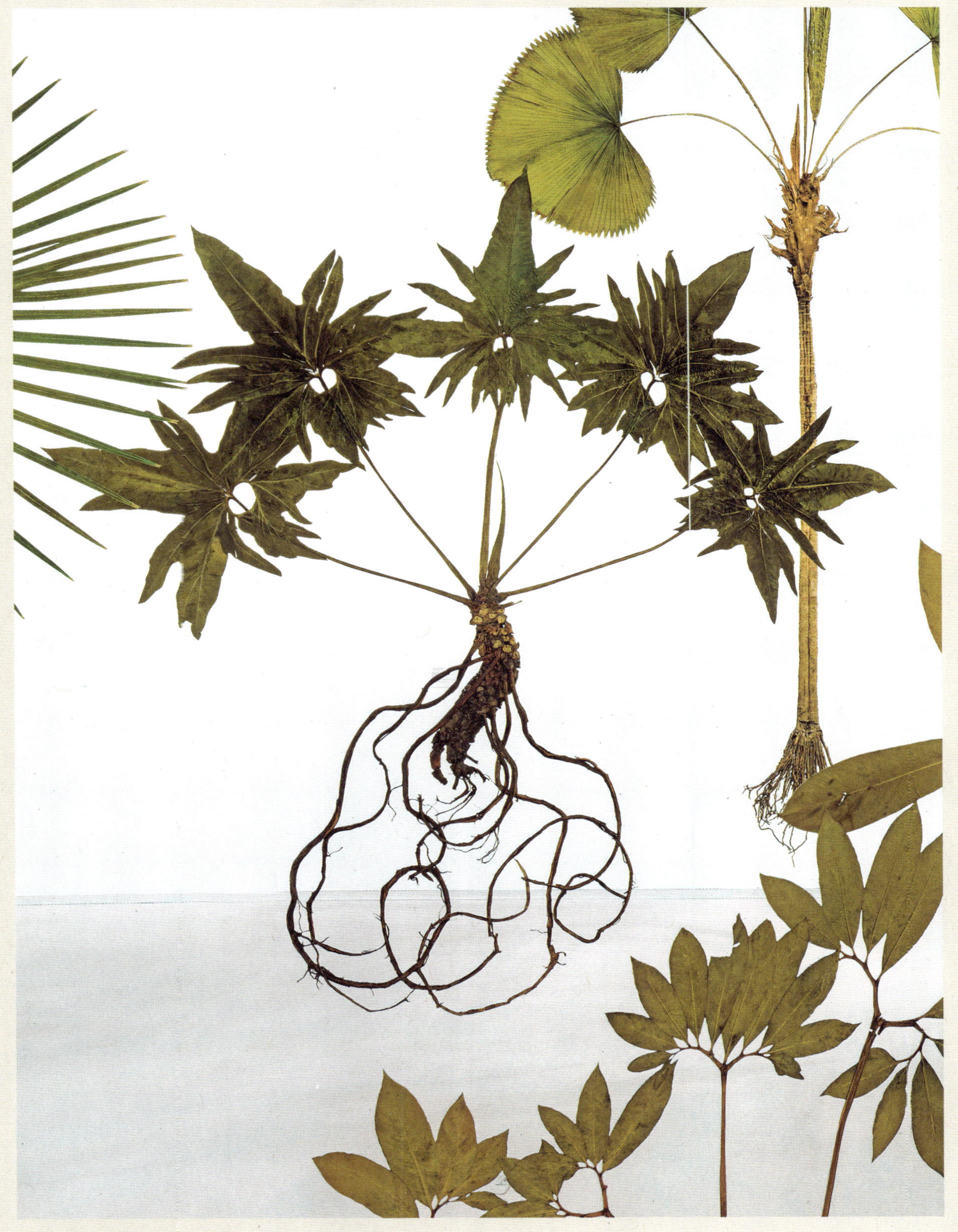

The Indigenous Perspective on Natural Habitats in Papua New Guinea – Stories from Managalas

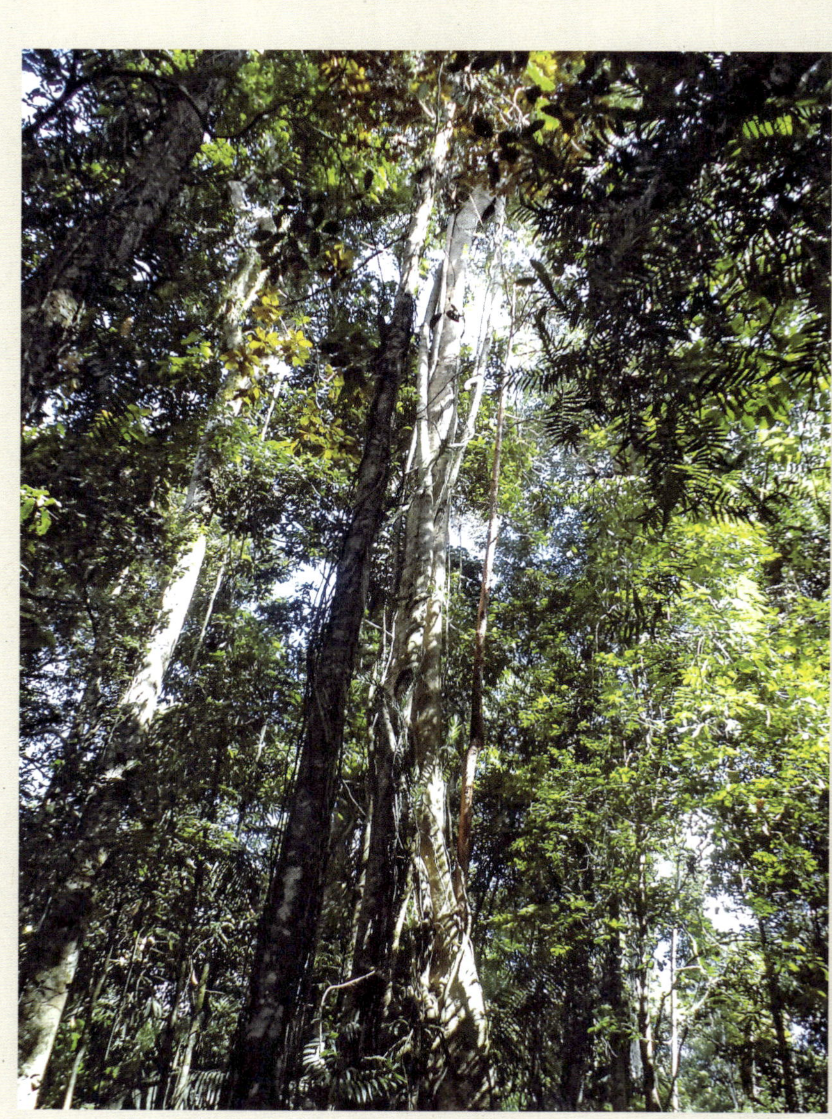

Jacinta Gure
and Chris Jamie

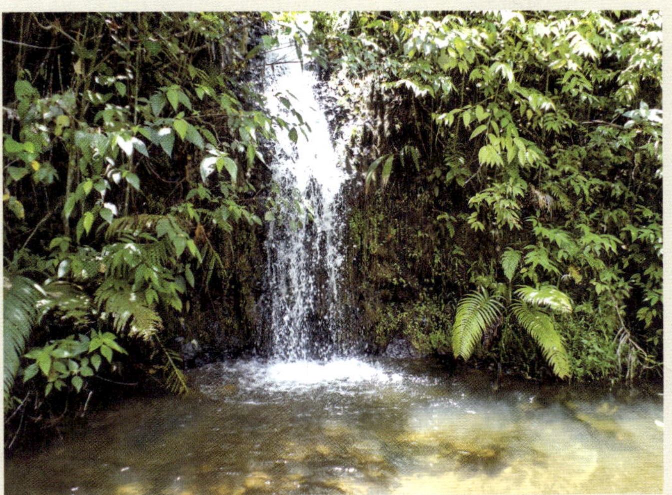

The depiction of a rainforest clearing and a waterfall symbolises the local communities' belief that land is a wellspring of resources and a sacred place.

The Island of Papua New Guinea (PNG) is located within the south-western Pacific Ocean, sharing the eastern half of the island with Indonesia. Its geographical landscape is incredibly diverse, featuring rugged mountains, dense rainforests, and extensive coastlines. This varied terrain supports a rich biodiversity with numerous endemic species of plants and animals including an estimated 150,000 species of insects, 314 species of freshwater fishes (82 endemic), 641 species of amphibians and reptiles (328 endemic), 740 species of birds (77 endemic), and 276 species of mammals (69 endemic).

PNG is celebrated for its remarkable cultural diversity and abundant natural resources. With over 850 languages spoken and numerous ethnic groups, each with unique traditions and customs, it stands as one of the most culturally diverse nations globally. This diversity is mirrored in its rich heritage, arts, and community practices. The country's natural wealth includes vast rainforests, rich mineral deposits, and extensive marine resources, housing up to 5 % of the world's plant and animal species. This unique blend of cultural and natural richness sets the stage for exploring Indigenous knowledge, which plays a crucial role in environmental stewardship. Local communities in PNG possess deep-rooted knowledge of their ecosystems, utilising sustainable practices that have been passed down through generations. This relationship between Indigenous knowledge and the environment highlights the importance of preserving both cultural heritage and biodiversity for future generations.

Indigenous perspectives on natural habitats in PNG are deeply rooted in a profound respect for the environment and a holistic understanding of the interconnectedness of all living things. For many local communities, the land is not just a resource but a sacred entity that sustains life and holds cultural and spiritual significance. Traditional ecological knowledge, passed down through generations, emphasises sustainable practices and careful stewardship of natural resources. This includes practices such as rotational farming, hunting and fishing regulations, and protection of sacred sites. The local people view themselves as custodians of the land, with a responsibility to maintain its health and balance for future generations. This perspective fosters a strong commitment to conservation and sustainable living, which is increasingly being recognised and integrated into broader environmental management and conservation efforts in the country.

The Managalas Conservation Area

The Managalas Conservation Area is located in the Ijivitari District, Oro Province. The Plateau is a low land tropical rain forest with volcanic soil and is home to approximately 20,000+ Managalasi people, living in over 75 villages, within 150 clans, speaking 3 languages and several dialects of the Managalas. Strong cultural linkage and daily livelihood is based on the land, forest, and the environment and is bonded by robust kinship and inter-marriages between the different clans and tribes on the Plateau.

The conservation area is also home to several endangered species which are found on the red list of the International Union for Conversation of Nature (ICUN), including; Queen Alexandra's Birdwing Butterfly, species of Doria's Tree Kangaroo, Long Beaked Echidna, Count Raggi's Bird-of-Paradise, the tiny Magnificent Bird-of-Paradise, Black-billed sicklebill Bird-of-Paradise, the Papuan Hornbill (known locally as Kokomo) and the non-venomous Black python, all endemic to the area. Biodiversity surveys have also identified animal species still unknown to science, which makes this area truly rich in diverse flora and fauna.

Traditional Ecological Knowledge

Traditional ecological knowledge systems include detailed understanding of local flora and fauna, weather patterns, and ecological relationships, passed down through generations. This knowledge informs the environmental practices and conservation effects in Managalas. As a result, every flora and fauna are identified with their names and uses (traditional forest inventory). The peoples' livelihood even today depends heavily on their environment for food, shelter, tools, local calendars, and even for spiritual importance. Such examples are certain plants that are grown on the edges of garden plots in order to prevent bad spirits from going near the crops, and this ensures a plentiful harvest. They are planted around the homes, too, for protection, whereas other plants and trees are considered a local calendar that the Managalas people employ in planning their individual activities such as gardening or fishing as well as larger community activities such as marriages and harvest feasts. Observing the different seasonal color change in leaves indicates the timing for specific activities such as hunting, planting or going into the forest and flowering or fruiting plants will indicate the presence of certain animals that can be hunted.

Certain natural features and landscapes are considered sacred and imbued with spiritual significance. For example, mountains, rivers, and forests may be revered as the homes of spirits of nature. These areas are considered sacred and taboo, not to be disturbed, otherwise bringing ill omen to the entire clan or tribe. From today's perspective we understand that that was a traditional conservation method used for resource management to ensure habitats were untouched and the animal population or water source remains plentiful for continuous use.

Cultural practices in Managalas reflect harmony with nature, including rituals, ceremonies, and seasonal activities that align with natural cycles and processes. For instance, a Yam festival known as 'Pondo' is held every year as an acknowledgement to the Mother Land (Mother Nature) and the spirits of the forefathers. The festival commences right after harvesting yam from gardens and lasts around two weeks with traditional dancing, singing and also marriage arrangements, peacemaking ceremonies and the marking of clan chiefs and leaders. One of the traditional dances is the 'Oro' dance which depicts the Queen Alexandra's Birdwing Butterfly as it holds spiritual significance due to its huge size.

The Indigenous of the Plateau value the land and natural environment highly and have ritual practices that honor the environment as their survival is dependent on it.

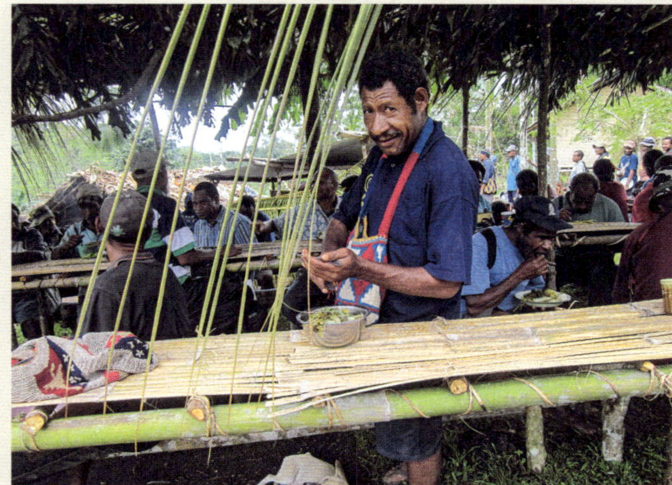

The rituals of the Indigenous population celebrate and honour their culture and life-giving nature.

Challenges

Whilst the Managalas Indigenous community share a harmonious existence with their environment, as human beings they still have need for basic government services such as health, education, connectivity to the outside world and means to earn money to pay for basic needs. And like most remote communities in PNG, government servicing facilities and institutions established are very run down and not in use.

The only road network to Managalas is from Popondetta, the capital of Oro Province and is for the most part a set of four-wheel drive tracks that is impassable during the rainy seasons. Because of that, return fares to town are about twenty-five US dollars which is excessive and unaffordable for locals.

The health clinic and schools on the Plateau are run-down and lack at most times adequate supplies and professionals to run the facilities. There is no presence of police but there are local level government councilors and peace officers elected locally who take on the role of keeping law and order along with traditional clan leaders.

Threats to the Conservation Area

Though the Managalas Conservation Area is relatively protected from outside threats through foreign private industries and resource extractions such as logging, there is still a threat as there is on-going illegal logging on the outskirts of the Managalas Conservation Area.

However, the real threat to the Conservation Areas (CAs) is from the locals themselves through gardening and agricultural practices. As local population increases, there is a need for newer and bigger farming land to increase food supply, not just for family consumption but also for selling to earn money in order to meet basic needs such as clothing, household supplies, and school fees. With the fast-fading beliefs in the traditional systems such as sacred grounds, the locals have to be educated on sustainable resource management.

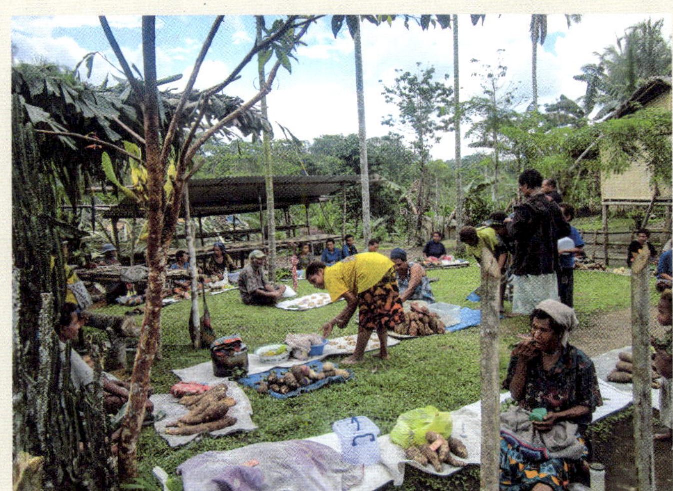

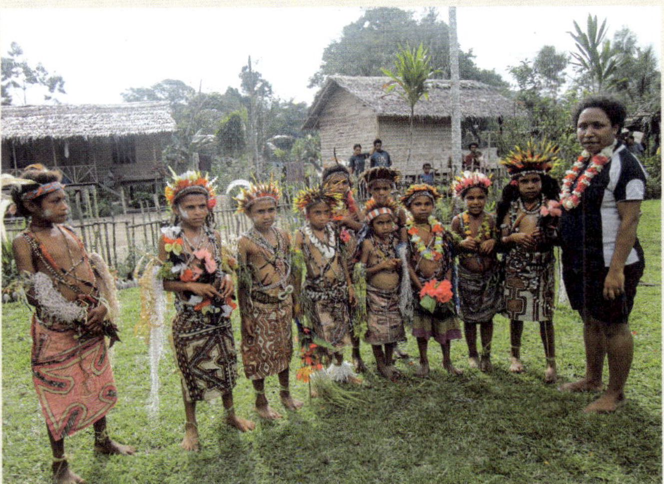

The connection between the various clans and tribes and their traditional knowledge forms a communal bond that is passed on from generation to generation and is characterised by the sustainable use of resources and traditions.

With all established CAs in PNG, there are policies and processes in place to assist the Indigenous communities in sustainably managing their CAs. As part of the process of attaining a CA there has to be in place a 'Conservation Area Management Committee' (CAMC) overseeing the management of the CA and a 'Conservation Area Management Plan' (CAMP) that acts as a guide to the management of the CA by setting out rules and land-use plans for the CA. These rules and plans come from the locals themselves with guidance from the relevant government authorities and other stakeholders such as local and international conservation NGOs and partners.

There is also on-going partnership with sustainability programs such as sustainable livelihood alternatives that are eco-friendly and bring in some form of income for the locals such as organic coffee, vanilla, and even venturing to carbon off-setting.

Conclusion

The Indigenous communities of Managalas have, due to its relative remoteness, not fully experienced the fast development phase of some parts of the country, and that has kept them in close contact with their environment, maintaining this mutual existence and harmony and still practising traditional wisdom and knowledge with the added bonus of having the status of a protected area.

However, they are not totally free from the external as well as internal environmental threats coupled with the ever-growing influence of the outside world, and they have to be better prepared to manage these threats.

Though the PNG governments' environment authority is working hard to improve its governance of environmental issues in the country, there is lacking a true consultation with the real resource owners who are the 95 % Indigenous population still living in remote, isolated communities, out of government reach.

The Managalas community, however, is at the crossroads of environmental development and is learning to balance traditional practices with modern western conservation concepts and government focused development.

These people whose daily existence is solely dependent on the land through subsistence farming, although the area is massive and the number of clans and villages are numerous, have learnt to work together to integrate traditional practices with the modern concept of owning a protected area. They continue their agricultural practices but within allocated land-use plans, and traditional knowledge is combined with scientific facts, awareness of conservation and climate change issues enhancing their ecological knowledge They are an empowered people who make informed decisions regarding the use of their natural resources ensuring sustainability for their children and children's children. ✦

Wetlands of International Importance as Nature-Based Solutions for Ensuring Life and Livelihoods

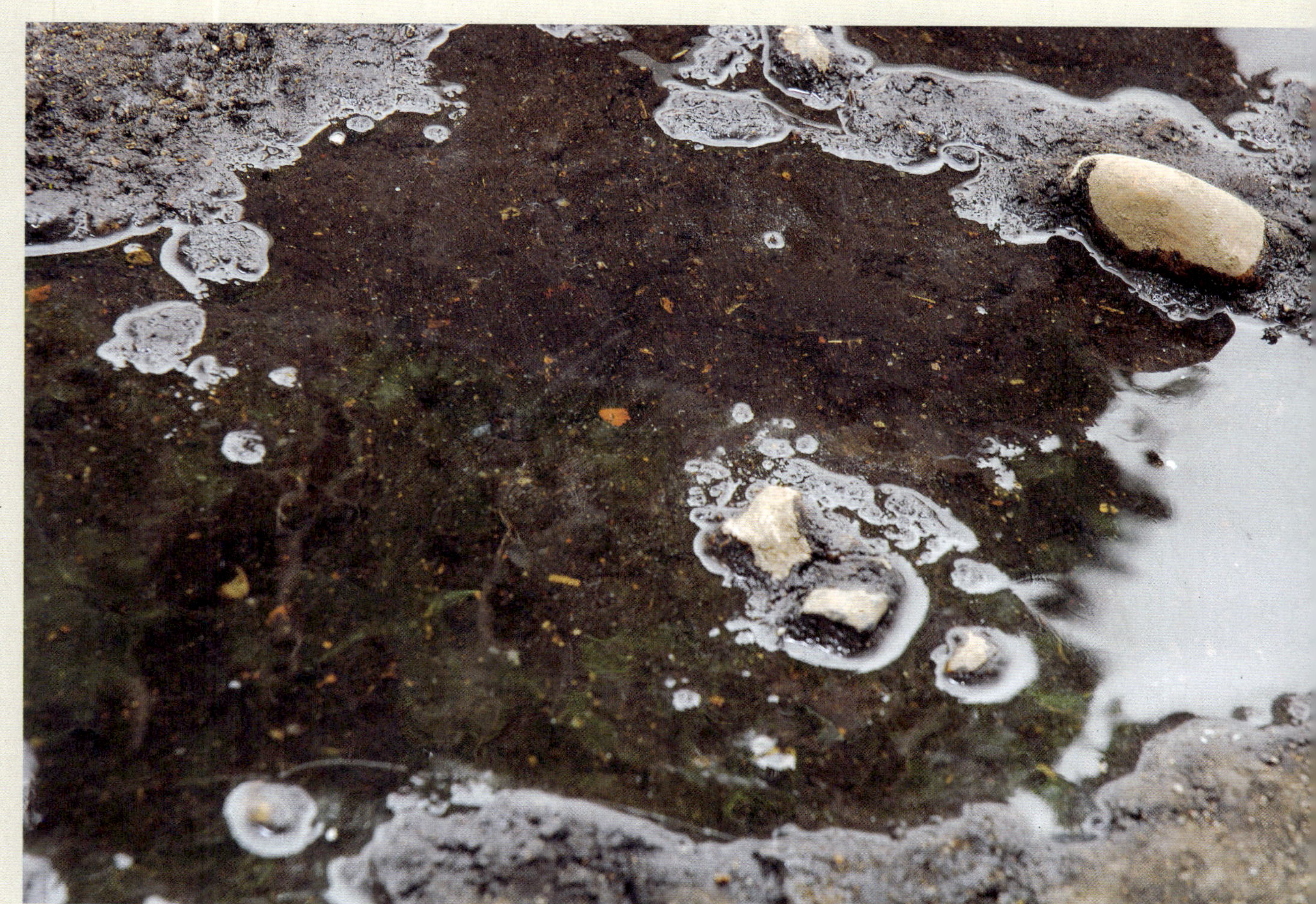

Musonda Mumba

Wetlands are not just patches of wet land; they are amazing ecosystems that help support biodiversity, mitigate climate change, and provide jobs and resources. Whether it's a marsh, swamp, peatland, estuary, or even coral reef, each wetland area is unique and invaluable. They are, all of them, living, breathing examples of how to reach a common goal: ensuring that wetlands benefit both people and the planet.

As the Secretary General of the Convention on Wetlands, I have seen first-hand how preserving these areas can lead to healthier environments, stronger economies, and better lives for hundreds of millions of people.

Understanding 'Wetlands of International Importance'

The Convention on Wetlands is the first intergovernmental treaty focused on protecting our environment. Established in 1971 for the conservation and wise use of wetlands, our Wetlands of International Importance ('Ramsar sites') are recognised for their significant ecological, hydrological, and socio-economic value.

Wetlands contribute directly to achieving many UN Sustainable Development Goals (SDGs), making them integral to global sustainability strategies. Wetlands act as natural water purifiers, filtering out pollutants and improving water quality, helping ensure clean water for all (SDG 6). They also store carbon which helps to tackle climate change by capturing greenhouse gases (SDG 13).

Coastal and marine wetlands, such as mangroves and coral reefs, support marine biodiversity and fisheries, proving food and livelihoods for many (SDG 14). Wetland ecosystems are rich in biodiversity and are home to numerous endemic or endangered plant and animal species (SDG 15).

Additionally, urban wetlands enhance urban resilience, manage stormwater, and provide green spaces that improve the quality of life in cities and reduce the risk of disasters in vulnerable areas (SDG 11).

Stefanie Bühler, *Puddles*, 2006, epoxy, earth, stones.

Wetlands as an Economic Driver

The benefits of wetlands extend well beyond the environment – they are also economic powerhouses. They play a role in mitigating climate change that is creating havoc for communities that rely on wetlands for their livelihoods.

Imagine a Senegalese woman harvesting water lilies to make a tasty local delicacy or a boatman in the Sundarbans delivering goods through marshy waters, serving as the only method of transportation for local communities. If wetlands disappear, so do these jobs – and many others.

On the environmental side, wetlands act as carbon sinks, reducing the amount of CO_2 in the atmosphere. This helps combat global warming and prevents climate-related health risks for plants, animals, and people, which can range from heatwaves to the spread of diseases, ultimately affecting human livelihoods.

Urbanisation and Wetlands

Urbanisation is dramatically altering human settlement patterns, with half of the world's population currently residing in urban areas – a figure expected to rise significantly by 2050. This trend poses a grave threat to wetland conservation. As cities expand and demand for land increases, wetlands are often viewed as prime space for development.

But when preserved and managed sustainably, urban wetlands offer many environmental, economic, and social benefits. They act as natural sponges during storms, reducing city flooding and preventing disaster-related costs. Dense vegetation in these wetlands filters domestic and industrial waste, improving water quality.

Recognising these benefits is crucial for integrating wetlands into urban planning and development. Cities like Colombo, Sri Lanka, and Kampala, Uganda, have taken the plunge, restoring and integrating urban wetlands to mitigate flooding and enhance water security.

Urban wetlands also provide recreational and educational opportunities for city dwellers. Green spaces and water bodies in urban areas offer residents a chance to connect with nature to promote mental and physical well-being.

Effects on the Global Economy

The economic impact of mental health and wellness issues like absenteeism, burnout, and depression costs the global economy billions of dollars each year. The International Labour Organization (ILO) estimates that the economic loss due to mental health problems, including absenteeism and decreased productivity, is around 4% of global GDP, or 2.5 trillion dollars annually.

Addressing mental health through nature-based solutions like preserving and promoting access to wetlands can have economic benefits. Imagine that a walk in a wetland area can lead to saving literally trillions of dollars. Pushing this idea forward, many cities have transformed urban wetlands into parks and nature reserves, with the added benefit of attracting tourists and boosting local economies.

Lima, Peru, has done just that with Los Pantanos de Villa. This tiny urban wetland, only 263 hectares in size, is a popular site for recreation, tourism, education, and scientific research, and represents an oasis in the sprawl of the capital.

Strategies for Saving Urban Wetlands

Conserving urban wetlands requires a comprehensive approach involving policy interventions, community engagement, and innovation.

One effective strategy is wetland-friendly urban planning and design. This includes incorporating wetlands into urban development plans, protecting existing wetlands from encroachment, and restoring those that are degraded. Cities like New York and Singapore have successfully integrated wetlands into their urban landscapes, demonstrating that development and conservation can indeed co-exist.

Community involvement is also crucial as local communities often have valuable knowledge and a vested interest in protecting their natural surroundings. Engaging residents in wetland restoration, offering educational programs, and promoting citizen science can foster a sense of ownership and stewardship. Near Mumbai, India, for example, the restoration of the Thane Creek Wetland has involved local communities in monitoring and managing the wetland, ensuring its long-term sustainability.

Constructed wetlands, which mimic the functions of natural wetlands, can be used to treat wastewater, manage stormwater, and create new green spaces in urban areas. The city of Hamburg, Germany, for example, has implemented constructed wetlands as part of its sustainable urban drainage system, improving water quality and enhancing biodiversity.

The Wetland City Accreditation Scheme

To recognise and promote the conservation of urban wetlands, the Convention on Wetlands administers the Wetland City Accreditation scheme. This initiative aims to highlight cities that have made significant steps toward the conservation and wise use of wetlands. Accredited cities can serve as models of best practices, showcasing how urban development and wetland conservation can indeed coexist.

The Wetland City Accreditation scheme has already recognised many cities for their exemplary efforts. In 2018, the inaugural list of 18 accredited cities included Changde in China, Colombo in Sri Lanka, and Dakar in Senegal, among others. Today, there are 43 accredited Wetland Cities with others continuing to apply for this prestigious status.

These cities have demonstrated strong commitment to wetland conservation through policies, projects, and community engagement. They have integrated wetlands into their urban planning, protected and restored wetland ecosystems, and raised awareness about the importance of wetlands.

The Wetland City Accreditation scheme shows the potential of urban wetlands to transform cities into more sustainable and liveable spaces. It is my hope that more cities will join the Wetland City Accreditation scheme, embracing the conservation of urban wetlands as a key component of their development agenda. Together, we can create a future where wetlands are valued and protected.

The Benefits of Wetland Conservation

Conserving wetlands, both in urban and rural areas, offers numerous benefits that extend beyond environmental sustainability. Wetlands support livelihoods by providing resources such as fish, plants, and clean water. They offer opportunities for sustainable agriculture and aquaculture, supporting food security and income generation. Wetlands also play a crucial role in disaster risk reduction, protecting communities from floods, storms, and droughts.

In addition to these tangible benefits, wetlands hold cultural and spiritual significance for many communities. They are often considered sacred places, associated with traditional practices and beliefs. Conserving wetlands helps preserve cultural heritage and promotes a sense of identity and belonging.

As we face the dual challenges of climate change and rapid urbanisation, the conservation of wetlands has never been more critical. The solution lies in conserving and restoring wetlands as nature-based solutions that support livelihoods, enhance resilience, and promote sustainable development.

In my role as Secretary General of the Convention on Wetlands, I am committed to advocating for the conservation and wise use of wetlands. I invite all stakeholders – governments, communities, businesses, and individuals – to join us in this mission. By working together, we can ensure that wetlands continue to provide their invaluable services – supporting livelihoods and sustaining life on our wondrous planet. ✦

Stefanie Bühler, *Puddles*, 2006, epoxy, earth, stones.

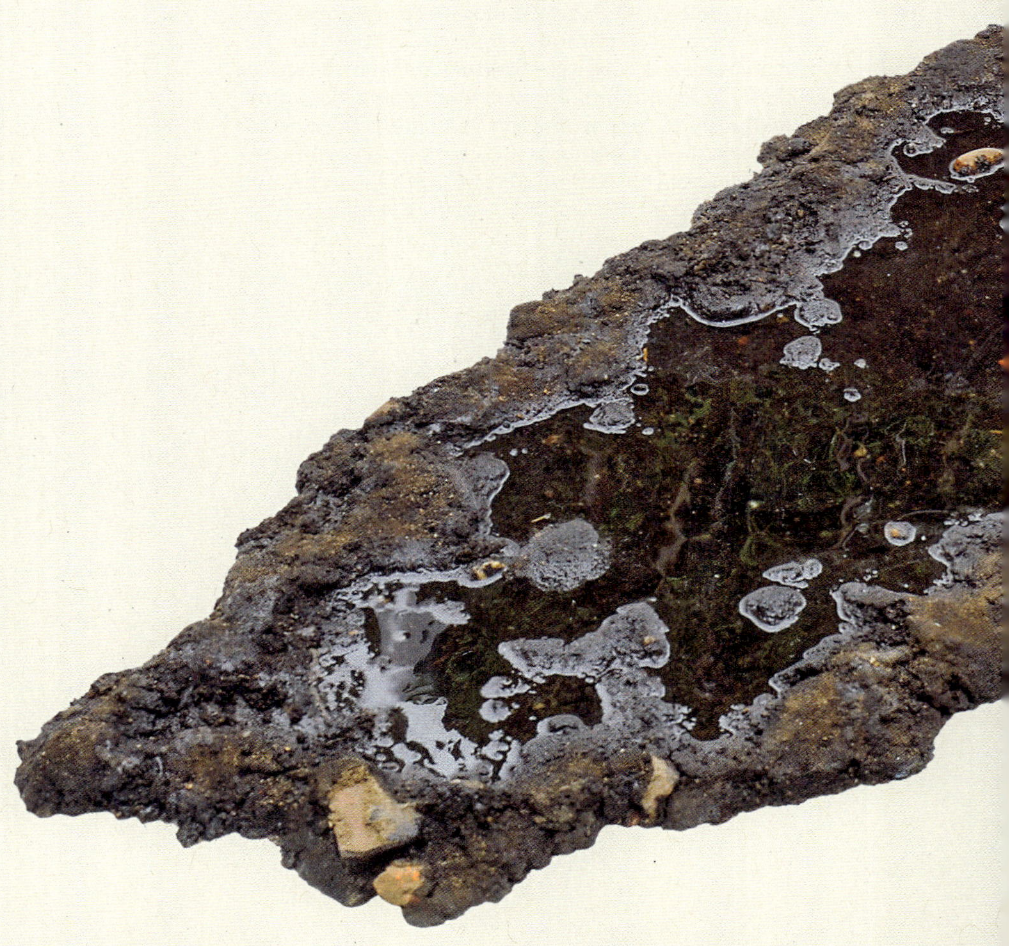

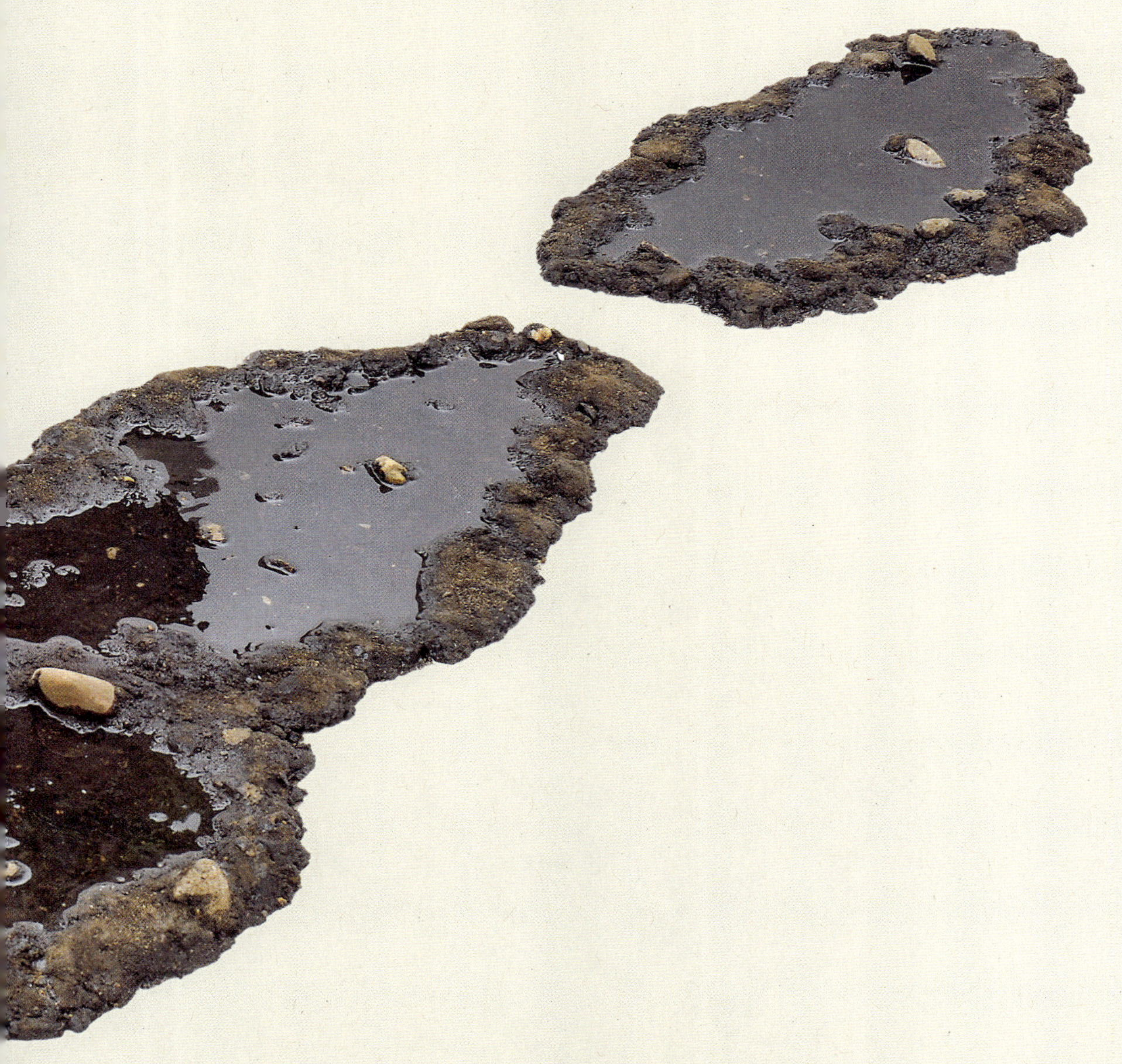

Jochen Hiltmann, *Mushroom Stone*, 1959. This work from the collection of the Kunstmuseum Bonn consists of steel wire and slag. The amorphous, flat structure has a rough surface. Round heads seem to push up from below like mushrooms. The slag provides the connection like a fungal network. Fungi make an important contribution to humus formation by breaking down organic substances and enriching the soil with minerals.

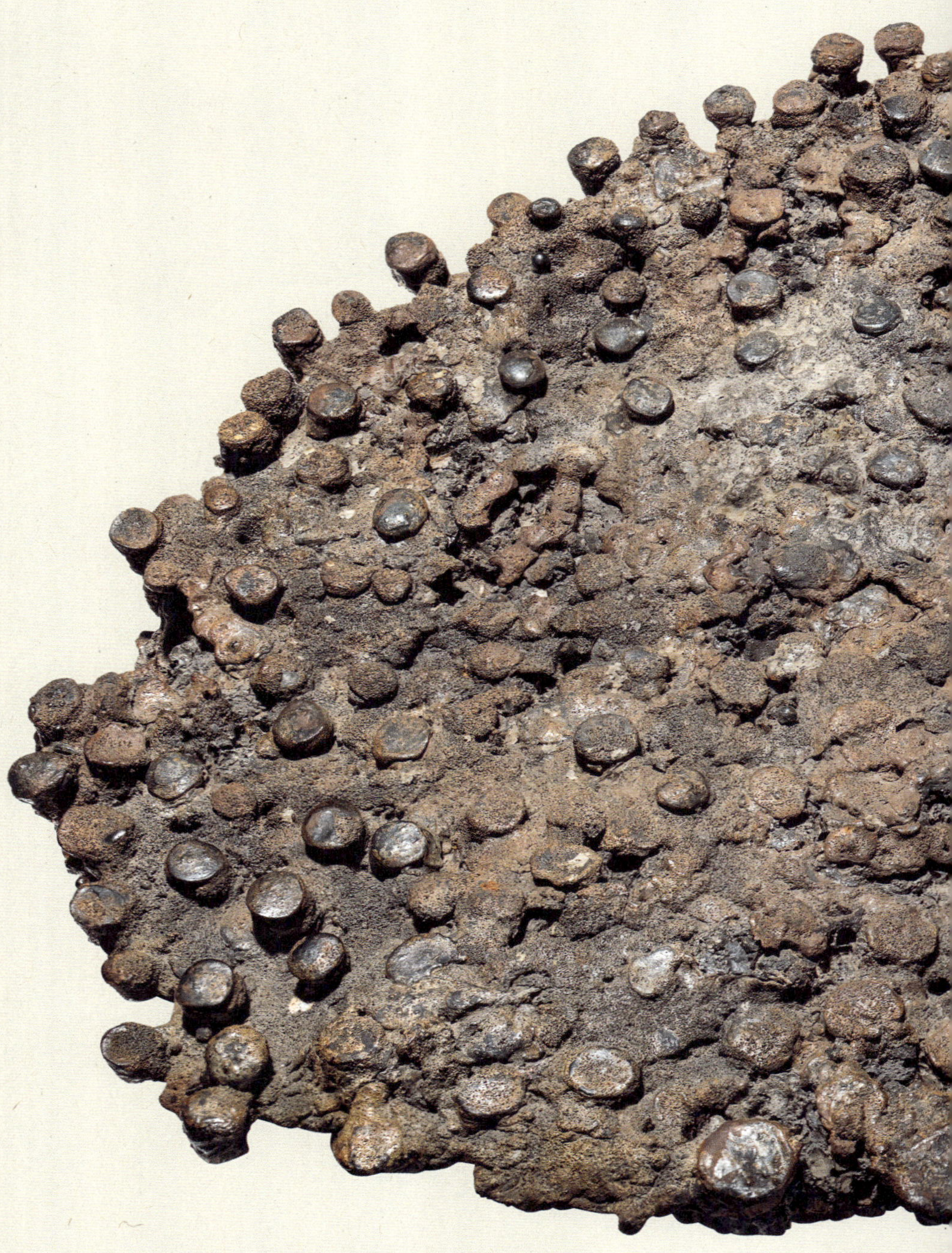

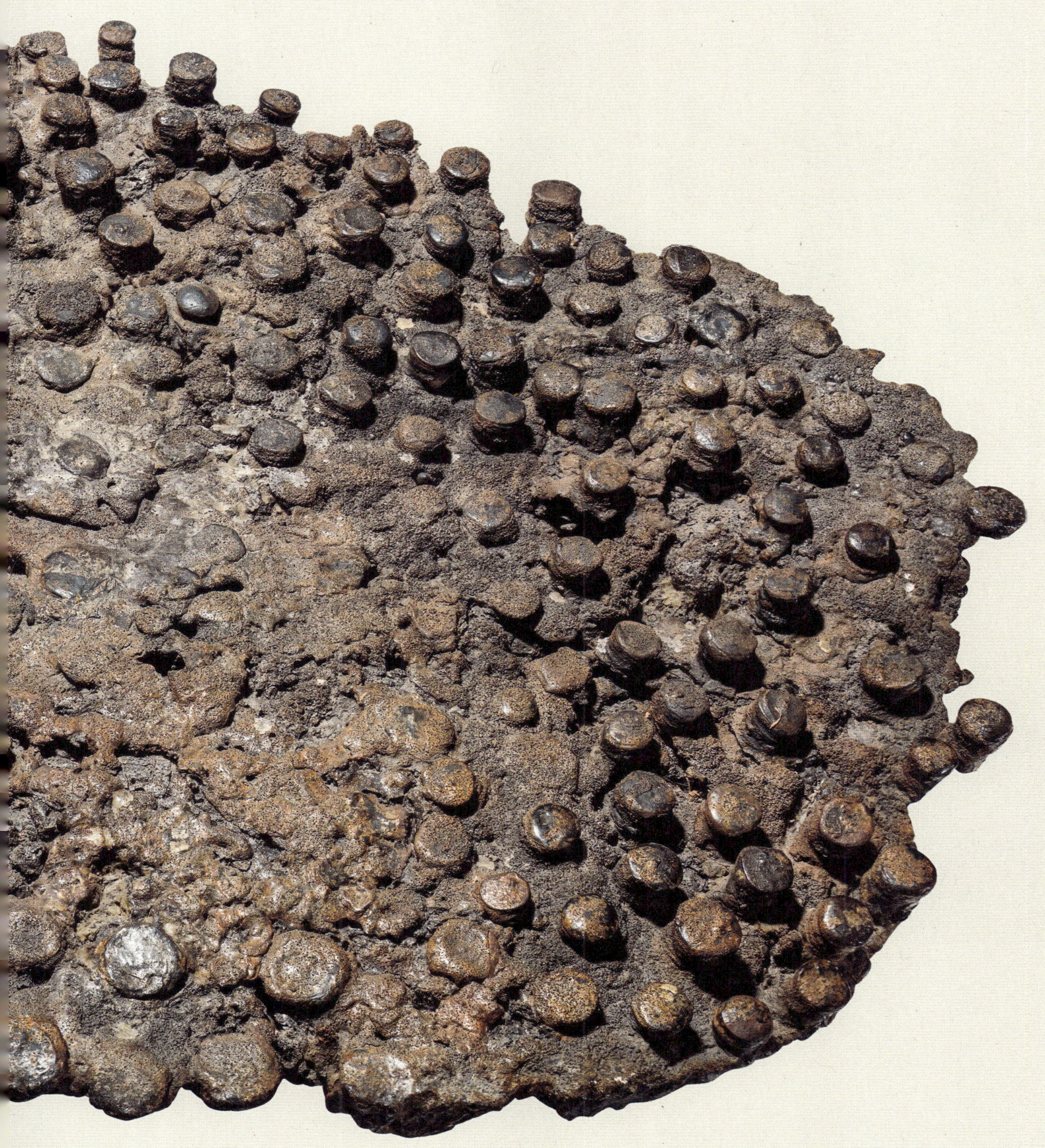

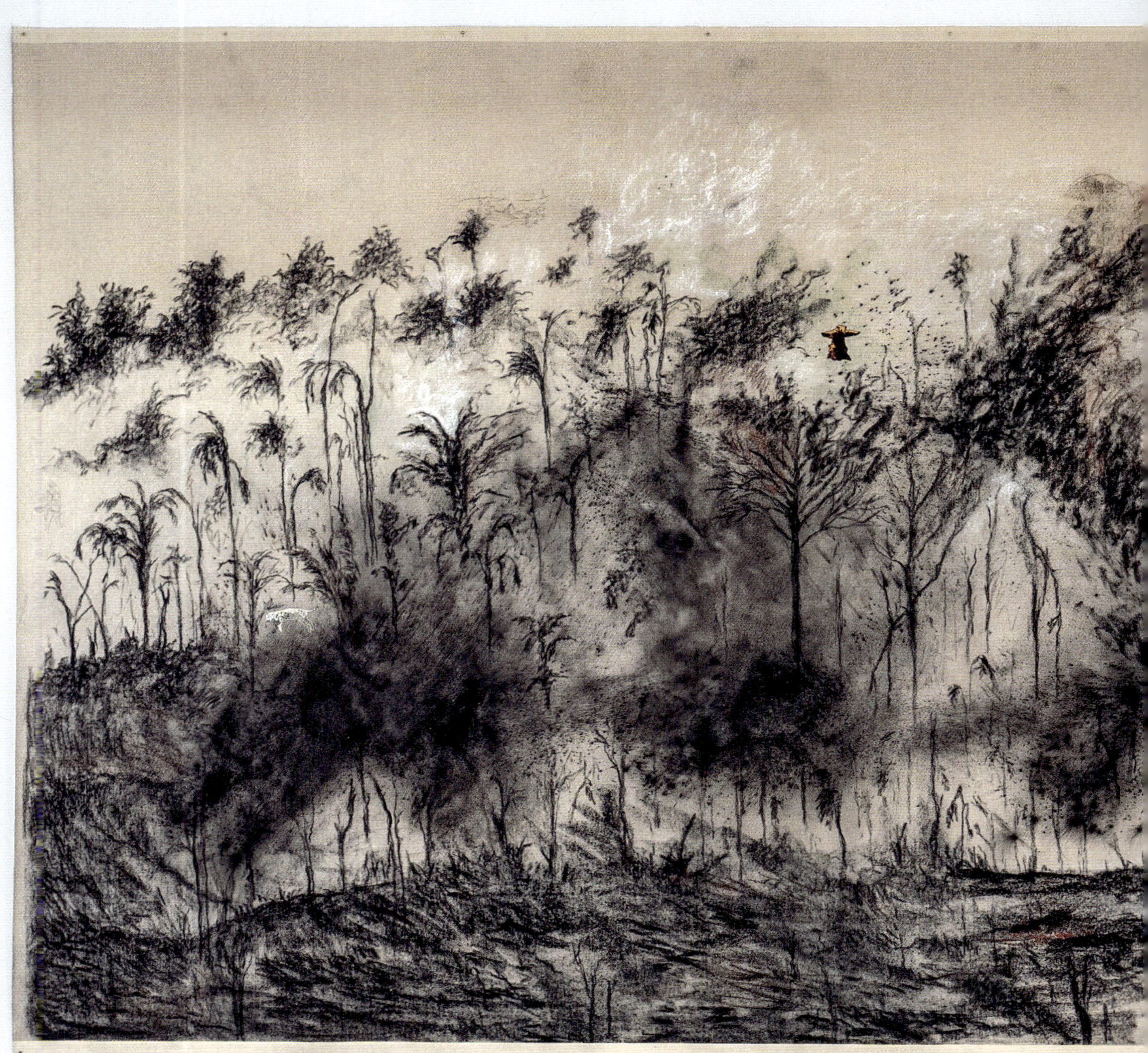

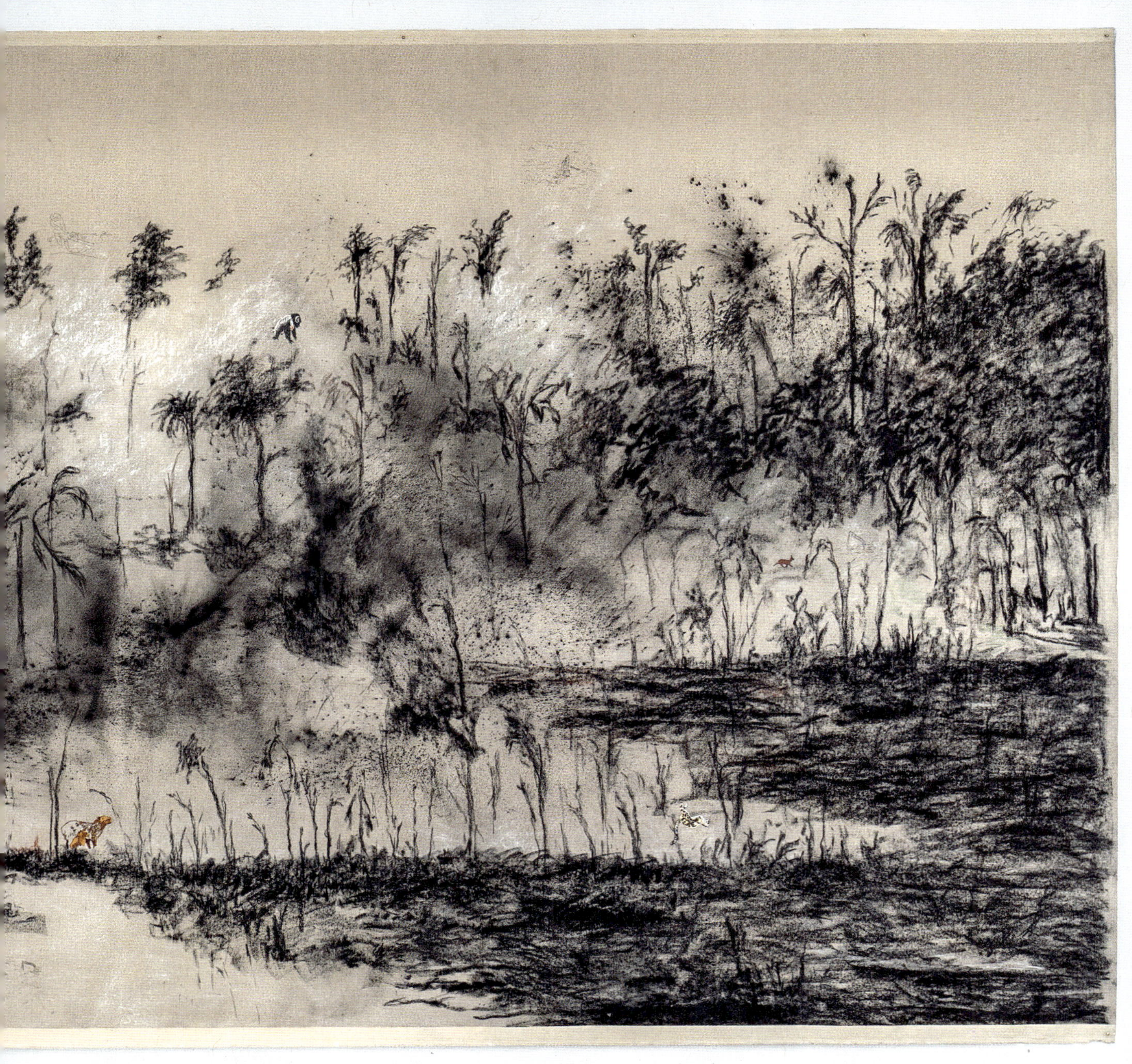

Nohemí Pérez, *La huida de la mama Chiguiro* (The Flight of Mama Chiguiro), 2023. The artist Nohemi Perez lives in Bogota, Colombia. The huge painting, painted with charcoal on canvas, is decorated with delicate embroidery. The title alludes to a native animal species; chiguiro is another name for the capybara in Colombia and Venezuela, where the animal also plays an important mythological role. In her works, Pérez thematises the conflictual relationship between humans and nature. Here she refers to the Catatumbo region on the border between Colombia and Venezuela, which has a very special natural and socio-cultural ecosystem. Illegal armed groups of the right and left, Indigenous tribes, evangelical missionaries, as well as multinational mining companies and drug trafficking organisations coexist in this jungle region.

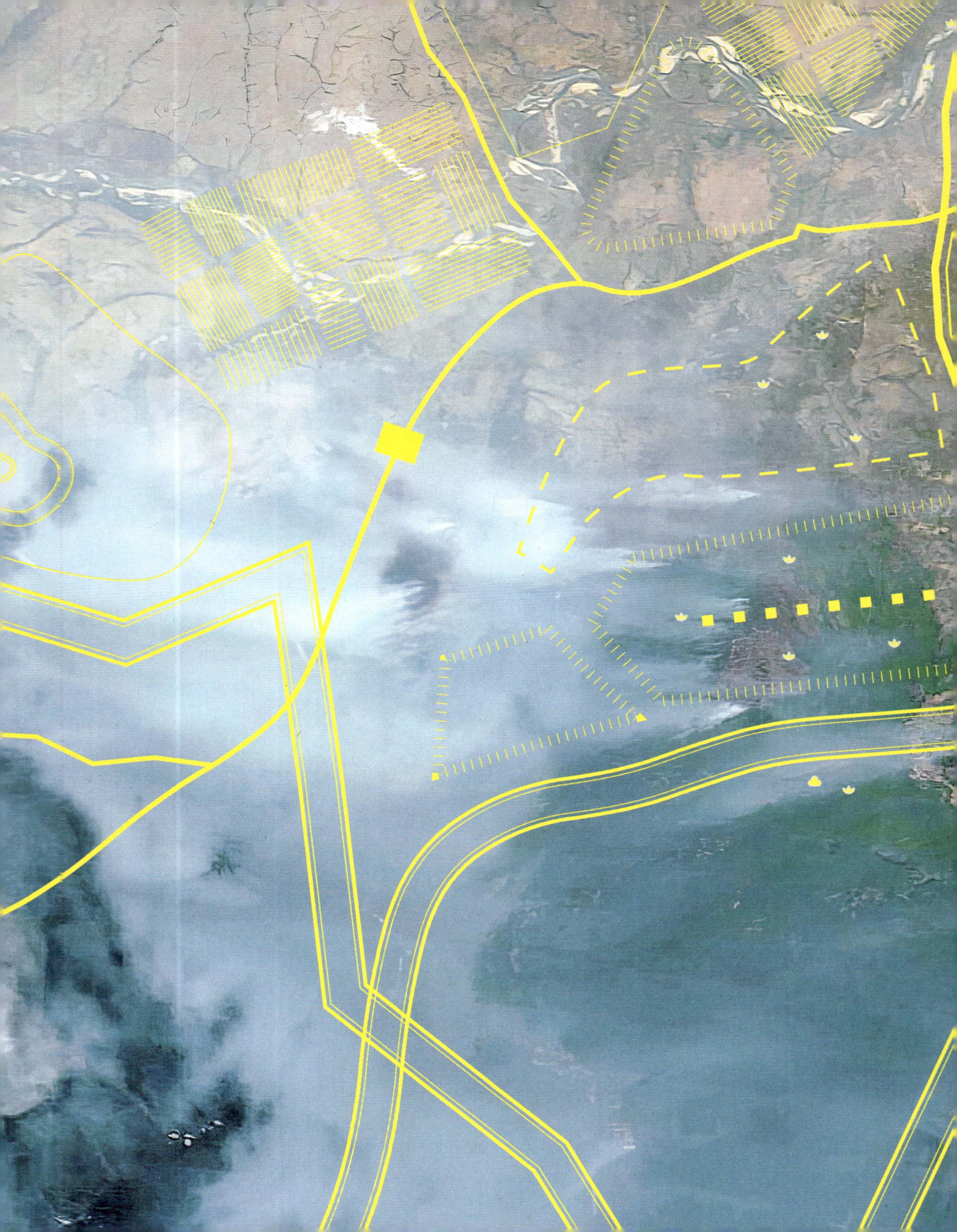

The Global Ambition

Up to 40 % of all land is already degraded and over 4 million km² of land are lost to degradation each year. To prevent, halt, and reverse land degradation, the G20 Land Initiative was launched in 2020. Under the supervision of the UNCCD, the aim is to reduce degraded land by 50 % by 2040. The global community has an interest in combating land degradation beyond its environmental and ecological effects. Worldwide 3.2 billion people (2 in 5) are affected by land degradation and the natural disasters, food and water insecurity, and political and economic instability they bring. The global economic loss is enormous, hitting the poorest regions the most. There are already global commitments from 115 countries to ecologically restore 1 billion hectares of land by 2030. Almost half of all restoration commitments are found in Sub-Saharan Africa. Restoration measures are estimated to be possible on 1.6 billion hectares of cropland, 2.2 billion hectares of grazing land, and 1.4 billion hectares of natural areas. But to achieve the biggest impact, we not only need to restore already degraded land, but also to halt all future conversion and protect the natural land. Governments, companies, and individuals must work together to halt the negative trend. Healthier land brings many benefits, such as local food, sufficient clean water, a more stable economy, and a more secure livelihood.

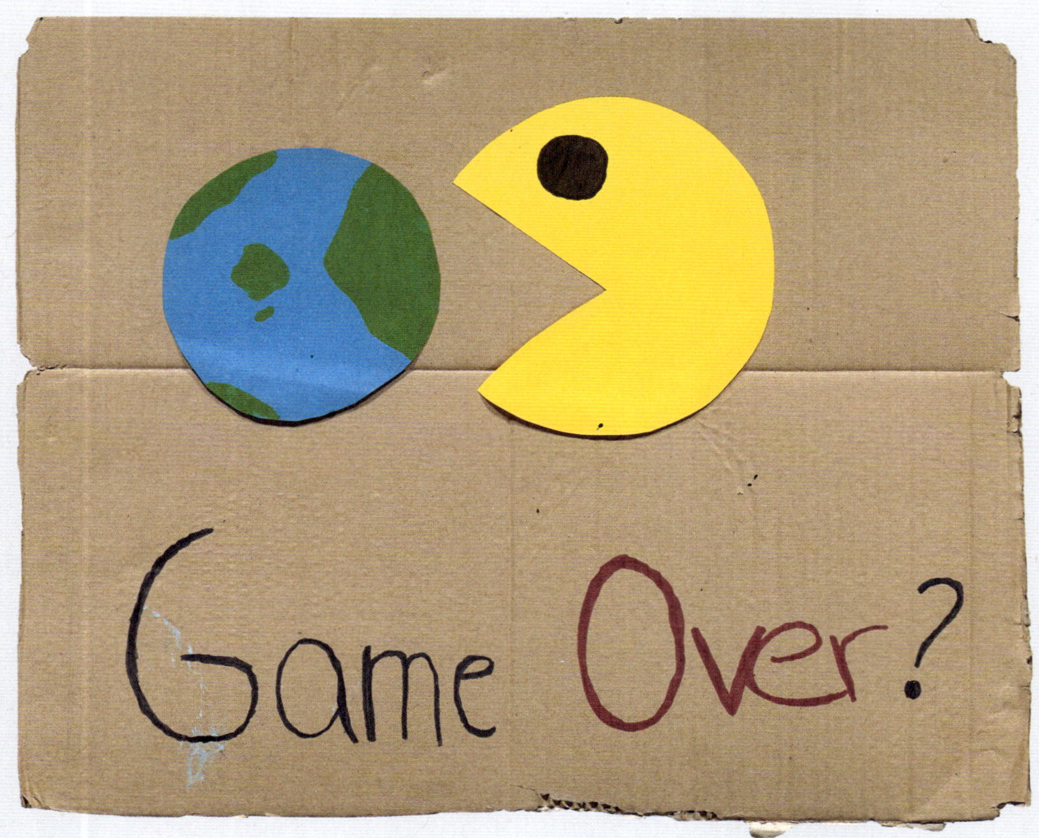

Demonstration sign: 'Game over?', Hürth Comprehensive School, 2019.

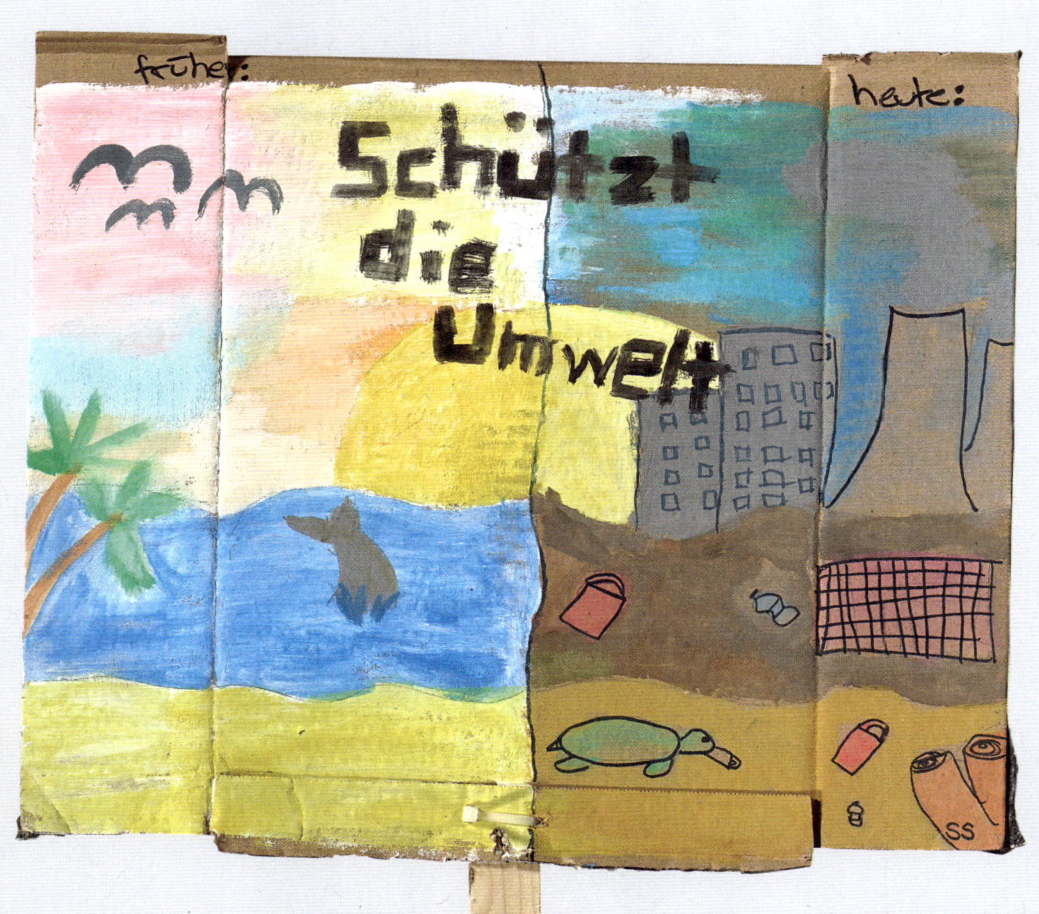

Demonstration sign: 'Protect the environment', Bonn 2018/2019.

8 Projects Introduce Themselves – Ideas and Inspirations

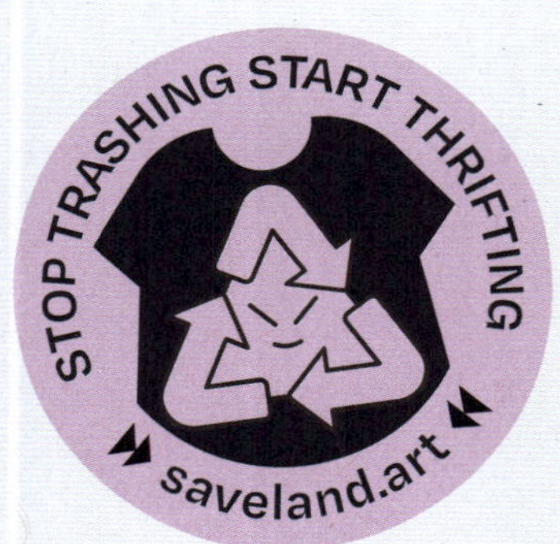

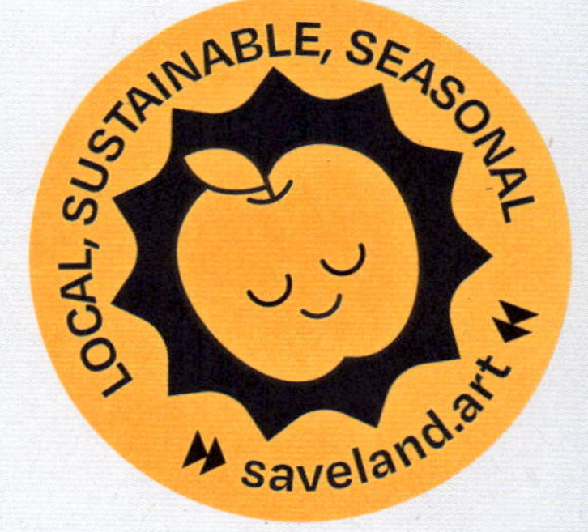

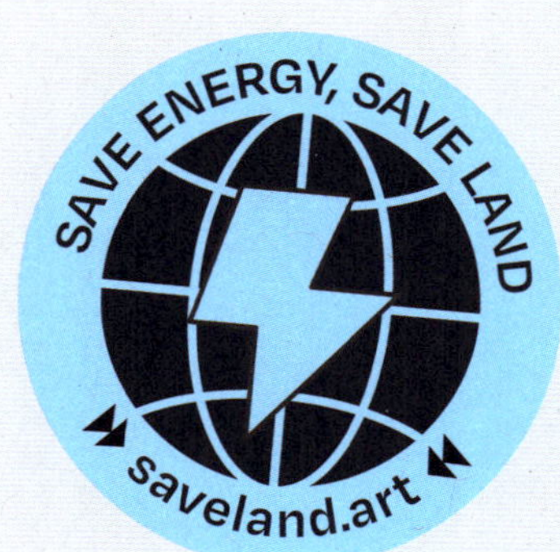

What does 'Take Action' actually mean? How can we get involved in the restoration of degraded land and make our lives more land-friendly? There are several possible step-by-step approaches: ❶ Raise your awareness of the issue and inform yourself. ❷ Discuss the issue with others and share experiences. ❸ Advocate for the issue, for example by taking part in campaigns or demonstrations. ❹ Change your behaviour and attitudes in everyday life. ❺ Become active in the restoration of damaged soils.

The following eight projects and stories present ideas that we can all implement as first steps, and they provide inspirations for what a more land-friendly life could look like in the future. They are divided into 4 categories. ❶ Fashion: Today's industrial production methods in the textile and fashion industry are considered to be particularly harmful to soils worldwide. ❷ Energy: An alternative to fossil fuels and a reduction in the mountains of waste worldwide would also benefit land areas. ❸ Food: Here, too, a shift towards more land-friendly production methods is needed, away from monocultures and towards regional biodiversity. ❹ Well-being: Apart from our food, countless medicines also have a natural origin, but nature does more than just sustain us physically. We also need its wholesome beauty mentally.

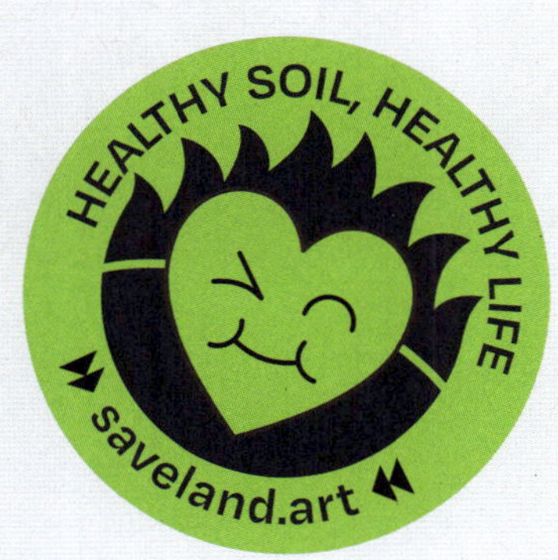

Fashion

STOP TRASHING START

saveland.art

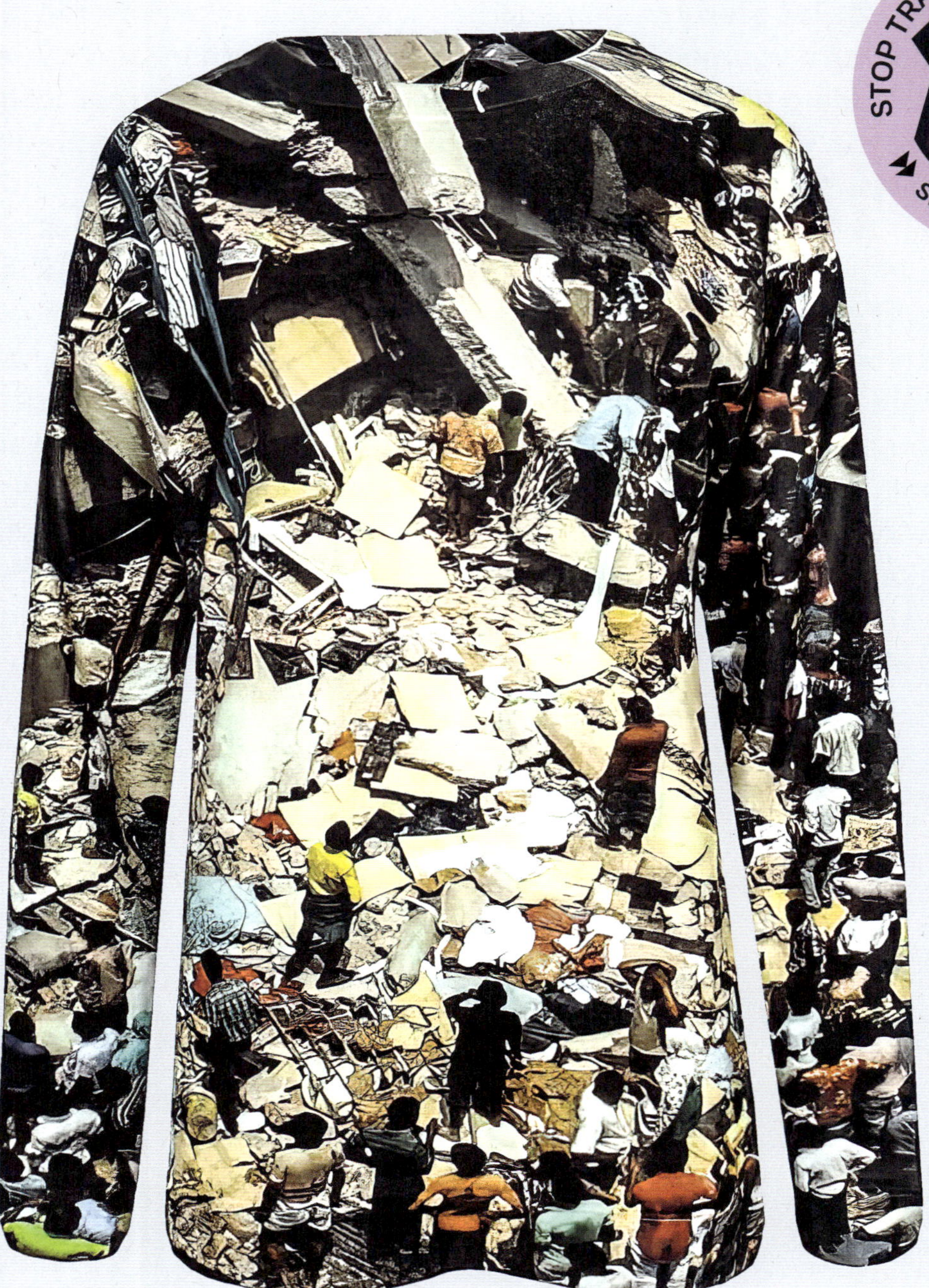

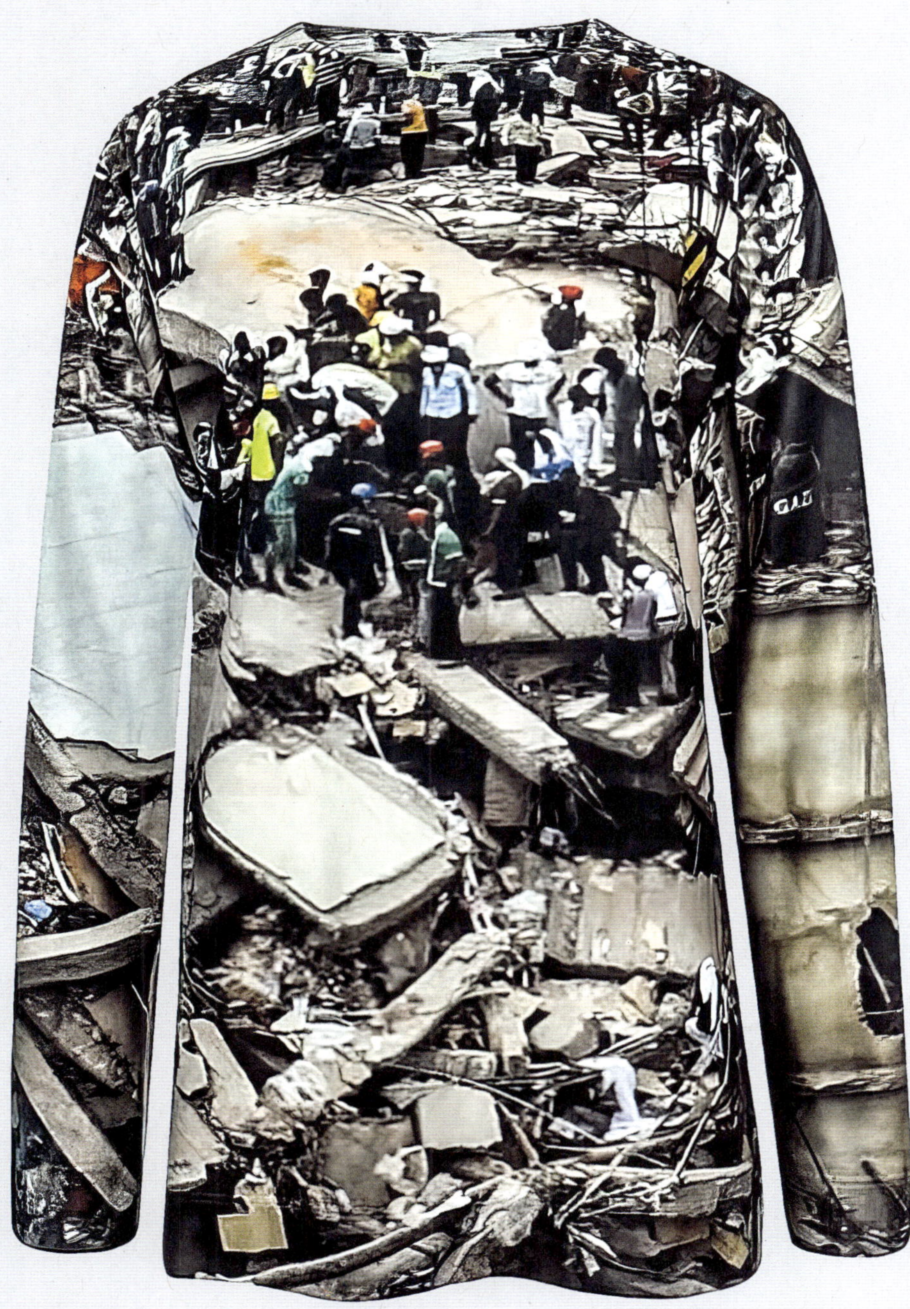

Manu Washaus, *Sweater: Study of the Possible II*, 2013. In April 2013, the Rana Plaza building in Bangladesh collapsed, claiming more than 1,000 lives. Manu Washaus utilises photos of the disaster on sweatshirts to openly address Western exploitation through tolerating problematic production conditions. The effects of the fast fashion industry on the environment are well known, but are nevertheless almost invisible in daily life in the rich countries of the Global North. The intensive use of chemicals pollutes the soil and impairs its fertility, while mountains of often artificial textile waste exacerbate the problem. The sweatshirts are intended to stimulate discussion about the ecological and social consequences of the fashion industry.

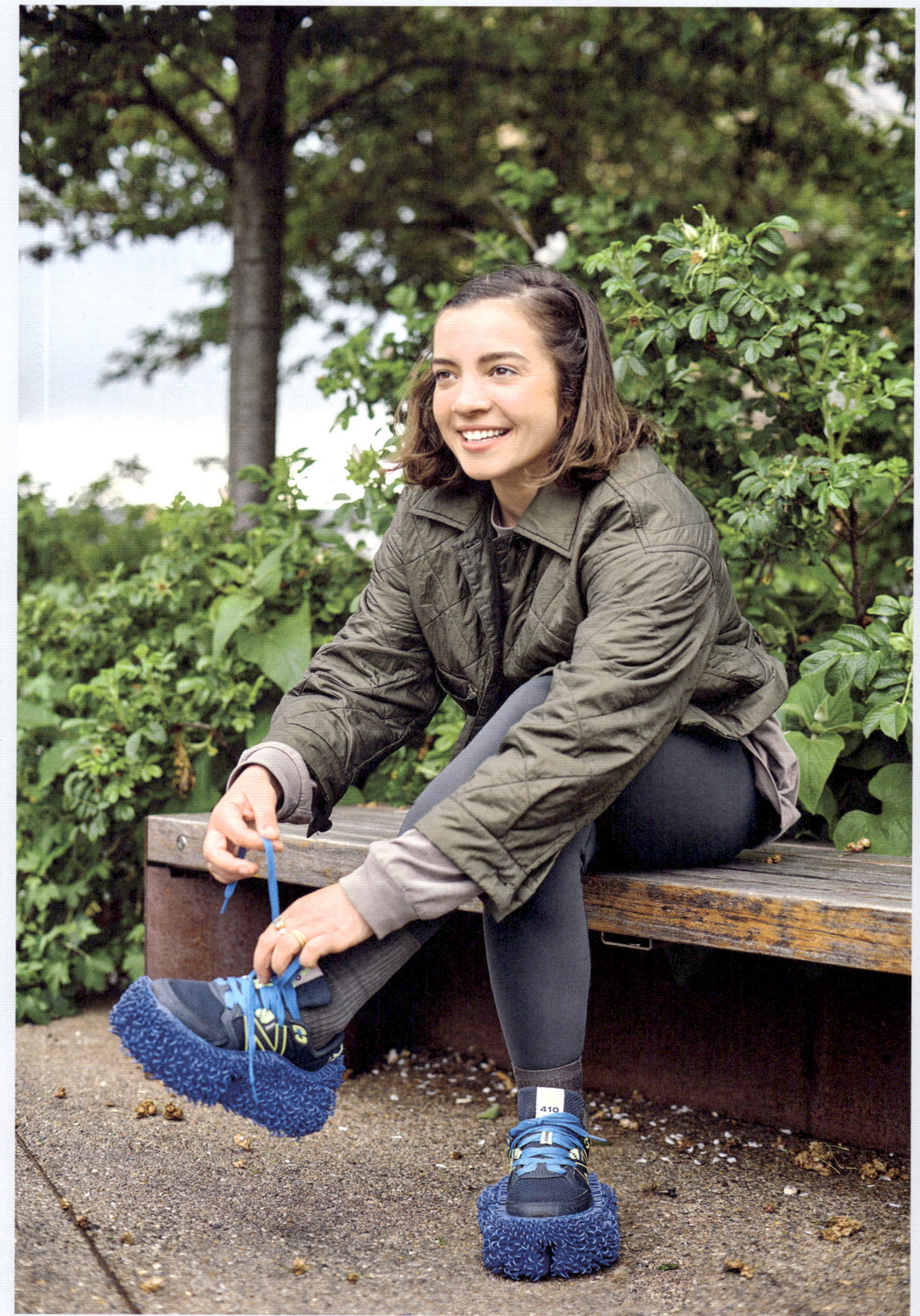
410

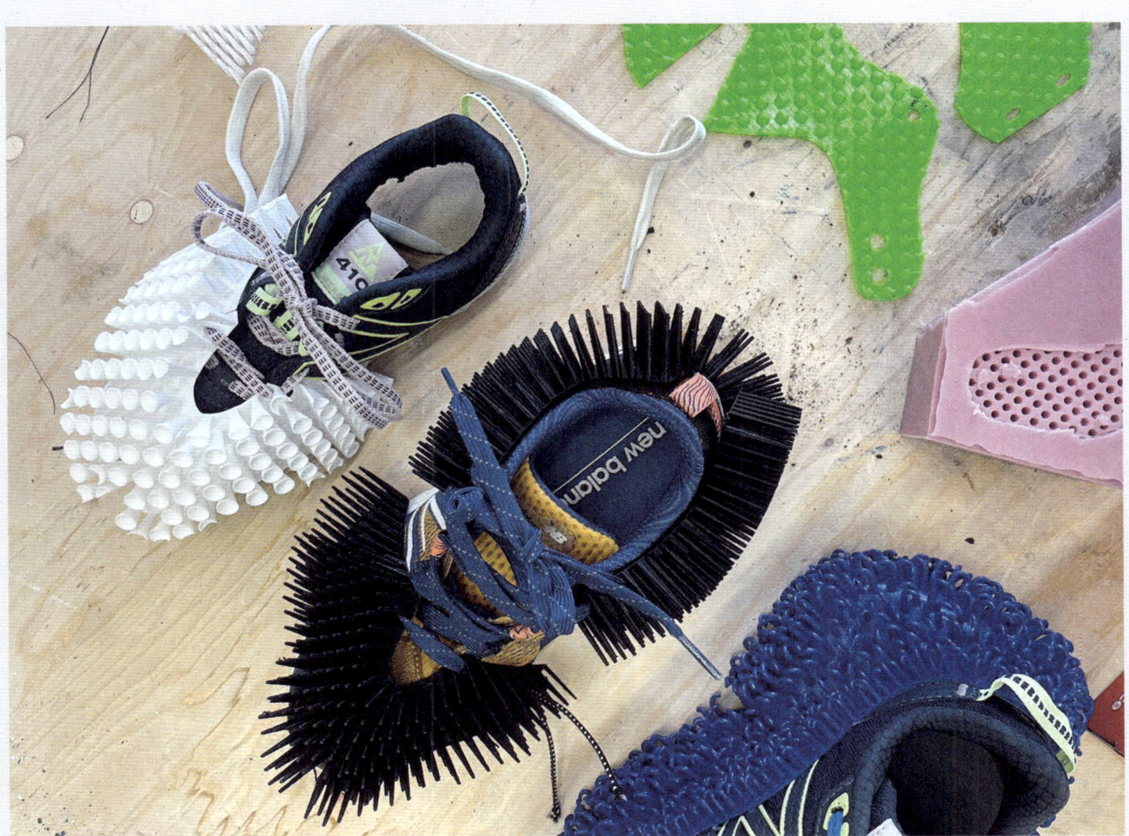

Kiki Grammatopoulos, *Rewild the Run (Part 2)*, 2024. In our cities, soils are being sealed, biodiversity is being reduced, and soil health is being compromised. As part of the *Rewild the Run* project, the artist developed shoe soles inspired by animal hooves to promote biodiversity in cities. The special sole structure – similar to that of insect hairs – is intended to gently loosen the soil and support plant growth and seed dispersal. In this way, people – by acting as pollinators – can actively contribute to the improvement of soil health and the conservation of nature in everyday urban living.

Energy

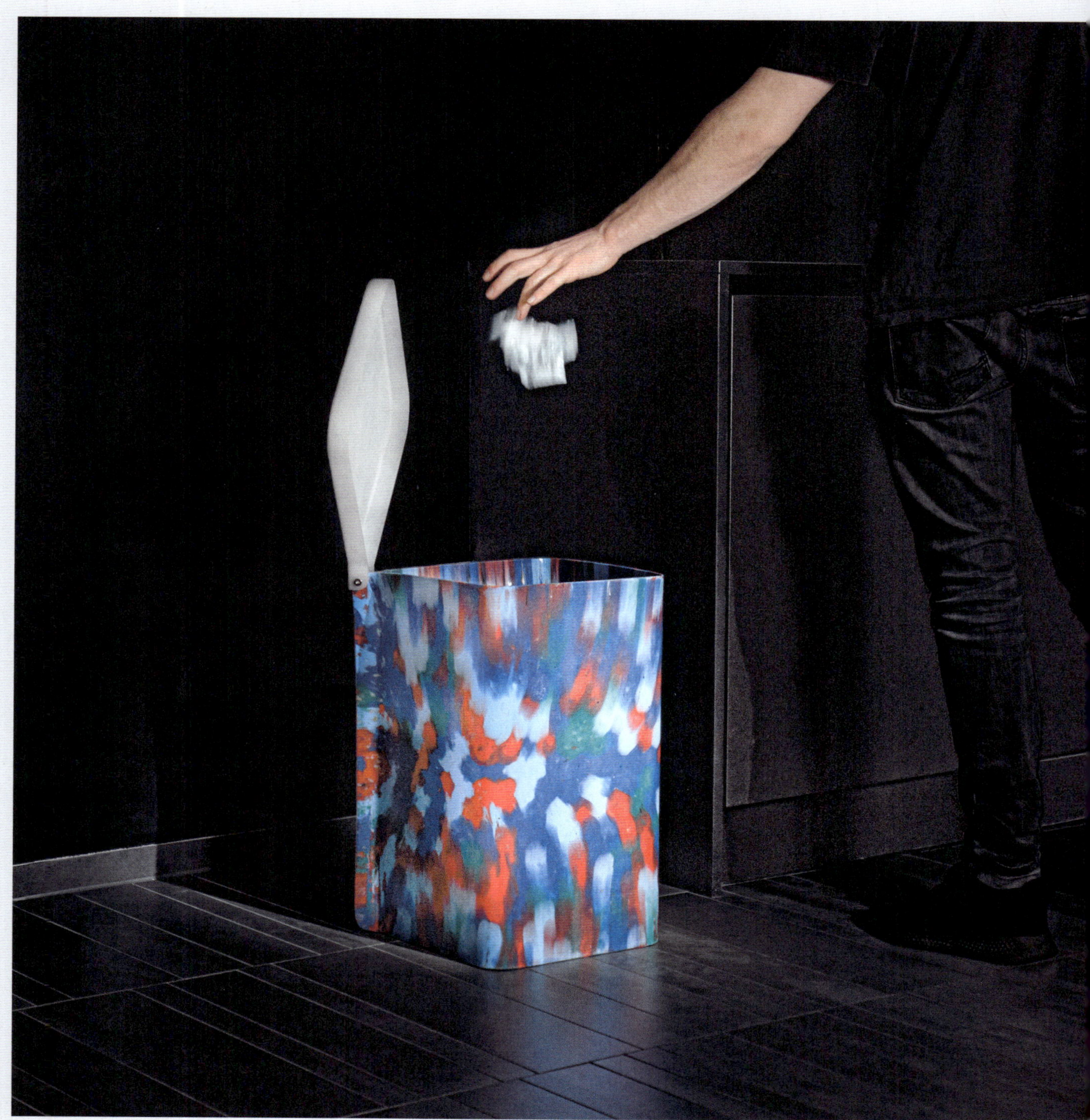

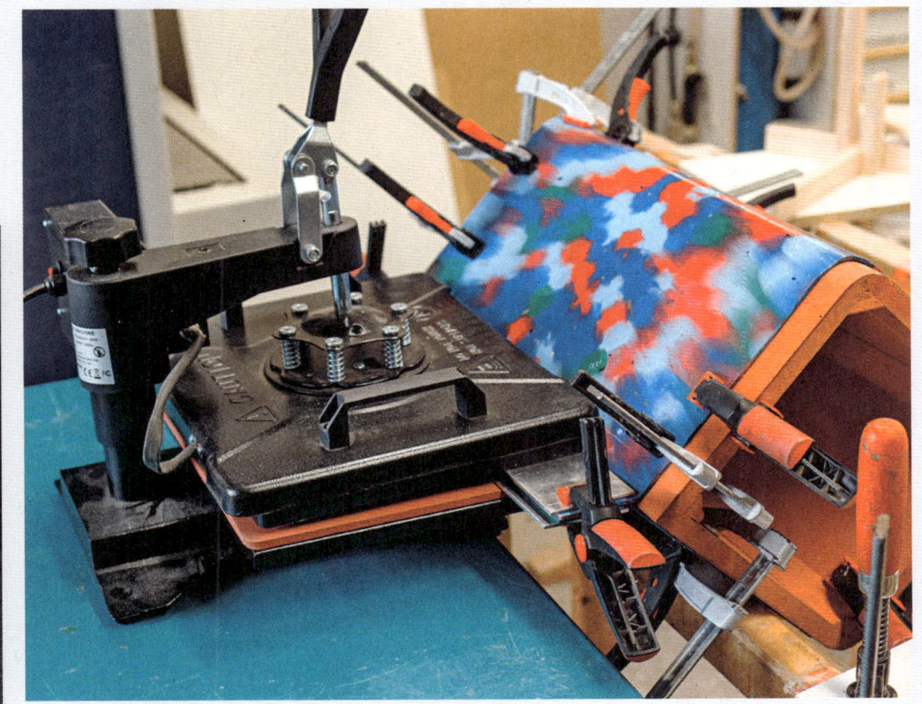

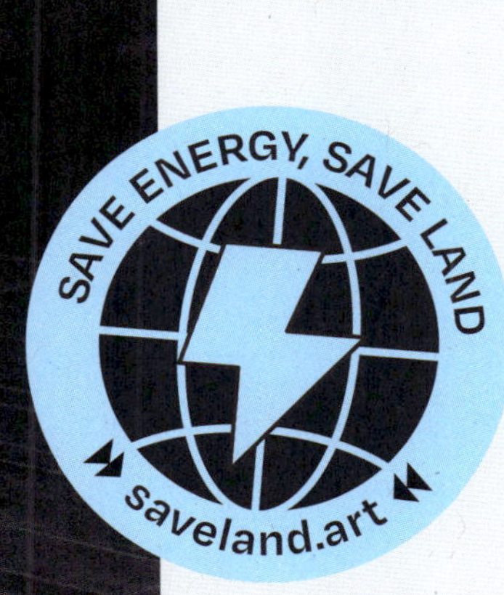
SAVE ENERGY, SAVE LAND
saveland.art

Jonathan Kuhlmann, *CapTon: Visual Recycling*, 2022. Waste often goes unnoticed into the trash bin and disappears from sight. But plastic, for example, decomposes slowly, polluting our soil and impairing its fertility. Furthermore, the production and disposal of plastic requires considerable amounts of energy and resources. The *Visual Recycling* project takes plastic waste out of this anonymity and gives it a clear visual presence. The result is *CapTon*, a recycling bin made from 1,060 bottle caps that makes consumption and hidden waste visible.

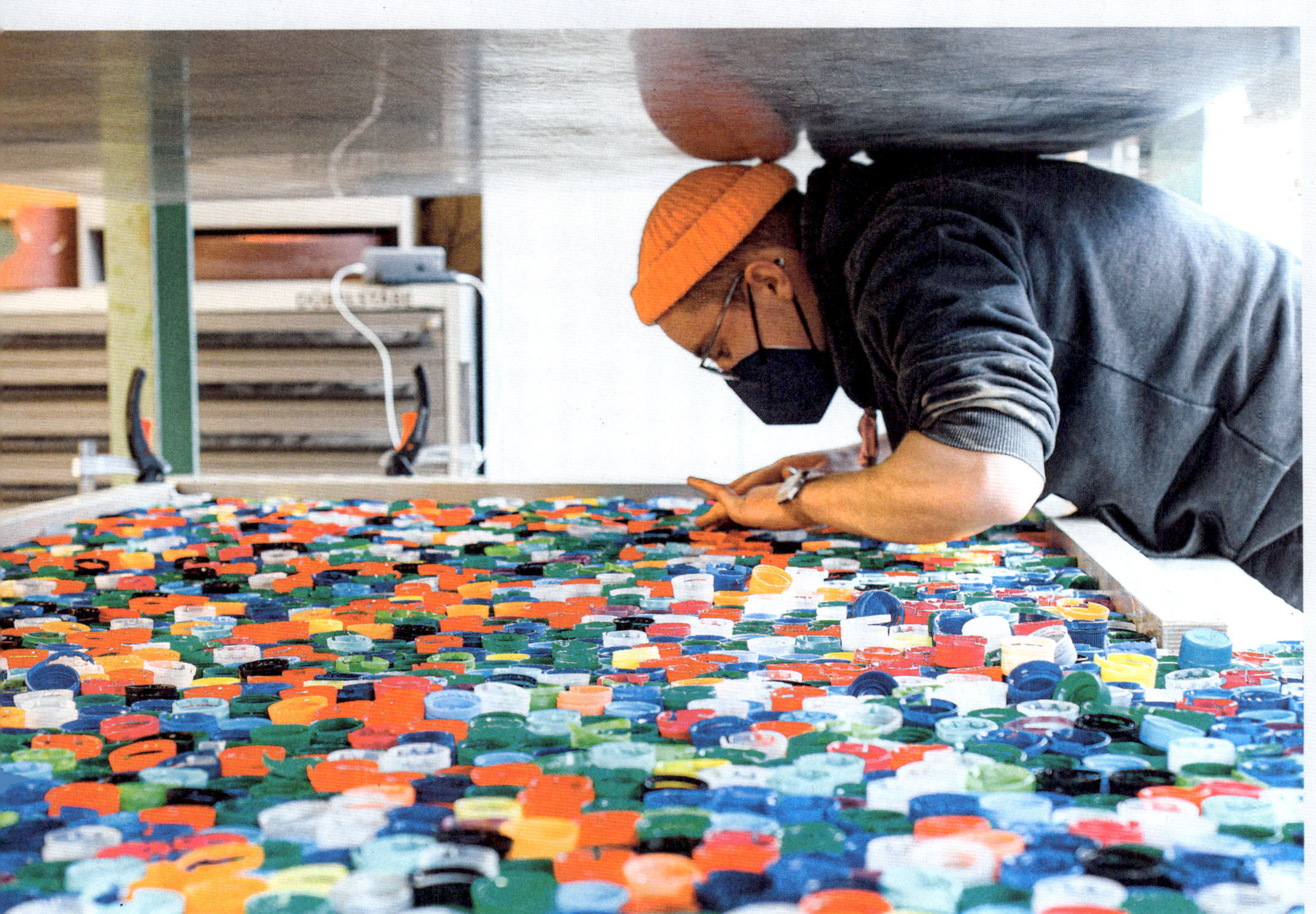

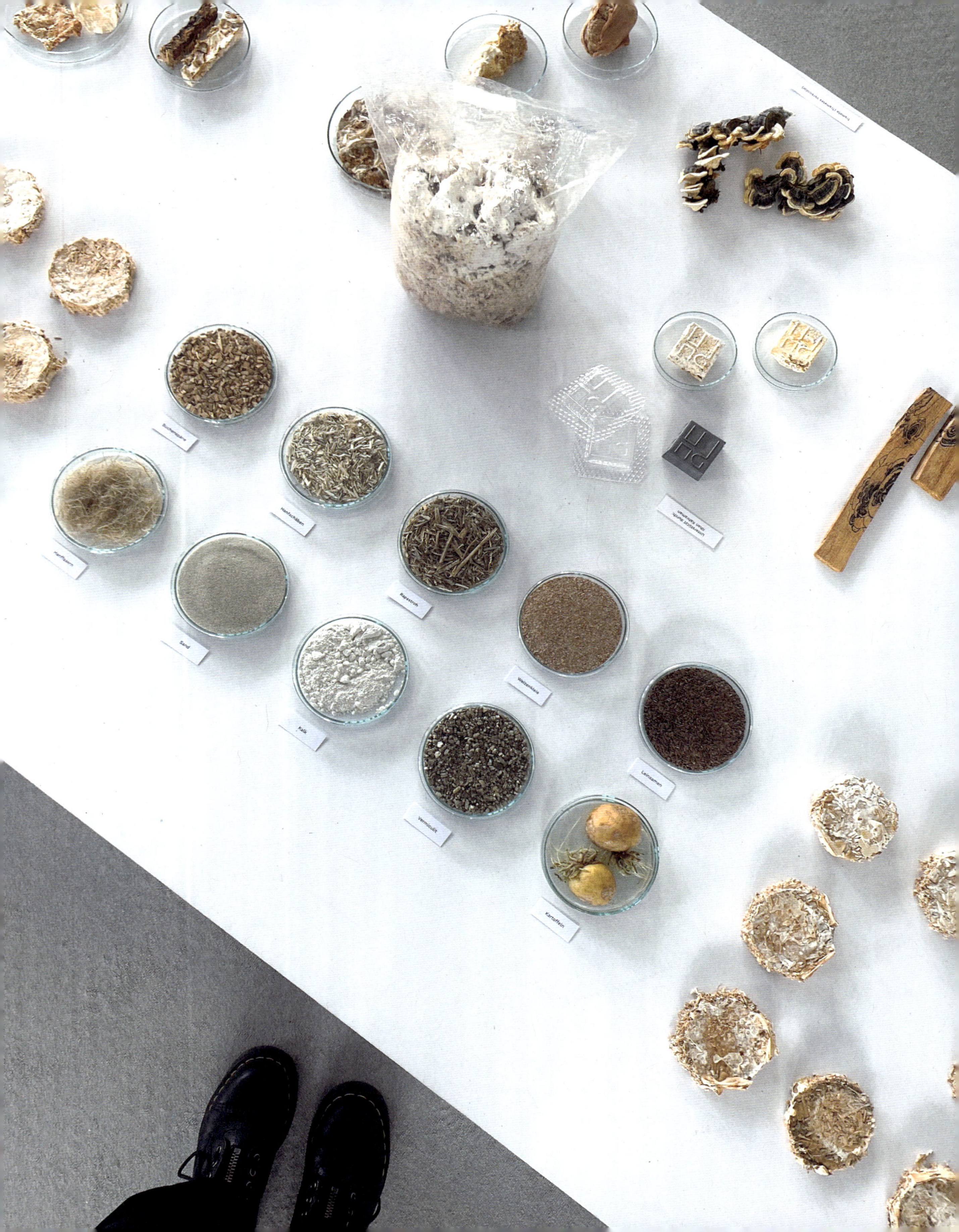
Hanfschäben
Rapsstroh
Sand
Kalk
Weizenkleie
Vermiculit
Leinsamen
Kartoffeln

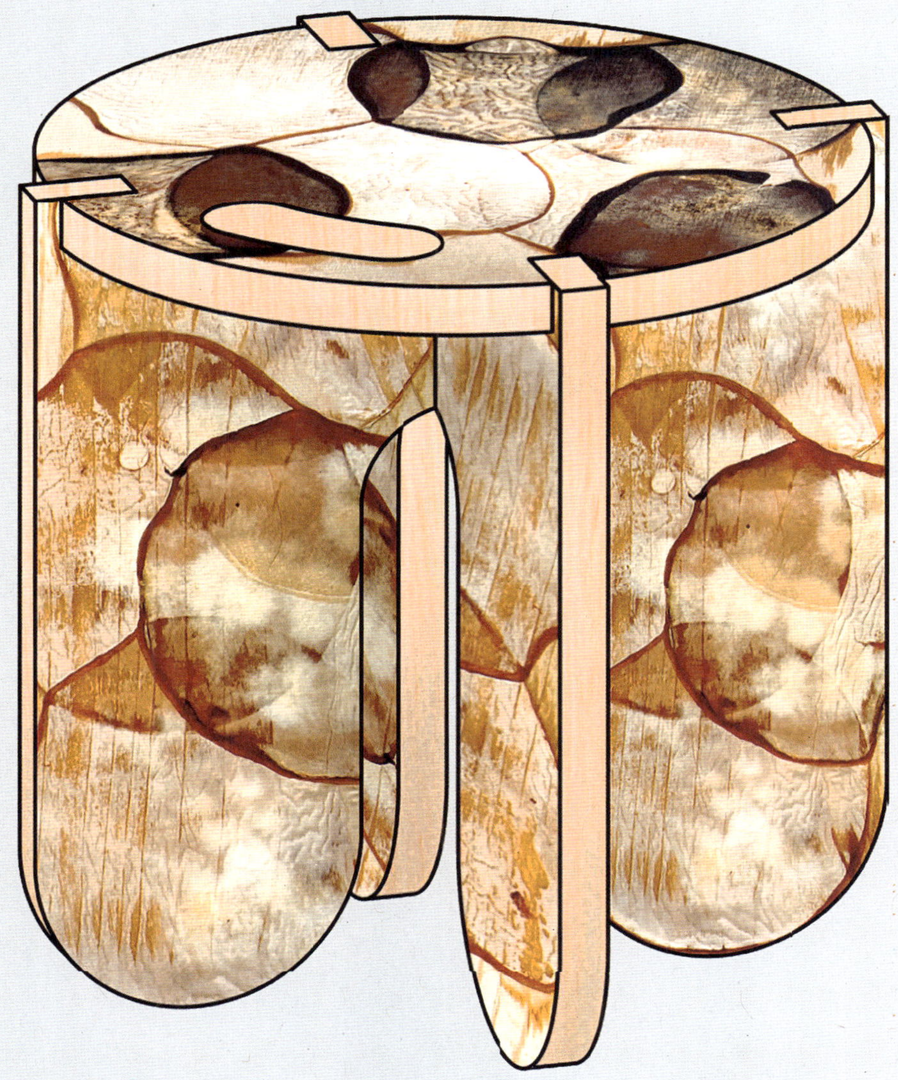

Paulina Heidlberger, *Fungiture: Compostable stool made from mycelium*, 2024. *Fungiture* is a seating element made from mycelium-based material. Mycelium consists of organic substances that have grown together and are firmly connected by a fungal network. The use of mycelium, which is completely compostable after use, conserves resources and minimises soil pollution. In contrast to conventional materials used in furniture construction, mycelium is returned to the natural cycle as a nutrient at the end of its life span.

Food

Ina Sistig-Heuken, *Natura Morta*, 2016. Meat consumption in Germany is problematically high. This is not only ethically, ecologically, and from a health perspective questionable, but also harmful to our soils, as intensive livestock farming leads to over-fertilisation and soil erosion. *Natura Morta* addresses the way meat is not recognised as a valuable commodity by photographing cheap meat in the stye of a classic still life. The project thus symbolises the absurdity of modern eating habits and the loss of quality and tradition. The project was awarded a prize by the North Rhine-Westphalia Consumer Advice Centre in the 'Well Done: Meat and Sustainability' competition.

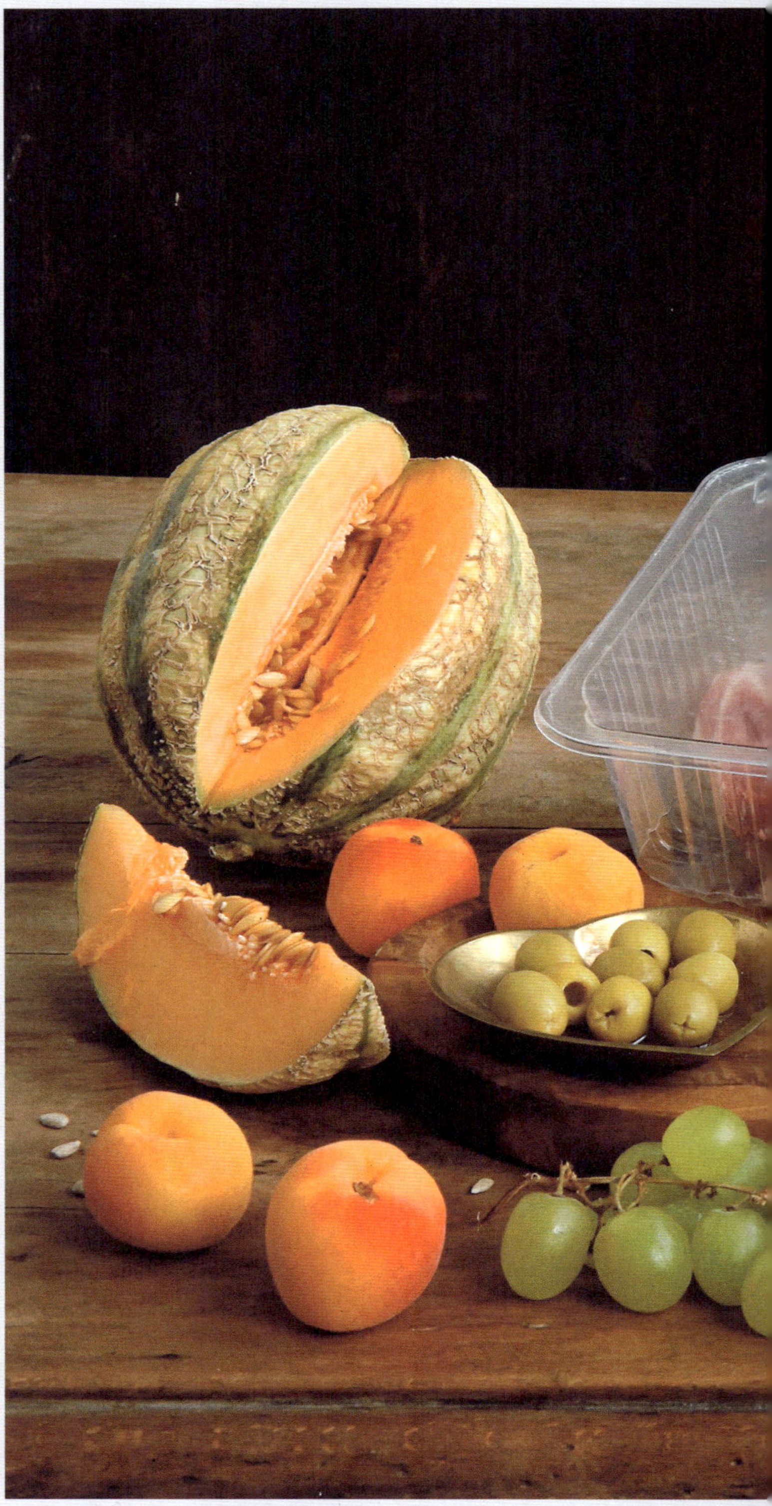

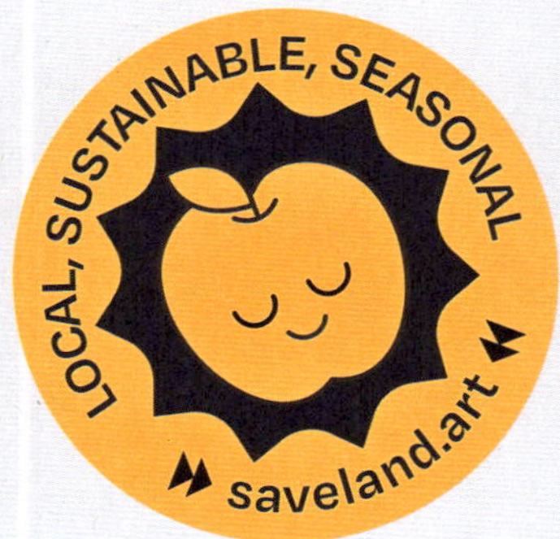

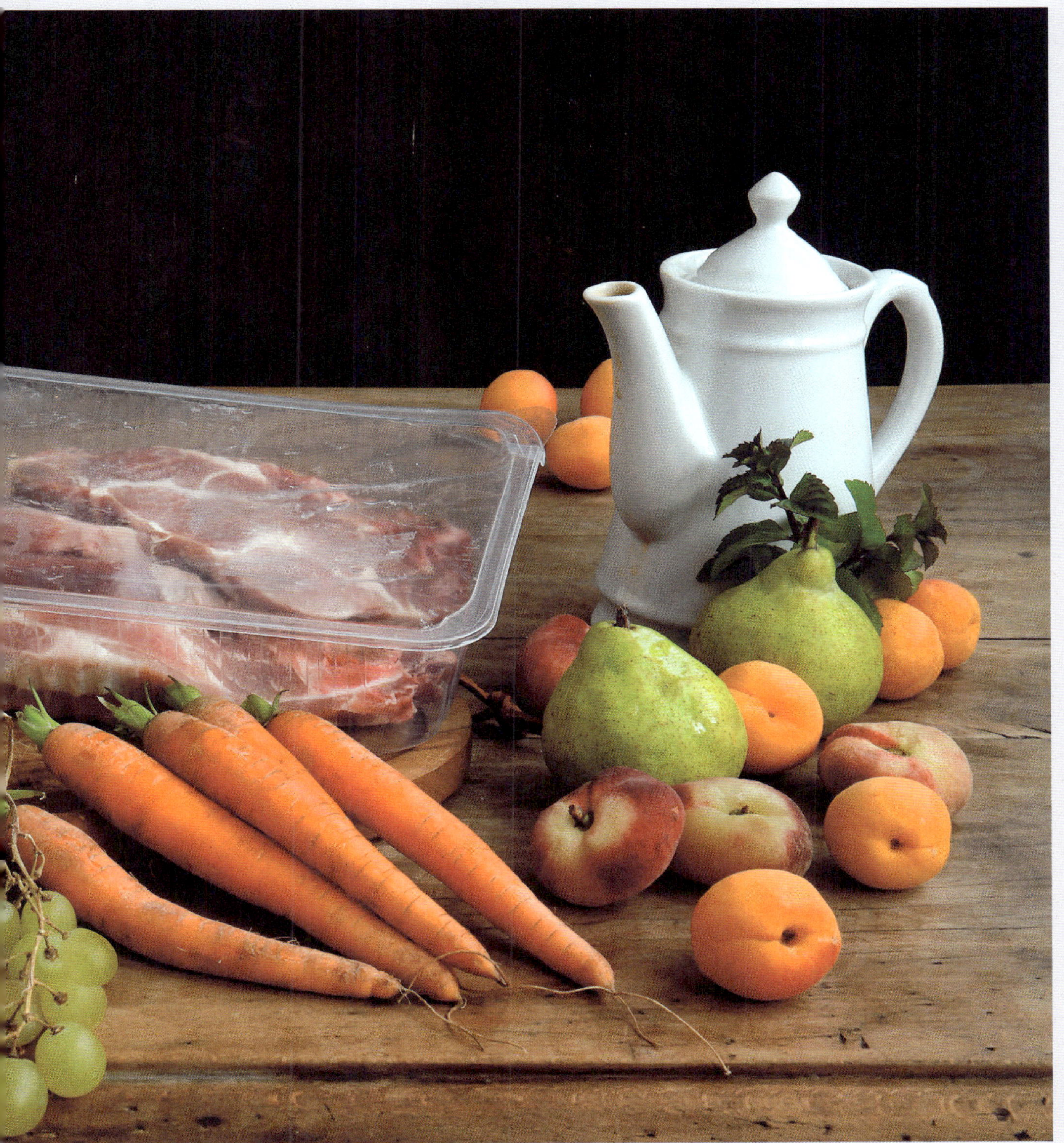

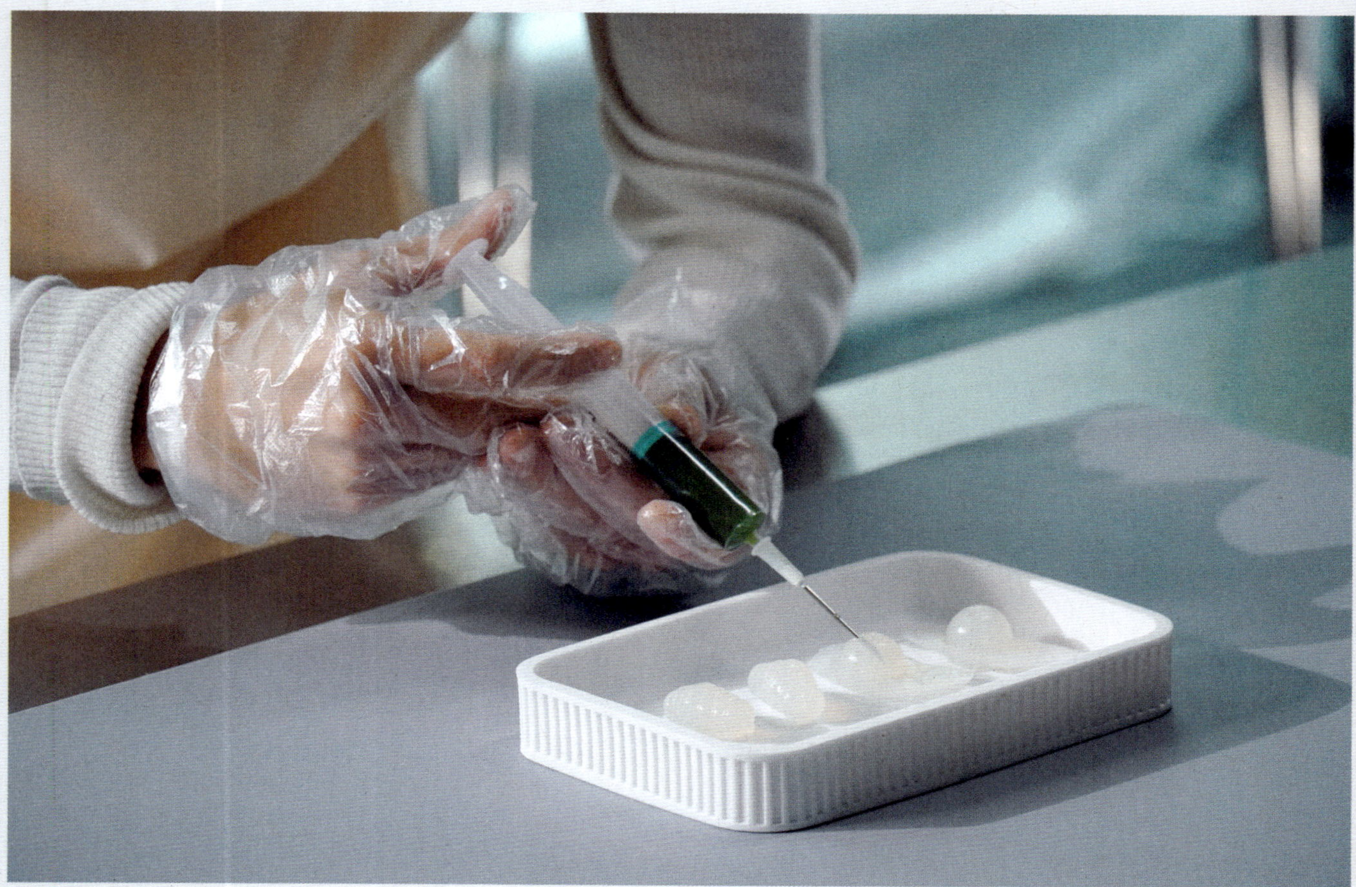

Malu Lücking, *Landless Food*, 2022. Microalgae strains cultivated on edible, gel-like objects, flavours: flower, crab, mussel. The project transports us to the year 2050, to a scenario in which overexploitation and erosion have made soils infertile, while human consumption and climate change have greatly reduced biodiversity. Overfishing and bee mortality have caused further crises, drastically limiting the natural flavour spectrum. With *Landless Food*, the food system is preserved by regenerating lost flavours based on microalgae. In fact, these algae offer diverse flavours that can be further refined through metabolic manipulation. Initial results include seafood aromas and a floral spice.

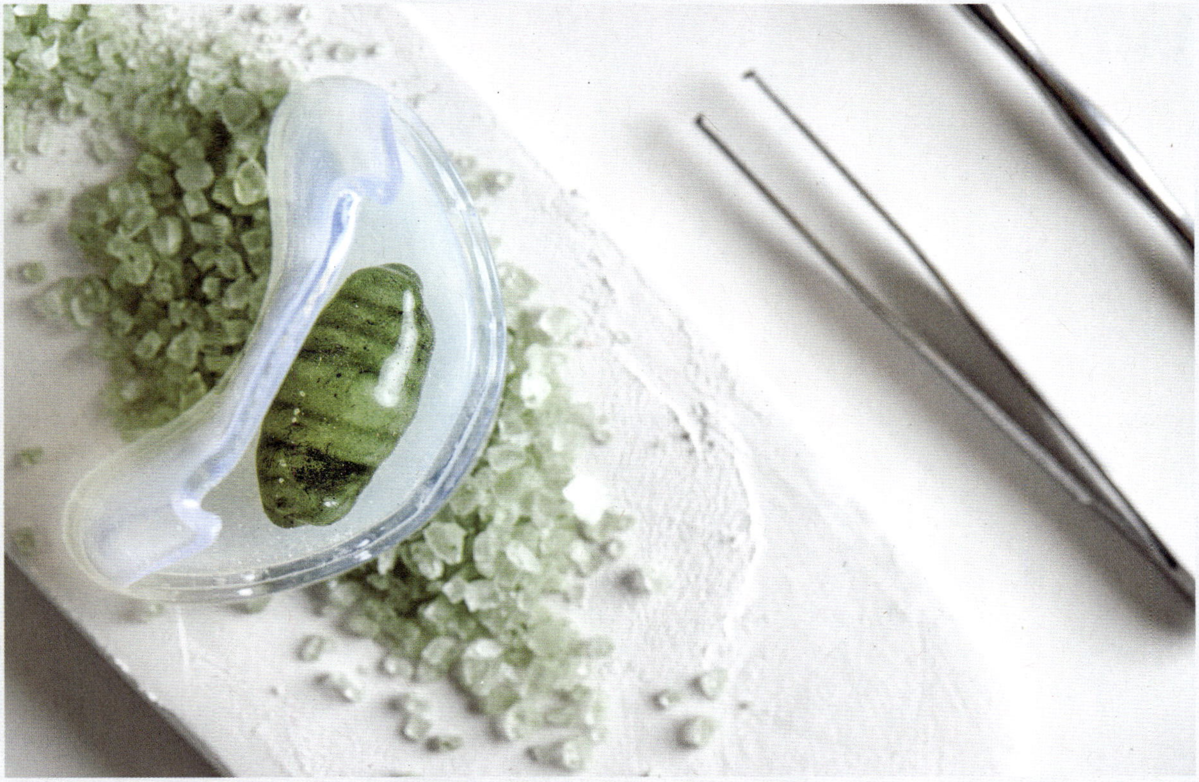

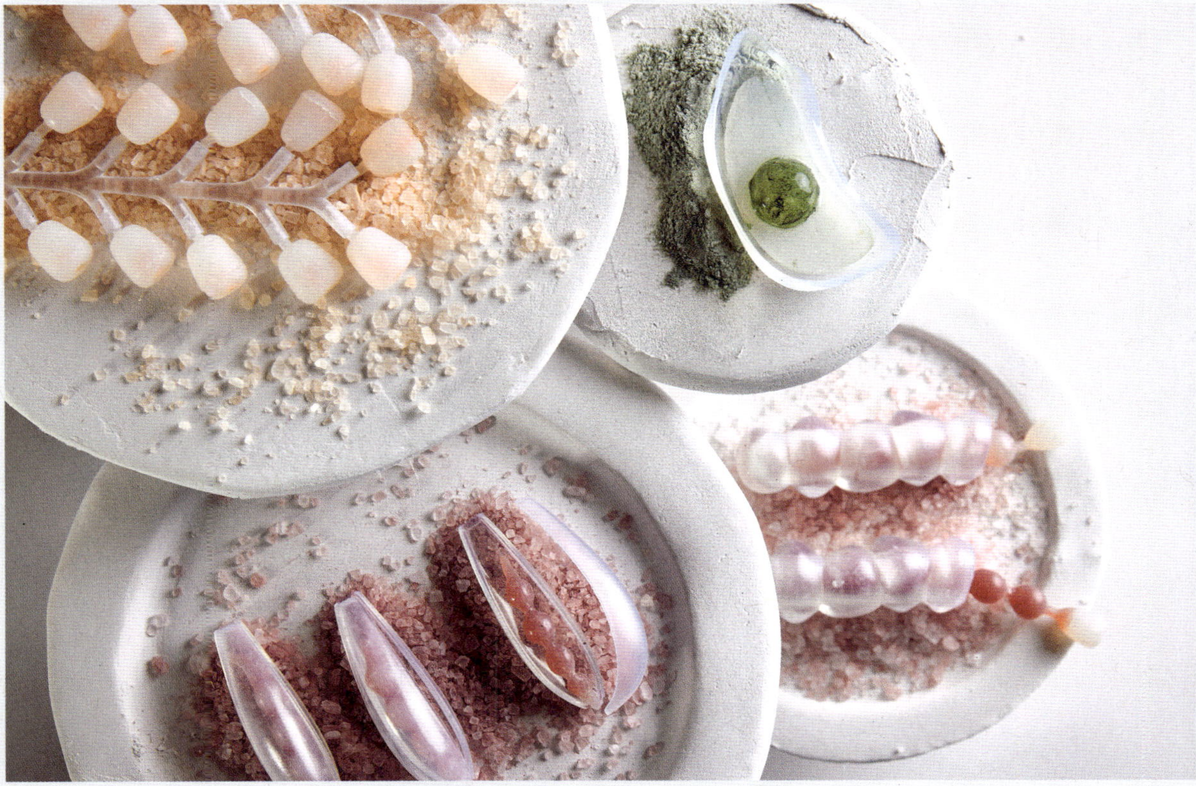

Well-being

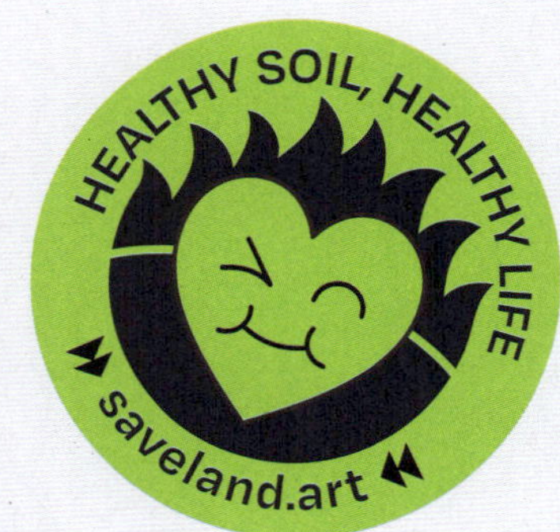

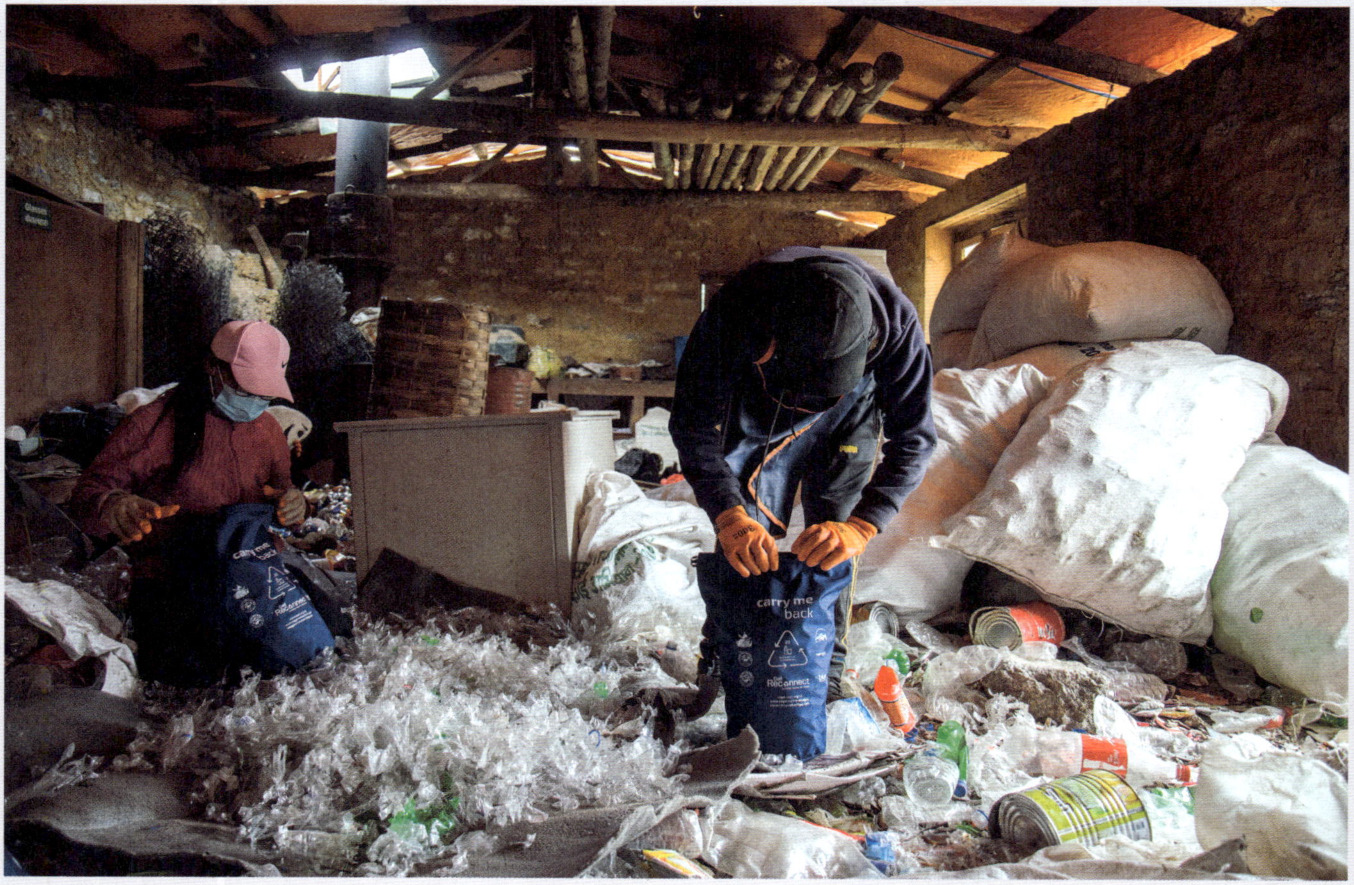

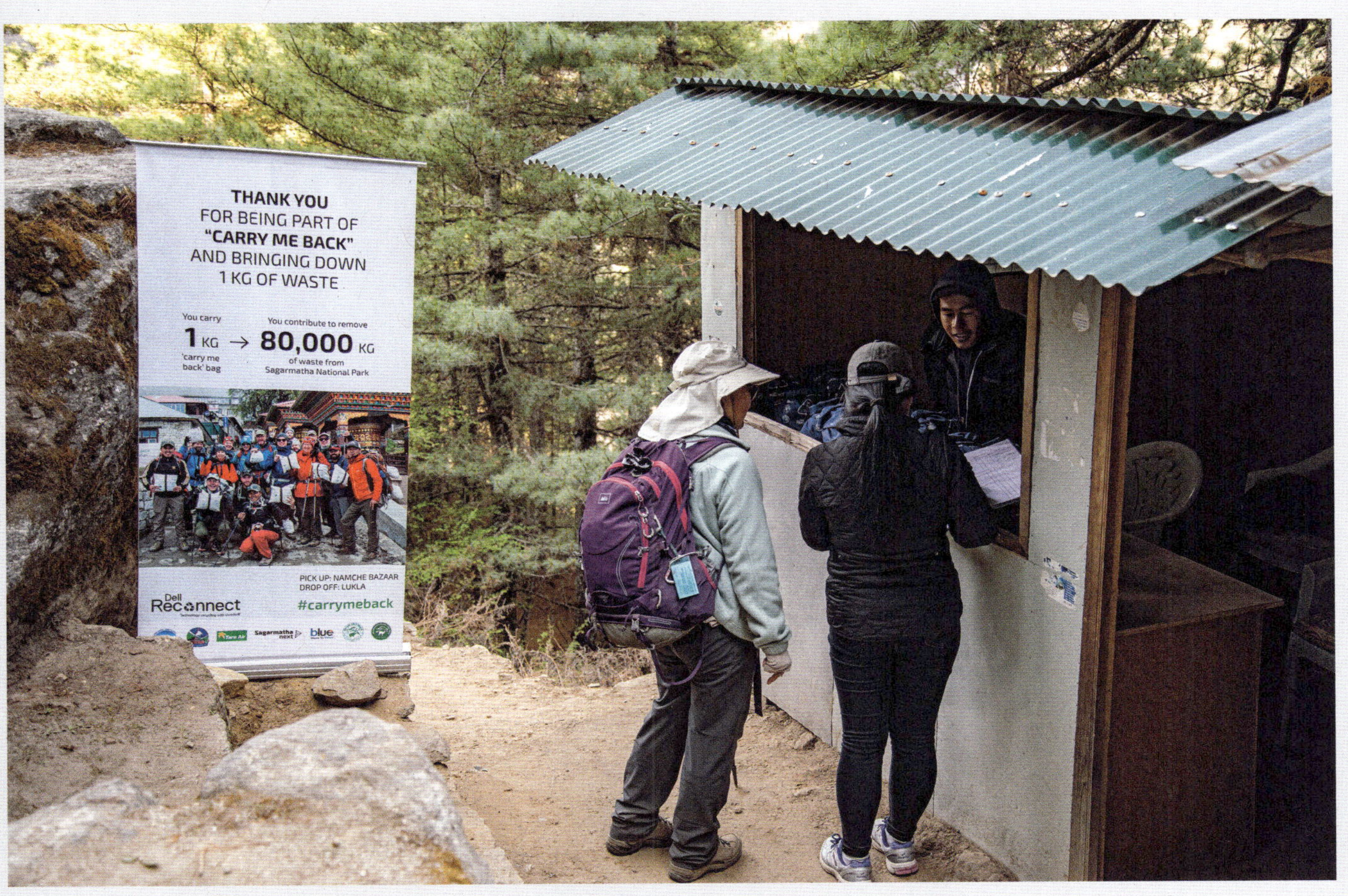

SuperLocal, Luc van Hoekel & Pim van Baarsen, *Carry Me Back – From the Himalayas*, Khumbu, Nepal, 2017. The Himalayas attract many visitors, but tourism leaves rubbish in the landscape, some of which is disposed of by incineration. However, this causes considerable damage to the soil. The *Carry Me Back* project addresses this problem by packaging collected rubbish in 1 kg bags (Carry Me Back Bag), which can be transported to the airport by hikers. Plastic lids are melted down on site and turned into souvenirs (rock or mountain-shaped key rings). In this way, the project not only promotes proper waste disposal, but also contributes to the protection and regeneration of the soil in the Himalayas.

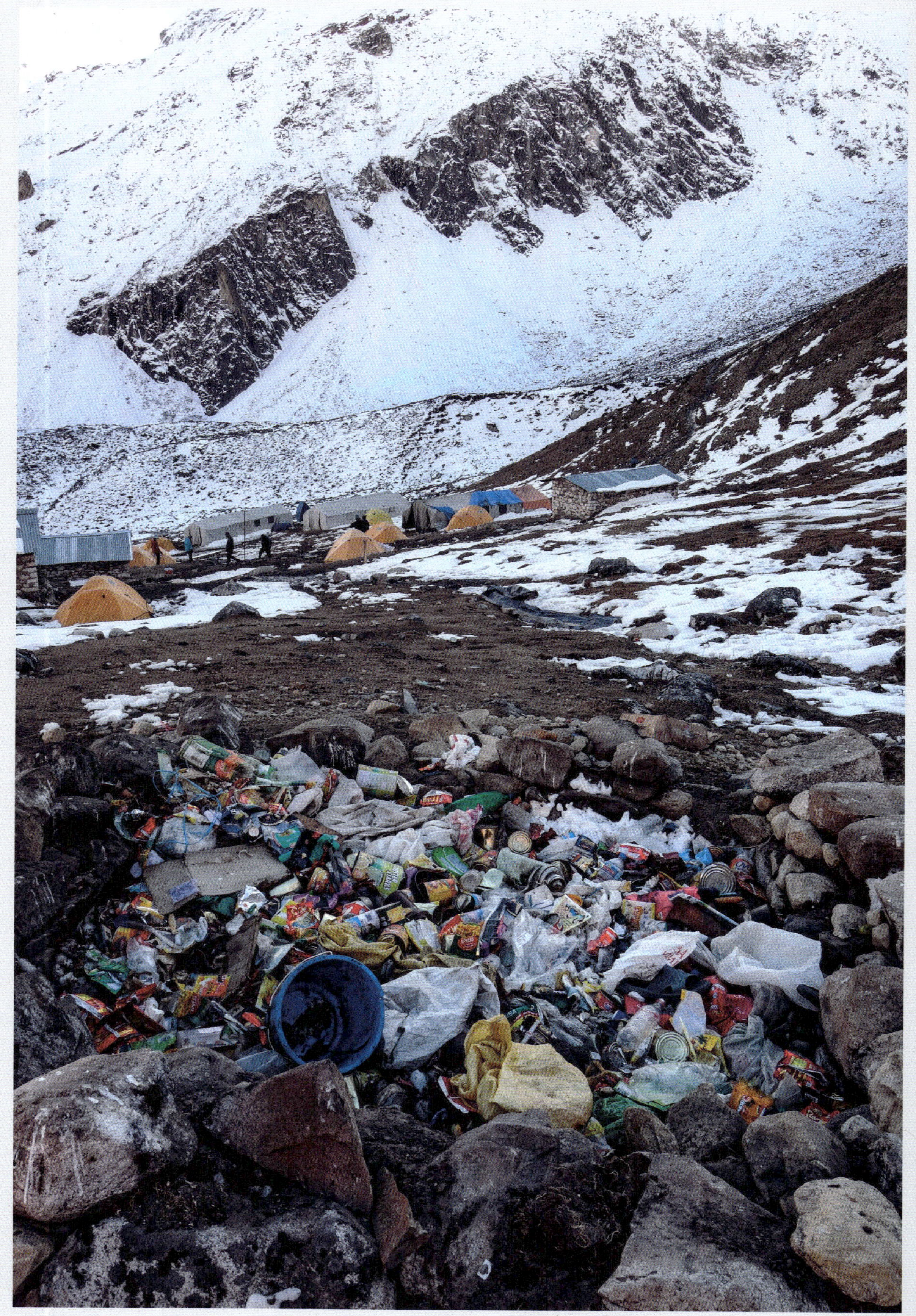

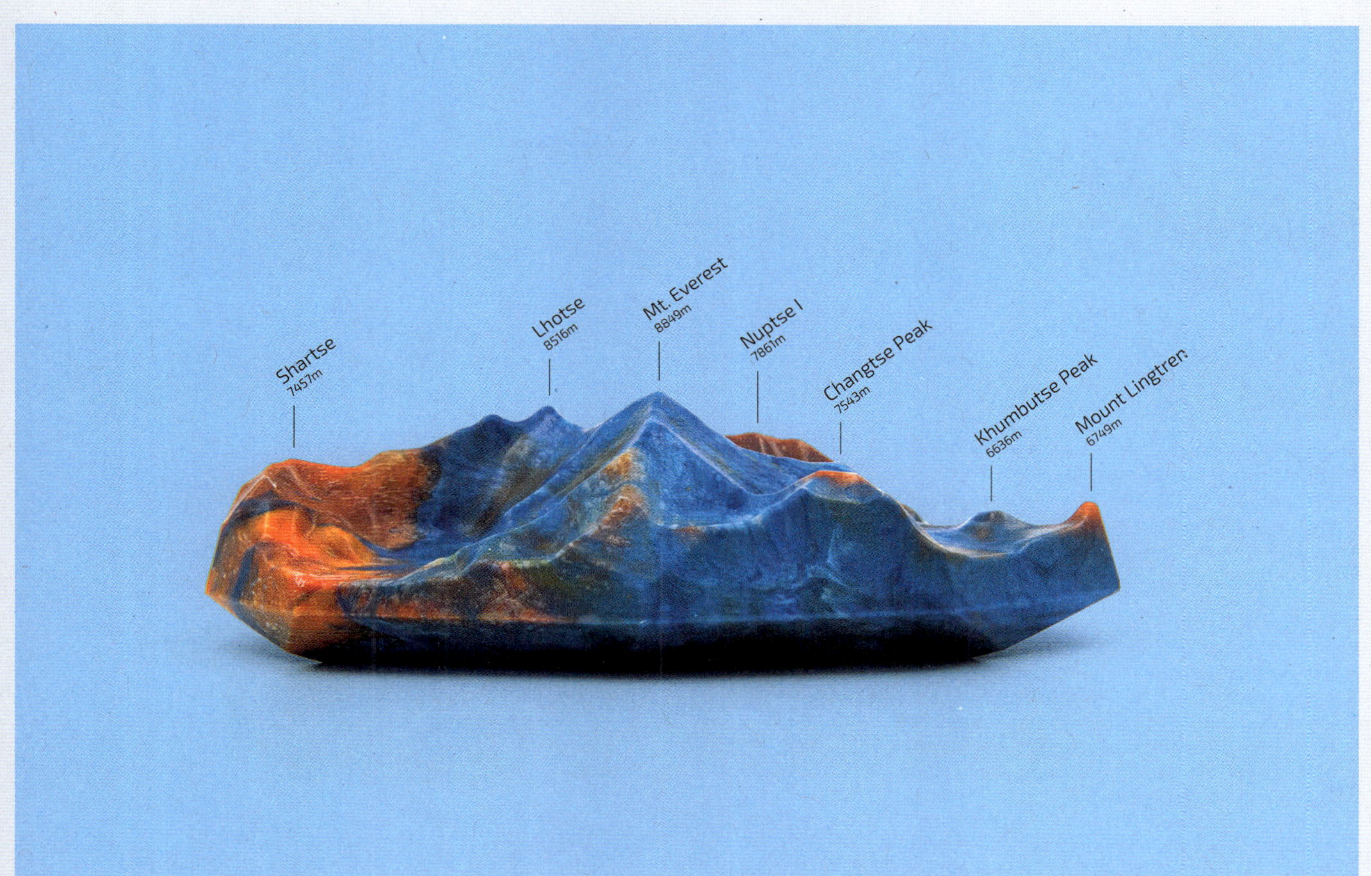
Shartse
7457m
Lhotse
8516m
Mt. Everest
8849m
Nuptse I
7861m
Changtse Peak
7543m
Khumbutse Peak
6636m
Mount Lingtren
6749m

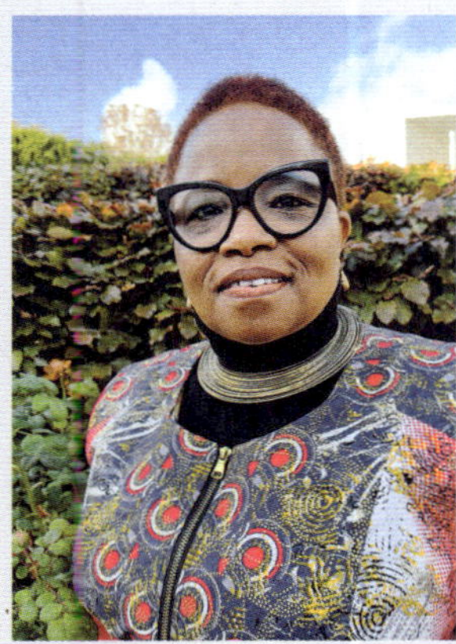

Wagaki Wischnewski, *Interview: Ferrous red soil,* 2024. In this interview, Wagaki Wischnewski, a member of the UNCCD-G20 Global Land Initiative from Kenya, talks about an extraordinary childhood experience that illustrates the healing effect of soil:

'The smell of red soil after a drizzle is glorious! The taste, just as glorious. So glorious, I couldn't resist eating it as a child, albeit in hiding. It melts like chocolate in your mouth. My mother was livid when she found out. But I couldn't stop. As a graduate student in the United States years later, I pleaded with friends to bring me just a handful of it. I found out I am not alone. Pregnant women in Kenya buy a particular type of stone to suck. I found out belatedly that my cravings were due to an iron deficiency. I turned to iron supplements, and although the red soil still smells good, there's no longer the urge to do the unthinkable.'

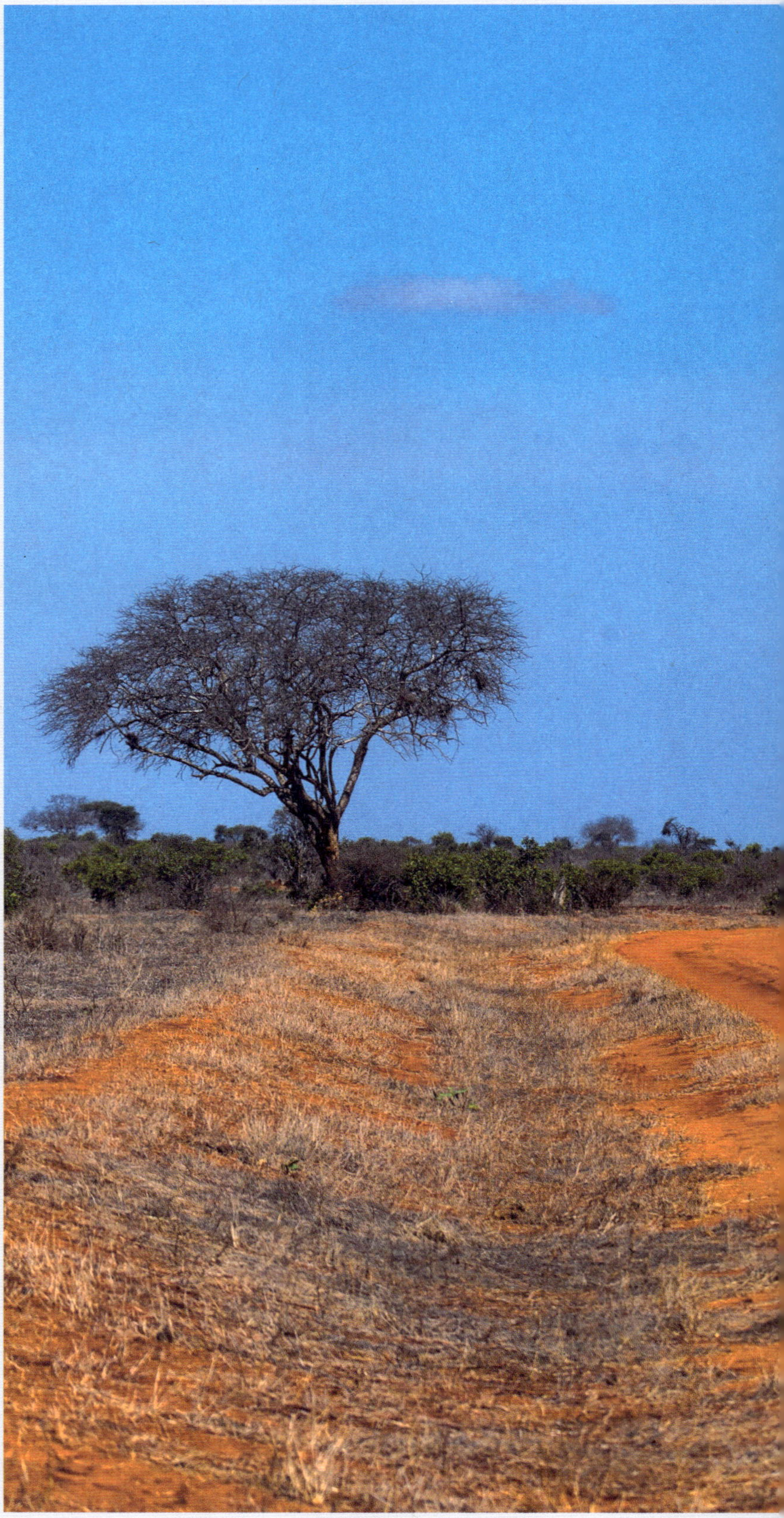

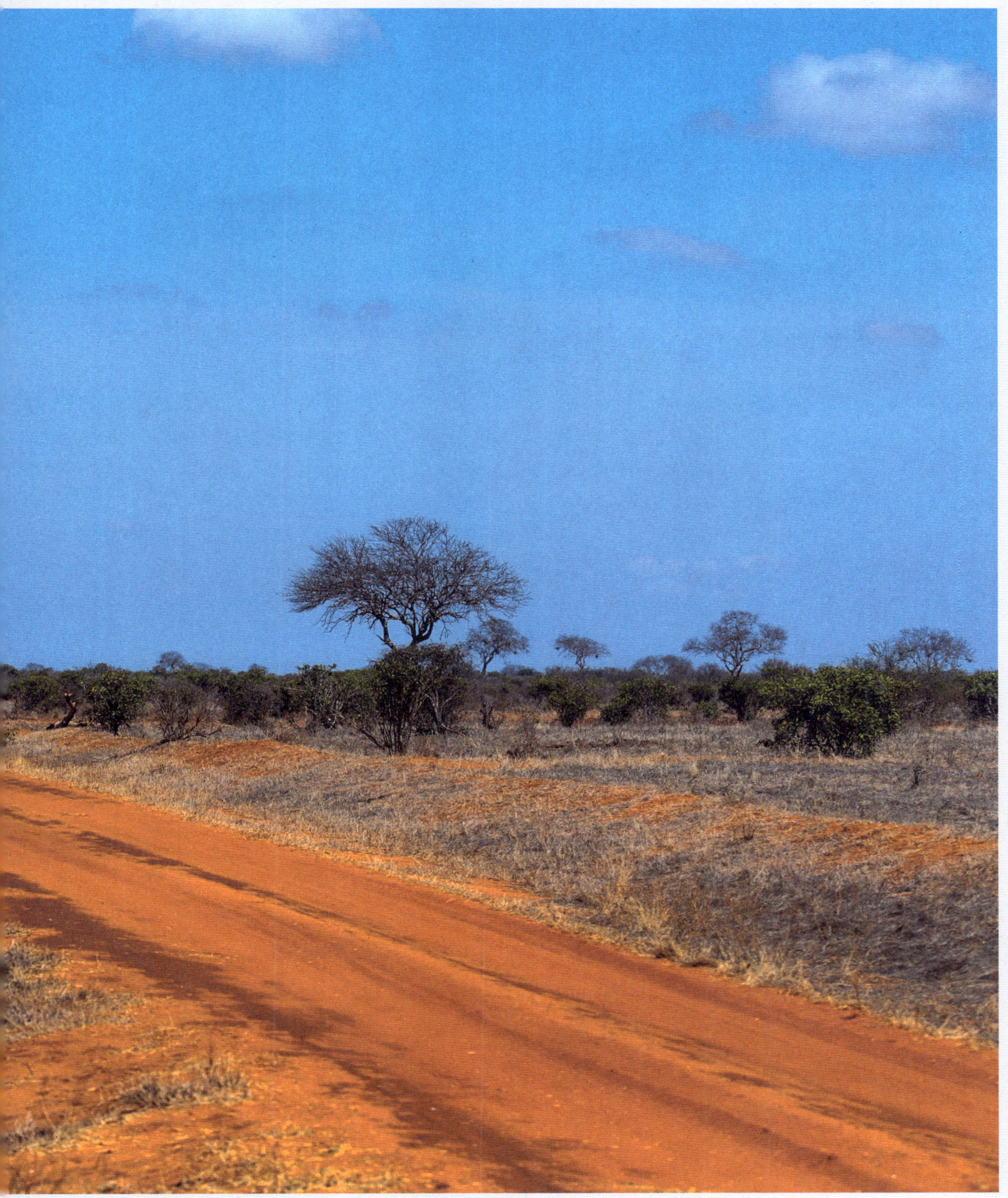

Stickers for Land

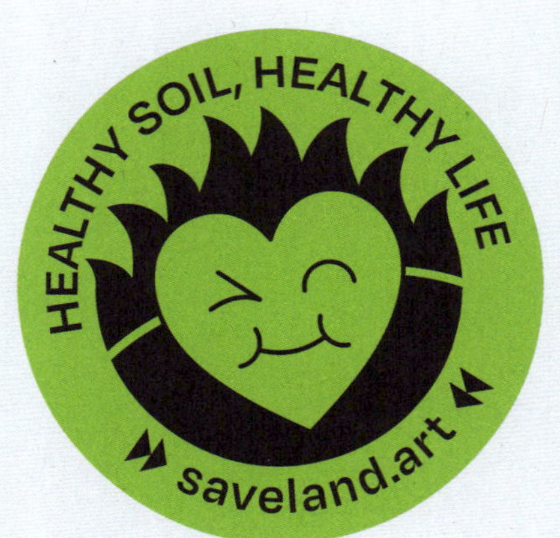

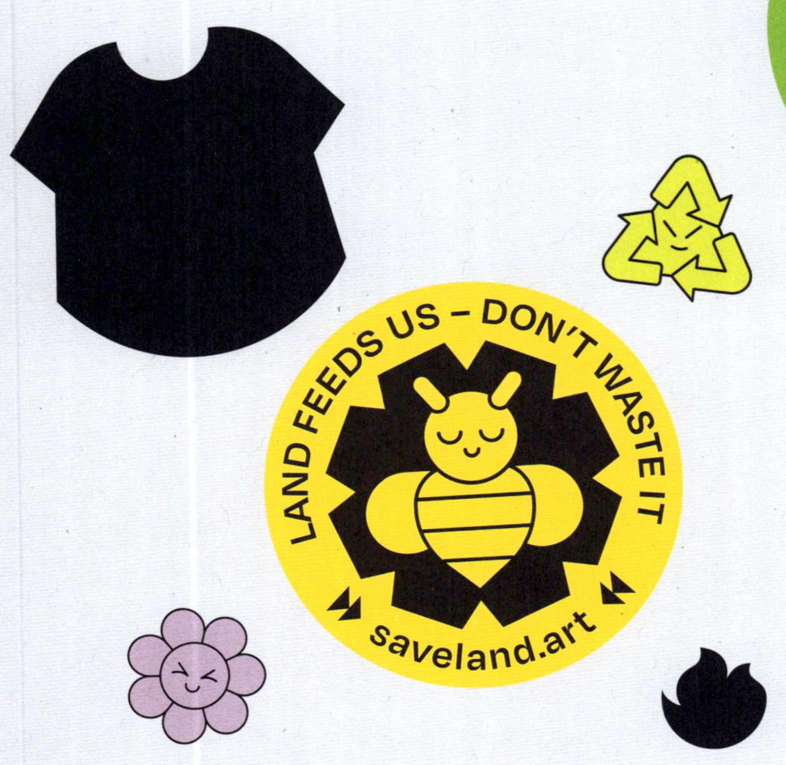

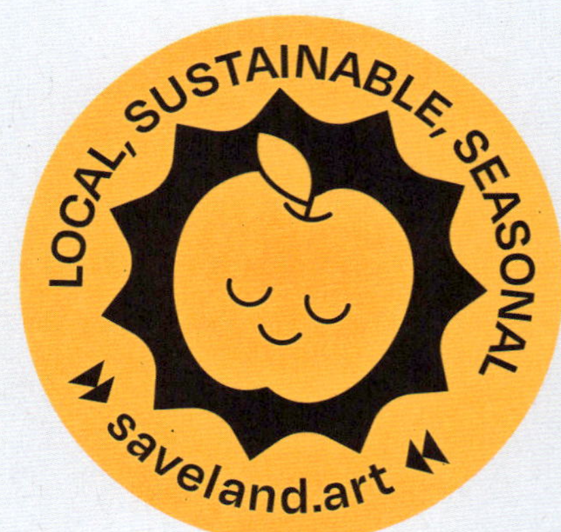

STATEMENT + BACKDROP + SYMBOL = STICKER

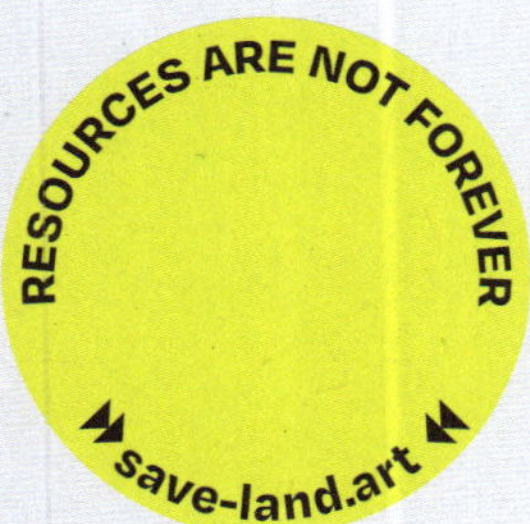

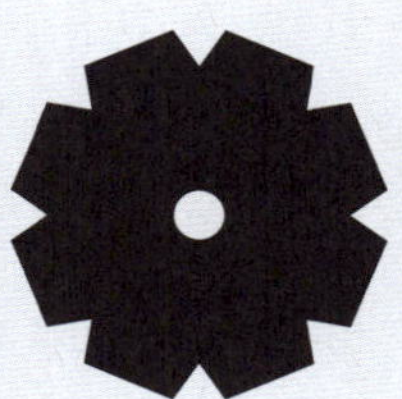

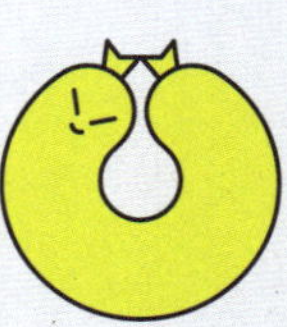

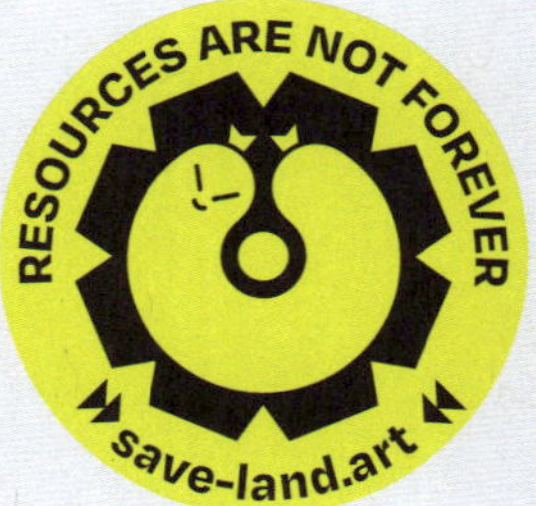

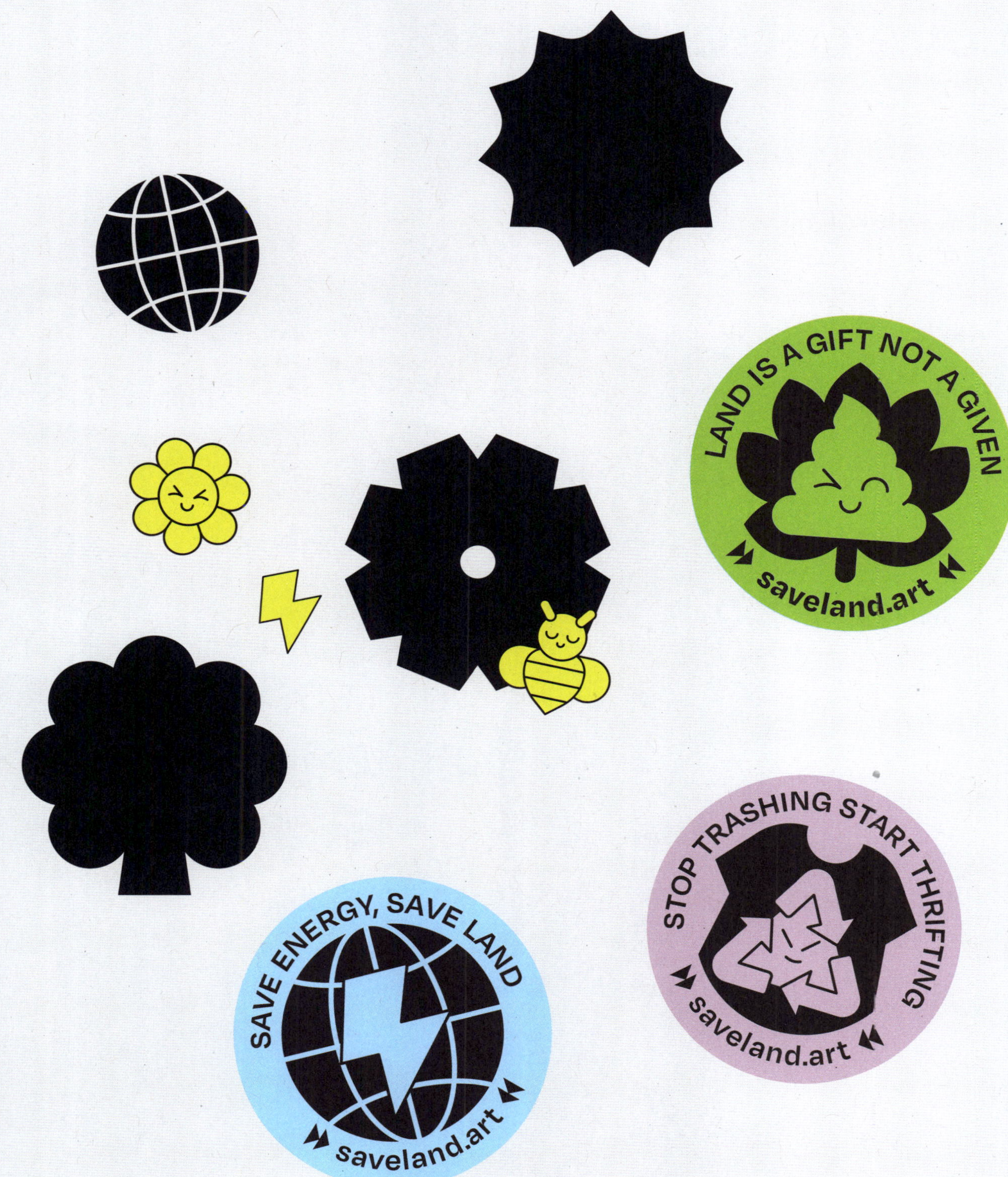

A sticker campaign has been developed for the *Save Land* exhibition. Using a sticker generator, you can design your own sticker. This generator is available digitally on the website www.saveland.art. The stickers can be downloaded and shared.

Love Letters to Land

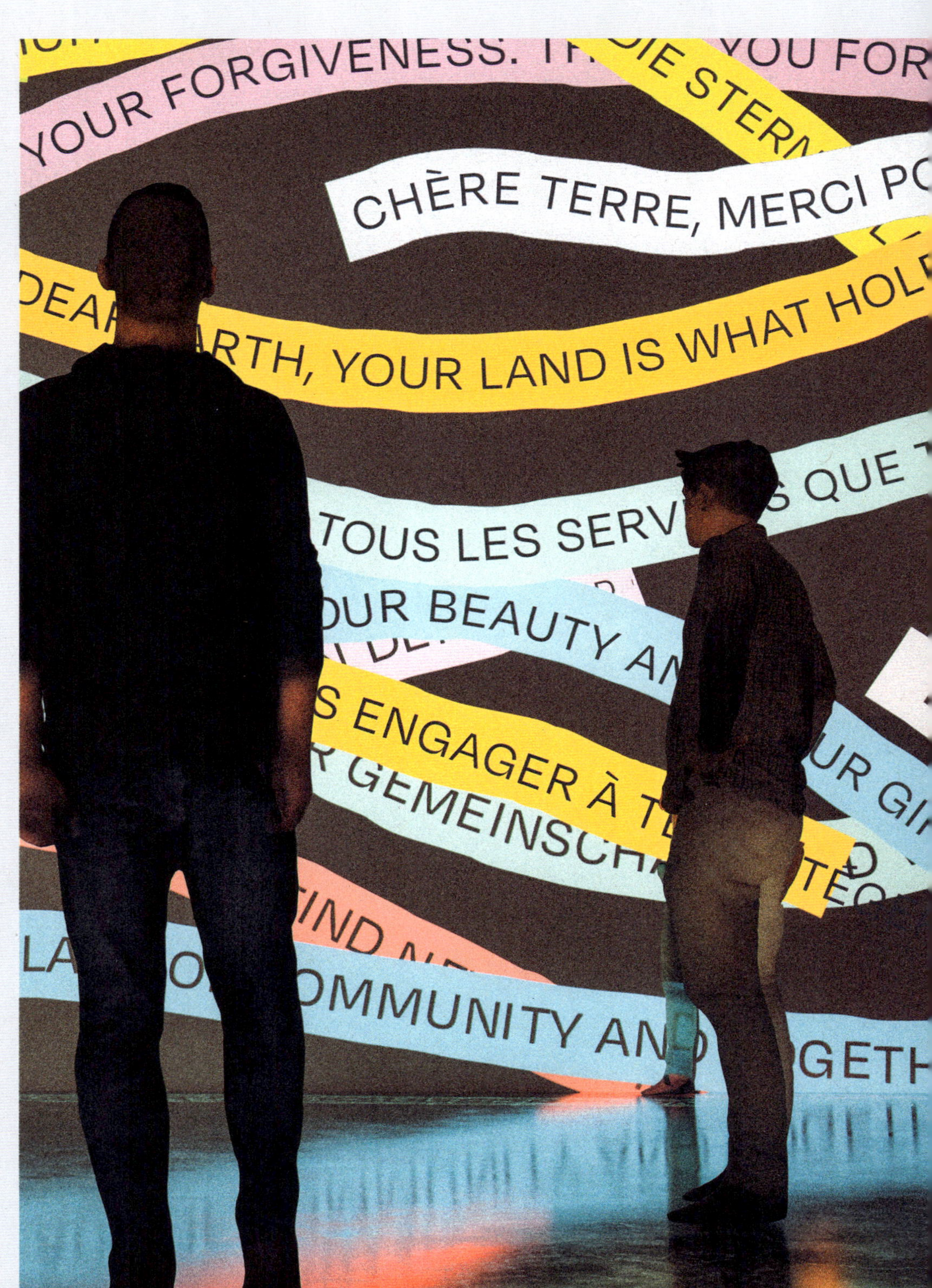

For the exhibition *Save Land. United for Land* in 2022/23, we collaborated with a group of Master's students on the Strategic Product and Innovation Development programme at the Faculty of Design & Art at the University of Wuppertal. To jointly develop the general objective of the show and possible narratives and exhibits, the students undertook extensive research in museums and exhibitions as well as on the streets of Wuppertal. They tested a series of campaigns to draw attention to the urgent issue of renaturalising degraded soils. One of these campaigns was called 'Love Letters to Land':

'With clipboards, pens, and a homemade letterbox in our bags, we set off on an expedition through the streets of Wuppertal city centre and the university campus. Our mission: to invite people to write a love letter to the land. We wanted to get people emotionally involved in an accessible way. This intervention reminded them of all the positive things they associate with the countryside. Most of the people we asked were willing to write a letter because it wasn't difficult to find kind words for nature, the earth, and the land. Most of them really enjoyed writing and put a lot of effort and love into it. Some needed a private space to think and write.'

BUNDESKUNSTHALLE /// STUDENTS FOR LAND

yo liebes Land,

ich als Städter habe immer wenig von dir gehalten. Doch du bist mehr als das endlose Warten an Bushaltestellen oder der penetrante Geruch von Gülle. Actually bist du ziemlich cool. Ich liebe deine Berge, deine Seen, deine Felder (solange sie gut riechen). An Mama's Apell „Geh doch mal an die frische Luft" ist auf jeden Fall was dran. Es ist schön bei dir zu sein, dich einzuatmen, dich zu genießen. Deswegen hoffe ich, dass du auch uns Städtern erhalten bleibst und Wege gefunden werden, dich noch mehr zu uns zu tragen.

hdgdl <3

Liebes Land,

Ich denke, dass man dich heutzutage gerne einmal vernachlässigt, weil du immer da bist; immer da und immer fest und etwas, auf das man wortwörtlich bauen kann.
Und im Zuge von immer mehr Nahrung, die in Chemielaboren rund um den Globus hergestellt wird, nehme ich an, ist es sehr leicht, zu vergessen, dass letztendlich alles aus dir kommt, was wir zum Leben brauchen.
Ich lebe in der Nähe des Tagebau Garzweiler. Ich bin schon oft an der tiefen Wunde vorbei gefahren, die man dort in dich gerissen hat.
Und während es weh tut, zu sehen, wie viel Leid an diesem Ort mit dir verbunden ist, und mit wie viel Rücksichtslosigkeit Menschen dich zerreißen und zerstückeln, um an die Teile von dir zu kommen, die sie haben wollen, erinnert es mich auch daran, wie vielschichtig du bist, wie viel Geschichte in dir und deinen Knochen steckt.
Das ist etwas, das mich mit tiefem Staunen erfüllt: Du dokumentierst, was geschehen ist, jede Katastrophe, jede Bitterkeit, du nimmst sie auf und schützt sie und erinnerst dich.

Dear Land,

In the age of climate change, many of challanges you face as well as strugle and difficulties. For who lives in tropical ecosystem, mangrove and peatlands are essential. I hope in the really near future more people and youth interest and engace to restore. you. More inovation and briliant ideas to restore is urgently needed. Let's put our briliant idea together. Semangat!!

Lina, Indonesia.

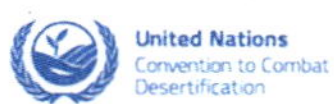

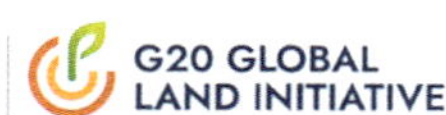

Photo: SEYED ALI HOSSEINY FAR / Beautiful Landscapes

Dear Earth,

Your land is what holds us and binds us. There's no place I'd rather be. Thank you for your beauty and your gifts and your forgiveness. Thank you for our home places- all of the forests across so many landscapes.- especially those of Puerto Rico, the most beautiful place on Earth.

♡ Sara

United States of America/
Puerto Rico

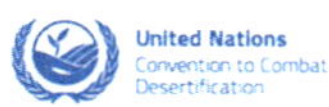

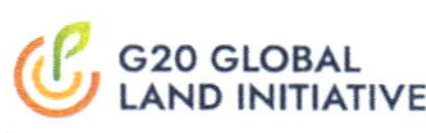

Photo: PYAE PHYO THET PAING / Beautiful Landscapes

This land is your land. This land is my land. From ocean to ocean, From forests to mountains. Let us take good care of the land, the forests + the water for the generations to come!

Anita Rosen

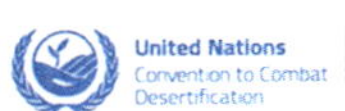

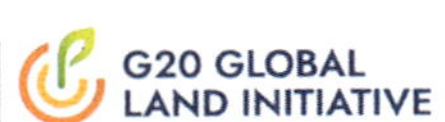

Photo: TRIKANSH SHARMA / Beautiful Landscapes

Chère Terre !

Merci pour tous les services que tu nous donnes, nous allons nous engager à te protéger !

YOBA ALENGA
DRC
28.06-2024

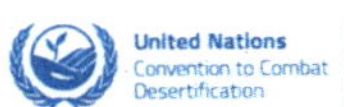

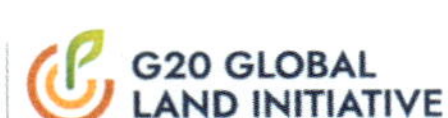

Photo: NEROZYA ALEKSANDR / Beautiful Landscapes

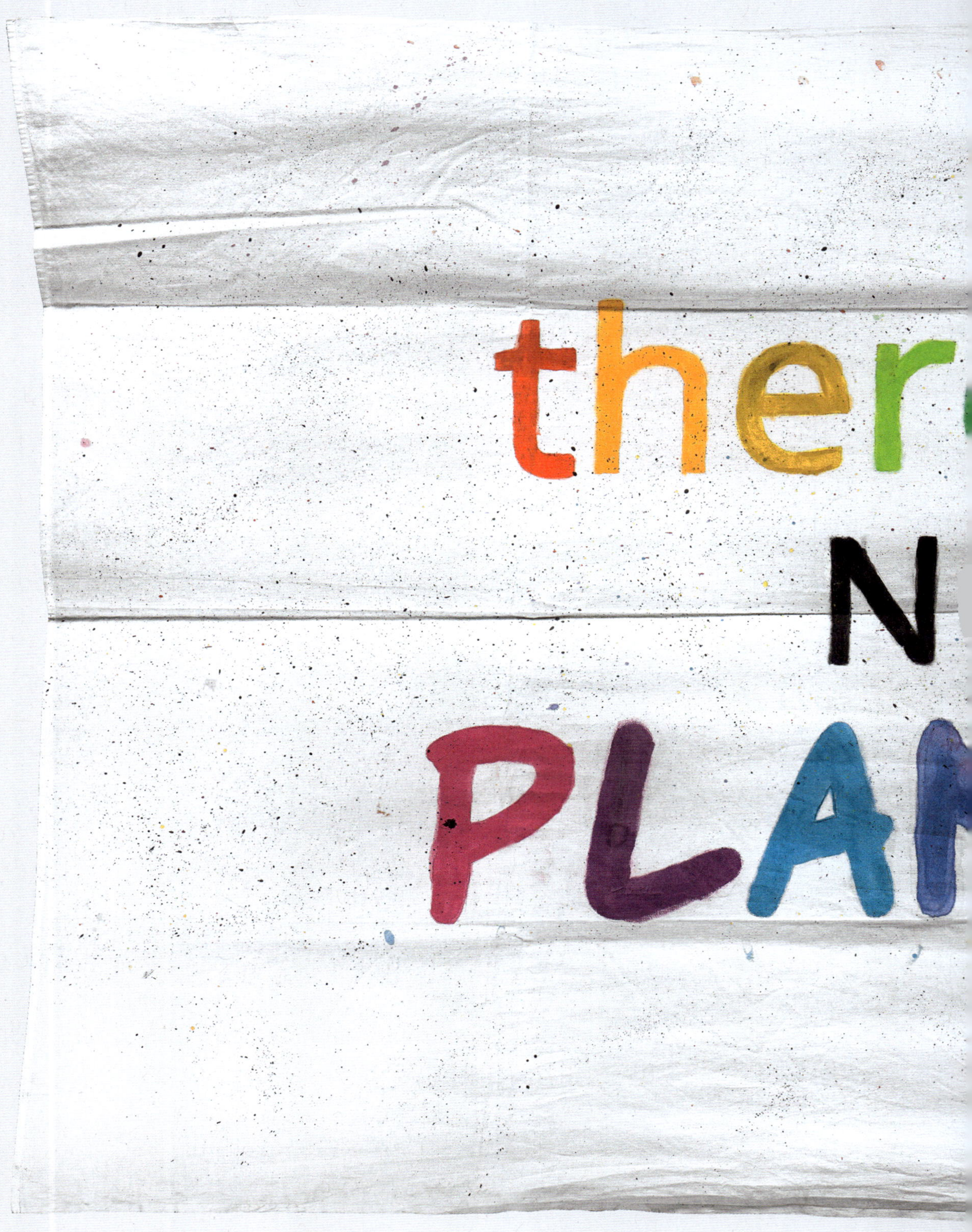

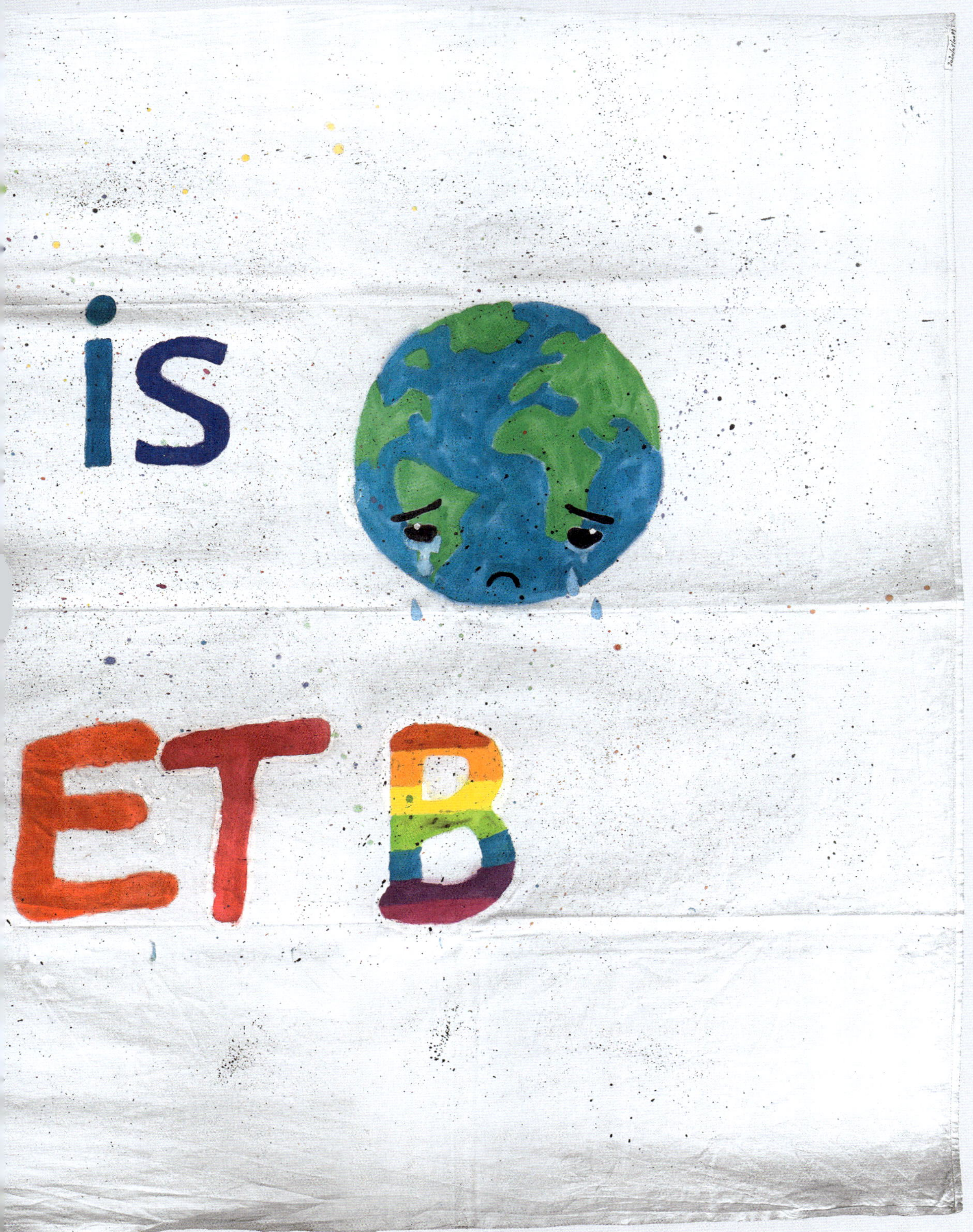

Banner: 'There is no planet B', Hürth Comprehensive School, 2019. The Fridays for Future movement began in 2018 when Swedish schoolgirl Greta Thunberg went on strike alone outside the parliament in Stockholm to demand that the government take more action against climate change. Her action soon attracted students from all over the world, who also took part in the school strikes. Today, Fridays for Future has become a global movement.

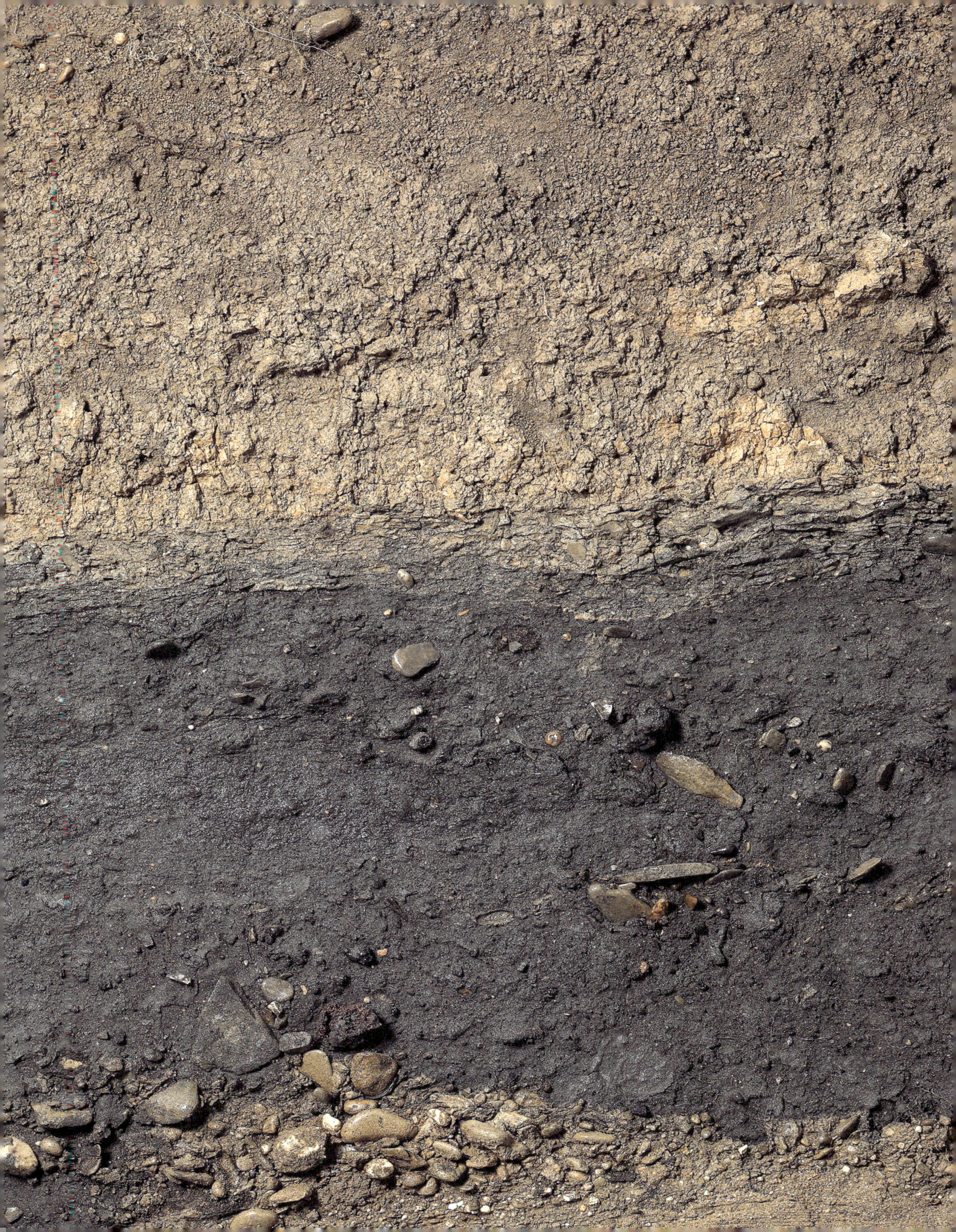

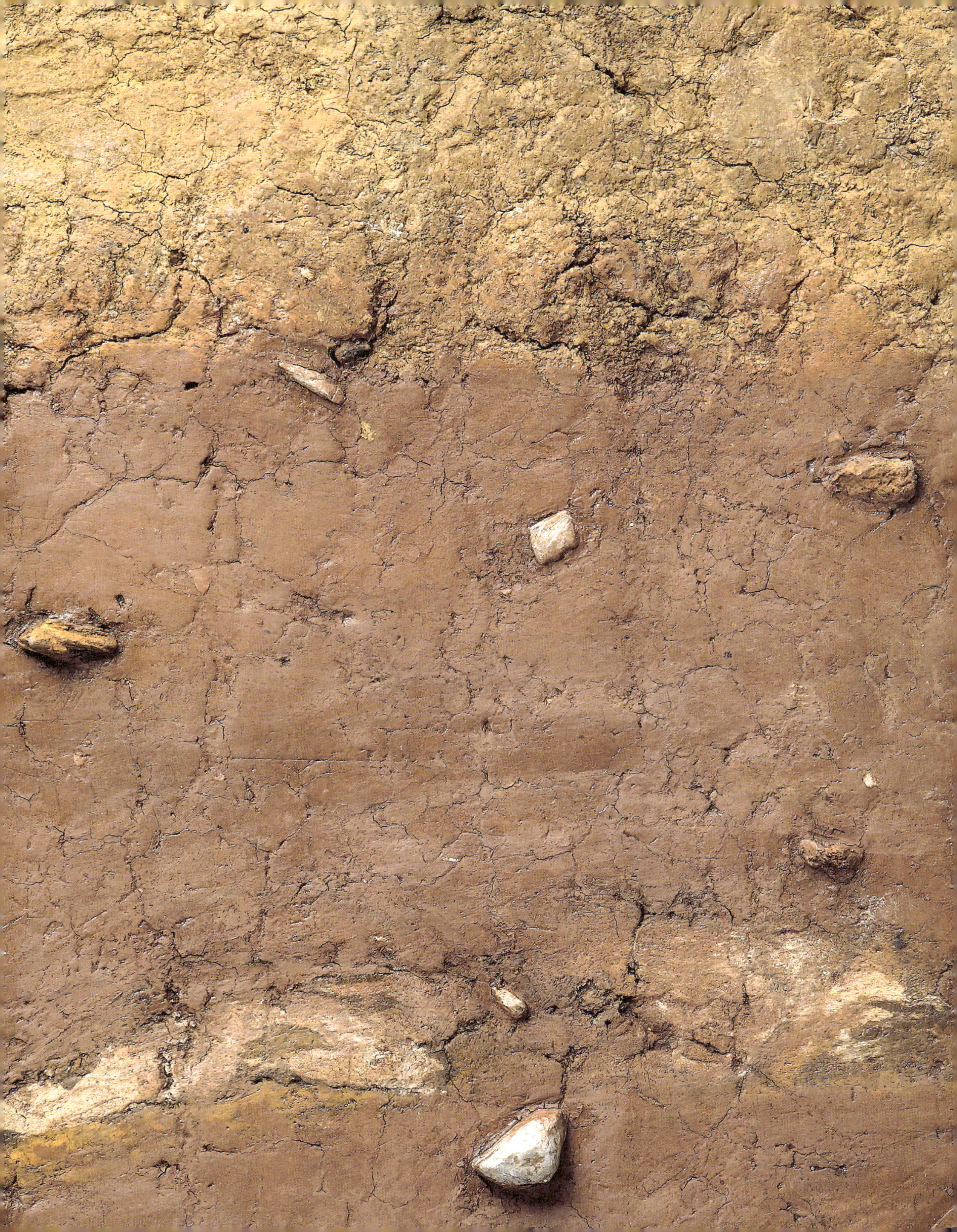

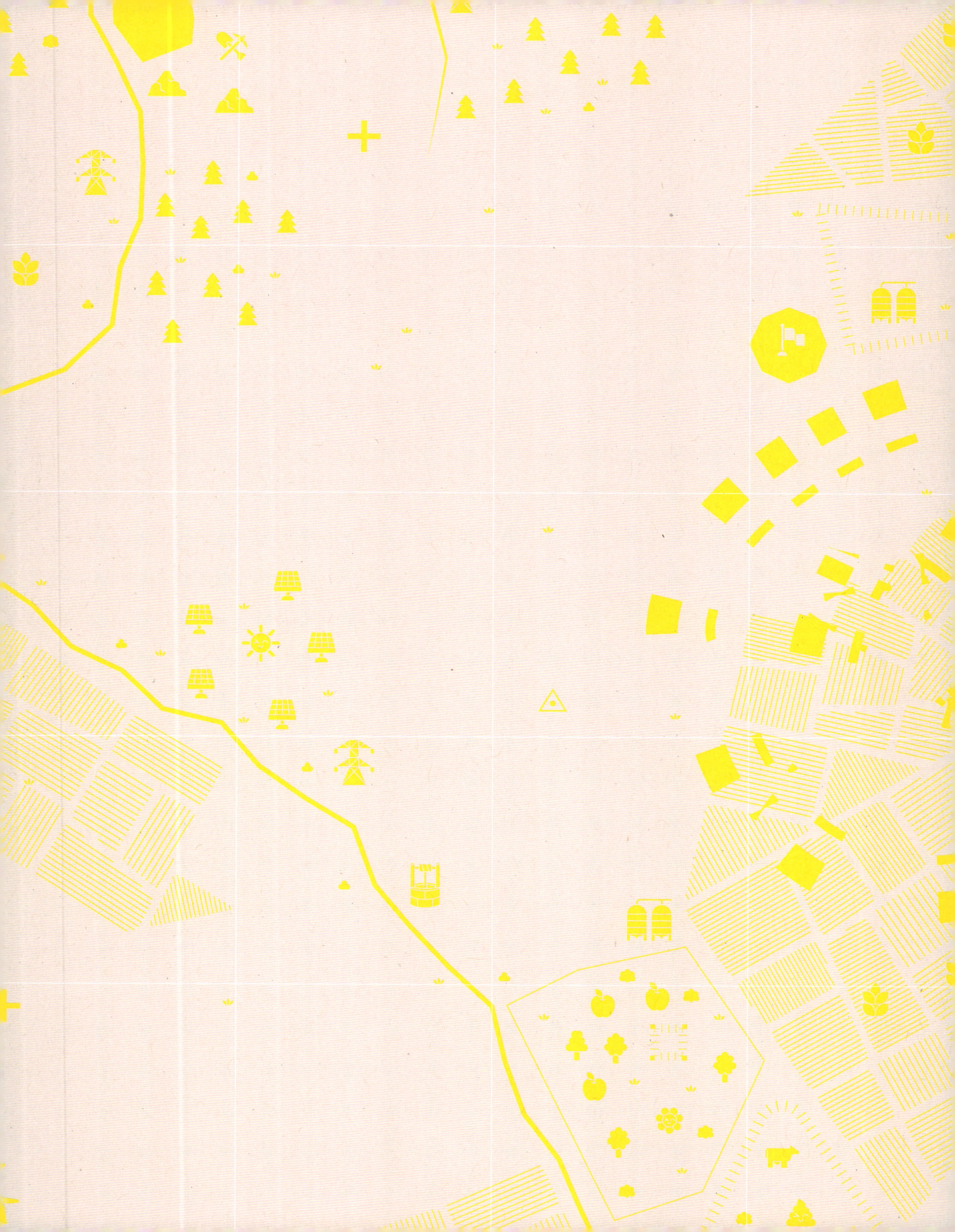

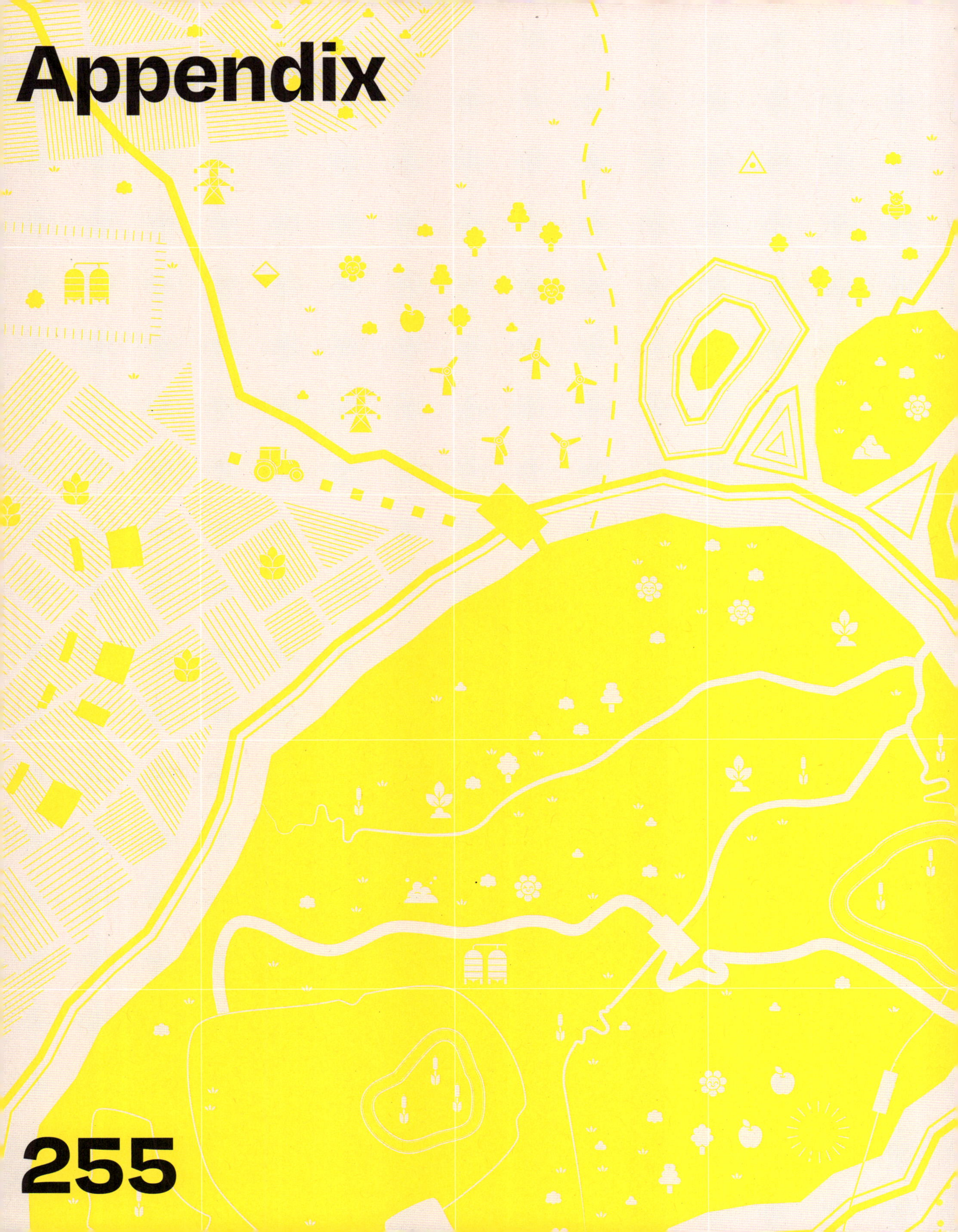

Appendix
255

Thanks to the lenders of the exhibition *Save Land. United for Land*

Amsterdam
- Collection Stedelijk Museum Amsterdam

Bad Honnef
- Henriette Pleiger

Basel
- Jan Hostettler

Berlin
- Stefanie Bühler
- Julius von Bismarck Studio
- Julian Charrière (Artist)
- Humboldt University of Berlin, Institute of Geography, PD Dr. Mohsen Makki
- Humboldt University of Berlin, Institute of Physics, Crystallographic Teaching Collection
- Museum Europäischer Kulturen, Staatliche Museen zu Berlin

Bonn
- Jan Karczewski
- Kunstmuseum Bonn
- Private Collection Bonn
- Stiftung Haus der Geschichte
- University of Bonn, Botanical Gardens

Dresden
- Technical University of Dresden, Institute of Cartography

Düsseldorf
- Kunstpalast
- Sies + Höke Gallery

Eslohe
- DampfLandLeute – Museum Eslohe

Germersheim
- Deutsches Straßenmuseum e.V.

Greifswald
- University of Greifswald, Institute of Botany and Landscape Ecology, Botanical Museum

Hamburg
- University of Hamburg, Centre for Natural History (CeNak), Department 'Invertebrates I', Earthworm Collection

Hünxe
- Paulina Heidlberger

Jena
- University of Jena, AG Biology Didactics

Katzenelnbogen
- Einrichmuseum

Cologne
- Gisela Capitain Gallery for Monika Sosnowska and Ximena Garrido-Lecca
- Ina Sistig-Heuken
- Michael & Eleonore Stoffel Foundation
- Museum Ludwig
- Rautenstrauch-Joest-Museum
- Private Collection Cologne

Krefeld
- Geological Service North Rhine-Westphalia

Leipzig
- Manu Washaus

London
- Alexandra Daisy Ginsberg
- Kiki Grammatopoulos
- Malu Lücking
- Grace Ndiritu

Los Angeles
- Cao Fei, 2024 Courtesy the artist, Sprüth Magers and Vitamin Creative Space
- Liam Young with VFX Supervisor Alexey Marfin

Munich
- Technical University of Munich, Institute for Wood Research

Münster
- University of Münster, Geological-Palaeontological Department, Geomuseum

Nairobi
- UNEP – UN Environment Programme

New York
- Leslie Tonkonow *Artworks + Projects*

Offenbach am Main
- Jonathan Kuhlmann

Overath
- Stephan Andreae

Rosenthal-Bielatal
- Private Collection

's-Hertogenbosch
- SuperLocal, Luc van Hoekel & Pim van Baarsen

Stuttgart
- Landesmuseum Württemberg, Stuttgart

Tübingen
- Museum of the Eberhard Karls University, Tübingen (MUT)

Vienna
- Andreas Pawlik

Image credits

Photo credits

- Courtesy the artist; alexander levy, Berlin; Sies + Höke, Dusseldorf, Photo: Roman März pp. 196–199
- Courtesy the artist, Sprüth Magers and Vitamin Creative Space pp. 105–107
- Auscape International PTY Ltd. /Alamy Stock Photo p. 75
- Purabi Bose pp. 80–83
- bpk / Antikensammlung, SMB / Johannes Laurentius p. 48
- Stefanie Bühler, Photo: Uwe Walter pp. 204, 208/209
- Courtesy Galerie Gisela Capitain, Cologne, Photo: Max Creasy pp. 148/149; Photo: Simon Vogel, Cologne pp. 97–99
- Julian Charrière pp. 168/169; Julian Charrière, Photo: Jens Ziehe pp. 170/171
- Rendering: Counterspace by Sumayya Vally pp. 112/113
- dform, Vienna pp. 30/31, 86–89, 128–131, 174–177, 242
- Deutsches Straßenmuseum e.V., Germersheim, Photographer: Matthias Granacher pp. 134, 172
- Angelica Francke p. 55
- Kazue Fujiwara p. 102
- Geologischer Dienst NRW Pre- and postscript, pp. 4, 5, 8, 9, 21, 62, 77, 250–253
- Alexandra Daisy Ginsberg Ltd., Courtesy the artist pp. 56/57, 59
- Kiki Grammatopoulos, Photo: 2023 Tom Mannion pp. 222, 223
- Paulina Heidlberger pp. 228, 229
- Jan Hostettler p. 53
- Imagebroker / Alamy Stock Photo p. 74 above
- Institut für Ur- und Frühgeschichte und Archäologie des Mittelalters, Abteilung für Ältere Urgeschichte und Quartärökologie, Eberhard Karls Universität Tübingen, Photo: Gregor Bader p. 52
- Illustrations: Matthäus Jandl for dform, Vienna pp. 218, 219, 220 above right, 225 bottom centre, 230 bottom left, 234 above right, 240/241
- Iyenemi Ibimina Kakulu pp. 164, 166, 167
- Jan Karczewski, Photo: David Ertl, Cologne p. 96
- Kristallographische Lehrsammlung, Institut für Physik, Humboldt-Universität zu Berlin p. 184
- Jonathan Kuhlmann, 2022 pp. 224/225, 227
- Kunstmuseum Bonn, Photo: David Ertl, Cologne pp. 210/211
- Kunstpalast – LVR-ZMB – Stefan Arendt – ARTOTHEK p. 79
- ERIC LAFFORGUE / Alamy Stock Photo pp. 238/239
- Landesmuseum Württemberg, Hendrik Zwietasch pp. 67–69, 162, 163
- Malu Lücking, Photo: Paul Cochrane pp. 232, 233
- LWZ, Vienna pp. 32–45
- V. Marquardt | Museum der Universität Tübingen MUT p. 54
- Museum Ludwig, Cologne; Photo: © Historisches Archiv der Stadt Köln mit Rheinischem Bildarchiv, rba_d033170 pp. 60/61
- Mutua Matheka, Courtesy of To.org pp. 108–110
- Anna-Lisa Miccoli-Bagkan, p. 238 above left
- Courtesy of Nagami Studio, 2021 p. 115
- NASA/JPL-Caltech p. 72
- Courtesy of Grace Ndiritu and LUX, London pp. 84/85
- Partners With Melanesians pp. 200–203
- picture alliance / JOKER/Ralf Gerard; JOKER/Hady Khandani; Imaginechina/ Sipa USA (composition) pp. 1–3
- picture alliance / Bildagentur-online/ Sigrid Wolf-Feix; JOKER/Hady Khandani; Zoonar/Andreas Muth; Zoonar/Andreas Völkel (composition) pp. 6–7
- picture alliance / blickwinkel/M. Woike; NurPhoto/Ambir Tolang; Zoonar/Galyna Andrushko (composition) pp. 10–11
- picture alliance / blickwinkel/M. Woike; CFOTO; ingo kutsche (composition) p. 12
- Scan: Andreas Pawlik pp. 158/159
- Private Collection Bonn, Photo: Reinhard Freyberg pp. 212/213
- Private Collection, Rosenthal-Bielatal, Photo: Uwe Walter p. 183
- Collage Manuel Radde p. 13; Collage Manuel Radde and aerial photographs from the National Agriculture Imagery Program (NAIP) of Chicago/Illinois and Northern Iowa/Worth County, USA pp. 46/47; and aerial photograph from the National Agriculture Imagery Program (NAIP) of Chicago/Illinois, USA pp. 90/91; and aerial photograph from the National Agriculture Imagery Program (NAIP) of Northern Iowa/Worth County, USA pp. 132/133; and aerial photograph 'Autumn along the Amur', September 30, 2019 – NASA Earth Observatory image by Joshua Stevens, using Landsat data from the U.S. Geological Survey pp. 178/179; and aerial photograph 'Smoke Blankets Venezuela', March 26, 2024 – NASA Earth Observatory image by Michala Garrison, using MODIS data from NASA EOSDIS LANCE and GIBS/Worldview pp. 214/215
- Rautenstrauch-Joest-Museum, Cologne, Photo: © Historisches Archiv der Stadt Köln mit Rheinischem Bildarchiv, Marc Weber, rba_d024836 p. 151, rba_d064782 p. 152, rba_d064781 p. 153
- Elke Seeber 2024, Botanisches Museum der Universität Greifswald, Institut für Botanik und Landschafts-ökologie pp. 142–146
- Ina Sistig-Heuken pp. 230/231
- Staatliche Museen zu Berlin, Museum Europäischer Kulturen / Christian Krug pp. 154, 173
- Collection Stedelijk Museum Amsterdam pp. 70/71, 192
- Super Local, Luc van Hoekel & Pim van Baarsen pp. 234, 235, 237
- TU Dresden, Institut für Kartographie p. 188
- Technische Universität München, Holzforschung München, Ralf Rosin pp. 138, 139
- Axel Thünker, Stiftung Haus der Geschichte pp. 92, 216, 217, 248/249
- Courtesy Leslie Tonkonow Artworks + Projects pp. 100/101
- Universität Bonn, Botanische Gärten, Photo: Volker Lannert p. 140
- Universität Jena, AG Biologiedidaktik pp. 141, 160, 161
- Manu Washaus, Photo: Konstantin Laschkow/Silk Relations pp. 220/221
- Leon Werdinger / Alamy Stock Photo p. 236
- Directed and Designed by Liam Young with VFX Supervisor Alexey Marfin pp. 121–127, 187–191
- Zoonar GmbH / Alamy Stock Photo p. 74 bottom

The assertion of claims pursuant to Section 60h UrhG for the reproduction of images of the exhibits/existing works is carried out by VG Bild-Kunst.

Despite intensive research, it was not possible in all cases to locate the rights holders of the images. Justified claims will of course be compensated within the framework of the usual agreements.

Imprint

This catalogue is published on the occasion of the exhibition: ***Save Land. United for Land***

6 December 2024–1 June 2025
Kunst- und Ausstellungshalle der Bundesrepublik Deutschland

An exhibition by the Bundeskunsthalle and UNCCD-G20 Global Land Initiative

EXHIBITION

Director Eva Kraus
Managing Director Oliver Hölken
Patron Ibrahim Thiaw
Advisory Board Martina Fineder-Hochmayr, Fabian Hemmert, Mark Nesbitt, Annette Scheersoi, Muralee Thummarukudy
Curators Henriette Pleiger, Tony Simons, Wagaki Wischnewski
Exhibition Manager Henriette Pleiger
Project Assistant Martin Hoffmann
Internships and Voluntary Social Year for Cultural Engagement Rebekah Caesar, Josephine Herzig, Benjamin Kerstan, Ronja Sturm, Dareen Syan
Exhibition Design Andreas Garber-Pawlik (head), Fanny Arnold, Matthäus Jandl, Lara Nellißen, Bernhard Poppe for dform, Vienna
Programming and technical realisation of the exhibition's interactive elements Benjamin Pokropek, Leonard Pokropek, Jürgen Haghofer, Beatriz Lacerda, Tim Peham, Achim Stromberger for BILDWERK MEDIA OG, Vienna

For more Information about the exhibition, please visit
www.saveland.art

Kunst- und Ausstellungshalle der Bundesrepublik Deutschland GmbH
Helmut-Kohl-Allee 4
D-53113 Bonn
T +49 228 9171 0
www.bundeskunsthalle.de

Supported by

Die Beauftragte der Bundesregierung für Kultur und Medien

CATALOGUE

Editors Kunst- und Ausstellungshalle der Bundesrepublik Deutschland, Bonn and UNCCD-G20 Global Land Initiative
Book concept Henriette Pleiger, Tony Simons, Wagaki Wischnewski
Authors Purabi Bose, Moustapha Cisse, Angela Churie Kallhauge, Eva Flinkerbusch, Kazue Fujiwara, Reinhard Geßl, Jacinta Gure, Brian Harris, Chris Jamie, Iyenemi Ibimina Kakulu, Eva Kraus, Eike Lüdeling, Florian Mayer, Nachson Mimran, Peter Minang, Musonda Mumba, Henriette Pleiger, Tony Simons, Ibrahim Thiaw, Muralee Thummarukudy, Susanne Wedlich, Wagaki Wischnewski
Catalogue coordination Donatella Cacciola
Copy editing Dorothee Dziewas, Taunusstein
Translations Lisa Contag, Berlin (English-German)
Olivia Parkes, Berlin (German-English)
Proofreading Dorothee Dziewas, Olivia Parkes, David Kenzler
Image rights clearance Eva Assenmacher
Project and production management
Hirmer Publishers Katja Durchholz with Hannes Halder
Graphic design and layout Manuel Radde, Vienna
Cover design Manuel Radde, Vienna
Main motif Bernhard Poppe and team dform, Vienna
Typeface Degular
Paper Inapa Enviropolar 100 g/m², Favini Crush Mais 100 g/m² (core), Favini Crush Mais 120 g/m² (endpapers), Peygreen 120 g/m² (cover)

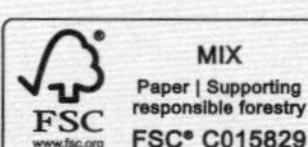

Except for pages 1–12, this book has been produced on the premium recycled paper enviro®polar in 100 g/m² made from 100 % recycled paper. The paper meets the strict requirements for environmentally friendly paper production and offers ecological savings in wood, energy, and water consumption as well as CO_2 emissions. The paper used for this book, enviro®polar by Lenzing Papier, has been awarded the C2C Certified® certificate at Silver level and has been awarded the EU Ecolabel certificate as well as the Blauer Engel certificate. Cradle to Cradle Certified® is a globally recognized standard for safe and circular products.
Reprographics Reproline mediateam GmbH & Co. KG, Unterföhring
Printing and Binding Printer Trento S.r.l., Trento, Italy
Printed in Italy

The Deutsche Nationalbibliothek lists this publication in the Deutsche Nationalbibliografie; detailed bibliographic data are available online at http:/dnb.d-nb.de

ISBN 978-3-7774-4508-3

Hirmer Verlag
Managing Director: Kerstin Ludolph
Bayerstraße 57–59
D-50835 Munich
www.hirmerverlag.de

Disclaimer
The designations employed and the presentation of materials in this information product do not imply the expression of any opinion whatsoever on the part of the United Nations Convention to Combat Desertification (UNCCD) concerning the legal or development status of any country, territory, city or area or its authorities, or concerning the delimitation of its frontiers or boundaries. The mention of specific companies or products of manufacturers does not imply that these have been endorsed or recommended by the UNCCD in preference to others of similar nature that are not mentioned. The views expressed in this Information product are those of the authors or contributors and do not necessarily reflect the views or policies of the UNCCD.

For more Information on the UNCCD and Global Land Initiative products, please visit:
www.unccd.int
www.G20land.org

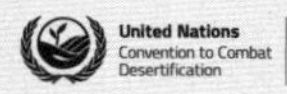

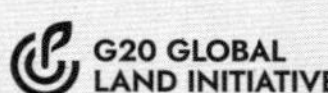

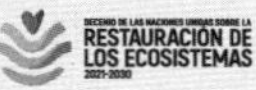

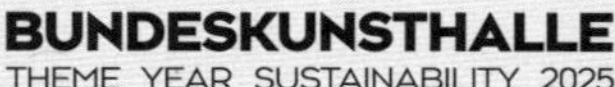

THEME YEAR SUSTAINABILITY 2025